COMPREHENSIVE

MICROSOFT® OFFICE 365™

ACCESS® 2016

For Microsoft® Office updates, go to sam.cengage.com

FRIEDRICHSEN

CENGAGE
Learning®

Australia • Brazil • Mexico • Singapore • United Kingdom • United States

Illustrated Microsoft® Office 365™ &
Access® 2016—Comprehensive
Lisa Friedrichsen

SVP, GM Skills & Global Product Management:
    Dawn Gerrain

Product Director: Kathleen McMahon

Senior Product Team Manager: Lauren Murphy

Product Team Manager: Andrea Topping

Associate Product Manager: Melissa Stehler

Senior Director, Development: Marah Bellegarde

Product Development Manager: Leigh Hefferon

Senior Content Developer: Christina Kling-Garrett

Developmental Editor: Lisa Ruffolo

Product Assistant: Erica Chapman

Marketing Director: Michele McTighe

Marketing Manager: Stephanie Albracht

Marketing Coordinator: Cassie Cloutier

Senior Production Director: Wendy Troeger

Production Director: Patty Stephan

Senior Content Project Manager: Stacey Lamodi

Art Director: Diana Graham

Text Designer: Joseph Lee, Black Fish Design

Cover Template Designer: Lisa Kuhn, Curio Press, LLC
    www.curiopress.com

Composition: GEX Publishing Services

For product information and technology assistance, contact us at
Cengage Learning Customer & Sales Support, 1-800-354-9706

For permission to use material from this text or product, submit all requests online at **www.cengage.com/permissions**
Further permissions questions can be emailed to
permissionrequest@cengage.com

Mac users: If you're working through this product using a Mac, some of the steps may vary. Additional information for Mac users is included with the Data Files for this product.

Some of the product names and company names used in this book have been used for identification purposes only and may be trademarks or registered trademarks of their respective manufacturers and sellers.

Windows® is a registered trademark of Microsoft Corporation. © 2012 Microsoft. Microsoft and the Office logo are either registered trademarks or trademarks of Microsoft Corporation in the United States and/or other countries. Cengage Learning is an independent entity from Microsoft Corporation and not affiliated with Microsoft in any manner. Microsoft product screenshots used with permission from Microsoft Corporation. Unless otherwise noted, all clip art is courtesy of openclipart.org.

Disclaimer: Any fictional data related to persons or companies or URLs used throughout this text is intended for instructional purposes only. At the time this text was published, any such data was fictional and not belonging to any real persons or companies.

Disclaimer: The material in this text was written using Microsoft Windows 10 Professional and Office 365 Professional Plus and was Quality Assurance tested before the publication date. As Microsoft continually updates the Windows 10 operating system and Office 365, your software experience may vary slightly from what is presented in the printed text.

Library of Congress Control Number: 2016932962
Soft-cover Edition ISBN: 978-1-305-87800-6
Loose-leaf Edition ISBN: 978-1-337-25097-9

Cengage Learning
20 Channel Center Street
Boston, MA 02210
USA

Cengage Learning is a leading provider of customized learning solutions with employees residing in nearly 40 different countries and sales in more than 125 countries around the world. Find your local representative at **www.cengage.com**

Cengage Learning products are represented in Canada by Nelson Education, Ltd.

For your course and learning solutions, visit **www.cengage.com**

Purchase any of our products at your local college store or at our preferred online store **www.cengagebrain.com**

Printed in the United States of America
Print Number: 01   Print Year: 2016

Contents

Productivity Apps for School and Work

OneNote
Sway
Office Mix
Edge

Corinne Hoisington

Lochlan keeps track of his class notes, football plays, and internship meetings with OneNote.

Zoe is using the annotation features of Microsoft Edge to take and save web notes for her research paper.

Nori is creating a Sway site to highlight this year's activities for the Student Government Association.

Hunter is adding interactive videos and screen recordings to his PowerPoint resume.

© Rawpixel/Shutterstock.com

Being computer literate no longer means mastery of only Word, Excel, PowerPoint, Outlook, and Access. To become technology power users, Hunter, Nori, Zoe, and Lochlan are exploring Microsoft OneNote, Sway, Mix, and Edge in Office 2016 and Windows 10.

In this Module

Learn to use productivity apps!
Links to companion **Sways**, featuring **videos** with hands-on instructions, are located on www.cengagebrain.com.

Introduction to OneNote 2016

notebook | section tab | To Do tag | screen clipping | note | template | Microsoft OneNote Mobile app | sync | drawing canvas | inked handwriting | Ink to Text

As you glance around any classroom, you invariably see paper notebooks and notepads on each desk. Because deciphering and sharing handwritten notes can be a challenge, Microsoft OneNote 2016 replaces physical notebooks, binders, and paper notes with a searchable, digital notebook. OneNote captures your ideas and schoolwork on any device so you can stay organized, share notes, and work with others on projects. Whether you are a student taking class notes as shown in **Figure 1** or an employee taking notes in company meetings, OneNote is the one place to keep notes for all of your projects.

Bottom Line
- OneNote is a note-taking app for your academic and professional life.
- Use OneNote to get organized by gathering your ideas, sketches, webpages, photos, videos, and notes in one place.

Figure 1: OneNote 2016 notebook

Each **notebook** is divided into sections, also called **section tabs**, by subject or topic.

Use **To Do tags**, icons that help you keep track of your assignments and other tasks.

Type on a page to add a **note**, a small window that contains text or other types of information.

Personalize a page with a **template**, or stationery.

Write or draw directly on the page using drawing tools.

Pages can include pictures such as **screen clippings**, images from any part of a computer screen.

Attach files and enter equations so you have everything you need in one place.

Creating a OneNote Notebook

OneNote is divided into sections similar to those in a spiral-bound notebook. Each OneNote notebook contains sections, pages, and other notebooks. You can use One-Note for school, business, and personal projects. Store information for each type of project in different notebooks to keep your tasks separate, or use any other organization that suits you. OneNote is flexible enough to adapt to the way you want to work.

When you create a notebook, it contains a blank page with a plain white background by default, though you can use templates, or stationery, to apply designs in categories such as Academic, Business, Decorative, and Planners. Start typing or use the buttons on the Insert tab to insert notes, which are small resizable windows that can contain text, equations, tables, on-screen writing, images, audio and video recordings, to-do lists, file attachments, and file printouts. Add as many notes as you need to each page.

Learn to use OneNote!
Links to companion **Sways**, featuring **videos** with hands-on instructions, are located on www.cengagebrain.com.

Syncing a Notebook to the Cloud

OneNote saves your notes every time you make a change in a notebook. To make sure you can access your notebooks with a laptop, tablet, or smartphone wherever you are, OneNote uses cloud-based storage, such as OneDrive or SharePoint. **Microsoft OneNote Mobile app**, a lightweight version of OneNote 2016 shown in **Figure 2**, is available for free in the Windows Store, Google Play for Android devices, and the AppStore for iOS devices.

If you have a Microsoft account, OneNote saves your notes on OneDrive automatically for all your mobile devices and computers, which is called **syncing**. For example, you can use OneNote to take notes on your laptop during class, and then open OneNote on your phone to study later. To use a notebook stored on your computer with your OneNote Mobile app, move the notebook to OneDrive. You can quickly share notebook content with other people using OneDrive.

Figure 2: Microsoft OneNote Mobile app

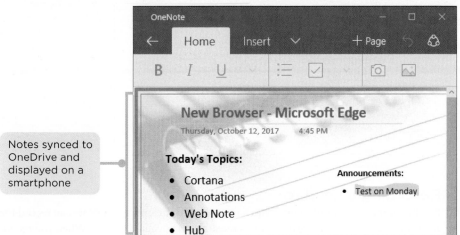

Notes synced to OneDrive and displayed on a smartphone

Taking Notes

Use OneNote pages to organize your notes by class and topic or lecture. Beyond simple typed notes, OneNote stores drawings, converts handwriting to searchable text and mathematical sketches to equations, and records audio and video.

OneNote includes drawing tools that let you sketch freehand drawings such as biological cell diagrams and financial supply-and-demand charts. As shown in **Figure 3**, the Draw tab on the ribbon provides these drawing tools along with shapes so you can insert diagrams and other illustrations to represent your ideas. When you draw on a page, OneNote creates a **drawing canvas**, which is a container for shapes and lines.

Figure 3: Tools on the Draw tab

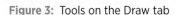

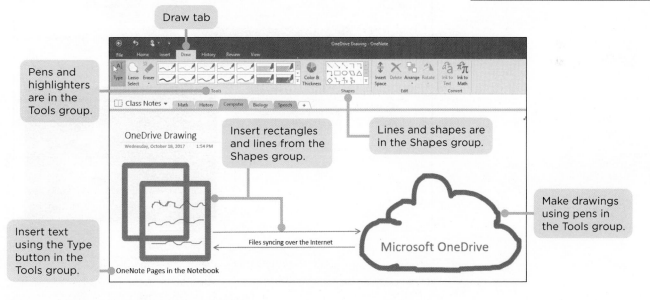

Draw tab

Pens and highlighters are in the Tools group.

Insert rectangles and lines from the Shapes group.

Lines and shapes are in the Shapes group.

Insert text using the Type button in the Tools group.

Make drawings using pens in the Tools group.

Converting Handwriting to Text

When you use a pen tool to write on a notebook page, the text you enter is called **inked handwriting**. OneNote can convert inked handwriting to typed text when you use the **Ink to Text** button in the Convert group on the Draw tab, as shown in **Figure 4**. After OneNote converts the handwriting to text, you can use the Search box to find terms in the converted text or any other note in your notebooks.

Figure 4: Converting handwriting to text

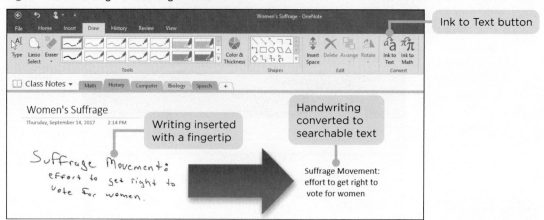

Ink to Text button

On the Job Now

Use OneNote as a place to brainstorm ongoing work projects. If a notebook contains sensitive material, you can password-protect some or all of the notebook so that only certain people can open it.

Recording a Lecture

If your computer or mobile device has a microphone or camera, OneNote can record the audio or video from a lecture or business meeting as shown in **Figure 5**. When you record a lecture (with your instructor's permission), you can follow along, take regular notes at your own pace, and review the video recording later. You can control the start, pause, and stop motions of the recording when you play back the recording of your notes.

Figure 5: Video inserted in a notebook

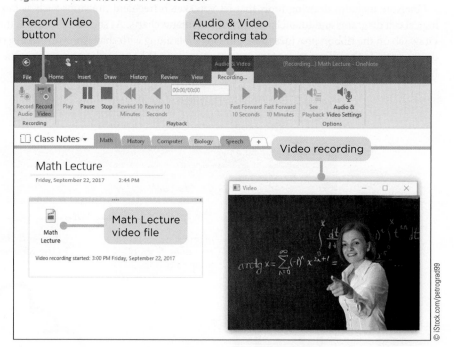

Try This Now

Learn to use OneNote!
Links to companion **Sways**, featuring **videos** with hands-on instructions, are located on www.cengagebrain.com.

1: Taking Notes for a Week

As a student, you can get organized by using OneNote to take detailed notes in your classes. Perform the following tasks:

a. Create a new OneNote notebook on your Microsoft OneDrive account (the default location for new notebooks). Name the notebook with your first name followed by "Notes," as in **Caleb Notes**.

b. Create four section tabs, each with a different class name.

c. Take detailed notes in those classes for one week. Be sure to include notes, drawings, and other types of content.

d. Sync your notes with your OneDrive. Submit your assignment in the format specified by your instructor.

2: Using OneNote to Organize a Research Paper

You have a research paper due on the topic of three habits of successful students. Use OneNote to organize your research. Perform the following tasks:

a. Create a new OneNote notebook on your Microsoft OneDrive account. Name the notebook **Success Research**.

b. Create three section tabs with the following names:

- **Take Detailed Notes**
- **Be Respectful in Class**
- **Come to Class Prepared**

c. On the web, research the topics and find three sources for each section. Copy a sentence from each source and paste the sentence into the appropriate section. When you paste the sentence, OneNote inserts it in a note with a link to the source.

d. Sync your notes with your OneDrive. Submit your assignment in the format specified by your instructor.

3: Planning Your Career

Note: This activity requires a webcam or built-in video camera on any type of device.

Consider an occupation that interests you. Using OneNote, examine the responsibilities, education requirements, potential salary, and employment outlook of a specific career. Perform the following tasks:

a. Create a new OneNote notebook on your Microsoft OneDrive account. Name the notebook with your first name followed by a career title, such as **Kara - App Developer**.

b. Create four section tabs with the names **Responsibilities, Education Requirements, Median Salary**, and **Employment Outlook**.

c. Research the responsibilities of your career path. Using OneNote, record a short video (approximately 30 seconds) of yourself explaining the responsibilities of your career path. Place the video in the Responsibilities section.

d. On the web, research the educational requirements for your career path and find two appropriate sources. Copy a paragraph from each source and paste them into the appropriate section. When you paste a paragraph, OneNote inserts it in a note with a link to the source.

e. Research the median salary for a single year for this career. Create a mathematical equation in the Median Salary section that multiplies the amount of the median salary times 20 years to calculate how much you will possibly earn.

f. For the Employment Outlook section, research the outlook for your career path. Take at least four notes about what you find when researching the topic.

g. Sync your notes with your OneDrive. Submit your assignment in the format specified by your instructor.

Introduction to Sway

Sway site | responsive design | Storyline | card | Creative Commons license | animation emphasis effects | Docs.com

Expressing your ideas in a presentation typically means creating PowerPoint slides or a Word document. Microsoft Sway gives you another way to engage an audience. Sway is a free Microsoft tool available at Sway.com or as an app in Office 365. Using Sway, you can combine text, images, videos, and social media in a website called a **Sway site** that you can share and display on any device. To get started, you create a digital story on a web-based canvas without borders, slides, cells, or page breaks. A Sway site organizes the text, images, and video into a **responsive design**, which means your content adapts perfectly to any screen size as shown in **Figure 6**. You store a Sway site in the cloud on OneDrive using a free Microsoft account.

Figure 6: Sway site with responsive design

You can display a Sway presentation in a web browser.

Sway uses responsive design to make sure pages fit perfectly on any device.

© iStock.com/marinello, © iStock.com/marekuliasz

Creating a Sway Presentation

You can use Sway to build a digital flyer, a club newsletter, a vacation blog, an informational site, a digital art portfolio, or a new product rollout. After you select your topic and sign into Sway with your Microsoft account, a **Storyline** opens, providing tools and a work area for composing your digital story. See **Figure 7**. Each story can include text, images, and videos. You create a Sway by adding text and media content into a Storyline section, or **card**. To add pictures, videos, or documents, select a card in the left pane and then select the Insert Content button. The first card in a Sway presentation contains a title and background image.

Figure 7: Creating a Sway site

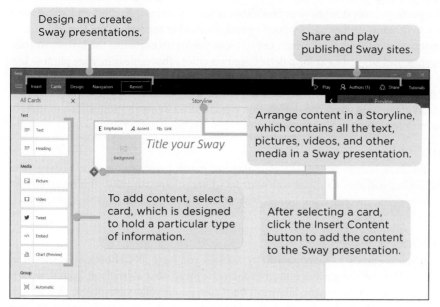

Design and create Sway presentations.

Share and play published Sway sites.

Arrange content in a Storyline, which contains all the text, pictures, videos, and other media in a Sway presentation.

To add content, select a card, which is designed to hold a particular type of information.

After selecting a card, click the Insert Content button to add the content to the Sway presentation.

Adding Content to Build a Story

As you work, Sway searches the Internet to help you find relevant images, videos, tweets, and other content from online sources such as Bing, YouTube, Twitter, and Facebook. You can drag content from the search results right into the Storyline. In addition, you can upload your own images and videos directly in the presentation. For example, if you are creating a Sway presentation about the market for commercial drones, Sway suggests content to incorporate into the presentation by displaying it in the left pane as search results. The search results include drone images tagged with a **Creative Commons license** at online sources as shown in **Figure 8**. A Creative Commons license is a public copyright license that allows the free distribution of an otherwise copyrighted work. In addition, you can specify the source of the media. For example, you can add your own Facebook or OneNote pictures and videos in Sway without leaving the app.

On the Job Now

If you have a Microsoft Word document containing an outline of your business content, drag the outline into Sway to create a card for each topic.

Figure 8: Images in Sway search results

Select the source of media objects

Information about Creative Commons licenses

Storyline title

The Market for Commercial Drones

Drag an image to the picture placeholder box

Suggested images in the search results

On the Job Now

If your project team wants to collaborate on a Sway presentation, click the Authors button on the navigation bar to invite others to edit the presentation.

Designing a Sway

Sway professionally designs your Storyline content by resizing background images and fonts to fit your display, and by floating text, animating media, embedding video, and removing images as a page scrolls out of view. Sway also evaluates the images in your Storyline and suggests a color palette based on colors that appear in your photos. Use the Design button to display tools including color palettes, font choices, **animation emphasis effects**, and style templates to provide a personality for a Sway presentation. Instead of creating your own design, you can click the Remix button, which randomly selects unique designs for your Sway site.

Publishing a Sway

Use the Play button to display your finished Sway presentation as a website. The Address bar includes a unique web address where others can view your Sway site. As the author, you can edit a published Sway site by clicking the Edit button (pencil icon) on the Sway toolbar.

Sharing a Sway

When you are ready to share your Sway website, you have several options as shown in **Figure 9**. Use the Share slider button to share the Sway site publically or keep it private. If you add the Sway site to the Microsoft **Docs.com** public gallery, anyone worldwide can use Bing, Google, or other search engines to find, view, and share your Sway site. You can also share your Sway site using Facebook, Twitter, Google+, Yammer, and other social media sites. Link your presentation to any webpage or email the link to your audience. Sway can also generate a code for embedding the link within another webpage.

Figure 9: Sharing a Sway site

Share button

| ▷ Play | ♟ Authors (1) | ♻ Share |

Share ⬤ Just me

Drag the slider button to Just me to keep the Sway site private

Share with the world

Docs.com - Your public gallery

Post the Sway site on Docs.com

Share with friends

Options differ depending on your Microsoft account

Send friends a link to the Sway site

https://sway.com/JQDFrUaxmg4lEbbk

◢ More options

☑ Viewers can duplicate this Sway

Stop sharing

Try This Now

1: Creating a Sway Resume

Learn to use Sway! Links to companion **Sways**, featuring **videos** with hands-on instructions, are located on www.cengagebrain.com.

Sway is a digital storytelling app. Create a Sway resume to share the skills, job experiences, and achievements you have that match the requirements of a future job interest. Perform the following tasks:

    a. Create a new presentation in Sway to use as a digital resume. Title the Sway Storyline with your full name and then select a background image.

    b. Create three separate sections titled **Academic Background, Work Experience**, and **Skills**, and insert text, a picture, and a paragraph or bulleted points in each section. Be sure to include your own picture.

    c. Add a fourth section that includes a video about your school that you find online.

    d. Customize the design of your presentation.

    e. Submit your assignment link in the format specified by your instructor.

2: Creating an Online Sway Newsletter

Newsletters are designed to capture the attention of their target audience. Using Sway, create a newsletter for a club, organization, or your favorite music group. Perform the following tasks:

    a. Create a new presentation in Sway to use as a digital newsletter for a club, organization, or your favorite music group. Provide a title for the Sway Storyline and select an appropriate background image.

    b. Select three separate sections with appropriate titles, such as Upcoming Events. In each section, insert text, a picture, and a paragraph or bulleted points.

    c. Add a fourth section that includes a video about your selected topic.

    d. Customize the design of your presentation.

    e. Submit your assignment link in the format specified by your instructor.

3: Creating and Sharing a Technology Presentation

To place a Sway presentation in the hands of your entire audience, you can share a link to the Sway presentation. Create a Sway presentation on a new technology and share it with your class. Perform the following tasks:

    a. Create a new presentation in Sway about a cutting-edge technology topic. Provide a title for the Sway Storyline and select a background image.

    b. Create four separate sections about your topic, and include text, a picture, and a paragraph in each section.

    c. Add a fifth section that includes a video about your topic.

    d. Customize the design of your presentation.

    e. Share the link to your Sway with your classmates and submit your assignment link in the format specified by your instructor.

Introduction to Office Mix

add-in | clip | slide recording | Slide Notes | screen recording | free-response quiz

Bottom Line
- Office Mix is a free PowerPoint add-in from Microsoft that adds features to PowerPoint.
- The Mix tab on the PowerPoint ribbon provides tools for creating screen recordings, videos, interactive quizzes, and live webpages.

To enliven business meetings and lectures, Microsoft adds a new dimension to presentations with a powerful toolset called Office Mix, a free add-in for PowerPoint. (An **add-in** is software that works with an installed app to extend its features.) Using Office Mix, you can record yourself on video, capture still and moving images on your desktop, and insert interactive elements such as quizzes and live webpages directly into PowerPoint slides. When you post the finished presentation to OneDrive, Office Mix provides a link you can share with friends and colleagues. Anyone with an Internet connection and a web browser can watch a published Office Mix presentation, such as the one in **Figure 10**, on a computer or mobile device.

Figure 10: Office Mix presentation

Learn to use Office Mix!
Links to companion **Sways**, featuring **videos** with hands-on instructions, are located on www.cengagebrain.com.

Adding Office Mix to PowerPoint

To get started, you create an Office Mix account at the website mix.office.com using an email address or a Facebook or Google account. Next, you download and install the Office Mix add-in (see **Figure 11**). Office Mix appears as a new tab named Mix on the PowerPoint ribbon in versions of Office 2013 and Office 2016 running on personal computers (PCs).

Figure 11: Getting started with Office Mix

Capturing Video Clips

A **clip** is a short segment of audio, such as music, or video. After finishing the content on a PowerPoint slide, you can use Office Mix to add a video clip to animate or illustrate the content. Office Mix creates video clips in two ways: by recording live action on a webcam and by capturing screen images and movements. If your computer has a webcam, you can record yourself and annotate the slide to create a **slide recording** as shown in **Figure 12**.

Figure 12: Making a slide recording

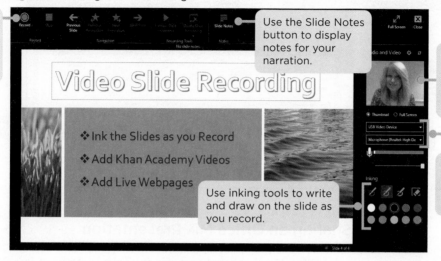

Record your voice; also record video if your computer has a camera.

Use the Slide Notes button to display notes for your narration.

For best results, look directly at your webcam while recording video.

Choose a video and audio device to record images and sound.

Use inking tools to write and draw on the slide as you record.

When you are making a slide recording, you can record your spoken narration at the same time. The **Slide Notes** feature works like a teleprompter to help you focus on your presentation content instead of memorizing your narration. Use the Inking tools to make annotations or add highlighting using different pen types and colors. After finishing a recording, edit the video in PowerPoint to trim the length or set playback options.

The second way to create a video is to capture on-screen images and actions with or without a voiceover. This method is ideal if you want to show how to use your favorite website or demonstrate an app such as OneNote. To share your screen with an audience, select the part of the screen you want to show in the video. Office Mix captures everything that happens in that area to create a **screen recording**, as shown in **Figure 13**. Office Mix inserts the screen recording as a video in the slide.

Figure 13: Making a screen recording

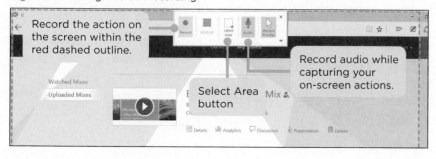

Record the action on the screen within the red dashed outline.

Record audio while capturing your on-screen actions.

Select Area button

Inserting Quizzes, Live Webpages, and Apps

To enhance and assess audience understanding, make your slides interactive by adding quizzes, live webpages, and apps. Quizzes give immediate feedback to the user as shown in **Figure 14**. Office Mix supports several quiz formats, including a **free-response quiz** similar to a short answer quiz, and true/false, multiple-choice, and multiple-response formats.

Figure 14: Creating an interactive quiz

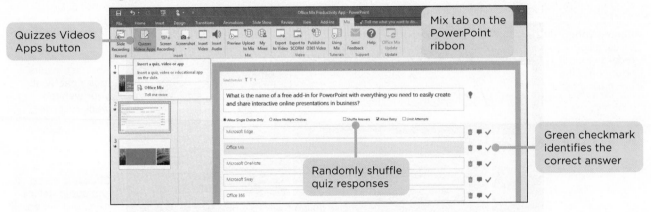

Quizzes Videos Apps button

Mix tab on the PowerPoint ribbon

Green checkmark identifies the correct answer

Randomly shuffle quiz responses

Sharing an Office Mix Presentation

When you complete your work with Office Mix, upload the presentation to your personal Office Mix dashboard as shown in **Figure 15**. Users of PCs, Macs, iOS devices, and Android devices can access and play Office Mix presentations. The Office Mix dashboard displays built-in analytics that include the quiz results and how much time viewers spent on each slide. You can play completed Office Mix presentations online or download them as movies.

Figure 15: Sharing an Office Mix presentation

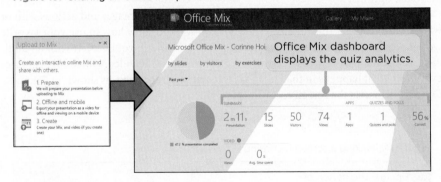

Office Mix dashboard displays the quiz analytics.

Try This Now

Learn to use Office Mix!

Links to companion **Sways**, featuring **videos** with hands-on instructions, are located on www.cengagebrain.com.

1: Creating an Office Mix Tutorial for OneNote

Note: This activity requires a microphone on your computer.

Office Mix makes it easy to record screens and their contents. Create PowerPoint slides with an Office Mix screen recording to show OneNote 2016 features. Perform the following tasks:

a. Create a PowerPoint presentation with the Ion Boardroom template. Create an opening slide with the title **My Favorite OneNote Features** and enter your name in the subtitle.

b. Create three additional slides, each titled with a new feature of OneNote. Open OneNote and use the Mix tab in PowerPoint to capture three separate screen recordings that teach your favorite features.

c. Add a fifth slide that quizzes the user with a multiple-choice question about OneNote and includes four responses. Be sure to insert a checkmark indicating the correct response.

d. Upload the completed presentation to your Office Mix dashboard and share the link with your instructor.

e. Submit your assignment link in the format specified by your instructor.

2: Teaching Augmented Reality with Office Mix

Note: This activity requires a webcam or built-in video camera on your computer.

A local elementary school has asked you to teach augmented reality to its students using Office Mix. Perform the following tasks:

a. Research augmented reality using your favorite online search tools.

b. Create a PowerPoint presentation with the Frame template. Create an opening slide with the title **Augmented Reality** and enter your name in the subtitle.

c. Create a slide with four bullets summarizing your research of augmented reality. Create a 20-second slide recording of yourself providing a quick overview of augmented reality.

d. Create another slide with a 30-second screen recording of a video about augmented reality from a site such as YouTube or another video-sharing site.

e. Add a final slide that quizzes the user with a true/false question about augmented reality. Be sure to insert a checkmark indicating the correct response.

f. Upload the completed presentation to your Office Mix dashboard and share the link with your instructor.

g. Submit your assignment link in the format specified by your instructor.

3: Marketing a Travel Destination with Office Mix

Note: This activity requires a webcam or built-in video camera on your computer.

To convince your audience to travel to a particular city, create a slide presentation marketing any city in the world using a slide recording, screen recording, and a quiz. Perform the following tasks:

a. Create a PowerPoint presentation with any template. Create an opening slide with the title of the city you are marketing as a travel destination and your name in the subtitle.

b. Create a slide with four bullets about the featured city. Create a 30-second slide recording of yourself explaining why this city is the perfect vacation destination.

c. Create another slide with a 20-second screen recording of a travel video about the city from a site such as YouTube or another video-sharing site.

d. Add a final slide that quizzes the user with a multiple-choice question about the featured city with five responses. Be sure to include a checkmark indicating the correct response.

e. Upload the completed presentation to your Office Mix dashboard and share your link with your instructor.

f. Submit your assignment link in the format specified by your instructor.

Introduction to Microsoft Edge

Reading view | Hub | Cortana | Web Note | Inking | sandbox

Microsoft Edge is the default web browser developed for the Windows 10 operating system as a replacement for Internet Explorer. Unlike its predecessor, Edge lets you write on webpages, read webpages without advertisements and other distractions, and search for information using a virtual personal assistant. The Edge interface is clean and basic, as shown in **Figure 16**, meaning you can pay more attention to the webpage content.

Figure 16: Microsoft Edge tools

Forward button · New tab button · Web address in the Address bar · Add to favorites or reading list button · Back button · Reading view button · More button · Refresh (F5) button · Hub (Favorites, reading list, history, and downloads) button · Share Web Note button · Make a Web Note button

Browsing the Web with Microsoft Edge

One of the fastest browsers available, Edge allows you to type search text directly in the Address bar. As you view the resulting webpage, you can switch to **Reading view**, which is available for most news and research sites, to eliminate distracting advertisements. For example, if you are catching up on technology news online, the webpage might be difficult to read due to a busy layout cluttered with ads. Switch to Reading view to refresh the page and remove the original page formatting, ads, and menu sidebars to read the article distraction-free.

Consider the **Hub** in Microsoft Edge as providing one-stop access to all the things you collect on the web, such as your favorite websites, reading list, surfing history, and downloaded files.

Locating Information with Cortana

Cortana, the Windows 10 virtual assistant, plays an important role in Microsoft Edge. After you turn on Cortana, it appears as an animated circle in the Address bar when you might need assistance, as shown in the restaurant website in **Figure 17**. When you click the Cortana icon, a pane slides in from the right of the browser window to display detailed information about the restaurant, including maps and reviews. Cortana can also assist you in defining words, finding the weather, suggesting coupons for shopping, updating stock market information, and calculating math.

Figure 17: Cortana providing restaurant information

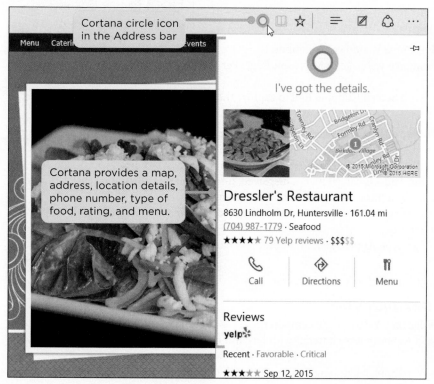

Cortana circle icon in the Address bar

Cortana provides a map, address, location details, phone number, type of food, rating, and menu.

I've got the details.

Dressler's Restaurant
8630 Lindholm Dr, Huntersville · 161.04 mi
(704) 987-1779 · Seafood
★★★★☆ 79 Yelp reviews · $$$$$

Call   Directions   Menu

Reviews
yelp⋆
Recent · Favorable · Critical
★★★☆☆ Sep 12, 2015

Annotating Webpages

One of the most impressive Microsoft Edge features are the **Web Note** tools, which you use to write on a webpage or to highlight text. When you click the Make a Web Note button, an **Inking** toolbar appears, as shown in **Figure 18**, that provides writing and drawing tools. These tools include an eraser, a pen, and a highlighter with different colors. You can also insert a typed note and copy a screen image (called a screen clipping). You can draw with a pointing device, fingertip, or stylus using different pen colors. Whether you add notes to a recipe, annotate sources for a research paper, or select a product while shopping online, the Web Note tools can enhance your productivity. After you complete your notes, click the Save button to save the annotations to OneNote, your Favorites list, or your Reading list. You can share the inked page with others using the Share Web Note button.

On the Job Now

To enhance security, Microsoft Edge runs in a partial sandbox, an arrangement that prevents attackers from gaining control of your computer. Browsing within the **sandbox** protects computer resources and information from hackers.

Figure 18: Web Note tools in Microsoft Edge

Inking toolbar with Web Note tools for making annotations

Writing and drawing created with the Pen tool

Highlighted text

Work anywhere

The integrated Kickstand features multiple positions so you can work comfortably whether you're on a plane, at your desk, or in front of the television.

I am considering purchasing the new Surface Pro for school

Save a copy of the webpage with annotations

Typed note

Try This Now

Learn to use Edge!
Links to companion **Sways**, featuring **videos** with hands-on instructions, are located on www.cengagebrain.com.

1: Using Cortana in Microsoft Edge

Note: This activity requires using Microsoft Edge on a Windows 10 computer.

Cortana can assist you in finding information on a webpage in Microsoft Edge. Perform the following tasks:

a. Create a Word document using the Word Screen Clipping tool to capture the following screenshots.

- Screenshot A—Using Microsoft Edge, open a webpage with a technology news article. Right-click a term in the article and ask Cortana to define it.
- Screenshot B—Using Microsoft Edge, open the website of a fancy restaurant in a city near you. Make sure the Cortana circle icon is displayed in the Address bar. (If it's not displayed, find a different restaurant website.) Click the Cortana circle icon to display a pane with information about the restaurant.
- Screenshot C—Using Microsoft Edge, type **10 USD to Euros** in the Address bar without pressing the Enter key. Cortana converts the U.S. dollars to Euros.
- Screenshot D—Using Microsoft Edge, type **Apple stock** in the Address bar without pressing the Enter key. Cortana displays the current stock quote.

b. Submit your assignment in the format specified by your instructor.

2: Viewing Online News with Reading View

Note: This activity requires using Microsoft Edge on a Windows 10 computer.

Reading view in Microsoft Edge can make a webpage less cluttered with ads and other distractions. Perform the following tasks:

a. Create a Word document using the Word Screen Clipping tool to capture the following screenshots.

- Screenshot A—Using Microsoft Edge, open the website **mashable.com**. Open a technology article. Click the Reading view button to display an ad-free page that uses only basic text formatting.
- Screenshot B—Using Microsoft Edge, open the website **bbc.com**. Open any news article. Click the Reading view button to display an ad-free page that uses only basic text formatting.
- Screenshot C—Make three types of annotations (Pen, Highlighter, and Add a typed note) on the BBC article page displayed in Reading view.

b. Submit your assignment in the format specified by your instructor.

3: Inking with Microsoft Edge

Note: This activity requires using Microsoft Edge on a Windows 10 computer.

Microsoft Edge provides many annotation options to record your ideas. Perform the following tasks:

a. Open the website **wolframalpha.com** in the Microsoft Edge browser. Wolfram Alpha is a well-respected academic search engine. Type **US$100 1965 dollars in 2015** in the Wolfram Alpha search text box and press the Enter key.

b. Click the Make a Web Note button to display the Web Note tools. Using the Pen tool, draw a circle around the result on the webpage. Save the page to OneNote.

c. In the Wolfram Alpha search text box, type the name of the city closest to where you live and press the Enter key. Using the Highlighter tool, highlight at least three interesting results. Add a note and then type a sentence about what you learned about this city. Save the page to OneNote. Share your OneNote notebook with your instructor.

d. Submit your assignment link in the format specified by your instructor.

Getting Started with Microsoft Office 2016

CASE ▶ This module introduces you to the most frequently used programs in Office, as well as common features they all share.

Module Objectives

After completing this module, you will be able to:

- Understand the Office 2016 suite
- Start an Office app
- Identify Office 2016 screen elements
- Create and save a file

- Open a file and save it with a new name
- View and print your work
- Get Help, close a file, and exit an app

Files You Will Need

OF 1-1.xlsx

Understand the Office 2016 Suite

Microsoft Office 2016 is a group of programs—which are also called applications or apps—designed to help you create documents, collaborate with coworkers, and track and analyze information. You use different Office programs to accomplish specific tasks, such as writing a letter or producing a presentation, yet all the programs have a similar look and feel. Microsoft Office 2016 apps feature a common, context-sensitive user interface, so you can get up to speed faster and use advanced features with greater ease. The Office apps are bundled together in a group called a **suite**. The Office suite is available in several configurations, but all include Word, Excel, PowerPoint, and OneNote. Some configurations include Access, Outlook, Publisher, Skype, and OneDrive. **CASE** *As part of your job, you need to understand how each Office app is best used to complete specific tasks.*

DETAILS

The Office apps covered in this book include:

• **Microsoft Word 2016**

When you need to create any kind of text-based document, such as a memo, newsletter, or multipage report, Word is the program to use. You can easily make your documents look great by using formatting tools and inserting eye-catching graphics. The Word document shown in **FIGURE 1-1** contains a company logo and simple formatting.

• **Microsoft Excel 2016**

Excel is the perfect solution when you need to work with numeric values and make calculations. It puts the power of formulas, functions, charts, and other analytical tools into the hands of every user, so you can analyze sales projections, calculate loan payments, and present your findings in a professional manner. The Excel worksheet shown in **FIGURE 1-1** tracks checkbook transactions. Because Excel automatically recalculates results whenever a value changes, the information is always up to date. A chart illustrates how the monthly expenses are broken down.

• **Microsoft PowerPoint 2016**

Using PowerPoint, it's easy to create powerful presentations complete with graphics, transitions, and even a soundtrack. Using professionally designed themes and clip art, you can quickly and easily create dynamic slide shows such as the one shown in **FIGURE 1-1**.

• **Microsoft Access 2016**

Access is a relational database program that helps you keep track of large amounts of quantitative data, such as product inventories or employee records. The form shown in **FIGURE 1-1** can be used to generate reports on customer invoices and tours.

Microsoft Office has benefits beyond the power of each program, including:

• **Note-taking made simple; available on all devices**

Use OneNote to take notes (organized in tabbed pages) on information that can be accessed on your computer, tablet, or phone. Share the editable results with others. Contents can include text, web page clips (using OneNote Clipper), email contents (directly inserted into a default section), photos (using Office Lens), and web pages.

• **Common user interface: Improving business processes**

Because the Office suite apps have a similar **interface**, your experience using one app's tools makes it easy to learn those in the other apps. Office documents are **compatible** with one another, so you can easily **integrate**, or combine, elements—for example, you can add an Excel chart to a PowerPoint slide, or an Access table to a Word document.

Most Office programs include the capability to incorporate feedback—called **online collaboration**—across the Internet or a company network.

FIGURE 1-1: Microsoft Office 2016 documents

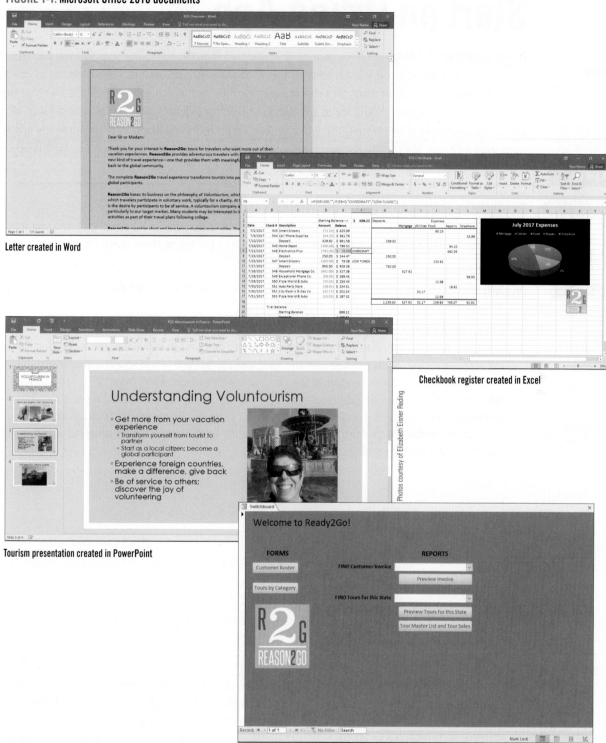

Letter created in Word

Checkbook register created in Excel

Tourism presentation created in PowerPoint

Form created in Access

Photos courtesy of Elizabeth Eisner Reding

What is Office 365?

Until recently, most consumers purchased Microsoft Office in a traditional way: by buying a retail package from a store or downloading it from Microsoft.com. You can still purchase Microsoft Office 2016 in this traditional way—but you can also now purchase it as a subscription service called Microsoft Office 365, which is available in a wide variety of configurations.

Depending on which configuration you purchase, you will always have access to the most up-to-date versions of the apps in your package and, in many cases, can install these apps on multiple computers, tablets, and phones. And if you change computers or devices, you can easily uninstall the apps from an old device and install them on a new one.

Start an Office App

Learning Outcomes
- Start an Office app
- Explain the purpose of a template
- Start a new blank document

To get started using Microsoft Office, you need to start, or **launch**, the Office app you want to use. An easy way to start the app you want is to press the Windows key, type the first few characters of the app name you want to search for, then click the app name In the Best match list. You will discover that there are many ways to accomplish just about any Windows task; for example, you can also see a list of all the apps on your computer by pressing the Windows key, then clicking All Apps. When you see the app you want, click its name. **CASE** ▶ *You decide to familiarize yourself with Office by starting Microsoft Word.*

STEPS

1. **Click the Start button ⊞ on the Windows taskbar**

   The Start menu opens, listing the most used apps on your computer. You can locate the app you want to open by clicking the app name if you see it, or you can type the app name to search for it.

2. **Type word**

   Your screen now displays "Word 2016" under "Best match", along with any other app that has "word" as part of its name (such as WordPad). See **FIGURE 1-2**.

3. **Click Word 2016**

   Word 2016 launches, and the Word **start screen** appears, as shown in **FIGURE 1-3**. The start screen is a landing page that appears when you first start an Office app. The left side of this screen displays recent files you have opened. (If you have never opened any files, then there will be no files listed under Recent.) The right side displays images depicting different templates you can use to create different types of documents. A **template** is a file containing professionally designed content and formatting that you can easily customize for your own needs. You can also start from scratch using the Blank Document template, which contains only minimal formatting settings.

Enabling touch mode

If you are using a touch screen with any of the Office 2016 apps, you can enable the touch mode to give the user interface a more spacious look, making it easier to navigate with your fingertips. Enable touch mode by clicking the Quick Access toolbar list arrow, then clicking Touch/Mouse Mode to select it. Then you'll see the Touch Mode button 👆 in the Quick Access toolbar. Click 👆, and you'll see the interface spread out.

Using shortcut keys to move between Office programs

You can switch between open apps using a keyboard shortcut. The [Alt][Tab] keyboard combination lets you either switch quickly to the next open program or file or choose one from a gallery. To switch immediately to the next open program or file, press [Alt][Tab]. To choose from all open programs and files, press and hold [Alt], then press and release [Tab] without releasing [Alt]. A gallery opens on screen, displaying the filename and a thumbnail image of each open program and file, as well as of the desktop. Each time you press [Tab] while holding [Alt], the selection cycles to the next open file or location. Release [Alt] when the program, file, or location you want to activate is selected.

FIGURE 1-2: **Searching for the Word app**

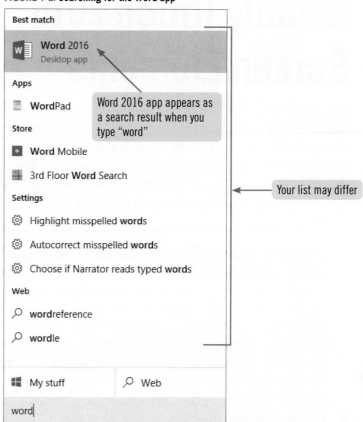

Best match

Word 2016
Desktop app

Apps

WordPad

Store

Word Mobile

3rd Floor Word Search

Settings

Highlight misspelled words

Autocorrect misspelled words

Choose if Narrator reads typed words

Web

wordreference

wordle

My stuff   Web

word

Word 2016 app appears as a search result when you type "word"

Your list may differ

FIGURE 1-3: **Word start screen**

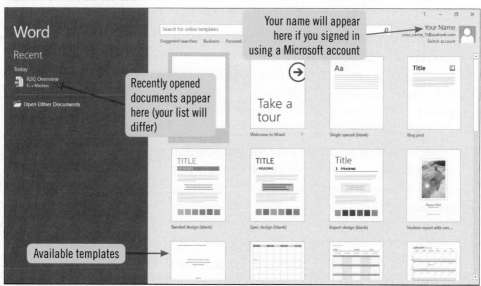

Word

Recent

Today

R2G Overview
C: » Masters

Open Other Documents

Search for online templates

Suggested searches: Business Personal

Take a tour

Welcome to Word

Single spaced (blank)

Blog post

Aa

Title

TITLE
HEADING

Banded design (blank)

TITLE
HEADING

Spec design (blank)

Title
1 HEADING

Report design (blank)

Student report with cov...

Your Name
your_name_15@outlook.com
Switch account

Your name will appear here if you signed in using a Microsoft account

Recently opened documents appear here (your list will differ)

Available templates

Office 2016

Using the Office Clipboard

You can use the Office Clipboard to cut and copy items from one Office program and paste them into others. The Office Clipboard can store a maximum of 24 items. To access it, open the Office Clipboard task pane by clicking the dialog box launcher [icon] in the Clipboard group on the Home tab. Each time you copy a selection, it is saved in the Office Clipboard. Each entry in the Office Clipboard includes an icon that tells you the program it was created in. To paste an entry, click in the document where you want it to appear, then click the item in the Office Clipboard. To delete an item from the Office Clipboard, right-click the item, then click Delete.

Identify Office 2016 Screen Elements

Learning Outcomes
- Identify basic components of the user interface
- Display and use Backstage view
- Adjust the zoom level

One of the benefits of using Office is that its apps have much in common, making them easy to learn and making it simple to move from one to another. All Office 2016 apps share a similar user interface, so you can use your knowledge of one to get up to speed in another. A **user interface** is a collective term for all the ways you interact with a software program. The user interface in Office 2016 provides intuitive ways to choose commands, work with files, and navigate in the program window. **CASE** *Familiarize yourself with some of the common interface elements in Office by examining the PowerPoint program window.*

STEPS

1. **Click the Start button 🖽 on the Windows taskbar, type** pow, **click** PowerPoint 2016, **then click** Blank Presentation

    PowerPoint starts and opens a new file, which contains a blank slide. Refer to FIGURE 1-4 to identify common elements of the Office user interface. The **document window** occupies most of the screen. At the top of every Office program window is a **title bar** that displays the document name and program name. Below the title bar is the **Ribbon**, which displays commands you're likely to need for the current task. Commands are organized onto **tabs**. The tab names appear at the top of the Ribbon, and the active tab appears in front. The **Share button** in the upper-right corner lets you invite other users to view your cloud-stored Word, Excel, or Powerpoint file.

2. **Click the** File tab

    The File tab opens, displaying **Backstage view**. It is called Backstage view because the commands available here are for working with the files "behind the scenes." The navigation bar on the left side of Backstage view contains commands to perform actions common to most Office programs.

3. **Click the** Back button ⬅ **to close Backstage view and return to the document window, then click the** Design tab **on the Ribbon**

    To display a different tab, click its name. Each tab contains related commands arranged into **groups** to make features easy to find. On the Design tab, the Themes group displays available design themes in a **gallery**, or visual collection of choices you can browse. Many groups contain a **launcher**, which you can click to open a dialog box or pane from which to choose related commands.

4. **Move the mouse pointer ⇱ over the** Ion Boardroom theme **in the Themes group as shown in** FIGURE 1-5, **but** *do not click* **the mouse button**

    The Ion Boardroom theme is temporarily applied to the slide in the document window. However, because you did not click the theme, you did not permanently change the slide. With the **Live Preview** feature, you can point to a choice, see the results, then decide if you want to make the change. Live Preview is available throughout Office.

5. **Move ⇱ away from the Ribbon and towards the slide**

    If you had clicked the Ion theme, it would be applied to this slide. Instead, the slide remains unchanged.

6. **Point to the** Zoom slider `– ——|—— + 100%` **on the status bar, then drag to the right until the Zoom level reads** 166%

    The slide display is enlarged. Zoom tools are located on the status bar. You can drag the slider or click the Zoom In or Zoom Out buttons to zoom in or out on an area of interest. **Zooming in** (a higher percentage), makes a document appear bigger on screen but less of it fits on the screen at once; **zooming out** (a lower percentage) lets you see more of the document at a reduced size.

7. **Click the** Zoom Out button `–` **on the status bar to the left of the Zoom slider until the Zoom level reads** 120%

FIGURE 1-4: PowerPoint program window

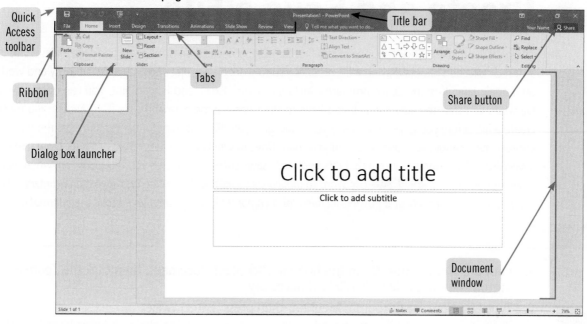

Quick Access toolbar

Ribbon

Dialog box launcher

Tabs

Title bar

Share button

Document window

Click to add title

Click to add subtitle

FIGURE 1-5: Viewing a theme with Live Preview

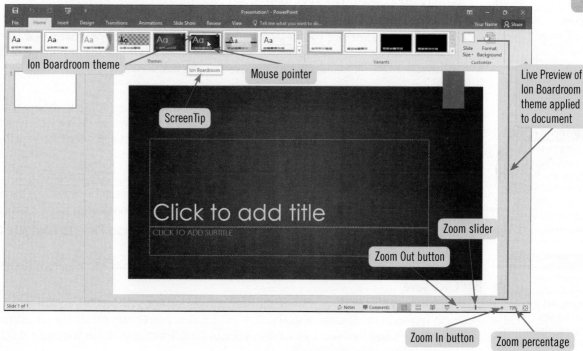

Ion Boardroom theme

Mouse pointer

ScreenTip

Click to add title

CLICK TO ADD SUBTITLE

Live Preview of Ion Boardroom theme applied to document

Zoom slider

Zoom Out button

Zoom In button

Zoom percentage

Using Backstage view

Backstage view in each Microsoft Office app offers "one stop shopping" for many commonly performed tasks, such as opening and saving a file, printing and previewing a document, defining document properties, sharing information, and exiting a program. Backstage view opens when you click the File tab in any Office app, and while features such as the Ribbon, Mini toolbar, and Live Preview all help you work *in* your documents, the File tab and Backstage view help you work *with* your documents. You can click commands in the navigation pane to open different places for working with your documents, such as the Open place, the Save place, and so on. You can return to your active document by clicking the Back button.

Create and Save a File

Learning Outcomes
• Create a file
• Save a file
• Explain OneDrive

When working in an Office app, one of the first things you need to do is to create and save a file. A **file** is a stored collection of data. Saving a file enables you to work on a project now, then put it away and work on it again later. In some Office programs, including Word, Excel, and PowerPoint, you can open a new file when you start the app, then all you have to do is enter some data and save it. In Access, you must create a file before you enter any data. You should give your files meaningful names and save them in an appropriate location, such as a folder on your hard drive or OneDrive so they're easy to find. **OneDrive** is a Microsoft cloud storage system that lets you easily save, share, and access your files from anywhere you have Internet access. **CASE** *Use Word to familiarize yourself with creating and saving a document. First you'll type some notes about a possible location for a corporate meeting, then you'll save the information for later use.*

STEPS

1. **Click the Word button 📘 on the taskbar, click Blank document, then click the Zoom In button ➕ until the level is 120%, if necessary**

2. **Type Locations for Corporate Meeting, then press [Enter] twice**
   The text appears in the document window, and the **insertion point** blinks on a new blank line. The insertion point indicates where the next typed text will appear.

QUICK TIP
A filename can be up to 255 characters, including a file extension, and can include upper- or lowercase characters and spaces, but not ?, ", /, \, <, >, *, |, or :.

3. **Type Las Vegas, NV, press [Enter], type Chicago, IL, press [Enter], type Seattle, WA, press [Enter] twice, then type your name**

4. **Click the Save button 💾 on the Quick Access toolbar**
   Because this is the first time you are saving this new file, the Save place in Backstage view opens, showing various options for saving the file. See **FIGURE 1-6**. Once you save a file for the first time, clicking 💾 saves any changes to the file *without* opening the Save As dialog box.

5. **Click Browse**
   The Save As dialog box opens, as shown in **FIGURE 1-7**, where you can browse to the location where you want to save the file. The Address bar in the Save As dialog box displays the default location for saving the file, but you can change it to any location. The File name field contains a suggested name for the document based on text in the file, but you can enter a different name.

QUICK TIP
Saving a file to the Desktop creates a desktop icon that you can double-click to both launch a program and open a document.

6. **Type OF 1-Possible Corporate Meeting Locations**
   The text you type replaces the highlighted text. (The "OF 1-" in the filename indicates that the file is created in Office Module 1. You will see similar designations throughout this book when files are named.)

7. **In the Save As dialog box, use the Address bar or Navigation Pane to navigate to the location where you store your Data Files**
   You can store files on your computer, a network drive, your OneDrive, or any acceptable storage device.

QUICK TIP
To create a new blank file when a file is open, click the File tab, click New on the navigation bar, then choose a template.

8. **Click Save**
   The Save As dialog box closes, the new file is saved to the location you specified, and the name of the document appears in the title bar, as shown in **FIGURE 1-8**. (You may or may not see the file extension ".docx" after the filename.) See **TABLE 1-1** for a description of the different types of files you create in Office, and the file extensions associated with each.

TABLE 1-1: Common filenames and default file extensions

file created in	is called a	and has the default extension
Word	document	.docx
Excel	workbook	.xlsx
PowerPoint	presentation	.pptx
Access	database	.accdb

FIGURE 1-6: Save place in Backstage view

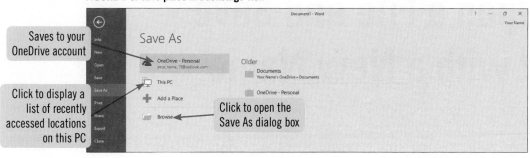

Saves to your OneDrive account

Click to display a list of recently accessed locations on this PC

Click to open the Save As dialog box

FIGURE 1-7: Save As dialog box

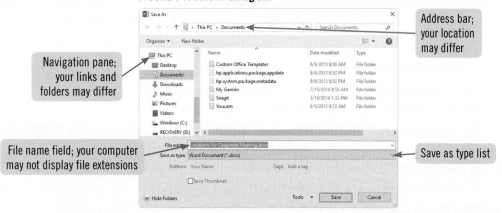

Navigation pane; your links and folders may differ

Address bar; your location may differ

File name field; your computer may not display file extensions

Save as type list

FIGURE 1-8: Saved and named Word document

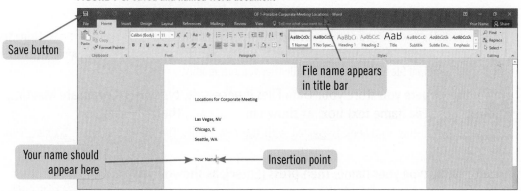

Save button

File name appears in title bar

Your name should appear here

Insertion point

Office 2016

Saving files to OneDrive

All Office programs include the capability to incorporate feedback—called **online collaboration**—across the Internet or a company network. Using **cloud computing** (work done in a virtual environment), you can store your work in the cloud. Using OneDrive, a file storage service from Microsoft, you and your colleagues can create and store documents in the cloud and make the documents available anywhere there is Internet access to whomever you choose. To use OneDrive, you need a Microsoft Account, which you obtain at onedrive.live.com. Pricing and storage plans vary based on the type of Microsoft account you have. When you are logged into your Microsoft account and you

save a file in any of the Office apps, the first option in the Save As screen is your OneDrive. Double-click your OneDrive option, and the Save As dialog box opens displaying a location in the address bar unique to your OneDrive account. Type a name in the File name text box, then click Save and your file is saved to your OneDrive. To sync your files with OneDrive, you'll need to download and install the OneDrive for Windows app. Then, when you open Explorer, you'll notice a new folder called OneDrive has been added to your folder. In this folder is a sub-folder called Documents. This means if your Internet connection fails, you can work on your files offline.

Getting Started with Microsoft Office 2016

Office 9

Open a File and Save It with a New Name

Learning
Outcomes
• Open an existing
  file
• Save a file with a
  new name

In many cases as you work in Office, you need to use an existing file. It might be a file you or a coworker created earlier as a work in progress, or it could be a complete document that you want to use as the basis for another. For example, you might want to create a budget for this year using the budget you created last year; instead of typing in all the categories and information from scratch, you could open last year's budget, save it with a new name, and just make changes to update it for the current year. By opening the existing file and saving it with the Save As command, you create a duplicate that you can modify to suit your needs, while the original file remains intact. **CASE** ▶ *Use Excel to open an existing workbook file, and save it with a new name so the original remains unchanged.*

STEPS

1. **Click the Start button ⊞ on the Windows taskbar, type exc, click Excel 2016, click Open Other Workbooks, This PC, then click Browse**

   The Open dialog box opens, where you can navigate to any drive or folder accessible to your computer to locate a file.

2. **In the Open dialog box, navigate to the location where you store your Data Files**

   The files available in the current folder are listed, as shown in FIGURE 1-9. This folder displays one file.

3. **Click OF 1-1.xlsx, then click Open**

   The dialog box closes, and the file opens in Excel. An Excel file is an electronic spreadsheet, so the new file displays a grid of rows and columns you can use to enter and organize data.

4. **Click the File tab, click Save As on the navigation bar, then click Browse**

   The Save As dialog box opens, and the current filename is highlighted in the File name text box. Using the Save As command enables you to create a copy of the current, existing file with a new name. This action preserves the original file and creates a new file that you can modify.

5. **Navigate to where you store your Data Files if necessary, type OF 1-Corporate Meeting Budget in the File name text box, as shown in FIGURE 1-10, then click Save**

   A copy of the existing workbook is created with the new name. The original file, OF 1-1.xlsx, closes automatically.

6. **Click cell A18, type your name, then press [Enter], as shown in FIGURE 1-11**

   In Excel, you enter data in cells, which are formed by the intersection of a row and a column. Cell A18 is at the intersection of column A and row 18. When you press [Enter], the cell pointer moves to cell A19.

7. **Click the Save button 🖫 on the Quick Access toolbar**

   Your name appears in the workbook, and your changes to the file are saved.

Exploring File Open options

You might have noticed that the Open button in the Open dialog box includes a list arrow to the right of the button. In a dialog box, if a button includes a list arrow you can click the button to invoke the command, or you can click the list arrow to see a list of related commands that you can apply to the currently selected file. The Open list arrow includes several related commands, including Open Read-Only and Open as Copy.

Clicking Open Read-Only opens a file that you can only save with a new name; you cannot make changes to the original file. Clicking Open as Copy creates and opens a copy of the selected file and inserts the word "Copy" in the file's title. Like the Save As command, these commands provide additional ways to use copies of existing files while ensuring that original files do not get changed by mistake.

FIGURE 1-9: Open dialog box

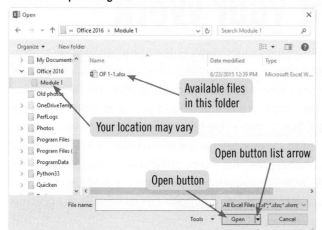

FIGURE 1-10: Save As dialog box

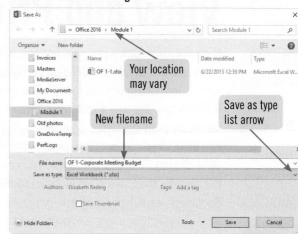

FIGURE 1-11: Your name added to the workbook

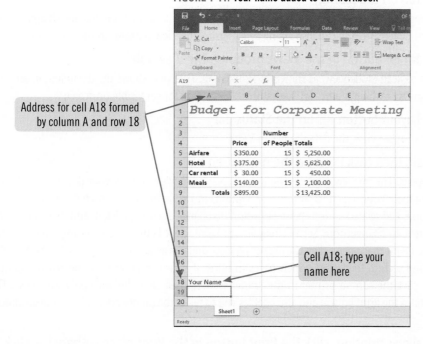

Working in Compatibility Mode

Not everyone upgrades to the newest version of Office. As a general rule, new software versions are **backward compatible**, meaning that documents saved by an older version can be read by newer software. To open documents created in older Office versions, Office 2016 includes a feature called Compatibility Mode. When you use Office 2016 to open a file created in an earlier version of Office, "Compatibility Mode" appears in the title bar, letting you know the file was created in an earlier but usable version of the program. If you are working with someone who

may not be using the newest version of the software, you can avoid possible incompatibility problems by saving your file in another, earlier format. To do this in an Office program, click the File tab, click Save As on the navigation bar, then click Browse. In the Save As dialog box, click the Save as type list arrow in the Save As dialog box, then click an option in the list. For example, if you're working in Excel, click Excel 97-2003 Workbook format in the Save as type list to save an Excel file so it can be opened in Excel 97 or Excel 2003.

View and Print Your Work

Learning Outcomes
- Describe and change views in an app
- Print a document

Each Microsoft Office program lets you switch among various **views** of the document window to show more or fewer details or a different combination of elements that make it easier to complete certain tasks, such as formatting or reading text. Changing your view of a document does not affect the file in any way, it affects only the way it looks on screen. If your computer is connected to a printer or a print server, you can easily print any Office document using the Print button in the Print place in Backstage view. Printing can be as simple as **previewing** the document to see exactly what the printed version will look like and then clicking the Print button. Or, you can customize the print job by printing only selected pages. You can also use the Share place in Backstage view or the Share button on the Ribbon (if available) to share a document, export to a different format, or save it to the cloud. **CASE** *Experiment with changing your view of a Word document, and then preview and print your work.*

STEPS

1. **Click the Word program button 🗗 on the taskbar**

   Word becomes active, and the program window fills the screen.

QUICK TIP

To minimize the display of the buttons and commands on tabs, click the Collapse the Ribbon button ⌃ on the lower-right end of the Ribbon.

2. **Click the View tab on the Ribbon**

   In most Office programs, the View tab on the Ribbon includes groups and commands for changing your view of the current document. You can also change views using the View buttons on the status bar.

3. **Click the Read Mode button in the Views group on the View tab**

   The view changes to Read Mode view, as shown in FIGURE 1-12. This view shows the document in an easy-to-read, distraction-free reading mode. Notice that the Ribbon is no longer visible on screen.

4. **Click the Print Layout button 🗐 on the Status bar**

   You return to Print Layout view, the default view in Word.

QUICK TIP

Office 2016 apps default to print to OneDrive.

5. **Click the File tab, then click Print on the navigation bar**

   The Print place opens. The preview pane on the right displays a preview of how your document will look when printed. Compare your screen to FIGURE 1-13. Options in the Settings section enable you to change margins, orientation, and related options before printing. To change a setting, click it, and then click a new setting. For instance, to change from Letter paper size to Legal, click Letter in the Settings section, then click Legal on the menu that opens. The document preview updates as you change the settings. You also can use the Settings section to change which pages to print. If your computer is connected to multiple printers, you can click the current printer in the Printer section, then click the one you want to use. The Print section contains the Print button and also enables you to select the number of copies of the document to print.

QUICK TIP

You can add the Quick Print button 🖶 to the Quick Access toolbar by clicking the Customize Quick Access Toolbar button, then clicking Quick Print. The Quick Print button prints one copy of your document using the default settings.

6. **If your school allows printing, click the Print button in the Print place (otherwise, click the Back button ⊙)**

   If you chose to print, a copy of the document prints, and Backstage view closes.

Customizing the Quick Access toolbar

You can customize the Quick Access toolbar to display your favorite commands. To do so, click the Customize Quick Access Toolbar button ▾ in the title bar, then click the command you want to add. If you don't see the command in the list, click More Commands to open the Quick Access Toolbar tab of the current program's Options dialog box. In the Options dialog box, use the Choose commands from list to choose a category, click the desired command in the list on the left, click Add to add it to the Quick Access toolbar, then click OK. To remove a button from the toolbar, click the name in the list on the right in the Options dialog box, then click Remove. To add a command to the Quick Access toolbar as you work, simply right-click the button on the Ribbon, then click Add to Quick Access Toolbar on the shortcut menu. To move the Quick Access toolbar below the Ribbon, click the Customize Quick Access Toolbar button, and then click Show Below the Ribbon.

FIGURE 1-12: Read Mode view

Print Layout button

View buttons on status bar

FIGURE 1-13: Print settings on the File tab

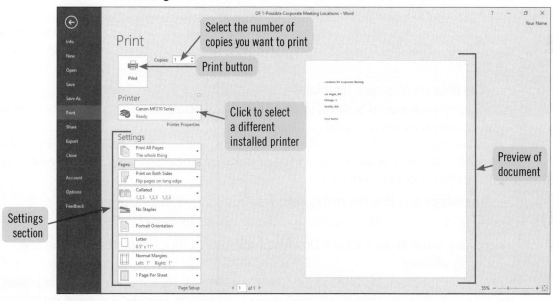

Select the number of copies you want to print

Print button

Click to select a different installed printer

Settings section

Preview of document

Creating a screen capture

A **screen capture** is a digital image of your screen, as if you took a picture of it with a camera. For instance, you might want to take a screen capture if an error message occurs and you want a Technical Support person to see exactly what's on the screen. You can create a screen capture using the Snipping Tool, an accessory designed to capture whole screens or portions of screens. To open the Snipping Tool, click the Start button on the Windows taskbar, type "sni", then click the Snipping Tool when it appears in the left panel. On the Snipping Tool toolbar, click New, then drag the pointer on the screen to select the area of the screen you want to capture. When you release the mouse button, the screen capture opens in the Snipping Tool window, and you can save, copy, or send it in an email. In Word, Excel, and PowerPoint 2016, you can capture screens or portions of screens and insert them in the current document using the Screenshot button in the Illustrations group on the Insert tab. Alternatively, you can create a screen capture by pressing [PrtScn]. (Keyboards differ, but you may find the [PrtScn] button in or near your keyboard's function keys.) Pressing this key places a digital image of your screen in the Windows temporary storage area known as the **Clipboard**. Open the document where you want the screen capture to appear, click the Home tab on the Ribbon (if necessary), then click the Paste button in the Clipboard group on the Home tab. The screen capture is pasted into the document.

Get Help, Close a File, and Exit an App

Learning Outcomes
- Display a ScreenTip
- Use Help
- Close a file
- Exit an app

You can get comprehensive help at any time by pressing [F1] in an Office app or clicking the Help button on the title bar. You can also get help in the form of a ScreenTip by pointing to almost any icon in the program window. When you're finished working in an Office document, you have a few choices for ending your work session. You close a file by clicking the File tab, then clicking Close; you exit a program by clicking the Close button on the title bar. Closing a file leaves a program running, while exiting a program closes all the open files in that program as well as the program itself. In all cases, Office reminds you if you try to close a file or exit a program and your document contains unsaved changes. **CASE** *Explore the Help system in Microsoft Office, and then close your documents and exit any open programs.*

STEPS

1. **Point to the Zoom button in the Zoom group on the View tab of the Ribbon**
   A ScreenTip appears that describes how the Zoom button works and explains where to find other zoom controls.

   QUICK TIP
   You can also open Help (in any of the Office apps) by pressing [F1].

2. **Click the Tell me box above the Ribbon, then type Choose a template**
   As you type in the Tell me box, a Smart list anticipates what you might want help with. If you see the task you want to complete, you can click it and Word will take you to the dialog box or options you need to complete the task. If you don't see the answer to your query, you can use the bottom two options to search the database.

   QUICK TIP
   If you are not connected to the Internet, the Help window displays on the Help content available on your computer.

3. **Click Get Help on "choose a template"**
   The Word Help window opens, as shown in FIGURE 1-14, displaying help results for choosing a template in Word. Each entry is a hyperlink you can click to open a list of topics. The Help window also includes a toolbar of useful Help commands such as printing and increasing the font size for easier readability, and a Search field. Office.com supplements the help content available on your computer with a wide variety of up-to-date topics, templates, and training.

4. **Click the Where do I find templates link in the results list Word Help window**
   The Word Help window changes, and a more detailed explanation appears below the topic.

   QUICK TIP
   You can print the entire current topic by clicking the Print button 🖶 on the Help toolbar, then clicking Print in the Print dialog box.

5. **If necessary, scroll down until the Download Microsoft Office templates topic fills the Word Help window**
   The topic is displayed in the Help window, as shown in FIGURE 1-15. The content in the window explains that you can create a wide variety of documents using a template (a pre-formatted document) and that you can get many templates free of charge.

6. **Click the Keep Help on Top button 📌 in the lower-right corner of the window**
   The Pin Help button rotates so the pin point is pointed towards the bottom of the screen: this allows you to read the Help window while you work on your document.

7. **Click the Word document window, notice the Help window remains visible**

8. **Click a blank area of the Help window, click 📌 to Unpin Help, click the Close button ✖ in the Help window, then click the Close button ✖ in the Word program window**
   Word closes, and the Excel program window is active.

9. **Click the Close button ✖ in the Excel program window, click the PowerPoint app button 📊 on the taskbar if necessary, then click the Close button ✖ to exit PowerPoint**
   Excel and PowerPoint both close.

FIGURE 1-14: Word Help window

Search field

Help toolbar

Word 2016 Help

Choose a template

Click to learn how to find templates

Where do I find templates?
In Microsoft templates all the formatting is complete; ... click My Templates or Personal, and then choose your template. ... Download Microsoft Office templates.

Edit templates
Edit templates. Whether you're starting from a built-in template or updating one of your own, Word's built-in tools help you update templates to suit your needs.

Create forms that users complete or print in Word
Create forms that users complete or print in Word. You can create a form in Microsoft Word by starting with a template and ... you want people to choose a ...

Zoom in or out of a document
Choose a particular zoom setting. You can choose how

Help topics are updated frequently; your list may differ

FIGURE 1-15: Create a document Help topic

Print button

Word 2016 Help

Choose a template

Download Microsoft Office templates

Do you want to create a resume, mailing label, budget, fax cover sheet, presentation, or invitation? To get free templates like these, go to **File** > **New** in your Office program, and then click a category under **Office.com Templates**, such as **Letters**, **Business**, or **Form** (In Office 2013 or Office 2016, try one of the **Suggested searches** links).

Or, type what you're looking for in the search box, such as **avery** for labels.

TIP If you're on the web, try the free online templates at templates.office.com. You can use them right in your browser, in the Office Online programs.

Drag scroll bar to read more

Keep Help on Top button

Using sharing features and co-authoring capabilities

If you are using Word, Excel, or PowerPoint, you can take advantage of the Share feature, which makes it easy to share your files that have been saved to OneDrive. When you click the Share button, you will be asked to invite others to share the file. To do this, type in the name or email addresses in the Invite people text box. When you invite others, you have the opportunity to give them different levels of permission. You might want some people to have read-only privileges; you might want others to be able to make edits. Also available in Word, Excel, and PowerPoint is real-time co-authoring capabilities for files stored on OneDrive. Once a file on OneDrive is opened and all the users have been given editing privileges, all the users can make edits simultaneously. On first use, each user will be prompted to automatically share their changes.

Recovering a document

Each Office program has a built-in recovery feature that allows you to open and save files that were open at the time of an interruption such as a power failure. When you restart the program(s) after an interruption, the Document Recovery task pane opens on the left side of your screen displaying both original and recovered versions of the files that were open. If you're not sure which file to open (original or recovered), it's usually better to open the recovered file because it will contain the latest information. You can, however, open and review all versions of the file that were recovered and save the best one. Each file listed in the Document Recovery task pane displays a list arrow with options that allow you to open the file, save it as is, delete it, or show repairs made to it during recovery.

Practice

Concepts Review

Label the elements of the program window shown in FIGURE 1-16**.**

FIGURE 1-16

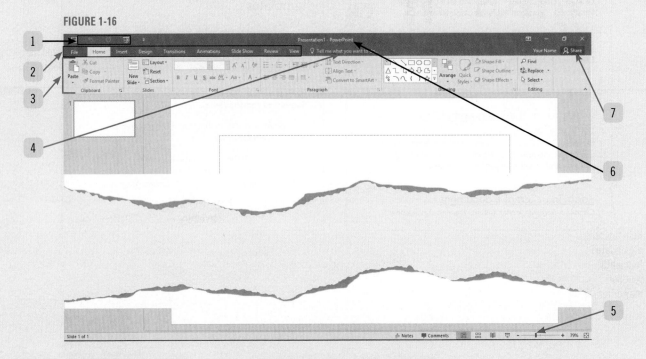

Match each project with the program for which it is best suited.

8. Microsoft PowerPoint
9. Microsoft Word
10. Microsoft Excel
11. Microsoft Access

a. Corporate convention budget with expense projections
b. Presentation for city council meeting
c. Business cover letter for a job application
d. Department store inventory

Independent Challenge 1

You just accepted an administrative position with a local independently owned insurance agent who has recently invested in computers and is now considering purchasing a subscription to Office 365. You have been asked to think of uses for the apps and you put your ideas in a Word document.

a. Start Word, create a new Blank document, then save the document as **OF 1-Microsoft Office Apps Uses** in the location where you store your Data Files.
b. Change the zoom factor to 120%, type **Microsoft Access**, press [Enter] twice, type **Microsoft Excel**, press [Enter] twice, type **Microsoft PowerPoint**, press [Enter] twice, type **Microsoft Word**, press [Enter] twice, then type your name.
c. Click the line beneath each program name, type at least two tasks you can perform using that program (each separated by a comma), then press [Enter].
d. Save the document, then submit your work to your instructor as directed.
e. Exit Word.

Getting Started with Access 2016

CASE Julia Rice is the developer for a new initiative at Reason 2 Go (R2G), a specialized type of travel company that combines volunteer opportunities and tourism into meaningful experiences for its customers. Julia has been asked to create products to meet a market demand for shorter experiences in the United States. Julia uses Microsoft Access 2016 to store, maintain, and analyze customer and trip information.

Module Objectives

After completing this module, you will be able to:

- Understand relational databases
- Explore a database
- Create a database
- Create a table
- Create primary keys
- Relate two tables
- Enter data
- Edit data

Files You Will Need

R2G-1.accdb
LakeHomes-1.accdb
Salvage-1.accdb

Contacts-1.accdb
Basketball-1.accdb

Understand Relational Databases

Learning
Outcomes
• Describe relational
database concepts
• Explain when to
use a database
• Compare a
relational database
to a spreadsheet

Microsoft Access 2016 is relational database software that runs on the Windows operating system. You use **relational database software** to manage data that is organized into lists, such as information about customers, products, vendors, employees, projects, or sales. Many small companies track customer, inventory, and sales information in a spreadsheet program such as Microsoft Excel. Although Excel offers some list management features, Access provides many more tools and advantages for managing data. Some advantages are due to Access using a relational database model whereas Excel manages data as a single list. TABLE 1-1 compares the two programs. **CASE** *You and Julia review the advantages of database software over spreadsheets for managing lists of information.*

DETAILS

The advantages of using Access for database management include the following:

- **Duplicate data is minimized**

  FIGURES 1-1 and 1-2 compare how you might store sales data in a single Excel spreadsheet list versus three related Access tables. With Access, you do not have to reenter information such as a customer's name and address or trip name every time a sale is made, because lists can be linked, or "related," in relational database software.

- **Information is more accurate, reliable, and consistent because duplicate data is minimized**

  The relational nature of data stored in an Access database allows you to minimize duplicate data entry, which creates more accurate, reliable, and consistent information. For example, customer data in a Customers table is entered only once, not every time a customer makes a purchase.

- **Data entry is faster and easier using Access forms**

  Data entry forms (screen layouts) make data entry faster, easier, and more accurate than entering data in a spreadsheet.

- **Information can be viewed and sorted in many ways using Access queries, forms, and reports**

  In Access, you can save multiple queries (questions about the data), data entry forms, and reports, allowing you to use them over and over without performing extra work to re-create a particular view of the data.

- **Information is more secure using Access passwords and security features**

  Access databases can be encrypted and password protected.

- **Several users can share and edit information at the same time**

  Unlike spreadsheets or word-processing documents, more than one person can enter, update, and analyze data in an Access database at the same time.

FIGURE 1-1: Using a spreadsheet to organize sales data

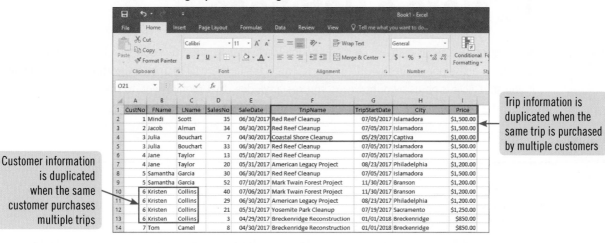

Customer information is duplicated when the same customer purchases multiple trips

Trip information is duplicated when the same trip is purchased by multiple customers

FIGURE 1-2: Using a relational database to organize sales data

TABLE 1-1: Comparing Excel with Access

feature	Excel	Access
Layout	Provides only a tabular spreadsheet layout	Provides tabular layouts as well as the ability to create customized data entry screens called forms
Storage	Restricted to a file's limitations	Virtually unlimited when coupled with the ability to use Microsoft SQL Server to store data
Linked tables	Manages single lists of information—no relational database capabilities	Relates lists of information to reduce data redundancy and create a powerful relational database
Reporting	Limited	Provides the ability to create an unlimited number of reports
Security	Limited to file security options such as marking the file "read-only" or protecting a range of cells	When used with SQL Server, provides extensive security down to the user and data level
Multiuser capabilities	Not allowed	Allows multiple users to simultaneously enter and update data
Data entry	Provides only one spreadsheet layout	Provides the ability to create an unlimited number of data entry forms

Explore a Database

Learning Outcomes
• Start Access and open a database
• Open and define Access objects

You can start Access in many ways. If you double-click an existing Access database icon or shortcut, that specific database opens directly within Access. This is the fastest way to open an existing Access database. If you start Access on its own, however, you see a window that requires you to make a choice between opening a database and creating a new database. **CASE** ▶ *Julia Rice has developed a database called R2G-1, which contains trip information. She asks you to start Access 2016 and review this database.*

STEPS

1. **Start Access**

   Access starts, as shown in **FIGURE 1-3**. This window allows you to open an existing database, create a new database from a template, or create a new blank database.

   TROUBLE
   If a yellow Security Warning bar appears below the Ribbon, click Enable Content.

2. **Click the Open Other Files link, navigate to the location where you store your Data Files, click the R2G-1.accdb database, click Open, then click the Maximize button ▣ if the Access window is not already maximized**

   The R2G-1.accdb Access database application contains five tables of data named Categories, Customers, Sales, States, and Trips. It also includes five queries, six forms, and four reports. Each of these items (table, query, form, and report) is a different type of **object** in an Access database application and is displayed in the **Navigation Pane**. The purpose of each object is defined in **TABLE 1-2**. To learn about an Access database application, you explore its objects.

   TROUBLE
   If the Navigation Pane is not open, click the Shutter Bar Open/Close Button ≫ to open it and view the database objects.

3. **In the Navigation Pane, double-click the Trips table to open it, then double-click the Customers table to open it**

   The Trips and Customers tables open in Datasheet View to display the data they store. A **table** is the fundamental building block of a relational database because it stores all of the data.

4. **In the Navigation Pane, double-click the TripSales query to open it, double-click any occurrence of Heritage in "American Heritage Tour," type Legacy, then click any other row**

   A **query** selects a subset of data from one or more tables. In this case, the TripSales query selects data from the Trips, Sales, and Customers tables. Entering or editing data in one object changes that information in every other object of the database, because all objects build on the same data stored only in the tables.

5. **Double-click the CustomerRoster form to open it, double-click Tour in "American Legacy Tour," type Project, then click any name in the middle part of the window**

   An Access **form** is a data entry screen. Users prefer forms for data entry (rather than editing and entering data in tables and queries) because forms can present information in any layout and include command buttons to make common tasks easy to perform.

6. **Double-click the TripSales report to open it**

   An Access **report** is a professional printout that can be distributed electronically or on paper. As shown in **FIGURE 1-4**, the edits made to the American Legacy Project name have carried through to the report, demonstrating the power and productivity of a relational database.

7. **Click the Close button ☒ in the upper-right corner of the window**

   Clicking the Close button in the upper-right corner of the window closes Access as well as the database on which you are working. Changes to data, such as the edits you made to the American Legacy Project record, are automatically saved as you work. Access will prompt you to save design changes to objects before it closes.

FIGURE 1-3: Opening the Microsoft Access 2016 window

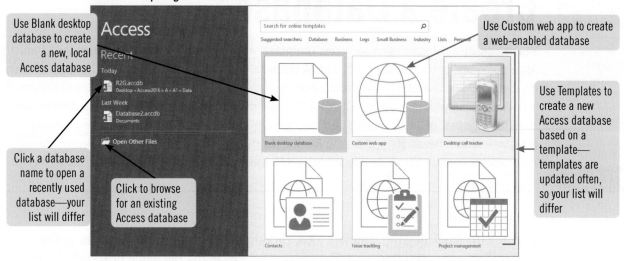

Use Blank desktop database to create a new, local Access database

Use Custom web app to create a web-enabled database

Use Templates to create a new Access database based on a template—templates are updated often, so your list will differ

Click a database name to open a recently used database—your list will differ

Click to browse for an existing Access database

FIGURE 1-4: Objects in the R2G-1 database

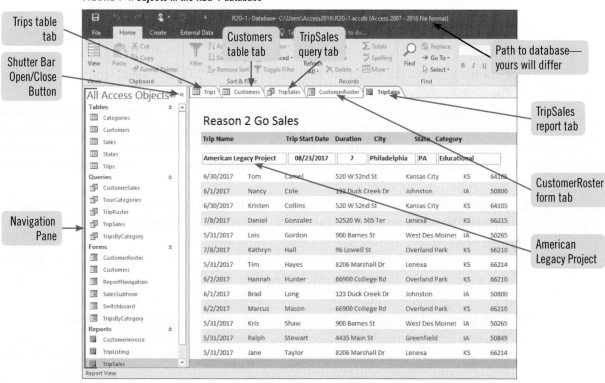

Trips table tab

Shutter Bar Open/Close Button

Customers table tab

TripSales query tab

Path to database—yours will differ

TripSales report tab

Navigation Pane

CustomerRoster form tab

American Legacy Project

TABLE 1-2: Access objects and their purpose

object	icon	purpose
Table		Contains all of the data within the database in a spreadsheet-like view called Datasheet View; tables are linked with a common field to create a relational database, which minimizes redundant data
Query		Allows you to select a subset of fields or records from one or more tables; create a query when you have a question about the data
Form		Provides an easy-to-use data entry screen
Report		Provides a professional presentation of data with headers, footers, graphics, and calculations on groups of records

Access 2016

Create a Database

Learning
Outcomes
• Create a database
• Create a table
• Define key
  database terms

You can create a database using an Access **template**, a sample database provided within the Microsoft Access program, or you can start with a blank database to create a database from scratch. Your decision depends on whether Access has a template that closely resembles the type of data you plan to manage. If it does, building your own database from a template might be faster than creating the database from scratch. Regardless of which method you use, you can always modify the database later, tailoring it to meet your specific needs. **CASE** ▶ *Julia Rice reasons that the best way for you to learn Access is to start a new database from scratch, so she asks you to create a new database that will track customer communication.*

STEPS

1. **Start Access**

2. **Click the Blank desktop database icon, click the Browse button ▣, navigate to the location where you store your Data Files, type R2G in the File name box, click OK, then click the Create button**

   A new database file with a single table named Table1 is created, as shown in FIGURE 1-5. Although you might be tempted to start entering data into the table, a better way to build a table is to first define the columns, or **fields**, of data that the table will store. **Table Design View** provides the most options for defining fields.

3. **Click the View button ☑ on the Fields tab to switch to Design View, type Customers in the Save As dialog box as the new table name, then click OK**

   The table name changes from Table1 to Customers, and you are positioned in Table Design View, a window you use to name and define the fields of a table. Access automatically created a field named ID with an AutoNumber data type. The **data type** is a significant characteristic of a field because it determines what type of data the field can store such as text, dates, or numbers. See TABLE 1-3 for more information about data types.

4. **Type CustID to rename ID to CustID, press [▾] to move to the first blank Field Name cell, type FirstName, press [▾], type LastName, press [▾], type Phone, press [▾], type Birthday, then press [▾]**

   Be sure to always separate a person's first and last names into two fields so that you can easily sort, find, and filter on either part of the name later. The Birthday field will only contain dates, so you should change its data type from Short Text (the default data type) to Date/Time.

5. **Click Short Text in the Birthday row, click the list arrow, then click Date/Time**

   With these five fields properly defined for the new Customers table, as shown in FIGURE 1-6, you're ready to enter data. You switch back to Datasheet View to enter or edit data. **Datasheet View** is a spreadsheet-like view of the data in a table. A **datasheet** is a grid that displays fields as columns and records as rows. The new **field names** you just defined are listed at the top of each column.

6. **Click the View button ▦ to switch to Datasheet View, click Yes when prompted to save the table, press [Tab] to move to the FirstName field, type *your* first name, press [Tab] to move to the LastName field, type *your* last name, press [Tab] to move to the Phone field, type 555-666-7777, press [Tab], type 1/32/1990, then press [Tab]**

   Because 1/32/1990 is not a valid date, Access does not allow you to make that entry and displays an error message, as shown in FIGURE 1-7. This shows that selecting the best data type for each field in Table Design View before entering data in Datasheet View helps prevent data entry errors.

7. **Press [Esc], edit the Birthday entry for the first record to 1/31/1990, press [Tab], enter two more sample records using realistic data, right-click the Customers table tab, then click Close to close the Customers table**

FIGURE 1-5: Creating a database with a new table

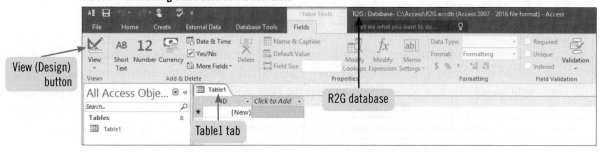

FIGURE 1-6: Defining field names and data types for the Customers table in Table Design View

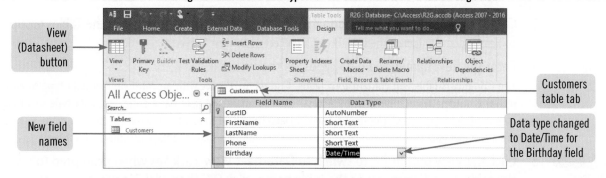

FIGURE 1-7: Entering your first record in the Customers table

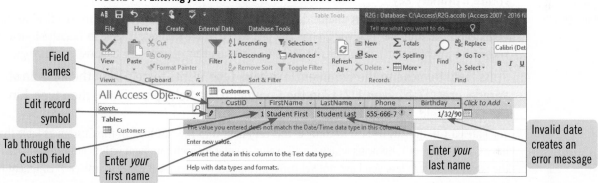

TABLE 1-3: Data types

data type	description of data
Short Text	Text or numbers not used in calculations such as a name, zip code, or phone number less than 255 characters
Long Text	Lengthy text greater than 255 characters, such as comments or notes
Number	Numeric data that can be used in calculations, such as quantities
Date/Time	Dates and times
Currency	Monetary values
AutoNumber	Sequential integers controlled by Access
Yes/No	Only two values: Yes or No
OLE Object	OLE (Object Linking and Embedding) objects such as an Excel spreadsheet or Word document
Hyperlink	Web and email addresses or links to local files
Attachment	Files such as .jpg images, spreadsheets, and documents
Calculated	Result of a calculation based on other fields in the table
Lookup Wizard	The Lookup Wizard helps you set Lookup properties, which display a drop-down list of values for the field; after using the Lookup Wizard, the final data type for the field is either Short Text or Number depending on the values in the drop-down list

Create a Table

Learning Outcomes
- Create a table in Table Design View
- Set appropriate data types for fields

After creating your database and first table, you need to create new, related tables to build a relational database. Creating a table consists of these essential tasks: defining the fields in the table, selecting an appropriate data type for each field, naming the table, and determining how the table will participate in the relational database. **CASE** *Julia Rice asks you to create another table to store customer comments. The new table will eventually be connected to the Customers table so each customer record in the Customers table may be related to many records in the Comments table.*

STEPS

1. **Click the Create tab on the Ribbon, then click the Table Design button in the Tables group**

   You create and manipulate the structure of an object in **Design View**.

2. **Enter the field names and data types, as shown in** FIGURE 1-8

   The Comments table will contain four fields. CommentID is set with an AutoNumber data type so each record is automatically numbered by Access. The CommentText field has a Long Text data type so a long comment can be recorded. CommentDate is a Date/Time field to identify the date of the comment. CustID has a Number data type and will be used to link the Comments table to the Customers table later.

   > **TROUBLE**
   > To rename an object, close it, right-click it in the Navigation Pane, and then click Rename.

3. **Click the View button** 📄 **to switch to Datasheet View, click Yes when prompted to save the table, type Comments as the table name, click OK, then click No when prompted to create a primary key**

   A **primary key field** contains unique data for each record. You'll identify a primary key field for the Comments table later. For now, you'll enter the first record in the Comments table in Datasheet View. A **record** is a row of data in a table. Refer to TABLE 1-4 for a summary of important database terminology.

4. **Press [Tab] to move to the CommentText field, type Wants to help with the Rose Bowl Parade, press [Tab], type 1/7/17 in the CommentDate field, press [Tab], then type 1 in the CustID field**

   You entered 1 in the CustID field to connect this comment with the customer in the Customers table that has a CustID value of 1. Knowing which CustID value to enter for each comment is difficult. After you relate the tables properly (a task you have not yet performed), Access can make it easier to link each comment to the correct customer.

   > **TROUBLE**
   > The CommentID field is an AutoNumber field, which will automatically increment to provide a unique value. If the number has already incremented beyond 1 for the first record, AutoNumber still works as intended.

5. **Point to the divider line between the CommentText and CommentDate field names, and then double-click the ↔ pointer to widen the CommentText field to read the entire comment, as shown in** FIGURE 1-9

6. **Right-click the Comments table tab, click Close, then click Yes if prompted to save the table**

Creating a table in Datasheet View

You can also create a new table in Datasheet View using the commands on the Fields tab of the Ribbon. However, if you use Design View to design your table before entering data, you will probably avoid some common data entry errors. Design View helps you focus on the appropriate data type for each field.

Selecting the best data type for each field before entering any data into that field helps prevent incorrect data and unintended typos. For example, if a field has a Number, Currency, or Date/Time data type, you will not be able to enter text into that field by mistake.

FIGURE 1-8: Creating the Comments table

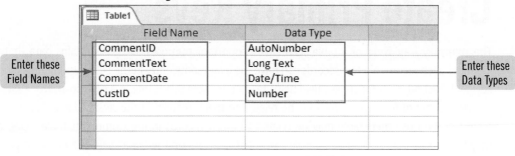

Enter these Field Names →

Enter these Data Types ←

Field Name	Data Type
CommentID	AutoNumber
CommentText	Long Text
CommentDate	Date/Time
CustID	Number

FIGURE 1-9: Entering a record in the Comments table

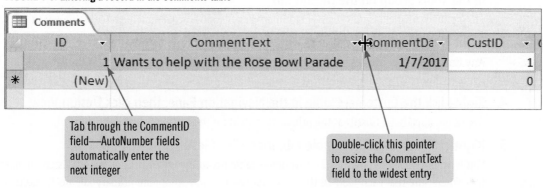

ID	CommentText	CommentDa	CustID
1	Wants to help with the Rose Bowl Parade	1/7/2017	1
* (New)			0

Tab through the CommentID field—AutoNumber fields automatically enter the next integer

Double-click this pointer to resize the CommentText field to the widest entry

TABLE 1-4: Important database terminology

term	description
Field	A specific piece or category of data such as a first name, last name, city, state, or phone number
Record	A group of related fields that describes a person, place, thing, or transaction such as a customer, location, product, or sale
Key field	A field that contains unique information for each record, such as a customer number for a customer
Table	A collection of records for a single subject such as Customers, Products, or Sales
Relational database	Multiple tables that are linked together to address a business process such as managing trips, sales, and customers at Reason 2 Go
Objects	The parts of an Access database that help you view, edit, manage, and analyze the data: tables, queries, forms, reports, macros, and modules

Create Primary Keys

Learning Outcomes
- Set the primary key field
- Define one-to-many relationships

The **primary key field** of a table serves two important purposes. First, it contains data that uniquely identifies each record. No two records can have the exact same entry in the field designated as the primary key field. Second, the primary key field helps relate one table to another in a **one-to-many relationship**, where one record from one table may be related to many records in the second table. For example, one record in the Customers table may be related to many records in the Comments table. (One customer may have many comments.) The primary key field is always on the "one" side of a one-to-many relationship between two tables. **CASE** > *Julia Rice asks you to check that a primary key field has been appropriately identified for each table in the new R2G database.*

STEPS

1. **Right-click the Comments table in the Navigation Pane, then click Design View**

   Table Design View for the Comments table opens. The field with the AutoNumber data type is generally the best candidate for the primary key field in a table because it automatically contains a unique number for each record.

   TROUBLE
   Make sure the Design tab is selected on the Ribbon.

2. **Click the CommentID field if it is not already selected, then click the Primary Key button in the Tools group on the Design tab**

   The CommentID field is now set as the primary key field for the Comments table, as shown in **FIGURE 1-10**.

   QUICK TIP
   You can also click the Save button 🖫 on the Quick Access Toolbar to save a table.

3. **Right-click the Comments table tab, click Close, then click Yes to save the table**

   Any time you must save design changes to an Access object such as a table, Access displays a dialog box to remind you to save the object.

4. **Right-click the Customers table in the Navigation Pane, then click Design View**

   Access has already set CustID as the primary key field for the Customers table, as shown in **FIGURE 1-11**.

5. **Right-click the Customers table tab, then click Close**

   You were not prompted to save the Customers table because you did not make any design changes. Now that you're sure that each table in the R2G database has an appropriate primary key field, you're ready to link the tables. The primary key field plays a critical role in this relationship.

Object views

Each object has a number of **views** that allow you to complete different tasks. For example, to enter and edit data into the database, use **Datasheet View** for tables and queries and **Form View** for forms. To change the structure of an object, you most often work in **Design View**. Use **Print Preview** to see how a report will appear on a physical piece of paper. Click the arrow at the bottom of the View button on the Design tab of the Ribbon to see all of the available views for an object.

Learning about field properties

Properties are the characteristics that define the field. Two properties are required for every field: Field Name and Data Type. Many other properties, such as Field Size, Format, Caption, and Default Value, are defined in the Field Properties pane in the lower half of a table's Design View. As you add more property entries, you are generally restricting the amount or type of data that can be entered in the field, which increases data entry accuracy. For example, you might change the Field Size property for a State field to 2 to eliminate an incorrect entry such as FLL. Field properties change depending on the data type of the selected field. For example, date fields do not have a Field Size property because Access controls the size of fields with a Date/Time data type.

FIGURE 1-10: Creating a primary key field for the Comments table

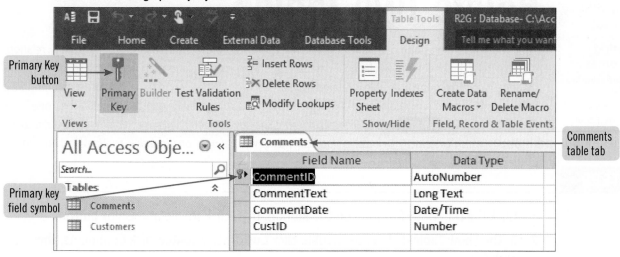

Primary Key button

Primary key field symbol

Comments table tab

FIGURE 1-11: Confirming the primary key field for the Customers table

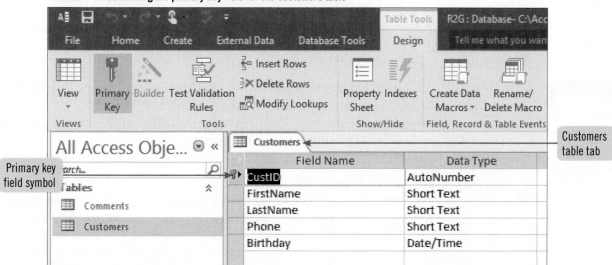

Primary key field symbol

Customers table tab

Relate Two Tables

After you create tables and set primary key fields, you must connect the tables in one-to-many relationships to enjoy the benefits of a relational database. A one-to-many relationship between two tables means that one record from the first table is related to many records in the second table. You use a common field to make this connection. The common field is always the primary key field in the table on the "one" side of the relationship. **CASE** *Julia Rice explains that she has new comments to enter into the R2G database. To identify which customer is related to each comment, you define a one-to-many relationship between the Customers and Comments tables.*

STEPS

1. **Click the Database Tools tab on the Ribbon, then click the Relationships button**

2. **In the Show Table dialog box, double-click Customers, double-click Comments, then click Close**

   Each table is represented by a small **field list** window that displays the table's field names. A **key symbol** identifies the primary key field in each table. To relate the two tables in a one-to-many relationship, you connect them using a common field, which is always the primary key field on the "one" side of the relationship.

3. **Drag CustID in the Customers field list to the CustID field in the Comments field list**

   The Edit Relationships dialog box opens, as shown in **FIGURE 1-12**. **Referential integrity**, a set of Access rules that governs data entry, helps ensure data accuracy.

4. **Click the Enforce Referential Integrity check box in the Edit Relationships dialog box, then click Create**

   The **one-to-many line** shows the link between the CustID field of the Customers table (the "one" side) and the CustID field of the Comments table (the "many" side, indicated by the **infinity symbol**), as shown in **FIGURE 1-13**. The linking field on the "many" side is called the **foreign key field**. Now that these tables are related, it is much easier to enter comments for the correct customer.

5. **Right-click the Relationships tab, click Close, click Yes to save changes, then double-click the Customers table in the Navigation Pane to open it in Datasheet View**

   When you relate two tables in a one-to-many relationship, expand buttons appear to the left of each record in the table on the "one" side of the relationship. In this case, the Customers table is on the "one" side of the relationship.

6. **Click the expand button ⊞ to the left of the first record**

   A **subdatasheet** shows the related comment records for each customer. In other words, the subdatasheet shows the records on the "many" side of a one-to-many relationship. The expand button ⊞ also changed to the collapse button ⊟ for the first customer. Widening the CommentText field allows you to see the entire entry in the Comments subdatasheet. Now the task of entering comments for the correct customer is much more straightforward.

7. **Enter two more comments, as shown in FIGURE 1-14**

   Interestingly, the CustID field in the Comments table (the foreign key field) is not displayed in the subdatasheet. Behind the scenes, Access is entering the correct CustID value in the Comments table, which is the glue that ties each comment to the correct customer.

8. **Close the Customers table, then click Yes if prompted to save changes**

FIGURE 1-12: Edit Relationships dialog box

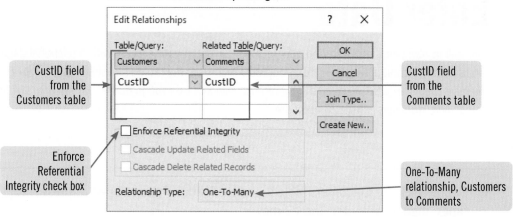

CustID field from the Customers table

CustID field from the Comments table

Enforce Referential Integrity check box

One-To-Many relationship, Customers to Comments

FIGURE 1-13: Linking the Customers and Comments tables

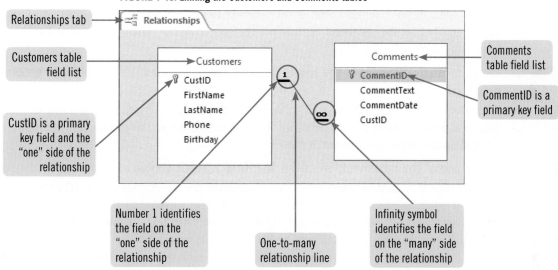

Relationships tab

Customers table field list

CustID is a primary key field and the "one" side of the relationship

Comments table field list

CommentID is a primary key field

Number 1 identifies the field on the "one" side of the relationship

One-to-many relationship line

Infinity symbol identifies the field on the "many" side of the relationship

---

FIGURE 1-14: Entering comments using the subdatasheet

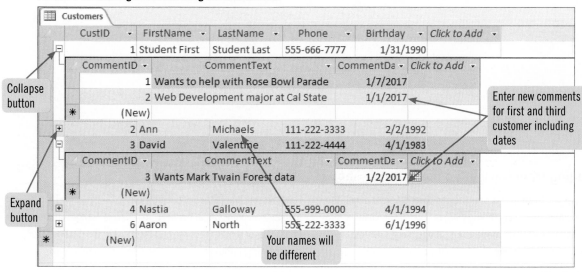

Collapse button

Expand button

Enter new comments for first and third customer including dates

Your names will be different

Enter Data

Learning Outcomes
• Navigate records in a datasheet
• Enter records in a datasheet

Your skill in navigating and entering new records is a key to your success with a relational database. You can use many techniques to navigate through the records in the table's datasheet. **CASE** *Even though you have already successfully entered some records, Julia Rice asks you to master this essential skill by entering several more customers in the R2G database.*

STEPS

1. **Double-click the Customers table in the Navigation Pane to open it, press [Tab] three times, then press [Enter] three times**

   The Customers table reopens. The Comments subdatasheets are collapsed. Both the [Tab] and [Enter] keys move the focus to the next field. The **focus** refers to which data you would edit if you started typing. When you navigate to the last field of the record, pressing [Tab] or [Enter] advances the focus to the first field of the next record. You can also use the Next record ▶ and Previous record ◀ **navigation buttons** on the navigation bar in the lower-left corner of the datasheet to navigate through the records. The **Current record** text box on the navigation bar tells you the number of the current record as well as the total number of records in the datasheet.

   QUICK TIP
   Press [Tab] in the CustID AutoNumber field.

2. **Click the FirstName field of the fourth record to position the insertion point to enter a new record**

   You can also use the New (blank) record button ▶✳ on the navigation bar to move to a new record. You enter new records at the end of the datasheet. You learn how to sort and reorder records later. A complete list of navigation keystrokes is shown in **TABLE 1-5**.

   QUICK TIP
   Access databases are multiuser with one important limitation: Two users cannot edit the same record at the same time. In that case, a message explains that the second user must wait until the first user moves to a different record.

3. **At the end of the datasheet, enter the last three records shown in FIGURE 1-15**

   The **edit record symbol** ✐ appears to the left of the record you are currently editing. When you move to a different record, Access saves the data. Therefore, Access never prompts you to save data because it performs that task automatically. Saving data automatically allows Access databases to be **multiuser** databases, which means that more than one person can enter and edit data in the same database at the same time.

   Your CustID values might differ from those in **FIGURE 1-15**. Because the CustID field is an **AutoNumber** field, Access automatically enters the next consecutive number into the field as it creates the record. If you delete a record or are interrupted when entering a record, Access discards the value in the AutoNumber field and does not reuse it. Therefore, AutoNumber values do not represent the number of records in your table. Instead, they provide a unique value per record, similar to check numbers.

Changing from Navigation mode to Edit mode

If you navigate to another area of the datasheet by clicking with the mouse pointer instead of pressing [Tab] or [Enter], you change from **Navigation mode** to Edit mode. In **Edit mode**, Access assumes that you are trying to make changes to the current field value, so keystrokes such as [Ctrl][End], [Ctrl][Home], [←], and [→] move the insertion point within the field. To return to Navigation mode, press [Tab] or [Enter] (thus moving the focus to the next field), or press [↑] or [↓] (thus moving the focus to a different record).

FIGURE 1-15: New records in the Customers table

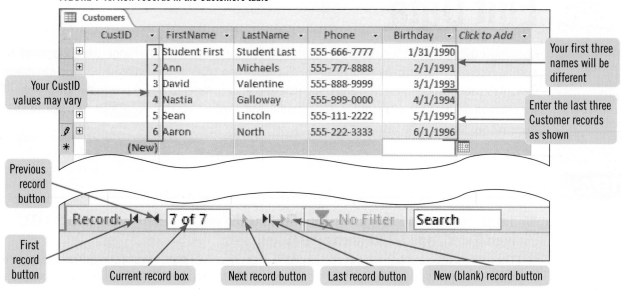

Your CustID values may vary →

Your first three names will be different

Enter the last three Customer records as shown

Previous record button

First record button

Current record box

Next record button

Last record button

New (blank) record button

Record: 7 of 7 · No Filter · Search

TABLE 1-5: Navigation mode keyboard shortcuts

shortcut key	moves to the
[Tab], [Enter], or [→]	Next field of the current record
[Shift][Tab] or [←]	Previous field of the current record
[Home]	First field of the current record
[End]	Last field of the current record
[Ctrl][Home] or [F5]	First field of the first record
[Ctrl][End]	Last field of the last record
[↑]	Current field of the previous record
[↓]	Current field of the next record

Access 2016

Cloud computing

Using **OneDrive**, a free service from Microsoft, you can store files in the "cloud" and retrieve them anytime you are connected to the Internet. Saving your files to the OneDrive is one example of cloud computing. **Cloud computing** means you are using an Internet resource to complete your work.

Edit Data

Learning Outcomes
- Edit data in a datasheet
- Delete records in a datasheet
- Preview and print a datasheet

Updating existing data in a database is another critical database task. To change the contents of an existing record, navigate to the field you want to change and type the new information. You can delete unwanted data by clicking the field and using [Backspace] or [Delete] to delete text to the left or right of the insertion point. Other data entry keystrokes are summarized in TABLE 1-6. **CASE** ▶ *Julia Rice asks you to correct two records in the Customers table.*

STEPS

1. **Select the phone number in the Phone field of the second record, type 111-222-3333, press [Enter], type 2/2/92, then press [Enter]**

   You changed the telephone number and birth date of the second customer. When you entered the last two digits of the year value, Access inserted the first two digits after you pressed [Enter]. You'll also update the third customer.

   QUICK TIP
   The ScreenTip for the Undo button ↶ displays the action you can undo.

2. **Press [Enter] enough times to move to the Phone field of the third record, type 111-222-4444, then press [Esc]**

   Pressing [Esc] once removes the current field's editing changes, so the Phone value changes back to the previous entry. Pressing [Esc] twice removes all changes to the current record. When you move to another record, Access saves your edits, so you can no longer use [Esc] to remove editing changes to the current record. You can, however, click the Undo button ↶ on the Quick Access Toolbar to undo changes to a previous record.

3. **Retype 111-222-4444, press [Enter], type 3/1/83 in the Birthday field, press [Enter], click the 3/1/83 date you just entered, click the Calendar icon 📅, then click April 1, 1983, as shown in FIGURE 1-16**

   When you are working in the Birthday field, which has a Date/Time data type, you can enter a date from the keyboard or use the **Calendar Picker**, a pop-up calendar, to find and select a date.

4. **Click the record selector for the fifth record (Sean Lincoln), click the Delete button in the Records group on the Home tab, then click Yes**

   A message warns that you cannot undo a record deletion. The Undo button ↶ is dimmed, indicating that you cannot use it. The Customers table now has five records, as shown in FIGURE 1-17. Keep in mind that your CustID values might differ from those in the figure because they are controlled by Access.

   QUICK TIP
   If requested to print the Customers datasheet by your instructor, click the Print button, then click OK.

5. **Click the File tab, click Print, then click Print Preview to review the printout of the Customers table before printing**

6. **Click the Close Print Preview button, then click the Close button ✕ in the upper-right corner of the window to close the R2G.accdb database and Access 2016**

FIGURE 1-16: Editing customer records

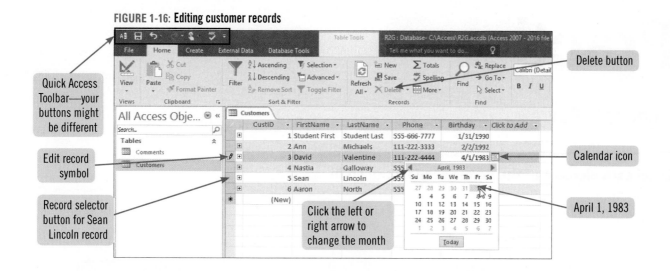

Quick Access Toolbar—your buttons might be different

Edit record symbol

Record selector button for Sean Lincoln record

Click the left or right arrow to change the month

Delete button

Calendar icon

April 1, 1983

FIGURE 1-17: Final Customers datasheet

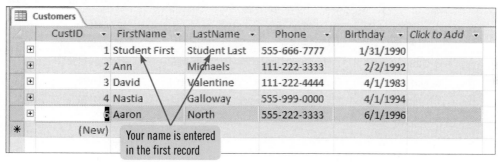

Your name is entered in the first record

TABLE 1-6: Edit mode keyboard shortcuts

editing keystroke	action
[Backspace]	Deletes one character to the left of the insertion point
[Delete]	Deletes one character to the right of the insertion point
[F2]	Switches between Edit and Navigation mode
[Esc]	Undoes the change to the current field
[Esc][Esc]	Undoes all changes to the current record
[F7]	Starts the spell-check feature
[Ctrl][']	Inserts the value from the same field in the previous record into the current field
[Ctrl][;]	Inserts the current date in a Date field

Resizing and moving datasheet columns

You can resize the width of a field in a datasheet by dragging the column separator, the thin line that separates the field names to the left or right. The pointer changes to ↔ as you make the field wider or narrower. Release the mouse button when you have resized the field. To adjust the column width to accommodate the widest entry in the field, double-click the column separator. To move a column, click the field name to select the entire column, then drag the field name left or right.

Practice

Concepts Review

Label each element of the Access window shown in FIGURE 1-18.

FIGURE 1-18

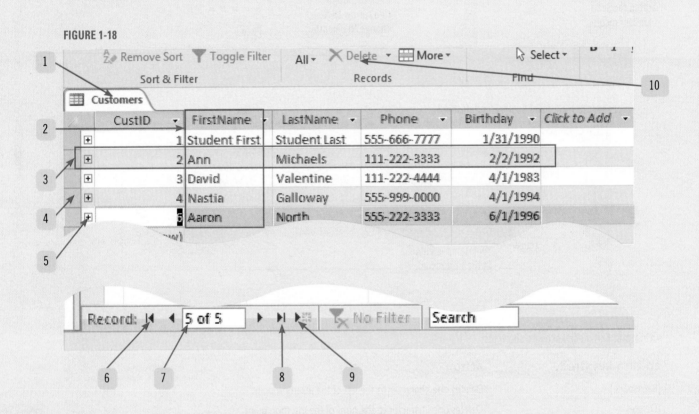

Match each term with the statement that best describes it.

11. Field
12. Record
13. Table
14. Datasheet
15. Query
16. Form
17. Report

a. A subset of data from one or more tables
b. A collection of records for a single subject, such as all the customer records
c. A professional printout of database information
d. A spreadsheet-like grid that displays fields as columns and records as rows
e. A group of related fields for one item, such as all of the information for one customer
f. A category of information in a table, such as a company name, city, or state
g. An easy-to-use data entry screen

Select the best answer from the list of choices.

18. **When you create a new database, which object is created first?**
    a. Module
    b. Query
    c. Table
    d. Form

19. **Which of the following is *not* a typical benefit of relational databases?**
    a. Minimized duplicate data entry
    b. More accurate data
    c. Tables automatically create needed relationships
    d. More consistent data

20. **Which of the following is *not* an advantage of managing data with relational database software such as Access versus spreadsheet software such as Excel?**
    a. Allows multiple users to enter data simultaneously
    b. Uses a single table to store all data
    c. Provides data entry forms
    d. Reduces duplicate data entry

Skills Review

1. **Understand relational databases.**
   a. Write down five advantages of managing database information in Access versus using a spreadsheet.
   b. Write a sentence to explain how the terms field, record, table, and relational database relate to one another.

2. **Explore a database.**
   a. Start Access.
   b. Open the LakeHomes-1.accdb database from the location where you store your Data Files. Click Enable Content if a yellow Security Warning message appears.
   c. Open each of the four tables to study the data they contain. Complete the following table:

table name	number of records	number of fields

   d. Double-click the ListingsByRealtor query in the Navigation Pane to open it. Change any occurrence of Gordon Bono to *your* name. Move to another record to save your changes.
   e. Double-click the RealtorsMainForm in the Navigation Pane to open it. Use the navigation buttons to navigate through the 13 realtors to observe each realtor's listings.
   f. Double-click the RealtorListingReport in the Navigation Pane to open it. The records are listed in ascending order by realtor last name. Scroll through the report to make sure your name is positioned correctly.
   g. Close the LakeHomes-1 database, then close Access 2016.

3. **Create a database.**
   a. Start Access, click the Blank desktop database icon, use the Browse button to navigate to the location where you store your Data Files, type **LakeHomeMarketing** as the filename, click OK, and then click Create to create a new database named LakeHomeMarketing.accdb.

Skills Review (continued)

b. Switch to Table Design View, name the table **Prospects**, then enter the following fields and data types:

field name	data type
ProspectID	AutoNumber
ProspectFirst	Short Text
ProspectLast	Short Text
Phone	Short Text
Email	Hyperlink
Street	Short Text
City	Short Text
State	Short Text
Zip	Short Text

c. Save the table, switch to Datasheet View, and enter two records using your name in the first record and your instructor's name in the second. Tab through the ProspectID field, an AutoNumber field.

d. Enter **TN** (Tennessee) as the value in the State field for both records. Use school or fictitious (rather than personal) data for all other field data, and be sure to fill out each record completely.

e. Widen each column in the Prospects table so that all data is visible, then save and close the Prospects table.

4. Create a table.

a. Click the Create tab on the Ribbon, click the Table Design button in the Tables group, then create a new table with the following two fields and data types:

field name	data type
State2	Short Text
StateName	Short Text

b. Save the table with the name **States**. Click No when asked if you want Access to create the primary key field.

5. Create primary keys.

a. In Table Design View of the States table, set the State2 field as the primary key field.

b. Save the States table and open it in Datasheet View.

c. Enter one state record, using **TN** for the State2 value and **Tennessee** for the StateName value to match the State value of TN that you entered for both records in the Prospects table.

d. Close the States table.

6. Relate two tables.

a. From the Database Tools tab, open the Relationships window.

b. Add the States, then the Prospects table to the Relationships window.

c. Drag the bottom edge of the Prospects table to expand the field list to display all of the fields.

d. Drag the State2 field from the States table to the State field of the Prospects table.

e. In the Edit Relationships dialog box, click the Enforce Referential Integrity check box, then click Create. Your Relationships window should look like **FIGURE 1-19**. If you connect the wrong fields by mistake, right-click the line connecting the two fields, click Delete, then try again.

f. Close the Relationships window, and save changes when prompted.

FIGURE 1-19

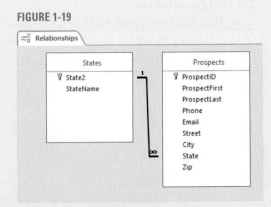

Skills Review (continued)

7. Enter data.

a. Open the States table and enter the following records:

State2 field	StateName field
CO	Colorado
IA	Iowa
KS	Kansas
MO	Missouri
NE	Nebraska
OK	Oklahoma
WI	Wisconsin
TX	Texas

b. Add three more state records of your choice for a total of 12 records in the States table using the correct two-character abbreviation for the state and the correctly spelled state name.

c. Close and reopen the States table. Notice that Access automatically sorts the records by the values in the primary key field, the State2 field.

8. Edit data.

a. Click the Expand button for the TN record to see the two related records from the Prospects table.

b. Enter two more prospects in the TN subdatasheet using any fictitious but realistic data, as shown in FIGURE 1-20. Notice that you are not required to enter a value for the State field, the foreign key field in the subdatasheet.

c. If required by your instructor, print the States datasheet and the Prospects datasheet.

d. Click the Close button in the upper-right corner of the Access window to close all open objects as well as the LakeHomeMarketing.accdb database and Access 2016. If prompted to save any design changes, click Yes.

FIGURE 1-20

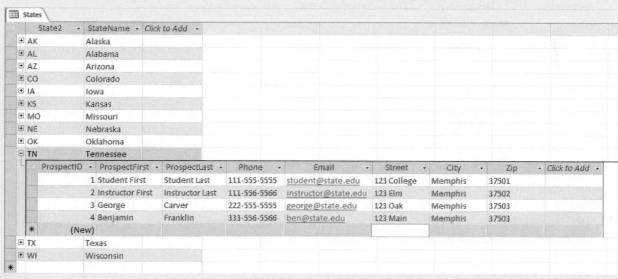

Independent Challenge 1

Consider the following twelve subject areas:

- Telephone directory
- Islands of the Caribbean
- Members of the U.S. House of Representatives
- College course offerings
- Physical activities
- Ancient wonders of the world
- Restaurant menu
- Shopping catalog items
- Vehicles
- Conventions
- Party guest list
- Movie listings

a. For each subject, build a Word table with 4–7 columns and three rows. In the first row, enter field names that you would expect to see in a table used to manage that subject.

b. In the second and third rows of each table, enter two realistic records. The first table, Telephone Directory, is completed as an example to follow.

TABLE: **Telephone Directory**

FirstName	LastName	Street	Zip	Phone
Marco	Lopez	100 Main Street	88715	555-612-3312
Christopher	Stafford	253 Maple Lane	77824	555-612-1179

c. Consider the following guidelines as you build the table:

Make sure each record represents one item in that table. For example, in the Restaurant Menu table, the following table is a random list of categories of food. The records do not represent one item in a restaurant menu.

Beverage	Appetizer	Meat	Vegetable	Dessert
Milk	Chicken wings	Steak	Carrots	Chocolate cake
Tea	Onion rings	Salmon	Potato	Cheesecake

A better example of records that describe an item in the restaurant menu would be the following:

Category	Description	Price	Calories	Spicy
Appetizer	Chicken wings	$10	800	Yes
Beverage	Milk	$2	250	No

Do not put first and last names in the same field. This prevents you from easily sorting, filtering, or searching on either part of the name later.

For the same reasons, break street, city, state, zip, and country data into separate fields as well.

Do not put values and units of measure such as 5 minutes, 4 lbs, or 6 sq. miles in the same field. This also prevents you from sorting and calculating on the numeric part of the information. Make your field names descriptive such as TimeInMinutes or AreaInSquareMiles so that each record's entries are consistent.

Do not put these tables in one Access database. Putting all of these tables in one Access database would be analogous to putting a letter to your Congressman, a creative poem, and a cover letter to a future employer all in the same Word file. Just as that wouldn't make organizational sense, these tables do not belong together in the same Access database either. Create your sample tables in a Word document to stay focused on proper field and record construction versus the task of building Access tables.

Independent Challenge 2

You are working with several civic groups to coordinate a community-wide recycling effort. You have started a database called Salvage-1, which tracks the clubs, their recyclable material deposits, and the collection centers that are participating.

a. Start Access, then open the Salvage-1.accdb database from the location where you store your Data Files. Enable content if prompted.

b. Open each table's datasheet to study the number of fields and records per table. Notice that there are no expand buttons to the left of any records because relationships have not yet been established between these tables.

c. In a Word document, re-create the following table and fill in the blanks:

table name	number of records	number of fields

d. Close all table datasheets, then open the Relationships window and create the following one-to-many relationships. Drag the tables from the Navigation Pane to the Relationships window, and drag the title bars and borders of the field lists to position them as shown in FIGURE 1-21.

field on the "one" side of the relationship	field on the "many" side of the relationship
ClubNumber in Clubs table	ClubNumber in Deposits table
CenterNumber in Centers table	CenterNumber in Deposits table

e. Be sure to enforce referential integrity on all relationships. If you create an incorrect relationship, right-click the line linking the fields, click Delete, and try again. Your final Relationships window should look like FIGURE 1-21.

f. Click the Relationship Report button on the Design tab, and if required by your instructor, click Print to print a copy of the Relationships for Salvage-1 report. To close the report, right-click the Relationships for Salvage-1 tab and click Close. Click Yes when prompted to save changes to the report with the name **Relationships for Salvage-1**. Save and close the Relationships window.

g. Open the Clubs table and add a new record with fictitious but realistic data in all of the fields. Enter **8** as the ClubNumber value and your name in the FName (first name) and LName (last name) fields.

h. Expand the subdatasheets for each record in the Clubs table to see the related records from the Deposits table. Which club made the most deposits? Be ready to answer in class. Close the Clubs table.

i. Open the Centers table and add a new record with fictitious but realistic data in all of the fields. Enter your first and last names in the CenterName field and enter **5** as the CenterNumber.

j. Expand the subdatasheets for each record in the Centers table to see the related records from the Deposits table. Which center made the most deposits? Be ready to answer in class. Close the Centers table.

k. Close the Salvage-1.accdb database, then exit Access 2016.

FIGURE 1-21

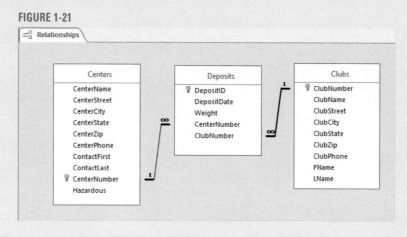

Independent Challenge 3

You are working for an advertising agency that provides social media consulting for small and large businesses in the mid-western United States. You have started a database called Contacts-1, which tracks your company's customers. (*Note*: To complete this Independent Challenge, make sure you are connected to the Internet.)

a. Start Access and open the Contacts-1.accdb database from the location where you store your Data Files. Enable content if prompted.

b. Add a new record to the Customers table, using any local business name, your first and last names, **$10,500** in the YTDSales field, and fictitious but reasonable entries for the rest of the fields.

c. Edit the Sprint Systems record (ID 1). Change the Company name to **A1 Cellular**, and change the Street value to **4455 Mastin St**.

d. Delete the record for EBC (ID 18), then close the Customers table.

e. Create a new table with two fields, **State2** and **StateName**. Assign both fields a Short Text data type. The State2 field will contain the two-letter abbreviation for state names. The StateName field will contain the Set the State2 field as the primary key field, then save the table as **States**.

f. Enter at least three records into the States table, making sure that all of the states used in the Customers datasheet are entered in the States table. This includes **KS Kansas**, **MO Missouri**, and any other state you entered in Step b when you added a new record to the Customers table.

g. Close all open tables. Open the Relationships window, add both the States and Customers field lists to the window, then expand the size of the Customers field list so that all fields are visible. (*Hint*: The field list will not show a vertical scroll bar when all fields in the list are visible.)

h. Build a one-to-many relationship between the States and Customers tables by dragging the State2 field from the States table to the State field of the Customers table to create a one-to-many relationship between the two tables. Enforce referential integrity on the relationship. If you are unable to enforce referential integrity, it means that a value in the State field of the Customers table doesn't have a perfect match in the State2 field of the States table. Open both table datasheets, making sure every state in the State field of the Customers table is also represented in the State2 field of the States table, close all datasheets, then reestablish the one-to-many relationship between the two tables with referential integrity.

i. Click the Relationship Report button on the Design tab, then if requested by your instructor, click Print to print the report.

j. Right-click the Relationships for Contacts-1 tab, then click Close. Click Yes when prompted to save the report with the name **Relationships for Contacts-1**.

k. Close the Relationships window, saving changes as prompted.

l. Close the Contacts-1.accdb database, then exit Access 2016.

Independent Challenge 4: Explore

Now that you've learned about Microsoft Access and relational databases, brainstorm how you might use an Access database in your daily life or career. Start by visiting the Microsoft website, and explore what's new in Access 2016.

(*Note*: To complete this Independent Challenge, make sure you are connected to the Internet.)

a. Using your favorite search engine, look up the keywords *benefits of a relational database* or *benefits of Microsoft Access* to find articles that discuss the benefits of organizing data in a relational database.

b. Read several articles about the benefits of organizing data in a relational database such as Access, identifying three distinct benefits. Use a Word document to record those three benefits. Also, copy and paste the website address of the article you are referencing for each benefit you have identified.

c. In addition, as you read the articles that describe relational database benefits, list any terminology unfamiliar to you, identifying at least five new terms.

d. Using a search engine or a website that provides a computer glossary such as www.whatis.com or www.webopedia.com, look up the definition of the new terms, and enter both the term and the definition of the term in your document as well as the website address where your definition was found.

e. Finally, based on your research and growing understanding of Access 2016, list three ways you could use an Access database to organize, enhance, or support the activities and responsibilities of your daily life or career. Type your name at the top of the document, and submit it to your instructor as requested.

Visual Workshop

Open the Basketball-1.accdb database from the location where you store your Data Files, then enable content if prompted. Open the Offense query datasheet, which lists offensive statistics by player by game. Modify any of the Matthew Douglas records to contain your first and last names, then move to a different record, observing the power of a relational database to modify every occurrence of that name throughout the database. Close the Offense query, then open the Players table. Note that there are no expand buttons to the left of the records, indicating that this table does not participate on the "one" side of a one-to-many relationship. Close the Players table and open the Relationships window. Drag the tables from the Navigation Pane and create the relationships with referential integrity, as shown in FIGURE 1-22. Note the one-to-many relationship between the Players and Stats table. Print the Relationships report if requested by your instructor and save it with the name **Relationships for Basketball-1**. Close the report and close and save the Relationships window. Now reopen the Players table noting the expand buttons to the left of each record. Expand the subdatasheet for your name and for several other players to observe the "many" records from the Stats table that are now related to each record in the Players table.

FIGURE 1-22

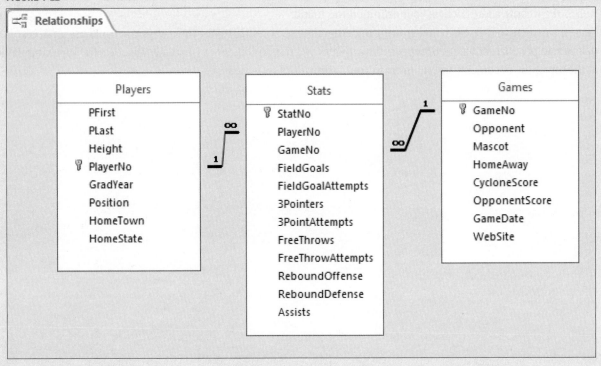

Building and Using Queries

CASE Julia Rice, trip developer for U.S. group travel at Reason 2 Go, has several questions about the customer and trip information in the R2G database. You'll develop queries to provide Julia with up-to-date answers.

Module Objectives

After completing this module, you will be able to:

- Use the Query Wizard
- Work with data in a query
- Use Query Design View
- Sort and find data
- Filter data
- Apply AND criteria
- Apply OR criteria
- Format a datasheet

Files You Will Need

R2G-2.accdb	HouseOfReps-2.accdb
Salvage-2.accdb	VetClinic-2.accdb
Service-2.accdb	Baseball-2.accdb

Use the Query Wizard

Learning Outcomes
• Describe the purpose for a query
• Create a query with the Simple Query Wizard

A **query** answers a question about the information in the database. A query allows you to select a subset of fields and records from one or more tables and then present the selected data as a single datasheet. A major benefit of working with data through a query is that you can focus on only the specific information you need, rather than navigating through all the fields and records from one or more large tables. You can enter, edit, and navigate data in a query datasheet just like a table datasheet. However, keep in mind that Access data is physically stored only in tables, even though you can select, view, and edit it through other Access objects such as queries and forms. Because a query doesn't physically store the data, a query data-sheet is sometimes called a **logical view** of the data. A query stores a set of **SQL (Structured Query Language)** instructions, but because you can use Access query tools such as Query Design View to create and modify the query, you are not required to write SQL statements to build or use Access queries. Access provides several tools to create a new query, one of which is the Simple Query Wizard. **CASE** *Julia Rice suggests that you use the Simple Query Wizard to create a query that displays fields from the Trips and Customers tables in one datasheet.*

STEPS

1. **Start Access, open the R2G-2.accdb database, enable content if prompted, then maximize the window**

   Access provides several tools to create a new query. One way is to use the **Simple Query Wizard**, which prompts you for the information it needs to create the query.

2. **Click the Create tab on the Ribbon, click the Query Wizard button in the Queries group, then click OK to start the Simple Query Wizard**

   The first Simple Query Wizard dialog box opens, prompting you to select the fields you want to view in the new query. You can select fields from one or more existing tables or queries.

3. **Click the Tables/Queries list arrow, click Table: Trips, double-click TripName, double-click City, double-click Category, then double-click Price**

   So far, you've selected four fields from the Trips table to display basic trip information in this query. You also want to add the first and last name information from the Customers table so you know which customers purchased each trip.

TROUBLE
Click the Remove Single Field button < if you need to remove a field from the Selected Fields list.

4. **Click the Tables/Queries list arrow, click Table: Customers, double-click FName, then double-click LName**

   You've selected four fields from the Trips table and two from the Customers table for your new query, as shown in **FIGURE 2-1**.

TROUBLE
Click the Back button if you need to move to a previous dialog box in the Simple Query Wizard.

5. **Click Next, click Next to select Detail, select Trips Query in the title text box, type TripCustomerList as the name of the query, then click Finish**

   The TripCustomerList datasheet opens, displaying four fields from the Trips table and two from the Customers table, as shown in **FIGURE 2-2**. The query can show which customers have purchased which Trips because of the one-to-many table relationships established in the Relationships window.

Simple Query Wizard

The **Simple Query Wizard** is a series of dialog boxes that prompt you for the information needed to create a Select query. A **Select query** selects fields from one or more tables in your database and is by far the most common type of query. The other query wizards—Crosstab, Find Duplicates, and Find Unmatched—are used to create queries that do specialized types of data analysis and are covered in Module 10 on advanced queries.

FIGURE 2-1: Selecting fields using the Simple Query Wizard

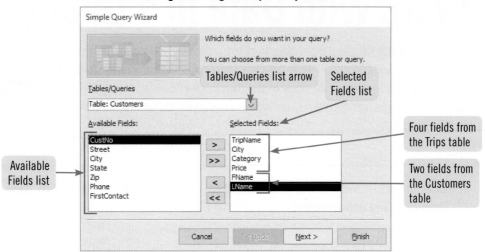

FIGURE 2-2: TripCustomerList datasheet

TripName	City	Category	Price	FName	LName
Stanley Bay Cleanup	Captiva	Eco	$750	Ralph	Stewart
Stanley Bay Cleanup	Captiva	Eco	$750	Lisa	Gomez
Breckenridge Reconstruction	Breckenridge	Eco	$850	Kristen	Collins
Stanley Bay Cleanup	Captiva	Eco	$750	Kris	Shaw
Stanley Bay Cleanup	Captiva	Eco	$750	Lois	Gordon
Stanley Bay Cleanup	Captiva	Eco	$750	Naresh	Blackwell
Coastal Shore Cleanup	Captiva	Family	$1,000	Julia	Bouchart
Breckenridge Reconstruction	Breckenridge	Eco	$850	Tom	Camel
Golden Hands Venture	Orlando	Family	$900	Shirley	Cruz
Golden Hands Venture	Orlando	Family	$900	Zohra	Bell
Golden Hands Venture	Orlando	Family	$900	Kathryn	Hall
Golden Hands Venture	Orlando	Family	$900	Jose	Edwards
Red Reef Cleanup	Islamadora	Eco	$1,500	Jane	Taylor
Stanley Bay Cleanup	Captiva	Eco	$750	Kori	James
American Heritage Tour	Philadelphia	Educational	$1,200	Sharol	Wood
American Heritage Tour	Philadelphia	Educational	$1,200	Lois	Gordon
American Heritage Tour	Philadelphia	Educational	$1,200	Tim	Hayes
American Heritage Tour	Philadelphia	Educational	$1,200	Frank	Torres
Yosemite Park Cleanup	Sacramento	Eco	$1,250	Tom	Camel
American Heritage Tour	Philadelphia	Educational	$1,200	Jane	Taylor
Yosemite Park Cleanup	Sacramento	Eco	$1,250	Kristen	Collins
American Heritage Tour	Philadelphia	Educational	$1,200	Kris	Shaw
American Heritage Tour	Philadelphia	Educational	$1,200	Ralph	Stewart
American Heritage Tour	Philadelphia	Educational	$1,200	Nancy	Cole
American Heritage Tour	Philadelphia	Educational	$1,200	Brad	Long

TripCustomerList query

Four fields from Trips table

Two fields from Customers table

Record: 1 of 106   No Filter   Search

106 records

Work with Data in a Query

Learning
Outcomes
• Edit records in
  a query
• Delete records in
  a query

You enter and edit data in a query datasheet the same way you do in a table datasheet. Because all data is stored in tables, any edits you make to data in a query datasheet are actually stored in the underlying tables and are automatically updated in all views of the data in other queries, forms, and reports. **CASE** ▶ *Julia Rice wants to change the name of one trip and update a city name. You can use the TripCustomerList query datasheet to make these edits.*

STEPS

TROUBLE
Be sure the final
TripName is *Captiva
Bay Cleanup*, not just
Captiva.

1. **Double-click Stanley in the TripName field of the first or second record, type Captiva, then click any other record**

   All occurrences of Stanley Bay Cleanup automatically update to Captiva Bay Cleanup because this TripName field value is stored only once in the Trips table. See **FIGURE 2-3**. The TripName is selected from the Trips table and displayed in the TripCustomerList query for each customer who purchased this trip.

2. **Double-click Orlando in the City field of any record for the Golden Hands Venture trip, type College Park, then click any other record**

   All occurrences of Orlando automatically update to College Park for the Golden Hands Venture trip because this value is stored only once in the City field of the Trips table for the Golden Hands Venture record. The Golden Hands Venture trip is displayed in the TripCustomerList query for each customer who purchased that trip.

3. **Click the record selector button to the left of the first record, click the Home tab, click the Delete button in the Records group, then click Yes**

   You can delete records from a query datasheet the same way you delete them from a table datasheet. Notice that the navigation bar now indicates you have 105 records in the datasheet, as shown in **FIGURE 2-4**.

4. **Right-click the TripCustomerList query tab, then click Close**

   Each time a query is opened, it shows a current view of the data. This means that as new trips, customers, or sales are recorded in the database, the next time you open this query, the information will include all updates.

Hiding and unhiding fields in a datasheet

To hide a field in a datasheet, right-click the field name at the top of the datasheet and click the Hide Fields option on the shortcut menu. To unhide a field, right-click any field name, click Unhide Fields, and check the hidden field's check box in the Unhide Columns dialog box.

Freezing and unfreezing fields in a datasheet

In large datasheets, you may want to freeze certain fields so that they remain on the screen at all times. To freeze a field, right-click its field name in the datasheet, and then click Freeze Fields. To unfreeze a field, right-click any field name and click Unfreeze All Fields.

FIGURE 2-3: Working with data in a query datasheet

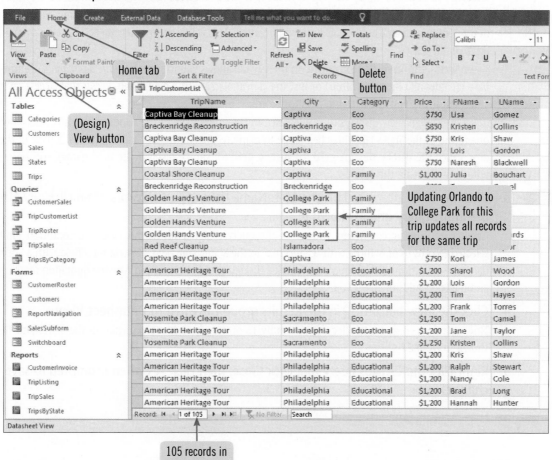

TripCustomerList

TripName	Record selector button for first record		City	Category	Price	FName	LName
Captiva Bay Cleanup			Captiva	Eco	$750	Ralph	Stewart
Captiva Bay Cleanup			Captiva	Eco	$750	Lisa	Gomez
Breckenridge Reconstruction			Breckenridge	Eco	$850	Kristen	Collins
Captiva Bay Cleanup			Captiva		$750	Kris	Shaw
Captiva Bay Cleanup	Updating Stanley to Captiva in one record updates all records with that TripName		Captiva		$750	Lois	Gordon
Captiva Bay Cleanup			Captiva		$750	Naresh	Blackwell
Coastal Shore Cleanup			Captiva		$1,000	Julia	Bouchart
Breckenridge Reconstruction			Brecken		$850	Tom	Camel
Golden Hands Venture			Orlando	Family	$900	Shirley	Cruz
Golden Hands Venture			Orlando	Family	$900	Zohra	Bell
Golden Hands Venture			Orlando	Family	$900	Kathryn	Hall
Golden Hands Venture			Orlando	Family	$900	Jose	Edwards
Red Reef Cleanup			Islamadora	Eco	$1,500	Jane	Taylor
Captiva Bay Cleanup			Captiva	Eco	$750	Kori	James
American Heritage Tour			Philadelphia	Educational	$1,200	Sharol	Wood

FIGURE 2-4: Final TripCustomerList datasheet

Use Query Design View

Learning Outcomes
• Work in Query Design View
• Add criteria to a query

You use **Query Design View** to add, delete, or move the fields in an existing query; to specify sort orders; or to add **criteria** to limit the number of records shown in the resulting datasheet. You can also use Query Design View to create a new query from scratch. In the upper pane, Query Design View presents the fields you can use for that query in small windows called **field lists**. If you use the fields of two or more related tables in the query, the relationship between two tables is displayed with a **join line** (also called a **link line**) identifying which fields are used to establish the relationship. **CASE** *Julia Rice asks you to produce a list of trips in California. You use Query Design View to modify the existing TripsByState query to meet her request.*

STEPS

1. **Double-click the TripsByState query in the Navigation Pane to review the datasheet, then click the View button ⬔ on the Home tab to switch to Query Design View**

   The TripsByState query contains the StateName field from the States table and the TripName, TripStartDate, and Price fields from the Trips table. This query contains two ascending sort orders: StateName and TripName. All records in California, for example, are further sorted by the TripName value.

   QUICK TIP
   Drag the lower edge of the field list to resize it to view all fields.

2. **Click the File tab, click Save As, click Save Object As, click the Save As button, type CATrips to replace Copy of TripsByState, then click OK**

   If you want to build a new query starting from an existing query, use the Save As command and give the new query a new name before you start working on it. This will prevent you from accidentally changing the original query.

   In Access, the **Save As command** on the File tab allows you to save the *entire database* (the entire database includes all objects within it) or just the *current object* with a new name. Recall that Access saves *data* automatically as you move from record to record.

   Query Design View displays the tables used in the upper pane of the window. The link line shows that one record in the States table may be related to many records in the Trips table. The lower pane of the window, called the **query design grid** (or **query grid** for short), displays the field names, sort orders, and criteria used within the query.

   QUICK TIP
   Query criteria are not case sensitive, so "California" equals "CALIFORNIA" equals "california".

3. **Click the first Criteria cell for the StateName field, type California, then click any other cell in the query grid as shown in FIGURE 2-5**

   Criteria are limiting conditions you set in the query design grid. In this case, the condition limits the selected records to only those with "California" in the StateName field. Criteria for a field with a Short Text data type are surrounded by "quotation marks" though you do not need to type the quotation marks. Access automatically adds them for you.

4. **Click the View button ▦ in the Results group to switch to Datasheet View**

   Now only 15 records are selected, because only 15 of the trips have "California" in the StateName field, as shown in FIGURE 2-6.

5. **Right-click the CATrips query tab, click Close, then click Yes when prompted to save changes**

Adding or deleting a table in a query

You might want to add a table's field list to the upper pane of Query Design View to select fields from that table for the query. To add a new table to Query Design View, drag it from the Navigation Pane to Query Design View, or click the Show Table button on the Design tab, then add the desired table(s). To delete an unneeded table from Query Design View, click its title bar, then press [Delete].

FIGURE 2-5: CATrips query in Design View

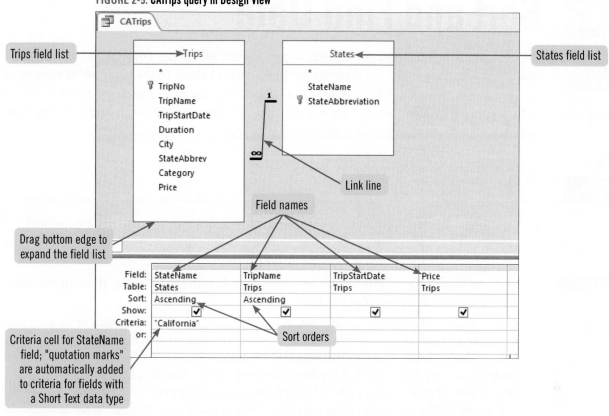

Trips field list

States field list

Trips

* TripNo
TripName
TripStartDate
Duration
City
StateAbbrev
Category
Price

States

* StateName
StateAbbreviation

Link line

Field names

Drag bottom edge to expand the field list

Field:	StateName	TripName	TripStartDate	Price
Table:	States	Trips	Trips	Trips
Sort:	Ascending	Ascending		
Show:	✔	✔	✔	✔
Criteria:	"California"			
or:				

Sort orders

Criteria cell for StateName field; "quotation marks" are automatically added to criteria for fields with a Short Text data type

FIGURE 2-6: CATrips query with California criterion

StateName	TripName	TripStartDate	Price
California	Bear Valley Adventures	08/18/2017	$800
California	Bigfoot Rafting Club	09/12/2017	$850
California	Black Sheep Hikers	08/25/2017	$3,000
California	Cactus Ecosystem	09/13/2017	$800
California	Golden State Trips	07/19/2017	$2,300
California	Japanese California Connection	08/18/2017	$900
California	Kings Canyon Bridge Builders	07/12/2017	$2,800
California	Langguth Environment	10/18/2017	$2,900
California	Monterey Mysteries	07/13/2017	$1,800
California	Oakland Museum of Science	07/19/2017	$1,000
California	Perfect Waves Project	06/26/2017	$800
California	Redwood Forest Lab	09/28/2017	$1,500
California	Silver Country Venture	07/12/2017	$3,500
California	Water Education Foundation	09/20/2017	$1,300
California	Yosemite Park Cleanup	07/19/2017	$1,250

TripName values are in ascending order

Only 15 California records are selected

Sort and Find Data

The Access sort and find features are handy tools that help you quickly organize and find data in a table or query datasheet. TABLE 2-1 describes the Sort and Find buttons on the Home tab. Besides using these buttons, you can also click the list arrow on the field name in a datasheet, and then click a sorting option. **CASE** *Julia asks you to provide a list of trips sorted by Category, and then by Price. You'll modify the TripsByCategory query to answer this request.*

STEPS

1. **Double-click the TripsByCategory query in the Navigation Pane to open its datasheet**

   The TripsByCategory query currently sorts Trips by Category, then by TripName. You'll add the Duration field to this query, then change the sort order for the records.

2. **Click the View button in the Views group to switch to Design View, then double-click the Duration field in the Trips field list**

   When you double-click a field in a field list, Access inserts it in the next available column in the query grid. You can also drag a field from a field list to a specific column of the query grid. To select a field in the query grid, you click its field selector. The **field selector** is the thin gray bar above each field in the query grid. To delete a field from a query, click its field selector, then press [Delete]. Deleting a field from a query does not delete it from the underlying table; the field is only deleted from the query.

   Currently, the TripsByCategory query is sorted by Category and then by TripName. Access evaluates sort orders from left to right. You want to change the sort order so that the records sort first by Category then by Price.

3. **Click Ascending in the TripName Sort cell, click the list arrow, click (not sorted), double-click the Price Sort cell, click the list arrow, then click Descending**

   The records are now set to be sorted in ascending order by Category, and within each Category, in a descending order by the Price field, as shown in FIGURE 2-7. Because sort orders always work from left to right, you might need to rearrange the fields before applying a sort order that uses more than one field. To move a field in the query design grid, click its field selector, then drag it left or right.

4. **Click the View button in the Results group to switch to Datasheet View**

   The new datasheet shows the Duration field in the fifth column. The records are now sorted in ascending order by the Category field, but for records in the same Category, they are further sorted in descending order by Price. Your next task is to replace all occurrences of "Tour" with "Trip" in the TripName field.

5. **Click in any TripName field, click the Replace button on the Home tab, type Tour in the Find What box, click in the Replace With box, type Trip, click the Match arrow button, then click Any Part of Field**

   The Find and Replace dialog box is shown in FIGURE 2-8.

6. **Click the Replace All button in the Find and Replace dialog box, click Yes to continue, then click Cancel to close the Find and Replace dialog box**

   Access replaced both occurrences of "Tour" with "Trip" in the TripName field, as shown in FIGURE 2-9.

7. **Right-click the TripsByCategory query tab, click Close, then click Yes if prompted to save changes**

FIGURE 2-7: Changing sort orders for the TripsByCategory query

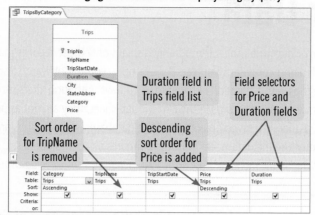

Duration field in
Trips field list

Field selectors
for Price and
Duration fields

Sort order
for TripName
is removed

Descending
sort order for
Price is added

Field:	Category	TripName	TripStartDate	Price	Duration
Table:	Trips	Trips	Trips	Trips	Trips
Sort:	Ascending			Descending	
Show:	☑	☑	☑	☑	☑
Criteria:					
or:					

FIGURE 2-8: Find and Replace dialog box

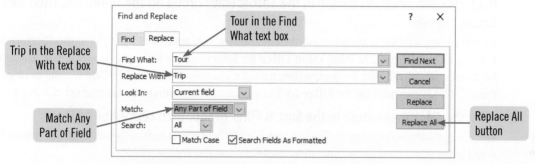

Trip in the Replace
With text box

Tour in the Find
What text box

Match Any
Part of Field

Replace All
button

FIGURE 2-9: Final TripsByCategory datasheet with new sort orders

Trip replaces
Tour in the
TripName field

Records with the
same Category are
further sorted in
descending order
by the Price field

Category	TripName	TripStartDate	Price	Duration
Educational	Bridgewater Country Study	08/06/2017	$2,000	10
Educational	Hummer Trail Study	05/29/2017	$1,250	7
Educational	American Heritage Trip	08/23/2017	$1,200	7
Educational	Broadway Workshops	08/23/2017	$1,000	7
Educational	Freedom Bionetwork	08/23/2017	$1,000	7
Educational	Oakland Museum of Science	07/19/2017	$1,000	7
Educational	Japanese California Connection	08/18/2017	$900	4
Educational	Great Fish Count	09/02/2017	$700	9
Family	Silver Country Venture	07/12/2017	$3,500	14
Family	Rocky Mountain Mission	08/10/2017	$1,700	3
Family	Blue Canyon Youth Project	06/30/2017	$1,400	7
Family	Missouri Bald Eagle Watch Club	08/12/2017	$1,100	7
Family	Coastal Shore Cleanup	05/29/2017	$1,000	7
Family	Golden Hands Venture	05/22/2017	$900	4
Service	Boy Scout Project	08/02/2017	$1,000	7
Service	Emmanuel Youth Club	06/30/2017	$900	7
Site Seeing	Golden State Trips	07/19/2017	$2,300	10
Site Seeing	Monterey Mysteries	07/13/2017	$1,800	7
Site Seeing	Patriots in Disneyland	06/11/2017	$1,500	7

TABLE 2-1: Sort and Find buttons

name	button	purpose
Ascending		Sorts records based on the selected field in ascending order (0 to 9, A to Z)
Descending		Sorts records based on the selected field in descending order (Z to A, 9 to 0)
Remove Sort		Removes the current sort order
Find		Opens the Find and Replace dialog box to find data
Replace		Opens the Find and Replace dialog box to find and replace data
Go To		Helps you navigate to the first, previous, next, last, or new record
Select		Helps you select a single record or all records in a datasheet

Filter Data

Learning Outcomes
• Apply and remove filters in a query
• Use wildcards in criteria

Filtering a table or query datasheet temporarily displays only those records that match given criteria. Recall that criteria are limiting conditions you set. For example, you might want to show only trips in the state of Missouri, or only trips with a duration of fewer than 14 days. Although filters provide a quick and easy way to display a temporary subset of records in the current datasheet, they are not as powerful or flexible as queries. Most important, a query is a saved object within the database, whereas filters are temporary. Access removes all filters when you close the datasheet. TABLE 2-2 compares filters and queries. **CASE** *Julia asks you to find all Family trips offered in the month of August. You can filter the Trips table datasheet to provide this information.*

STEPS

QUICK TIP
You can also apply a sort or filter by clicking the Sort and filter arrow to the right of the field name and choosing the sort order or filter values you want.

1. **Double-click the Trips table to open it, click any occurrence of Family in the Category field, click the Selection button in the Sort & Filter group on the Home tab, then click Equals "Family"**

   Six records are selected as shown in FIGURE 2-10. A filter icon appears to the right of the Category field. Filtering by the selected field value, called **Filter By Selection**, is a fast and easy way to filter the records for an exact match. To filter for comparative data (for example, where TripStartDate is equal to or greater than 7/1/2017), you must use the **Filter By Form** feature. Filter buttons are summarized in TABLE 2-3.

2. **Click the Advanced button in the Sort & Filter group, then click Filter By Form**

   The Filter by Form window opens. The previous Filter By Selection criterion, "Family" in the Category field, is still in the grid. Access places "quotation marks" around text criteria.

QUICK TIP
To clear previous criteria, click the Advanced button, then click Clear All Filters.

3. **Click the TripStartDate cell, then type 8/*/2017 as shown in FIGURE 2-11**

   Filter By Form also allows you to apply two or more criteria at the same time. An asterisk (*) in the day position of the date criterion works as a wildcard, selecting any date in the month of August in the year 2017.

QUICK TIP
Be sure to remove existing filters before applying a new filter, or the new filter will apply to the current subset of records instead of the entire datasheet.

4. **Click the Toggle Filter button in the Sort & Filter group**

   The datasheet selects one record that matches both filter criteria, as shown in FIGURE 2-12. Note that filter icons appear next to the TripStartDate and Category field names as both fields are involved in the filter.

5. **Close the Trips datasheet, then click Yes when prompted to save the changes**

   Saving changes to the datasheet saves the last sort order and column width changes. *Filters are not saved.*

Using wildcard characters

To search for a pattern, you can use a **wildcard** character to represent any character in the condition entry. Use a question mark (?) to search for any single character and an asterisk (*) to search for any number of characters. Wildcard characters are often used with the **Like** operator. For example, the criterion Like "12/*/17" would find all dates in December of 2017, and the criterion Like "F*" would find all entries that start with the letter F.

FIGURE 2-10: Filtering the Trips table

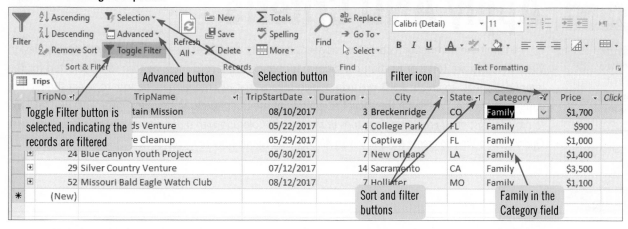

FIGURE 2-11: Filtering by Form criteria

FIGURE 2-12: Results of filtering by form

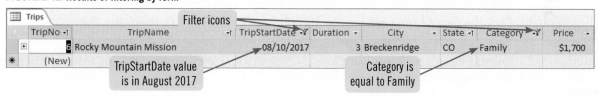

TABLE 2-2: Filters vs. queries

characteristics	filters	queries
Are saved as an object in the database		•
Can be used to select a subset of records in a datasheet	•	•
Can be used to select a subset of fields in a datasheet		•
Resulting datasheet used to enter and edit data	•	•
Resulting datasheet used to sort, filter, and find records	•	•
Commonly used as the source of data for a form or report		•
Can calculate sums, averages, counts, and other types of summary statistics across records		•
Can be used to create calculated fields		•

TABLE 2-3: Filter buttons

name	button	purpose
Filter	▼	Provides a list of values in the selected field that can be used to customize a filter
Selection	▼	Filters records that equal, do not equal, or are otherwise compared with the current value
Advanced		Provides advanced filter features such as Filter By Form, Save As Query, and Clear All Filters
Toggle Filter		Applies or removes the current filter

Apply AND Criteria

Learning Outcomes
- Enter AND criteria in a query
- Define criteria syntax
- Use comparison operators with criteria

You can limit the number of records that appear on a query datasheet by entering criteria in Query Design View. **Criteria** are tests, or limiting conditions, for which the record must be true to be selected for the query datasheet. To create **AND criteria**, which means that *all* criteria must be true to select the record, enter two or more criteria on the *same* Criteria row of the query design grid. **CASE** ▸ *Julia Rice asks you to provide a list of all Eco (ecological) trips in the state of Colorado with a duration of seven days or more. Use Query Design View to create the query with AND criteria to meet her request.*

STEPS

1. **Click the Create tab on the Ribbon, click the Query Design button, double-click Trips, then click Close in the Show Table dialog box**

   You want four fields from the Trips table in this query.

2. **Drag the bottom edge of the Trips field list down to display all of the fields, double-click TripName, double-click Duration, double-click StateAbbrev, then double-click Category to add these fields to the query grid**

   First add criteria to select only those records in Colorado. Because you are using the StateAbbrev field, you need to use the two-letter state abbreviation for Colorado, CO, as the Criteria entry.

3. **Click the first Criteria cell for the StateAbbrev field, type CO, then click the View button 🔲 to display the results**

   Querying for only those trips in the state of Colorado selects seven records. Next, you add criteria to select only the trips in the Eco category.

4. **Click the View button 🔲, click the first Criteria cell for the Category field, type Eco, then click the View button 🔲 in the Results group**

   Criteria added to the same line of the query design grid are AND criteria. When entered on the same line, each criterion must be true for the record to appear in the resulting datasheet. Querying for both CO and Eco trips narrows the selection to three records. Every time you add AND criteria, you narrow the number of records that are selected because the record must be true for all criteria.

5. **Click the View button 🔲, click the first Criteria cell for the Duration field, then type >=7, as shown in FIGURE 2-13**

   Access assists you with **criteria syntax**, rules that specify how to enter criteria. Access automatically adds "quotation marks" around text criteria in Short Text and Long Text fields ("CO" and "Eco") and pound signs (#) around date criteria in Date/Time fields. The criteria in the Number, Currency, and Yes/No fields are not surrounded by any characters. See **TABLE 2-4** for more information about comparison operators such as >= (greater than or equal to).

6. **Click the View button 🔲 in the Results group**

   The third AND criterion further narrows the number of records selected to two, as shown in **FIGURE 2-14**.

7. **Click the Save button 🔲 on the Quick Access Toolbar, type EcoCO7 as the query name, click OK, then close the query**

   The query is saved with the new name, EcoCO7, as a new object in the R2G-2 database. Criteria entered in Query Design View are permanently saved with the query (as compared to filters in the previous lesson, which are temporary and not saved with the object).

FIGURE 2-13: Query Design View with AND criteria

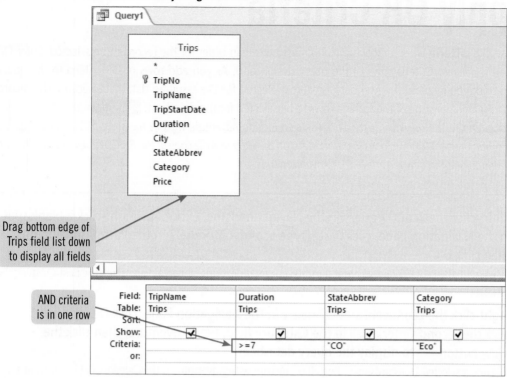

Drag bottom edge of Trips field list down to display all fields

AND criteria is in one row

FIGURE 2-14: Final datasheet of EcoCO7 query

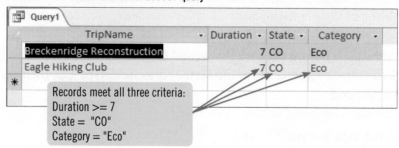

Records meet all three criteria:
Duration >= 7
State = "CO"
Category = "Eco"

TABLE 2-4: Comparison operators

operator	description	expression	meaning
>	Greater than	>500	Numbers greater than 500
>=	Greater than or equal to	>=500	Numbers greater than or equal to 500
<	Less than	<"Elder"	Names from A to Elder, but not Elder
<=	Less than or equal to	<="Buehler"	Names from A through Buehler, inclusive
<>	Not equal to	<>"Bridgewater"	Any name except for Bridgewater

Searching for blank fields

Is Null and Is Not Null are two other types of common criteria. The **Is Null** criterion finds all records where no entry has been made in the field. **Is Not Null** finds all records where there is any entry in the field, even if the entry is 0. Primary key fields cannot have a null entry.

Apply OR Criteria

Learning Outcomes
• Enter OR criteria in a query
• Rename a query

You use **OR criteria** when *any one criterion* must be true in order for the record to be selected. Enter OR criteria on *different* Criteria rows of the query design grid. As you add rows of OR criteria to the query design grid, you increase the number of records selected for the resulting datasheet because the record needs to match only one of the Criteria rows to be selected for the datasheet. **CASE** ▶ *Julia Rice asks you to add criteria to the previous query. She wants to include Adventure trips in the state of Colorado that are greater than or equal to seven days in duration. To do this, you make a copy of the EcoCO7 query to modify with OR criteria to add the new records for the Adventure trips.*

STEPS

1. **Right-click the EcoCO7 query in the Navigation Pane, click Copy, right-click a blank spot in the Navigation Pane, click Paste, type EcoAdventureCO7 in the Paste As dialog box, then click OK**

   By copying the EcoCO7 query before starting your modifications, you avoid changing the EcoCO7 query by mistake.

2. **Right-click the EcoAdventureCO7 query in the Navigation Pane, click Design View, click the second Criteria cell in the Category field, type Adventure, then click the View button ▦ to display the query datasheet**

   The query selected 11 records including all of the trips with Adventure in the Category field. Note that some of the Duration values are less than seven and some of the StateAbbrev values are not CO. Because each row of the query grid is evaluated separately, *all* Adventure trips are selected regardless of criteria in any other row. In other words, the criteria in one row have no effect on the criteria of other rows. To make sure that the Adventure trips are also in Colorado and have a duration of greater than or equal to seven days, you need to modify the second row of the query grid (the "or" row) to add that criteria.

QUICK TIP
Datasheet View ▦,
Design View ☑,
and other view buttons are also located in the lower-right corner of the Access window.

3. **Click the View button ☑, click the second Criteria cell in the Duration field, type >=7, click the second Criteria cell in the StateAbbrev field, type CO, then click in any other cell of the grid**

   Query Design View should look like **FIGURE 2-15**.

4. **Click the View button ▦**

   Three records are selected that meet all three criteria as entered in row one or row two of the query grid, as shown in **FIGURE 2-16**.

5. **Right-click the EcoAdventureCO7 query tab, click Close, then click Yes to save and close the query datasheet**

FIGURE 2-15: Query Design View with OR criteria

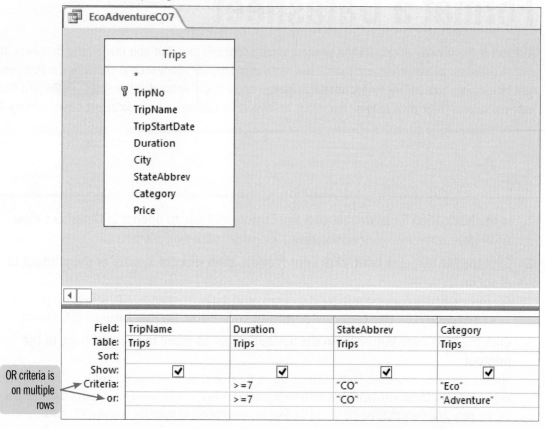

OR criteria is on multiple rows →

Field:	TripName	Duration	StateAbbrev	Category
Table:	Trips	Trips	Trips	Trips
Sort:				
Show:	☑	☑	☑	☑
Criteria:		>=7	"CO"	"Eco"
or:		>=7	"CO"	"Adventure"

FIGURE 2-16: Final datasheet of EcoAdventureCO7 query

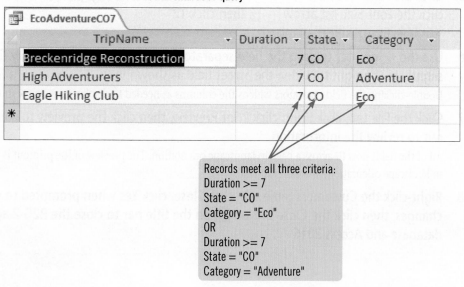

TripName	Duration	State.	Category
Breckenridge Reconstruction	7	CO	Eco
High Adventurers	7	CO	Adventure
Eagle Hiking Club	7	CO	Eco

Records meet all three criteria:
Duration >= 7
State = "CO"
Category = "Eco"
OR
Duration >= 7
State = "CO"
Category = "Adventure"

Format a Datasheet

A report is the primary Access tool to create a professional printout, but you can print a datasheet as well. A datasheet allows you to apply some basic formatting modifications such as changing the font size, font face, colors, and gridlines. All formatting changes apply to the entire datasheet. **CASE** *Julia Rice asks you to print a list of customers. You decide to format the Customers table datasheet before printing it for her.*

Learning Outcomes
- Zoom in print preview
- Format a datasheet
- Change page orientation

STEPS

1. **In the Navigation Pane, double-click the Customers table to open it in Datasheet View**

   Before applying new formatting enhancements, you preview the default printout.

2. **Click the File tab, click Print, click Print Preview, then click the header of the printout to zoom in**

   The preview window displays the layout of the printout, as shown in FIGURE 2-17. By default, the printout of a datasheet contains the object name and current date in the header. The page number is in the footer.

3. **Click the Next Page button ▶ in the navigation bar to move to the next page of the printout**

   The last two fields, Phone and FirstContact, print on the second page because the first is not wide enough to accommodate them. You decide to switch the report to landscape orientation so that all of the fields print on one page, and then increase the size of the font before printing to make the text easier to read.

4. **Click the Landscape button on the Print Preview tab to switch the report to landscape orientation, then click the Close Print Preview button**

   You return to Datasheet View where you can make font face, font size, font color, gridline color, and background color choices.

5. **Click the Font list arrow | Calibri (Detail) | in the Text Formatting group, click Arial Narrow, click the Font Size list arrow | 11 |, then click 12**

   You decide to widen the Street column.

6. **Use the ↔ pointer to drag the field separator between the Street and City field names slightly to the right to widen the Street field as shown in FIGURE 2-18**

   Double-clicking the field separators widens the columns as needed to display every entry in those fields.

   QUICK TIP
   If you need a printout of this datasheet, add your name as a new record to the Customers table, then print it.

7. **Click the File tab, click Print, click Print Preview, then click the preview to zoom in and out to review the information**

   All of the fields now fit across a page in landscape orientation. The preview of the printout is two pages, and in landscape orientation, it is easier to read.

8. **Right-click the Customers table tab, click Close, click Yes when prompted to save changes, then click the Close button ✕ on the title bar to close the R2G-2.accdb database and Access 2016**

FIGURE 2-17: Preview of Customers datasheet

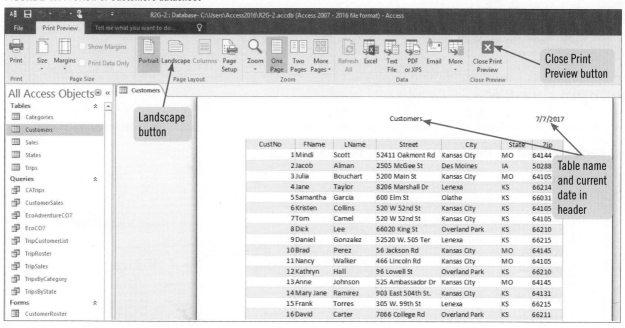

Landscape button

Close Print Preview button

Table name and current date in header

FIGURE 2-18: Formatting the Customers datasheet

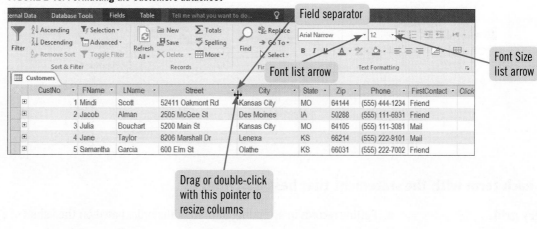

Field separator

Font list arrow

Font Size list arrow

Drag or double-click with this pointer to resize columns

Practice

Concepts Review

Label each element of the Access window shown in FIGURE 2-19.

FIGURE 2-19

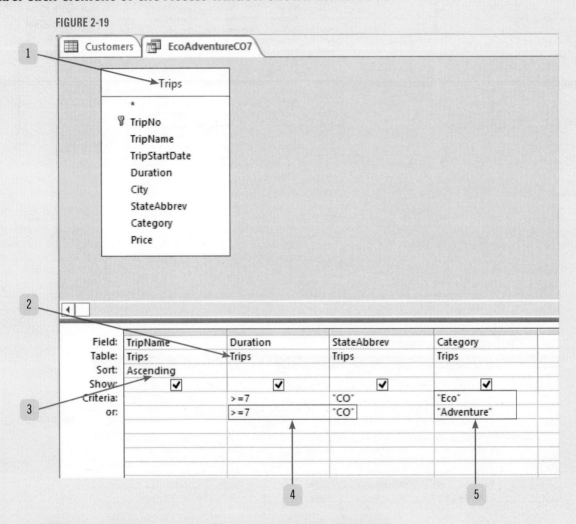

Match each term with the statement that best describes it.

6. **Query grid**
7. **Field selector**
8. **Filter**
9. **Filter By Selection**
10. **Field lists**
11. **Sorting**
12. **Join line**
13. **Criteria**
14. **Syntax**
15. **Wildcard**

a. Putting records in ascending or descending order based on the values of a field
b. Limiting conditions used to restrict the number of records that are selected in a query
c. The thin gray bar above each field in the query grid
d. Creates a temporary subset of records
e. Small windows that display field names
f. Rules that determine how criteria are entered
g. Used to search for a pattern of characters
h. The lower pane in Query Design View
i. Identifies which fields are used to establish a relationship between two tables
j. A fast and easy way to filter the records for an exact match

Select the best answer from the list of choices.

16. AND criteria:
   a. determine sort orders.
   b. must all be true for the record to be selected.
   c. determine fields selected for a query.
   d. help set link lines between tables in a query.

17. SQL stands for which of the following?
   a. Structured Query Language
   b. Standard Query Language
   c. Special Query Listing
   d. Simple Query Listing

18. A query is sometimes called a logical view of data because:
   a. you can create queries with the Logical Query Wizard.
   b. queries contain logical criteria.
   c. query naming conventions are logical.
   d. queries do not store data—they only display a view of data.

19. Which of the following describes OR criteria?
   a. Selecting a subset of fields and/or records to view as a datasheet from one or more tables
   b. Using two or more rows of the query grid to select only those records that meet given criteria
   c. Reorganizing the records in either ascending or descending order based on the contents of one or more fields
   d. Using multiple fields in the query design grid

20. Which of the following is *not* true about a query?
   a. A query is the same thing as a filter.
   b. A query can select fields from one or more tables in a relational database.
   c. A query can be created using different tools.
   d. An existing query can be modified in Query Design View.

Skills Review

1. **Use the Query Wizard.**
   a. Open the Salvage-2.accdb database from the location where you store your Data Files. Enable content if prompted.
   b. Create a new query using the Simple Query Wizard. Select the CenterName field from the Centers table, the DepositDate and Weight fields from the Deposits table, and the ClubName field from the Clubs table. Select Detail, and enter **CenterDeposits** as the name of the query.
   c. Open the query in Datasheet View, then change any record with the Johnson Recycling value to a center name that includes your last name.

2. **Work with data in a query.**
   a. Delete the first record (A1 Salvage Center with a DepositDate value of 2/4/2014).
   b. Change any occurrence of JavaScript KC in the ClubName field to **Bootstrap Club**.
   c. Click any value in the DepositDate field, then click the Descending button on the Home tab to sort the records in descending order on the DepositDate field.
   d. Use the Calendar Picker to choose the date of **1/30/17** for the first record.
   e. Save and close the CenterDeposits query.

3. **Use Query Design View.**
   a. Click the Create tab, click the Query Design button, double-click Clubs, double-click Deposits, and then click Close to add the Clubs and Deposits tables to Query Design View.
   b. Drag the bottom edge of both field lists down as needed to display all of the field names in both tables.
   c. Add the following fields from the Clubs table to the query design grid in the following order: FName, LName, ClubName. Add the following fields from the Deposits table in the following order: DepositDate, Weight. View the results in Datasheet View, observing the number of records that are selected in the record navigation bar at the bottom of the datasheet.
   d. In Design View, enter criteria to display only those records with a Weight value of **>=100**, then observe the number of records that are selected in Datasheet View.
   e. Save the query with the name **100PlusDeposits**.

4. **Sort and find data.**
   a. In Query Design View of the 100PlusDeposits query, choose an ascending sort order for the ClubName field and a descending sort order for the Weight field.
   b. Display the query in Datasheet View, noting how the records have been resorted.
   c. In the ClubName field, change any occurrence of Boy Scout Troop 324 to Boy Scout Troop **6**.
   d. In the FName field, change any occurrence of Trey to *your* initials and save the query.

5. **Filter data.**
   a. Filter the 100PlusDeposits datasheet for only those records where the ClubName equals **Access Users Group**.
   b. Apply an advanced Filter By Form and use the >= operator to further narrow the records so that only the deposits with a DepositDate value on or after 1/1/2015 are selected.
   c. Apply the filter to see the datasheet and, if requested by your instructor, print the filtered 100PlusDeposits datasheet.
   d. Save and close the 100PlusDeposits query. Reopen the 100PlusDeposits query to confirm that filters are temporary (not saved), and then close the 100PlusDeposits query again.

Skills Review (continued)

6. **Apply AND criteria.**
   a. Right-click the 100PlusDeposits query, copy it, and then paste it as **100PlusDeposits2016**.
   b. Open the 100PlusDeposits2016 query in Query Design View.
   c. Modify the criteria to select all of the records with a DepositDate in **2016** and a Weight value **greater than or equal to 100**. (*Hint:* To select all records with a DepositDate in 2016, use a wildcard character for the month and day positions of the date criterion.)
   d. Display the results in Datasheet View. If requested by your instructor, print the 100PlusDeposits2016 datasheet, then save and close it.

7. **Apply OR criteria.**
   a. Right-click the 100PlusDeposits query, copy it, then paste it as **100PlusDeposits2Clubs**.
   b. Open the 100PlusDeposits2Clubs query in Design View, then add criteria to select the records with a ClubName of **Social Media Club** and a Weight value **greater than or equal to 100**.
   c. Add criteria to also include the records with a ClubName of **Access Users Group** with a Weight value **greater than or equal to 100**. FIGURE 2-20 shows the results.
   d. If requested by your instructor, print the 100PlusDeposits2Clubs datasheet, then save and close it.

FIGURE 2-20

Your initials will be in the FName field

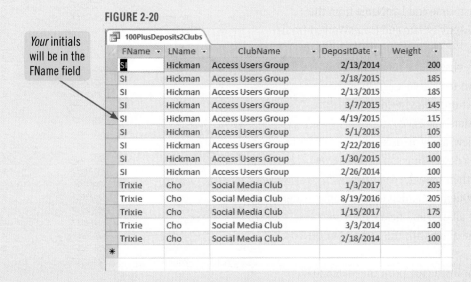

FName	LName	ClubName	DepositDate	Weight
SI	Hickman	Access Users Group	2/13/2014	200
SI	Hickman	Access Users Group	2/18/2015	185
SI	Hickman	Access Users Group	2/13/2015	185
SI	Hickman	Access Users Group	3/7/2015	145
SI	Hickman	Access Users Group	4/19/2015	115
SI	Hickman	Access Users Group	5/1/2015	105
SI	Hickman	Access Users Group	2/22/2016	100
SI	Hickman	Access Users Group	1/30/2015	100
SI	Hickman	Access Users Group	2/26/2014	100
Trixie	Cho	Social Media Club	1/3/2017	205
Trixie	Cho	Social Media Club	8/19/2014	205
Trixie	Cho	Social Media Club	1/15/2017	175
Trixie	Cho	Social Media Club	3/3/2014	100
Trixie	Cho	Social Media Club	2/18/2014	100

8. **Format a datasheet.**
   a. In the Centers table datasheet, apply the Times New Roman font and a 14-point font size.
   b. Resize all columns so that all data and field names are visible.
   c. Display the Centers datasheet in Print Preview, switch the orientation to landscape, click the Margins button in the Page Size group, then click Narrow.
   d. If requested by your instructor, print the Centers datasheet.
   e. Save and close the Centers table, then close Access 2016.

Independent Challenge 1

You have built an Access database to track membership in a community service club. The database tracks member names and addresses as well as their community service hours.

a. Open the Service-2.accdb database from the location where you store your Data Files, enable content if prompted, then open the Activities, Members, and Zips tables to review their datasheets.

b. In the Zips table, click the expand button to the left of the 64111, Kansas City, MO record to display the two members linked to that zip code. Click the expand button to the left of the Jeremiah Hopper record to display the three activity records linked to Jeremiah.

c. Close all three datasheets, click the Database Tools tab, then click the Relationships button. The Relationships window shows you that one record in the Zips table is related to many records in the Members table through the common ZipCode field, and that one record in the Members table is related to many records in the Activities table through the common MemberNo field.

d. Click the Relationship Report button, then if requested by your instructor, print the Relationship report. Close and save the report with the default name **Relationships for Service-2**. Close the Relationships window.

e. Using Query Design View, build a query with the following fields: FirstName and LastName from the Members table and ActivityDate and HoursWorked from the Activities table.

f. View the datasheet, observe the number of records selected, then return to Query Design View.

g. Add criteria to select only those records where the ActivityDate is in March of 2017.

h. In Query Design View, apply an ascending sort order to the LastName and a descending sort order to the ActivityDate field, then view the datasheet.

i. Change the name Quentin Garden to your name, widen all columns so that all data and field names are visible, and save the query with the name **March2017**, as shown in FIGURE 2-21.

j. If requested by your instructor, print the March2017 datasheet, then close the March2017 query and close Access 2016.

FIGURE 2-21

FirstName	LastName	ActivityDate	HoursWorked
Rhea	Alman	3/23/2017	4
Micah	Ati	3/23/2017	4
Evan	Bouchart	3/24/2017	8
Forrest	Browning	3/23/2017	5
Patch	Bullock	3/21/2017	4
Angela	Cabriella	3/23/2017	5
Andrea	Collins	3/25/2017	8
Student First	Student Last	3/25/2017	8
Student First	Student Last	3/23/2017	4
Gabriel	Hammer	3/23/2017	5
Jeremiah	Hopper	3/21/2017	4
Heidi	Kalvert	3/23/2017	4
Karla	Larson	3/23/2017	5
Katrina	Margolis	3/23/2017	4
Jose	Martin	3/24/2017	8
Jon	Maxim	3/24/2017	4
Harvey	McCord	3/24/2017	4
Mallory	Olson	3/25/2017	8
Jana	Pence	3/24/2017	10
Allie	Pitt	3/23/2017	4
Su	Vogue	3/24/2017	8
Taney	Wilson	3/24/2017	8

Record: I◄ ◄ 23 of 23 ► ►I ► No Filter   Search

Independent Challenge 2

You work for a nonprofit agency that tracks voting patterns. You have developed an Access database with contact information for members of the House of Representatives. The director of the agency has asked you to create several state lists of representatives. You will use queries to extract this information.

a. Open the HouseOfReps-2.accdb database from the location where you store your Data Files, then enable content if prompted.

b. Open the Representatives and the States tables. Notice that one state is related to many representatives as evidenced by the expand buttons to the left of the records in the States tables.

c. Close both datasheets, then using Query Design View, create a query with the StateAbbrev, StateName, and Capital fields from the States table (in that order) as well as the FName and LName fields from the Representatives table.

d. Sort the records in ascending order on the StateName field, then in ascending order on the LName field.

e. Add criteria to select the representatives from Ohio or Pennsylvania. Use the StateAbbrev field to enter your criteria, using the two-character state abbreviations of **OH** and **PA**.

f. Save the query with the name **OhioAndPenn**, view the results, shown in FIGURE 2-22, then change the last name of Butterfield in the second record to *your* last name. Resize the columns as needed to view all the data and field names.

g. Print the OhioAndPenn datasheet if requested by your instructor, then close it and exit Access 2016.

FIGURE 2-22

StateAbbrev	StateName	Capital	FName	LName
OH	Ohio	Columbus	Luis	Boehner
OH	Ohio	Columbus	Ed	Student Last Name
OH	Ohio	Columbus	Sue	Crowley
OH	Ohio	Columbus	Totoro	Engel
OH	Ohio	Columbus	Dana	Higgins
OH	Ohio	Columbus	Chaka	Hinchey
OH	Ohio	Columbus	Dave	Israel
OH	Ohio	Columbus	Roger	Maloney
OH	Ohio	Columbus	Gil	McCarthy
OH	Ohio	Columbus	Mookie	McHugh
OH	Ohio	Columbus	Dennis	McNulty
OH	Ohio	Columbus	Alan	Pearce
OH	Ohio	Columbus	John	Reynolds
OH	Ohio	Columbus	Vic	Serrano
OH	Ohio	Columbus	Nydia	Slaughter
OH	Ohio	Columbus	Carter	Towns
OH	Ohio	Columbus	Chuck	Udall
OH	Ohio	Columbus	Joe	Velázquez
PA	Pennsylvania	Harrisburg	Jon	Blumenauer
PA	Pennsylvania	Harrisburg	Artur	Coble
PA	Pennsylvania	Harrisburg	Ron	Etheridge
PA	Pennsylvania	Harrisburg	Denny	Foxx
PA	Pennsylvania	Harrisburg	John	Gillmor
PA	Pennsylvania	Harrisburg	Spencer	Hayes
PA	Pennsylvania	Harrisburg	David	Jones

Record: 3 of 37   No Filter   Search

Independent Challenge 3

You have built an Access database to track the veterinarian clinics in your area.

a. Open the VetClinic-2.accdb database from the location where you store your Data Files, then enable content if prompted.

b. Open the Vets table and then the Clinics table to review the data in both datasheets.

c. Click the expand button next to the Animal Haven record in the Clinics table, then add your name as a new record to the Vets subdatasheet.

d. Close both datasheets.

e. Using the Simple Query Wizard, select the VetLast and VetFirst fields from the Vets table, and select the ClinicName and Phone fields from the Clinics table. Title the query **ClinicVetListing**, then view the datasheet.

f. Update any occurrence of Animal Haven in the ClinicName field to **Animal Emergency Shelter**.

g. In Query Design View, add criteria to select only **Animal Emergency Shelter** or **Veterinary Specialists** in the ClinicName field, then view the datasheet.

h. In Query Design View, move the ClinicName field to the first column, then add an ascending sort order on the ClinicName and VetLast fields.

i. Display the ClinicVetListing query in Datasheet View, resize the fields as shown in FIGURE 2-23, then print the datasheet if requested by your instructor.

j. Save and close the ClinicVetListing datasheet, then exit Access 2016.

FIGURE 2-23

Independent Challenge 4: Explore

An Access database is an excellent tool to help record and track job opportunities. For this exercise, you'll create a database from scratch that you can use to enter, edit, and query data in pursuit of a new job or career.

a. Create a new desktop database named **Jobs.accdb**.

b. Create a table named **Positions** with the following field names, data types, and descriptions:

Field name	Data type	Description
PositionID	AutoNumber	Primary key field
Title	Short Text	Title of position such as Accountant, Assistant Court Clerk, or Web Developer
CareerArea	Short Text	Area of the career field such as Accounting, Government, or Information Systems
AnnualSalary	Currency	Annual salary
Desirability	Number	Desirability rating of 1 = low to 5 = high to show how desirable the position is to you
EmployerID	Number	Foreign key field to the Employers table

c. Create a table named **Employers** with the following field names, data types, and descriptions:

Field name	Data type	Description
EmployerID	AutoNumber	Primary key field
CompanyName	Short Text	Company name of the employer
EmpStreet	Short Text	Employer's street address
EmpCity	Short Text	Employer's city
EmpState	Short Text	Employer's state
EmpZip	Short Text	Employer's zip code
EmpPhone	Short Text	Employer's phone, such as 111-222-3333

d. Be sure to set EmployerID as the primary key field in the Employers table and the PositionID as the primary key field in the Positions table.

e. Link the Employers and Positions tables together in a one-to-many relationship using the common EmployerID field. One employer record will be linked to many position records. Be sure to enforce referential integrity.

f. Using any valid source of potential employer data, enter five records into the Employers table.

g. Using any valid source of job information, enter five records into the Positions table by using the subdatasheets from within the Employers datasheet.

Because one employer may have many positions, all five of your Positions records may be linked to the same employer, you may have one position record per employer, or any other combination.

h. Build a query that selects CompanyName from the Employers table, and the Title, CareerArea, AnnualSalary, and Desirability fields from the Positions table. Sort the records in descending order based on Desirability. Save the query as **JobList**, and print it if requested by your instructor.

i. Close the JobList datasheet, then exit Access 2016.

Visual Workshop

Open the Baseball-2.accdb database from the location where you store your Data Files, and enable content if prompted. Create a query in Query Design View based on the Players and Teams tables, as shown in FIGURE 2-24. Add criteria to select only those records where the PlayerPosition field values are equal to 1 or 2 (representing pitchers and catchers). In Query Design View, set an ascending sort order on the TeamName and PlayerPosition fields. In the results, change the name of Aaron Campanella to your name. Save the query with the name **PitchersAndCatchers**, then compare the results with FIGURE 2-24, making changes and widening columns to display all of the data. Print the datasheet if requested by your instructor. Save and close the query and the Baseball-2.accdb database, then exit Access 2016.

FIGURE 2-24

TeamName	PlayerFirst	PlayerLast	Positic
Brooklyn Beetles	Student First	Student Last	1
Brooklyn Beetles	Cy	Young	2
Mayfair Monarchs	Luis	Durocher	1
Mayfair Monarchs	Carl	Mathewson	2
Rocky's Rockets	Andrew	Spalding	1
Rocky's Rockets	Sanford	Koufax	2
Snapping Turtles	Charles	Ford	1
Snapping Turtles	Greg	Perry	2

Building and Using Queries

Using Forms

CASE ▸ Julia Rice, a trip developer at Reason 2 Go, asks you to create forms to make trip information easier to access, enter, and update.

Module Objectives

After completing this module, you will be able to:

- Use the Form Wizard
- Create a split form
- Use Form Layout View
- Add fields to a form

- Modify form controls
- Create calculations
- Modify tab order
- Insert an image

Files You Will Need

R2G-3.accdb
R2GLogo.jpg
LakeHomes-3.accdb
LakeHome.jpg
Scuba-3.accdb

Service-3.accdb
Salvage-3.accdb
Jobs-3.accdb
Baseball-3.accdb

Use the Form Wizard

Learning Outcomes
- Create a form with the Form Wizard
- Sort data in a form
- Describe form terminology and views

A **form** is an easy-to-use data entry and navigation screen. A form allows you to arrange the fields of a record in any layout so a database **user** can quickly and easily find, enter, edit, and analyze data. The database **designer** or **application developer** is the person responsible for building and maintaining tables, queries, forms, and reports for all of the users. **CASE** *Julia Rice asks you to build a form to enter and maintain trip information.*

STEPS

1. **Start Access, open the R2G-3.accdb database from the location where you store your Data Files, then enable content if prompted**

   You can use many methods to create a new form, but the Form Wizard is a fast and popular tool that helps you get started. The **Form Wizard** prompts you for information it needs to create a form, such as the fields, layout, and title for the form.

2. **Click the Create tab on the Ribbon, then click the Form Wizard button in the Forms group**

   The Form Wizard starts, prompting you to select the fields for this form. You want to create a form to enter and update data in the Trips table.

3. **Click the Tables/Queries list arrow, click Table: Trips, then click the Select All Fields button** >>

   You could now select fields from other tables, if necessary, but in this case, you have all of the fields you need.

4. **Click Next, click the Columnar option button, click Next, type Trips Entry Form as the title, then click Finish**

   The Trips Entry Form opens in **Form View**, as shown in FIGURE 3-1. Access provides three different views of forms, as summarized in TABLE 3-1. Each item on the form is called a **control**. A **label control** is used to describe the data shown in other controls such as text boxes. A label is also used for the title of the form, Trips Entry Form. A **text box** is used to display the data as well as enter, edit, find, sort, and filter the data. A **combo box** is a combination of two controls: a text box and a list. The Category data is displayed in a combo box control. You click the arrow button on a combo box control to display a list of values, or you can edit data directly in the combo box itself.

   QUICK TIP
   Click in the text box of the field you want to sort before clicking a sort button.

5. **Click Stanley Bay Cleanup in the TripName text box, click the Ascending button in the Sort & Filter group, then click the Next record button** ▶ **in the navigation bar to move to the second record**

   The Bass Habitat Project trip is the second record when the records are sorted in ascending order on the TripName data. Information about the current record number and total number of records appears in the navigation bar, just as it does in a datasheet.

6. **Click the Previous record button** ◀ **in the navigation bar to move back to the first record, click the TripName text box, then change American Legacy Project to American Heritage Project**

   Your screen should look like FIGURE 3-2. Forms displayed in Form View are the primary tool for database users to enter, edit, and delete data in an Access database.

7. **Right-click the Trips Entry Form tab, then click Close**

   When a form is closed, Access automatically saves any edits made to the current record.

FIGURE 3-1: Trips Entry Form in Form View

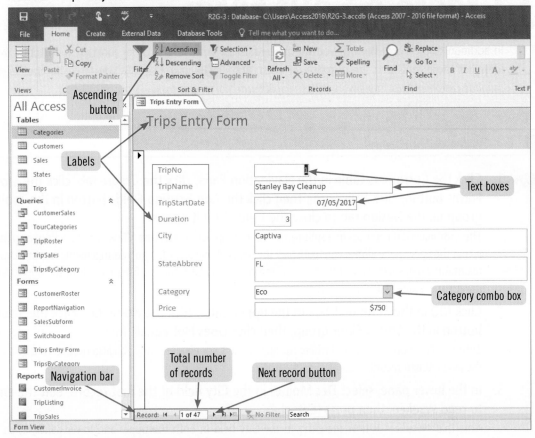

FIGURE 3-2: Editing data in Form View

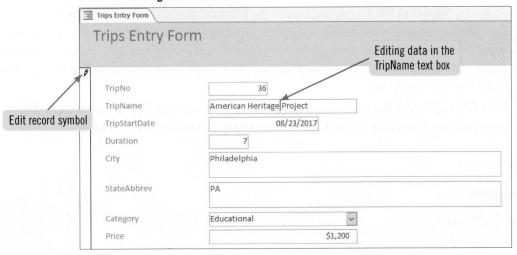

TABLE 3-1: Form views

view	primary purpose
Form	To find, sort, enter, and edit data
Layout	To modify the size, position, or formatting of controls; shows data as you modify the form, making it the tool of choice when you want to change the appearance and usability of the form while viewing data
Design	To modify the Form Header, Detail, and Footer section, or to access the complete range of controls and form properties; Design View does not display data

Create a Split Form

Learning
Outcomes
• Create a split form
• Enter and edit
  data in a form

In addition to the Form Wizard, you should be familiar with several other form creation tools. TABLE 3-2 identifies those tools and the purpose for each. **CASE** *Julia Rice asks you to create another form to manage customer data. You'll work with the Split Form tool for this task.*

STEPS

QUICK TIP
Layout View allows you to view and filter the data, but not edit it.

1. **Click the Customers table in the Navigation Pane, click the Create tab, click the More Forms button, click Split Form, then click the Add Existing Fields button in the Tools group on the Design tab to close the Field List if it opens**

   The Customers data appears in a split form with the top half in **Layout View**. The benefit of a **split form** is that the upper pane allows you to display the fields of one record in any arrangement, and the lower pane maintains a datasheet view of the first few records. If you edit, sort, or filter records in the upper pane, the lower pane is automatically updated, and vice versa.

2. **Click MO in the State text box in the upper pane, click the Home tab, click the Selection button in the Sort & Filter group, then click Does Not Equal "MO"**

   Thirty-seven records are filtered where the State field is not equal to MO. You also need to change a value in the Jacob Alman record.

TROUBLE
Make sure you edit the record in the datasheet in the lower pane.

3. **In the lower pane, select Des Moines in the City field of the first record, edit the entry to read Waukee, then press [Enter]**

   Note that "Waukee" is now the entry in the City field in both the upper and lower panes, as shown in FIGURE 3-3.

4. **Click the record selector for the Kristen Collins record in the lower pane as shown in FIGURE 3-4, then click the Delete button in the Records group on the Home tab**

   You cannot delete this record because it contains related records in the Sales table. This is a benefit of referential integrity on the one-to-many relationship between the Customers and Sales tables. Referential integrity prevents the creation of **orphan records**, records on the many side of a relationship that do not have a match on the one side.

5. **Click OK, right-click the Customers form tab, click Close, click Yes when prompted to save changes, then click OK to save the form with Customers as the name**

TABLE 3-2: Form creation tools

tool	icon	creates a form
Form		with one click based on the selected table or query
Form Design		from scratch in Form Design View
Blank Form		from scratch in Form Layout View
Form Wizard		by answering a series of questions provided by the Form Wizard dialog boxes
Navigation		used to navigate or move between different areas of the database
More Forms		based on Multiple Items, Datasheet, Split Form, or Modal Dialog arrangements
Split Form		with two panes, the upper showing one record at a time and the lower displaying a datasheet of many records

FIGURE 3-3: Customers table in a split form

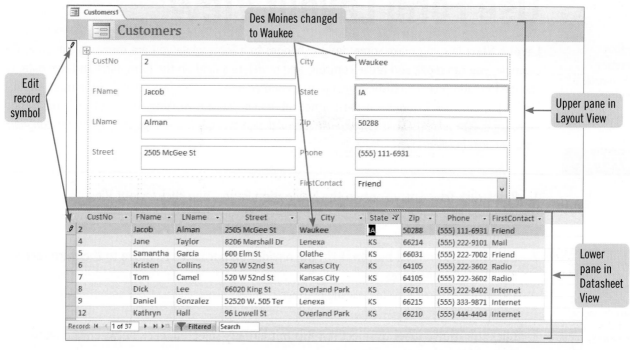

Edit record symbol

Des Moines changed to Waukee

Upper pane in Layout View

Lower pane in Datasheet View

FIGURE 3-4: Editing data in a split form

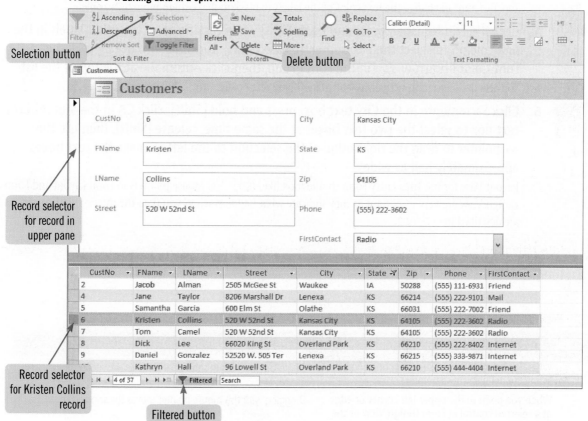

Selection button

Delete button

Record selector for record in upper pane

Record selector for Kristen Collins record

Filtered button

Use Form Layout View

Learning
Outcomes
• Resize controls in
  Layout View
• Format controls in
  Layout View

Layout View lets you make some design changes to a form while you are browsing the data. For example, you can move and resize controls, add or delete a field on the form, filter and sort data, or change formatting characteristics, such as fonts and colors. TABLE 3-4 lists several of the most popular formatting commands found on the Format tab when you are working in Layout or Form Design View. **CASE** *Julia Rice asks you to make several design changes to the Trips Entry Form. You can make these changes in Layout View.*

STEPS

1. **Right-click Trips Entry Form in the Navigation Pane, then click Layout View**

   In Layout View, you can move through the records, but you cannot enter or edit the data as you can in Form View.

   TROUBLE
   If your third record is not Bear Valley Adventures, sort the records in ascending order on the TripName field.

2. **Click the Next record button ▶ in the navigation bar twice to move to the third record, Bear Valley Adventures**

   You often use Layout View to make minor design changes, such as editing labels and changing formatting characteristics.

3. **Click the TripNo label to select it if it is not already selected, click between the words Trip and No, then press [Spacebar]**

   You also want to edit a few more labels.

   TROUBLE
   Be sure to modify the labels in the left column instead of the text boxes on the right.

4. **Continue editing the labels, as shown in** FIGURE 3-5

   You also want to change the text color of the labels to black to make them more noticeable.

5. **Click the Trip No label, press and hold [Shift] while clicking all of the other labels in the first column to select them together, release [Shift], click the Format tab, click the Font Color list arrow A · in the Font group, then click Automatic at the top of the list**

   You also decide to narrow the City and StateAbbrev text boxes.

   TROUBLE
   Be sure to modify the text boxes in the right column instead of the labels on the left.

6. **Click Sacramento in the City text box, press and hold [Shift], click CA in the StateAbbrev text box to select the two text boxes at the same time, release [Shift], then use the ↔ pointer to drag the right edge of the selection to the left to make the text boxes approximately half as wide**

   Layout View for the Trips Entry Form should look like FIGURE 3-5. Mouse pointers in Form Layout and Form Design View are very important as they indicate what happens when you drag the mouse. Mouse pointers are described in TABLE 3-3.

TABLE 3-3: Mouse pointer shapes

shape	when does this shape appear?	action
▷	When you point to any unselected control on the form (the default mouse pointer)	Single-clicking with this mouse pointer selects a control
✛	When you point to the upper-left corner or edge of a selected control in Form Design View or the middle of the control in Form Layout View	Dragging with this mouse pointer moves the selected control(s)
↕ ↔ ⤡ ⤢	When you point to any sizing handle (except the larger one in the upper-left corner in Form Design View)	Dragging with one of these mouse pointers resizes the control

Using Forms

FIGURE 3-5: Using Layout View to modify controls on the Trips Entry Form

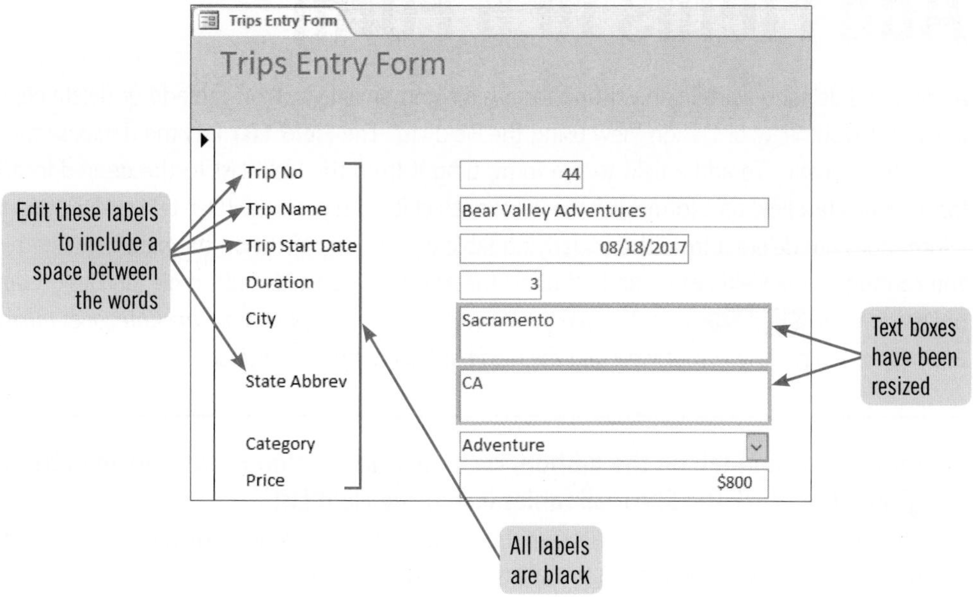

Edit these labels to include a space between the words

Trip No   44

Trip Name   Bear Valley Adventures

Trip Start Date   08/18/2017

Duration   3

City   Sacramento

State Abbrev   CA

Category   Adventure

Price $800

Text boxes have been resized

All labels are black

TABLE 3-4: Useful formatting commands

button	button name	description
B	Bold	Toggles bold on or off for the selected control(s)
I	Italic	Toggles italic on or off for the selected control(s)
U	Underline	Toggles underline on or off for the selected control(s)
A	Font Color	Changes the text color of the selected control(s)
	Background Color or Shape Fill	Changes the background color of the selected control(s)
	Align Left	Left-aligns the selected control(s) within its own border
	Center	Centers the selected control(s) within its own border
	Align Right	Right-aligns the selected control(s) within its own border
	Alternate Row Color	Changes the background color of alternate records in the selected section
	Shape Outline	Changes the border color, thickness, or style of the selected control(s)
	Shape Effects	Changes the special visual effect of the selected control(s)

Table layouts

Layouts provide a way to group several controls together on a form or report to more quickly add, delete, rearrange, resize, or align controls. To insert a layout into a form or report, select the controls you want to group together, then choose the Stacked or Tabular button on the Arrange tab in Layout View. Each option applies a table layout to the controls so that you can insert, delete, merge, or split the cells in the layout to quickly rearrange or edit the controls in the layout. To remove a layout, use the Remove Layout button on the Arrange tab in Form Design View.

Access 2016

Add Fields to a Form

Learning Outcomes
• Add fields to a form
• Define bound and unbound controls

Adding and deleting fields in an existing form is a common activity. You can add or delete fields in a form in either Layout View or Design View using the Field List. The **Field List** lists the database tables and the fields they contain. To add a field to the form, drag it from the Field List to the desired location on the form. To delete a field on a form, click the field to select it, then press the [Delete] key. Deleting a field from a form does not delete it from the underlying table or have any effect on the data contained in the field. You can toggle the Field List on and off using the Add Existing Fields button on the Design tab in Layout or Design View. **CASE** ▶ *Julia Rice asks you to add the Trip description from the Categories table to the Trips Entry Form. You can use Layout View and the Field List to accomplish this goal.*

STEPS

TROUBLE
If you don't see the Design tab on the Ribbon, switch to Layout View.

1. **Click the Design tab on the Ribbon, click the Add Existing Fields button in the Tools group, then click the Show all tables link in the Field List**

   The Field List opens in Layout View, as shown in FIGURE 3-6. Notice that the Field List is divided into sections. The upper section shows the tables currently used by the form, the middle section shows directly related tables, and the lower section shows other tables in the database. The expand/collapse button to the left of the table names allows you to expand (show) the fields within the table or collapse (hide) them. The Description field is in the Categories table in the middle section.

   To move the Field List, drag its title bar. Double-click the title bar of the Field List to dock it to the right.

TROUBLE
In Design View, adding the Description field creates a text box instead of a combo box.

2. **Click the expand button ⊞ to the left of the Categories table, drag the Description field to the form, then use the ⬚ pointer to drag the new Description combo box and label below the Price text box**

   When you add a new field to a form, two controls are usually created: a label and a text box. The label contains the field name and the text box displays the data in the field. The Categories table moved from the middle to the top section of the Field List. You also want to align and format the new controls with others already on the form.

QUICK TIP
If you make a mistake, click the Undo button ↺ and try again.

3. **Click the Description label, click the Format tab on the Ribbon, then click the Font color button 𝐀 ▾ to change the text color from gray to black**

   With the new controls in position and formatted, you want to enter a new record. You must switch to Form View to edit, enter, or delete data.

TROUBLE
Your Trip No value might not match FIGURE 3-7. As an AutoNumber value, the value is inserted automatically and is controlled by Access.

4. **Click the Home tab, click the View button ▦ to switch to Form View, click the New (blank) record button ▶✴ in the navigation bar, click the TripName text box, then enter a new record in the updated form, as shown in FIGURE 3-7**

   Be sure to enter the correct value for each field and note that when you select a value in the Category combo box, the Description is automatically updated. This is due to the one-to-many relationship between the Categories and Trips tables in the Relationships window.

FIGURE 3-6: Field List in Form Layout View

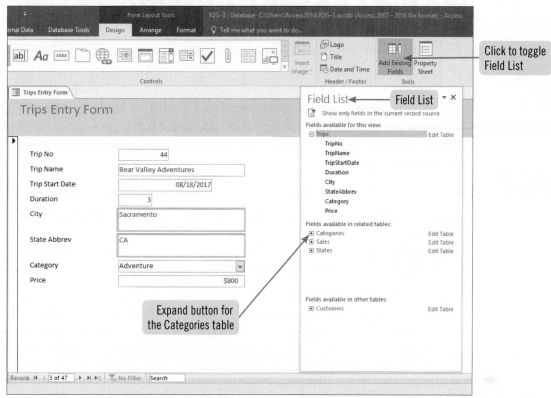

FIGURE 3-7: Entering a record in the updated Trips Entry Form in Form View

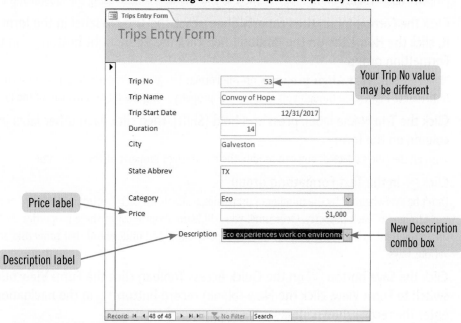

Bound versus unbound controls

Controls are either bound or unbound. **Bound controls** display values from a field such as text boxes and combo boxes. **Unbound controls** do not display data; unbound controls describe data or enhance the appearance of the form. Labels are the most common type of unbound control, but other types include lines, images, tabs, and command buttons. Another way to distinguish bound from unbound controls is to observe the form as you move from record to record. Because bound controls display data, their contents change as you move through the records, displaying data from the field of the current record. Unbound controls such as labels and lines do not change as you move through the records in a form.

Modify Form Controls

You have already made many modifications to form controls, such as changing the font color of labels and the size of text boxes. Labels and text boxes are the two most popular form controls. Other common controls are listed in TABLE 3-5. When you modify controls, you change their **properties** (characteristics). All of the control characteristics you can modify are stored in the control's **Property Sheet**. **CASE** *Because R2G is now focused on Eco (ecological) trips, you decide to use the Property Sheet of the Category field to modify the default value to be "Eco." Julia asks you to use the Property Sheet to make other control modifications to better size and align the controls.*

STEPS

1. **Right-click the Trips Entry Form tab, click Layout View, then click the Property Sheet button in the Tools group**

   The Property Sheet opens, replacing the Field List and showing you all of the properties for the selected item. Drag the title bar of the Property Sheet to move it. Double-click the title bar to dock it to the right.

2. **Click the Category combo box on the form, click the Data tab in the Property Sheet (if it is not already selected), click the Default Value box, type Eco, then press [Enter]**

   The Property Sheet should look like FIGURE 3-8. Access often helps you with the **syntax** (rules) of entering property values. In this case, Access added quotation marks around "Eco" to indicate that the default entry is text. Properties are categorized in the Property Sheet with the Format, Data, Event, and Other tabs. The All tab is a complete list of all the control's properties. You can use the Property Sheet to make all control modifications, although you'll probably find that some changes are easier to make using the Ribbon. The property values change in the Property Sheet as you modify a control using the Ribbon and vice versa.

   > **TROUBLE**
   > Be sure to click the Trip No label on the left, not the TripNo text box on the right.

3. **Click the Format tab in the Property Sheet, click the Trip No label in the form to select it, click the Home tab on the Ribbon, then click the Align Right button ☰ in the Text Formatting group**

   Notice that the **Text Align property** on the Format tab in the Property Sheet is automatically updated from Left to Right even though you changed the property using the Ribbon instead of the Property Sheet.

4. **Click the Trip Name label, press and hold [Shift], then click each other label in the first column on the form**

   With all the labels selected, you can modify their Text Align property at the same time.

   > **TROUBLE**
   > You may need to click ☰ twice.

5. **Click ☰ in the Text Formatting group**

   Don't be overwhelmed by the number of properties available for each control on the form or the number of ways to modify each property. Over time, you will learn about most of these properties. At this point, it's only important to know the purpose of the Property Sheet and understand that properties are modified in various ways.

   > **TROUBLE**
   > Your Trip No value might not match FIGURE 3-9. It is an AutoNumber value, controlled by Access.

6. **Click the Save button 🖫 on the Quick Access Toolbar, click the Form View button 🔲 to switch to Form View, click the New (blank) record button ▶* in the navigation bar, then enter the record shown in FIGURE 3-9**

   For new records, "Eco" is provided as the default value for the Category combo box, but you can change it by typing a new value or selecting one from the list. With the labels right-aligned, they are much closer to the data in the text boxes that they describe.

FIGURE 3-8: Using the Property Sheet

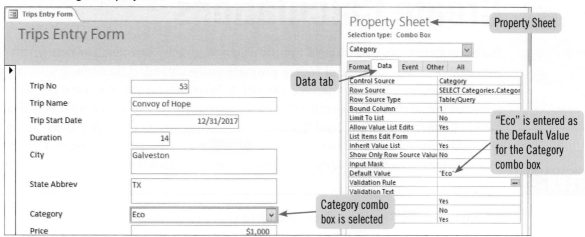

FIGURE 3-9: Modified Trips Entry Form

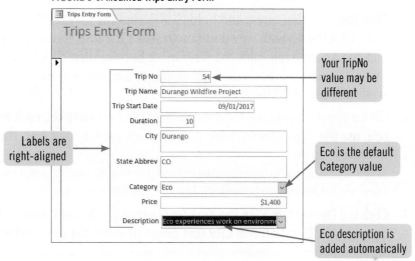

TABLE 3-5: Common form controls

name	used to	bound	unbound
Label	Provide consistent descriptive text as you navigate from record to record; the label is the most common type of unbound control and can also be used as a hyperlink to another database object, external file, or webpage		•
Text box	Display, edit, or enter data for each record from an underlying record source; the text box is the most common type of bound control	•	
List box	Display a list of possible data entries	•	
Combo box	Display a list of possible data entries for a field, and provide a text box for an entry from the keyboard; combines the list box and text box controls	•	
Tab control	Create a three-dimensional aspect on a form		•
Check box	Display "yes" or "no" answers for a field; if the box is checked, it means "yes"	•	
Toggle button	Display "yes" or "no" answers for a field; if the button is pressed, it means "yes"	•	
Option button	Display a choice for a field	•	
Option group	Display and organize choices (usually presented as option buttons) for a field	•	
Line and Rectangle	Draw lines and rectangles on the form		•
Command button	Provide an easy way to initiate a command or run a macro		•

Create Calculations

Learning Outcomes
• Build calculations on a form
• Move controls on a form

Text boxes are generally used to display data from underlying fields. The connection between the text box and field is defined by the **Control Source property** on the Data tab of the Property Sheet for that text box. A text box control can also display a calculation. To create a calculation in a text box, you enter an expression instead of a field name in the Control Source property. An **expression** is a combination of field names, operators (such as +, −, /, and *), and functions (such as Sum, Count, or Avg) that results in a single value. Sample expressions are shown in TABLE 3-6. **CASE** ▶ *Julia Rice asks you to add a text box to the Trips Entry Form to calculate the trip end date. You can add a text box in Form Design View to accomplish this.*

STEPS

1. **Right-click the Trips Entry Form tab, then click Design View**

   You want to add the trip end date calculation just below the Duration text box. First, you'll resize the City and State Abbrev fields.

2. **Click the City label, press and hold [Shift], click the City text box, click the State Abbrev label, click the StateAbbrev text box to select the four controls together, release [Shift], click the Arrange tab, click the Size/Space button, then click To Shortest**

   With the City and StateAbbrev fields resized, you're ready to move them to make room for the new control to calculate the tour end date.

3. **Click a blank spot on the form to deselect the four controls, click the StateAbbrev text box, use the ⬚ pointer to move it down, click the City text box, then use the ⬚ pointer to move it down**

   To add the calculation to determine the trip end date (the trip start date plus the duration), start by adding a new text box to the form between the Duration and City text boxes.

4. **Click the Design tab, click the Text Box button ⓐⓑ in the Controls group, then click between the Duration and City text boxes to insert the new text box**

   Adding a new text box automatically adds a new label to the left of the text box.

5. **Double-click Text23, type Trip End Date, click the Home tab, click the Font Color button ⒜ ·, then press [Enter]**

   With the label updated to correctly identify the text box to the right, you're ready to enter the expression to calculate the tour end date.

6. **Click the new text box to select it, click the Data tab in the Property Sheet, click the Control Source property, type =[TripStartDate]+[Duration], then press [Enter] to update the form as shown in FIGURE 3-10**

   All expressions entered in a control must start with an equal sign (=). When referencing a field name within an expression, [square brackets]—(not parentheses) and not {curly braces}—surround the field name. In an expression, you must type the field name exactly as it was created in Table Design View, but you do not need to match the capitalization.

7. **Click the View button ▦ to switch to Form View, tab three times to the Duration field, type 5, then press [Enter]**

   Note that the trip end date, calculated by an expression, automatically changed to five days after the trip start date to reflect the new duration value. The updated Trips Entry Form with the trip end date calculation for the Bikers for Ecology is shown in FIGURE 3-11.

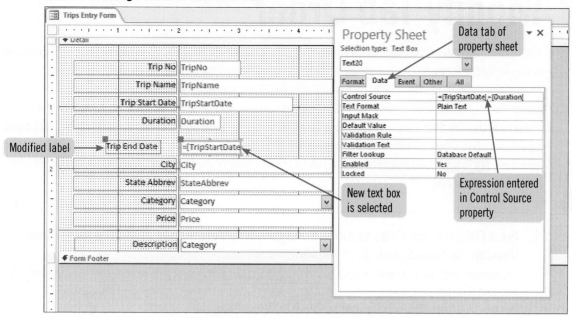

FIGURE 3-10: Adding a text box to calculate a value

Modified label → Trip End Date

Data tab of property sheet

New text box is selected

Expression entered in Control Source property

FIGURE 3-11: Displaying the results of a calculation in Form View

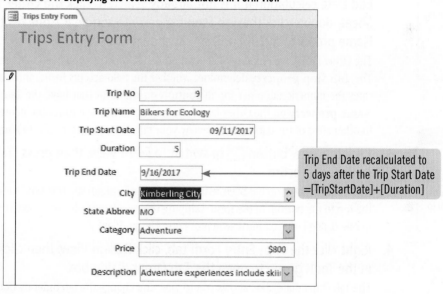

Trip End Date recalculated to 5 days after the Trip Start Date =[TripStartDate]+[Duration]

TABLE 3-6: Sample expressions

sample expression	description
=Sum([Salary])	Uses the **Sum** function to add the values in the Salary field
=[Price] * 1.05	Multiplies the Price field by 1.05 (adds 5% to the Price field)
=[Subtotal] + [Shipping]	Adds the value of the Subtotal field to the value of the Shipping field
=Avg([Freight])	Uses the **Avg** function to display an average of the values in the Freight field
=Date()	Uses the **Date** function to display the current date in the form of mm-dd-yy
="Page " &[Page]	Displays the word Page, a space, and the result of the [Page] field, an Access field that contains the current page number
=[FirstName]& " " &[LastName]	Displays the value of the FirstName and LastName fields in one control, separated by a space
=Left([ProductNumber],2)	Uses the **Left** function to display the first two characters in the ProductNumber field

Modify Tab Order

After positioning all of the controls on the form, you should check the tab order and tab stops. **Tab order** is the order the focus moves as you press [Tab] in Form View. A **tab stop** refers to whether a control can receive the focus in the first place. By default, the Tab Stop property for all text boxes and combo boxes is set to Yes, but some text boxes, such as those that contain expressions, will not be used for data entry. Therefore, the Tab Stop property for a text box that contains a calculation should be set to No. Unbound controls such as labels and lines do not have a Tab Stop property because they cannot be used to enter or edit data. **CASE** *Julia suggests that you check the tab order of the Trips Entry Form, then change tab stops and tab order as necessary.*

STEPS

1. **Press [Tab] enough times to move through several records, watching the focus move through the bound controls of the form**

   Because the Trip End Date text box is a calculated field, you don't want it to receive the focus. To prevent the Trip End Date text box from receiving the focus, you set its Tab Stop property to No using its Property Sheet. You can work with the Property Sheet in either Layout or Design View.

2. **Right-click the Trips Entry Form tab, click Design View, click the text box with the Trip End Date calculation if it is not already selected, click the Other tab in the Property Sheet, double-click the Tab Stop property to toggle it from Yes to No, then change the Name property to TripEndDate, as shown in** FIGURE 3-12

   The Other tab of the Property Sheet contains the properties you need to change the tab stop and tab order. The **Tab Stop property** determines whether the field accepts focus, and the **Tab Index property** indicates the numeric tab order for all controls on the form that have the Tab Stop property set to Yes. The **Name property** on the Other tab is also important as it identifies the name of the control, which is used in other areas of the database. To review your tab stop changes, return to Form View.

3. **Click the View button 📋 to switch to Form View, then press [Tab] nine times to move to the next record**

   Now that the tab stop has been removed from the TripEndDate text box, the tab order flows correctly from the top to the bottom of the form, skipping the calculated field. To review the tab order for the entire form in one dialog box, you must switch to Form Design View.

4. **Right-click the Trips Entry Form tab, click Design View, then click the Tab Order button in the Tools group to open the Tab Order dialog box**

   The Tab Order dialog box allows you to view and change the tab order by dragging fields up or down using the **field selector** to the left of the field name. Moving fields up and down in this list also renumbers the Tab Index property for the controls in their respective Property Sheets. If you want Access to create a top-to-bottom and left-to-right tab order, click **Auto Order**.

5. **Click the Auto Order button to make sure your tab order goes top to bottom as shown in** FIGURE 3-13**, click OK to close the Tab Order dialog box, click the Property Sheet button to toggle it off, click the Save button 🖫 on the Quick Access Toolbar to save your work, then click a blank spot on the form to deselect the text box**

FIGURE 3-12: Using the Property Sheet to set tab properties

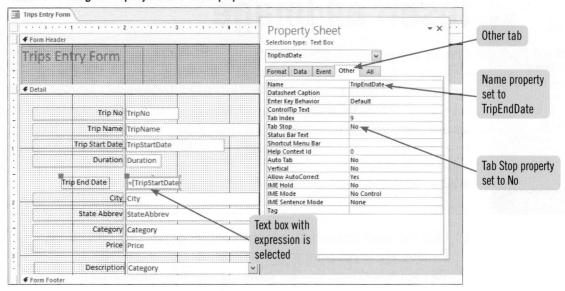

FIGURE 3-13: Tab Order dialog box

Form layouts

A **layout** helps you keep the controls on a form organized as a group. You can apply a stacked or tabular layout to the controls on your form by clicking the Stacked or Tabular buttons on the Arrange tab in Form Design View. Remove a layout by clicking the Remove Layout button. You can also modify a layout by modifying the margins, padding, and anchoring options of the layout using buttons found in the Position group on the Arrange tab in Form Design View. **Margin** refers to the space between the outer edge of the control and the data displayed inside the control. **Padding** is the space between the controls. **Anchoring** allows you to tie controls together so you can work with them as a group. Some of the Form Wizards automatically apply a layout to the controls that you can modify or remove as needed.

Insert an Image

Learning Outcomes
• Insert an image on a form
• Modify form sections
• Print a selected record

Graphic images, such as pictures, logos, or clip art, can add style and professionalism to a form. The form section in which you place the images is significant. **Form sections** determine where controls are displayed and printed; they are described in TABLE 3-7. For example, if you add a company logo to the Form Header section, the image appears at the top of the form in Form View as well as at the top of a printout. If you add the same image to the Detail section, it prints next to each record in the printout because the Detail section is printed for every record. **CASE** *Julia Rice suggests that you add the R2G logo to the top of the Trips Entry Form. You can add the control in either Layout or Design View, but if you want to place it in the Form Header section, you have to work in Design View.*

STEPS

1. **Click the** Insert Image button **in the Controls group, click** Browse, **then navigate to the location where you store your Data Files**
   The Insert Picture dialog box opens, prompting you for the location of the image.

2. **Click the** Web-Ready Image Files button, **click** All Files, **double-click** R2GLogo.jpg, **then click at the top of the Form Header section at about the 3" mark on the ruler**
   The R2GLogo image is added to the right side of the Form Header section. When an image or control is selected in Design View, you can use **sizing handles**, which are small squares at the corners of the selection box. Drag a handle to resize the image or control. You use the ⚓ pointer to move a control.

3. **Use the** ⚓ **pointer to move the logo to the top edge of the Form Header section, then drag the** top edge **of the Detail section up using the** ✛ **pointer**
   You also want to align the Trip End Date label with the other labels in the first column.

TROUBLE
You may need to continue to move or slightly adjust the controls to fit them all on the screen.

4. **Click the** Trip End Date label, **click the** Home tab **on the Ribbon, click the** Align Right button ▤, **press and hold [Shift], click the** Duration label, **click the** Arrange tab **on the Ribbon, click the** Align button, **then click** Right **as shown in** FIGURE 3-14
   With the form completed, you open it in Form View to observe the changes.

5. **Click the** Save button ▣ **on the Quick Access Toolbar, click the** Home tab, **then click the** View button ▤ **to switch to Form View**
   You decide to add one more record with your final Trips Entry Form.

6. **Click the** New (blank) record button ▸▪ **in the navigation bar, then enter the new record shown in** FIGURE 3-15, **using your last name in the Trip Name field**
   Now print only this single new record.

TROUBLE
If you do not click the Selected Record(s) option button, you will print all records, which creates a very long printout.

7. **Click the** File tab, **click** Print **in the navigation bar, click** Print, **click the** Selected Record(s) option button, **then click** OK

8. **Close the Trips Entry Form, click** Yes **if prompted to save it, close the R2G-3.accdb database, then exit Access 2016**

FIGURE 3-14: Adding an image to the Form Header section

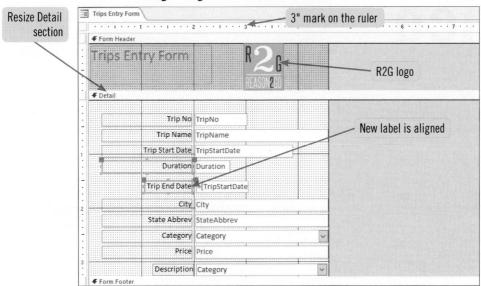

Resize Detail section

3" mark on the ruler

R2G logo

New label is aligned

FIGURE 3-15: Final Trips Entry Form with new record

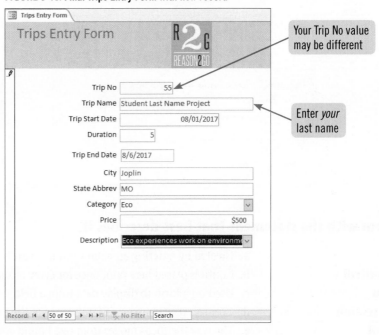

Your Trip No value may be different

Enter *your* last name

TABLE 3-7: Form sections

section	controls placed in this section print
Form Header	Only once at the top of the first page of the printout
Detail	Once for every record
Form Footer	Only once at the end of the last page of the printout

Applying a background image

A **background image** is an image that fills the entire form or report, appearing "behind" the other controls. A background image is sometimes called a watermark image. To add a background image, use the Picture property for the form or report to browse for the image that you want to use in the background.

Using Forms

Practice

Concepts Review

Label each element of Form Design View shown in FIGURE 3-16.

FIGURE 3-16

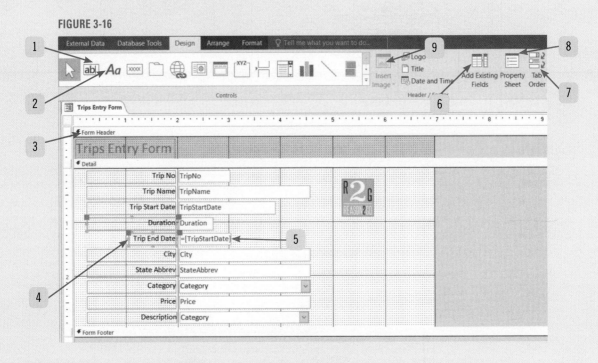

Match each term with the statement that best describes it.

10. **Tab order**
11. **Calculated control**
12. **Detail section**
13. **Form Footer section**
14. **Bound control**
15. **Database designer**

a. Created by entering an expression in a text box
b. Controls placed here print once for every record in the underlying record source
c. Used on a form to display data from a field
d. Controls placed here print only once at the end of the printout
e. The way the focus moves from one bound control to the next in Form View
f. Responsible for building and maintaining tables, queries, forms, and reports

Select the best answer from the list of choices.

16. **Every element on a form is called a(n):**
    a. property.
    b. item.
    c. control.
    d. tool.

17. **Which of the following is probably *not* a graphic image?**
    a. Logo
    b. Clip art
    c. Calculation
    d. Picture

18. The most common bound control is the:

 a. combo box.

 b. label.

 c. list box.

 d. text box.

19. The most common unbound control is the:

 a. text box.

 b. combo box.

 c. label.

 d. command button.

20. Which form view cannot be used to view data?

 a. Layout

 b. Design

 c. Datasheet

 d. Preview

Skills Review

1. Use the Form Wizard.

 a. Start Access and open the LakeHomes-3.accdb database from the location where you store your Data Files. Enable content if prompted.

 b. Click the Create tab, then use the Form Wizard to create a form based on all of the fields in the Realtors table. Use a Columnar layout and type **Realtor Entry Form** to title the form.

 c. Add a *new record* with your name in the RFirst and RLast text boxes. Note that the RealtorNo field is an AutoNumber field that is automatically incremented as you enter your first and last names. Enter your school's telephone number for the RPhone field value, and enter **4** as the AgencyNo field value.

 d. Save and close the Realtor Entry Form.

2. Create a split form.

 a. Click the Agencies table in the Navigation Pane, click the Create tab, click the More Forms button, then click Split Form.

 b. Close the Property Sheet if it opens then switch to Form View.

 c. Click the record selector in the lower pane for AgencyNo 3, Green Mountain Realty, then click the Delete button in the Records group to delete this realtor. Click OK when prompted that you cannot delete this record because there are related records in the Realtors table.

 d. Navigate to the AgencyNo 4 record, Shepherd of the Hills Realtors, in either the upper or lower pane of the split form. Change 7744 Pokeberry Lane to **800 Lake Shore Drive**.

 e. Right-click the Agencies form tab, click Close, click Yes when prompted to save changes, type **Agencies Split Form** as the name of the form, then click OK.

3. Use Form Layout View.

 a. Open the Realtor Entry Form in Layout View.

 b. Modify the labels on the left to read: **Realtor Number**, **Realtor First Name**, **Realtor Last Name**, **Realtor Cell**, **Agency Number**.

 c. Modify the text color of the labels to be black.

 d. Resize all of the text boxes on the right to be the same width as the RealtorNo text box.

 e. Save the Realtor Entry Form.

4. Add fields to a form.

 a. Open the Field List, show all the tables, then expand the Agencies table to display its fields.

 b. Drag the AgencyName field to the form, then move the AgencyName label and combo box below the Agency Number controls.

 c. Modify the AgencyName label to read **Agency Name**.

 d. Modify the text color of the Agency Name label to black.

 e. Close the Field List and save and close the Realtor Entry Form.

Skills Review (continued)

5. Modify form controls.

  a. Reopen the Realtor Entry Form in Layout View, then select all of the labels in the left column and use the Align Right button on the Home tab to right-align them.

  b. Save the form, switch to Form View, navigate to Realtor No 5 (Jane Ann Welch), then use the Agency Name combo box to change the Agency Name to **Big Cedar Realtors**.

  c. In Layout View, resize and align all controls so that the labels are lined up on the left and the text boxes are lined up on the right, as shown in FIGURE 3-17.

FIGURE 3-17

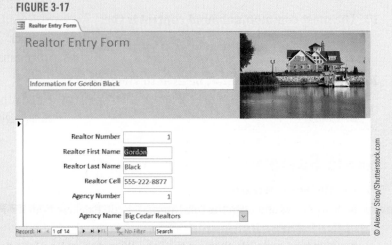

6. Create calculations.

  a. Switch to Form Design View, expand the size of the Form Header section by dragging the top edge of the Detail section down about 0.5", then add a text box at about the 1" mark below the Realtor Entry Form label in the Form Header section.

  b. Delete the Text14 label that is created when you add a new text box. The number in your label is based on previous work done to the form, so it might vary.

  c. Widen the text box to be almost as wide as the entire form, then enter the following expression into the text box, which will add the words *Information for* to the realtor's first name, a space, and then the realtor's last name.

    ="Information for "&[RFirst]&" "&[RLast]

  d. Save the form, then view it in Form View. Be sure the new text box correctly displays a space before and after the realtor's first name. If #Name? appears, which indicates that the expression was entered incorrectly, return to Design View to correct the expression.

  e. In Form View, change the Realtor Last Name for Realtor Number 1 from Bono to **Black**. Tab to the RPhone text box to observe how the expression in the Form Header automatically updates.

  f. Tab through several records, observing the expression in the Form Header section.

7. Modify tab order.

  a. Switch to Form Design View, then open the Property Sheet.

  b. Select the new text box with the expression in the Form Header section, then change the Tab Stop property from Yes to **No**.

  c. Select the RealtorNo text box in the Detail section, then change the Tab Stop property from Yes to **No**. (AutoNumber fields cannot be edited, so they do not need to have a tab stop.)

  d. Close the Property Sheet.

  e. Open the Tab Order dialog box and click the Auto Order button to make sure the focus moves from top to bottom through the form.

  f. Save the form and view it in Form View. Tab through the form to make sure that the tab order is sequential and skips the expression in the Form Header as well as the Realtor Number text box. Use the Tab Order button on the Design tab in Form Design View to modify the tab order, if necessary.

Skills Review (continued)

8. Insert an image.

    a. Switch to Design View, then click the Form Header section bar.

    b. Add the LakeHome.jpg image to the right side of the Form Header, then resize the image to be about 2.5" × 1.5". Remember to search for All files.

    c. Remove the extra blank space in the Form Header section by dragging the top edge of the Detail section up as far as possible.

    d. Drag the right edge of the form as far as possible to the left.

    e. Save the form, then switch to Form View as shown in **FIGURE 3-17**. Move through the records, observing the calculated field from record to record to make sure it is calculating correctly.

    f. Find the record with your name, and if requested by your instructor, print only that record.

    g. Close the Realtor Entry Form, close the LakeHomes-3.accdb database, then exit Access.

Independent Challenge 1

As a volunteer for a scuba divers' club, you have developed a database to help manage scuba dives. In this exercise, you'll create a data entry form to manage the dive trips.

    a. Start Access, then open the Scuba-3.accdb database from the location where you store your Data Files. Enable content if prompted.

    b. Using the Form Wizard, create a form that includes all the fields in the DiveTrips table and uses the Columnar layout, then type **Dive Trip Entry** as the title of the form.

    c. Switch to Layout View, then delete the ID text box and label.

    d. Using Form Design View, use the [Shift] key to select all of the text boxes except the last one for TripReport, then resize them to the shortest size using the To Shortest option on the Size/Space button on the Arrange tab.

    e. Using Form Design View, resize the Location, City, State/Province, Country, and Lodging text boxes to be no wider than the Rating text box.

    f. Using Form Design View, move and resize the controls, as shown in **FIGURE 3-18**. This will require several steps. Once the controls are resized, drag the top of the Form Footer section up to remove the extra blank space in the Detail section.

    g. Using Form Layout View, modify the labels and alignment of the labels, as shown in **FIGURE 3-18**. Note that there are spaces between the words in the labels, the labels are right-aligned, and the text boxes are left-aligned.

    h. In Form View, sort the records in ascending order on the Dive Master ID field, which will order the Great Barrier Reef tour as the first record. Edit the Certification Diving and Trip Report fields, as shown in **FIGURE 3-18** for the TripReport field using your name.

    i. Save the form, then if requested by your instructor, print only the record with your name.

    j. Close the Dive Trip Entry form, close the Scuba-3.accdb database, then exit Access 2016.

FIGURE 3-18

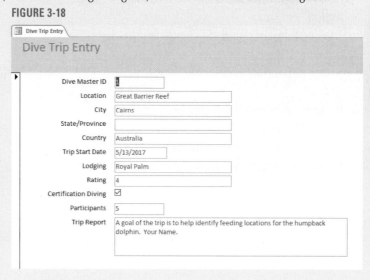

Independent Challenge 2

You have built an Access database to track membership in a community service club. The database tracks member names and addresses as well as their status in the club.

   a. Start Access, then open the Service-3.accdb database from the location where you store your Data Files. Enable content if prompted.

   b. Using the Form Wizard, create a form based on all of the fields of the Members table and the DuesOwed field in the Status table.

   c. View the data by Members, use a Columnar layout, then enter **Member Information** as the title of the form.

   d. Enter a new record with your name and the school name, and address of your school for the Company and address fields. Give yourself a StatusNo entry of **1**. In the DuesPaid field, enter **50**. The DuesOwed field automatically displays 100 because that value is pulled from the Status table and is based on the entry in the StatusNo field, which links the Members table to the Status table.

   e. In Layout View, add a text box to the form and move it below the DuesOwed text box.

   f. Open the Property Sheet for the new text box, display the Data tab, and in the Control Source property of the new text box, enter **=[DuesOwed]-[DuesPaid]**, the expression that calculates the balance between DuesOwed and DuesPaid.

   g. Open the Property Sheet for the new label, and change the Caption property on the Format tab for the new label to **Balance**. Resize the label to be as wide as the labels above it.

   h. Right-align all of the labels in the first column.

   i. Set the Tab Stop property for the text box that contains the calculated Balance to **No**.

   j. In Layout or Design View, resize DuesPaid and DuesOwed text boxes to be the same width as the new Balance text box, then right-align all data within the three text boxes because numbers are clearer when they align on the decimal point.

FIGURE 3-19

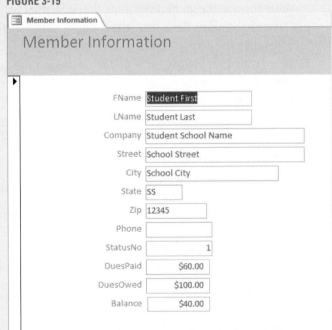

   k. Make sure that the Format property on the Format tab is Currency for the DuesPaid, DuesOwed, and Balance expression text boxes. Close the Property Sheet.

   l. In Form Design View, make sure that the right edge of the form is at or less than the 7" mark on the horizontal ruler. The horizontal ruler is located just above the Form Header section.

   m. Save the form, find the record with your name, change the DuesPaid value to **60**, then move and resize controls as necessary to match **FIGURE 3-19**.

   n. If requested by your instructor, print only the record with your name.

   o. Save and close the Member Information form, then close the Service-3.accdb database and exit Access 2016.

Independent Challenge 3

You have built an Access database to organize the deposits at a salvage and recycling center. Various clubs regularly deposit recyclable material, which is measured in pounds when the deposits are made.

a. Open the Salvage-3.accdb database from the location where you store your Data Files. Enable content if prompted.

b. Using the Form Wizard, create a form based on all of the fields in the CenterDeposits query. View the data by Deposits, use the Columnar layout, and title the form **Deposit Listing**.

c. Switch to Layout View, then make each label bold.

d. Modify the labels so that CenterName is **Center Name**, DepositDate is **Deposit Date**, and ClubName is **Club Name**.

e. Switch to Form Design View and resize the CenterName and ClubName text boxes so they are the same height and width as the Weight text box, as shown in FIGURE 3-20.

f. Switch to Form View, find and change any entry of A1 Salvage Center to *your* last name, then print one record with your name if requested by your instructor.

g. Using Form View of the Deposit Listing form, filter for all records with your last name in the CenterName field.

h. Using Form View of the Deposit Listing form, sort the filtered records in descending order on the DepositDate field.

i. In Form Design View, narrow the form by dragging the right edge as far left as possible.

j. Preview the first record, as shown in FIGURE 3-20. If requested by your instructor, print the first record.

k. Save and close the Deposit Listing form, close the Salvage-3.accdb database, then exit Access.

FIGURE 3-20

Independent Challenge 4: Explore

One way you can use an Access database on your own is to record and track your job search efforts. In this exercise, you will develop a form to help you enter data into your job-tracking database.

    a. Start Access and open the Jobs-3.accdb database from the location where you store your Data Files. Enable content if prompted.

    b. Click the Create tab, then use the Form Wizard to create a new form based on all the fields of both the Employers and Positions tables.

    c. View the data by Employers, use a Datasheet layout for the subform, accept the default names for the form and subform, then open the form to view information.

    d. Use Layout View and Design View to modify the form labels, text box positions, alignment, and sizes, as shown in FIGURE 3-21. Also note that the columns within the subform have been resized to display all of the data in the subform.

FIGURE 3-21

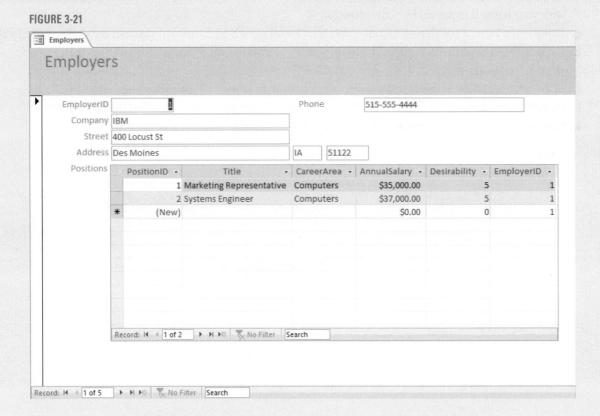

Independent Challenge 4: Explore (continued)

e. Change the CompanyName of IBM in the first record to *Your* **Last Name Software**, and if instructed to create a printout, print only that record. Close the Employers form.

f. Click the Employers table in the Navigation Pane, then use the Split Form option on the More Forms button of the Create tab to create a split form on the Employers table. Close and save the split form with the name **Employers Split Form**.

g. Open the Employers Split Form in Form View, change the address and phone number information for EmployerID 1 to your school's address and phone information, as shown in FIGURE 3-22.

h. Navigate through all five records, then back to EmployerID 1, observing both the upper and lower panes of the split form as you move from record to record.

i. Open the Employers form and navigate forward and backward through all five records to study the difference between the Employers form, which uses a form/subform versus the Employers Split Form. Even though both the Employers form and Employers Split Form show datasheets in the bottom halves of the forms, they are fundamentally very different. The split form is displaying the records of only the Employers table, whereas the Employers form is using a subform to display related records from the Positions table in the lower datasheet. You will learn more about forms and subforms in later modules.

j. Close the Jobs-3.accdb database, then exit Access.

FIGURE 3-22

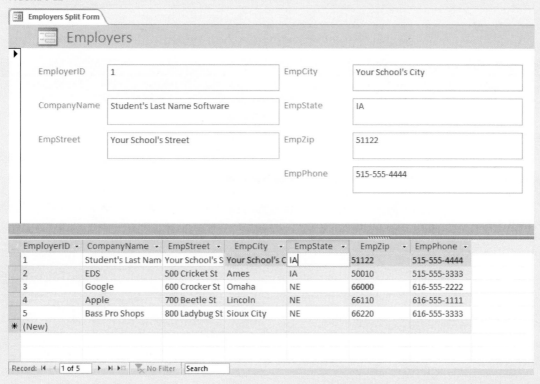

Visual Workshop

Open the Baseball-3.accdb database, enable content if prompted, then use the Split Form tool to create a form named **Players**, as shown in FIGURE 3-23, based on the Players table. Switch to Form Design View, remove the layout, and resize the controls as shown. Modify the labels as shown and note that they are all right-aligned. View the data in Form View, and sort the records in ascending order by last name. Change the first, last, and nickname of the John Bench record in the first record to your name, and if instructed to create a printout, print only that record. Save and close the Players form, close the Baseball-3.accdb database, then exit Access.

FIGURE 3-23

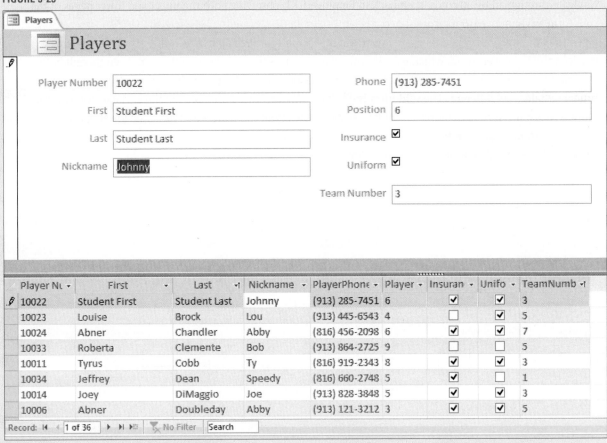

Using Reports

CASE ▶ Julia Rice, a trip developer at Reason 2 Go, asks you to produce some reports to help her share and analyze data. A report is an Access object that creates a professional-looking printout.

Module Objectives

After completing this module, you will be able to:

- Use the Report Wizard
- Use Report Layout View
- Review report sections
- Apply group and sort orders

- Add subtotals and counts
- Resize and align controls
- Format a report
- Create mailing labels

Files You Will Need

R2G-4.accdb
LakeHomes-4.accdb
Conventions-4.accdb
Service-4.accdb

Salvage-4.accdb
JobSearch-4.accdb
Basketball-4.accdb

Use the Report Wizard

A **report** is the primary object you use to print database content because it provides the most formatting, layout, and summary options. A report may include various fonts and colors, clip art and lines, and multiple headers and footers. A report can also calculate subtotals, averages, counts, and other statistics for groups of records. You can create reports in Access by using the **Report Wizard**, a tool that asks questions to guide you through the initial development of the report. Your responses to the Report Wizard determine the record source, style, and layout of the report. The **record source** is the table or query that defines the fields and records displayed on the report. The Report Wizard also helps you sort, group, and analyze the records. **CASE** *Julia Rice asks you to use the Report Wizard to create a report to display the trips within each state.*

STEPS

1. **Start Access, open the R2G-4.accdb database, enable content if prompted, click the Create tab on the Ribbon, then click the Report Wizard button in the Reports group**

   The Report Wizard starts, prompting you to select the fields you want on the report. You can select fields from one or more tables or queries.

2. **Click the Tables/Queries list arrow, click Table: States, double-click the StateName field, click the Tables/Queries list arrow, click Table: Trips, click the Select All Fields button >> , click StateAbbrev in the Selected Fields list, then click the Remove Field button <**

   By selecting the StateName field from the States table, and all fields from the Trips table except the StateAbbrev field, you have all of the fields you need for the report, as shown in **FIGURE 4-1**.

3. **Click Next, then click by States if it is not already selected**

   Choosing "by States" groups the records for each state. In addition to record-grouping options, the Report Wizard later asks if you want to sort the records within each group. You can use the Report Wizard to specify up to four fields to sort in either ascending or descending order.

4. **Click Next, click Next again to include no additional grouping levels, click the first sort list arrow, click TripName, then click Next**

   The last questions in the Report Wizard deal with report appearance and the report title.

5. **Click the Stepped option button, click the Landscape option button, click Next, type State Trips for the report title, then click Finish**

   The State Trips report opens in **Print Preview**, which displays the report as it appears when printed, as shown in **FIGURE 4-2**. The records are grouped by state, the first state being California, and then sorted in ascending order by the TripName field within each state. Reports are **read-only** objects, meaning you can use them to read and display data but not to change (write to) data. As you change data using tables, queries, or forms, reports constantly display those up-to-date edits just like all of the other Access objects.

6. **Scroll down to see the second grouping section on the report for the state of Colorado, then click the Next Page button ▶ in the navigation bar to see the second page of the report**

   Even in **landscape orientation** (11" wide by 8.5" tall as opposed to **portrait orientation**, which is 8.5" wide by 11" tall), the fields on the State Trips report may not fit on one sheet of paper. The labels in the column headings and the data in the columns need to be resized to improve the layout. Depending on your monitor, you might need to scroll to the right to display all the fields on this page.

FIGURE 4-1: Selecting fields for a report using the Report Wizard

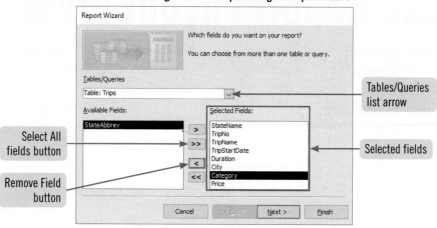

Tables/Queries list arrow

Select All fields button

Remove Field button

Selected fields

FIGURE 4-2: State Trips report in Print Preview

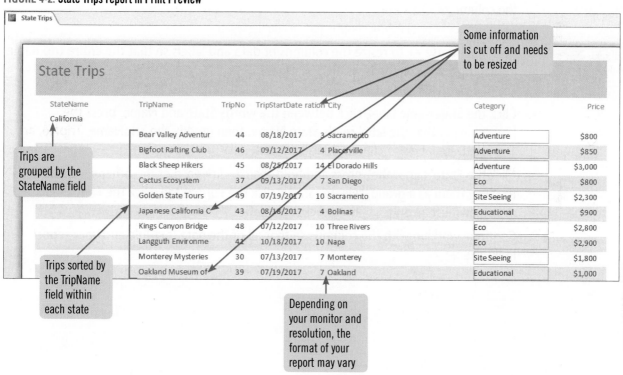

Some information is cut off and needs to be resized

Trips are grouped by the StateName field

Trips sorted by the TripName field within each state

Depending on your monitor and resolution, the format of your report may vary

Changing page orientation

To change page orientation from Portrait (8.5" wide by 11" tall) to Landscape (11" wide by 8.5" tall) and vice versa, click the Portrait or Landscape button on the Print Preview tab when viewing the report in Print Preview. To switch to Print Preview, right-click the report in the Navigation Pane, and then choose Print Preview on the shortcut menu.

Use Report Layout View

Learning Outcomes
• Move and resize controls in Layout View
• Modify labels

Reports have multiple views that you use for various report-building and report-viewing activities. Although some tasks can be accomplished in more than one view, each view has a primary purpose to make your work with reports as easy and efficient as possible. The different report views are summarized in TABLE 4-1. **CASE** *Julia Rice asks you to modify the State Trips report so that all of the fields fit comfortably across one sheet of paper in landscape orientation.*

STEPS

TROUBLE
If the Field List or Property Sheet window opens, close it.

1. **Right-click the State Trips report tab, then click Layout View**

   Layout View opens and applies a grid to the report that helps you resize, move, and position controls. You decide to narrow the City column to make room for the Price data.

2. **Click Sacramento (or any value in the City column), then use the ↔ pointer to drag the left edge of the City column to the right to narrow it to about half of its current size, as shown in FIGURE 4-3**

   By narrowing the City column, you create extra space in the report.

QUICK TIP
If you select the entire row, just click again directly on the label to select it.

3. **Click the City label, then use ↔ to drag the left edge to the right to position it above the column of City data**

   You use the extra room to better display the data on the report.

QUICK TIP
You can use the Undo button ↩ to undo multiple actions in Layout View.

4. **Continue to use ↔ to resize the columns of data and labels so that the entire trip name in the TripName column is visible**

   The TripName column now has more space to completely display the trip names.

5. **Click the StateName label, click between the words State and Name, press the [Spacebar] so that the label reads State Name, then modify the TripName, TripNo, and TripStartDate labels to contain spaces as well**

6. **Click the StateName label, press and hold [Shift], click each of the other seven labels to select them as a group, release [Shift], click the Format tab, click the Font Color drop-down list arrow A ·, then click Automatic**

7. **Continue working with the columns so that all of the data is visible and your report looks like FIGURE 4-4**

FIGURE 4-3: Modifying the column width in Report Layout View

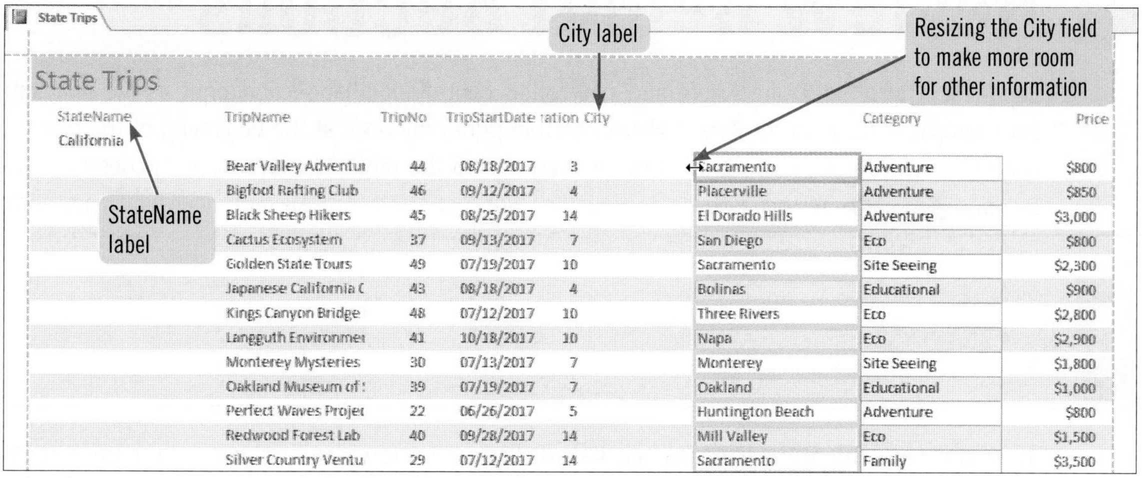

City label

Resizing the City field to make more room for other information

StateName label

FIGURE 4-4: Final State Trips report in Report Layout View

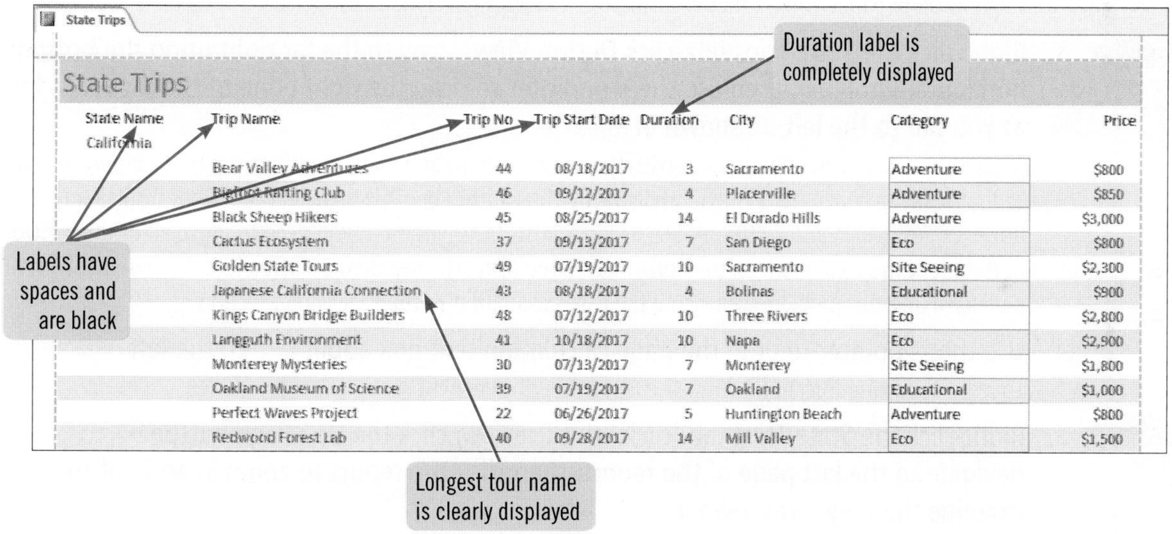

Duration label is completely displayed

Labels have spaces and are black

Longest tour name is clearly displayed

TABLE 4-1: Report views

view	primary purpose
Report View	To quickly review the report without page breaks
Print Preview	To review each page of an entire report as it will appear if printed
Layout View	To modify the size, position, or formatting of controls; shows live data as you modify the report, making it the tool of choice when you want to change the appearance and positioning of controls on a report while also reviewing live data
Design View	To work with report sections or to access the complete range of controls and report properties; Design View does not display data

Review Report Sections

Learning
Outcomes
• Navigate through
  report sections
  and pages
• Resize the width of
  the report
• Work with error
  indicators

Report **sections** determine where and how often controls in that section print in the final report. For example, controls in the Report Header section print only once at the beginning of the report, but controls in the Detail section print once for every record the report displays. TABLE 4-2 describes report sections. **CASE** You and Julia Rice preview the State Trips report to review and understand report sections.

STEPS

1. **Right-click the State Trips tab, click Print Preview, then scroll up as needed and click the light blue bar at the top of the report above the Trip Start Date label until you display the first page of the report, as shown in** FIGURE 4-5

   The first page shows four report sections: Report Header, Page Header, StateAbbreviation Header, and Detail.

2. **Click the Next Page button ▶ on the navigation bar to move to the second page of the report**

   If the second page of the report does not contain data, it means that the report may be too wide to fit on a single sheet of paper. You fix that problem in Report Design View.

QUICK TIP
If your report is too wide, you will see a green error indicator in the upper-left corner of the report. Pointing to the error icon ⚠ ▾ displays a message about the error.

3. **Right-click the State Trips tab, click Design View, scroll to the far right using the bottom horizontal scroll bar, then use the ↔ pointer to drag the right edge of the report as far as you can to the left, as shown in** FIGURE 4-6

   In Report Design View, you can work with the report sections and make modifications to the report that you cannot make in other views, such as narrowing the width. Report Design View does not display any data, however. For your report to fit on one page in landscape orientation, you need to move all of the controls to the left of the 10.5" mark on the horizontal **ruler** using the default 0.25" left and right margins. You will practice fixing this problem by moving the page calculation in the Page Footer section.

4. **Use the ⬉ pointer to drag the page calculation text box about 0.5" to the left**

   To review your modifications, show the report in Print Preview.

QUICK TIP
You can also use the View buttons in the lower-right corner of a report to switch views.

5. **Right-click the State Trips tab, click Print Preview, click the Last Page button ▶| to navigate to the last page of the report, then click the report to zoom in and out to examine the page, as shown in** FIGURE 4-7

   Previewing each page of the report helps you confirm that no blank pages are created and allows you to examine how the different report sections print on each page.

TABLE 4-2: Report sections

section	where does this section print?
Report Header	At the top of the first page
Page Header	At the top of every page (but below the Report Header on the first page)
Group Header	Before every group of records
Detail	Once for every record
Group Footer	After every group of records
Page Footer	At the bottom of every page
Report Footer	At the end of the report

FIGURE 4-5: State Trips in Print Preview

FIGURE 4-5: State Trips in Print Preview

FIGURE 4-6: State Trips report in Design View

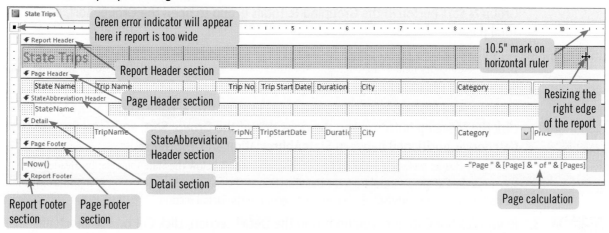

FIGURE 4-7: Last page of State Trips report in Print Preview

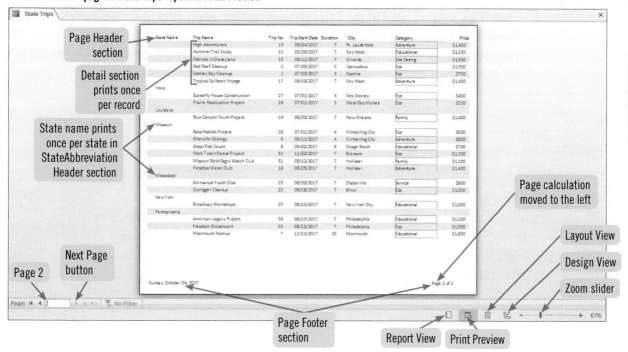

Apply Group and Sort Orders

Learning
Outcomes
• Group and sort
  records in a report
• Cut and paste
  controls

Grouping means to sort records by a particular field plus provide a header and/or footer section before or after each group of sorted records. For example, if you group records by the StateAbbreviation field, the Group Header is called the StateAbbreviation Header and the Group Footer is called the StateAbbreviation Footer. The StateAbbreviation Header section appears once for each state in the report, immediately before the records in that state. The StateAbbreviation Footer section also appears once for each state in the report, immediately after the records for that state. **CASE** *The records in the State Trips report are currently grouped by the StateAbbreviation field. Julia Rice asks you to further group the records by the Category field (Adventure, Eco, Educational, and Family, for example) within each state.*

STEPS

1. **Click the Close Print Preview button to return to Report Design View, then click the Group & Sort button in the Grouping & Totals group to open the Group, Sort, and Total pane**

   Currently, the records are grouped by the StateAbbreviation field and further sorted by the TripName field. To add the Category field as a grouping field within each state, you work with the Group, Sort, and Total pane in Report Design View.

2. **Click the Add a group button in the Group, Sort, and Total pane, click Category, then click the Move up button ⬆ on the right side of the Group, Sort, and Total pane so that Category is positioned between StateAbbreviation and TripName**

   A Category Header section is added to Report Design View just below the StateAbbreviation Header section. You move the Category control from the Detail section to the Category Header section so it prints only once for each new Category instead of once for each record in the Detail section.

3. **Right-click the Category combo box in the Detail section, click Cut on the shortcut menu, right-click the Category Header section, click Paste, then use the ⬚ pointer to drag the Category combo box to the right to position it as shown in FIGURE 4-8**

   Now that you've moved the Category combo box to the Category Header, it will print only once per category within each state. You no longer need the Category label in the Page Header section.

4. **Click the Category label in the Page Header section, press [Delete], then switch to Print Preview and zoom to 100%**

   The State Trips report should look like **FIGURE 4-9**. Notice that the records are now grouped by category within state. Detail records are further sorted in ascending order by the TripName field value.

FIGURE 4-8: Group, Sort, and Total pane and new Category Header section

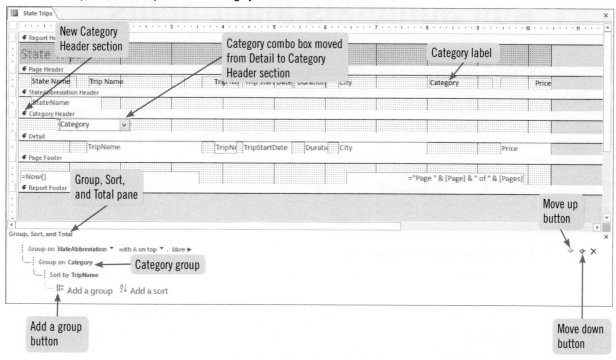

FIGURE 4-9: State Trips report grouped by category within state

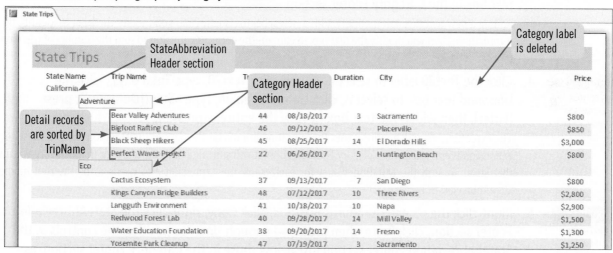

Record Source Property

The **Record Source property** of a report or form determines what fields and records that report or form will display. It is the first property on the Data tab of the Property Sheet for a report or form. The value of the Record Source property may be the name of a table or query. The Record Source property can also be a SELECT statement, which is SQL (Structured Query Language) code. In the Property Sheet for a report, click the Record Source property, and then click the Build button ⟦...⟧ to enter Query Design View, where you can change the Record Source property or save it as a query object within the database.

Add Subtotals and Counts

In a report, you create a **calculation** by entering an expression into a text box. When a report is previewed or printed, the expression is evaluated and the resulting calculation is placed on the report. An **expression** is a combination of field names, operators (such as +, −, /, and *), and functions that results in a single value. A **function** is a built-in formula, such as Sum or Count, that helps you quickly create a calculation. Notice that every expression starts with an equal sign (=), and when it uses a function, the arguments for the function are placed in (parentheses). **Arguments** are the pieces of information that the function needs to create the final answer. When an argument is a field name, the field name must be surrounded by [square brackets]. **CASE** ▶ *Julia Rice asks you to add a calculation to the State Trips report to sum the total number of trip days within each category and within each state.*

STEPS

1. **Switch to Report Design View**

   A logical place to add subtotals for each group is right after that group of records prints, in the Group Footer section. You use the Group, Sort, and Total pane to open Group Footer sections.

2. **Click the More button for the StateAbbreviation field in the Group, Sort, and Total pane, click the without a footer section list arrow, click with a footer section, then do the same for the Category field, as shown in FIGURE 4-10**

   With the StateAbbreviation Footer and Category Footer sections open, you're ready to add controls to calculate the total number of trip days within each category and within each state. You use a text box control with an expression to make this calculation.

3. **Click the Text Box button 📄 in the Controls group, then click just below the Duration text box in the Category Footer section**

   Adding a new text box automatically adds a new label to its left. First, you modify the label to identify the information; then you modify the text box to contain the correct expression to sum the number of trip days for that category.

4. **Click the Text20 label to select it, double-click Text20, type Total days:, click the Unbound text box to select it, click Unbound again, type =Sum([Duration]), press [Enter], then widen the text box to view the entire expression**

   The expression =Sum([Duration]) uses the Sum function to add the days in the Duration field. Because the expression is entered in the Category Footer section, it will sum all Duration values for that category within that state. To sum the Duration values for each state, the expression also needs to be inserted in the StateAbbreviation Footer.

5. **Right-click the =Sum([Duration]) text box, click Copy, right-click the StateAbbreviation Footer section, click Paste, then press [→] enough times to position the controls in the StateAbbreviation Footer section just below those in the Category Footer section, as shown in FIGURE 4-11**

   With the expression copied to the StateAbbreviation Footer section, you're ready to preview your work.

6. **Switch to Print Preview, navigate to the last page of the report, then click to zoom so you can see all of the Pennsylvania trips**

   As shown in **FIGURE 4-12**, seven trip days are totaled for the Eco category, and 17 for the Educational category, which is a total of 24 trip days for the state of Pennsylvania. The summary data would look better if it were aligned more directly under the trip Duration values. You resize and align controls in the next lesson.

FIGURE 4-10: Opening group footer sections

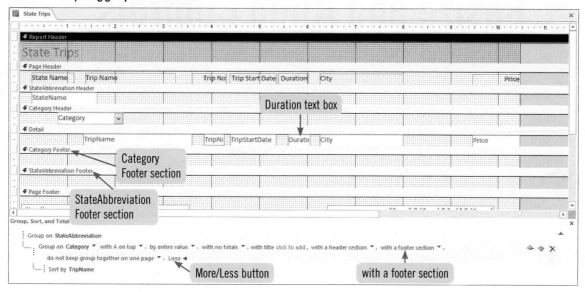

FIGURE 4-11: Adding subtotals to group footer sections

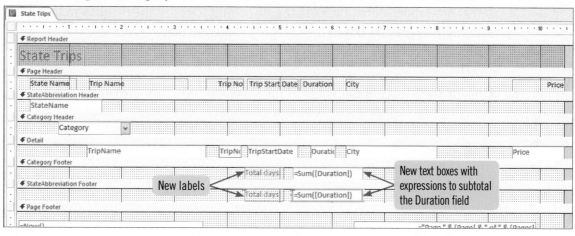

FIGURE 4-12: Previewing the new group footer calculations

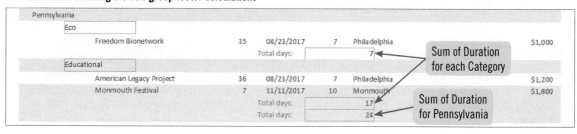

Resize and Align Controls

After you add information to the appropriate section of a report, you might also want to align the data in precise columns and rows to make the information easier to read. To do so, you can use two different types of **alignment** commands. You can left-, right-, or center-align a control within its own border using the Align Left 🔲, Center 🔲, and Align Right 🔲 buttons on the Home tab. You can also align the edges of controls with respect to one another using the Left, Right, Top, and Bottom commands on the Align button of the Arrange tab in Report Design View. **CASE** ▶ *You decide to resize and align several controls to improve the readability of the State Trips report. Layout View is a good choice for these tasks.*

STEPS

1. **Switch to Layout View, click the Design tab on the Ribbon, then click the Group & Sort button to toggle off the Group, Sort, and Total pane**

   You decide to align the expressions that subtotal the number of trip days for each category within the Duration column to make the report easier to read and more professional.

2. **Click the Total days text box in the Category Footer, then use the ↔ pointer to resize the text box so that the data is aligned in the Duration column, as shown in FIGURE 4-13**

   If the value in your Total days text box is not right-aligned, click the Align Right button (shown in FIGURE 4-13). With the calculation formatted as desired in the Category Footer, you can quickly apply those modifications to the calculation in the StateAbbreviation Footer as well.

3. **Scroll down the report far enough to find and then click the Total days text box in the StateAbbreviation Footer, then use the ↔ pointer to resize the text box so that it is the same width as the text box in the Category Footer section**

   With both expressions resized so they line up under the Duration values in the Detail section, they are easier to read on the report.

4. **Scroll the report so you can see all of the Colorado trips, as shown in FIGURE 4-14**

   You can apply resize, alignment, or formatting commands to more than one control at a time. TABLE 4-3 provides techniques for selecting more than one control at a time in Report Design View.

Precisely moving and resizing controls

You can move and resize controls using the mouse or other pointing device, but you can move controls more precisely using the keyboard. Pressing the arrow keys while holding [Ctrl] moves selected controls one **pixel** (picture element) at a time in the direction of the arrow. Pressing the arrow keys while holding [Shift] resizes selected controls one pixel at a time.

FIGURE 4-13: Resizing controls in Layout View

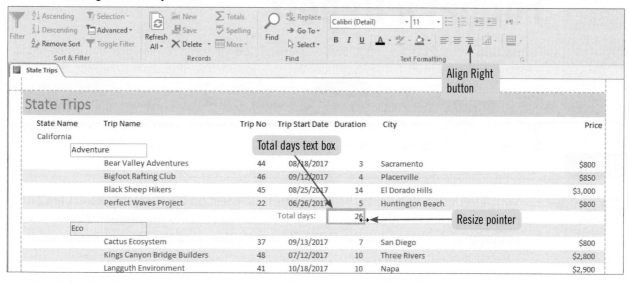

FIGURE 4-14: Reviewing the aligned and resized controls

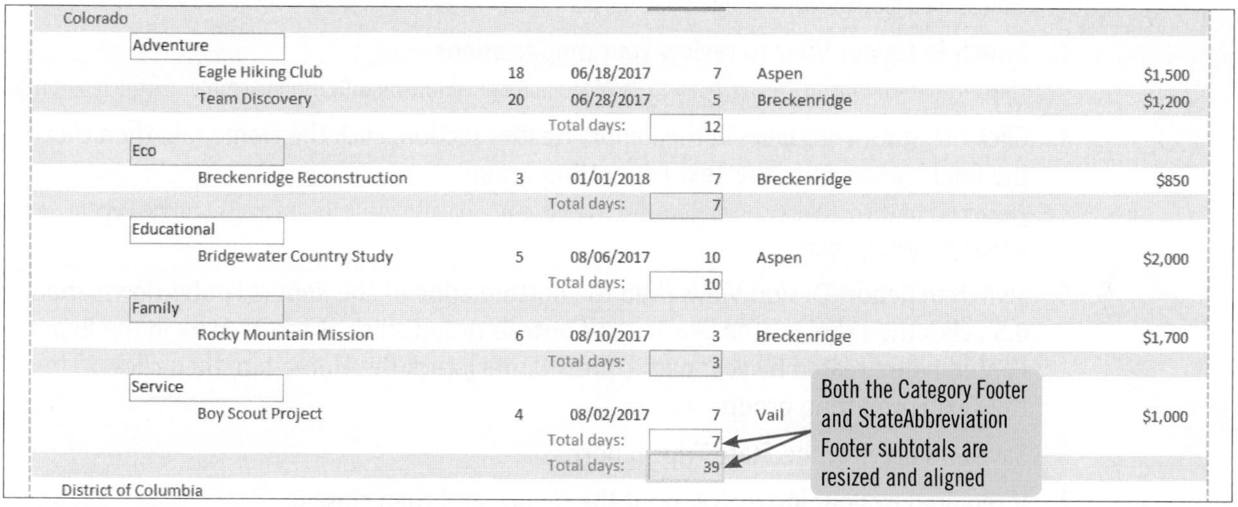

TABLE 4-3: Selecting more than one control at a time in Report Design View

technique	description
Click, [Shift]+click	Click a control, and then press and hold [Shift] while clicking other controls; each one is selected
Drag a selection box	Drag a selection box (an outline box you create by dragging the pointer in Report Design View); every control that is in or is touched by the edges of the box is selected
Click in the ruler	Click in either the horizontal or vertical ruler to select all controls that intersect the selection line
Drag in the ruler	Drag through either the horizontal or vertical ruler to select all controls that intersect the selection line as it is dragged through the ruler

Format a Report

Learning Outcomes
• Format controls and sections of a report
• Add labels to a report

Formatting refers to enhancing the appearance of the information. Although the Report Wizard automatically applies many formatting embellishments, you often want to change the appearance of the report to fit your particular needs. **CASE** *When reviewing the State Trips report with Julia, you decide to change the background color of some of the report sections to make the data easier to read. The Report Wizard applied alternating formats, which you want to change. You want to shade each Category Header and Category Footer section using the same color. To make changes to entire report sections, you work in Report Design View.*

STEPS

QUICK TIP
The quick keystroke for Undo is [Ctrl][Z]. The quick keystroke for Redo is [Ctrl][Y].

1. **Switch to Design View, click the** Category Header **section bar, click the** Format **tab on the Ribbon, click the** Alternate Row Color **button arrow, click the** Maroon 2 color square **as shown in** FIGURE 4-15, **click the** Shape Fill **button, then click the** Maroon 2 color square

   Make a similar modification by applying a different fill color to the Category Footer section.

2. **Click the** Category Footer **section bar, click the** Alternate Row Color **button arrow, click the** Maroon 1 color square **(just above Maroon 2 in the Standard Colors section), click the** Shape Fill **button, then click the** Maroon 1 color square

   When you use the Alternate Row Color and Shape Fill buttons, you're actually modifying the **Back Color** and **Alternate Back Color** properties in the Property Sheet of the section or control you selected. Background shades can help differentiate parts of the report, but be careful with dark colors, as they may print as solid black on some printers and fax machines.

3. **Switch to Layout View to review your modifications**

   The category sections are clearer, but you decide to make one more modification to emphasize the report title.

4. **Click the** State Trips label **in the Report Header section, click the** Home **tab, then click the** Bold button B **in the Text Formatting group**

   The report in Layout View should look like FIGURE 4-16. You also want to add a label to the Report Footer section to identify yourself.

5. **Switch to Report Design View, drag the** bottom edge of the Report Footer **down about 0.5", click the** Label button Aa **in the Controls group, click at the 1" mark in the Report Footer, type** Created by *your* name, **press [Enter], click the** Home **tab, then click** B **in the Text Formatting group**

6. **Save and preview the State Trips report**

7. **If required by your instructor, print the report, and then close it**

FIGURE 4-15: Formatting section backgrounds

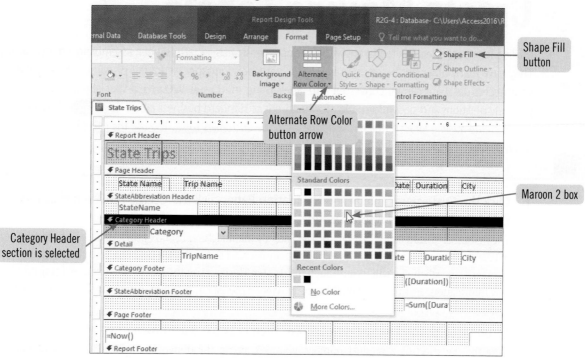

FIGURE 4-16: Final formatted State Trips report

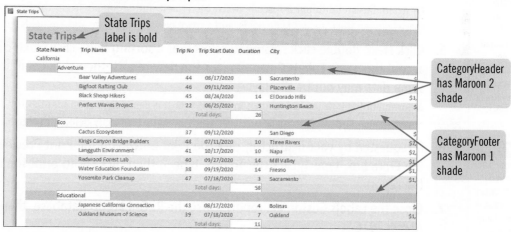

Create Mailing Labels

Learning Outcomes
- Create a report of labels
- Print specific pages of a report

Mailing labels are often created to apply to envelopes, postcards, or letters when assembling a mass mailing. They have many other business purposes too, such as labels for paper file folders or name tags. Any data in your Access database can be converted into labels using the **Label Wizard**, a special report wizard that precisely positions and sizes information for hundreds of standard business labels. **CASE** ▸ *Julia Rice asks you to create mailing labels for all of the addresses in the Customers table. You use the Label Wizard to handle this request.*

STEPS

1. **Click the Customers table in the Navigation Pane, click the Create tab, then click the Labels button in the Reports group**

   The first Label Wizard dialog box opens. The Filter by manufacturer list box provides over 30 manufacturers of labels. Avery is the default choice. With the manufacturer selected, your next task is to choose the product number of the labels you will feed through the printer. The cover on the box of labels you are using provides this information. In this case, you'll be using Avery 5160 labels, a common type of sheet labels used for mailings and other purposes.

2. **Scroll through the Product number list, then click 5160 as shown in** FIGURE 4-17

   Note that by selecting a product number, you also specify the dimensions of the label and number of columns.

3. **Click Next, then click Next again to accept the default font and color choices**

   The third question of the Label Wizard asks how you want to construct your label. You'll add the fields from the Customers table with spaces and line breaks to pattern a standard mailing format.

4. **Double-click FName, press [Spacebar], double-click LName, press [Enter], double-click Street, press [Enter], double-click City, type a comma (,) and press [Spacebar], double-click State, press [Spacebar], then double-click Zip**

   If your prototype label doesn't look exactly like FIGURE 4-18, delete the fields in the Prototype label box and try again. Be careful to put a space between the FName and LName fields in the first row, a comma and a space between the City and State fields, and a space between the State and Zip fields.

QUICK TIP

In this case, all data is displayed. This message reminds you to carefully preview the data to make sure long names and addresses are fully displayed within the constraints of the 5160 label dimensions.

5. **Click Next, double-click LName to select it as a sorting field, click Next, click Finish to accept the name Labels Customers for the new report, then click OK if prompted that some data may not be displayed**

   A portion of the new report is shown in FIGURE 4-19. It is generally a good idea to print the first page of the report on standard paper to make sure everything is aligned correctly before printing on labels.

QUICK TIP

To include your name on the printout, change Jacob Alman to your own name in the Customers table, and then close and reopen the Labels Customers report.

6. **If requested by your instructor, click the Print button on the Print Preview tab, click the From box, type 1, click the To box, type 1, then click OK to print the first page of the report**

7. **Close the Labels Customers report, close the R2G-4.accdb database, then exit Access 2016**

FIGURE 4-17: Label Wizard dialog box

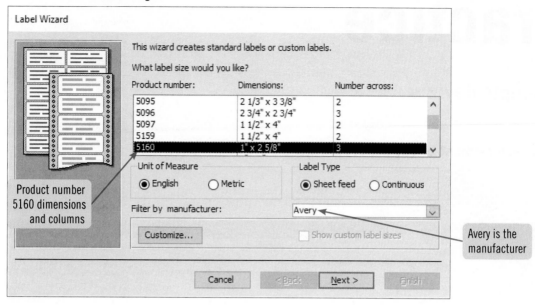

FIGURE 4-18: Building a prototype label

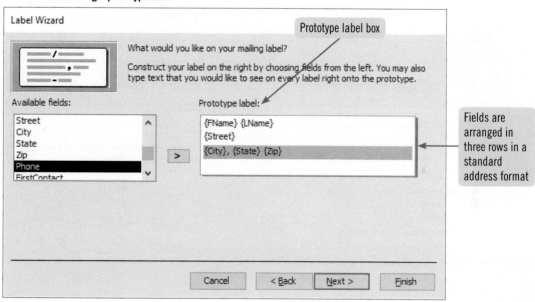

FIGURE 4-19: Labels Customers report

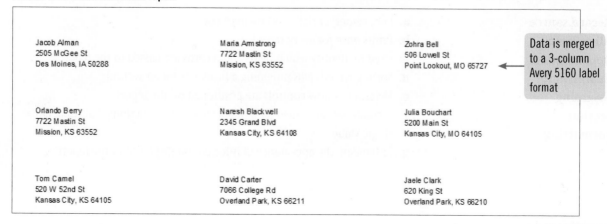

Practice

Concepts Review

Label each element of the Report Design View window shown in FIGURE 4-20.

FIGURE 4-20

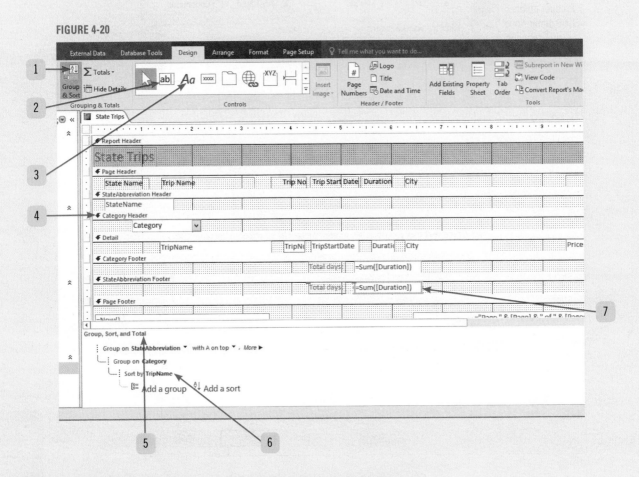

Match each term with the statement that best describes it.

8. **Record source**
9. **Alignment**
10. **Detail section**
11. **Expression**
12. **Grouping**
13. **Section**
14. **Formatting**

a. Left, center, or right are common choices
b. Prints once for every record
c. Used to identify which fields and records are passed to the report
d. Sorting records *plus* providing a header or footer section
e. Determines how controls are positioned on the report
f. A combination of field names, operators, and functions that results in a single value
g. Enhancing the appearance of information displayed in the report

Select the best answer from the list of choices.

15. Which type of control is most commonly placed in the Detail section?
a. Image
b. Line
c. Text box
d. Label

16. Which of the following is not a valid report view?
a. Print Preview
b. Section View
c. Layout View
d. Design View

17. A title for a report would most commonly be placed in which report section?
a. Group Footer
b. Detail
c. Report Header
d. Report Footer

18. A calculated expression that presents page numbering information would probably be placed in which report section?
a. Report Header
b. Detail
c. Group Footer
d. Page Footer

19. To align the edges of several controls with each other, you use the alignment commands on the:
a. Formatting tab.
b. Design tab.
c. Print Preview tab.
d. Arrange tab.

20. Which of the following expressions counts the number of records using the FirstName field?
a. =Count([FirstName])
b. =Count[FirstName]
c. =Count((FirstName))
d. =Count{FirstName}

21. What is the difference between grouping and sorting in a report?
a. Grouping allows you to add a Group Header and/or Group Footer section to a report.
b. Grouping means to sort in ascending order.
c. Grouping means to sort by more than one field.
d. You can have more than one grouping field, but you can only have one sorting field.

Skills Review

1. Use the Report Wizard.
   a. Start Access and open the LakeHomes-4.accdb database from the location where you store your Data Files. Enable content if prompted.
   b. Use the Report Wizard to create a report based on the RLast and RPhone fields from the Realtors table and the Type, SqFt, BR, Bath, and Asking fields from the Listings table. (*Hint*: Make sure your fields are added in the order listed.)
   c. View the data by Realtors, do not add any more grouping levels, and sort the records in descending order by the Asking field. (*Hint*: Click the Ascending button to toggle it to Descending.)
   d. Use a Stepped layout and a Landscape orientation. Title the report **Listings by Realtor**.
   e. Preview the first and second pages of the new report.

2. Use Report Layout View.
   a. Switch to Layout View and close the Field List and Property Sheet if they are open.
   b. Drag the right edge of the Asking column and label to the left to provide a little more space between the Asking column and Type column.
   c. Modify the RLast label to read **Realtor**, the RPhone label to read **Cell**, the SqFt label to read **Square Ft**, the BR label to read **Bedrooms**, and the Bath label to read **Baths**.
   d. Switch to Print Preview to review your changes.

Skills Review (continued)

3. **Review report sections.**
   a. Switch to Report Design View.
   b. Drag the text box that contains the Page calculation in the lower-right corner of the Page Footer section to the left so that it is to the left of the 9" mark on the horizontal ruler.
   c. Drag the right edge of the entire report to the left as far as possible.
   d. Preview the report and make sure there are no blank pages between printed pages. You may need to move or narrow more controls and narrow the report again in order to accomplish this.

4. **Apply group and sort orders.**
   a. Open the Group, Sort, and Total pane.
   b. Add the Type field as a grouping field between the RealtorNo grouping field and Asking sort field. Make sure the sort order on the Asking field is in descending order (from largest to smallest). (*Hint*: Use the Move up button to move the Type field between the RealtorNo and Asking fields in the Group, Sort, and Total pane.)
   c. Cut and paste the Type combo box from its current position in the Detail section to the Type Header section.
   d. Move the Type combo box in the Type Header section so its left edge is at about the 1" mark on the horizontal ruler.
   e. Delete the Type label in the Page Header section.
   f. Switch to Layout View, and resize the Asking, Square Ft, Bedrooms, and Baths columns as needed so they are more evenly spaced across the page.

5. **Add subtotals and counts.**
   a. Switch to Report Design View, then open the RealtorNo Footer section. (*Hint*: Use the More button on the RealtorNo field in the Group, Sort, and Total pane.)
   b. Add a text box control to the RealtorNo Footer section, just below the Asking text box in the Detail section. Change the label to read **Subtotal:**, and enter the expression **=Sum([Asking])** in the text box.
   c. Drag the bottom edge of the Report Footer section down about 0.25" to add space to the Report Footer.
   d. Copy and paste the new expression in the RealtorNo Footer section to the Report Footer section. Position the new controls in the Report Footer section directly below the controls in the RealtorNo Footer section.
   e. Modify the Subtotal: label in the Report Footer section to read **Grand Total:**.
   f. Preview the last page of the report to view the new subtotals in the RealtorNo Footer and Report Footer sections.

6. **Resize and align controls.**
   a. Switch to Design View, then click the Group & Sort button on the Design tab to close the Group, Sort, and Total pane if it is open.
   b. Click the Asking text box in the Detail section, press and hold [Shift], and then click the expression in the RealtorNo Footer as well as the Report Footer sections to select the three text boxes at the same time. Click the Arrange tab on the Ribbon, click the Align button, then click Right to right-align the edges of the three text boxes.
   c. With all three text boxes still selected, click the Format tab on the Ribbon, click the Apply Comma Number Format button, and click the Decrease Decimals button twice so that the values appear as whole dollar amounts without cents.
   d. Preview the report to view the alignment and format on the Asking data and subtotals.

7. **Format a report.**
   a. In Report Design View, change the Alternate Row Color of the Detail section to No Color.
   b. Change the Alternate Row Color of the Type Header, the RealtorNo Header, and the RealtorNo Footer sections to No Color.
   c. Change the Shape Fill color of the RealtorNo Header section to Green 2. (*Hint*: The Shape Fill button will change the Back Color property in the Property Sheet.)

Skills Review (continued)

d. Select the RLast and RPhone text boxes in the RealtorNo Header section, and change the Shape Fill color to Green 2 to match the RealtorNo Header section.

e. Bold the title of the report, which is the **Listings by Realtor** label in the Report Header, and resize it to make it a little wider to accommodate the bold text.

f. Change the font color of each label in the Page Header section to Automatic (black).

g. Save and preview the report in Print Preview. It should look like FIGURE 4-21. The report should fit on three pages, and the grand total for all Asking values should be 7,957,993. If there are blank pages between printed pages, return to Report Design View and drag the right edge of the report to the left.

FIGURE 4-21

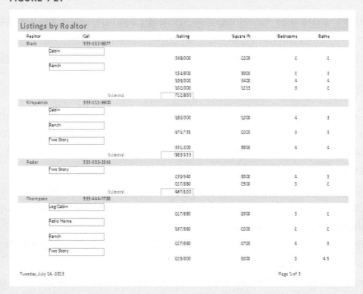

h. In Report Design View, add a label to the left side of the Report Footer section with your name. Be sure to add a label and not a text box control. Make sure that your name is displayed clearly on the last page only in Print Preview.

i. Print the report if requested by your instructor, then save and close the Listings by Realtor report.

8. Create mailing labels.

a. Click the Agencies table in the Navigation Pane, then start the Label Wizard.

b. Choose Avery 5160 labels and the default text appearance choices.

c. Build a prototype label with the AgencyName on the first line, Street on the second line, and City, State, and Zip on the third line with a comma and space between City and State, and a space between State and Zip.

d. Sort by AgencyName, and name the report **Labels Agencies**.

e. Preview then save and close the report. Click OK if a warning dialog box appears regarding horizontal space. The data in your label report does not exceed the dimensions of the labels.

f. Open the Agencies table and change the name of Big Cedar Realtors to *Your Last Name* **Realtors**. Close the Agencies table, reopen the Labels Agencies report, then print it if requested by your instructor.

g. Close the Labels Agencies report, close the LakeHomes-4.accdb database, then exit Access 2016.

Independent Challenge 1

As the office manager of an international convention planning company, you have created a database to track convention, enrollment, and company data. Your goal is to create a report of up-to-date attendee enrollments.

a. Start Access, then open the Conventions-4.accdb database from the location where you store your Data Files. Enable content if prompted.

b. Use the Report Wizard to create a report with the AttendeeLast and AttendeeFirst fields from the Attendees table, the CompanyName field from the Companies table, and the ConventionName and CountryName from the Conventions table. Add the fields in the order listed.

c. View your data by Conventions, add the CompanyName as a second grouping field, then sort in ascending order by AttendeeLast.

d. Use the Block layout and Portrait orientation, then name the report **Convention Attendees**.

e. In Layout View, change the labels in the Page Header section from ConventionName to **Convention** and CompanyName to **Company**. Delete the CountryName, AttendeeLast, and AttendeeFirst labels in the Page Header section.

f. In Report Design View, open the Group, Sort, and Total pane, then open the ConventionNo Footer section.

g. In Report Design View, add a text box to the ConventionNo Footer section just below the AttendeeLast text box in the Detail section. The purpose of the text box is to count the number of people enrolled for each convention. The label should read **Count of Attendees:**, and the expression in the text box should be **=Count([AttendeeLast])**.

h. Resize the new label and text box as needed to make their contents clearly visible.

i. Copy and paste the new label and expression to the Report Footer section. Move and align the controls so they are at the same horizontal position on the page.

j. Change the text color of all labels to Automatic (black). (*Hint:* There are labels in the Report Header, Page Header, ConventionNo Footer, and Report Footer sections.)

k. Preview the report and make sure there are no blank pages between pages. Resize controls in Layout View and narrow the report in Report Design view as needed to remove blank pages.

l. Preview the last page of the report to make sure the subtotal count for each convention and grand total count for the report are aligned as shown in FIGURE 4-22.

m. Add a label with your name to the left side of the Report Footer section, change the text color to Automatic (black), and then print the last page if required by your instructor.

n. Save and close the Convention Attendees report, close the Conventions-4.accdb database, then exit Access 2016.

FIGURE 4-22

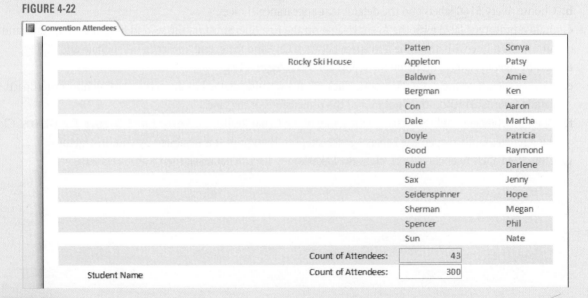

Independent Challenge 2

You have built an Access database to track membership in a community service club. The database tracks member names and addresses as well as their status and rank in the club and their hours of service to the community.

a. Start Access and open the Service-4.accdb database from the location where you store your Data Files. Enable content if prompted.

b. Open the Members table, find and change the name of Micah Ati to *your* name, then close the Members table.

c. Use the Report Wizard to create a report using the FirstName, LastName, and Dues fields from the Members table and the ActivityDate and HoursWorked fields from the Activities table, all in that order.

d. View the data by Members. Do not add any more grouping fields, and sort the records in ascending order by ActivityDate.

e. Use a Stepped layout and Portrait orientation, title the report **Activity Log**, then preview the report.

f. Use Report Layout View to resize the controls to fit the available space and display all data clearly.

g. Change the FirstName label to **First Name**. Change the LastName label to **Last Name**. Change the ActivityDate label to **Date**. Change the HoursWorked label to **Hours**.

h. Switch to Report Design View, then use the Group, Sort, and Total pane to open the MemberNo Footer section.

i. Add a text box to the MemberNo Footer section, just below the HoursWorked text box in the Detail section. Change the label to **Total:** and the expression in the text box to **=Sum([HoursWorked])**.

j. Open the Report Footer section, then copy and paste the **=Sum([HoursWorked])** text box to the Report Footer section. Change the label in the Report Footer section to read **Grand Total:**.

k. Align the HoursWorked text box in the Detail section and the two expressions in the MemberNo Footer and Report Footer sections so that the numbers are perfectly aligned. Be sure to preview the last page of the report to make sure all three controls are aligned as shown in FIGURE 4-23.

l. Add a label to the left edge of the Report Footer section with your name.

m. Preview each page of the report to make sure there are no blank pages. If there are, narrow the controls and the right edge of the report in Report Design View to fix this problem.

n. Print the last page of the report if requested to do so by your instructor.

o. Close the Activity Log report, close the Service-4.accdb database, then exit Access.

FIGURE 4-23

| Total: | 13 |
| Grand Total: | 476 |

Independent Challenge 3

You have built an Access database to organize the deposits at a salvage center. Various clubs regularly deposit material, which is measured in pounds when the deposits are made.

a. Start Access and open the Salvage-4.accdb database from the location where you store your Data Files. Enable content if prompted.

b. Open the Centers table, change **A1 Salvage Center** to **Your Last Name Salvage**, then close the table.

c. Use the Report Wizard to create a report with the CenterName field from the Centers table, the DepositDate and Weight fields from the Deposits table, and the ClubName field from the Clubs table.

d. View the data by Centers, do not add any more grouping levels, and sort the records in ascending order by DepositDate.

e. Use a Stepped layout and a Portrait orientation, then title the report **Deposit Log**.

f. In Layout View, resize the Weight label and Weight data to better position the data across the report. Rename the DepositDate label to **Date**.

g. Add spaces to the labels so that CenterName becomes **Center Name**, and ClubName becomes **Club Name**.

h. In Report Design View, open the Group, Sort, and Total pane and then open the CenterNumber Footer section.

i. Add a text box to the CenterNumber Footer section just below the Weight text box with the expression **=Sum([Weight])**.

j. Rename the new label to be **Subtotal:**.

k. Copy the new text box and paste it back to the CenterNumber Footer section. Change the new label to **Count:** and the expression to **=Count([Weight])**. Align the new controls directly below the Subtotal and =Sum([Weight]) expression.

l. Paste the controls a second time to the CenterNumber Footer section, and change the new label to **Average:** and the expression to **=Avg([Weight])**.

m. Change the Format property of the =Avg([Weight]) expression to **Standard**, and change the Decimal Places property to **0**. (*Hint*: Open the Property Sheet for the text box and click the Format tab to find the Format and Decimal Places properties.)

n. Expand the Report Footer section, then copy and paste the three text boxes from the CenterNumber Footer section to the Report Footer section.

o. Move and align the text boxes in the CenterNumber Footer and Report Footer sections to be positioned directly under the Weight text box in the Detail section. (*Hint*: You may need to both right-align the text boxes as well as align the right edges of the text boxes.)

p. Change the Subtotal label in the Report Footer section to **Total Sum:**. Change the Count label in the Report Footer section to **Total Count:** and also left-align the labels in the CenterNumber Footer and Report Footer sections.

q. Add a label to the left edge of the Report Footer section with your name and preview the last page of the report, a portion of which is shown in FIGURE 4-24. Your numbers should match.

r. Continue to improve the report as needed to align all numbers and labels and to remove any extra blank space in the report by making your sections as vertically short as possible in Report Design View.

s. Save and close the Deposit Log report, close the Salvage-4.accdb database, then exit Access.

FIGURE 4-24

	1/16/2017	85	Access Users Group
	1/21/2017	150	Boy Scout Troop 324
	Subtotal:	3315	
	Count:	36	
	Average:	92	
	Total Sum:	11360	
Student Name	Total Count:	118	
	Average:	96	

Independent Challenge 4: Explore

One way you can use an Access database on your own is to record and track your job search efforts. In this exercise, you create a report to help read and analyze data in your job-tracking database.

a. Start Access and open the JobSearch-4.accdb database from the location where you store your Data Files. Enable content if prompted.

b. Open the Employers table, and enter five more records to identify five more potential employers.

c. Use subdatasheets in the Employers table to enter five more potential jobs. You may enter all five jobs for one employer, one job for five different employers, or any combination thereof. Be sure to check the spelling of all data entered. For the Desirability field, enter a value from **1** to **5**, 1 being the least desirable and 5 being the most desirable. Close the Employers table.

d. Use the Report Wizard to create a report that lists the CompanyName, EmpCity, and EmpState fields from the Employers table, and the Title, AnnualSalary, and Desirability fields from the Positions table.

e. View the data by Employers, do not add any more grouping levels, and sort the records in descending order by Desirability.

f. Use an Outline layout and a Portrait orientation, then title the report **Jobs**.

g. In Design View, revise the labels in the EmployerID Header section from CompanyName to **Company**, EmpCity to **City**, EmpState to **State**, and AnnualSalary to **Salary**.

h. Right-align the text within the Company, City, and State labels so they are closer to the text boxes they describe.

i. In Report Layout View, resize the Desirability, Title, and Salary labels and text boxes to space the controls evenly across the report.

j. Preview the report, then switch to Report Design View to remove any extra space in the report sections. This will involve moving the controls in the EmployerID Header section as far to the top of that section as possible, then dragging the top edge of the Detail section up.

k. Preview the report, making sure all controls fit within the width of portrait orientation. If not, switch to Report Design View and fix this problem.

l. Print the first page if requested by your instructor.

m. Close the Jobs report, close the JobSearch-4.accdb database, then exit Access 2016.

Visual Workshop

Open the Basketball-4.accdb database from the location where you store your Data Files and enable content if prompted. Open the Players table, change the name of Matthew Douglas to *your* name, then close the table. Your goal is to create the report shown in FIGURE 4-25. Use the Report Wizard, and select the PFirst, PLast, HomeTown, and HomeState fields from the Players table. Select the FieldGoals, 3Pointers, and FreeThrows fields from the Stats table. View the data by Players, do not add any more grouping levels, and do not add any more sorting levels. Use a Block layout and a Portrait orientation, then title the report **Scoring Report**. In Layout View, resize all of the columns so that they fit on a single piece of portrait paper, and change the labels in the Page Header section as shown. In Design View, open the PlayerNo Footer section and add text boxes with expressions to sum the FieldGoals, 3Pointers, and FreeThrows fields and bold those controls. Drag the top edge of the Page Footer section down a little to add a little space between the subtotals in the PlayerNo Footer section and the next set of records for the next player. Move, modify, align, and resize all controls as needed to match FIGURE 4-25. (*Hint*: Change the Shape Outline of the text boxes in the PlayerNo Footer section to Transparent to remove the outline.) Be sure to print preview the report to make sure that it fits within the width of one sheet of paper. Modify the report to narrow it in Report Design View if needed.

FIGURE 4-25

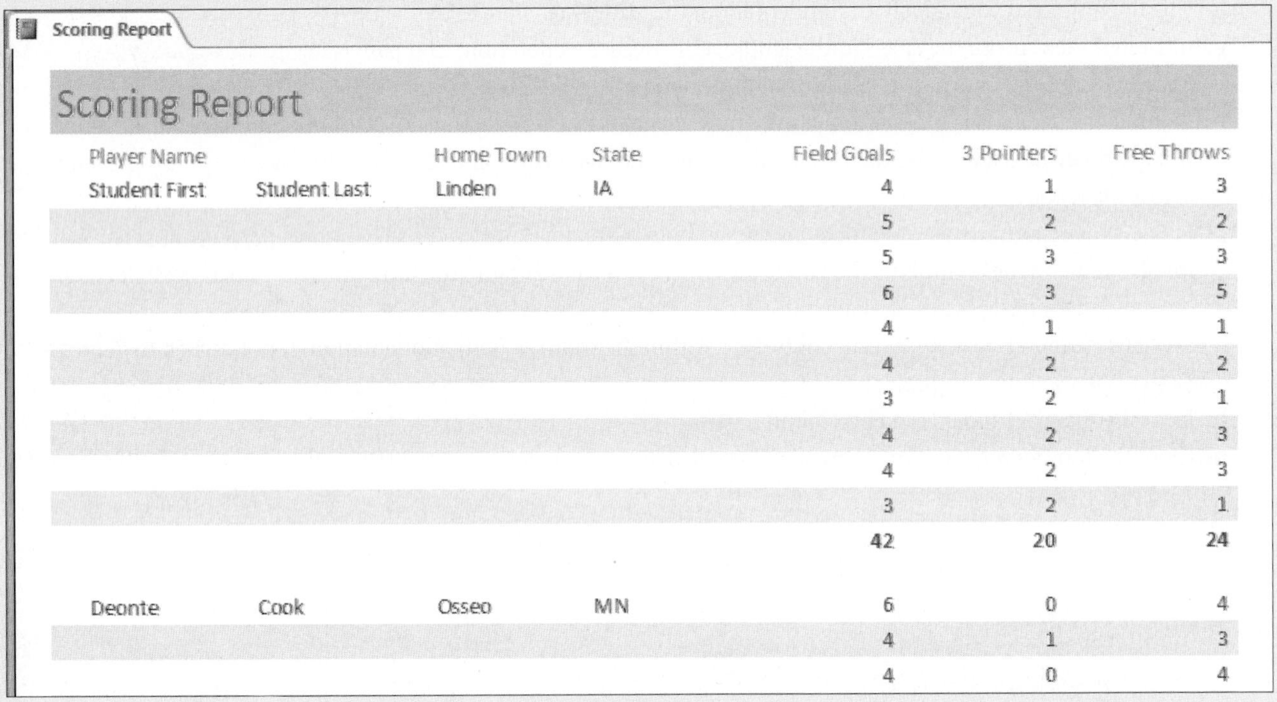

| Scoring Report | | | | | | |

Scoring Report

Player Name		Home Town	State	Field Goals	3 Pointers	Free Throws
Student First	Student Last	Linden	IA	4	1	3
				5	2	2
				5	3	3
				6	3	5
				4	1	1
				4	2	2
				3	2	1
				4	2	3
				4	2	3
				3	2	1
				42	20	24
Deonte	Cook	Osseo	MN	6	0	4
				4	1	3
				4	0	4

Modifying the Database Structure

CASE Working with Julia Rice, the trip developer for U.S. travel at Reason 2 Go, you are developing an Access database to track trips, customers, sales, and payments. The database consists of multiple tables that you link, modify, and enhance to create a relational database.

Module Objectives

After completing this module, you will be able to:

- Examine relational databases
- Design related tables
- Create one-to-many relationships
- Create Lookup fields
- Modify Short Text fields

- Modify Number and Currency fields
- Modify Date/Time fields
- Modify validation properties
- Create Attachment fields

Files You Will Need

R2G-5.accdb
JAlman.jpg
Member1.jpg

Jobs-5.accdb
Training-5.accdb

Examine Relational Databases

Learning Outcomes
• Design tables and fields
• Design primary and foreign key fields
• Analyze one-to-many relationships

The purpose of a relational database is to organize and store data in a way that minimizes redundancy and maximizes your flexibility when querying and analyzing data. To accomplish these goals, a relational database uses related tables rather than a single large table of data. At one time, the Sales Department at Reason 2 Go tracked information about its trip sales and payments using a single Access table called Sales, shown in FIGURE 5-1. This created data redundancy problems because of the duplicate trip, customer, and payment information entered into a single table. **CASE** *You decide to study the principles of relational database design to help R2G reorganize these fields into a correctly designed relational database.*

DETAILS

To redesign a list into a relational database, follow these principles:

- **Design each table to contain fields that describe only one subject**

  Currently, the table in FIGURE 5-1 contains four subjects—trips, sales, customers, and payments—which creates redundant data. For example, the trip name must be duplicated for each sale of that trip. The customer's name must be reentered every time that customer purchases a trip or makes a payment. The problems of redundant data include extra data entry work; more data entry inconsistencies and errors; larger physical storage requirements; and limitations on your ability to search for, analyze, and report on the data. You minimize these problems by implementing a properly designed relational database.

- **Identify a primary key field for each table**

  A **primary key field** is a field that contains unique information for each record. For example, in a customer table, the customer number field usually serves this purpose. Although using the customer's last name as the primary key field might work in a small database, names are generally a poor choice for a primary key field because the primary key cannot accommodate two customers who have the same name.

- **Build one-to-many relationships**

  To tie the information from one table to another, a field must be common to each table. This linking field is the primary key field on the "one" side of the relationship and the **foreign key field** on the "many" side of the relationship. Recall that a primary key field stores unique information for each record in that table. For example, a CustomerNo field acting as the primary key field in the Customers table would link to a CustomerNo foreign key field in a Sales table to join one customer to many sales. You are not required to give the primary and foreign key fields the same name, although doing so does clarify which fields are used to link two tables in a one-to-many relationship.

  The revised design for the database is shown in FIGURE 5-2. One customer can purchase many trips, so the Customers and Sales tables have a one-to-many relationship based on the linking CustNo field. One trip can be purchased many times, so the Trips and Sales tables have a one-to-many relationship (TripNo in the Sales table and TripNo in the Trips table). One sale may have many payments, creating a one-to-many relationship between the Sales and Payments tables based on the common SalesNo field.

Using many-to-many relationships

As you design your database, you might find that two tables have a **many-to-many relationship**, which means that a record in one table may be related to many records in the other table and vice versa. To join them, you must establish a third table called a **junction table**, which contains two foreign key fields to serve on the "many" side of separate one-to-many relationships with the two original tables. The Customers and Trips tables have a many-to-many relationship because one customer can purchase many trips and one trip can have many customers purchase it. The Sales table serves as the junction table to link the three tables together.

Modifying the Database Structure

FIGURE 5-1: Single Sales table results in duplicate data

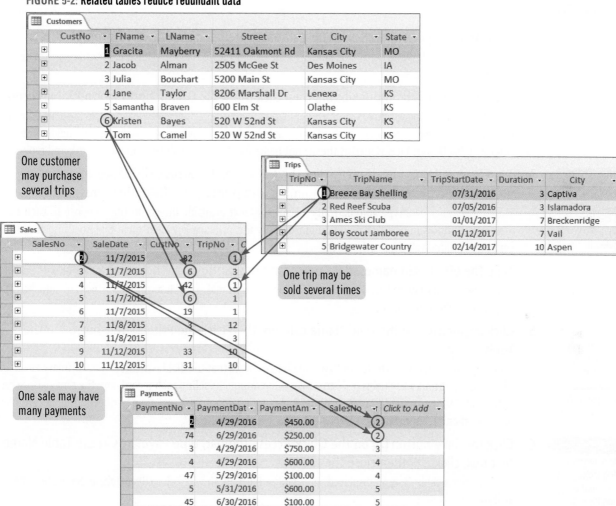

FIGURE 5-2: Related tables reduce redundant data

Enforcing referential integrity

Referential integrity is a set of rules that helps reduce invalid entries and orphan records. An **orphan record** is a record in the "many" table that doesn't have a matching entry in the linking field of the "one" table. With **referential integrity** enforced on a one-to-many relationship, you cannot enter a value in a foreign key field of the "many" table that does not have a match in the linking field of the "one" table. Referential integrity also prevents you from deleting a record in the "one" table if a matching entry exists in the foreign key field of the "many" table. You should enforce referential integrity on all one-to-many relationships if possible. If you are working with a database that already contains orphan records, you cannot enforce referential integrity on that relationship until the orphan records are either corrected or deleted, a process called **scrubbing** the database.

Design Related Tables

After you develop a valid relational database design, you are ready to create the tables in Access. Using **Table Design View**, you can specify all characteristics of a table, including field names, data types, field descriptions, field properties, Lookup properties, and primary key field designations. **CASE** *Using the new database design, Julia Rice asks you to create the Payments table for Reason 2 Go.*

STEPS

1. **Start Access, open the R2G-5.accdb database, then enable content if prompted**

   The Customers, Sales, and Trips tables have already been created in the database. You need to create the Payments table.

2. **Click the Create tab on the Ribbon, then click the Table Design button in the Tables group**

   Table Design View opens, where you can enter field names and specify data types and field properties for the new table. Field names should be as short as possible but long enough to be descriptive. The field name you enter in Table Design View is used as the default name for the field in all later queries, forms, and reports.

3. **Type PaymentNo, press [Enter], click the Data Type list arrow, click AutoNumber, press [Tab], type Unique payment number and primary key field, then press [Enter]**

   The AutoNumber data type automatically assigns the next available integer in the sequence to each new record. The AutoNumber data type is often used as the primary key field for a table because it always contains a unique value for each record.

4. **Type the other field names, data types, and descriptions, as shown in FIGURE 5-3**

   Field descriptions entered in Table Design View are optional, but they provide a way to add helpful information about the field.

5. **Click PaymentNo in the Field Name column, then click the Primary Key button in the Tools group**

   A **key symbol** appears to the left of PaymentNo to indicate that this field is defined as the primary key field for this table. Primary key fields have two roles: They uniquely define each record, and they may also serve as the "one" side of a one-to-many relationship between two tables. **TABLE 5-1** describes common examples of one-to-many relationships.

6. **Click the Save button 🖫 on the Quick Access Toolbar, type Payments in the Table Name text box, click OK, then close the table**

   The Payments table is now displayed as a table object in the R2G-5.accdb database Navigation Pane, as shown in **FIGURE 5-4**.

Specifying the foreign key field data type

A foreign key field in the "many" table must have the same data type (Short Text or Number) as the primary key it is related to in the "one" table. An exception to this rule is when the primary key field in the "one" table has an AutoNumber data type. In this case, the linking foreign key field in the "many" table must have a Number data type. Also note that a Number field used as a foreign key field must have a Long Integer Field Size property to match the Field Size property of the AutoNumber primary key field.

FIGURE 5-3: Table Design View for the new Payments table

Field Name	Data Type	Description (Optional)
PaymentNo	AutoNumber	Unique payment number and primary key field
PaymentDate	Date/Time	Date the payment is made
PaymentAmt	Currency	Amount of the payment
SalesNo	Number	Foreign key field to the Sales table

Field names   Data types   Descriptions

FIGURE 5-4: Payments table in R2G-5 database Navigation Pane

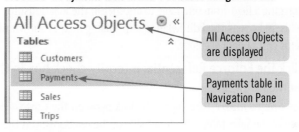

All Access Objects are displayed

Payments table in Navigation Pane

TABLE 5-1: Common one-to-many relationships

table on "one" side	table on "many" side	linking field	description
Products	Sales	ProductID	A ProductID field must have a unique entry in a Products table, but it is listed many times in a Sales table
Students	Enrollments	StudentID	A StudentID field must have a unique entry in a Students table, but it is listed many times in an Enrollments table as the student enrolls in multiple classes
Employees	Promotions	EmployeeID	An EmployeeID field must have a unique entry in an Employees table, but it is listed many times in a Promotions table as the employee is promoted over time

Create One-to-Many Relationships

Learning Outcomes
• Enforce referential integrity on a one-to-many relationship
• Create a Relationship report

After creating the tables you need, you link them together in appropriate one-to-many relationships using the primary key field in the "one" table and the foreign key field in the "many" table. To avoid time-consuming rework, be sure that your table relationships are finished before building queries, forms, or reports using fields from multiple tables. **CASE** *Julia asks you to define the one-to-many relationships between the tables of the R2G-5.accdb database.*

STEPS

QUICK TIP
Drag the table's title bar to move the field list.

1. **Click the Database Tools tab on the Ribbon, click the Relationships button, click the Show Table button, double-click Customers, double-click Sales, double-click Trips, double-click Payments, then click Close in the Show Table dialog box**

   The four table field lists appear in the Relationships window. The primary key fields are identified with a small key symbol to the left of the field name. With all of the field lists in the Relationships window, you're ready to link them in proper one-to-many relationships.

QUICK TIP
Drag the bottom border of the field list to display all of the fields.

2. **Click CustNo in the Customers table field list, then drag it to the CustNo field in the Sales table field list**

   Dragging a field from one table to another in the Relationships window links the two tables by the selected fields and opens the Edit Relationships dialog box, as shown in FIGURE 5-5. Recall that referential integrity helps ensure data accuracy.

TROUBLE
Right-click a relationship line then click Delete if you need to delete a relationship and start over.

3. **Click the Enforce Referential Integrity check box in the Edit Relationships dialog box, then click Create**

   The **one-to-many line** shows the link between the CustNo field of the Customers table and the CustNo field of the Sales table. The "one" side of the relationship is the unique CustNo value for each record in the Customers table. The "many" side of the relationship is identified by an infinity symbol pointing to the CustNo field in the Sales table. You also need to link the Trips table to the Sales table.

4. **Click TripNo in the Trips table field list, drag it to TripNo in the Sales table field list, click the Enforce Referential Integrity check box, then click Create**

   Finally, you need to link the Payments table to the Sales table.

5. **Click SalesNo in the Sales table field list, drag it to SalesNo in the Payments table field list, click the Enforce Referential Integrity check box, click Create, then drag the Trips title bar down so all links are clear**

   The updated Relationships window should look like FIGURE 5-6.

TROUBLE
Click the Landscape button on the Print Preview tab if the report is too wide for portrait orientation.

6. **Click the Relationship Report button in the Tools group, click the Print button on the Print Preview tab, then click OK**

   A printout of the Relationships window, called the **Relationship report**, shows how your relational database is designed and includes table names, field names, primary key fields, and one-to-many relationship lines. This printout is helpful as you later create queries, forms, and reports that use fields from multiple tables. Note that it is not necessary to directly link each table to every other table.

7. **Right-click the Relationships for R2G-5 report tab, click Close, click Yes to save the report, then click OK to accept the default report name**

   The Relationships for R2G-5 report is saved in your database, as shown in the Navigation Pane.

8. **Close the Relationships window, then click Yes if prompted to save changes**

FIGURE 5-5: Edit Relationships dialog box

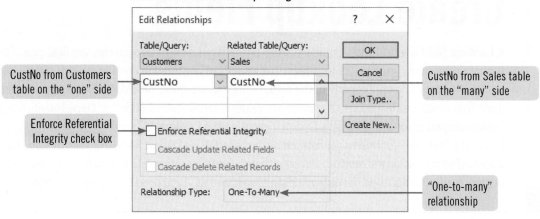

CustNo from Customers table on the "one" side

CustNo from Sales table on the "many" side

Enforce Referential Integrity check box

"One-to-many" relationship

FIGURE 5-6: Final Relationships window

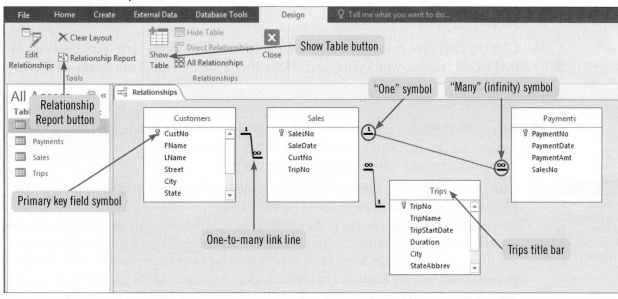

Relationship Report button

Show Table button

"One" symbol

"Many" (infinity) symbol

Primary key field symbol

One-to-many link line

Trips title bar

More on enforcing referential integrity

Recall that referential integrity is a set of rules to help ensure that no orphan records are entered or created in the database. An orphan record is a record in the "many" table (also called the **child table**) that doesn't have a matching entry in the linking field of the "one" table (also called the **parent table**). Referential integrity prevents orphan records in multiple ways. Referential integrity will not allow you to make an entry in the foreign key field of the child table that does not have a matching value in the linking field of the parent table. (So you can't make a sale to a customer who doesn't first exist in the Customers table, for example.) Referential integrity

also prevents you from deleting a record in the parent table that has related records in the child table. (So you can't delete a customer from the Customers table who already has related sales records in the Sales table, for example.) You should enforce referential integrity on all one-to-many relationships if possible. Unfortunately, if you are working with a database that already contains orphan records, you cannot enforce this powerful set of rules unless you find and fix the data so that orphan records no longer exist. The process of removing and fixing orphan records is commonly called **scrubbing data** or **data cleansing**.

Create Lookup Fields

Learning Outcomes
- Modify field Lookup properties
- Edit data in a Lookup field

A **Lookup field** is a field that contains Lookup properties. **Lookup properties** are field properties that supply a drop-down list of values for a field. The values can be stored in another table or directly stored in the **Row Source** Lookup property of the field. Fields that are good candidates for Lookup properties are those that contain a defined set of appropriate values such as State, Gender, or Department. You can set Lookup properties for a field in Table Design View using the **Lookup Wizard**. **CASE** ▶ *The FirstContact field in the Customers table identifies how the customer first made contact with R2G, such as being referred by a friend (Friend), finding the company through the web (Web), or responding to a radio advertisement (Radio). Because the FirstContact field has only a handful of valid entries, it is a good Lookup field candidate.*

STEPS

1. **Right-click the** Customers table **in the Navigation Pane, then click** Design View

   The Lookup Wizard is included in the Data Type list.

2. **Click the** Short Text data type **for the FirstContact field, click the** Data Type list arrow, **then click** Lookup Wizard

   The Lookup Wizard starts and prompts you for information about where the Lookup column will get its values.

3. **Click the** I will type in the values that I want option button, **click** Next, **click the** first cell in the Col1 column, type Friend, press [Tab], **then type the rest of the values, as shown in** FIGURE 5-7

   These are the values for the drop-down list for the FirstContact field.

4. **Click** Next, **then click** Finish **to accept the default label and complete the Lookup Wizard**

   Note that the data type for the FirstContact field is still Short Text. The Lookup Wizard is a process for setting Lookup property values for a field, not a data type itself.

QUICK TIP
The right side of the Field Properties pane displays a short description for the selected property.

5. **Click the** Lookup tab **in the Field Properties pane to observe the new Lookup properties for the FirstContact field, as shown in** FIGURE 5-8

   The Lookup Wizard helped you enter Lookup properties for the FirstContact field, but you can always enter or edit them directly, too. Some of the most important Lookup properties include Row Source, Limit To List, and Allow Value List Edits. The **Row Source** property stores the values that are provided in the drop-down list for a Lookup field. The **Limit To List** Lookup property determines whether you can enter a new value into a field with other Lookup properties, or whether the entries are limited to the drop-down list. The **Allow Value List Edits** property determines whether users can add or edit the list of items.

QUICK TIP
To quickly remove all Lookup properties, change the Display Control property to Text Box.

6. **Click the** View button **to switch to Datasheet View, click** Yes **when prompted to save the table, press [Tab] eight times to move to the FirstContact field, then click the** FirstContact list arrow, **as shown in** FIGURE 5-9

   The FirstContact field now provides a list of four values for this field. To edit the list in Datasheet View, click the **Edit List Items button** below the list.

7. **Close the Customers table**

Creating multivalued fields

Multivalued fields allow you to make more than one choice from a drop-down list for a field. As a database designer, multivalued fields allow you to select and store more than one choice without having to create a more advanced database design. To create a multivalued field, enter Yes in the **Allow Multiple Values** Lookup property.

FIGURE 5-7: Entering a list of values in the Lookup Wizard

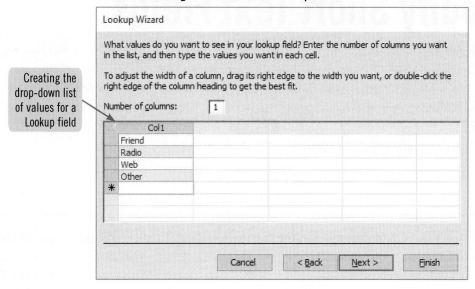

Creating the drop-down list of values for a Lookup field

FIGURE 5-8: Viewing Lookup properties

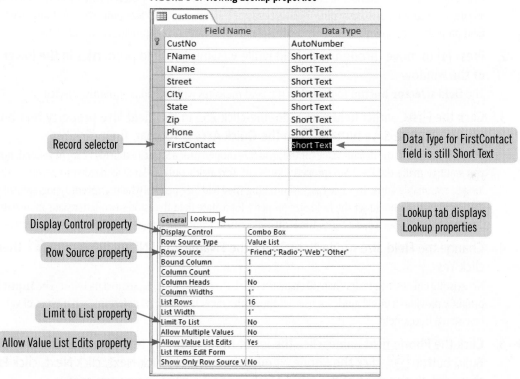

Record selector

Data Type for FirstContact field is still Short Text

Lookup tab displays Lookup properties

Display Control property

Row Source property

Limit to List property

Allow Value List Edits property

FIGURE 5-9: Using a Lookup field in a datasheet

Drop-down list for Lookup field

Edit List Items button

Modify Short Text Fields

Field properties are the characteristics that describe each field, such as Field Size, Format, Input Mask, Caption, or Default Value. These properties help ensure database accuracy and clarity because they restrict the way data is entered, stored, and displayed. You modify field properties in Table Design View. See **TABLE 5-2** for more information on Short Text field properties. (*Note:* The "Short Text" data type was called the "Text" data type in some previous versions of Access.) **CASE** ▶ *After reviewing the Customers table with Julia Rice, you decide to change field properties for several Short Text fields in that table.*

STEPS

1. **Right-click the Customers table in the Navigation Pane, then click Design View on the shortcut menu**

   Field properties appear on the General tab on the lower half of the Table Design View window called the **Field Properties pane**, and they apply to the selected field. Field properties change depending on the field's data type. For example, when you select a field with a Short Text data type, you see the **Field Size property**, which determines the number of characters you can enter in the field. However, when you select a field with a Date/Time data type, Access controls the size of the data, so the Field Size property is not displayed. Many field properties are optional, but for those that require an entry, Access provides a default value.

2. **Press [↓] to move through each field while viewing the field properties in the lower half of the window**

   The **field selector button** to the left of the field indicates which field is currently selected.

3. **Click the FirstContact field name, double-click 255 in the Field Size property text box, type 6, click the Save button 🖫 on the Quick Access Toolbar, then click Yes**

   The maximum and the default value for the Field Size property for a Short Text field is 255. In general, however, you want to make the Field Size property for Short Text fields only as large as needed to accommodate the longest reasonable entry. In some cases, shortening the Field Size property helps prevent typographical errors. For example, you should set the Field Size property for a State field that stores two-letter state abbreviations to 2 to prevent typos such as TXX. For the FirstContact field, your longest entry is "Friend"—6 characters.

4. **Change the Field Size property to 30 for the FName and LName fields, click 🖫, then click Yes**

   No existing entries are greater than 30 characters for either of these fields, so no data is lost. The **Input Mask** property provides a visual guide for users as they enter data. It also helps determine what types of values can be entered into a field.

5. **Click the Phone field name, click the Input Mask property text box, click the Build button [···], click the Phone Number input mask, click Next, click Next, click Finish, then click to the right of the Input Mask property value so you can read it**

   Table Design View of the Customers table should look like **FIGURE 5-10**, which shows the Input Mask property created for the Phone field by the Input Mask Wizard.

6. **Right-click the Customers table tab, click Datasheet View, click Yes to save the table, press [Tab] enough times to move to the Phone field for the first record, type 5551118888, then press [Enter]**

   The Phone Input Mask property creates an easy-to-use visual guide to facilitate accurate data entry.

7. **Close the Customers table**

FIGURE 5-10: Changing Short Text field properties

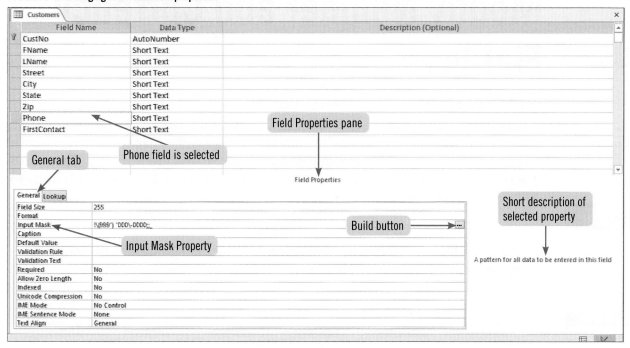

TABLE 5-2: Common Short Text field properties

property	description	sample field	sample property entry
Field Size	Controls how many characters can be entered into the field	State	2
Format	Controls how information will be displayed and printed	State	> (displays all characters in uppercase)
Input Mask	Provides a pattern for data to be entered	Phone	!(999) 000-0000;1;_
Caption	Describes the field in the first row of a datasheet, form, or report; if the Caption property is not entered, the field name is used to label the field	EmpNo	Employee Number
Default Value	Displays a value that is automatically entered in the given field for new records	City	Kansas City
Required	Determines if an entry is required for this field	LastName	Yes

Working with the Input Mask property

The Input Mask property provides a pattern for data to be entered, using three parts separated by semicolons. The first part provides a pattern for what type of data can be entered. For example, 9 represents an optional number, 0 a required number, ? an optional letter, and L a required letter. The second part determines whether all displayed characters (such as dashes in a phone number) are stored in the field. For the second part of the input mask, a 0 entry stores all characters, such as 555-1199, and a 1 entry stores only the entered data, 5551199. The third part of the input mask determines which character Access uses to guide the user through the mask. Common choices are the asterisk (*), underscore (_), or pound sign (#).

Access 2016
Module 5

Learning
Outcomes
• Modify the Field
  Size property for
  Number fields
• Modify the
  Decimal Places
  property

Modify Number and Currency Fields

Although some properties for Number and Currency fields are the same as the properties of Short Text fields, each data type has its own list of valid properties. Number and Currency fields have similar properties because they both contain numeric values. Currency fields store values that represent money, and Number fields store values that represent values such as quantities, measurements, and scores. **CASE** *The Trips table contains both a Number field (Duration) and a Currency field (Price). Julia wants you to modify the properties of these two fields.*

STEPS

1. **Right-click the Trips table in the Navigation Pane, click Design View on the shortcut menu, then click the Duration field name**

   The default Field Size property for a Number field is **Long Integer**. See **TABLE 5-3** for more information on the Field Size property and other common properties for a Number field. Access sets the size of Currency fields to control the way numbers are rounded in calculations, so the Field Size property isn't available for Currency fields.

QUICK TIP
The list arrow for
each property is on
the far right side of
the property box.

2. **Click Integer in the Field Size property text box, click the Field Size list arrow, then click Byte**

   Choosing a **Byte** value for the Field Size property allows entries from 0 to 255, so it greatly restricts the possible values and the storage requirements for the Duration field.

QUICK TIP
Double-click a
property name to
toggle through the
choices.

3. **Click the Price field name, click Auto in the Decimal Places property text box, click the Decimal Places list arrow, click 0, then press [Enter]**

   Your Table Design View should look like **FIGURE 5-11**. Because all of R2G's trips are priced at a round dollar value, you do not need to display cents in the Price field.

TROUBLE
If values appear as
#####, it means the
column needs to be
widened to see all of
the data.

4. **Save the table, then switch to Datasheet View**

   You won't lose any data because none of the current entries in the Duration field is greater than 255, the maximum value allowed by a Number field with a Byte Field Size property. You want to test the new property changes.

5. **Press [Tab] three times to move to the Duration field for the first record, type 300, then press [Tab]**

   Because 300 is larger than what the Byte Field Size property allows (0–255), an Access error message appears, indicating that the value isn't valid for this field.

6. **Click OK, press [Esc] to remove the inappropriate entry in the Duration field, then press [Tab] four times to move to the Price field**

   The Price field is set to display zero digits after the decimal point.

7. **Type 750.99 in the Price field of the first record, press [Tab], then click $751 in the Price field of the first record to see the full entry**

   Although the Decimal Places property for the Price field specifies that entries in the field are formatted to display zero digits after the decimal point, 750.99 is the actual value stored in the field. Modifying the Decimal Places property does not change the actual data. Rather, the Decimal Places property only changes the way the data is *presented*.

8. **Close the Trips table**

FIGURE 5-11: Changing Currency and Number field properties

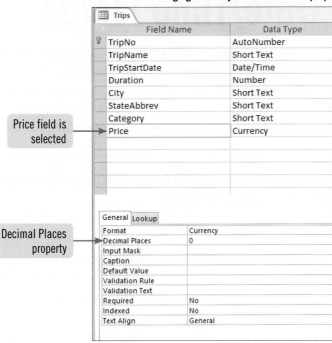

TABLE 5-3: Common Number field properties

property	description
Field Size	Determines the largest number that can be entered in the field, as well as the type of data (e.g., integer or fraction)
Byte	Stores numbers from 0 to 255 (no fractions)
Integer	Stores numbers from –32,768 to 32,767 (no fractions)
Long Integer	Stores numbers from –2,147,483,648 to 2,147,483,647 (no fractions)
Single	Stores numbers (including fractions with six digits to the right of the decimal point) times 10 to the –38th to +38th power
Double	Stores numbers (including fractions with more than 10 digits to the right of the decimal point) in the range of 10 to the –324th to +324th power
Decimal Places	The number of digits displayed to the right of the decimal point

Modifying fields in Datasheet View

When you work in Table Datasheet View, the Fields tab on the Ribbon provides many options to modify fields and field properties. For example, you can add and delete fields, change a field name or data type, and modify many field properties such as Caption, Default Value, and Format.

Table Design View, however, gives you full access to all field properties such as all of the Lookup properties. In Datasheet View, an **Autofilter** arrow is displayed to the right of each field name. Click the Autofilter arrow to quickly sort or filter by that field.

Modify Date/Time Fields

Many properties of the Date/Time field, such as Input Mask, Caption, and Default Value, work the same way as they do in fields with a Short Text or Number data type. One difference, however, is the **Format** property, which helps you format dates in various ways such as January 25, 2017; 25-Jan-17; or 01/25/2017. **CASE** *You want to change the format of Date/Time fields in the Trips table to display two digits for the month and day values and four digits for the year, as in 05/06/2017.*

STEPS

1. **Right-click the Trips table in the Navigation Pane, click Design View on the shortcut menu, then click the TripStartDate field name**

   You want the trip start dates to appear with two digits for the month and day, such as 07/05/2017, instead of the default presentation of dates, 7/5/2017.

2. **Click the Format property box, then click the Format list arrow**

   Although several predefined Date/Time formats are available, none matches the format you want. To define a custom format, enter symbols that represent how you want the date to appear.

3. **Type mm/dd/yyyy then press [Enter]**

   The updated Format property for the TripStartDate field shown in FIGURE 5-12 sets the date to appear with two digits for the month, two digits for the day, and four digits for the year. The parts of the date are separated by forward slashes.

4. **Save the table, display the datasheet, then click the New (blank) record button ▶ on the navigation bar**

   To test the new Format property for the TripStartDate field, you can add a new record to the table.

5. **Press [Tab] to move to the TripName field, type Mississippi Cleanup, press [Tab], type 5/6/17, press [Tab], type 7, press [Tab], type Dubuque, press [Tab], type IA, press [Tab], type Eco, press [Tab], type 1000, then press [Tab]**

   The new record you entered into the Trips table should look like FIGURE 5-13. The Format property for the TripStartDate field makes the entry appear as 05/06/2017, as desired.

FIGURE 5-12: Changing Date/Time field properties

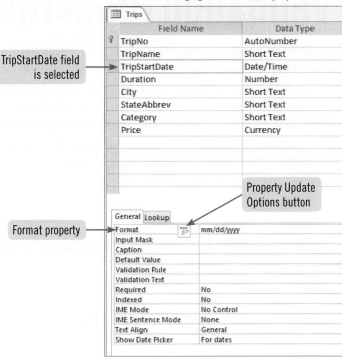

TripStartDate field is selected

Property Update Options button

Format property

Field Name	Data Type
TripNo	AutoNumber
TripName	Short Text
TripStartDate	Date/Time
Duration	Number
City	Short Text
StateAbbrev	Short Text
Category	Short Text
Price	Currency

General | Lookup

Format	mm/dd/yyyy
Input Mask	
Caption	
Default Value	
Validation Rule	
Validation Text	
Required	No
Indexed	No
IME Mode	No Control
IME Sentence Mode	None
Text Align	General
Show Date Picker	For dates

FIGURE 5-13: Testing the Format property

⊞	48	Kings Canyon Bridge Builders	07/12/2017	10	Three Rivers	CA	Eco	$2,800
⊞	49	Golden State Tours	07/19/2017	10	Sacramento	CA	Site Seeing	$2,300
⊞	51	Mark Twain Forest Project	11/30/2017	7	Branson	MO	Eco	$1,200
⊞	52	Missouri Bald Eagle Watch Club	08/12/2017	7	Hollister	MO	Family	$1,100
⊞	53	Mississippi Cleanup	05/06/2017	7	Dubuque	IA	Eco	$1,000
*	(New)						

Record: 1 of 48   No Filter   Search

Custom mm/dd/yyyy Format property applied to TripStartDate field

Using Smart Tags

Smart Tags are buttons that automatically appear in certain conditions. They provide a small menu of options to help you work with the task at hand. Access provides the **Property Update Options** Smart Tag to help you quickly apply property changes to other objects of the database that use the field.

The **Error Indicator** Smart Tag helps identify potential design errors. For example, if you are working in Report Design View and the report is too wide for the paper, the Error Indicator appears in the upper-left corner by the report selector button to alert you to the problem.

Modify Validation Properties

Learning
Outcomes
• Modify the
  Validation Rule
  property
• Modify the
  Validation Text
  property
• Define Validation
  Rule expressions

The **Validation Rule** property determines what entries a field can accept. For example, a validation rule for a Date/Time field might require date entries on or after a particular date. A validation rule for a Currency field might indicate that valid entries fall between a minimum and maximum value. You use the **Validation Text** property to display an explanatory message when a user tries to enter data that breaks the validation rule. Therefore, the Validation Rule and Validation Text field properties help you prevent unreasonable data from being entered into the database. **CASE** *Julia Rice reminds you that all new R2G trips must be scheduled to start before January 1, 2021. You can use the validation properties to establish this rule for the TripStartDate field in the Trips table.*

STEPS

1. **Right-click the Trips table tab, click Design View, click the TripStartDate field, click the Validation Rule property box, then type <1/1/2021**

    R2G is currently not scheduling any trips in the year 2021 or beyond. This entry forces all dates in the TripStartDate field to be less than 1/1/2021. See **TABLE 5-4** for more examples of Validation Rule expressions. The Validation Text property provides a helpful message to the user when the entry in the field breaks the rule entered in the Validation Rule property.

2. **Click the Validation Text box, then type Date must be before 1/1/2021**

    Design View of the Trips table should now look like **FIGURE 5-14**. Access modifies a property to include additional syntax by changing the entry in the Validation Rule property to <#1/1/2021#. Pound signs (#) are used to surround date criteria.

3. **Save the table, then click Yes when asked to test the existing data with new data integrity rules**

    Because no dates in the TripStartDate field are later than 1/1/2021, Access finds no date errors in the current data and saves the table. You now want to test that the Validation Rule and Validation Text properties work when entering data in the datasheet.

4. **Click the View button [icon] to display the datasheet, press [Tab] twice to move to the TripStartDate field, type 1/1/21, then press [Tab]**

    Because you tried to enter a date that was not true for the Validation Rule property for the TripStartDate field, a dialog box opens and displays the Validation Text entry, as shown in **FIGURE 5-15**.

5. **Click OK to close the validation message**

    You now know that the Validation Rule and Validation Text properties work properly.

6. **Press [Esc] to reject the invalid date entry in the TripStartDate field**

7. **Close the Trips table**

FIGURE 5-14: Entering Validation properties

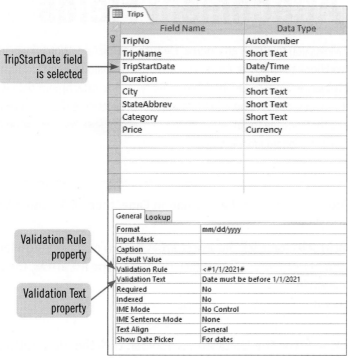

TripStartDate field is selected

Validation Rule property

Validation Text property

FIGURE 5-15: Validation Text message

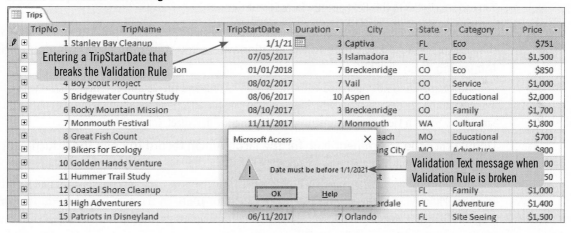

Entering a TripStartDate that breaks the Validation Rule

Validation Text message when Validation Rule is broken

TABLE 5-4: Validation Rule expressions

data type	validation rule expression	description
Number or Currency	>0	The number must be positive
Number or Currency	>10 And <100	The number must be greater than 10 and less than 100
Number or Currency	10 Or 20 Or 30	The number must be 10, 20, or 30
Short Text	"AZ" Or "CO" Or "NM"	The entry must be AZ, CO, or NM
Date/Time	>=#7/1/17#	The date must be on or after 7/1/2017
Date/Time	>#1/1/10# And <#1/1/2030#	The date must be greater than 1/1/2010 and less than 1/1/2030

Access 2016

Create Attachment Fields

Learning Outcomes
- Create an Attachment field
- Attach and view a file in an Attachment field

An **Attachment field** allows you to attach an external file such as a picture, Word document, PowerPoint presentation, or Excel workbook to a record. Earlier versions of Access allowed you to link or embed external data using the **OLE** (object linking and embedding) data type. The Attachment data type stores more file formats such as JPEG images, requires no additional software to view the files from within Access, and allows you to attach more than one file to the Attachment field. **CASE** *You can use an Attachment field to store JPEG images for customer photo identification.*

STEPS

1. **Right-click the Customers table in the Navigation Pane, then click Design View**

   You can insert a new field anywhere in the list.

2. **Click the Street field selector, click the Insert Rows button on the Design tab, click the Field Name cell, type Photo, press [Tab], click the Data Type list arrow, then click Attachment, as shown in FIGURE 5-16**

   Now that you've created the new Attachment field named Photo, you're ready to add data to it in Datasheet View.

3. **Click the Save button 🖫 on the Quick Access Toolbar, click the View button 🏢 on the Design tab to switch to Datasheet View, then press [Tab] three times to move to the new Photo field**

   An Attachment field cell displays a small paperclip icon with the number of files attached to the field in parentheses. You have not attached any files to this field yet, so each record shows zero (0) file attachments. You can attach files to this field directly from Datasheet View.

4. **Double-click the attachment icon 📎 for the Jacob Alman record to open the Attachments dialog box, click Add, navigate to the location where you store your Data Files, double-click JAlman.jpg, then click OK**

   The JAlman.jpg file is now included with the second record, and the datasheet reflects that one (1) file is attached to the Photo field. You can add more than one file attachment and different types of files to the same field. You can view file attachments directly from the datasheet, form, or report.

5. **Double-click the attachment icon for the Jacob Alman record to open the Attachments dialog box shown in FIGURE 5-17, then click Open**

   The image opens in the program that is associated with the .jpg extension on your computer such as Windows Photo Viewer. The **.jpg** file extension is short for **JPEG**, an acronym for **Joint Photographic Experts Group**. This group defines the standards for the compression algorithms that make JPEG files very efficient to use in databases and on webpages.

6. **Close the window that displays the JAlman.jpg image, click Cancel in the Attachments dialog box, close the Customers table, close the R2G-5.accdb database, then exit Access**

FIGURE 5-16: Adding an Attachment field

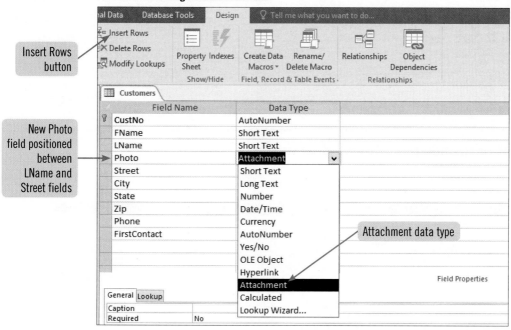

FIGURE 5-17: Opening an attached file

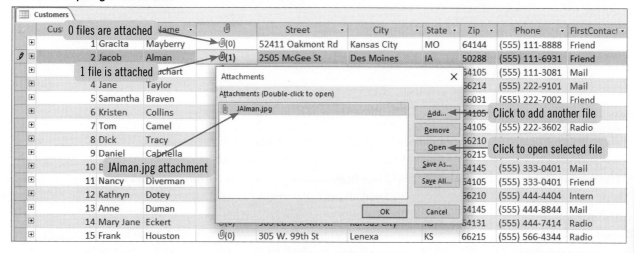

Working with database file types

When you create a new database in Microsoft Access 2016, Access gives the file an **.accdb** extension and saves it as an Access 2007-2016 database file type as shown in the Access title bar. Saving the database as an Access 2007-2016 file type allows users of Access 2007, 2010, 2013, and 2016 to share the same database. Access 2007-2016 databases are not readable by earlier versions of Access such as Access 2000, Access 2002 (XP), or Access 2003. If you need to share your database with people using Access 2000, 2002, or 2003, you can use the Save As command on the File tab to save the database with an Access 2000 or 2002-2003 file type, which applies an **.mdb** file extension to the database. Databases with an Access 2000 file type can be used by any version of Access from Access 2000 through 2016, but some features, such as multivalued fields and Attachment fields, are only available when working with an Access 2007-2016 database.

Practice

Concepts Review

Identify each element of the Relationships window shown in FIGURE 5-18.

FIGURE 5-18

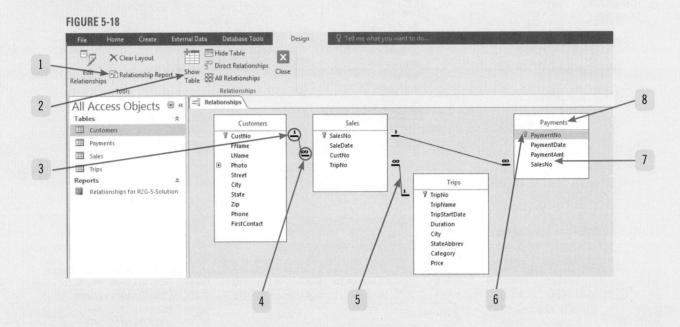

Match each term with the statement that best describes it.

9. **Table Design View**
10. **Row Source**
11. **Attachment field**
12. **Limit To List**
13. **Validation Rule**
14. **Input Mask**
15. **Lookup properties**
16. **Primary key field**
17. **Multivalued field**

a. Field that allows you to store external files such as a Word document, PowerPoint presentation, Excel workbook, or JPEG image

b. Field that holds unique information for each record in the table

c. Field that allows you to make more than one choice from a drop-down list

d. Determines whether you can enter a new value into a field

e. Field properties that allow you to supply a drop-down list of values for a field

f. Access window in which all characteristics of a table, such as field names and field properties, are defined

g. Field property that provides a visual guide as you enter data

h. Field property that prevents unreasonable data entries for a field

i. Lookup property that determines where the Lookup field gets its list of values

Select the best answer from the list of choices.

18. **The linking field in the "many" table is called the:**
    a. Attachment field.
    b. Child field.
    c. Foreign key field.
    d. Primary key field.

19. **Which of the following problems most clearly indicates that you need to redesign your database?**
    a. Referential integrity is enforced on table relationships.
    b. The Input Mask Wizard has not been used.
    c. There is duplicated data in several records of a table.
    d. Not all fields have Validation Rule properties.

20. **Which of the following is not done in Table Design View?**
    a. Creating file attachments
    b. Defining field data types
    c. Specifying the primary key field
    d. Setting Field Size properties

21. **What is the purpose of enforcing referential integrity?**
    a. To require an entry for each field of each record
    b. To prevent incorrect entries in the primary key field
    c. To prevent orphan records from being created
    d. To force the application of meaningful validation rules

22. **To create a many-to-many relationship between two tables, you must create:**
    a. Foreign key fields in each table.
    b. A junction table.
    c. Two primary key fields in each table.
    d. Two one-to-one relationships between the two tables, with referential integrity enforced.

23. **The default filename extension for a database created in Access 2016 is:**
    a. .accdb.
    b. .acc16.
    c. .mdb.
    d. .mdb16.

24. **If the primary key field in the "one" table is an AutoNumber data type, the linking field in the "many" table will have which data type?**
    a. Number
    b. Short Text
    c. AutoNumber
    d. Attachment

25. **Which symbol is used to identify the "many" field in a one-to-many relationship in the Relationships window?**
    a. Arrow
    b. Triangle
    c. Key
    d. Infinity

26. **The process of removing and fixing orphan records is commonly called:**
    a. Relating tables.
    b. Designing a relational database.
    c. Scrubbing the database.
    d. Analyzing performance.

Skills Review

1. Examine relational databases.

a. List the fields needed to create an Access relational database to manage volunteer hours for the members of a philanthropic club or community service organization.

b. Identify fields that would contain duplicate values if all of the fields were stored in a single table.

c. Group the fields into subject matter tables, then identify the primary key field for each table.

d. Assume that your database contains two tables: Members and ServiceHours. If you did not identify these two tables earlier, regroup the fields within these two table names, then identify the primary key field for each table, the foreign key field in the ServiceHours table, and how the tables would be related using a one-to-many relationship.

2. Design related tables.

a. Start Access 2016, then create a new blank desktop database named **Service-5** in the location where you store your Data Files.

b. Use Table Design View to create a new table with the name **Members** and the field names, data types, descriptions, and primary key field, as shown in FIGURE 5-19. Close the Members table.

FIGURE 5-19

	Field Name	Data Type	Description
⚷	MemberNo	AutoNumber	Member Number. Unique number for each member
	FirstName	Short Text	Member's first name
	LastName	Short Text	Member's last name
	City	Short Text	Member's city
	Phone	Short Text	Member's best phone number
	Email	Short Text	Member's best email address
	Birthdate	Date/Time	Member's birthdate
	Gender	Short Text	Member's gender: male, female, unknown

c. Use Table Design View to create a new table named **ServiceHours** with the field names, data types, descriptions, and primary key field shown in FIGURE 5-20. Close the ServiceHours table.

FIGURE 5-20

	Field Name	Data Type	Description (Optional)
⚷	ServiceNo	AutoNumber	Unique number to identify each ServiceHours record
	MemberNo	Number	Foreign key field to Members table. One member may have many ServiceHours records
	ServiceDate	Date/Time	Date that the service occurred
	Location	Short Text	Location where the service occurred
	Description	Short Text	Description of the service activity
	ServiceHours	Number	Number of hours spent on service activity
	ServiceValue	Currency	Monetary value of the service activity

Modifying the Database Structure

Skills Review (continued)

3. Create one-to-many relationships.

a. Open the Relationships window, double-click Members, then double-click ServiceHours to add the two tables to the Relationships window. Close the Show Table dialog box.

b. Resize all field lists by dragging the bottom border down so that all fields are visible, then drag the MemberNo field from the Members table to the MemberNo field in the ServiceHours table.

c. Enforce referential integrity, and create the one-to-many relationship between Members and ServiceHours. See **FIGURE 5-21**.

FIGURE 5-21

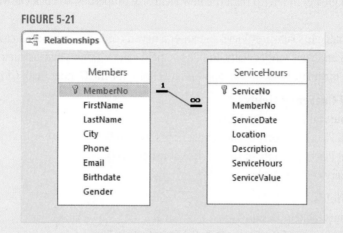

d. Create a Relationship report for the Service-5 database, add your name as a label to the Report Header section of the report in Report Design View, save the Relationship report with the default name **Relationships for Service-5**, then preview it.

e. Print the report if requested by your instructor, close the Relationship report, then save and close the Relationships window.

4. Create Lookup fields.

a. Open the Members table in Design View, then start the Lookup Wizard for the Gender field.

b. Select the option that allows you to enter your own values, then enter **Female**, **Male**, and **Unknown** as the values for the Lookup column in the Col1 list.

c. Use the default **Gender** label, click the Limit To List check box, then click Finish to finish the Lookup Wizard.

d. Save the Members table, display it in Datasheet View, and enter your name in the FirstName and LastName fields for the first record. Enter your school's city, **5551112233** in the Phone field, your school email address in the Email field, **1/1/1991** in the Birthdate field, and any valid choice in the Gender field.

e. Type **Test** in the Gender field, then press [Tab] to test the Limit To List property. If it worked properly, you should receive an error message that states that the text you entered isn't an item on the list. Click OK in that dialog box, make a choice from the Gender drop-down list, then press [Tab] to finish the record. (*Hint*: If you were allowed to enter Test in the Gender field, it means that the Limit To List property is set to No instead of Yes. If that's the case, delete the Test entry, then switch to Table Design View. Modify the Limit To List Lookup property in the Lookup properties for the Gender field from No to Yes, save the table, then switch back to Datasheet View. Retest the property change by repeating Step e.)

f. Resize fields in Datasheet View as needed to clearly see all entries.

Skills Review (continued)

5. Modify Short Text fields.

  a. Open the Members table in Design View.

  b. Use the Input Mask Wizard to create an Input Mask property for the Phone field. Choose the Phone Number Input Mask. Accept the other default options provided by the Input Mask Wizard. (*Hint*: If the Input Mask Wizard is not installed on your computer, type **!(999) 000-0000;;_** for the Input Mask property for the Phone field.)

  c. Change the Field Size property of the FirstName, LastName, and City fields to **25**. Change the Field Size property of the Phone field to **10**. Change the Field Size property of the Gender field to **7**. Save the Members table. None of these fields has data greater in length than the new Field Size properties, so click OK when prompted that some data may be lost.

  d. Open the Members table in Datasheet View, and enter a new record with your instructor's name in the FirstName and LastName fields and your school's City and Phone field values. Enter your instructor's email address, **1/1/1975** for the Birthdate field, and an appropriate choice for the Gender field. Close the Members table.

6. Modify Number and Currency fields.

  a. Open the ServiceHours table in Design View.

  b. Change the Decimal Places property of the ServiceHours field to **0**.

  c. Change the Decimal Places property of the ServiceValue field to **0**.

  d. Save and close the ServiceHours table.

7. Modify Date/Time fields.

  a. Open the ServiceHours table in Design View.

  b. Change the Format property of the ServiceDate field to Medium Date.

  c. Save and close the ServiceHours table.

  d. Open the Members table in Design View.

  e. Change the Format property of the Birthdate field to Medium Date.

  f. Save and close the Members table.

8. Modify validation properties.

  a. Open the Members table in Design View.

  b. Click the Birthdate field name, click the Validation Rule text box, then type **<Date()**. (Note that Date() is a built-in Access function that returns today's date.)

  c. Click the Validation Text box, then type **Birthdate must not be in the future**.

  d. Save and accept the changes, then open the Members table in Datasheet View.

  e. Test the Validation Text and Validation Rule properties by tabbing to the Birthdate field and entering a date in the future. (*Note*: You must enter dates in a m/d/yy pattern regardless of the Medium Date format property.) Click OK when prompted with the Validation Text message, press [Esc] to remove the invalid Birthdate field entry, then enter **1/1/91** as the Birthdate value for your record. (*Note*: Be sure your Validation Text message is spelled properly. If not, correct it in Table Design View.)

9. Create Attachment fields.

  a. Open the Members table in Design View, then add a new field after the Gender field with the field name **Photo** and an Attachment data type. Enter **Member's picture** for the Description. Save the Members table.

  b. Display the Members table in Datasheet View, then attach a .jpg file of yourself to the record. If you do not have a .jpg file of yourself, use the **Member1.jpg** file provided in the location where you store your Data Files.

  c. Close the Members table.

  d. Use the Form Wizard to create a form based on all of the fields in the Members table. Use a Columnar layout, and title the form **Member Entry Form**.

  e. If requested by your instructor, print the first record in the Members Entry Form that shows the picture you just entered in the Photo field, then close the form.

  f. Close the Service-5.accdb database, then exit Access.

Independent Challenge 1

As the manager of a music store's instrument rental program, you decide to create a database to track rentals to schoolchildren. The fields you need to track are organized with four tables: Instruments, Rentals, Students, and Schools.

a. Start Access, then create a new blank desktop database called **Rentals-5** in the location where you store your Data Files.

b. Use Table Design View or the Fields tab on the Ribbon of Table Datasheet View to create the four tables in the Rentals-5 database using the field names, data types, descriptions, and primary keys shown in FIGURES 5-22, 5-23, 5-24, and 5-25.

FIGURE 5-22

Schools

Field Name	Data Type	Description
SchoolName	Short Text	Full name of school
SchoolID	Short Text	Unique three character id for each school

FIGURE 5-23

Students

Field Name	Data Type	Description (Optional)
FirstName	Short Text	Student's first name
LastName	Short Text	Student's last name
Street	Short Text	Student's street
City	Short Text	Student's city
State	Short Text	Student's state
Zip	Short Text	Student's zip code
StudentNo	AutoNumber	Unique number to identify each student
SchoolID	Short Text	Three character school id for that student

FIGURE 5-24

Instruments

Field Name	Data Type	Description
SerialNo	Short Text	Unique serial number on each instrument
Description	Short Text	Description of the instrument
MonthlyFee	Currency	Monthly rental fee

FIGURE 5-25

Rentals

Field Name	Data Type	Description (Optional)
RentalNo	AutoNumber	Unique rental number for each record
StudentNo	Number	Foreign key field to Students table. One student can be linked to many rentals
SerialNo	Short Text	Foreign key field to Instruments table. One instrument can be linked to many rentals
RentalStartDate	Date/Time	Date the rental starts

Independent Challenge 1 (continued)

  c. In Design View of the Rentals table, enter **>1/1/2016** as the Validation Rule property for the RentalStartDate field. This change allows only dates later than 1/1/2016, the start date for this business, to be entered into this field.

  d. Enter **Rental start dates must be after January 1, 2016** as the Validation Text property to the RentalStartDate field of the Rentals table. Note that Access adds pound signs (#) to the date criteria entered in the Validation Rule as soon as you tab out of the Validation Text property.

  e. Save and close the Rentals table.

  f. Open the Relationships window, then add the Schools, Students, Rentals, and Instruments tables to the window. Expand the Students field list to view all fields. Create one-to-many relationships, as shown in FIGURE 5-26. Be sure to enforce referential integrity on each relationship.

FIGURE 5-26

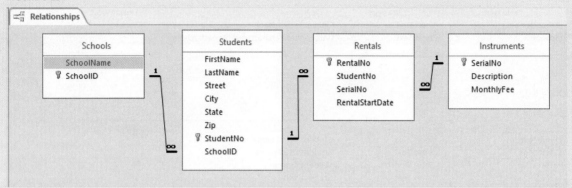

  g. Preview the Relationship report, add your name as a label to the Report Header section, then save the report with the default name **Relationships for Rentals-5**. If requested by your instructor, print the report and then close it.

  h. Save and close the Relationships window.

  i. Close the Rentals-5.accdb database, then exit Access.

Independent Challenge 2

You want to create a database that documents blood drive donations by the employees of your company. You want to track information such as employee name, blood type, date of donation, and the hospital where the employee chooses to send the donation. You also want to track basic hospital information, such as the hospital name and address.

a. Start Access, then create a new, blank desktop database called **BloodDrive-5** in the location where you store your Data Files.

b. Create an **Employees** table with appropriate field names, data types, and descriptions to record the automatic employee ID, employee first name, employee last name, and blood type. Make the EmployeeID field the primary key field. Use FIGURE 5-27 as a guide for appropriate field names.

FIGURE 5-27

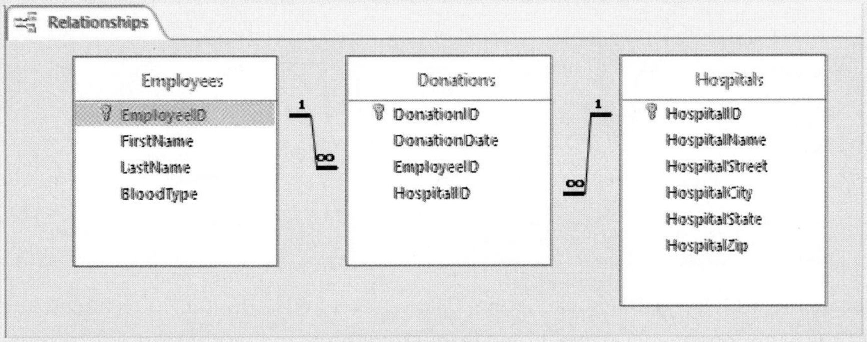

c. Add Lookup properties to the blood type field in the Employees table to provide only valid blood type entries of **A+, A–, B+, B–, O+, O–, AB+**, and **AB–** for this field.

d. Create a **Donations** table with appropriate field names, data types, and descriptions to record an automatic donation ID, date of the donation, employee ID field, and hospital ID field. Make the donation ID the primary key field. Use FIGURE 5-27 as a guide for appropriate field names.

e. Create a **Hospitals** table with fields and appropriate field names, data types, and descriptions to record a hospital ID, hospital name, street, city, state, and zip. Make the hospital ID field the primary key field. Use FIGURE 5-27 as a guide for appropriate field names.

f. In the Relationships window, create one-to-many relationships with referential integrity between the tables in the database, as shown in FIGURE 5-27. One employee may make several donations over time. Each donation is marked for a particular hospital, so each hospital may receive many donations over time.

g. Preview the Relationship report, add your name as a label to the Report Header section, then save the report with the default name **Relationships for BloodDrive-5**. If requested by your instructor, print the report and then close it.

h. Save and close the Relationships window.

i. Close the BloodDrive-5.accdb database, then exit Access.

Independent Challenge 3

You're a member and manager of a recreational baseball team and decide to create an Access database to manage player information, games, and batting statistics.

a. Start Access, then create a new, blank desktop database called **Baseball-5** in the location where you store your Data Files.

b. Create a **Players** table with appropriate field names, data types, and descriptions to record the uniform number, player first name, player last name, and position. Make the uniform number field the primary key field. Use FIGURE 5-28 as a guide for appropriate field names.

FIGURE 5-28

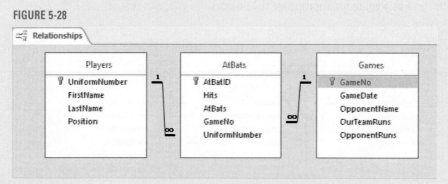

c. Create a **Games** table with appropriate field names, data types, and descriptions to record an automatic game number, date of the game, opponent's name, home team's total runs, and visitor team's total runs. Make the game number field the primary key field. Use FIGURE 5-28 as a guide for appropriate field names.

d. Create an **AtBats** table with appropriate field names, data types, and descriptions to record hits, at bats, game number, and uniform number of each player. The game number and uniform number fields will both be foreign key fields. Create an AtBatID AutoNumber field to server as the primary key field. Use FIGURE 5-28 as a guide for appropriate field names.

e. In the Relationships window, create one-to-many relationships with referential integrity between the tables shown in FIGURE 5-28. The AtBats table contains one record for each player that plays in each game to record his hitting statistics—hits and at bats—for each game. Therefore, one player record is related to many records in the AtBats table, and one game record is related to many records in the AtBats table.

f. Preview the Relationship report, add your name as a label to the Report Header section, then save the report with the default name **Relationships for Baseball-5**. If requested by your instructor, print the report and then close it.

g. Save and close the Relationships window.

h. Close the Baseball-5.accdb database, then exit Access.

Modifying the Database Structure

Independent Challenge 4: Explore

An Access database can help record and track your job search efforts. In this exercise, you will modify two fields in the Positions table in your Jobs database with Lookup properties to make data entry easier, more efficient, and more accurate.

a. Start Access, open the Jobs-5.accdb database from the location where you store your Data Files, then enable content if prompted.

b. Open the Positions table in Design View. Click the EmployerID field, then start the Lookup Wizard.

c. In this situation, you want the EmployerID field in the Positions table to look up both the EmployerID and the CompanyName fields from the Employers table, so leave the "I want the lookup field to get the values from another table or query" option button selected.

d. The Employers table contains the fields you want to display in this Lookup field. Select both the EmployerID field and the CompanyName fields. Sort the records in ascending order by the CompanyName field.

e. Deselect the "Hide key column" check box so that you can see the data in both the EmployerID and CompanyName fields.

f. Choose EmployerID as the field in which to store values, choose **EmployerID** as the label for the Lookup field, click the Enable Data Integrity check box, then click Finish to finish the Lookup Wizard. Click Yes when prompted to save the table.

g. Switch to Datasheet View of the Positions table and tab to the EmployerID field for the first record. Click the EmployerID list arrow. You should see both the EmployerID value and the CompanyName in the drop-down list, as shown in FIGURE 5-29.

FIGURE 5-29

h. Return to Design View of the Positions table, click the Desirability field, and start the Lookup Wizard. This field stores the values 1 through 5 as a desirability rating. You will manually enter those values, so choose the "I will type in the values that I want" option button.

i. Enter **1**, **2**, **3**, **4**, and **5** in the Col1 column; accept the Desirability label for the Lookup field; click the Limit To List check box; then click Finish to finish the Lookup Wizard.

Independent Challenge 4: Explore (continued)

j. Save the table, and test the Desirability field for the first record in Datasheet View. You should see a drop-down list with the values 1, 2, 3, 4, and 5, as shown in **FIGURE 5-30**.

FIGURE 5-30

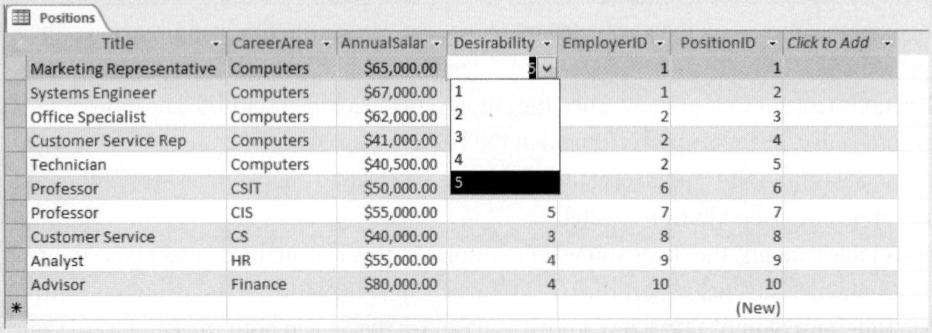

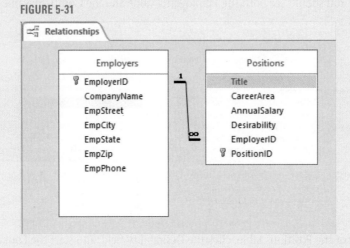

k. Save the table, and test the Desirability and EmployerID fields. You should not be able to make any entries in those fields that are not presented in the list.

l. Close the Positions table, and open the Relationships window. Your Relationships window should look like **FIGURE 5-31**. The Lookup Wizard created the relationship between the Employers and Positions table when you completed Step f. Save and close the Relationships window.

FIGURE 5-31

Modifying the Database Structure

Independent Challenge 4: Explore (continued)

m. Use the Form Wizard and select all of the fields from both the Employers and Positions tables. View the data by Employers, and use a Datasheet layout for the subform.

n. Title the form **Job Entry Form** and the subform **Job Subform**. View the form in Form View.

o. In Form Design View, use your skills to move, resize, align, and edit the controls, and find the record for IBM as shown in FIGURE 5-32. Be sure to resize the columns of the subform as well. Enter a fictitious but realistic new job for IBM, and if requested by your instructor, print only that record in the Job Entry Form.

p. Save and close the Job Entry Form, close the Jobs-5.accdb database, and exit Access.

FIGURE 5-32

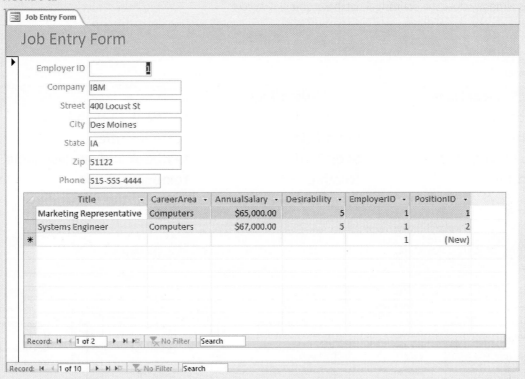

Visual Workshop

Open the Training-5.accdb database from the location where you store your Data Files, then enable content if prompted. Create a new table called **Textbooks** using the Table Design View shown in FIGURE 5-33 to determine field names, data types, and descriptions. Make the following property changes: Change the Field Size property of the TextbookISBN field to **13**, the TextTitle field to **30**, and TextAuthorLastName field to **20**. Change the Field Size property of the TextEdition field to Byte. Be sure to specify that the TextbookISBN field is the primary key field. Relate the tables in the Training-5 database, as shown in FIGURE 5-34, which will require you to first add a foreign key field named **Textbook** with a Short Text data type to the Courses table. View the Relationship report in landscape orientation. Add your name as a label to the Report Header section to document the Relationship report, then print it if requested by your instructor. Save the Relationship report with the default name of **Relationships for Training-5**, close the report, save and close the Relationships window, close the Training-5 database, and exit Access.

FIGURE 5-33

Field Name	Data Type	
TextbookISBN	Short Text	Textbook 13-digit ISBN
TextTitle	Short Text	Textbook title
TextAuthorLastName	Short Text	Textbook author's last name
TextEdition	Number	Textbook edition

FIGURE 5-34

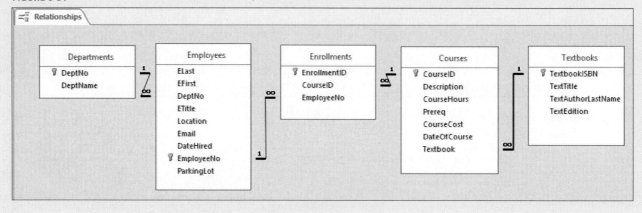

Modifying the Database Structure

Improving Queries

CASE ▸ The Reason 2 Go database has been updated to contain more customers, trips, and sales. You help Julia Rice, an R2G trip developer for U.S. travel, create queries to analyze this information.

Module Objectives

After completing this module, you will be able to:

- Create multitable queries
- Apply sorts and view SQL
- Develop AND criteria
- Develop OR criteria

- Create calculated fields
- Build summary queries
- Build crosstab queries
- Create a report on a query

Files You Will Need

R2G-6.accdb	LakeHomes-6.accdb
Service-6.accdb	Scholarships-6.accdb
Music-6.accdb	Training-6.accdb

Create Multitable Queries

A **select query**, the most common type of query, selects fields from related tables and displays records in a datasheet where you can view, enter, edit, or delete data. You can create select queries by using the Simple Query Wizard, or you can start from scratch in Query Design View. **Query Design View** gives you more options for selecting and presenting information. When you open (or **run**) a query, the fields and records that you selected for the query are presented in **Query Datasheet View**, also called a **logical view** of the data. **CASE** ▶ *Julia Rice asks you to create a query to analyze customer payments. You select fields from the Customers, Trips, Sales, and Payments tables to complete this analysis.*

STEPS

1. **Start Access, open the R2G-6.accdb database** from the location where you store your Data Files, then enable content if prompted

2. **Click the Create tab on the Ribbon, then click the Query Design button in the Queries group**

   The Show Table dialog box opens and lists all the tables in the database.

3. **Double-click Customers, double-click Sales, double-click Trips, double-click Payments, then click Close**

   Recall that the upper pane of Query Design View displays the fields for each of the selected tables in field lists. The name of the table is shown in the field list title bar. Primary key fields are identified with a small key icon. Relationships between tables are displayed with **one-to-many join lines** that connect the linking fields. You select the fields you want by adding them to the query design grid.

4. **Double-click the FName field in the Customers table field list to add this field to the first column of the query design grid, double-click LName, double-click TripName in the Trips field list, scroll then double-click Price in the Trips field list, double-click PaymentDate in the Payments field list, then double-click PaymentAmt, as shown in FIGURE 6-1**

   When you double-click a field in a field list, it is automatically added as the next field in the query grid. When you drag a field to the query design grid, any existing fields move to the right to accommodate the new field.

5. **Click the View button 📊 in the Results group to run the query and display the query datasheet**

   The resulting datasheet looks like **FIGURE 6-2**. The datasheet shows the six fields selected in Query Design View: FName and LName from the Customers table, TripName and Price from the Trips table, and PaymentDate and PaymentAmt from the Payments table. The datasheet displays 78 records because 78 different payments have been made. Some of the payments are from the same customer. For example, Kristen Collins has made payments on multiple trips (records 2 and 20). Kristen's last name has changed to Lang.

6. **Double-click Collins in the LName field of the second record, type Lang, then click any other record**

   Because Kristen's data is physically stored in only one record in the Customers table (but selected multiple times in this query because Kristen has made more than one payment), changing any occurrence of her last name updates all other selections of that data in this query and throughout all other queries, forms, and reports in the database, too. Note that Kristen's name has been updated to Kristen Lang in record 20, as shown in **FIGURE 6-2**.

Improving Queries

FIGURE 6-1: Query Design View with six fields in the query design grid

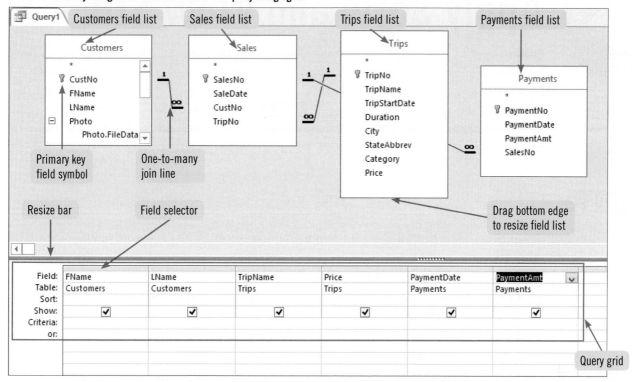

FIGURE 6-2: Query datasheet

Deleting a field from the query grid

If you add the wrong field to the query design grid, you can delete it by clicking the **field selector**, the thin gray bar above each field name, then pressing [Delete]. Deleting a field from the query design grid removes it from the logical view of this query's datasheet, but does not delete the field from the database. A field is defined and the field's contents are stored in a table object only.

Apply Sorts and View SQL

Sorting refers to reordering records in either ascending or descending order based on the values in a field. You can specify more than one sort field in Query Design View. Sort orders are evaluated from left to right, meaning that the sort field on the far left is the primary sort field. Sort orders defined in Query Design View are saved with the query object. **CASE** *Julia Rice wants to list the records in alphabetical order based on the customer's last name. If the customer has made more than one payment, Julia asks you to further sort the records by the payment date.*

STEPS

1. **Click the View button 🔽 on the Home tab to return to Query Design View**

   To sort the records by last name then by payment date, the LName field must be the primary sort field, and the PaymentDate field must be the secondary sort field.

2. **Click the LName field Sort cell in the query design grid, click the Sort list arrow, click Ascending, click the PaymentDate field Sort cell in the query design grid, click the Sort list arrow, then click Ascending**

   The resulting query design grid should look like **FIGURE 6-3**.

3. **Click the View button 🖿 in the Results group to display the query datasheet**

   The records of the datasheet are now listed in ascending order based on the values in the LName field. When the same value appears in the LName field, the records are further sorted by the secondary sort field, PaymentDate, as shown in **FIGURE 6-4**. Jacob Alman made two payments, one on 7/25/2017 and the next on 8/31/2017. Julia Bouchart made many payments and they are all listed in ascending order on the PaymentDate field.

4. **Click the Save button 🖫 on the Quick Access Toolbar, type CustPayments in the Save As dialog box, then click OK**

   When you save a query, you save a logical view of the data, a selection of fields and records from underlying tables. Technically, when you save a query, you are saving a set of instructions written in **Structured Query Language (SQL)**. You can view the SQL code for any query by switching to **SQL View**.

5. **Click the View button list arrow, click SQL View, then click in the lower part of the SQL window to deselect the code**

   The SQL statements shown in **FIGURE 6-5** start with the **SELECT** keyword. Field names follow SELECT, and how the tables are joined follow the **FROM** keyword. The **ORDER BY** keyword determines how records are sorted. Fortunately, you do not have to write or understand SQL to use Access or select data from multiple tables. The easy-to-use Query Design View gives you a way to select and sort data from underlying tables without being an SQL programmer.

6. **Close the CustPayments query**

FIGURE 6-3: Specifying multiple sort orders in Query Design View

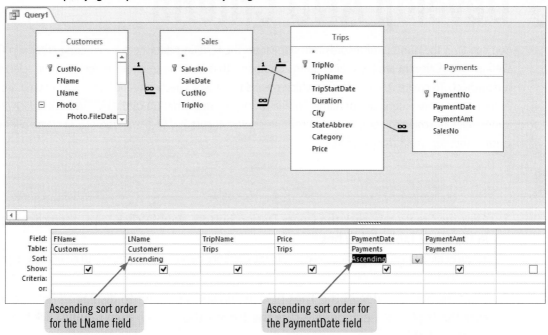

Ascending sort order for the LName field

Ascending sort order for the PaymentDate field

FIGURE 6-4: Records sorted by LName, then by PaymentDate

FName	LName	TripName	Price	PaymentDat	PaymentAm
Jacob	Alman	Red Reef Cleanup	$1,500	7/25/2017	$300.00
Jacob	Alman	Red Reef Cleanup	$1,500	8/31/2017	$100.00
Julia	Bouchart	Coastal Shore Cleanup	$1,000	5/31/2017	$600.00
Julia	Bouchart	Coastal Shore Cleanup	$1,000	6/30/2017	$200.00
Julia	Bouchart	Red Reef Cleanup	$1,500	7/21/2017	$300.00
Julia	Bouchart	anup	$1,000	7/31/2017	$200.00
Julia	Bouchart		$1,500	8/20/2017	$100.00
Julia	Bouchart	Coastal Shore Cleanup	$1,000	8/31/2017	$200.00

Secondary sort order

Primary sort order

FIGURE 6-5: SQL View

CustPayments

SELECT keyword

SELECT Customers.FName, Customers.LName, Trips.TripName, Trips.Price, Payments.PaymentDate, Payments.PaymentAmt
FROM Trips INNER JOIN (Customers INNER JOIN Sales ON Customers.CustNo = Sales.CustNo) ON Trips.TripNo = Sales.TripNo) INNER JOIN Payments ON Sales.SalesNo = Payments.SalesNo
ORDER BY Customers.LName, Payments.PaymentDate;

FROM keyword

ORDER BY keyword

Specifying a sort order different from the field order in the datasheet

If your database has several customers with the same last name, you can include a secondary sort on the first name field to distinguish the customers. If you want to display the fields in a different order from which they are sorted, you can use the solution shown in **FIGURE 6-6**. Add a field to the query design grid twice, once to select for the datasheet, and once to use as a sort order. Use the Show check box to deselect the field used as a sort order.

FIGURE 6-6: Sorting on a field that is not displayed

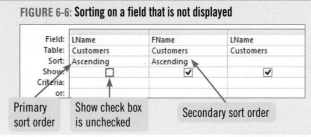

Field:	LName	FName	LName
Table:	Customers	Customers	Customers
Sort:	Ascending	Ascending	
Show:		✓	✓
Criteria:			
or:			

Primary sort order

Show check box is unchecked

Secondary sort order

Improving Queries

Develop AND Criteria

Learning Outcomes
- Use the Like operator in query criteria
- Define advanced comparison operators

You can limit the number of records that appear on the resulting datasheet by entering criteria in Query Design View. **Criteria** are tests, or limiting conditions, that must be true for the record to be selected for a datasheet. To create **AND criteria**, which means the query selects a record only if all criteria are true, enter two or more criteria on the same Criteria row of the query design grid. **CASE** *Julia Rice predicts strong sales for ecological (Eco) trips that start on or after August 1, 2018. She asks you to create a list of the existing trips that meet those criteria.*

STEPS

1. **Click the Create tab, click the Query Design button, double-click Trips, then click Close in the Show Table dialog box**

   To query for ecological trips, you need to add the Category field to the query grid. In addition, you want to know the trip name and start date.

2. **Drag the bottom edge of the Trips field list down to resize it to display all fields, double-click the TripName field, double-click the TripStartDate field, then double-click the Category field**

   To find trips in the Eco category, you need to add a criterion for the Category field in the query grid.

3. **Click the first Criteria cell for the Category field, then type Eco**

   To find all trips that start on or after August 1st, use the >= (greater than or equal to) operator.

4. **Click the first Criteria cell for the TripStartDate field, type >=8/1/2018, then press [↓]**

   As shown in **FIGURE 6-7**, Access assists you with criteria syntax, rules by which criteria need to be entered. Access automatically adds quotation marks around text criteria in Short Text fields, such as "Eco" in the Category field, and pound signs around date criteria in Date/Time fields, such as #8/1/2018# in the TripStartDate field. The criteria in Number, Currency, and Yes/No fields are not surrounded by any characters. See **TABLE 6-1** for more information on common Access comparison operators and criteria syntax.

5. **Click the Save button [🖫] on the Quick Access Toolbar, type EcoAugust2018 in the Save As dialog box, click OK, then click the View button [▦] to view the query results**

   The query results are shown in **FIGURE 6-8**.

6. **Close the EcoAugust2018 datasheet**

FIGURE 6-7: Entering AND criteria on the same row

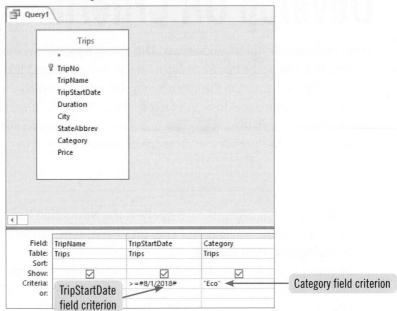

TripStartDate field criterion

Category field criterion

FIGURE 6-8: Datasheet for EcoAugust2018 records

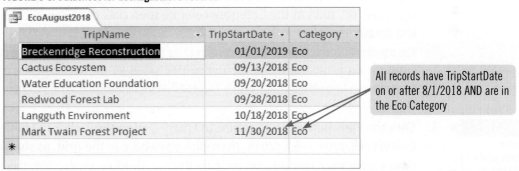

All records have TripStartDate on or after 8/1/2018 AND are in the Eco Category

TABLE 6-1: Common comparison operators

operator	description	example	result
>	Greater than	>500	Value exceeds 500
>=	Greater than or equal to	>=500	Value is 500 or greater
<	Less than	<500	Value is less than 500
<=	Less than or equal to	<=500	Value is 500 or less
<>	Not equal to	<>500	Value is any number other than 500
Between...And	Finds values between two numbers or dates	Between #2/2/2017# And #2/2/2020#	Dates between 2/2/2017 and 2/2/2020, inclusive
In	Finds a value that is one of a list	In ("NC","SC","TN")	Value equals NC or SC or TN
Null	Finds records that have no entry in a particular field	Null	No value has been entered in a field
Is Not Null	Finds records that have any entry in a particular field	Is Not Null	Any value has been entered in a field
Like	Finds records that match the criterion, used with the * (asterisk) wildcard character	Like "C*"	Value starts with C
Not	Finds records that do not match the criterion	Not 100	Numbers other than 100

Develop OR Criteria

Learning Outcomes
• Use AND and OR criteria in the same query
• Define advanced wildcard characters

As you experienced in the previous lesson, AND criteria narrow the number of records in the datasheet by requiring that a record be true for multiple criteria. You also learned that AND criteria are entered on the same row. OR criteria work in the opposite way. **OR criteria** expand the number of records in the datasheet because a record needs to be true for only one of the criteria. You enter OR criteria in the query design grid on different criteria rows. **CASE** *Julia Rice asks you to modify the EcoAugust2018 query to expand the number of records to include trips in the Service category that start on or after 8/1/2018 as well.*

STEPS

1. **Right-click the EcoAugust2018 query in the Navigation Pane, click Copy, right-click a blank spot in the Navigation Pane, click Paste, type EcoServiceAugust2018 in the Paste As dialog box, then click OK**

   By making a copy of the EcoAugust2018 query before modifying it, you won't change the EcoAugust2018 query by mistake. To add OR criteria, you enter criteria in the next available "or" row of the query design grid. By default, the query grid displays eight rows for additional OR criteria, but you can add even more rows using the Insert Rows button on the Design tab.

2. **Right-click the EcoServiceAugust2018 query, click Design View, type Service in the next row (the "or" row) of the Category column, then click the View button ▦ to display the datasheet**

   The datasheet expands from 6 to 10 records because four trips with a Category of Service were added to the datasheet. But notice that two of the TripStartDate values for the Service records are prior to 8/1/2018. To select only those Service trips with a TripStartDate on or after 8/1/2018, you need to add more criteria to Query Design View.

QUICK TIP
The criterion >7/31/2018 would work the same as >=8/1/2018.

3. **Click the View button ▨ to return to Query Design View, click the next TripStartDate Criteria cell, type >=8/1/2018, then click elsewhere in the grid, as shown in FIGURE 6-9**

   Criteria in one row do not affect criteria in another row. Therefore, to select only those trips that start on or after 8/1/2018, you must put the same TripStartDate criterion in both rows of the query design grid.

4. **Click ▦ to return to Datasheet View**

   The resulting datasheet selects 8 records, as shown in **FIGURE 6-10**. When no sort order is applied, the records are sorted by the primary key field of the first table in the query (in this case, TripNo, which is not selected for this query). All of the records have a Category of Eco or Service and a TripStartDate value greater than or equal to 8/1/2018.

5. **Save and close the EcoServiceAugust2018 query**

   The R2G-6.accdb Navigation Pane displays the three queries you created plus the RevByState query that was already in the database.

FIGURE 6-9: Entering OR criteria on different rows

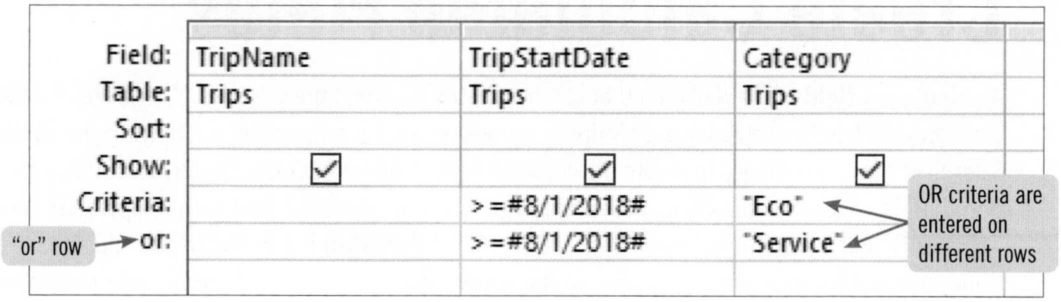

Field:	TripName	TripStartDate	Category	
Table:	Trips	Trips	Trips	
Sort:				
Show:	☑	☑	☑	
Criteria:		>=#8/1/2018#	"Eco"	
or:		>=#8/1/2018#	"Service"	

"or" row → or:

OR criteria are entered on different rows

FIGURE 6-10: Datasheet for EcoServiceAugust2018 query

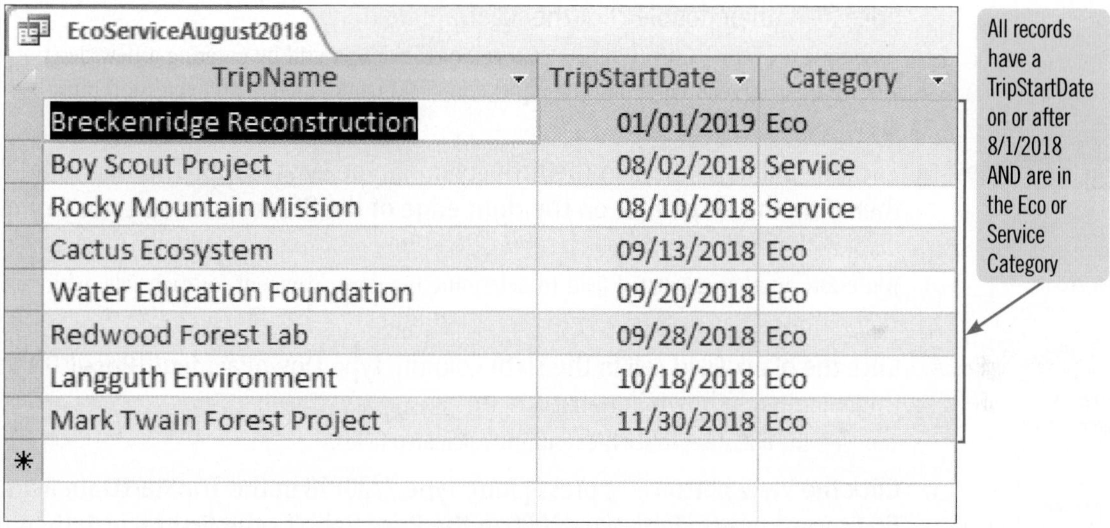

EcoServiceAugust2018

TripName	TripStartDate	Category
Breckenridge Reconstruction	01/01/2019	Eco
Boy Scout Project	08/02/2018	Service
Rocky Mountain Mission	08/10/2018	Service
Cactus Ecosystem	09/13/2018	Eco
Water Education Foundation	09/20/2018	Eco
Redwood Forest Lab	09/28/2018	Eco
Langguth Environment	10/18/2018	Eco
Mark Twain Forest Project	11/30/2018	Eco

All records have a TripStartDate on or after 8/1/2018 AND are in the Eco or Service Category

Using wildcard characters in query criteria

To search for a pattern, use a **wildcard character** to represent any character in the criteria entry. Use a **question mark (?)** to search for any single character, and an **asterisk (*)** to search for any number of characters. Wildcard characters are often used with the Like operator. For example, the criterion Like "10/*/2017" finds all dates in October of 2017, and the criterion Like "F*" finds all entries that start with the letter F.

Create Calculated Fields

Learning
Outcomes
• Create calculated
  fields in queries
• Define functions
  and expressions

A **calculated field** is a field of data that can be created based on the values of other fields. For example, you can calculate the value for a discount, commission, or tax amount by multiplying the value of the Sales field by a percentage. To create a calculated field, define it in Query Design View using an expression that describes the calculation. An **expression** is a combination of field names, operators (such as +, −, /, and *), and functions that result in a single value. A **function** is a predefined formula that returns a value such as a subtotal, count, average, or the current date. See TABLE 6-2 for more information on arithmetic operators and TABLE 6-3 for more information on functions. **CASE** ▶ *Julia Rice asks you to find the number of days between the sale date and the trip start date. To determine this information, you create a calculated field called DaysToTrip that subtracts the SaleDate from the TripStartDate. You create another calculated field to determine the down payment amount for each trip sale.*

STEPS

1. **Click the** Create tab **on the Ribbon, click the** Query Design button, **double-click** Trips, **double-click** Sales, **then click** Close **in the Show Table dialog box**
   First, you add the fields to the grid that you want to display in the query.

2. **Double-click the** TripName **field, double-click the** TripStartDate **field, double-click the** Price field, **then double-click the** SaleDate field
   You create a calculated field in the Field cell of the design grid by entering a new descriptive field name followed by a colon, followed by an expression. Field names used in an expression must be surrounded by square brackets.

3. **Click the blank Field cell in the fifth column, type** DaysToTrip:[TripStartDate]-[SaleDate], **then drag the ↔ pointer on the right edge of the fifth column selector to the right to display the entire entry**
   You create another calculated field to determine the down payment for each sale, which is calculated as 10% of the Price field.

4. **Click the blank Field cell in the sixth column, type** DownPayment:[Price]*0.1, **then widen the column, as shown in** FIGURE 6-11
   You view the datasheet to see the resulting calculated fields.

5. **Click the** View button **🖻, press [Tab], type** 7/20/18 **in the TripStartDate field for the first record, press [Tab], type** 1000 **in the Price field for the first record, then press [↓]**
   A portion of the resulting datasheet, with two calculated fields, is shown in FIGURE 6-12. The DaysToTrip field is automatically recalculated, showing the number of days between the SaleDate and the TripStartDate. The DownPayment field is also automatically recalculated, multiplying the Price value by 10%.

6. **Click the** Save button **🖫 on the Quick Access Toolbar, type** TripCalculations **in the Save As dialog box, click** OK, **then close the datasheet**

FIGURE 6-11: **Creating calculated fields**

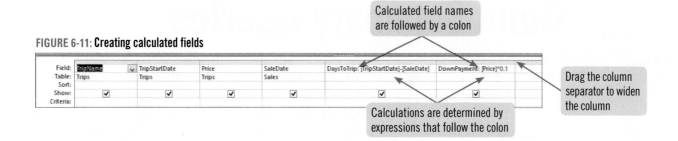

Calculated field names are followed by a colon

Drag the column separator to widen the column

Calculations are determined by expressions that follow the colon

FIGURE 6-12: **Viewing and testing calculated fields**

DownPayment equals Price * 10%

DaysToTrip equals the days between the SaleDate and TripStartDate

Updated to 7/20/18

Updated to $1000

TABLE 6-2: **Arithmetic operators**

operator	description
+	Addition
–	Subtraction
*	Multiplication
/	Division
^	Exponentiation

TABLE 6-3: **Common functions**

function	sample expression and description
DATE	DATE()-[BirthDate] Calculates the number of days between today and the date in the BirthDate field; Access expressions are not case sensitive, so DATE()-[BirthDate] is equivalent to date()-[birthdate] and DATE()-[BIRTHDATE]; therefore, use capitalization in expressions in any way that makes the expression easier to read
PMT	PMT([Rate],[Term],[Loan]) Calculates the monthly payment on a loan where the Rate field contains the monthly interest rate, the Term field contains the number of monthly payments, and the Loan field contains the total amount financed
LEFT	LEFT([LastName],2) Returns the first two characters of the entry in the LastName field
RIGHT	RIGHT([PartNo],3) Returns the last three characters of the entry in the PartNo field
LEN	LEN([Description]) Returns the number of characters in the Description field

Build Summary Queries

Learning Outcomes
• Create a summary query
• Define aggregate functions

A **summary query** calculates statistics for groups of records. To create a summary query, you add the **Total row** to the query design grid to specify how you want to group and calculate the records using aggregate functions. **Aggregate functions** calculate a statistic such as a subtotal, count, or average on a field in a group of records. Some aggregate functions, such as Sum or Avg (Average), work only on fields with Number or Currency data types. Other functions, such as Min (Minimum), Max (Maximum), or Count, also work on Short Text fields. TABLE 6-4 provides more information on aggregate functions. A key difference between the statistics displayed by a summary query and those displayed by calculated fields is that summary queries provide calculations that describe a group of records, whereas calculated fields provide a new field of information for each record. **CASE** *Julia Rice asks you to calculate total sales for each trip category. You build a summary query to provide this information.*

STEPS

QUICK TIP
In Query Design View, drag a table from the Navigation Pane to add it to the query.

1. **Click the Create tab on the Ribbon, click the Query Design button, double-click Sales, double-click Trips, then click Close in the Show Table dialog box**

   It doesn't matter in what order you add the field lists to Query Design View, but it's important to move and resize the field lists as necessary to clearly see all field names and relationships.

2. **Double-click the Category field in the Trips field list, double-click the Price field in the Trips field list, double-click the SalesNo field in the Sales field list, then click the View button ▦ to view the datasheet**

   One hundred and one records are displayed, representing all 101 records in the Sales table. You can add a Total row to any datasheet to calculate grand total statistics for that datasheet.

3. **Click the Totals button in the Records group, click the Total cell below the Price field, click the Total list arrow, click Sum, then use ↔ to widen the Price column to display the entire total**

   The Total row is added to the bottom of the datasheet and displays the sum total of the Price field, $129,550. Other Total row statistics you can select include Average, Count, Maximum, Minimum, Standard Deviation, and Variance. To create subtotals per Category, you need to modify the query in Query Design View.

4. **Click the View button ▨ to return to Query Design View, click the Totals button in the Show/Hide group, click Group By in the Price column, click the list arrow, click Sum, click Group By in the SalesNo column, click the list arrow, then click Count**

   The Total row is added to the query grid below the Table row. To calculate summary statistics for each category, the Category field is the Group By field, as shown in FIGURE 6-13. With the records grouped together by Category, you subtotal the Price field using the Sum operator to calculate a subtotal of revenue for each Category of trip sales and count the SalesNo field using the Count operator to calculate the number of sales in each category.

5. **Click ▦ to display the datasheet, widen each column as necessary to view all field names, click in the Total row for the SumOfPrice field, click the list arrow, click Sum, then click another row in the datasheet to remove the selection**

   The Eco category leads all others with a count of 42 sales totaling $47,450. The total revenue for all sales is still $129,550, as shown in FIGURE 6-14, but now each record represents a subtotal for each Category instead of an individual sale.

TROUBLE
To delete or rename any object, close it, then right-click it in the Navigation Pane and click Delete or Rename on the shortcut menu.

6. **Click the Save button ▤ on the Quick Access Toolbar, type CategorySales, click OK, then close the datasheet**

Improving Queries

FIGURE 6-13: Summary query in Design View

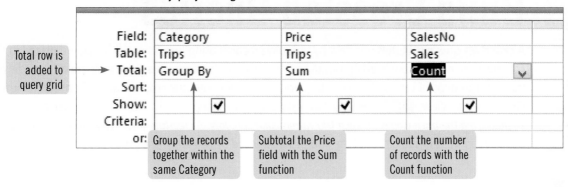

Total row is added to query grid →

Field:	Category	Price	SalesNo	
Table:	Trips	Trips	Sales	
Total:	Group By	Sum	Count	▾
Sort:				
Show:	✔	✔	✔	
Criteria:				
or:				

Group the records together within the same Category

Subtotal the Price field with the Sum function

Count the number of records with the Count function

FIGURE 6-14: Summary query datasheet

Group By the Category field →

Query1		
Category ▾	SumOfPrice ▾	CountOfSalesNo ▾
Adventure	$12,500.00	10
Cultural	$12,600.00	7
Eco	$47,450.00	42
Educational	$36,800.00	27
Family	$1,000.00	1
Service	$19,200.00	14
Total	$129,550.00	

Count the SalesNo field

Sum the Price field

Grand total for the Price field

TABLE 6-4: Aggregate functions

aggregate function	used to find the
Sum	Total of values in a field
Avg	Average of values in a field
Min	Minimum value in a field
Max	Maximum value in a field
Count	Number of values in a field (not counting null values)
StDev	Standard deviation of values in a field
Var	Variance of values in a field
First	Field value from the first record in a table or query
Last	Field value from the last record in a table or query

Build Crosstab Queries

A **crosstab query** subtotals one field by grouping records using two other fields that are placed in the column heading and row heading positions. You can use the **Crosstab Query Wizard** to guide you through the steps of creating a crosstab query, or you can build the crosstab query from scratch using Query Design View. **CASE** *Julia Rice asks you to continue your analysis of prices per category by summarizing the price values for each trip within each category. A crosstab query works well for this request because you want to subtotal the Price field as summarized by two other fields, TripName and Category.*

STEPS

1. **Click the Create tab on the Ribbon, click the Query Design button, double-click Trips, double-click Sales, then click Close in the Show Table dialog box**

   The fields you need for your crosstab query come from the Trips table, but you also need to include the Sales table in this query to select trip information for each record (sale) in the Sales table.

2. **Double-click the TripName field, double-click the Category field, then double-click the Price field**

   The first step in creating a crosstab query is to create a select query with the three fields you want to use in the crosstabular report.

3. **Click the View button [image] to review the unsummarized datasheet of 101 records, then click the View button [image] to return to Query Design View**

   To summarize these 101 records in a crosstabular report, you need to change the current select query into a crosstab query.

4. **Click the Crosstab button in the Query Type group**

   Note that two new rows are added to the query grid—the Total row and the Crosstab row. The **Total row** helps you determine which fields group or summarize the records, and the **Crosstab row** identifies which of the three positions each field takes in the crosstab report: Row Heading, Column Heading, or Value. The **Value field** is typically a numeric field, such as Price, that can be summed or averaged.

5. **Click the Crosstab cell for the TripName field, click the list arrow, click Row Heading, click the Crosstab cell for the Category field, click the list arrow, click Column Heading, click the Crosstab cell for the Price field, click the list arrow, click Value, click Group By in the Total cell of the Price field, click the list arrow, then click Sum**

   The completed Query Design View should look like FIGURE 6-15. Note the choices made in both the Total and Crosstab rows of the query grid.

6. **Click [image] to review the crosstab datasheet**

   The final crosstab datasheet is shown in FIGURE 6-16. The datasheet summarizes all 101 sales records by the Category field used as the column headings and by the TripName field used in the row heading position. Although you can switch the row and column heading fields without changing the numeric information on the crosstab datasheet, you should generally place the field with the most entries (in this case, TripName has more values than Category) in the row heading position so that the printout is taller than it is wide.

7. **Click the Save button [image] on the Quick Access Toolbar, type TripCrosstab as the query name, click OK, then close the datasheet**

   Crosstab queries appear with a crosstab icon to the left of the query name in the Navigation Pane.

FIGURE 6-15: **Query Design View of crosstab query**

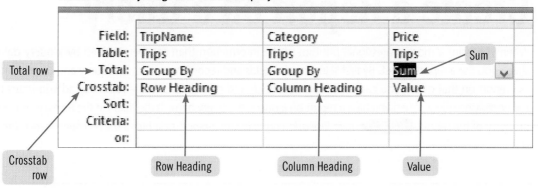

Total row → Total:
Crosstab row → Crosstab:

Row Heading   Column Heading   Value

FIGURE 6-16: **Crosstab query datasheet**

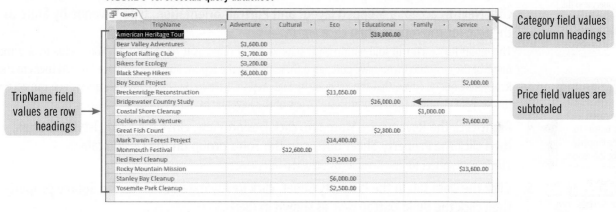

TripName field values are row headings

Category field values are column headings

Price field values are subtotaled

Using query wizards

Four query wizards are available to help you build queries including the Simple (which creates a select query), Crosstab, Find Duplicates, and Find Unmatched Query Wizards. Use the **Find Duplicates Query Wizard** to determine whether a table contains duplicate values in one or more fields. Use the **Find Unmatched Query Wizard** to find records in one table that do not have related records in another table. To use the query wizards, click the Query Wizard button on the Create tab.

Create a Report on a Query

When you want a more professional printout of the information than can be provided by a query datasheet, you use a report object. By first selecting the fields and records you want in a query and then basing the report on that query, you can easily add new fields and calculations to the report by adding them to the underlying query. When you base a report on a query, the query name is identified in the **Record Source** property of the report. **CASE** *Julia Rice asks you to create a report to subtotal the revenue for each trip.*

STEPS

1. **Double-click the RevByState query in the Navigation Pane to open its datasheet**

   The RevByState query contains the customer state, trip name, and price of each trip sold. Analyzing which trips are the most popular in various states will help focus marketing expenses. Creating a query to select the fields and records needed on a report is the first step in creating a report that can be easily modified later.

2. **Close the RevByState query, click the Create tab on the Ribbon, click the Report Wizard button, click the Select All button `>>` to select all fields in the RevByState query, then click Next**

   The Report Wizard wants to group the records by the State field. This is also how you want to analyze the data.

3. **Click Next, click TripName, then click the Select Field button `>` to add the TripName field as a second grouping level, click Next, click Next to not choose any sort orders, click Next to accept a Stepped layout and Portrait orientation, type Revenue by State as the title for the report, then click Finish**

   The report lists each trip sold within each state as many times as it has been sold. You decide to add the name of the customers who have purchased these trips to the report. First, you will need to add them to the RevByState query. Given that the Revenue by State report is based on the RevByState query, you can access the RevByState query from Report Design View of the Revenue by State report.

4. **Right-click the Revenue by State tab, click Design View, close the Field List if it is open, then click the Property Sheet button in the Tools group on the Design tab**

   The Property Sheet for the Revenue by State report opens.

5. **Click the Data tab in the Property Sheet, click RevByState in the Record Source property, then click the Build button `...`, as shown in FIGURE 6-17**

   The RevByState query opens in Query Design View.

6. **Double-click the FName field, double-click the LName field, click the Close button on the Design tab, then click Yes when prompted to save the changes**

   Now that the FName and LName fields have been added to the RevByState query, they are available to the report.

7. **Click the Design tab on the Ribbon, click the Text Box button `ab|`, click to the left of the Price text box in the Detail section, click the Text13 label, press [Delete], click Unbound in the text box, type =[FName] &" "&[LName], then press [Enter]**

   You could have added the FName and LName fields directly to the report but the information looks more professional as the result of one expression that calculates the entire name.

8. **Switch to Layout View, resize the new text box as shown in FIGURE 6-18 to see the entire name, save and close the Revenue by State report, close the R2G-6.accdb database, then exit Access**

FIGURE 6-17: Modifying a query from the Record Source property

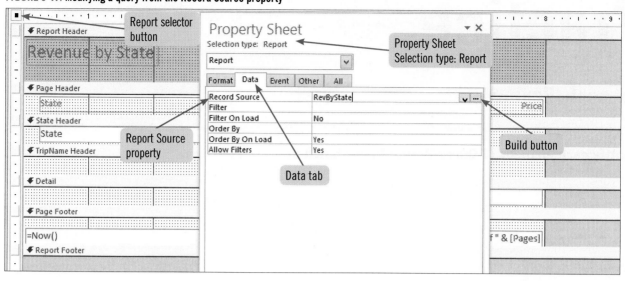

FIGURE 6-18: Final State Revenue Report

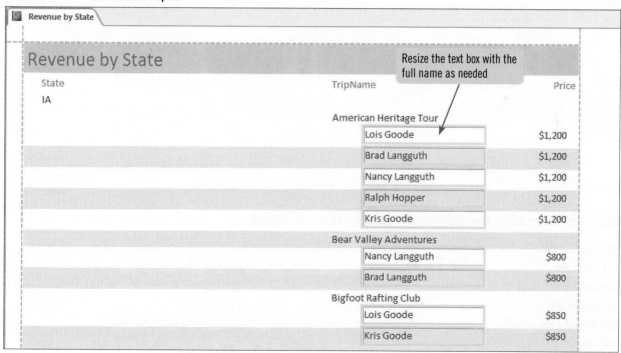

Practice

Concepts Review

Identify each element of Query Design View shown in FIGURE 6-19.

FIGURE 6-19

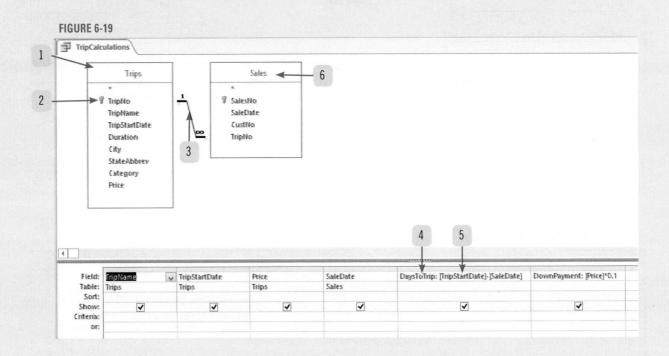

Match each term with the statement that best describes it.

7. **AND criteria**
8. **OR criteria**
9. **Record Source**
10. **Select query**
11. **Wildcard character**
12. **Sorting**

a. Placing the records of a datasheet in a certain order
b. Entered on more than one row of the query design grid
c. Report property that determines what fields and records the report will display
d. Asterisk (*) or question mark (?) used in query criteria
e. Retrieves fields from related tables and displays records in a datasheet
f. Entered on one row of the query design grid

Select the best answer from the list of choices.

13. The query datasheet can best be described as a:

   a. Logical view of the selected data from underlying tables.

   b. Duplication of the data in the underlying table's datasheet.

   c. Separate file of data.

   d. Second copy of the data in the underlying tables.

14. Queries may not be used to:

   a. Calculate new fields of data.

   b. Enter or update data.

   c. Set the primary key field for a table.

   d. Sort records.

15. When you update data in a table that is also selected in a query:

   a. You must relink the query to the table to refresh the data.

   b. The updated data is automatically displayed in the query.

   c. You must also update the data in the query datasheet.

   d. You can choose whether to update the data in the query.

16. Which of the following is *not* an aggregate function available to a summary query?

   a. Avg

   b. Count

   c. Subtotal

   d. Max

17. The order in which records in a query are sorted is determined by:

   a. The order in which the fields are defined in the underlying table.

   b. The importance of the information in the field.

   c. The alphabetic order of the field names.

   d. The left-to-right position of the fields in the query design grid that contain a sort order choice.

18. A crosstab query is generally constructed with how many fields?

   a. 1

   b. 2

   c. 3

   d. More than 5

19. In a crosstab query, which field is the most likely candidate for the Value position?

   a. FName

   b. Cost

   c. Department

   d. Country

20. Which property determines the fields and records available to a report?

   a. Field List

   b. Underlying Query

   c. Data

   d. Record Source

Skills Review

1. Create multitable queries.

a. Start Access and open the Service-6.accdb database from the location where you store your Data Files, then enable content if prompted.

b. Create a new select query in Query Design View using the Names and Zips tables.

c. Add the following fields to the query design grid in this order:
- FirstName and LastName from the Names table
- City, State, and Zip from the Zips table

d. In Datasheet View, replace the LastName value in the Martha Robison record with your last name.

e. Save the query as **MemberList**, print the datasheet if requested by your instructor, then close the query.

2. Apply sorts and view SQL.

a. Open the MemberList query in Query Design View.

b. Drag the FirstName field from the Names field list to the third column in the query design grid to make the first three fields in the query design grid FirstName, LastName, and FirstName.

c. Add an ascending sort to the *second* and *third* fields in the query design grid, and uncheck the Show check box in the *third* column. The query is now sorted in ascending order by LastName, then by FirstName, though the order of the fields in the resulting datasheet still appears as FirstName, LastName.

d. Click the File tab, click Save As, then use Save Object As to save the query as **SortedMemberList**. View the datasheet, print the datasheet if requested by your instructor, then close the SortedMemberList query.

3. Develop AND criteria.

a. Right-click the SortedMemberList query in the Navigation Pane, click Copy, right-click a blank spot in the Navigation Pane, click Paste, then type **KansasB** as the name for the new query.

b. Open the KansasB query in Design View, then type **B*** (the asterisk is a wildcard) in the LastName field Criteria cell to choose all people whose last name starts with B. Access assists you with the syntax for this type of criterion and enters Like "B*" in the cell when you click elsewhere in the query design grid.

c. Enter **KS** as the AND criterion for the State field. Be sure to enter the criterion on the same line in the query design grid as the Like "B*" criterion.

d. View the datasheet. It should select only those people from Kansas with a last name that starts with the letter B.

e. Enter your hometown in the City field of the first record to uniquely identify the printout.

f. Save the KansasB query, print the datasheet if requested by your instructor, then close the KansasB query.

4. Develop OR criteria.

a. Right-click the KansasB query in the Navigation Pane, click Copy, right-click a blank spot in the Navigation Pane, click Paste, then type **KansasBC** as the name for the new query.

b. Open the KansasBC query in Design View, then enter **C*** in the second Criteria row (the or row) of the LastName field.

c. Enter **KS** as the criterion in the second Criteria row (the or row) of the State field so that those people from KS with a last name that starts with the letter C are added to this query.

d. View the datasheet. It should select only those people from Kansas with a last name that starts with the letter B or C. Print the datasheet if requested by your instructor, then save and close the query.

5. Create calculated fields.

a. Create a new select query in Query Design View using only the Names table.

b. Add the following fields to the query design grid in this order: FirstName, LastName, Birthday.

c. Create a calculated field called Age in the fourth column of the query design grid by entering the expression: **Age: Int((Now()-[Birthday])/365)** to determine the age of each person in years based on the information in the Birthday field. The Now() function returns today's date. Now()-[Birthday] determines the number of days a person has lived. Dividing that value by 365 determines the number of years a person has lived. The Int() function is used to return the integer portion of the answer. So if a person has lived 23.5 years, Int(23.5) = 23.

Skills Review (continued)

d. Sort the query in descending order on the calculated Age field.

e. Save the query with the name **AgeCalc**, view the datasheet, print the datasheet if requested by your instructor, then close the query.

6. **Build summary queries.**

a. Create a new select query in Query Design View using the Names and Activities tables.

b. Add the following fields: FirstName and LastName from the Names table, and Hours from the Activities table.

c. Add the Total row to the query design grid, then change the aggregate function for the Hours field from Group By to Sum.

d. Sort in descending order by Hours.

e. Save the query as **HoursSum**, view the datasheet, widen all columns so that all data is clearly visible, print the datasheet if requested by your instructor, then save and close the query.

7. **Build crosstab queries.**

a. Use Query Design View to create a select query with the City and State fields from the Zips table and the Dues field from the Names table. Save the query as **DuesCrosstab**, then view the datasheet.

b. Return to Query Design View, then click the Crosstab button to add the Total and Crosstab rows to the query design grid.

c. Specify City as the crosstab row heading, State as the crosstab column heading, and Dues as the summed value field within the crosstab datasheet.

d. View the datasheet as shown in FIGURE 6-20, print the datasheet if requested by your instructor, then save and close the DuesCrosstab query.

FIGURE 6-20

City	IA	KS	MO
Blue Springs			$50.00
Bridgewater	$50.00		
Buehler		$50.00	
Clear Water		$100.00	
Des Moines	$25.00		
Dripping Springs		$25.00	
Flat Hills		$50.00	
Fontanelle	$50.00		
Greenfield	$50.00		
Kansas City		$50.00	$100.00
Langguth		$25.00	
Leawood			$50.00
Lee's Summit			$75.00
Lenexa		$25.00	
Manawatta		$25.00	
Manhattan		$25.00	
Overland Park		$100.00	
Red Bridge		$425.00	
Running Deer			$25.00
Student Hometown		$200.00	

Skills Review (continued)

8. Create a report on a query.

   a. Use the Report Wizard to create a report on all of the fields of the SortedMemberList query. View the data by Names, add State as a grouping level, add LastName then FirstName as the ascending sort orders, use a Stepped layout and Landscape orientation, then title the report **Members by State**.

   b. In Design View, open the Property Sheet for the report, then open the SortedMemberList query in Design View using the Build button on the Record Source property.

   c. Add the Birthday field to the SortedMemberList query then close the query.

   d. To the left of the LastName field in the Detail section, add a text box bound to the Birthday field. (*Hint*: Type **Birthday** in place of Unbound or modify the text box's Control Source property to be Birthday.) Delete the label that is automatically created to the left of the text box.

   e. In Layout View, resize the City and Zip columns so that all data is clearly visible, as shown in FIGURE 6-21. Be sure to preview the report to make sure it fits on the paper.

   f. If requested by your instructor, print the first page of the Members by State report, save and close it, close the Service-6.accdb database, then exit Access.

FIGURE 6-21

State		LastName	FirstName	City	Zip
Members by State					
IA					
	1/1/1954	Cabriella	Angela	Greenfield	50265
	10/6/1961	Goode	Loraine	Des Moines	52240
	12/25/1970	Pitt	Allie	Fontanelle	50033
	9/5/1959	Student Last	Student First	Bridgewater	50022
KS					
	6/4/1979	Alman	Rhea	Student Hometown	64145
	8/20/1985	Ati	Micah	Student Hometown	64145
	9/6/1961	Bogard	Young	Student Hometown	64145
	5/5/1960	Bouthart	Evan	Red Bridge	66210

Independent Challenge 1

As the manager of a music store's instrument rental program, you have created a database to track rentals to elementary through high school students. Now that several rentals have been made, you want to query the database and produce different datasheet printouts to analyze school information.

   a. Start Access and open the Music-6.accdb database from the location where you store your Data Files, then enable content if prompted.

   b. In Query Design View, create a query with the following fields in the following order:
- SchoolName field from the Schools table
- RentalDate field from the Rentals table
- Description field from the Instruments table

(*Hint*: Although you don't use any fields from the Students table, you need to add the Students table to this query to make the connection between the Schools table and the Rentals table.)

   c. Sort in ascending order by SchoolName, then in ascending order by RentalDate.

   d. Save the query as **SchoolActivity**, view the datasheet, replace Lincoln Elementary with your elementary school name, print the datasheet if requested by your instructor, then close the datasheet.

   e. Copy and paste the SchoolActivity query as **SchoolSummary**, then open the SchoolSummary query in Query Design View.

Independent Challenge 1 (continued)

f. Modify the SchoolSummary query by deleting the Description field. Use the Totals button to group the records by SchoolName and to count the RentalDate field. Print the datasheet if requested by your instructor, then save and close the SchoolSummary query.

g. Create a crosstab query named **SchoolCrosstab** based on the SchoolActivity query. (*Hint*: Select the SchoolActivity query in the Show Table dialog box.) Use Description as the column heading position and SchoolName in the row heading position. Count the RentalDate field.

h. View the SchoolCrosstab query in Datasheet View. Resize each column to best fit the data in that column, then print the datasheet if requested by your instructor. Save and close the SchoolCrosstab query.

i. Copy and paste the SchoolActivity query as **HSRentals**. Modify the HSRentals query in Query Design View so that only those schools with the words **"High School"** in the SchoolName field are displayed. (*Hint*: You have to use wildcard characters in the criteria.)

j. View the HSRentals query in Datasheet View, print it if requested by your instructor, then save and close the datasheet.

k. Close the Music-6.accdb database, then exit Access.

Independent Challenge 2

As the manager of a music store's instrument rental program, you have created a database to track rentals to elementary through high school students. You can use queries to analyze customer and rental information.

a. Start Access and open the Music-6.accdb database from the location where you store your Data Files, then enable content if prompted.

b. In Query Design View, create a query with the following fields in the following order:
- Description and MonthlyFee fields from the Instruments table
- LastName, Zip, and City fields from the Students table

(*Hint*: Although you don't need any fields from the Rentals table in this query's datasheet, you need to add the Rentals table to this query to make the connection between the Customers table and the Instruments table.)

c. Add the Zip field to the first column of the query grid, and specify an ascending sort order for this field. Uncheck the Show check box for the first Zip field so that it does not appear in the datasheet.

d. Add an ascending sort order to the Description field.

e. Save the query as **RentalsByZipCode**.

f. View the datasheet, replace Johnson with your last name in the LastName field, print the datasheet if requested by your instructor, then save and close the datasheet. (*Note*: If you later view this query in Design View, note that Access changes the way the sort orders are specified but in a way that gives you the same results in the datasheet.)

g. In Query Design View, create a query with the following fields in the following order:
- Description and MonthlyFee fields from the Instruments table
- LastName, Zip, and City fields from the Students table

(*Hint*: You'll need to add the Rentals table.)

h. Add criteria to find the records where the Description is equal to **cello**. Sort in ascending order based on the Zip then City fields. Save the query as **Cellos**, view the datasheet, print it if requested by your instructor, then close the datasheet.

i. Copy and paste the Cellos query as **CellosAndAnkeny**, then modify the CellosAndAnkeny query with AND criteria to further specify that the City must be **Ankeny**. View the datasheet, print it if requested by your instructor, then save and close the datasheet.

Independent Challenge 2 (continued)

j. Copy and paste the CellosAndAnkeny query as **CellosOrAnkeny**, then modify the CellosOrAnkeny query so that all records with a Description equal to Cello *or* a City value of **Ankeny** are selected. View the datasheet, print it if requested by your instructor, then save and close the datasheet.

k. Close the MusicStore-6.accdb database, then exit Access.

Independent Challenge 3

As a real estate agent, you use an Access database to track residential real estate listings in your area. You can use queries to answer questions about the real estate properties and to analyze home values.

a. Start Access and open the LakeHomes-6.accdb database from the location where you store your Data Files, then enable content if prompted.

b. In Query Design View, create a query with the following fields in the following order:
  • AgencyName from the Agencies table
  • RFirst and RLast from the Realtors table
  • SqFt and Asking from the Listings table

c. Sort the records in descending order by the SqFt field.

d. Save the query as **BySqFt**, view the datasheet, enter your last name instead of Schwartz for the listing with the largest SqFt value, then print the datasheet if requested by your instructor.

e. In Query Design View, modify the BySqFt query by creating a calculated field that determines price per square foot. The new calculated field's name should be **PerSqFt**, and the expression should be the asking price divided by the square foot field, or **[Asking]/[SqFt]**.

f. Remove any former sort orders, sort the records in descending order based on the PerSqFt calculated field, and view the datasheet. Save and close the BySqFt query. ###### means the data is too wide to display in the column. You can make the data narrower and also align it by applying a Currency format.

g. Reopen the BySqFt query in Query Design View, right-click the calculated PerSqFt field, click Properties, then change the Format property to Currency. View the datasheet, print it if requested by your instructor, then save and close the BySqFt query.

h. Copy and paste the BySqFt query as **CostSummary**.

i. In Design View of the CostSummary query, delete the RFirst, RLast, and SqFt fields.

j. View the datasheet, then change the Big Cedar Realtors agency name to *your last name* followed by **Realtors**.

k. In Design View, add the Total row, then sum the Asking field and use the Avg (Average) aggregate function for the PerSqFt calculated field.

l. In Datasheet View, add the Total row and display the sum of the SumOfAsking field. Widen all columns as needed, as shown in FIGURE 6-22.

m. If requested by your instructor, print the CostSummary query, then save and close it.

n. Close the LakeHomes-6.accdb database, then exit Access.

FIGURE 6-22

AgencyName	SumOfAsking	PerSqFt
Sunset Cove Realtors	$2,628,840.00	$113.87
Student Last Name Realtors	$3,835,214.40	$113.51
Green Mountain Realty	$1,493,940.00	$83.12
Total	$7,957,994.40	

Independent Challenge 4: Explore

You're working with the local high school guidance counselor to help her with an Access database used to manage college scholarship opportunities. You help her with the database by creating several queries. (*Note*: To complete this Independent Challenge, make sure you are connected to the Internet.)

a. Start Access, open the Scholarships-6.accdb database from the location where you store your Data Files, then enable content if prompted.

b. Conduct research on the Internet or at your school to find at least five new scholarships relevant to your major, and enter them into the Scholarships table.

c. Conduct research on the Internet or at your school to find at least one new scholarship relevant to a Computer Science major, and enter the two records into the Scholarships table. Enter **Computer Science** in the Major field.

d. Create a query called **ComputerScience** that displays all fields from the Scholarships table and selects all records with a **Computer Science** major. If requested by your instructor, print the ComputerScience query then save and close it.

e. Copy and paste the ComputerScience query as **BusinessOrCS**. Add OR criteria to the BusinessOrCS query to add all scholarships in the **Business** major to the existing scholarships in the Computer Science major. If requested by your instructor, print the BusinessOrCS query then save and close it.

f. Create a new query that selects the ScholarshipName, DueDate, and Amount from the Scholarships table, and sorts the records in ascending order by DueDate, then descending order by Amount. Name the query **AllScholarshipsByDueDate**. If requested by your instructor, print the AllScholarshipsByDueDate query then save and close it.

g. Use the Report Wizard to create a report on the AllScholarshipsByDueDate query, do not add any grouping levels or additional sort orders, use a Tabular layout and a Portrait orientation, and title the report **All Scholarships by Due Date**.

h. In Design View of the All Scholarships by Due Date report, open the Property Sheet, and use the Record Source Build button to open the AllScholarshipsByDueDate query in Design View. Add the Major field to the query, save and close it.

i. In Report Design View, open the Group, Sort, and Total pane, add the Major field as a grouping field. Add DueDate as a sort order from newest to oldest, then add Amount as a sort field from largest to smallest.

j. Add a text box to the Major Header section, and bind it to the Major field. (*Hint*: Type **Major** in place of Unbound or modify the text box's Control Source property to be Major.) Delete the label that is automatically created to the left of the text box. Preview the report, modify the ScholarshipName and DueDate labels in the Page Header section to show spaces between the words, and move and resize any controls as needed to match FIGURE 6-23. Print the report if requested by your instructor.

k. Save and close the All Scholarships by Due Date report, close the Scholarships-6.accdb database, then exit Access.

FIGURE 6-23

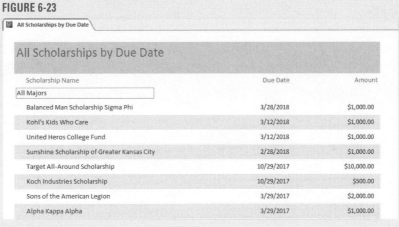

Visual Workshop

Open the Training-6.accdb database from the location where you store your Data Files, then enable content if prompted. In Query Design View, create a new select query with the DeptName field from the Departments table, the CourseCost field from the Courses table, and the Description field from the Courses table. (*Hint*: You will also have to add the Employees and Enrollments tables to Query Design View to build relationships from the Departments table to the Courses table.) Save the query with the name **DeptCrosstab,** then display it as a crosstab query, as shown in FIGURE 6-24. Print the DeptCrosstab query if requested by your instructor, save and close it, then close the Training-6.accdb database.

FIGURE 6-24

Description	Accounting	Book	Human Resc	Information	Marketing	Operations	Shipping	Training	Warehouse
Access Case Problems	$400.00	$600.00			$200.00	$200.00		$200.00	$400.00
Computer Fundamentals	$200.00	$800.00	$400.00	$200.00	$600.00		$400.00	$400.00	$800.00
Dynamite Customer Service Skills		$100.00	$100.00	$100.00	$200.00				$200.00
Employee Benefits Made Clear		$150.00	$100.00	$50.00	$150.00	$50.00	$100.00	$50.00	$200.00
Excel Case Problems	$200.00		$200.00			$400.00	$400.00	$200.00	$400.00
Intermediate Access	$800.00	$1,200.00			$400.00	$400.00		$400.00	$800.00
Intermediate Excel	$400.00	$200.00	$200.00			$400.00	$400.00	$200.00	$400.00
Intermediate Internet Explorer	$400.00	$800.00	$400.00	$200.00	$400.00	$200.00	$200.00	$400.00	$600.00
Intermediate Phone Skils	$300.00	$300.00				$300.00		$150.00	$300.00
Intermediate PowerPoint	$400.00	$600.00	$200.00		$200.00	$200.00	$200.00	$400.00	$600.00
Intermediate Tax Planning	$100.00	$50.00	$50.00	$50.00		$50.00	$100.00	$50.00	$200.00
Intermediate Windows		$200.00	$400.00	$200.00	$400.00		$400.00	$200.00	$600.00
Intermediate Word		$200.00	$200.00	$200.00	$400.00				$400.00
Internet Fundamentals		$600.00	$400.00	$200.00	$600.00		$400.00	$400.00	$800.00
Introduction to Access	$400.00	$600.00	$200.00		$400.00	$200.00		$200.00	$400.00
Introduction to Excel	$400.00	$200.00	$200.00			$400.00	$400.00	$200.00	$800.00
Introduction to Insurance Planning	$150.00	$225.00	$75.00		$75.00	$75.00	$150.00	$150.00	$225.00
Introduction to Internet Explorer	$400.00	$800.00	$400.00	$200.00	$600.00	$200.00	$200.00	$400.00	$1,000.00
Introduction to Networking		$400.00	$400.00	$200.00	$600.00		$400.00	$200.00	$800.00
Introduction to Outlook	$400.00	$600.00	$400.00		$400.00	$400.00	$400.00	$400.00	$400.00
Introduction to Phone Skills	$300.00	$450.00			$150.00	$300.00	$150.00	$150.00	$450.00
Introduction to PowerPoint	$400.00	$800.00	$400.00	$200.00	$600.00	$200.00	$200.00	$400.00	$600.00
Introduction to Project	$1,200.00	$2,000.00	$400.00		$1,600.00	$1,600.00	$1,600.00	$1,200.00	$3,200.00
Introduction to Tax Planning	$100.00	$100.00	$50.00	$50.00	$50.00	$50.00	$100.00	$50.00	$200.00
Introduction to Windows		$600.00	$400.00	$200.00	$600.00	$200.00	$400.00	$400.00	$800.00

Record: 1 of 31   No Filter   Search

Enhancing Forms

CASE Julia Rice wants to improve the usability of the forms in the Reason 2 Go database. You will build and improve forms by working with subforms, combo boxes, option groups, and command buttons to enter, find, and filter data.

Module Objectives

After completing this module, you will be able to:

- Use Form Design View
- Add subforms
- Align control edges
- Add a combo box for data entry
- Add a combo box to find records
- Add command buttons
- Add option groups
- Add tab controls

Files You Will Need

R2G-7.accdb	LakeHomes-7.accdb
Service-7.accdb	Scholarships-7.accdb
Music-7.accdb	Baseball-7.accdb

Use Form Design View

Learning Outcomes
- Create a form in Form Design View
- Modify the Record Source property
- Add fields to a form with the Field List

A **form** is a database object designed to make data easy to find, enter, and edit. You create forms by using **controls**, such as labels, text boxes, combo boxes, and command buttons, which help you manipulate data more quickly and reliably than working in a datasheet. A form that contains a **subform** allows you to work with related records in an easy-to-use screen arrangement. For example, using a form/subform combination, you can display customer data and all of the orders placed by that customer at the same time. **Design View** of a form is devoted to working with the detailed structure of a form. The purpose of Design View is to provide full access to all of the modifications you can make to the form. **CASE** ▶ *Julia Rice asks you to create a customer entry form. You create this form from scratch in Form Design View.*

STEPS

1. **Start Access, then open the R2G-7.accdb database from the location where you store your Data Files, enable content if prompted, click the Create tab on the Ribbon, then click the Form Design button in the Forms group**

   A blank form is displayed in Design View. Your first step is to connect the blank form to an underlying **record source**, a table or query that contains the data you want to display on the form. The fields in the record source populate the **Field List**, a small window that lists the fields in the record source. The Customers table should be the record source for the CustomerEntry form.

   QUICK TIP
   Click the Build button ⬚ in the Record Source property to build or edit a query as the record source for a form.

2. **Double-click the form selector button ▪ to open the form's Property Sheet, click the Data tab in the Property Sheet, click the Record Source list arrow, then click Customers**

   The Record Source property lists all existing tables and queries, or you could use the Build button ⬚ to create a query for the form. With the record source selected, you're ready to add controls to the form. Recall that bound controls, such as text boxes and combo boxes, display data from the record source, and unbound controls, such as labels and lines, clarify information.

3. **Click the Add Existing Fields button in the Tools group to open the Field List, click CustNo in the Field List, press and hold [Shift], click FirstContact in the Field List, then drag the selection to the form at about the 1" mark on the horizontal ruler**

   The fields of the Customers table are added to the form, as shown in **FIGURE 7-1**. The FirstContact field is added as a combo box because it has Lookup properties. The other fields are text boxes except for the Photo field, which is inserted as an **Attachment** control given the Photo field has an Attachment data type. Labels are created for each bound control and are captioned with the field name. You can rearrange the controls by moving them.

   QUICK TIP
   In a column of controls, labels are on the left and text boxes are on the right.

4. **Click the form to deselect all controls, click the Street text box, press and hold [Ctrl], click the City, State, Zip, and Phone text boxes as well as the FirstContact combo box to add them to the selection, then release [Ctrl]**

   Selected controls will move as a group.

   TROUBLE
   If your form doesn't look like FIGURE 7-2, switch to Design View to fix it.

5. **Use the 🖑 pointer to drag the selected controls up and to the right of the name controls, then click the View button ▤ to switch to Form View**

   The new form in Form View is shown in **FIGURE 7-2**. You will improve and enhance it in later lessons.

6. **Click the Save button 🖫 on the Quick Access Toolbar, type CustomerEntry as the form name, click OK, then close the CustomerEntry form**

FIGURE 7-1: Adding fields in Form Design View

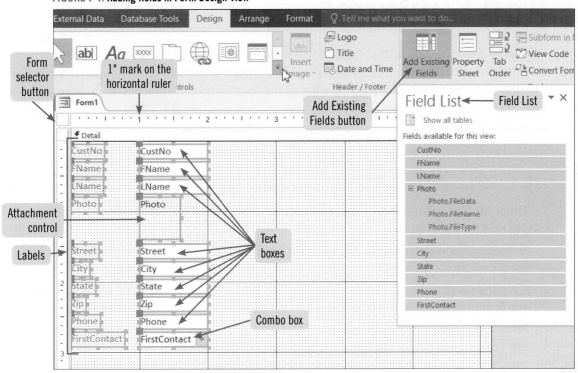

FIGURE 7-2: New form in Form View

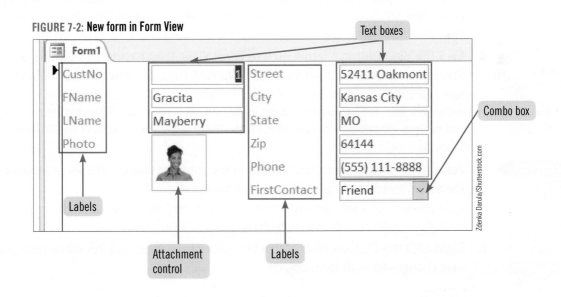

Add Subforms

Learning Outcomes
• Add a subform to a form
• Resize columns in a subform
• Define form layouts

A **subform** is a form within a form. The form that contains the subform is called the **main form**. A main form/subform combination displays the records of two tables that are related in a one-to-many relationship. The main form shows data from the table on the "one" side of the relationship, and the subform shows the records from the table on the "many" side of the relationship. **CASE** *Julia asks you to add a subform to the CustomerEntry form to show related sales for each customer.*

STEPS

1. **Open the CustomerEntry form in Design View, then close the Field List and Property Sheet if they are open**

   You add new controls to a form by dragging fields from the Field List or selecting the control on the Design tab of the Ribbon.

TROUBLE
If the SubForm Wizard doesn't start, click the More button ⟱ in the Controls group, then click Use Control Wizards 🔲 to toggle it on.

2. **Click the More button ⟱ in the Controls group to view all of the form controls, click the Subform/Subreport button 🔳, then click below the Photo label in the form, as shown in FIGURE 7-3**

   The Subform Wizard opens to help you add a subform control to the form.

QUICK TIP
To remove a form layout, you must work in Form Design View.

3. **Click Next to use existing Tables and Queries as the data for the subform, click the Tables/Queries list arrow, click Query: SalesData, click the Select All Fields button >> , click Next, click Next to accept the option Show SalesData for each record in Customers using CustNo, then click Finish to accept SalesData subform as the name for the new subform control**

   A form **layout** is the general way that the data and controls are arranged on the form. By default, subforms display their controls in a columnar arrangement in Design View, but their **Default View property** is set to Datasheet. See **TABLE 7-1** for a description of form layouts. The subform layout is apparent when you view the form in Form View.

TROUBLE
You may need to shorten the subform to see its navigation bar in Form View.

4. **Click the View button 🔲 to switch to Form View, then navigate to CustNo 6, Kristen Lang, who has purchased four different trips, as shown in the subform**

   Sales information appears in the subform in a datasheet layout. As you move through the customer records of the main form, the information changes in the subform to reflect sales for each customer. The main form and subform are linked by the common CustNo field. Resize the columns of the subform to make the information easier to read.

QUICK TIP
Double-click the line between field names to automatically adjust the width of the column to the widest field entry.

5. **Point to the line between field names in the subform and use the ↔ pointer to resize the column widths of the subform, as shown in FIGURE 7-4**

   The CustomerEntry form now displays two navigation bars. The inside bar is for the subform records, and the outside bar is for the main form records.

6. **Right-click the CustomerEntry form tab, click Close, then click Yes when prompted to save changes to both form objects**

Linking the form and subform

If the form and subform do not appear to be correctly linked, examine the subform's Property Sheet, paying special attention to the **Link Child Fields** and **Link Master Fields** properties on the Data tab. These properties tell you which field serves as the link between the main form and subform.

FIGURE 7-3: Adding a subform control

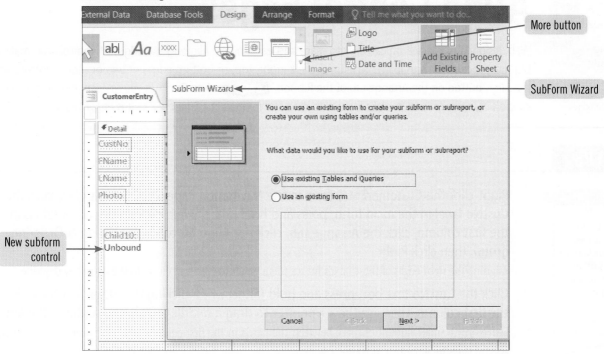

FIGURE 7-4: CustomerEntry form and SalesData subform

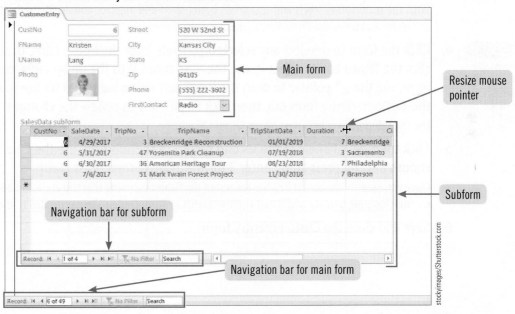

TABLE 7-1: Form layouts

layout	description
Columnar	Default view for main forms; each field appears on a separate row with a label to its left
Tabular	Each field appears as an individual column, and each record is presented as a row
Datasheet	Default view for subforms; fields and records are displayed as they appear in a table or query datasheet

Align Control Edges

Learning Outcomes
- Select multiple controls together
- Align the edges of controls

Well-designed forms are logical, easy to read, and easy to use. Aligning the edges of controls can make a big difference in form usability. To align the left, right, top, or bottom edges of two or more controls, use the Align button on the Arrange tab of the Ribbon. **CASE** *Julia Rice asks you to align and rearrange the controls in the main form to make it easier to read and to resize the Photo box so it is much larger.*

STEPS

QUICK TIP

To select multiple controls, click the first control, then press and hold either [Ctrl] or [Shift] to add more controls to the selection.

1. **Right-click the CustomerEntry form in the Navigation Pane, click Design View, click the CustNo label in the main form, press and hold [Shift] while clicking the other labels in the first column, click the Arrange tab, click the Align button in the Sizing & Ordering group, then click Right**

   Aligning the right edges of these labels makes them easier to read and closer to the data they describe.

2. **Click the CustNo text box, press and hold [Shift] while clicking the other text boxes in the first column, then use the ↔ pointer to drag a middle-left sizing handle to the left**

   Leave only a small amount of space between the labels in the first column and the bound controls in the second column, as shown in **FIGURE 7-5**.

3. **Click the form to deselect the selected controls, press and hold [Shift] and click to select the six labels in the third column of the main form, click the Align button in the Sizing & Ordering group, then click Right**

   With the main form's labels and text boxes better sized and aligned, you decide to delete the Photo label and move and resize the Photo box to make it much larger.

TROUBLE

The Undo button ↩ will undo multiple actions in Form Design View.

4. **Click the form to deselect any selected controls, click the Photo label, press [Delete], click the Photo box to select it, use the ⬚ to move it to the upper-right corner of the form, use the ↗ pointer to drag the lower-left sizing handle to fill the space, right-click the CustomerEntry form tab, then click Form View to review the changes**

   Use the subform to enter a new sale to Gracita Mayberry.

5. **Click the SaleDate field in the second record of the subform, use the Calendar Picker to choose 8/1/18, press [Tab], enter 3 for the TripNo, then press [Tab]**

   Once you identify the correct TripNo, the rest of the fields describing that trip are automatically added to the record. Continue to make additional enhancements in Form Design View as needed to match **FIGURE 7-6**.

6. **Save and close the CustomerEntry form**

Anchoring, margins, and padding

Anchoring means to position and tie a control to other controls so they move or are resized together. The control margin is the space between the content inside the control and the outside border of the control. Control **padding** is the space between the outside borders of adjacent controls. To apply anchoring, margins, or padding, work in Form Design View. Click the Arrange tab, select the control(s) you want to modify, and choose the Control Margins, Control Padding, or Anchoring buttons in the Position group.

FIGURE 7-5: Aligning and resizing controls

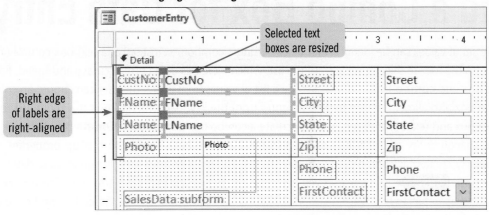

Right edge of labels are right-aligned

Selected text boxes are resized

FIGURE 7-6: Updated CustomerEntry form

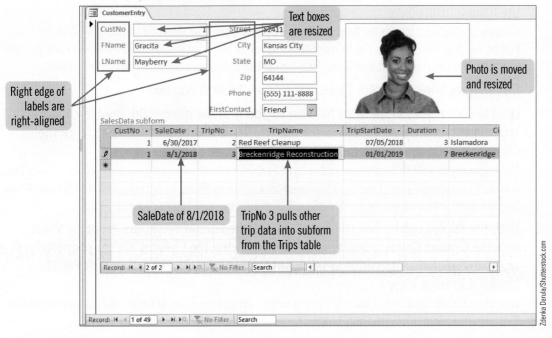

Right edge of labels are right-aligned

Text boxes are resized

Photo is moved and resized

SaleDate of 8/1/2018

TripNo 3 pulls other trip data into subform from the Trips table

Zdenka Darula/Shutterstock.com

Add a Combo Box for Data Entry

Learning
Outcomes
• Add a combo box
  to a form
• Modify combo
  box properties
• Use a combo box
  for data entry

If a finite set of values can be identified for a field, using a combo box instead of a text box control on a form allows the user to select a value from the list, which increases data entry accuracy and speed. Both the **list box** and **combo box** controls provide a list of values from which the user can choose an entry. A combo box also allows the user to type an entry from the keyboard; therefore, it is a "combination" of the list box and text box controls. You can create a combo box by using the **Combo Box Wizard**, or you can change an existing text box or list box into a combo box. Fields with Lookup properties are automatically created as combo boxes on new forms. Foreign key fields are also good candidates for combo boxes. **CASE** *Julia Rice asks you to change the TripNo field in the subform of the CustomerEntry form into a combo box so that when a customer purchases a new trip, users can choose the trip from a list instead of entering the TripNo value from the keyboard.*

STEPS

1. **Open the CustomerEntry form in Design View, click the TripNo text box in the subform to select it, right-click the TripNo text box, point to Change To on the shortcut menu, then click Combo Box**

   Now that the control has been changed from a text box to a combo box, you need to populate the list with the appropriate values.

2. **With the combo box still selected, click the Property Sheet button in the Tools group, click the Data tab in the Property Sheet, click the Row Source property box, then click the Build button** ⋯

   Clicking the Build button for the **Row Source property** opens the Show Table dialog box and the Query Builder window, which allows you to select the field values you want to display in the combo box list. You want to select the TripNo and TripName fields for the list, which are both stored in the Trips table.

3. **Double-click Trips, then click Close in the Show Table dialog box**

4. **Double-click TripNo in the Trips field list to add it to the query grid, double-click TripName, click the Sort list arrow for the TripName field, click Ascending, click the Close button on the Design tab, then click Yes to save the changes**

   The beginning of a SELECT statement is displayed in the Row Source property, as shown in **FIGURE 7-7**. This is an SQL (Structured Query Language) statement and can be modified by clicking the Build button. If you save the query with a name, the query name will appear in the Row Source property.

5. **With the TripNo combo box still selected, click the Format tab in the Property Sheet, click the Column Count property, change 1 to 2, click the Column Widths property, type 0.5;2, click the List Width property and change Auto to 2.5, save the form, then display it in Form View**

   Entering 0.5;2 sets the width of the first column to 0.5 inch and the width of the second column to 2 inches. To test the new combo box, you add another new sales record in the subform.

6. **Move to the second record for CustNo 2, click the TripNo list arrow in the second record in the subform, scroll as needed and click TripID 9 Bikers for Ecology on the list, press [Tab], enter 9/1/18 as the SaleDate value, then press [Enter]**

   The new record is entered as shown in **FIGURE 7-8**. Selecting a specific TripNo automatically fills in the correct Trip fields for that TripNo number.

FIGURE 7-7: Changing the TripNo field to a combo box

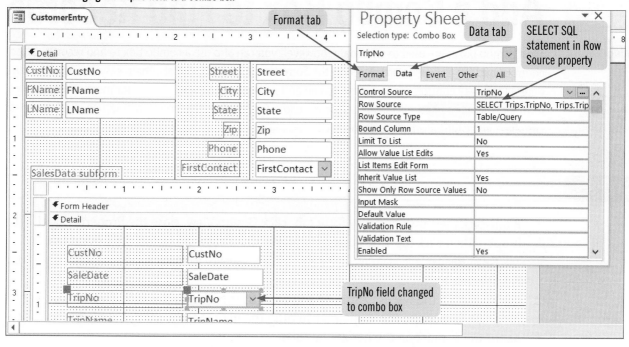

FIGURE 7-8: Using the TripNo combo box to enter a new record

Choosing between a combo box and a list box

The list box and combo box controls are very similar, but the combo box is more popular for two reasons. While both provide a list of values from which the user can choose to make an entry in a field, the combo box also allows the user to make a unique entry from the keyboard (unless the **Limit To List property** is set to Yes). More important, however, is that most users like the drop-down list action of the combo box.

Add a Combo Box to Find Records

Most combo boxes are used to enter data; however, you can also use a combo box to find records. Often, controls used for navigation are placed in the Form Header section to make them easy to find. **Sections** determine where controls appear on the screen and print on paper. See TABLE 7-2 for more information on form sections. **CASE** *Julia suggests that you add a combo box to the Form Header section to quickly locate customers in the CustomerEntry form.*

STEPS

1. **Right-click the CustomerEntry form tab, click Design View, close the Property Sheet if it is open, then click the Title button in the Header/Footer group on the Design tab**

   The **Form Header** section opens and displays a label captioned with the name of the form. You modify and resize the label.

2. **Click between the words Customer and Entry in the label in the Form Header, press the [Spacebar], then use the ↔ pointer to drag the middle-right sizing handle to the left to about the 3" mark on the horizontal ruler**

   Now you have space on the right side of the Form Header section to add a combo box to find records.

3. **Click the Combo Box button 🔲 in the Controls group, click in the Form Header at about the 5" mark on the horizontal ruler, click the Find a record option button in the Combo Box Wizard, click Next, double-click LName, double-click FName, click Next, click Next to accept the column widths and hide the key column, type Find Customer: as the label for the combo box, then click Finish**

   The new combo box is placed in the Form Header section, as shown in FIGURE 7-9. Because a combo box can be used for data entry or to find a record, a clear label to identify its purpose is very important. You modify the label to make it easier to read and widen the combo box.

4. **Click the Find Customer: label, click the Home tab, click the Font Color button arrow ▲⏷, click the Dark Blue, Text 2 color box (top row, fourth from the left), click the Unbound combo box, use the ↔ pointer to drag the middle-right sizing handle to the right edge of the form to widen the combo box, then click the View button 🖼**

   You test the combo box in Form View.

5. **Click the Find Customer: list arrow, then click Lang, Kristen**

   The combo box finds the customer named Kristen Lang, but the combo box list entries are not in alphabetical order. You fix this in Form Design View by working with the Property Sheet of the combo box.

6. **Right-click the CustomerEntry form tab, click Design View, double-click the edge of the Unbound combo box in the Form Header to open its Property Sheet, click the Data tab, click SELECT in the Row Source property, then click the Build button 🔲**

   The Query Builder opens, allowing you to modify the fields or sort order of the values in the combo box list.

7. **Click Ascending in the Sort cell for LName, click Ascending in the Sort cell for FName, click the Close button on the Design tab, click Yes when prompted to save changes, click the View button 🖼, then click the Find Customer: list arrow**

   This time, the combo box list is sorted in ascending order by last name, then by first name, as shown in FIGURE 7-10.

8. **Scroll, click Alman, Jacob to test the combo box again, then save and close the CustomerEntry form**

   To modify the number of items displayed in the list, use the **List Rows property** on the Format tab.

Enhancing Forms

FIGURE 7-9: Adding a combo box to find records

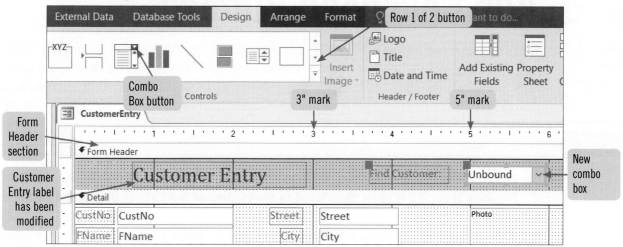

FIGURE 7-10: Using a combo box to find customers

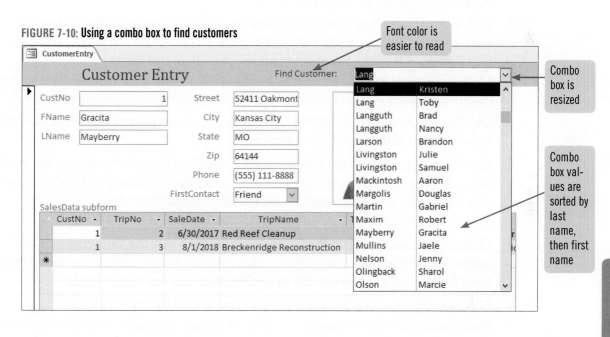

TABLE 7-2: Form sections

section	description
Detail	Appears once for every record
Form Header	Appears at the top of the form and often contains command buttons or a label with the title of the form
Form Footer	Appears at the bottom of the form and often contains command buttons or a label with instructions on how to use the form
Page Header	Appears at the top of a printed form with information such as page numbers or dates
Page Footer	Appears at the bottom of a printed form with information such as page numbers or dates

Add Command Buttons

Learning
Outcomes
• Add a command
button to a form

You use a **command button** to perform a common action in Form View such as printing the current record, opening another form, or closing the current form. Command buttons are often added to the Form Header or Form Footer sections. **CASE** *Julia Rice asks you to add command buttons to the Form Footer section of the CustomerEntry form to help other Reason 2 Go employees print the current record and close the form.*

STEPS

1. **Right-click the CustomerEntry form in the Navigation Pane, click Design View, close the Property Sheet if it is open, then scroll to the bottom of the form to display the Form Footer section**

   Good form design gives users everything they need in a logical location. You decide to use the Form Footer section for all of your form's command buttons.

2. **Click the Button button ⌷ⁱⁱⁱⁱ in the Controls group, then click in the Form Footer at the 1" mark**

   The Command Button Wizard opens, listing 28 of the most popular actions for the command button, organized within six categories, as shown in **FIGURE 7-11**.

3. **Click Record Operations in the Categories list, click Print Record in the Actions list, click Next, click the Text option button, click Next to accept the default text of Print Record, type PrintRecord as the meaningful button name, then click Finish**

   Adding a command button to print only the current record prevents the user from using the Print option on the File tab, which prints *all* records. You also want to add a command button to close the form.

4. **Click the Button button ⌷ⁱⁱⁱⁱ in the Controls group, then click to the right of the Print Record button in the Form Footer section**

5. **Click Form Operations in the Categories list, click Close Form in the Actions list, click Next, click the Text option button, click Next to accept the default text of Close Form, type CloseForm as the meaningful button name, then click Finish**

   To test your command buttons, you switch to Form View.

6. **Click the Save button 🖫 on the Quick Access Toolbar, click the View button 🖩 to review the form as shown in FIGURE 7-12, click the Print Record button you added in the Form Footer section, then click OK to confirm that only one record prints**

7. **Click the Close Form button in the Form Footer section to close the form**

   Using a command button to close a form prevents the user from unintentionally closing the entire Access application.

Shape effects

Shape effects provide a special visual impact (such as shadow, glow, soft edges, and bevel) to command buttons. To apply a shape effect, work in Form Design View. Click the Format tab, select the command button you want to modify, then click the Shape Effects button in the Control Formatting group to display the options.

Enhancing Forms

FIGURE 7-11: Command Button Wizard

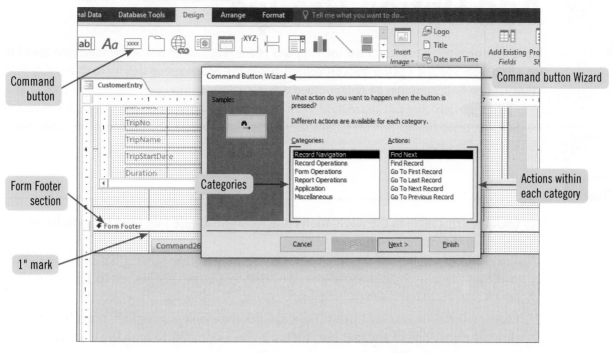

FIGURE 7-12: Final Customer Entry form with two command buttons

Access 2016

Add Option Groups

Learning Outcomes
• Add an option group to a form
• Add option buttons to an option group
• Use option buttons to edit data

An **option group** is a bound control used in place of a text box when only a few values are available for a field. You add one **option button** control within the option group box for each possible field value. Option buttons within an option group are mutually exclusive; only one can be chosen at a time. **CASE** ▶ *Julia Rice asks you to build a new form to view trips and sales information. You decide to use an option group to work with the data in the Duration field because R2G trips have only a handful of possible duration values.*

STEPS

1. **Click the Trips table in the Navigation Pane, click the Create tab, then click the Form button in the Forms group**

   A form/subform combination is created and displayed in Layout View, showing trip information in the main form and sales records in the subform. You delete the Duration text box and resize the controls to provide room for an option group.

   TROUBLE
   The blank placeholder is where the Duration text box formerly appeared.

2. **Click the Duration text box, press [Delete], click the blank placeholder, press [Delete], click the right edge of any text box, then use the ↔ pointer to drag the right edge of the controls to the left so they are about half as wide**

   You add the Duration field back to the form as an option group control using the blank space on the right that you created.

3. **Right-click the Trips form tab, click Design View, click the Design tab on the Ribbon, click the Option Group button [XYZ] in the Controls group, then click to the right of the TripNo text box**

   The Option Group Wizard starts and prompts for label names. All the trips sold by R2G have a duration of 3, 5, 7, 10, or 14 days, so the labels and values will describe this data.

   TROUBLE
   FIGURE 7-13 shows the Option Group Wizard at the end of Step 4.

4. **Enter the Label Names shown in FIGURE 7-13, click Next, click the No, I don't want a default option button, click Next, then enter the Values to correspond with their labels, as shown in FIGURE 7-13**

   The Values are entered into the field and correspond with the **Option Value property** of each option button. The Label Names are clarifying text.

   QUICK TIP
   Option buttons commonly present mutually exclusive choices for an option group. Check boxes commonly present individual Yes/No fields.

5. **Click Next, click the Store the value in this field list arrow, click Duration, click Next, click Next to accept Option buttons in an Etched style, type Duration as the caption for the option group, then click Finish**

   View and work with the new option group in Form View.

6. **Click the View button [▦] to switch to Form View, click the Next record button [▶] in the navigation bar for the main form three times to move to the Boy Scout Project record, then click the 10 days option button**

   Your screen should look like FIGURE 7-14. You changed the duration of this trip from 7 to 10 days.

7. **Right-click the Trips form tab, click Close, click Yes when prompted to save changes, then click OK to accept Trips as the form name**

FIGURE 7-13: **Option Group Label Names and Values**

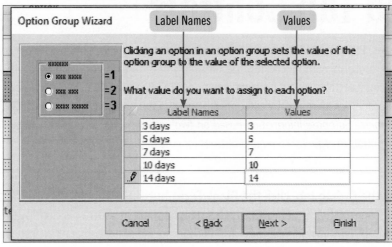

FIGURE 7-14: **Trips form with option group for Duration field**

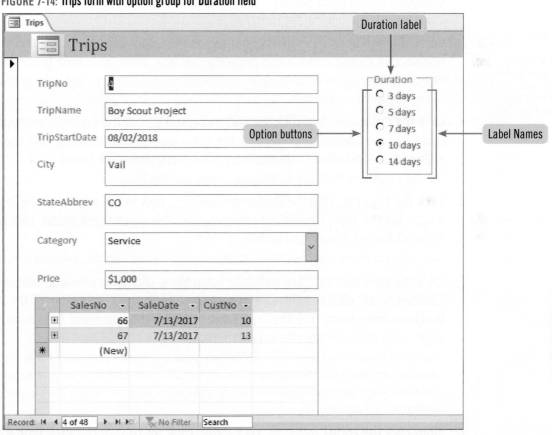

Protecting data

You may not want to allow all users who view a form to change all the data that appears on that form. You can design forms to limit access to certain fields by changing the Enabled and Locked properties of a control. The **Enabled property** specifies whether a control can have the focus in Form View. The **Locked property** specifies whether you can edit data in a control in Form View.

Add Tab Controls

Learning Outcomes
• Add a tab control to a form
• Modify tab control properties

You use the **tab control** to create a three-dimensional aspect to a form so that many controls can be organized and displayed by clicking the tabs. You have already used tab controls because many Access dialog boxes use tabs to organize information. For example, the Property Sheet uses tab controls to organize properties identified by categories: Format, Data, Event, Other, and All. **CASE** ▶ *Julia Rice asks you to organize database information based on two categories: Trips and Customers. You create a new form with tab controls to organize command buttons for easy access to trip and customer information.*

STEPS

1. **Click the Create tab, click the Blank Form button in the Forms group, close the Field List if it is open, click the Tab Control button 🗔 in the Controls group, then click the form**
   A new tab control is automatically positioned in the upper-left corner of the new form with two tabs. You rename the tabs to clarify their purpose.

2. **Click the Page1 tab to select it, click the Property Sheet button in the Tools group, click the Other tab in the Property Sheet, double-click Page1 in the Name property, type Customers, then press [Enter]**
   You also give Page2 a meaningful name.

3. **Click Page2 to open its Property Sheet, click the Other tab (if it is not already selected), double-click Page2 in the Name property text box, type Trips, then press [Enter]**
   Now that the tab names are meaningful, you're ready to add controls to each page. In this case, you add command buttons to each page.

4. **Click the Customers tab, click the Button button ⌗ in the Controls group, click in the middle of the Customers page, click the Form Operations category, click the Open Form action, click Next, click CustomerEntry, click Next, then click Finish**
   You add a command button to the Trips tab to open the Trips form.

5. **Click the Trips tab, click the Button button ⌗, click in the middle of the Trips page, click the Form Operations category, click the Open Form action, click Next, click Trips, click Next, then click Finish**
   Your new form should look like FIGURE 7-15. To test your command buttons, you must switch to Form View.

6. **Click the View button 🗔 to switch to Form View, click the command button on the Customers tab, click the Close Form command button at the bottom of the CustomerEntry form, click the Trips page tab, click the command button on the Trips page, right-click the Trips form tab, then click Close**
   Your screen should look like FIGURE 7-16. The two command buttons opened the CustomerEntry and Trips forms and are placed on different pages of a tab control in the form. In a fully developed database, you would add many more command buttons to make other database objects (tables, queries, forms, and reports) easy to find and open.

7. **Right-click the Form1 form tab, click Close, click Yes to save changes, type R2G Navigation as the form name, click OK, then close the R2G-7.accdb database**

FIGURE 7-15: Adding command buttons to a tab control

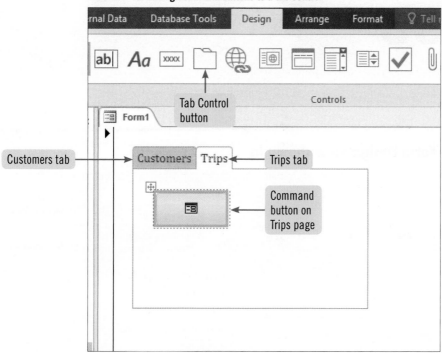

FIGURE 7-16: Form Navigation form

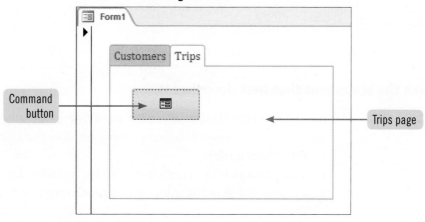

Practice

Concepts Review

Identify each element of Form Design View shown in FIGURE 7-17.

FIGURE 7-17

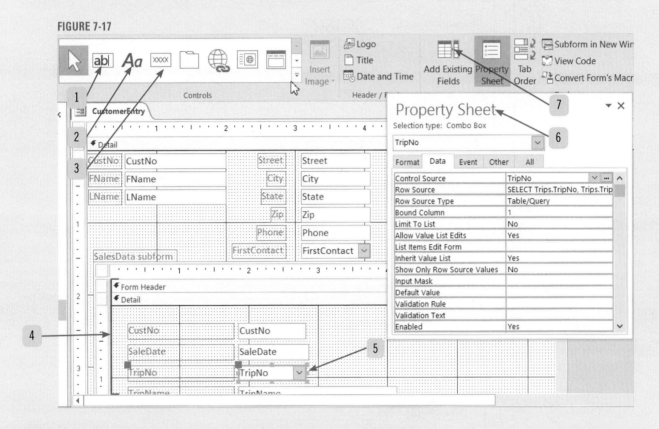

Match each term with the statement that best describes it.

8. **Combo box**
9. **Command button**
10. **Option group**
11. **Subform**
12. **Tab control**

a. A bound control that displays a few mutually exclusive entries for a field
b. A control that is used to organize other controls to give a form a three-dimensional quality
c. A bound control that is really both a list box and a text box
d. A control that shows records that are related to one record shown in the main form
e. An unbound control that executes an action when it is clicked

Select the best answer from the list of choices.

13. Which control works best to display three choices—1, 2, or 3—for a Rating field?

  a. Text box

  b. Label

  c. Command button

  d. Option group

14. Which control would you use to initiate a print action?

  a. Text box

  b. Option group

  c. Command button

  d. List box

15. Which control would you use to display a drop-down list of 50 states?

  a. List box

  b. Check box

  c. Combo box

  d. Field label

16. To view many related records within a form, use a:

  a. Design template.

  b. Subform.

  c. Link control.

  d. List box.

17. Which of the following form properties defines the fields and records that appear on a form?

  a. Record Source

  b. Row Source

  c. Default View

  d. List Items Edit Form

18. Which is a popular layout for a main form?

  a. Datasheet

  b. Global

  c. Justified

  d. Columnar

19. Which is a popular layout for a subform?

  a. Justified

  b. Columnar

  c. Global

  d. Datasheet

20. To align controls on their left edges, first:

  a. Click the Layout tab on the Ribbon.

  b. Click the Design tab on the Ribbon.

  c. Select the controls whose edges you want to align.

  d. Align the data within the controls.

21. Which control is most commonly used within an option group?

  a. Check box

  b. Command button

  c. Option button

  d. Toggle button

Skills Review

1. Use Form Design View.

  a. Start Access and open the Service-7.accdb database from the location where you store your Data Files. Enable content if prompted.

  b. Create a new form in Form Design View, open the Property Sheet for the new form, then choose the Members table as the Record Source.

  c. Open the Field List, then add all fields from the Members table to Form Design View to the upper-left corner of the form.

  d. Move the Birthday, Dues, MemberNo, and CharterMember controls to the right of the FirstName, LastName, Street, and Zip fields.

  e. Save the form with the name **MemberHours**.

2. Add subforms.

  a. In Form Design View of the MemberHours form, use the SubForm Wizard to create a subform below the Zip label.

  b. Use all three fields in the Activities table for the subform. Show Activities for each record in Members using MemberNo, and name the subform **ActivityHours**.

  c. Drag the bottom edge of the form up to just below the subform control.

  d. View the MemberHours form in Form View, and move through several records. Note that the form could be improved with better alignment and that the Street text box is too narrow to display the entire value in the field.

Skills Review (continued)

3. Align control edges.

a. Switch to Form Design View, then edit the FirstName, LastName, MemberNo, and CharterMember labels in the main form to read **First Name**, **Last Name**, **Member No**, and **Charter Member**.

b. Select the four labels in the first column (First Name, Last Name, Street, and Zip) together, and align their right edges.

c. Move the Charter Member label to the left of the check box, below the Member No label. (*Hint*: Point to the upper-left corner of the Charter Member label to move the label without moving its associated check box.)

d. Select the four labels in the third column (Birthday, Dues, Member No, and Charter Member) together, and align their right edges.

e. Select the First Name label, the FirstName text box, the Birthday label, and the Birthday text box together. Align their top edges.

f. Select the Last Name label, the LastName text box, the Dues label, and the Dues text box together. Align their top edges.

g. Select the Street label, the Street text box, the Member No label, and the MemberNo text box together. Align their top edges.

h. Select the Zip label, the Zip text box, the Charter Member label, and the CharterMember check box together. Align their top edges.

i. Select the FirstName text box, the LastName text box, the Street text box, and the Zip text box together. Align their left edges and resize them to be wider and closer to the corresponding labels in the first column.

j. Align the left edges of the Birthday, Dues, and MemberNo text box controls.

k. Resize the Street text box to be about twice as wide as its current width.

l. Save the MemberHours form.

4. Add a combo box for data entry.

a. In Form Design View, right-click the Zip text box, then change it to a combo box control.

b. In the Property Sheet of the new combo box, click the Row Source property, then click the Build button.

c. Select only the Zips table for the query, then double-click the Zip, City, and State fields to add them to the query grid.

d. Close the Query Builder window, and save the changes.

e. On the Format tab of the Property Sheet for the Zip combo box, change the Column Count property to **3**, the Column Widths property to **0.5;2;0.5**, the List Width property to **3**, and the List Rows property from 16 to **50**.

f. Close the Property Sheet, then save and view the MemberHours form in Form View.

g. In the first record for Rhea Alman, change the Zip to **66205** using the new combo box.

5. Add a combo box to find records.

a. Display the MemberHours form in Design View.

b. Open the Form Header section by clicking the Title button in the Header/Footer section on the Design tab.

c. Modify the label to read **Member Activity Hours**, then narrow the width of the label to be only as wide as needed.

d. Add a combo box to the right side of the Form Header, and choose the "Find a record on my form..." option in the Combo Box Wizard.

e. Choose the MemberNo, LastName, and FirstName fields in that order.

f. Hide the key column.

g. Label the combo box **FIND MEMBER:**.

h. Move and widen the new combo box to be at least 2" wide, change the FIND MEMBER: label text color to black so it is easier to read, save the MemberHours form, then view it in Form View.

i. Use the FIND MEMBER combo box to find the Aaron Love record. Notice that the entries in the combo box are not alphabetized by last name.

j. Return to Form Design View, and use the Row Source property and Build button for the FIND MEMBER combo box to open the Query Builder. Add an ascending sort order to the LastName and FirstName fields.

Skills Review (continued)

k. Close the Query Builder, saving changes. View the MemberHours form in Form View, and find the record for Holly Cabriella. Note that the entries in the combo box list are now sorted in ascending order first by the LastName field, then by the FirstName field.

6. Add command buttons.

a. Display the MemberHours form in Design View.

b. Use the Command Button Wizard to add a command button to the middle of the Form Footer section.

c. Choose the Print Record action from the Record Operations category.

d. Choose the Text option button, type **Print Current Record**, then use **PrintButton** for the meaningful name for the button.

e. Use the Command Button Wizard to add a command button to the right of the other command button in the Form Footer section.

f. Choose the Close Form action from the Form Operations category.

g. Choose the Text option button, type **Close**, then use **CloseButton** for the meaningful name for the button.

h. Select both command buttons then align their top edges.

i. Save the form, display it in Form View, navigate through the first few records, then close the MemberHours form using the new Close command button.

7. Add option groups.

a. Open the MemberHours form in Form Design View.

b. Because the dues are always $25 or $50, the Dues field is a good candidate for an option group control. Delete the existing Dues text box and label.

c. Click the Option Group button in the Controls group on the Design tab, then click the form just to the right of the Birthday text box.

d. Type **$25** and **$50** for Label Names, do not choose a default value, and enter **25** and **50** for corresponding Values.

e. Store the value in the Dues field, use option buttons, use the Flat style, and caption the option group **Dues:**.

f. Save the MemberHours form, and view it in Form View. Move and align the other form controls as needed to match FIGURE 7-18.

g. Use the FIND MEMBER: combo box to find the record for Derek Camel, change his first and last names to your name, then change the Dues to $25 using the new option group. Print this record if requested by your instructor.

h. Use the Close command button to close and save the MemberHours form.

FIGURE 7-18

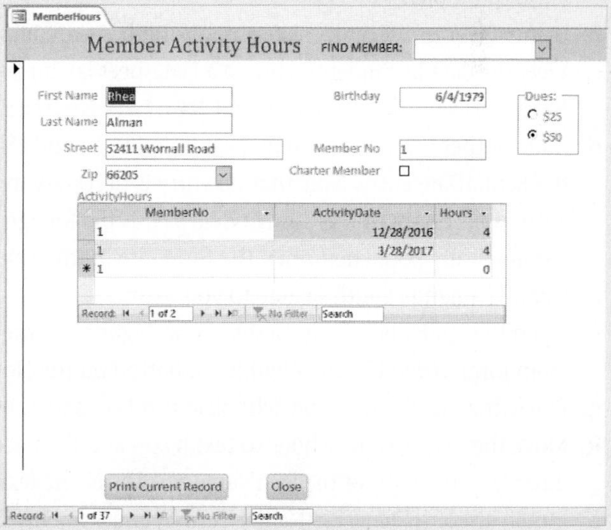

8. Add tab controls.

a. Create a new blank form, and add a tab control to it.

b. Open the Property Sheet, then use the Name property to rename Page1 to **Members** and Page2 to **Activities**. (*Hint*: Be sure to select the tab for the page and not the entire tab control.)

c. Right-click the Activities tab, click Insert Page, and use the Name property to rename the third page to **Dues**.

d. Save the form with the name **Navigation**.

Skills Review (continued)

e. On the Members page, add a command button with the Preview Report action from the Report Operations category. Choose the MemberRoster report, choose Text on the button, type **Preview Member Roster Report** as the text, and name the button **MemberRosterReportButton**.

f. On the Activities page, add a command button with the Open Form action from the Form Operations category. Choose the MemberHours form, choose to open the form and show all the records, choose Text on the button, type **Open Member Hours Form** as the text, and name the button **MemberHoursFormButton**.

g. On the Activities page, add a second command button below the first with the Preview Report action from the Report Operations category. Choose the ActivityListing report, choose Text on the button, type **Preview Activity Listing Report** as the text, and name the button **ActivityListingReportButton**.

h. Widen the command buttons on the Activities page as needed so that all of the text on the command buttons is clearly visible and the buttons are the same size. Also align the buttons as shown in FIGURE 7-19.

i. On the Dues page, add a command button with the Preview Report action from the Report Operations category. Choose the DuesByState report, choose Text on the button, type **Preview Dues by State Report** as the text, and name the button **DuesByStateReportButton**.

j. Save the Navigation form, then view it in Form View.

k. Test each button on each tab of the Navigation form to make sure it works as intended.

l. Close all open objects, then close the Service-7.accdb database.

FIGURE 7-19

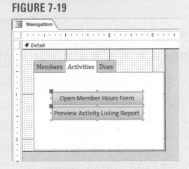

Independent Challenge 1

As the manager of a music store's instrument rental program, you have created a database to track instrument rentals to students. You want to build a form for fast, easy data entry.

a. Start Access, then open the database Music-7.accdb from the location where you store your Data Files. Enable content if prompted.

b. Using the Form Wizard, create a new form based on all of the fields in the Students and Rentals tables.

c. View the data by Students, choose a Datasheet layout for the subform, then accept the default form titles of **Students** for the main form and **Rentals Subform** for the subform.

d. Add another record to the rental subform for Amanda Smith by typing **7711** as the SerialNo entry and **8/2/17** as the RentalDate entry. Note that no entry is necessary in the RentalNo field because it is an AutoNumber field. No entry is necessary in the CustNo field as it is the foreign key field that connects the main form to the subform and is automatically populated when the forms are in this arrangement.

e. Change Amanda Smith's name to your name.

f. Open the Students form in Design View. Right-align the text within each label control in the first column of the main form. (*Hint*: Use the Align Right button on the Home tab.)

g. Resize the Zip, CustNo, and SchoolNo text boxes to as wide as the State text box.

h. Move the CustNo and SchoolNo text boxes and their accompanying labels to the upper-right portion of the form, directly to the right of the FirstName and LastName text boxes.

i. Modify the FirstName, LastName, CustNo, and SchoolNo labels to read First Name, Last Name, Cust No, and School No.

j. Delete the RentalNo and CustNo fields from the subform.

k. Open the Field List, and drag the Description field from the Instruments table to the subform above the existing text boxes. (*Hint*: Show all tables, then look in the Fields available in related tables section of the Field List.)

Independent Challenge 1 (continued)

l. Shorten and move the subform up, and continue moving and resizing fields as needed so that your form in Form View looks similar to **FIGURE 7-20**.

m. Save and close the Students form, close the Music-7.accdb database, then exit Access.

FIGURE 7-20

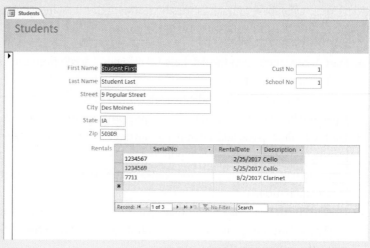

Independent Challenge 2

As the manager of a community effort to provide better access to residential real estate listings for a lake community, you have developed a database to track listings by realtor and real estate agency. You want to develop a form/subform system to see all listings within each realtor as well as within each real estate agency.

a. Start Access, then open the database LakeHomes-7.accdb from the location where you store your Data Files. Enable content if prompted.

b. Using the Form Wizard, create a new form based on all of the fields in the Agencies, Realtors, and Listings tables.

c. View the data by Agencies, choose a Datasheet layout for each of the subforms, and accept the default titles of **Agencies**, **Realtors Subform**, and **Listings Subform**.

d. In Form Design View, use the Combo Box Wizard to add a combo box to the Form Header to find a record. Choose the AgencyName field, hide the key column, widen the AgencyName column to see the entries clearly, and enter the label **FIND AGENCY:**.

e. Change the text color of the FIND AGENCY: label to black, and widen the combo box to about twice its current size.

f. Add a command button to a blank spot on the main form to print the current record. Use the Print Record action from the Record Operations category. Use a picture on the button, and give the button the meaningful name of **PrintButton**.

g. Use your skills to modify, move, resize, align text, and align control edges, as shown in **FIGURE 7-21**. Note that several labels have been modified, and many controls have been moved, resized, and aligned. Note that the subforms have also been resized and moved and that the ListingNo and RealtorNo fields in the Listings subform have been hidden. (*Hint*: To hide a field, right-click the fieldname in Form View and then click Hide Fields.)

h. Save the form, view it in Form View, then use the combo box to find Sunset Cove Realtors.

i. Resize the columns of the subforms to view as much data as possible, as shown in **FIGURE 7-21**, change Trixie Angelina's name in the Realtors subform to your name, then if requested by your instructor, print only the current record using the new command button.

j. Save and close the Agencies form, close the LakeHomes-7.accdb database, and exit Access.

FIGURE 7-21

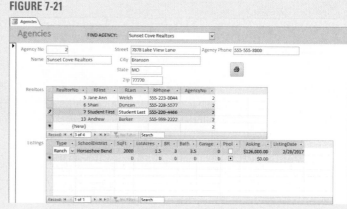

Independent Challenge 3

As the manager of a community effort to provide better access to residential real estate listings for a lake community, you have developed a database to track listings by realtor and real estate agency. You want to develop a navigation form to help find queries and reports in your database much faster.

a. Start Access, then open the database LakeHomes-7.accdb from the location where you store your Data Files. Enable content if prompted.

b. Create a new blank form, and add a tab control to it.

c. Open the Property Sheet and use the Name property to rename Page1 to **Realtors** and Page2 to **Listings**.

d. On the Realtors page, add a command button with the Preview Report action from the Report Operations category. Choose the RealtorsByAgency report, choose Text on the button, type **Preview Realtors by Agency** as the text, and name the button **cmdRealtors**. (Note that cmd is the three-character prefix sometimes used to name command buttons.)

e. On the Listings page, add a command button with the Run Query action from the Miscellaneous category. Choose the SchoolDistricts query, choose Text on the button, type **Open School Districts Query** as the text, and name the button **cmdSchools**.

f. On the Listings page, add a second command button with the Preview Report action from the Report Operations category. Choose the ListingsByType report, choose Text on the button, type **Preview Listing Report** as the text, and name the button **cmdListingReport**.

g. Save the form with the name **Lake Homes Navigation System**, then view it in Form View. The new form with the Listings tab selected should look like FIGURE 7-22.

h. Test each command button on both the Realtors and Listings pages.

i. Close all open objects, then close the LakeHomes-7.accdb database and exit Access.

FIGURE 7-22

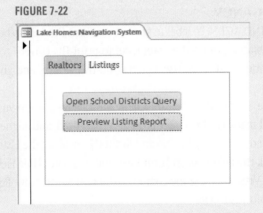

Independent Challenge 4: Explore

You have created an Access database to help manage college scholarship opportunities. You can keep the database updated more efficiently by creating some easy-to-use forms.

a. Start Access and open the Scholarships-7.accdb database from the location where you store your Data Files. Enable content if prompted.

b. Create a split form for the Scholarships table. Save and name the form **ScholarshipEntry**.

c. In Form Design View, narrow the label in the Form Header section to about half of its current size, then use the Combo Box Wizard to add a combo box to the Form Header section to find a scholarship based on the ScholarshipName field. Hide the key column, and use the label **FIND SCHOLARSHIP:**.

d. In Form Design View, widen the combo box as necessary so that all of the scholarship names in the list are clearly visible in Form View. Change the color of the FIND SCHOLARSHIP: text to black, and move and resize the label and combo box as necessary to clearly view them. Switch between Form View and Form Design View to test the new combo box control.

e. In Form Design View, change the combo box's List Rows property (on the Format tab) to **50** and use the Build button to modify the Row Source property to add an ascending sort order based on the ScholarshipName field. (*Hint*: The ID field needs to remain in the query, but it is hidden in the combo box as evidenced by the value in the Column Widths property of the combo box.)

f. Save the form, and in Form View, use the combo box to find the Papa Johns Scholarship. Change Papa Johns to your name as shown in **FIGURE 7-23**, then, if requested by your instructor, print only that record by using the Selected Record(s) option on the Print dialog box.

g. Save and close the ScholarshipEntry form, close the Scholarships-7.accdb database, then exit Access.

FIGURE 7-23

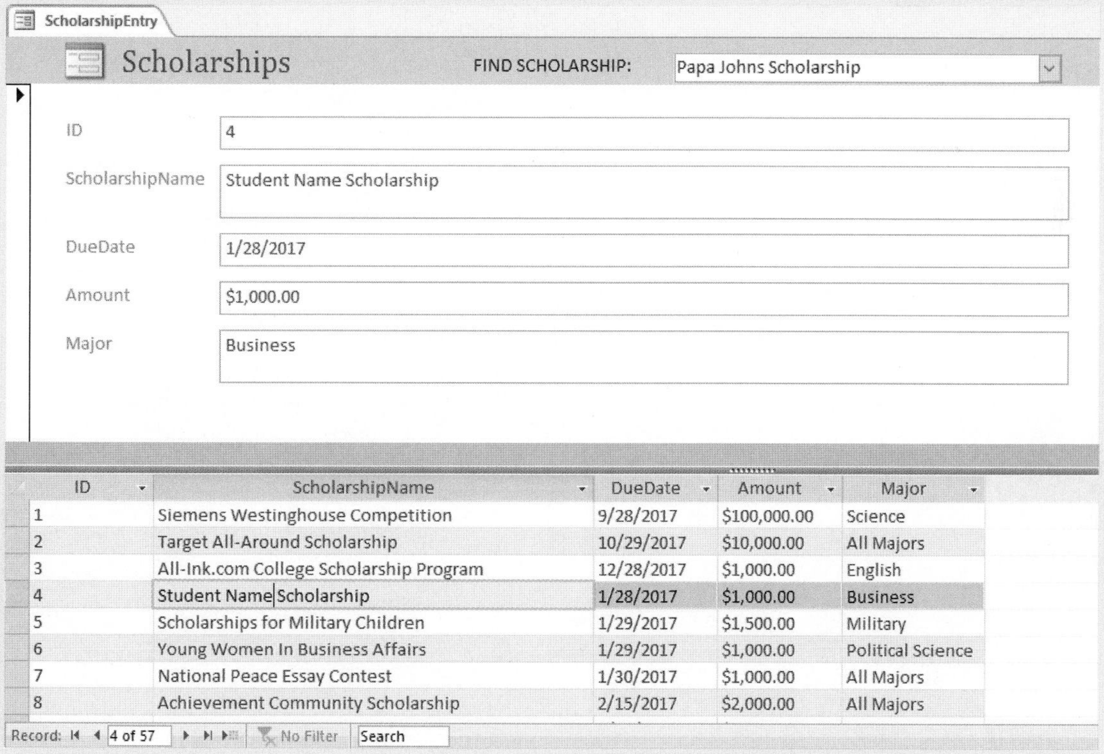

Visual Workshop

Open the Baseball-7.accdb database from the location where you store your Data Files. Enable content if prompted. Use Form Design View to create a form based on the Players table named **PlayersEntry**. Use your skills to modify, move, resize, align text, and align control edges as shown in FIGURE 7-24. Note that both the PlayerPosition as well as the TeamNo fields are presented as option groups. The values that correspond with each Position label can be found in the Field Description of the PlayerPosition field in Table Design View of the Players table. The Position option group is tied to the PlayerPosition field. The values that correspond with each Team label can be found by reviewing the TeamNo and TeamName fields of the Teams table. The Team option group is tied to the TeamNo field. Do not choose default values for either option group. Change Hank Aaron's name to your name, change the Position value to Pitcher, and change the Team to Dexter Cardinals. If requested by your instructor, print only that record.

FIGURE 7-24

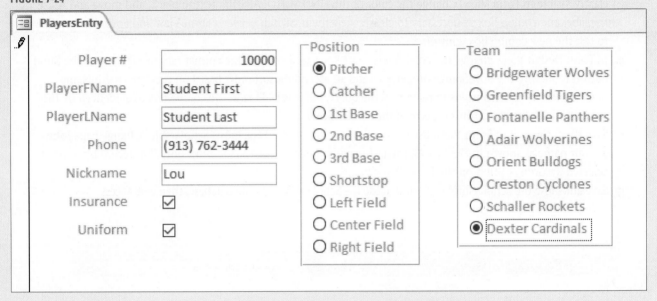

Analyzing Data with Reports

CASE ▶ Julia Rice asks you to create and enhance reports to analyze, clarify, and format important information at Reason 2 Go.

Module Objectives

After completing this module, you will be able to:

- Use Report Design View
- Create parameter reports
- Apply conditional formatting
- Add lines

- Use the Format Painter and themes
- Add subreports
- Modify section properties
- Create summary reports

Files You Will Need

R2G-8.accdb
LakeHomes-8.accdb
Music-8.accdb

Scholarships-8.accdb
Baseball-8.accdb

Use Report Design View

Learning Outcomes
• Modify report properties
• Modify group and sort orders

Although you can print data in forms and datasheets, **reports** give you more control over how data is printed and greater flexibility in presenting summary information. To create a report, you include text boxes to display data and use calculations and labels, lines, and graphics to clarify the data. **Report Design View** allows you to work with a complete range of report, section, and control properties. Because Report Design View gives you full control of all aspects of a report, it is well worth your time to master. **CASE** ▶ *Julia Rice asks you to build a report that shows all trips grouped by category and sorted in descending order by price. You use Report Design View to build this report.*

STEPS

1. **Start Access, open the R2G-8.accdb database from the location where you store your Data Files, enable content if prompted, click the Create tab, then click the Report Design button in the Reports group**

   The first step to building a report in Report Design View is identifying the record source.

2. **If the Property Sheet is not open, click the Property Sheet button in the Tools group, click the Data tab in the Property Sheet, click the Record Source list arrow, then click Trips**

   The Record Source can be an existing table, query, or SQL SELECT statement. The **Record Source** identifies the fields and records that the report can display. To build a report that shows trips grouped by category, you'll need to add a Category Header section. See TABLE 8-1 for a review of report sections.

3. **Use the ╬ pointer to drag the top edge of the Page Footer section up to about the 1″ mark on the vertical ruler, then click the Group & Sort button in the Grouping & Totals group to open the Group, Sort, and Total pane if it is not already open**

   Use the Group, Sort, and Total pane to specify grouping and sorting fields and open group headers and footers.

4. **Click the Add a group button in the Group, Sort, and Total pane; click Category; click the Add a sort button in the Group, Sort, and Total pane; click Price; click the from smallest to largest button arrow; then click from largest to smallest, as shown in FIGURE 8-1**

   With the grouping and sorting fields specified, you're ready to add controls to the report.

5. **Click the Add Existing Fields button in the Tools group, click TripNo in the Field List, press and hold [Shift] as you click Price in the Field List to select all fields in the Trips table, drag the selected fields to the Detail section of the report, then close the Field List window**

   Next, you move the Category controls to the Category Header section.

6. **Click the report to remove the current selection, right-click the Category combo box, click Cut on the shortcut menu, right-click the Category Header section, then click Paste on the shortcut menu**

   If the data on a report is self-explanatory, it doesn't need descriptive labels. Delete the labels, and position the text boxes across the page to finalize the report.

7. **Click each label and press [Delete] to delete the Category label as well as each label in the first column of the Detail section, then move and resize the remaining text boxes and shorten the Detail section, as shown in FIGURE 8-2**

8. **Click the Save button 🖫 on the Quick Access Toolbar, type TripsByCategory as the new report name, click OK, preview the first page of the report, as shown in FIGURE 8-3, then close the report**

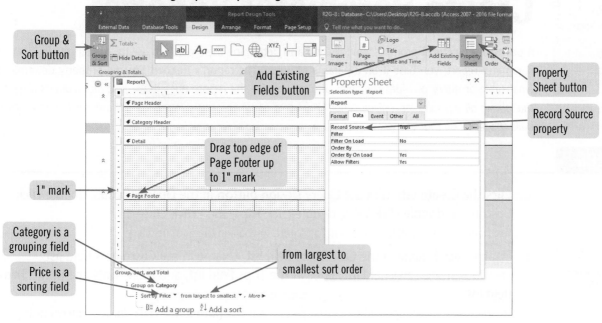

FIGURE 8-1: Creating a report in Report Design View

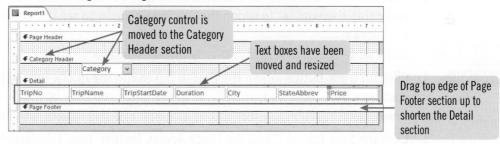

FIGURE 8-2: Moving and resizing the text box controls in the Detail section

FIGURE 8-3: Previewing the TripsByCategory report

TABLE 8-1: Review of report sections

section	where does this section print?	what is this section most commonly used for?
Report Header	At the top of the first page of the report	To print a title or logo
Page Header	At the top of every page (but below the Report Header on page 1)	To print titles, dates, or page numbers
Group Header	Before every group of records	To display the grouping field value
Detail	Once for every record	To display data for every record
Group Footer	After every group of records	To calculate summary statistics on groups of records
Page Footer	At the bottom of every page	To print dates or page numbers

Create Parameter Reports

Learning Outcomes
- Enter parameter criteria
- Create a parameter report

A **parameter report** prompts you for criteria to determine the records to use for the report. To create a parameter report, you base it on a parameter query. The report's **Record Source** property determines what table or query provides the fields and records for the report. **CASE** ▸ *Julia Rice requests a report that shows all trip sales for a given period. You use a parameter query to prompt the user for the dates, then build the report on that query.*

STEPS

1. **Click the Create tab, click the Query Design button in the Queries group, double-click Customers, double-click Sales, double-click Trips, then click Close**

   You want fields from all three tables in the report, so you add them to the query.

   TROUBLE
   Resize the Trips field list to see all fields, or scroll down to find the Price field.

2. **Double-click FName in the Customers field list, LName in the Customers field list, SaleDate in the Sales field list, Price in the Trips field list, and then TripName in the Trips field list**

   To select only those trips sold in a given period, you add **parameter criteria**, text entered in [square brackets] that prompts the user for an entry each time the query is run, to the SaleDate field.

3. **Click the Criteria cell for the SaleDate field, type Between [Enter start date] and [Enter end date], then use ↔ to widen the SaleDate column to see the entire entry, as shown in** FIGURE 8-4

   To test the query, run it and enter dates in the parameter prompts.

   QUICK TIP
   You can also click the Run button to run a Select query, which displays it in Datasheet View.

4. **Click the View button 🖳 on the Design tab to run the query, type 6/1/17 in the Enter start date box, click OK, type 6/30/17 in the Enter end date box, then click OK**

   Fifteen records are displayed in the datasheet, each with a SaleDate value in June 2017.

5. **Click the Save button 🖫 on the Quick Access Toolbar, type SalesDateParam as the new query name, click OK, then close the SalesDateParam query**

   You use the Report button on the Create tab to quickly build a report on the SalesDateParam query.

6. **Click the SalesDateParam query in the Navigation Pane, click the Create tab, click the Report button in the Reports group, type 6/1/17 in the Enter start date box, click OK, type 6/30/17 in the Enter end date box, then click OK**

   The report is displayed in Layout View with records in June 2017. You decide to preview and save the report.

   QUICK TIP
   The Page buttons in the navigation bar are dim if the report contains only one page.

7. **Work in Layout View to narrow the controls (including the page number control) so that they fit within the margins of a single page, use Design View to drag the right edge of the report to the left, save the report with the name SalesDateParameter, then preview it as shown in** FIGURE 8-5, **entering 6/1/17 as the start date and 6/30/17 as the end date**

FIGURE 8-4: Entering parameter criteria in a query

FIGURE 8-4: Entering parameter criteria in a query

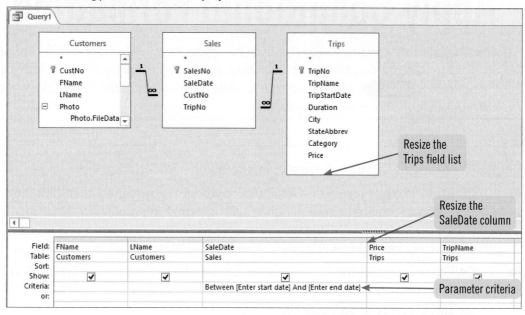

FIGURE 8-5: Previewing the SalesDateParameter report

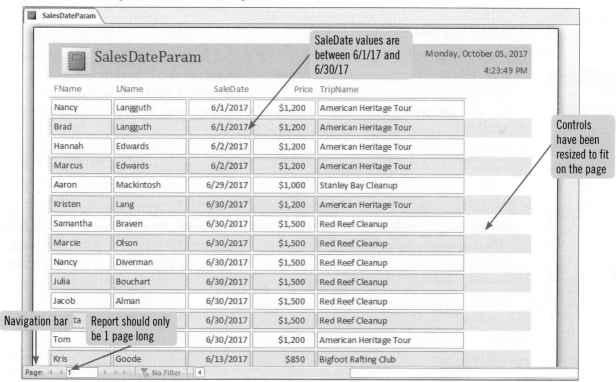

Parameter criteria

In Query Design View, you must enter parameter criteria within [square brackets]. Each parameter criterion you enter appears as a prompt in an Enter Parameter Value dialog box. The entry you make in the Enter Parameter Value box is used as the criterion for the field that contains the parameter criteria.

Access 2016

Apply Conditional Formatting

Conditional formatting allows you to change the appearance of a control on a form or report based on criteria you specify. Conditional formatting helps you highlight important or exceptional data on a form or report. **CASE** *Julia Rice asks you to apply conditional formatting to the SalesDateParameter report to emphasize different trip Price levels.*

STEPS

1. **Right-click the** SalesDateParameter report tab, **then click** Design View

TROUBLE

Be sure the Price text box (not Price label) is selected.

2. **Click the** Price text box **in the Detail section, click the** Format tab, **then click the** Conditional Formatting button **in the Control Formatting group**

   The Conditional Formatting Rules Manager dialog box opens, asking you to define the conditional formatting rules. You want to format Price values between 500 and 1000 with a yellow background color.

QUICK TIP

Between...and criteria include both values in the range.

3. **Click** New Rule, **click the** text box to the right of the between arrow, **type** 500, **click the** and box, **type** 1000, **click the** Background color button arrow ⬛▾, **click the** Yellow box **on the bottom row, then click** OK

   You add the second conditional formatting rule to format Price values greater than 1000 with a light green background color.

4. **Click** New Rule, **click the** between list arrow, **click** greater than, **click the** value box, **type** 1000, **click the** Background color button arrow ⬛▾, **click the** Light Green box **on the bottom row, then click** OK

   The Conditional Formatting Rules Manager dialog box with two rules should look like **FIGURE 8-6**.

QUICK TIP

The text box in the Report Footer section was automatically added when you used the Report button to create the report.

5. **Click** OK **in the Conditional Formatting Rules Manager dialog box, right-click the** SalesDateParameter report tab, **click** Print Preview, **type** 7/12/17 **in the Enter start date box, click** OK, **type** 7/13/17 **in the Enter end date box, then click** OK

   Conditional formatting rules applied a light green background color to the Price text box for two sales because the Price value is greater than 1000. Conditional formatting applied a yellow background color to the Price text box for seven sales because the Price value is between 500 and 1000.

   The text box in the Report Footer needs to be taller to display the information clearly.

6. **Right-click the** report tab, **click** Design View, **use the** ↕ **pointer to increase the height of the text box in the Report Footer section to clearly display the expression, right-click the** SalesDateParameter report tab, **click** Print Preview, **type** 7/12/17 **in the Enter start date box, click** OK, **type** 7/13/17 **in the Enter end date box, click** OK, **then click the report to zoom in as shown in** FIGURE 8-7

7. **Save, then close the** SalesDateParameter report

FIGURE 8-6: Conditional Formatting Rules Manager dialog box

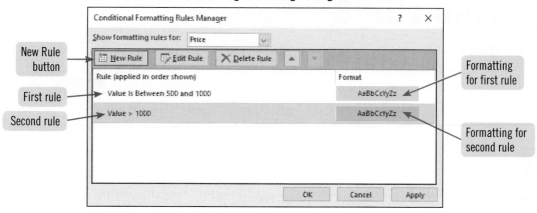

New Rule button → New Rule

First rule → Value is Between 500 and 1000

Second rule → Value > 1000

Formatting for first rule → AaBbCcYyZz

Formatting for second rule → AaBbCcYyZz

FIGURE 8-7: Conditional formatting applied to SalesDateParameter report

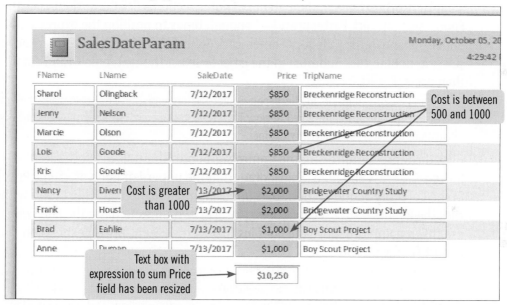

Cost is between 500 and 1000

Cost is greater than 1000

Text box with expression to sum Price field has been resized → $10,250

Conditional formatting using data bars

A feature of Access allows you to compare the values of one column to another with small data bars. To use this feature, use the "Compare to other records" rule type option in the New Formatting Rule dialog box, as shown in **FIGURE 8-8**.

FIGURE 8-8: Conditional formatting with data bars

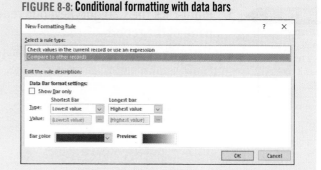

Add Lines

Learning Outcomes
- Add grand totals to a report
- Add lines to a report

Lines are often added to a report to highlight information or enhance its clarity. For example, you might want to separate the Report Header and Page Header information from the rest of the report with a horizontal line. You can also use short lines to indicate subtotals and grand totals. **CASE** *Julia Rice likes the data on the CategoryRevenue report, which has already been created in the R2G-8 database, but she asks you to enhance the report by adding a grand total calculation and separating the categories more clearly. Lines will help clarify the information.*

STEPS

QUICK TIP
Recall that Report View does not show page margins or individual pages of the report.

1. **Double-click the CategoryRevenue report in the Navigation Pane to open it in Report View, then scroll to the end of the report**

   The report could be improved if lines were added to separate the trip categories and to indicate subtotals. You also want to add a grand total calculation on the last page of the report. You use Report Design View to make these improvements and start by adding the grand total calculation to the Report Footer section.

2. **Right-click the CategoryRevenue report tab, click Design View, right-click the =Sum([Price]) text box in the Category Footer section, click Copy, right-click the Report Footer section, click Paste, press [→] enough times to position the expression directly under the one in the Category Footer, click Subtotal: in the Report Footer section to select it, double-click Subtotal: in the label to select the text, type Grand Total, then press [Enter]**

   The =Sum([Price]) expression in the Report Footer section sums the Price values for the entire report, whereas the same expression in the Category Footer section sums Price values for each category. With the calculations in place, you add clarifying lines.

TROUBLE
Lines can be difficult to find in Report Design View. See the "Line troubles" box in this lesson for tips on working with lines.

3. **Click the More button ⯆ in the Controls group to show all controls, click the Line button ╲, press and hold [Shift], drag from the upper-left edge of =Sum([Price]) in the Category Footer section to its upper-right edge, press [Ctrl][C] to copy the line, click the Report Footer section, press [Ctrl][V] two times to paste the line twice, then use the ⬧ pointer to move the lines just below the =Sum([Price]) expression in the Report Footer section**

   Pressing [Shift] while drawing a line makes sure that the line remains perfectly horizontal or vertical. The single line above the calculation in the Category Footer section indicates that the calculation is a subtotal. Double lines below the calculation in the Report Footer section indicate that it is a grand total. You also want to add a line to visually separate the categories.

QUICK TIP
Use the Rectangle button ▭ to insert a rectangle control on a form or report.

4. **Click the More button ⯆ in the Controls group to show all controls, click the Line button ╲, press and hold [Shift], then drag along the bottom of the Category Footer section**

   The final CategoryRevenue report in Report Design View is shown in **FIGURE 8-9**.

QUICK TIP
As a final report creation step, print preview a report to make sure it fits on the paper.

5. **Right-click the CategoryRevenue report tab, click Print Preview, then navigate to the last page of the report**

   The last page of the CategoryRevenue report shown in **FIGURE 8-10** displays the Category Footer section line as well as the subtotal and grand total lines.

FIGURE 8-9: Adding lines to a report

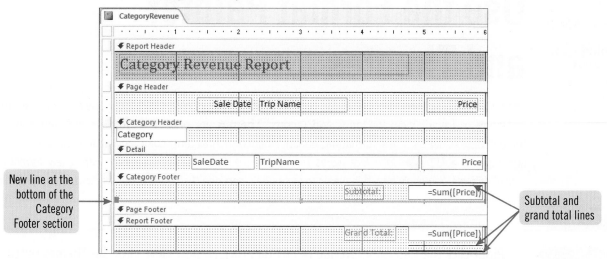

New line at the bottom of the Category Footer section

Subtotal and grand total lines

FIGURE 8-10: Previewing the last page of the CategoryRevenue report

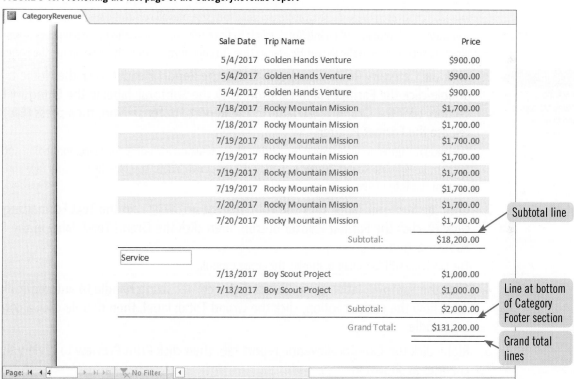

Subtotal line

Line at bottom of Category Footer section

Grand total lines

Line troubles

Sometimes lines are difficult to find in Report Design View because they are placed against the edge of a section or the edge of other controls. To find lines that are positioned next to the edge of a section, drag the section bar to expand the section and expose the line. Recall that to draw a perfectly horizontal line, you hold [Shift] while creating or resizing the line. It is easy to accidentally widen a line beyond the report margins, thus creating extra unwanted pages in your printout. To fix this problem, narrow any controls that extend beyond the margins of the printout, and drag the right edge of the report to the left. Note that the default left and right margins for an 8.5 x 11-inch sheet of paper are often 0.25 inches each, so a report in portrait orientation must be no wider than 8 inches, and a report in landscape orientation must be no wider than 10.5 inches.

Use the Format Painter and Themes

The **Format Painter** is a tool you use to copy multiple formatting properties from one control to another in Design or Layout View for forms and reports. **Themes** are predefined formats that you apply to the database to set all of the formatting enhancements, such as font, color, and alignment, on all forms and reports. **CASE** *Julia Rice wants to improve the CategoryRevenue report with a few formatting embellishments. You apply a built-in theme to the entire report and then use the Format Painter to quickly copy and paste formatting characteristics from one label to another.*

STEPS

1. **Right-click the CategoryRevenue report tab, click Design View, click the Themes button, point to several themes to observe the changes in the report, then click Ion, as shown in** FIGURE 8-11

   The Ion theme gives the Report Header section a light turquoise background. All text now has a consistent font face, controls in the same section are the same font size, and all controls have complementary font colors. You want the Subtotal: and Grand Total: labels to have the same formatting characteristics as the Category Revenue Report label in the Report Header section. To copy formats quickly, you will use the Format Painter.

2. **Click the Category Revenue Report label in the Report Header, click the Home tab, double-click the Format Painter button, click the Subtotal: label in the Category Footer section, click the Grand Total: label in the Report Footer section, then press [Esc] to release the Format Painter**

   The Format Painter applied several formatting characteristics, including font face, font color, and font size from the label in the Report Header section to the other two labels. You like the new font face and color, but the font size is too large.

3. **Click the Subtotal: label, click the Font Size list arrow** 18 ⁻ **in the Text Formatting group, click 12, click the Format Painter button, then click the Grand Total: label in the Report Footer section**

   The labels are still too small to display the entire caption.

4. **Click the Subtotal: label, then double-click a corner sizing handle to automatically resize it to show the entire caption, click the Grand Total: label, then double-click a corner sizing handle**

5. **Right-click the CategoryRevenue report tab, then click Print Preview to review the changes as shown in** FIGURE 8-12

6. **Save and close the CategoryRevenue report**

Analyzing Data with Reports

FIGURE 8-11: Applying a theme to a report

Themes button →

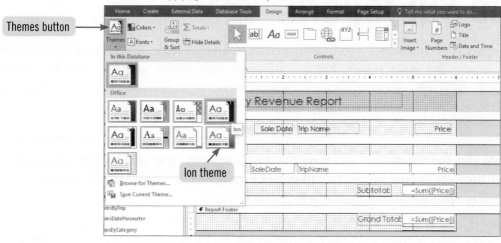

Ion theme

FIGURE 8-12: Ion theme applied to the CategoryRevenue report

Add Subreports

A **subreport** control displays a report within another report. The report that contains the subreport control is called the **main report**. You can use a subreport control when you want to connect two reports. **CASE** ▶ *You want the CategoryRevenue report to automatically print at the end of the TripsByCategory report. You use a subreport in the Report Footer section to accomplish this.*

STEPS

1. **Right-click the TripsByCategory report in the Navigation Pane, click Design View, right-click the Page Header section bar, then click Report Header/Footer on the shortcut menu to open the Report Header and Footer sections**

   With the Report Footer section open, you're ready to add the CategoryRevenue subreport.

   > **TROUBLE**
   > Be sure to put the subreport in the Report Footer section versus the Page Footer section.

2. **Click the More button ⤓ in the Controls group, click the Subform/Subreport button, then click the left edge of the Report Footer to start the SubReport Wizard, as shown in FIGURE 8-13**

   The SubReport Wizard asks what data you want to use for the subreport.

   > **TROUBLE**
   > You may need to scroll to find the None option in the list.

3. **Click the Use an existing report or form option button in the SubReport Wizard, click CategoryRevenue if it is not already selected, click Next, scroll and click None when asked how you want the reports to be linked, click Next, then click Finish to accept the default name**

   The Report Footer section contains the CategoryRevenue report as a subreport. Therefore, the CategoryRevenue report will print after the TripsByCategory report prints. You don't need the label that accompanies the subreport, so you delete it.

   > **TROUBLE**
   > You may need to move the subreport control to see the CategoryRevenue label.

4. **Click the new CategoryRevenue label associated with the subreport, press [Delete], then drag the top part of the Report Footer bar up to close the Page Footer section**

   Report Design View should look similar to FIGURE 8-14. If the subreport pushes the right edge of the main report beyond the 8" mark on the ruler, you may see a green error indicator in the report selector button because the report width is greater than the page width. To narrow a report, drag the right edge of a report to the left. Preview your changes.

5. **Right-click the TripsByCategory report tab, click Print Preview, then navigate through the pages of the report**

   The TripsByCategory report fills the first two pages. The CategoryRevenue subreport starts at the top of page three. There should be no blank pages between the printed pages of the report.

6. **Save and close the TripsByCategory report**

FIGURE 8-13: SubReport Wizard dialog box

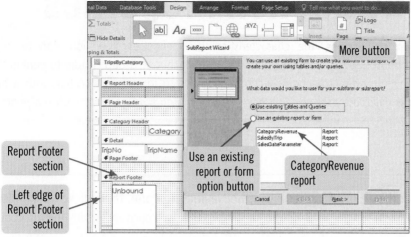

More button

Use an existing report or form option button

CategoryRevenue report

Report Footer section

Left edge of Report Footer section

FIGURE 8-14: Subreport in Report Design View

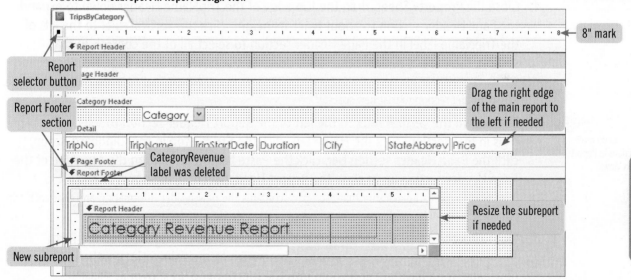

8" mark

Report selector button

Report Footer section

Drag the right edge of the main report to the left if needed

CategoryRevenue label was deleted

Resize the subreport if needed

New subreport

Modify Section Properties

Learning
Outcomes
• Modify section
properties
• Use rulers to select
controls in Report
Design View

Report **section properties**, the characteristics that define each section, can be modified to improve report printouts. For example, you might want each new Group Header to print at the top of a page. Or, you might want to modify section properties to format that section with a background color. **CASE** ► *Julia Rice asks you to modify the SalesByTrip report so that each trip prints at the top of a page.*

STEPS

1. **Right-click the SalesByTrip report in the Navigation Pane, then click Design View**
   To force each new trip to start printing at the top of a page, you open and modify the TripName Footer.

2. **Click the Group & Sort button to open the Group, Sort, and Total pane if it is not open; click the TripName More Options button in the Group, Sort, and Total pane; click the without a footer section list arrow; click with a footer section; then double-click the TripName Footer section bar to open its Property Sheet**
   You modify the **Force New Page** property of the TripName Footer section to force each trip name to start printing at the top of a new page.

QUICK TIP
You can double-click
a property in the
Property Sheet to
toggle through the
available options.

3. **Click the Format tab in the Property Sheet, click the Force New Page property list arrow, then click After Section, as shown in** FIGURE 8-15
   You also move the Report Header controls into the Page Header so they print at the top of every page. First, you need to create space in the upper half of the Page Header section to hold the controls.

4. **Close the Property Sheet, drag the top edge of the TripName Header down to expand the Page Header section to about twice its height, click the vertical ruler to the left of the TripName label in the Page Header section to select all of the controls in that section, then use ⬚↖ to move the labels down to the bottom of the Page Header section**
   With space available in the top half of the Page Header section, you cut and paste the controls from the Report Header section to that new space.

TROUBLE
You can undo multi-
ple actions in Report
Design View.

5. **Drag down the vertical ruler to the left of the Report Header section to select all controls in that section, click the Home tab, click the Cut button in the Clipboard group, click the Page Header section bar, click the Paste button, then drag the top edge of the Page Header section up to close the Report Header section, as shown in** FIGURE 8-16
   Preview the report to make sure that each page contains the new header information and that each trip prints at the top of its own page.

6. **Right-click the SalesByTrip report tab, click Print Preview, navigate back and forth through several pages to prove that each new TripName value prints at the top of a new page, then navigate and zoom into the fourth page, as shown in** FIGURE 8-17
   Each trip now starts printing at the top of a new page, and the former Report Header section controls now print at the top of each page too, because they were moved to the Page Header section.

7. **Save and close the SalesByTrip report**

FIGURE 8-15: Changing section properties

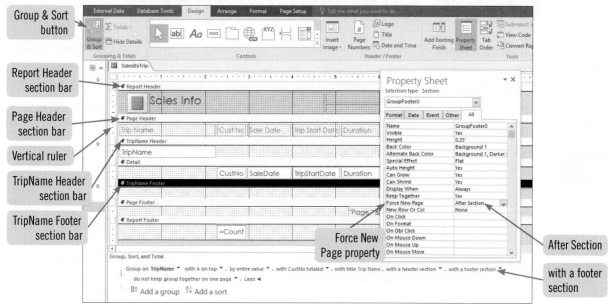

- Group & Sort button
- Report Header section bar
- Page Header section bar
- Vertical ruler
- TripName Header section bar
- TripName Footer section bar
- Force New Page property
- After Section
- with a footer section

FIGURE 8-16: Moving controls from the Report Header to the Page Header

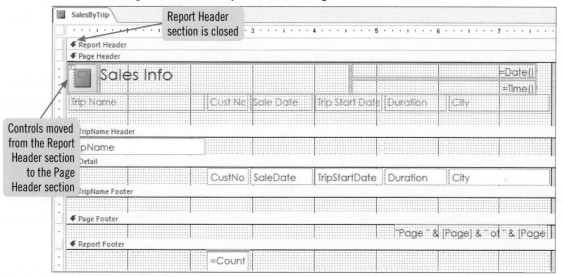

- Report Header section is closed
- Controls moved from the Report Header section to the Page Header section

FIGURE 8-17: Fourth page of SalesByTrip report

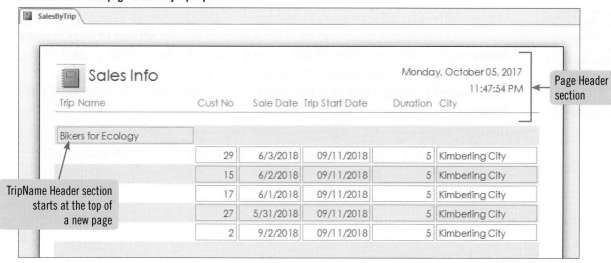

- Page Header section
- TripName Header section starts at the top of a new page

Create Summary Reports

Learning Outcomes
• Resize report sections
• Add calculations to Group Footer sections

Summary reports are reports that show statistics on groups of records rather than details for each record. You create summary reports by using Access functions such as Sum, Count, or Avg in expressions that calculate the desired statistic. These expressions are entered in text boxes most commonly placed in the Group Footer section. **CASE** ▶ *Julia Rice asks for a report to summarize the revenue for each trip category. You create a copy of the CategoryRevenue report and modify it to satisfy this request.*

STEPS

1. **Right-click the CategoryRevenue report in the Navigation Pane, click Copy on the shortcut menu, right-click below the report objects in the Navigation Pane, click Paste, type CategorySummary as the report name, then click OK**

   Summary reports may contain controls in the Group Header and Group Footer sections, but because they provide summary statistics instead of details, they do not contain controls in the Detail section. You delete the controls in the Detail section and close it.

2. **Right-click the CategorySummary report in the Navigation Pane, click Design View, click the vertical ruler to the left of the Detail section to select all controls in the Detail section, press [Delete], then drag the top of the Category Footer section bar up to close the Detail section**

   You can also delete the labels in the Page Header section.

3. **Click the vertical ruler to the left of the Page Header section to select all controls in the Page Header section, press [Delete], then drag the top of the Category Header section bar up to close the Page Header section**

   Because the Page Header and Page Footer sections do not contain any controls, those section bars can be toggled off to simplify Report Design View.

4. **Right-click the Report Header section bar, then click Page Header/Footer on the shortcut menu to remove the Page Header and Page Footer section bars from Report Design View**

   With the unneeded controls and sections removed, as shown in FIGURE 8-18, you preview the final summary report.

5. **Right-click the CategorySummary report tab, then click Print Preview**

   You could make this report look even better by moving the Category text box into the Category Footer section and deleting the Subtotal label and line.

QUICK TIP
Be sure to review all reports in Print Preview to make sure that the report is not too wide and that all labels, numbers, and dates are clearly visible.

6. **Right-click the CategorySummary report tab, click Design View, use the ⟨ᵏ⟩ pointer to drag the Category text box down from the Category Header section to the Category Footer section, click the Subtotal label in the Category Footer section, press [Delete], click the subtotal line just above the =Sum([Price]) text box in the Category Footer section, press [Delete], right-click the CategorySummary report tab, then click Print Preview**

   The summarized revenue for each category is shown in the one-page summary report in FIGURE 8-19.

7. **Save and close the CategorySummary report, then close R2G-8.accdb and exit Access**

FIGURE 8-18: Design View of the CategorySummary report

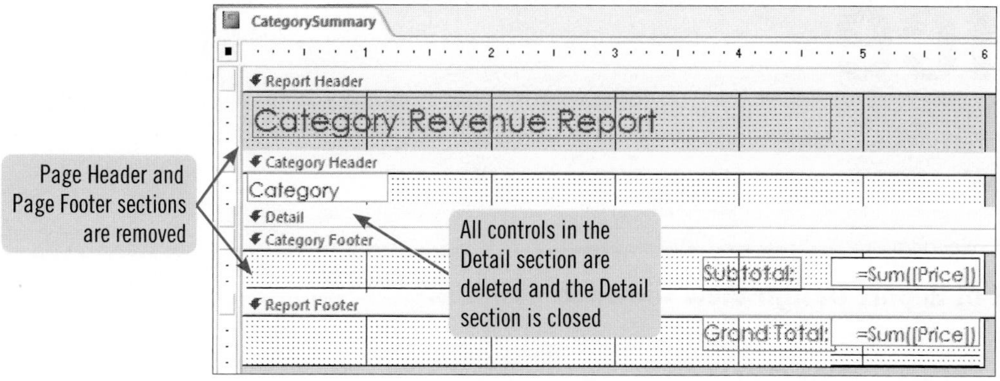
CategorySummary
Report Header
Category Revenue Report
Category Header
Category
Detail
Category Footer
Subtotal:
=Sum([Price])
Report Footer
Grand Total:
=Sum([Price])
Page Header and Page Footer sections are removed
All controls in the Detail section are deleted and the Detail section is closed

FIGURE 8-19: Preview of the CategorySummary report

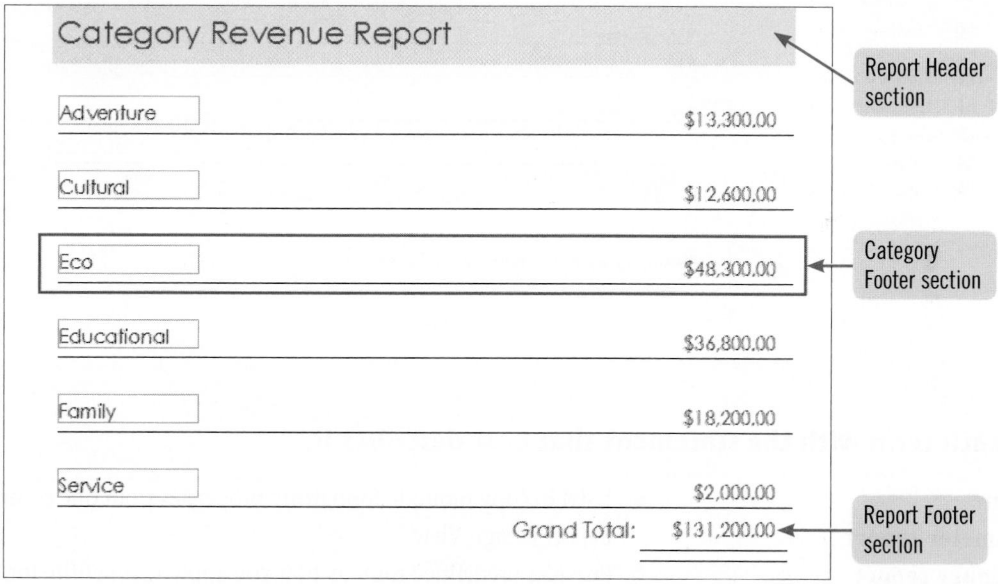
Category Revenue Report
Adventure
$13,300.00
Cultural
$12,600.00
Eco
$48,300.00
Educational
$36,800.00
Family
$18,200.00
Service
$2,000.00
Grand Total:
$131,200.00
Report Header section
Category Footer section
Report Footer section

Access 2016

Practice

Concepts Review

Identify each element of Report Design View shown in FIGURE 8-20.

FIGURE 8-20

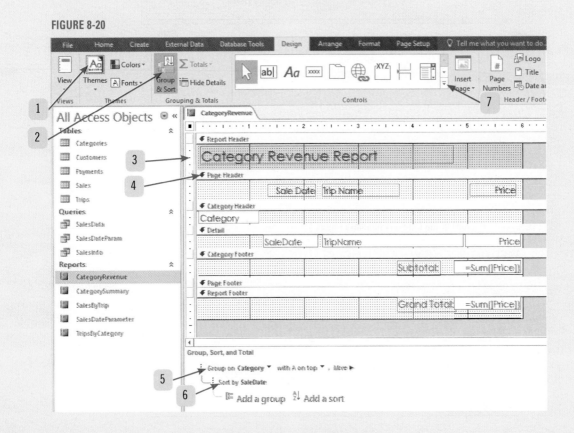

Match each term with the statement that best describes it.

8. Theme
9. Parameter report
10. Summary report
11. Conditional formatting
12. Format Painter

a. Used to copy multiple formatting properties from one control to another in Report Design View

b. Provides predefined formats that you apply to an entire form or report

c. Prompts the user for the criteria for selecting the records for the report

d. A way to change the appearance of a control on a form or report based on criteria you specify

e. Used to show statistics on groups of records

Select the best answer from the list of choices.

13. Which control would you use to visually separate groups of records on a report?
a. Image
b. Line
c. Bound Object Frame
d. Option group

14. Which property would you use to force each group of records to print at the top of the next page?
a. Paginate
b. Force New Page
c. Calculate
d. Display When

15. What feature allows you to apply the formatting characteristics of one control to another?
a. Theme
b. AutoContent Wizard
c. Format Painter
d. Report Layout Wizard

16. Which key do you press when creating a line to make it perfectly horizontal?
a. [Alt]
b. [Shift]
c. [Home]
d. [Ctrl]

17. Which feature allows you to apply the same formatting characteristics to all the controls in a report at once?
a. AutoPainting
b. Themes
c. Format Wizard
d. Palletizing

18. In a report, an expression used to calculate values is entered in which type of control?
a. Label
b. Text Box
c. Combo Box
d. Command Button

19. Which section most often contains calculations for groups of records?
a. Page Header
b. Page Footer
c. Group Footer
d. Detail

20. Which control would you use to combine two reports?
a. List Box
b. Subreport
c. Combo Box
d. Group & Sort Control

Skills Review

1. Use Report Design View.

a. Open the LakeHomes-8.accdb database from where you store your Data Files and enable content if prompted.

b. Open the RealtorList query, and then change Phil Kirkpatrick to your name. Close the query.

c. Create a new report in Report Design View based on the RealtorList query.

d. In the Group, Sort, and Total pane, select AgencyName as a grouping field and RLast as a sort field.

e. Add the AgencyName field to the AgencyName Header. Delete the accompanying AgencyName label, position the AgencyName text box on the left side of the AgencyName Header, then resize it to be about 3" wide.

f. Add the RealtorNo, RFirst, RLast, and RPhone fields to the Detail section. Delete all labels and position the text boxes horizontally across the top of the Detail section.

g. Drag the top edge of the Page Footer section up to remove the blank space in the Detail section.

h. Save the report with the name **RealtorList**, then preview it, as shown in FIGURE 8-21. The width and spacing of the controls in your report may differ. Use Layout View to resize each control so it is wide enough to view all data.

i. Save and close the RealtorList report.

FIGURE 8-21

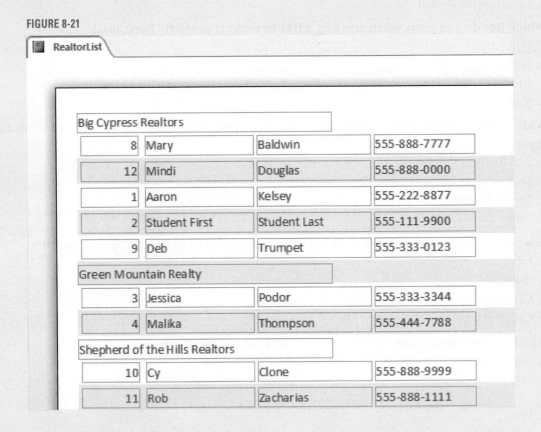

2. Create parameter reports.

a. Create a query in Query Design View, including the RFirst, RLast, and RPhone fields from the Realtors table. Include the Type, SchoolDistrict, SqFt, and Asking fields from the Listings table.

b. In the Asking field, include the following parameter criteria: **<=[Enter maximum asking price]**.

c. Test the query by switching to Datasheet View, enter **300,000** in the Enter maximum asking price box, then click OK. The query should display 25 records, all with an asking price of less than or equal to $300,000. Save the query as **PriceParameter**, then close it.

Skills Review (continued)

d. Click the PriceParameter query in the Navigation Pane, then click Report on the Create tab. Enter **300,000** in the Enter maximum asking price box, then click OK.

e. Work in Layout View to narrow each column to be only as wide as necessary and to fit all columns across a single sheet of paper in portrait orientation.

f. In Report Design View, narrow the PriceParameter label to be about half as wide, then add a label with your name to the right side of the Report Header section.

g. In Report Design View, drag the right edge of the report to the left to make sure the report is no wider than 8 inches. This may include moving controls in the Page Footer or Report Footer to the left as well.

h. Preview the report again to make sure it is not too wide to fit on the paper, enter **300,000** in the prompt, then print the report if requested by your instructor.

i. Save the report with the name **PriceParameter**, then close it.

3. **Apply conditional formatting.**

a. Open the PriceParameter report in Report Design View, click the Asking text box, then open the Conditional Formatting Rules Manager dialog box.

b. Add a rule to format all Asking field values between **0** and **199999** with a light green background color.

c. Add a rule to format all Asking field values between **200000** and **300000** with a yellow background color.

d. Add a rule to format all Asking field values greater than **300000** with a red background color.

e. Test the report in Print Preview, entering a value of **500,000** when prompted. Make sure the conditional formatting colors are working as intended.

4. **Add lines.**

a. Open the PriceParameter report in Design View, then use the Group, Sort, and Total pane to add a sort order. Sort the fields in descending (largest to smallest) order on the Asking field.

b. Add a label to the Report Footer section directly to the left of the =Sum([Asking]) text box. Enter **Grand Total:** as the label text.

c. Expand the vertical size of the Report Footer section to about twice its current height and resize the =Sum([Asking]) text box in the Report Footer to better read the contents.

d. Draw two short horizontal lines just below the =Sum([Asking]) calculation in the Report Footer section to indicate a grand total.

e. Widen the Asking column if needed to display the values clearly, but be careful to stay within the margins of the report. Save the report, then switch to Print Preview to review the changes using a value of **300,000** when prompted. You should only see green and yellow background colors on the Asking field values.

5. **Use the Format Painter and themes.**

a. Open the PriceParameter report in Design View.

b. Change the PriceParameter label in the Report Header section to **Asking Price Analysis**.

c. Apply the Facet theme.

d. Change the font color of the RFirst label in the Page Header section to Automatic (black).

e. Use the Format Painter to copy the format from the RFirst label to the RLast, RPhone, Type, and SchoolDistrict labels in the Page Header section.

f. Change the font color of the SqFt label in the Page Header section to red.

g. Use the Format Painter to copy the format from the SqFt label to the Asking label.

h. Save and close the PriceParameter report.

Skills Review (continued)

6. Add subreports.

a. Open the ListingReport and RealtorList reports in Print Preview. If needed, resize and align any text boxes that are not wide enough to show all data. Be careful to not extend the right edge of the report beyond one sheet of paper.

b. Close the RealtorList report and display the ListingReport in Design View. Expand the Report Footer section, and add the RealtorList report as a subreport using the SubReport Wizard. Choose None when asked to link the main form to the subform (you may have to scroll), and accept the default name of RealtorList.

c. Delete the extra RealtorList label in the Report Footer. (*Hint*: It will be positioned near the upper-left corner of the subreport, but it may be mostly hidden by the subreport.)

d. Preview each page of the report to make sure all data is clearly visible. Widen any controls that do not clearly display information, again being careful not to extend the report beyond the right margin.

e. Narrow the width of the report if necessary in Report Design View, then save and close it.

7. Modify section properties.

a. In Report Design View of the ListingReport, modify the Realtors.RealtorNo Footer section's Force New Page property to After Section. (Note: The RealtorNo field is included in two tables, Realtors and Listings. Access uses the table-name.fieldname convention to specify that this RealtorNo field is from the Realtors table.)

b. Open the Page Footer section, and add a label, **Created by Your Name**.

c. Save and preview the ListingReport to make sure that the new section property forces each new realtor group of records to print on its own page, as shown in FIGURE 8-22. Also check that a label identifying you as the report creator appears at the bottom of each page. Remember that you must print preview the report (rather than display it in Report View) to see how the report prints on each page.

d. Print the report if requested by your instructor, then save and close the report.

FIGURE 8-22

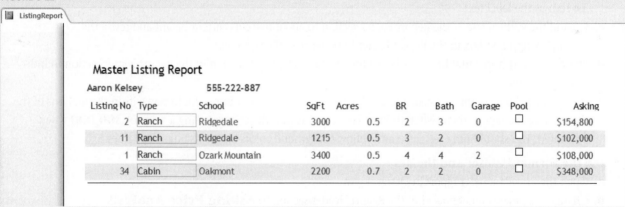

Skills Review (continued)

8. Create summary reports.

a. Right-click the ListingReport, click Copy, right-click the Navigation Pane, click Paste, then type **ListingSummary**.

b. Open the ListingSummary report in Design View, then delete the subreport from the Report Footer, all the controls in the Detail section, and all the labels in the Realtors.RealtorNo Header section. (*Hint*: Be careful not to delete the two text boxes in the Realtors.RealtorNo Header section.)

c. Close the extra space in the Report Footer, Detail, and Realtors.RealtorNo Header sections.

d. Expand the size of the Realtors.RealtorNo Footer section about 0.5", move the line to the bottom of that section, then add a text box to the right side of the section with the following expression: **=Sum([Asking])**.

e. Modify the new label to read **Subtotal of Asking Price:**, then move and resize the controls as needed so that both the label and text box can be clearly read in Report Design View.

f. Open the Property Sheet for the =Sum([Asking]) text box, click the Format tab, then choose **Currency** for the Format property and **0** for the Decimal Places property.

g. Expand the Report Footer section about 0.5 inches, copy the =Sum([Asking]) text box to the Report Footer section, move it directly under the =Sum([Asking]) text box in the Realtors.RealtorNo Footer section, then change the label to be **Grand Total:**.

h. Draw two short lines under the =Sum([Asking]) text box in the Report Footer section to indicate a grand total.

i. Change the Force New Page property of the Realtors.RealtorNo Footer section to None.

j. Move the two text boxes in the Realtors.RealtorNo Header section directly down to the Realtors.RealtorNo Footer section and then close the Realtors.RealtorNo Header section.

k. Position all controls within the 10.5" mark on the ruler so that the width of the paper is no wider than 10.5". Drag the right edge of the report as far to the left as possible so that it does not extend beyond 10.5".

l. Preview the report. Resize sections and move controls in Design View so the report matches FIGURE 8-23. Print the report if requested by your instructor, then save and close the report.

m. Close the LakeHomes-8.accdb database, and exit Access.

FIGURE 8-23

Master Listing Report			
Aaron Kelsey	555-222-8877	Subtotal of Asking Price:	$712,800
Student First Student Last	555-111-9900	Subtotal of Asking Price:	$985,936
Jessica Podor	555-333-3344	Subtotal of Asking Price:	$467,820
Malika Thompson	555-444-7788	Subtotal of Asking Price:	$1,026,120
Jane Ann Welch	555-223-0044	Subtotal of Asking Price:	$603,360
Shari Duncan	555-228-5577	Subtotal of Asking Price:	$144,000
Trixie Angelina	555-220-4466	Subtotal of Asking Price:	$126,000
Mary Baldwin	555-888-7777	Subtotal of Asking Price:	$914,279
Mindi Douglas	555-888-0000	Subtotal of Asking Price:	$1,222,200
Andrew Barker	555-999-2222	Subtotal of Asking Price:	$1,785,480
		Grand Total:	$7,987,994

Page: 1 ▶ ▶▌ No Filter ◀

Independent Challenge 1

As the manager of a music store's instrument rental program, you created a database to track instrument rentals. Now that several instruments have been rented, you need to create a report listing the rental transactions for each instrument.

a. Start Access, open the Music-8.accdb database from where you store your Data Files, and enable content if prompted.

b. Use the Report Wizard to create a report based on the FirstName and LastName fields in the Students table, the RentalDate field from the Rentals table, and the Description and MonthlyFee fields from the Instruments table.

c. View the data by Instruments, do not add any more grouping levels, sort the data in ascending order by RentalDate, use a Stepped layout and Portrait orientation, and title the report **Instrument Rentals**.

d. Open the report in Design View, change the first grouping level from SerialNo to Description so that all instruments with the same description are grouped together, and open the Description Footer section.

e. Add a new text box to the Description Footer section with the expression **=Count([LastName])**. Change the label to **Number of Rentals:**, and position the controls close to the right side of the report.

f. Change the Force New Page property of the Description Footer section to After Section.

g. Add your name as a label to the Report Header section, and use the Format Painter to copy the formatting from the Instrument Rentals label to your name. Double-click a corner sizing handle of the label with your name to resize it to show your entire name, and align the top edges of both labels in the Report Header.

h. Save and preview the report, as shown in FIGURE 8-24. Move, resize, and align controls as needed to match the figure, make sure all controls fit within the margins of one sheet of paper, then print the report if requested by your instructor.

i. Save and close the Instrument Rentals report, close the Music-8.accdb database, then exit Access.

FIGURE 8-24

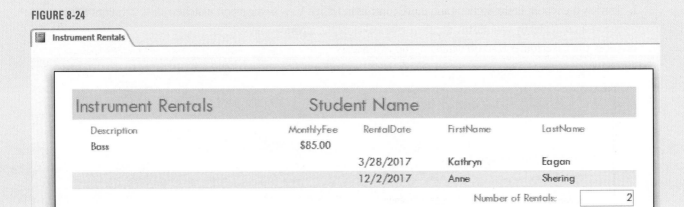

Independent Challenge 2

As the manager of a music store's instrument rental program, you have created a database to track instrument rentals. Now that the rental program is under way, you need to create a summary report that shows how many instruments have been rented by each school.

a. Start Access, open the Music-8.accdb database from the location where you store your Data Files, and enable content if prompted.

b. Build a query in Query Design View with the following fields: SchoolName from the Schools table and RentalDate from the Rentals table. (*Hint*: Include the Students table to build the proper relationships between the Schools and the Rentals table.) Save the query with the name **SchoolSummary**, then close it.

c. Create a new report in Report Design View. Use the SchoolSummary query as the Record Source property.

d. Add SchoolName as a grouping field, and add the SchoolName field to the left side of the SchoolName Header section. Delete the SchoolName label, and widen the SchoolName text box to about 4".

e. Drag the top edge of the Page Footer section up to completely close the Detail section.

f. Add a label to the Page Header section with your name. Format the label with an Arial Black font and a 14-point font size. Resize the label to display all the text.

g. Open the Report Header section, and add a label to the Report Header section that reads **New student musicians per school**. Format the label with Automatic (black) font color.

h. Add a text box to the right side of the SchoolName Header section with the expression **=Count([RentalDate])**. Delete the accompanying label.

i. Align the top edges of the two text boxes in the SchoolName Header.

j. Use the Format Painter to copy the formatting from the label with your name to the new label in the Report Header section, the SchoolName text box, and the =Count([RentalDate]) expression in the SchoolName Header section. Switch back and forth between Print Preview and Design View to resize the text boxes in the SchoolName Header section as needed to show all information in each box.

k. Open the Report Footer section, then copy and paste the =Count([RentalDate]) text box to the Report Footer section. Right-align the right edges of the =Count([RentalDate]) controls in the SchoolName Header and Report Footer sections.

l. Add one short line above and two short lines below the =Count([RentalDate]) text box in the Report Footer section to indicate a subtotal and grand total.

m. Save the report with the name **SchoolSummary**, then preview it, as shown in FIGURE 8-25.

n. Close the SchoolSummary report, close the Music-8.accdb database, then exit Access.

FIGURE 8-25

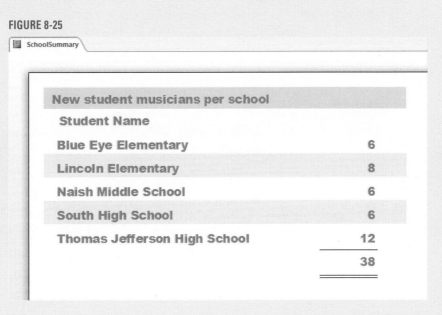

Independent Challenge 3

As the manager of a music store's instrument rental program, you have created a database to track instrument rentals. Now that the rental program is under way, you need to create a parameter report for each instrument type.

a. Start Access, open the Music-8.accdb database from where you store your Data Files, and enable content if prompted.

b. Create a query with the RentalDate field from the Rentals table, the Description and MonthlyFee fields from the Instruments table, and the FirstName and LastName fields from the Students table.

c. Enter the parameter criteria **Between [Enter start date] And [Enter end date]** for the RentalDate field and **[Enter instrument type such as cello]** for the Description field.

d. Save the query with the name **RentalParameter**, then test it with the dates **3/1/17** and **3/31/17** and the type **bass**. These criteria should select one record. Close the RentalParameter query.

e. Use the Report Wizard to create a report on all fields in the RentalParameter query. View the data by Instruments, do not add any more grouping levels, sort the records in ascending order by RentalDate, and use an Outline layout and a Portrait orientation. Title the report **Instrument Lookup**.

f. To respond to the prompts, enter **1/1/17** for the start date and **6/30/17** for the end date. Enter **viola** for the instrument type prompt.

g. In Report Design View, apply the Integral theme.

h. Add your name as a label to the Report Header section. Change the font color to black so that it is clearly visible.

i. Add spaces between all words in the labels in the Description Header section: MonthlyFee, RentalDate, FirstName, and LastName to change them to **Monthly Fee**, **Rental Date**, **First Name**, and **Last Name**. Be sure to change the label controls and not the text box controls.

j. Open the Description Footer section.

k. Add a text box to the Description Footer section that contains the expression **=Count([LastName])*[MonthlyFee]**. Change the accompanying label to read **Monthly Revenue:**, then move the text box with the expression below the LastName text box and resize both so that their contents are clearly visible.

l. Open the Property Sheet for the new expression. On the Format tab, change the Format property to **Currency** and the Decimal Places property to **0**.

m. Display the report for RentalDates **1/1/17** through **4/30/17**, instrument type **viola**. Your report should look like FIGURE 8-26.

n. Save the Instrument Lookup report, print it if requested by your instructor, close the Music-8.accdb database, then exit Access.

FIGURE 8-26

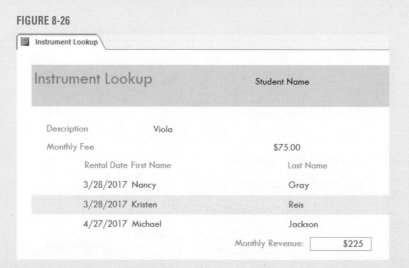

Independent Challenge 4: Explore

You have created an Access database to help manage college scholarship opportunities. You analyze scholarships by building a report with conditional formatting.

a. Start Access and open the Scholarships-8.accdb database from the location where you store your Data Files. Enable content if prompted.

b. Use the Report Wizard to create a report based on the Scholarships table. Include all of the fields. Add Major then Amount as the grouping levels, then click the Grouping Options button in the Report Wizard. Choose 5000s as the Grouping interval for the Amount field. Sort the records by DueDate in descending order. Use a Stepped layout and a Landscape orientation. Title the report **Scholarships by Major**.

c. Preview the report, then add your name as a label next to the report title.

d. In Layout View, add spaces to the DueDate and ScholarshipName labels to read **Due Date** and **Scholarship Name**.

e. Resize and narrow the columns to fit on a single sheet of landscape paper, then drag the right edge of the report to the left in Report Design View to make sure it is within the 10.5" mark on the horizontal ruler.

f. Expand the Page Header section to about twice its height, move the labels in the Page Header section to the bottom of the Page Header section, move the labels from the Report Header section to the top of the Page Header section, then close up the Report Header section.

g. Open the Major Footer section, then change the Force New Page property of the Major Footer section to After Section.

h. Click the Amount text box in the Detail section, then apply a new rule of conditional formatting. Use the Compare to other records rule type, and change the Bar color to light green.

i. Preview page 4 of the report for the Computer Science majors, as shown in FIGURE 8-27.

j. Save and close the Scholarships by Major report and the Scholarships-8.accdb database.

FIGURE 8-27

Visual Workshop

Open the Baseball-8.accdb database from the location where you store your Data Files and enable content if prompted. Using the Report Wizard, build a report on the PlayerLName field from the Players table and the AtBats and Hits fields from the PlayerStats table. View the data by Players, do not add any more grouping or sorting fields, and use a Stepped layout and Portrait orientation. Enter **Batting Average** as the name of the report. In Report Design View, open the PlayerNo Footer section and move the PlayerLName text box down to the same position in the PlayerNo Footer section. Add new text boxes to the PlayerNo Footer section to sum the AtBats, sum the Hits, and calculate the overall batting average per player. The expression to find the batting average is **=Sum([Hits])/Sum([AtBats])**. Delete any extra labels that are created when you add the text boxes, and delete all of the controls in the Detail section. Close the PlayerNo Header and Detail sections, and resize the PlayerNo Footer section to remove blank space. Modify the Decimal Places property of the batting average calculation to show **3** digits to the right of the decimal point, and modify the Format property to be Standard. Apply a conditional format to the batting average expression so that if it is greater than or equal to **0.5**, the text is bold and red. Add a label to the Page Header section to identify the batting average, add a label to the Report Header section with your name, and then edit the labels and align the controls, as shown in FIGURE 8-28. As a final step, change the Group on field from PlayerNo to PlayerLName so the records are sorted by player last name, change the Alternate Back Color of the PlayerLName Footer section to Background 1, and add a line at the bottom of the PlayerLName Footer section as shown in FIGURE 8-28. Save the Batting Average report, print the report if requested by your instructor, and then close it.

FIGURE 8-28

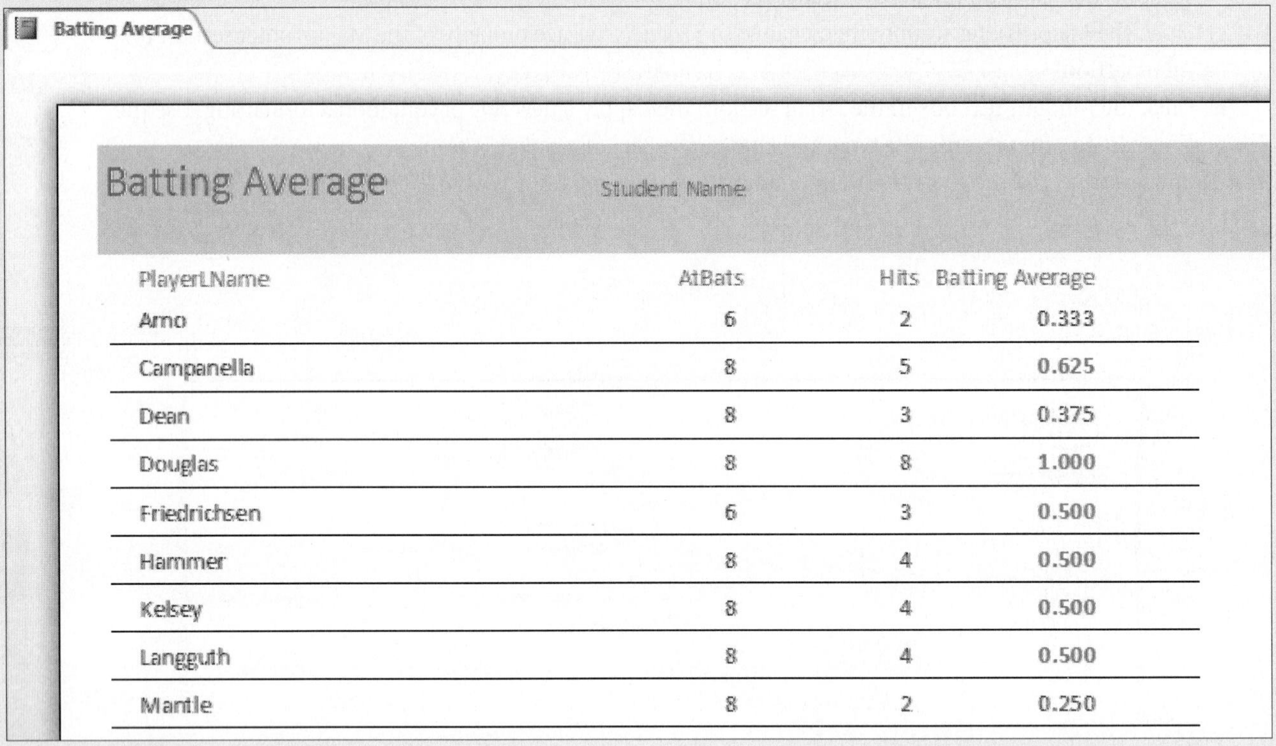

Importing and Exporting Data

CASE At Reason 2 Go, David Fox, director of staff development, has asked you to develop an Access database that tracks professional staff continuing education. First, you will work with Access tools that allow you to share Access data with other software programs so that each R2G department can have the necessary data in a format it can use. You will also explore the Access templates for creating a new database.

Module Objectives

After completing this module, you will be able to:

- Import data from Excel
- Link data
- Export data to Excel
- Publish data to Word
- Merge data with Word
- Export data to PDF
- Create objects using database templates
- Create objects using Application Parts

Files You Will Need

Training-9.accdb
Departments.xlsx
Materials.xlsx
Machinery-9.accdb
MachineryEmployees.xlsx

Vendors.xlsx
Basketball-9.accdb
2018-2019Schedule.xlsx
Languages-9.accdb

Import Data from Excel

Learning Outcomes
- Import data from Excel
- Describe other data import options

Access can share data with many other Microsoft Office programs. **Importing** enables you to quickly copy data from an external file into an Access database. You can import data from many sources, such as another Access database; Excel spreadsheet; SharePoint site; Outlook email; or text files in an HTML, XML, or delimited text file format. A **delimited text file** stores one record on each line. Field values are separated by a common character, the **delimiter**, such as a comma, tab, or dash. A **CSV (comma-separated value)** file is a common example of a delimited text file. An **XML file** is a text file containing **Extensible Markup Language (XML)** tags that identify field names and data. One of the most common file formats from which to import data into an Access database is **Microsoft Excel**, the spreadsheet program in the Microsoft Office suite. **CASE** ▶ *David Fox gives you an Excel spreadsheet that contains a list of supplemental materials used for various courses and asks you to import the information into the new internal training database.*

STEPS

1. **Start Access, open the Training-9.accdb database from the location where you store your Data Files, enable content if prompted, click the External Data tab, click the Excel button in the Import & Link group, click the Browse button, navigate to the location where you store your Data Files, then double-click Materials.xlsx**

   The **Get External Data - Excel Spreadsheet** dialog box opens. You can import the records, **append** the records (add the records to an existing table), or link to the data source. In this case, you want to import the records into a new table.

2. **Click OK**

   The **Import Spreadsheet Wizard** helps you import data from Excel into Access and presents a sample of the data to be imported, as shown in FIGURE 9-1.

3. **Click Next, click the First Row Contains Column Headings check box, click Next, click Next to accept the default field options, click Next to allow Access to add a primary key field, type Materials in the Import to Table box, click Finish, then click Close**

   To save the import steps so that they can be easily repeated, click the Save import steps check box on the last step of the import process. You run a saved import process by clicking the **Saved Imports** button on the External Data tab.

   One record in the Courses table can be related to many records in the Materials table.

4. **Click the Database Tools tab, click the Relationships button, drag the Materials table from the Navigation Pane to the right of the Courses table, drag the CourseID field in the Courses table to the CourseID field in the Materials table, click the Enforce Referential Integrity check box, then click Create**

   The final Relationships window is shown in FIGURE 9-2. One employee record is related to many enrollments. One course record is related to many enrollments and to many materials.

5. **Click the Close button, then click Yes to save the changes to the database relationships**

FIGURE 9-1: Import Spreadsheet Wizard

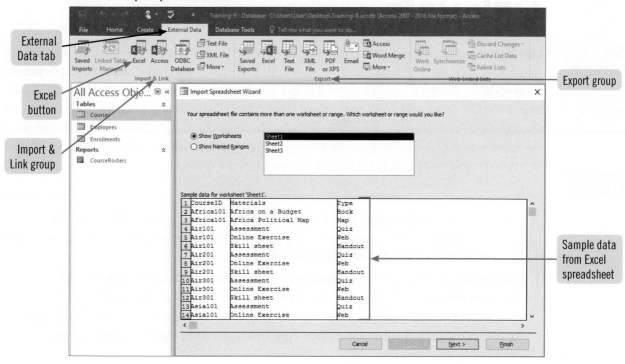

FIGURE 9-2: Relationships window with imported Materials table

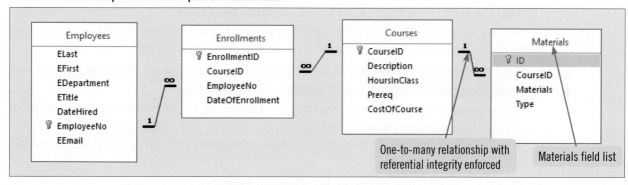

Referential integrity cascade options

When connecting tables in one-to-many relationships, apply referential integrity whenever possible. This feature prevents orphan records from being created in the database and lets you select cascade options. **Cascade Update Related Fields** means that if a value in the primary key field (the field on the "one" side of a one-to-many relationship) is modified, all values in the foreign key field (the field on the "many" side of a one-to-many relationship) are automatically updated as well.

Cascade Delete Related Records means that if a record on the "one" side of a one-to-many relationship is deleted, all related records in the "many" table are also deleted. Because both of these options automatically change or delete data in the "many" table behind the scenes, they should be used carefully. Often these features are not employed as standard options, but are used temporarily to correct a problem in the database.

Link Data

Linking connects an Access database to data in an external file such as another Access database, an Excel spreadsheet, a text file, an HTML file, an XML file, or other data sources that support **ODBC (Open Database Connectivity)** standards. Linking is different from importing in that linked data is not copied into the database. If you link, data is only stored and updated in the original file. Importing, in contrast, makes a copy of the data in the Access database. **CASE** *David Fox has created a small spreadsheet with information about the departments at R2G. He wants to use the information in the Training-9 database while maintaining it in Excel. He asks you to help create a link to this Excel file from the Training-9 database.*

STEPS

1. **Click the External Data tab, then click the Excel button in the Import & Link group**

   The Get External Data - Excel Spreadsheet dialog box opens. This dialog box allows you to choose whether you want to import, append, or link to the data source.

2. **Click Browse, navigate to the location where you store your Data Files, double-click Departments.xlsx, click the Link to the data source by creating a linked table option button, as shown in FIGURE 9-3, click OK, click Next to accept the default range selection, click Next to accept the default column headings, type Departments as the linked table name, click Finish, then click OK**

   The **Link Spreadsheet Wizard** guides you through the process of linking to a spreadsheet. The linked Departments table appears in the Navigation Pane with a linking Excel icon, as shown in FIGURE 9-4. Like any other table, in order for the linked table to work with the rest of a database, a one-to-many relationship between it and another table should be created.

3. **Click the Database Tools tab, click the Relationships button, drag the Departments table from the Navigation Pane to the left of the Employees table**

   The Dept field in the Departments table is used to create a one-to-many relationship with the EDepartment field in the Employees table. One department may be related to many employees.

4. **Drag the Dept field in the Departments table to the EDepartment field in the Employees table, then click Create in the Edit Relationships dialog box**

   Your Relationships window should look like FIGURE 9-5. A relationship is established between the Departments and Employees tables, but you cannot establish referential integrity with a linked table. Now that the linked Departments table is related to the rest of the database, it can participate in queries, forms, and reports that select fields from multiple tables.

5. **Click the Close button, then click Yes when prompted to save changes**

   You work with a linked table just as you work with any other table. The data in a linked table can be edited through either the source program (in this case, Excel) or in the Access database, even though the data is only physically stored in the original source file.

FIGURE 9-3: Get External Data - Excel Spreadsheet dialog box

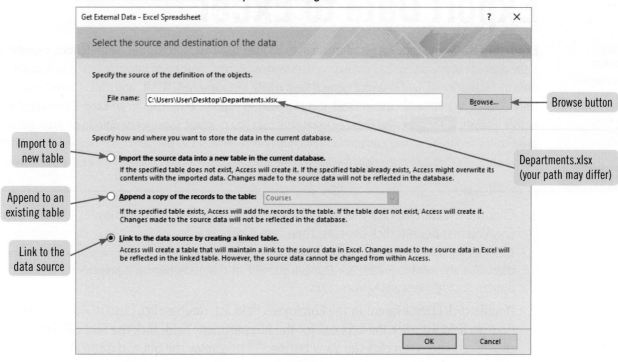

Browse button

Departments.xlsx (your path may differ)

Import to a new table

Append to an existing table

Link to the data source

FIGURE 9-4: Departments table is linked from Excel

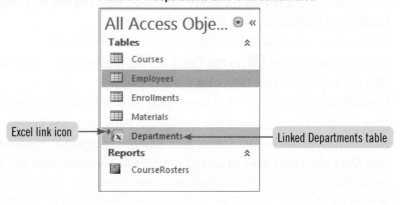

Excel link icon

Linked Departments table

FIGURE 9-5: Relationships window with linked Departments table

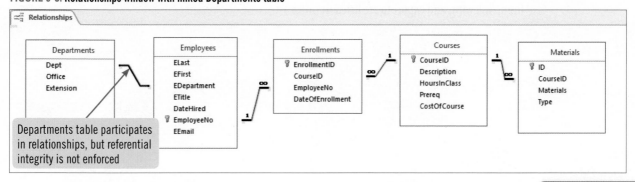

Departments table participates in relationships, but referential integrity is not enforced

Importing and Exporting Data

Export Data to Excel

Learning Outcomes
- Export data to Excel
- Describe other data export options

Exporting is a way to copy Access information to another database, spreadsheet, or file format. Exporting is the opposite of importing. You can export data from an Access database to other file types, such as those used by Excel or Word, and in several general file formats, including text, HTML, and XML. Given the popularity of analyzing numeric data in Excel, it is common to export Access data to an Excel spreadsheet for further analysis. **CASE** *The Finance Department asks you to export some Access data to an Excel spreadsheet so the finance personnel can use Excel to analyze how increases in the cost of the courses would affect departments. You can gather the fields needed in an Access query, then export the query to an Excel spreadsheet.*

STEPS

1. **Click the Create tab, click the Query Design button, double-click Employees, double-click Enrollments, double-click Courses, then click Close**

    The fields you want to export to Excel—EDepartment and CostOfCourse—are in the Employees and Courses tables. You also need to include the Enrollments table in this query because it provides the connection between the Employees and Courses tables.

2. **Double-click EDepartment in the Employees field list, double-click CostOfCourse in the Courses field list, click the Sort cell for the EDepartment field, click the Sort cell list arrow, click Ascending, then click the View button ⊞ to display the query datasheet**

    The resulting datasheet has 388 records. You want to summarize the costs by department before exporting this to Excel.

3. **Click the View button ⊠ to return to Design View, click the Totals button in the Show/Hide group, click the Group By list arrow for the CostOfCourse field, click Sum, click the View button ⊞ to display the query datasheet, then use the ↔ pointer to widen the SumOfCostOfCourse column, as shown in FIGURE 9-6**

    Save the query with a meaningful name to prepare to export it to Excel.

4. **Click the Save button 🖫 on the Quick Access Toolbar, type DeptCosts, click OK, right-click the DeptCosts tab, then click Close**

    Before you start an export process, be sure to select the object you want to export in the Navigation Pane.

5. **Click the DeptCosts query in the Navigation Pane, click the External Data tab, click the Excel button in the Export group, click Browse, navigate to the location where you store your Data Files, click Save to accept the default filename, click OK, then click Close**

    The data in the DeptCosts query has now been exported to an Excel spreadsheet file named DeptCosts and saved in the location where you store your Data Files. As with imports, you can save and then repeat the export process by saving the export steps when prompted by the last dialog box in the Export Wizard. Run the saved export process using the **Saved Exports** button on the External Data tab or by assigning the export process to an Outlook task.

    Access can work with data in a wide variety of file formats. Other file formats that Access can import from, link with, and export to are listed in **TABLE 9-1**.

FIGURE 9-6: New query selects and summarizes data to export to Excel

Records are grouped by EDepartment field →

Drag to resize column

Records are summed by CostOfCourse field

EDepartment	SumOfCostOfCourse
Africa	$13,295.00
Asia	$13,640.00
Australia	$6,580.00
Europe	$11,130.00
Finance	$6,685.00
Information Systems	$11,145.00
Marketing	$20,460.00
North America	$12,490.00
Operations	$12,345.00
Personnel	$12,180.00
South America	$12,800.00
USA	$9,510.00

TABLE 9-1: File formats that Access can link to, import, and export

file format	import	link	export
Access	•	•	•
Excel	•	•	•
Word			•
SharePoint site	•	•	•
Email file attachments			•
Outlook folder	•	•	
ODBC database (such as SQL Server)	•	•	•
dBASE	•	•	•
HTML document	•	•	•
PDF or XPS file			•
Text file (delimited or fixed width)	•	•	•
XML file	•		•

Publish Data to Word

Learning Outcomes
- Export data to Word
- Describe techniques to share Access data

Microsoft Word, the word-processing program in the Microsoft Office suite, is a premier program for entering, editing, and formatting text. You can easily export data from an Access table, query, form, or report into a Word document. This is helpful when you want to use Word's superior text-editing features to combine the information in a Word document with Access data. **CASE** ▶ *David Fox asks you to write a memo to the management committee describing departmental costs for continuing education. You export an Access query with this data to a Word document, where you finish the memo.*

STEPS

1. **Click the** DeptCosts query **in the Navigation Pane, click the** External Data tab**, click the** More button **in the Export group, click** Word**, click the** Open the destination file after the export operation is complete check box**, click** Browse**, navigate to the location where you store your Data Files, click** Save **to accept the default filename** DeptCosts.rtf**, then click** OK

   The data in the DeptCosts query is exported as an **RTF (Rich Text Format)** file and is opened in Word. Currently, the document contains only a table of information—the data you exported from the DeptCosts query. Use Word to add the memo information.

2. **Press [Enter], then type the following text, pressing [Tab] after typing each colon**

   To: Executive Committee

   From: *Your Name*

   Re: Analysis of Continuing Education Courses

   Date: *Today's date*

   The following information shows the overall cost for continuing education subtotaled by department. The information shows that the Marketing Department is the highest consumer of continuing education.

3. **Proofread your document, which should now look like** FIGURE 9-7**, then preview and print it**

   The **word wrap** feature in Word determines when a line of text extends into the right margin of the page and automatically forces the text to the next line without your needing to press [Enter]. This allows you to enter and edit large paragraphs of text in Word very efficiently.

4. **Save and close the document, then exit Word**

   In addition to exporting data, TABLE 9-2 lists other techniques you can use to copy Access data to other applications.

FIGURE 9-7: **Word document with Access data**

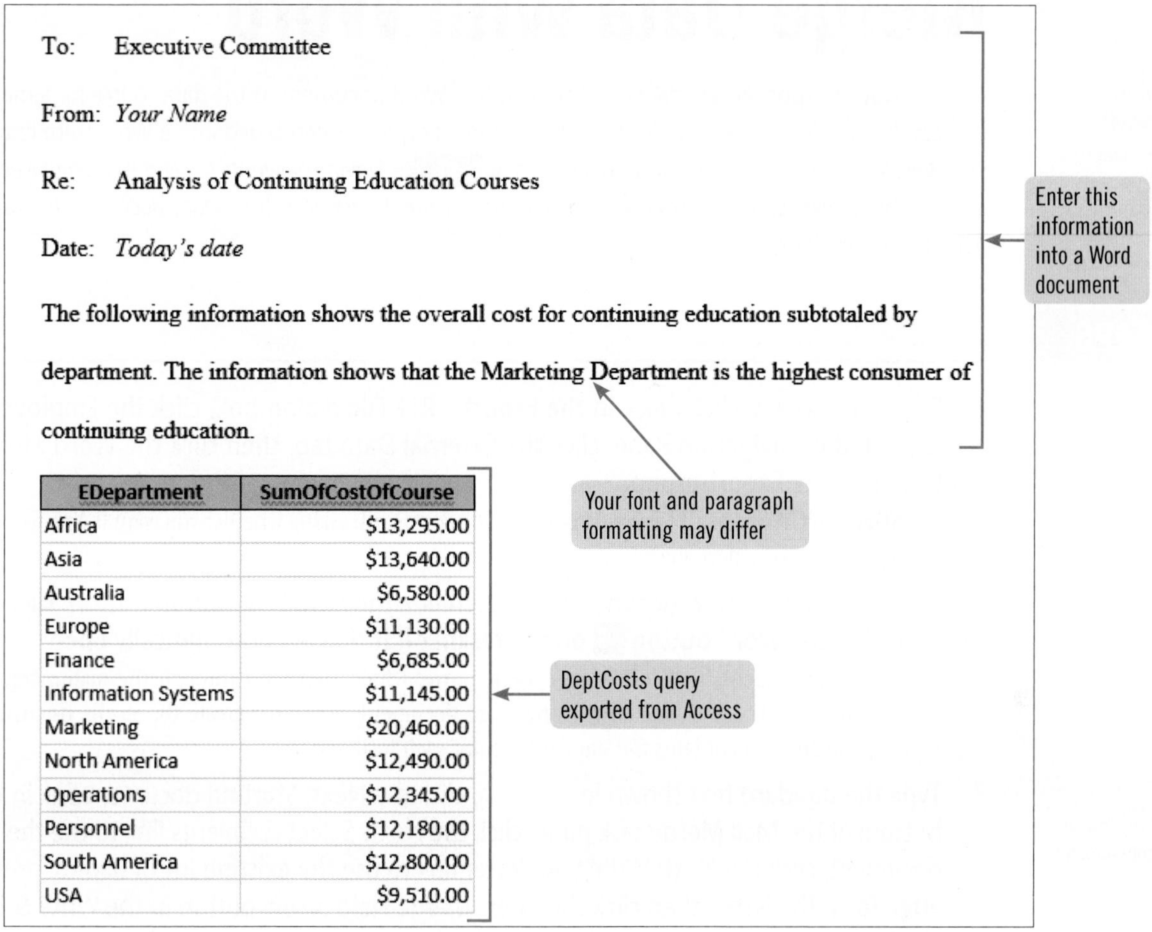

To: Executive Committee

From: *Your Name*

Re: Analysis of Continuing Education Courses

Date: *Today's date*

The following information shows the overall cost for continuing education subtotaled by

department. The information shows that the Marketing Department is the highest consumer of

continuing education.

EDepartment	SumOfCostOfCourse
Africa	$13,295.00
Asia	$13,640.00
Australia	$6,580.00
Europe	$11,130.00
Finance	$6,685.00
Information Systems	$11,145.00
Marketing	$20,460.00
North America	$12,490.00
Operations	$12,345.00
Personnel	$12,180.00
South America	$12,800.00
USA	$9,510.00

Enter this information into a Word document

Your font and paragraph formatting may differ

DeptCosts query exported from Access

Access 2016

TABLE 9-2: **Techniques to copy Access data to other applications**

technique	button or menu option	description
Drag and drop	Resize the Access window so that the target location (Word or Excel, for example) can also be seen on the screen	With both windows visible, drag the Access table, query, form, or report object icon from the Access window to the target (Excel or Word) window
Export	Use the buttons in the Export group on the External Data tab	Copy information from an Access object into a different file format
Office Clipboard	Copy and Paste	Click the Copy button to copy selected data to the Office Clipboard (the Office Clipboard can hold multiple items), open a Word document or Excel spreadsheet, click where you want to paste the data, then click the Paste button

Merge Data with Word

Learning
Outcomes
• Merge data to a
Word document
• Save a main
document with
merge fields

Another way to export Access data is to merge it to a Word document as the data source for a mail-merge process. In a **mail merge**, data from an Access table or query is combined into a Word form letter, label, or envelope to create mass mailing documents. **CASE** ▸ *David Fox wants to send R2G employees a letter announcing a new continuing education course. You merge Access data to a Word document to customize a letter to each employee.*

STEPS

1. **Return to Access, click** Close **in the Export – RTF File dialog box, click the** Employees table **in the Navigation Pane, click the** External Data tab, **then click the** Word Merge button **in the Export group**

   The **Microsoft Word Mail Merge Wizard** dialog box opens, asking whether you want to link to an existing document or create a new one.

2. **Click the** Create a new document and then link the data to it option button, **click** OK, **then click the** Word button 📰 **on the taskbar if it doesn't automatically open**

   Word starts and opens the **Mail Merge task pane**, which steps you through the mail-merge process. Before you merge the Access data with the Word document, you must create the **main document**, the Word document that contains the standard text for each form letter.

3. **Type the standard text shown in** FIGURE 9-8, **click the** Next: Starting document link **in the bottom of the Mail Merge task pane, click the** Next: Select recipients link **to use the current document, click the** Next: Write your letter link **to use the existing list of names, press [Tab] after To: in the letter, then click the** Insert Merge Field arrow button **in the Write & Insert Fields group on the Mailings tab**

   The Insert Merge Field drop-down list shows all of the fields in the original data source, the Employees table. You use this list to insert **merge fields**, codes that are replaced with the values in the field that the code represents when the mail merge is processed.

4. **Click** EFirst, **press [Spacebar], click the** Insert Merge Field arrow button, **click** ELast, **then click the** Next: Preview your letters link

   With the main document and merge fields inserted, you are ready to complete the mail merge.

5. **Click the** Next: Complete the merge link, **click the** Edit individual letters link **as shown in** FIGURE 9-9 **to view the letters on the screen, then click** OK

   The mail-merge process combines the EFirst and ELast field values from the Employees table with the main document, creating a 26-page document, as shown in the Word status bar. Each page is a customized letter for each record in the Employees table. The first page is a letter to David Fox. "David" is the field value for the EFirst field in the first record in the Employees table, and "Fox" is the field value for the ELast field.

6. **Press [Page Down] several times to view several pages of the final merged document, then close the merged document, Letters1, without saving it**

   You generally don't need to save the final, large merged document. Saving the one-page main document, however, is a good idea in case you need to repeat the merge process.

7. **Click the** Save button 💾 **on the Quick Access Toolbar, click the** Browse button, **navigate to the location where you store your Data Files, enter** NewCourse **in the File name text box, click** Save, **then close Word**

FIGURE 9-8: Creating the main document in Word

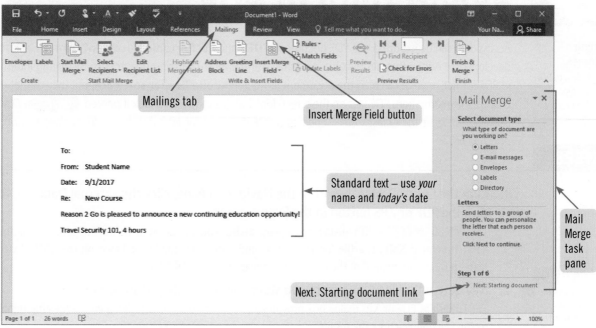

FIGURE 9-9: Inserting merge fields

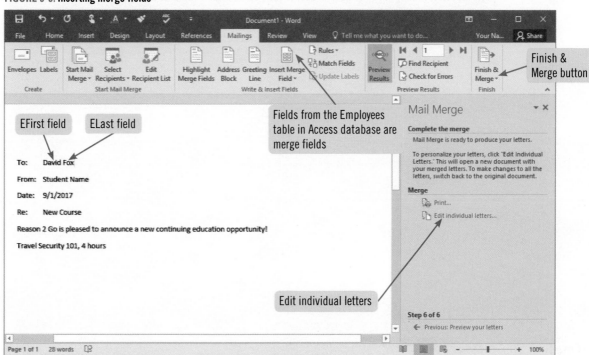

Export Data to PDF

Learning Outcomes
- Publish data to PDF
- Export a report as an email attachment

Access data can be exported to a PDF document. **PDF** stands for **Portable Document Format**, a file format developed by Adobe that has become a standard format for exchanging documents. By sharing information in PDF format, anyone can read the document using free **Adobe Reader software**, but they cannot edit or change the information. PDF files on the screen look just like they would look if printed. **CASE** ▸ *David Fox asks you to export the CourseRosters report to a PDF document for later distribution to employees as an email attachment.*

STEPS

1. **Click the CourseRosters report in the Navigation Pane, click the External Data tab, then click the PDF or XPS button in the Export group**

   The Publish as PDF or XPS dialog box opens, asking you to choose a name and location for the file. **XPS** (structured XML) is a file format that is similar to a PDF file but is based on the **XML** (Extensible Markup Language) instead of the PostScript language used by PDF files.

   TROUBLE
   Be sure the Open file after publishing check box is selected.

2. **Navigate to the location where you store your Data Files, as shown in** FIGURE 9-10

   The Publish as PDF or XPS dialog box provides a check box to automatically open the file after publishing so you can double-check the results.

   TROUBLE
   You may be prompted to select a program to open the PDF file. Select a PDF reader or a browser.

3. **Click Publish to save the file with the default name CourseRosters.pdf**

   The CourseRosters.pdf file automatically opens, as shown in FIGURE 9-11.

4. **Close the PDF window, return to the Access window, then click Close to close the Export - PDF dialog box**

   The CourseRosters.pdf file is now available for you to attach to an email. Because it is a PDF file, users can open, view, and print the report even if they don't have Access on their computers.

5. **Close the Training-9.accdb database and Access 2016**

Emailing an Access report

Another way to email an Access report (or any other Access object) as a PDF file is to click the report in the Navigation Pane, then click the Email button in the Export group of the External Data tab on the Ribbon. You are presented with the Send Object As dialog box that allows you to choose the desired file format, such as .xlsx, .pdf, .htm, or .rtf, for the report. Once you select the desired file format and click OK, Outlook opens with the report attached to the email in the chosen file format. You must have Microsoft Outlook installed and configured to use this option.

FIGURE 9-10: Publish as PDF or XPS dialog box

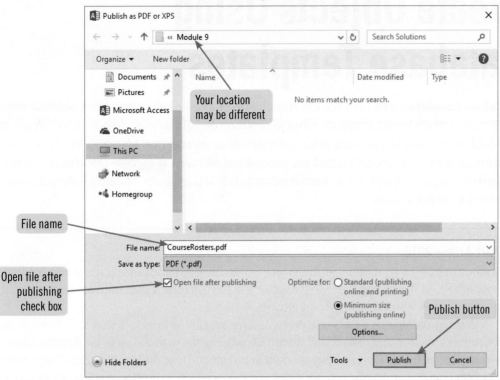

FIGURE 9-11: Previewing the CourseRosters.pdf file

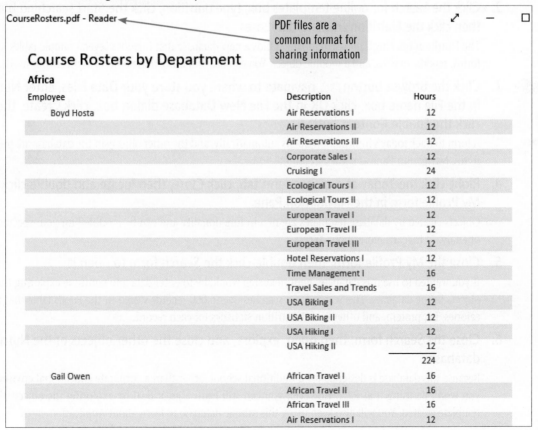

Learning
Outcomes
• Create a database
from a template
• Set a startup form

Create Objects Using Database Templates

A **database template** is a tool that you use to quickly create a new database based on a particular subject, such as assets, contacts, events, or projects. When you install Access 2016 on your computer, Microsoft provides many database templates for you to use. Additional templates are available from Microsoft Office Online, where they are organized by category, such as business, personal, and education. **CASE** ▶ *David Fox, director of staff development, asks you to develop a new Access database to help R2G employees. You explore Microsoft database templates to see what is available.*

STEPS

1. **Start Access 2016**

   As shown in **FIGURE 9-12**, Microsoft provides many web and desktop database templates to help you create a new database. An **Access app** is an Access database that you publish to a SharePoint server and is available to users who work with a browser over the Internet.

   A **desktop database** is a traditional Access database available to users who work with Access on their computers over a local area network and is often identified by the word *desktop* in the template name. All templates are **online**, meaning that they are available to download from the Microsoft Office Online website. Templates change over time as more are added and enhancements to existing templates are provided by Microsoft. The database you want to create should track employees and the continuing education courses they have completed, so you search for database templates using "nutrition" as the search phrase.

2. **Click the Search for online templates box, type nutrition, click the Start searching button, then click the Nutrition tracking database**

   The Nutrition tracking database template builds a new database that includes several sample tables, queries, forms, reports, macros, and a module object. You can use or modify these objects to meet your needs.

TROUBLE
Templates are constantly changing, so if you cannot find the Nutrition database or if it has changed, explore another desktop database template of your choice.

3. **Click the Browse button 📁, navigate to where you store your Data Files, enter Nutrition in the File name box, click OK in the File New Database dialog box, click Create, then click the Enable Content button**

   A form to track today's information opens automatically, and the other objects in the database are presented in the Navigation Pane as shown in **FIGURE 9-13**.

4. **Right-click the Today at a glance form tab, click Close, then locate and double-click the My Profile form in the Navigation Pane**

   Objects created by database templates are rich in functionality and can be modified for your specific needs or analyzed to learn more about Access.

5. **Close the My Profile form, then double-click the Search form to open it**

   If you wanted to use this database, your next step would be to enter data and continue exploring the other objects in the database. The Search form searches over 6,000 records stored in the Foods table that records calories, fat, protein, and other useful nutrition statistics for each record.

6. **Close the Search form, then open, explore, and close the other objects of the Nutrition database**

   Because this database is designed for a traditional school rather than a corporate educational environment, you won't be using it at R2G. However, you can still learn a great deal by exploring the objects that the template created. You will also keep using this sample database to learn about Application Parts.

FIGURE 9-12: **Creating a database from a template**

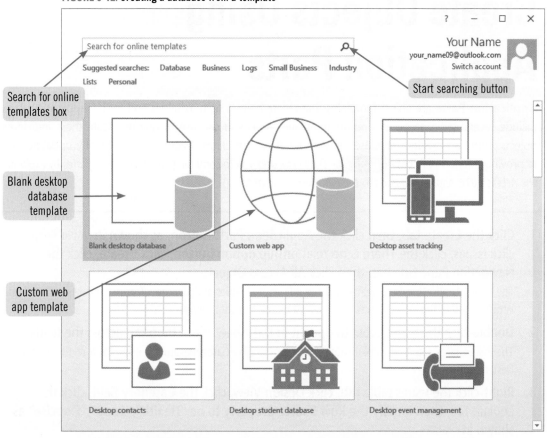

FIGURE 9-13: **Nutrition desktop database template**

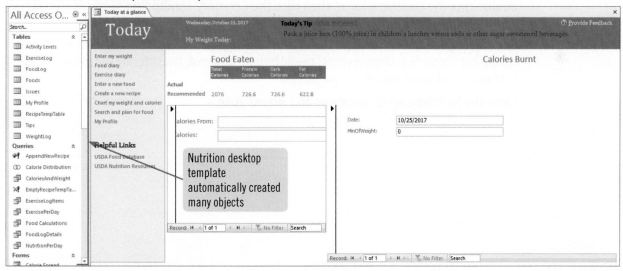

Setting a startup form

To specify that a particular form automatically opens when the database opens, click the File tab, click Options, then click the Current Database category in the Access Options dialog box. Use the Display Form drop-down list to specify which form should automatically open when the database is started. Another way to set startup options is to create an AutoExec macro. Macros will be covered in a later module.

Access 2016

Create Objects Using Application Parts

Application Parts are object templates that create objects such as tables and forms. Application Parts include several table, form, and report templates, tools you can use to quickly create these individual objects within an existing database. As with database templates, Microsoft is constantly updating and improving this part of Access. **CASE** *David Fox asks you to continue your study of templates by exploring the Access 2016 Application Parts in the Nutrition database.*

STEPS

1. **Click the Create tab, then click the Application Parts button, as shown in FIGURE 9-14, click Issues, click the There is no relationship option button, click Create, click the Navigation Pane title bar, then click All Access Objects**

   The Issues Application Part created a new table named Issues and two new forms named IssueDetail and IssueNew. All of the other objects were created by the Nutrition template.

2. **Double-click the Issues table to open it in Datasheet View, then tab across the fields**

   The Issues table has four Lookup fields: Status, Priority, Category, and Project. Explore them in Table Design View.

3. **Right-click the Issues table tab, click Design View, click the Category field, click the Lookup tab, then modify the Row Source property to be "Health","Food","Exercise" as shown in FIGURE 9-15**

   Modifying the Lookup properties of a field in Table Design View will impact the forms based on that table.

4. **Right-click the Issues table tab, click Close, click Yes when prompted to save the table, double-click the IssueNew form, then click the Category combo box arrow as shown in FIGURE 9-16**

   Access database templates and Application Parts provide powerful tools to build databases and objects quickly. You can use or modify the objects created by them as desired. Templates are also an exciting way to learn more about Access features and possibilities.

5. **Close the Nutrition.accdb database and Access 2016**

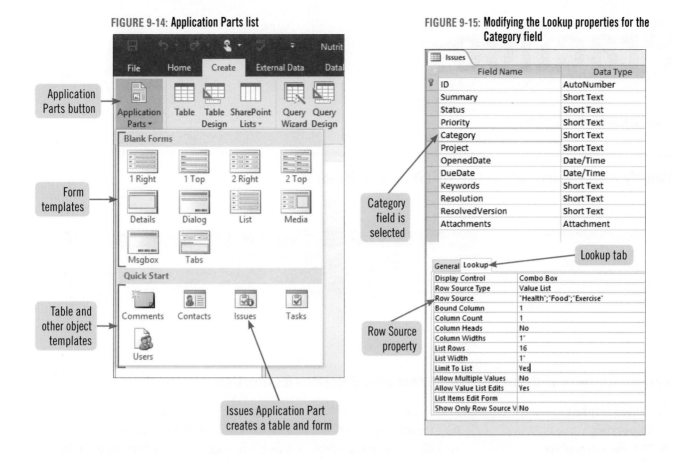

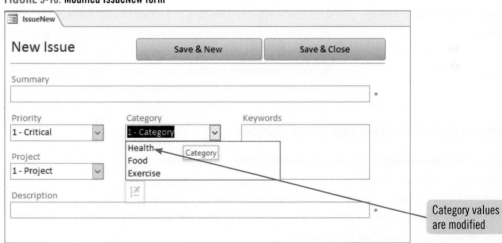

FIGURE 9-16: Modified IssueNew form

Importing from another database

If you import from an Access database using the Access button on the External Data tab, you are presented with a dialog box that allows you to import selected objects from the database. This provides an excellent way to develop new queries, forms, and reports in an external "development" database and then import them into the "production" database only after they have been fully developed and tested.

Practice

Concepts Review

Identify each element of the External Data tab shown in FIGURE 9-17.

FIGURE 9-17

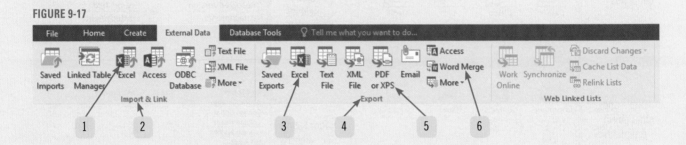

Match each term with the statement that best describes its function.

7. **Table template**
8. **Importing**
9. **Database template**
10. **Mail merge**
11. **Exporting**
12. **Main document**
13. **Delimited text file**
14. **Linking**

a. A tool used to quickly create a single table within an existing database
b. A file used to determine how a letter and Access data will be combined
c. A file that stores one record on each line, with the field values separated by a common character such as a comma, tab, or dash
d. A way to copy Access information to another database, spreadsheet, or file format
e. The process of converting data from an external source into an Access database
f. A way to connect to data in an external source without copying it
g. A tool used to quickly create a new database based on a particular subject, such as assets, contacts, events, or projects
h. To combine data from an Access table or query into a Word form letter, label, or envelope to create mass mailing documents

Select the best answer from the list of choices.

15. **Which of the following is not true about database templates?**
    a. They analyze the data on your computer and suggest database applications.
    b. They cover a wide range of subjects, including assets, contacts, events, or projects.
    c. Microsoft provides online templates in areas such as business and personal database applications.
    d. They create multiple database objects.

16. **Which of the following is not true about exporting?**
    a. Access data can be exported to Word.
    b. Access data can be exported into Excel.
    c. Exporting creates a copy of data.
    d. Exporting retains a link between the original and target data files.

17. **Which of the following is not a file format that Access can import?**
    a. Access
    b. Word
    c. Excel
    d. HTML

18. **Which of the following file formats allows you to send information that cannot be modified?**
   a. RTF
   b. HTM
   c. XLS
   d. PDF

19. **Which is not true about enforcing referential integrity?**
   a. It is required for all one-to-many relationships.
   b. It prevents orphan records.
   c. It prevents records that have matching records on the "many" side from being deleted on the "one" side of a one-to-many relationship.
   d. It prevents records that do not have a matching record on the "one" side from being created on the "many" side of a one-to-many relationship.

20. **Which of the following is not true about linking?**
   a. Access can link to data in an Excel spreadsheet.
   b. Linking copies data from one data file to another.
   c. Access can link to data in an HTML file.
   d. You can edit linked data in Access.

Skills Review

1. **Import data from Excel.**
   a. Open the Machinery-9.accdb database from the location where you store your Data Files. Enable content if prompted.
   b. Import the MachineryEmployees.xlsx spreadsheet from the location where you store your Data Files to a new table in the current database using the Import Spreadsheet Wizard to import the data. Make sure that the first row is specified as the column headings.
   c. Choose the EmployeeNo field as the primary key, and import the data to a table named **Employees**. Do not save the import steps.
   d. In Table Design View of the Employees table, change the Field Size of the EmployeeNo field to Long Integer. Save and close the Employees table.

2. **Link data from Excel.**
   a. Link to the Vendors.xlsx Excel file in the location where you store your Data Files.
   b. In the Link Spreadsheet Wizard, specify that the first row contains column headings.
   c. Name the linked table **Vendors**.
   d. Open the Relationships window and display all five field lists in the window. Link the tables together with one-to-many relationships, as shown in FIGURE 9-18. Be sure to enforce referential integrity on all relationships except for the relationship between Products and the linked Vendors table.
   e. Save and close the Relationships window.

FIGURE 9-18

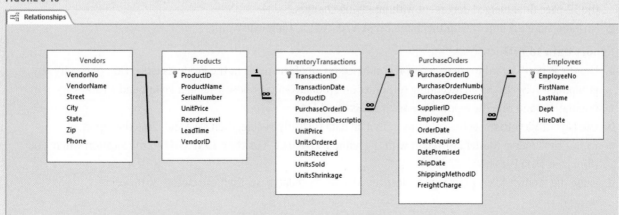

Skills Review (continued)

3. **Export data to Excel.**

   a. Open the Products table to view the datasheet, then close it.

   b. Export the Products table data to an Excel spreadsheet named **ProductList.xlsx**. Save the spreadsheet to the location where you store your Data Files. Do not save the export steps.

4. **Publish data to Word.**

   a. In the Machinery-9.accdb database, export the Products table to a Word document named **ProductList.rtf**. Save the ProductList.rtf file in the location where you store your Data Files. Do not save the export steps.

   b. Start Word, then open the ProductList.rtf document from the location where you store your Data Files. Press [Enter] twice, press [Ctrl][Home] to return to the top of the document, then type the following text:

   INTERNAL MEMO

From:	**Your Name**
To:	**Sales Staff**
Date:	**Today's date**

   Do not forget to check the lead times on the Back Hoe and Thatcher. We typically do not keep these items in stock.

   c. Proofread the document, then save and print it. Close the document, then exit Word.

5. **Merge data with Word.**

   a. In the Machinery-9.accdb database, merge the data from the Employees table to a new Word document.

   b. Use the "Create a new document and then link the data to it" option in the Microsoft Word Mail Merge Wizard dialog box. In the Word document, enter the following text as the main document for the mail merge:

Date:	**Today's date**
To:	
From:	**Your Name**
Re:	**First Aid Training**

   The annual First Aid Training session will be held on Friday, February 1, 2017. Please sign up for this important event in the lunchroom. Friends and family who are at least 18 years old are also welcome.

   c. To the right of To:, press [Spacebar] to position the insertion point at the location for the first merge field.

   d. Click the Insert Merge Field button arrow, click FirstName, press [Spacebar], click the Insert Merge Field button arrow, then click LastName.

   e. Click the links at the bottom of the Mail Merge task pane to move through the steps of the mail-merge process, Steps 1 through 6, click Edit individual letters, then click OK to make sure that your final document has 12 pages for the 12 records in your Access Employees table.

   f. Print the first page of the merged document if required by your instructor (the letter to Melissa Lenox), then close the 12-page final merged document without saving changes.

   g. Save the main document with the name **FirstAid.docx**, then exit Word.

6. **Export data to PDF.**

   a. Use the Report Wizard to create a new report based on all of the fields in the Products table. Do not specify any grouping levels, choose an ascending sort order on ProductName, choose a Tabular layout and a Landscape orientation, and title the report **Product Master List**.

   b. Use Layout View to resize the columns so that all data is clearly visible, then save and close the report.

   c. Export the Product Master List report with the name **Product Master List.pdf** to the location where you store your Data Files.

   d. Close the Product Master List report, close the Machinery-9 database, then exit Access 2016.

Skills Review (continued)

7. Create objects using database templates.

  a. Start Access 2016 and use the Desktop customer service template to build a new Access database. Save the database with the name **CustomerService** in the location where you store your Data Files.

  b. Enable content if prompted, then explore the forms in the database by opening and closing the Case Details form, the Case List form, and the Report Center form.

  c. Close all open forms, and then explore the relationships between tables by opening the Relationships window. Expand, move, and resize the field lists as needed to view all fields as shown in FIGURE 9-19.

FIGURE 9-19

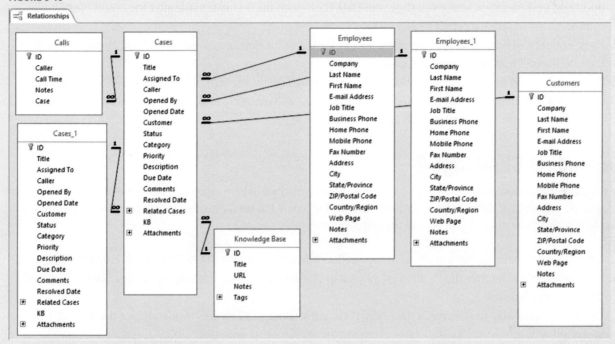

  d. Note that the Employees table is related to the Cases table twice, once to the Assigned To field and a second time to the Opened By field. Also, the Cases table is related to itself via the Related Cases field. Create a Relationships report in landscape orientation. If all of the field lists don't fit on a single piece of paper, keep working with the field lists in the Relationships window or narrow the left and right margins until the report fits on a single piece of paper.

  e. Add a label to the Report Header section with your name, and change the font color of the new label to black. Save the report with the default name **Relationships for CustomerService**, then close it.

8. Create objects using Application Parts.

  a. Use the Comments table template in Application Parts to create a new table in the CustomerService.accdb database named **Comments**. Choose "There is no relationship."

  b. Open the Comments table to view the fields. Using your Relationships report, decide how you think the Comments table would be connected to the rest of the relational database. What tables and fields would be used to create the one-to-many relationship? Be prepared to explain your answer in class or submit your answer as requested by the instructor.

  c. Save and close all open objects, and then close the CustomerService.accdb database.

Independent Challenge 1

As the manager of a women's college basketball team, you have created a database called Basketball-9 that tracks the players, games, and player statistics. You want to export a report to a Word document.

   a. Open the database Basketball-9.accdb from the location where you store your Data Files. Enable content if prompted.

   b. In the Relationships window, connect the Games and Stats tables with a one-to-many relationship based on the common GameNo field. Connect the Players and Stats tables with a one-to-many relationship based on the common PlayerNo field. Be sure to enforce referential integrity on both relationships. Save and close the Relationships window.

   c. Export the Player Statistics report to a Word file with the name **PlayerStats.rtf**. Save the PlayerStats.rtf document in the location where you store your Data Files. Open the destination file after the export operation is complete. Do not save the export steps.

   d. Press [Enter] three times to enter three blank lines at the top of the document, then press [Ctrl][Home] to position the insertion point at the top of the document.

   e. Type *your name* on the first line of the document, enter *today's date* as the second line, then read the information and write a sentence or two that explains the data that follows. Save, print, and close the PlayerStats.rtf document.

   f. Exit Word. Close the Basketball-9.accdb database, then exit Access.

Independent Challenge 2

As the manager of a women's college basketball team, you have created a database called Basketball-9 that tracks the players, games, and player statistics. The 2018–2019 basketball schedule has been provided to you as an Excel spreadsheet file. You will import that data and append it to the current Games table.

   a. Open the database Basketball-9.accdb from the location where you store your Data Files. Enable content if prompted.

   b. If the relationships haven't already been established in this database, create relationships as described in Step b of Independent Challenge 1.

   c. Open the Games table to observe the datasheet. It currently contains 22 records with scores for the 2017–2018 basketball season.

   d. Start Excel and open the 2018–2019Schedule.xlsx file from the location where you store your Data Files. Note that it contains 22 rows of data indicating the opponent, mascot, home or away status, and date of the games for the 2018–2019 season. You have been told that the data will import more precisely if it is identified with the same field names as have already been established in the Games table in Access, so you'll insert those field names as a header row in the Excel spreadsheet.

   e. Click anywhere in row 1 of the 2018–2019Schedule.xlsx spreadsheet, click the Insert button arrow in the Cells group, then click Insert Sheet Rows to insert a new blank row.

   f. In the new blank row 1, enter the field names that correspond to the field names in the Games table for the same data above each column: **Opponent**, **Mascot**, **Home-Away**, and **GameDate**. Be careful to enter the names precisely as shown.

   g. Save and close the 2018–2019Schedule.xlsx spreadsheet, exit Excel, and return to the Basketball-9.accdb database.

   h. Close the Games table, click the External Data tab, click the Excel button in the Import & Link group, browse for the 2018–2019Schedule.xlsx spreadsheet in your Data Files, then choose the Append a copy of the records to the table option button. Be sure that Games is selected as the table to use for the append process.

Independent Challenge 2 (continued)

i. Follow the steps of the Import Spreadsheet Wizard process through completion (do not save the import steps), then open the Games table. It should contain the original 22 records for the 2017–2018 season plus 22 more from the 2018–2019Schedule.xlsx spreadsheet with default values of 0 for both the CycloneScore and OpponentScore fields.

j. Change the Opponent value in the first record to *your last name's* **College**, then print the first page of the Games table if requested by your instructor.

k. Save and close the Games table, close the Basketball-9.accdb database, then exit Access.

Independent Challenge 3

You have been asked by a small engineering firm to build a database that tracks projects. You decide to explore Microsoft database templates to see if there is a template that could help you get started.

a. Start Access and start a new database with the *Desktop* project management template. (*Hint*: Do not use the *Access App* Project management template.) Save and name the database **ProjectMgmt.accdb**, store it in the location where you store your Data Files, then enable content if prompted.

b. Open the Navigation Pane, click the Navigation Pane title bar, then choose Object Type to organize the objects in this database by type.

c. Open and review the Relationships window. Rearrange the field lists as shown in FIGURE 9-20. Add a label to the Report Header section with your name, and change the font color of the new label to black. Save the report with the default name **Relationships for Project Mgmt**, print it if requested by your instructor, then close it.

FIGURE 9-20

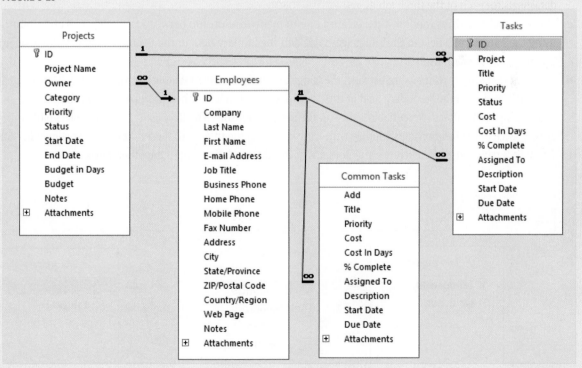

Independent Challenge 3 (continued)

d. Save and close the Relationships window.

e. Open the Project List form (if it's not already open), and enter the following data: Project Name: **Mobile Website**, Owner: **Your Name**.

f. Click Yes to add your name to the list, then enter your school's Business Phone, Address, City, State/Province, Zip/Postal Code, Country/Region, and your school Email information in the Employee Details form.

g. Close the Employee Details form and the Project List form.

h. Open the Employee List form, and add another record for your instructor. Enter your instructor's school email address, school phone, and school name for the E-mail Address, Business Phone, and Company fields. Enter **Professor** in the Job Title field for your instructor.

i. Close the Employee List form, then open the Employee Address Book report. If requested by your instructor, print the report and then close it.

j. Explore the other objects of the ProjectMgmt database, close the database, then exit Access.

Independent Challenge 4: Explore

Learning common phrases in a variety of foreign languages is extremely valuable if you travel or interact with people from other countries. As a volunteer with the foreign student exchange program at your college, you have created a database that documents the primary and secondary languages used by foreign countries. The database also includes a table of common words and phrases that you can use to practice basic conversation skills. (*Note*: To complete this Independent Challenge, make sure you are connected to the Internet.)

a. Open the Languages-9.accdb database from the location where you store your Data Files. Enable content if prompted.

b. Open the datasheets for each of the three tables to familiarize yourself with the fields and records. The Primary and Secondary fields in the Countries table represent the primary and secondary languages for that country. Close the datasheets for each of the three tables.

c. Open the Relationships window, then create a one-to-many relationship between the Languages and Countries table using the LanguageID field in the Languages table and the Primary field in the Countries table. Enforce referential integrity on the relationship.

d. Create a one-to-many relationship between the Languages and Countries tables using the LanguageID field in the Languages table and the Secondary field in the Countries table. Click No when prompted to edit the existing relationship, and enforce referential integrity on the new relationship. The field list for the Languages table will appear twice in the Relationships window with Languages_1 as the title for the second field list, as shown in FIGURE 9-21. The Words table is used for reference and does not have a direct relationship to the other tables.

FIGURE 9-21

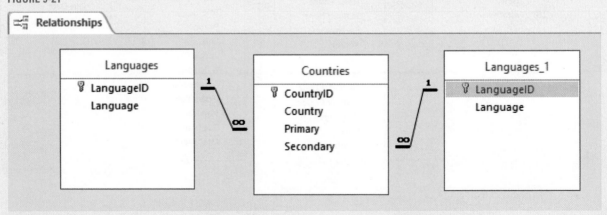

Independent Challenge 4: Explore (continued)

e. Create a Relationships report, then display it in Design View.

f. Add a label to the Report Header section with your name, change the font color of the new label to black, then save the report with the name **Relationships for Language-9**.

g. Print the report if requested by your instructor, then save and close it.

h. Connect to the Internet and go to www.ask.com, www.about.com, or any search engine. Your goal is to find a website that translates English to other languages and to print the home page of that website.

i. Add a new field to the Words table with a new language that isn't already represented. Use the website to translate the existing six words into the new language.

j. Add three new words or phrases to the Words table as shown in FIGURE 9-22, making sure that the translation is made in all of the represented languages: English, French, Spanish, German, Italian, Portuguese, Polish, and the new language you added.

FIGURE 9-22

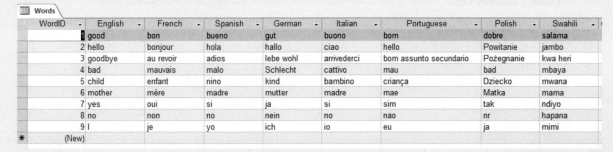

WordID	English	French	Spanish	German	Italian	Portuguese	Polish	Swahili
1	good	bon	bueno	gut	buono	bom	dobre	salama
2	hello	bonjour	hola	hallo	ciao	hello	Powitanie	jambo
3	goodbye	au revoir	adios	lebe wohl	arrivederci	bom assunto secundario	Pożegnanie	kwa heri
4	bad	mauvais	malo	Schlecht	cattivo	mau	bad	mbaya
5	child	enfant	nino	kind	bambino	criança	Dziecko	mwana
6	mother	mère	madre	mutter	madre	mae	Matka	mama
7	yes	oui	si	ja	si	sim	tak	ndiyo
8	no	non	no	nein	no	nao	nr	hapana
9	I	je	yo	ich	io	eu	ja	mimi
* (New)								

k. If requested by your instructor, print the updated datasheet for the Words table, close the Words table, close the Languages-9.accdb database, then exit Access.

Visual Workshop

Start Access and open the Basketball-9.accdb database from the location where you store your Data Files. Enable content if prompted. Merge the information from the Players table to a new Word form letter. The first page of the merged document is shown in FIGURE 9-23. Notice that the player's first and last names have been merged to the first line and that the player's first name is merged a second time in the first sentence of the letter. Be very careful to correctly add spaces as needed around the merge fields. Print the last page of the merged document if requested by your instructor, close the 13-page final merged document without saving it, save the main document as **Uniforms.docx**, then close it.

FIGURE 9-23

To: Sydney Freesen

From: *Your Name*

Date: *Current Date*

Re: New Uniforms

Sydney, during our first week of practice please check in with our manager to help her finalize our uniform order. She will be available right after practice ends. Our new uniforms are awesome!

Creating Advanced Queries

CASE You use advanced query techniques to help David Fox handle the requests for information about data stored in the Training database for Reason 2 Go.

Module Objectives

After completing this module, you will be able to:

- Query for top values
- Create a parameter query
- Modify query properties
- Create a Make Table query
- Create an Append query
- Create a Delete query
- Create an Update query
- Specify join properties
- Find unmatched records

Files You Will Need

Training-10.accdb   Basketball-10.accdb

Seminar-10.accdb   Candy-10.accdb

Query for Top Values

After you enter a large number of records into a database, you may want to select only the most significant records by choosing a subset of the highest or lowest values from a sorted query. Use the **Top Values** feature in Query Design View to specify a number or percentage of sorted records that you want to display in the query's datasheet. **CASE** ▶ *Employee attendance at continuing education classes has grown at Reason 2 Go. To help plan future classes, David Fox wants a listing of the top five classes, sorted in descending order by the number of attendees for each class. You can create a summary query to find and sort the total number of attendees for each class and then use the Top Values feature to find the five most attended classes.*

STEPS

1. **Start Access, open the Training-10.accdb database, enable content if prompted, click the Create tab, then click the Query Design button in the Queries group**

   You need fields from both the Enrollments and the Courses tables.

2. **Double-click Enrollments, double-click Courses, then click Close in the Show Table dialog box**

   Query Design View displays the field lists of the two related tables in the upper pane of the query window.

3. **Double-click Description in the Courses field list, double-click EnrollmentID in the Enrollments field list, then click the View button ⊞ to switch to Datasheet View**

   The datasheet shows 388 total records. You want to know how many people took each course, so you need to group the records by the Description field and count the EnrollmentID field.

4. **Click the View button ⊠ to switch to Query Design View, click the Totals button in the Show/Hide group, click Group By for the EnrollmentID field, click the Group By list arrow, then click Count**

   Sorting is required in order to find the top values.

5. **Click the EnrollmentID field Sort list arrow, then click Descending**

   Your screen should look like **FIGURE 10-1**. Choosing a descending sort order lists the courses with the highest count value (the most attended courses) at the top of the datasheet.

6. **Click the Top Values list arrow in the Query Setup group, then click 5**

   The number or percentage specified in the Top Values list box determines which records the query returns, starting with the first record on the sorted datasheet. This is why you must sort your records before applying the Top Values feature. See **TABLE 10-1** for more information on Top Values options.

7. **Click ⊞ to display the resulting datasheet, then use the ⟷ pointer to widen the second column to show the complete field name**

   Your screen should look like **FIGURE 10-2**. The datasheet shows the 8 most-attended continuing education courses. The query selected the top 8 rather than the top 5 courses because there are 5 courses with 17 enrollments tied for fourth and fifth place.

8. **Click the Save button ⊟ on the Quick Access Toolbar, type TopEnrollments, click OK, then close the datasheet**

   As with all queries, if you enter additional enrollment records into this database, the statistics in the TopEnrollments query are automatically updated.

FIGURE 10-1: Designing a summary query for top values

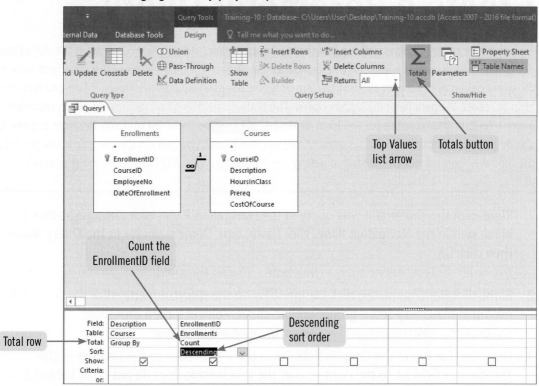

FIGURE 10-2: Top Values datasheet

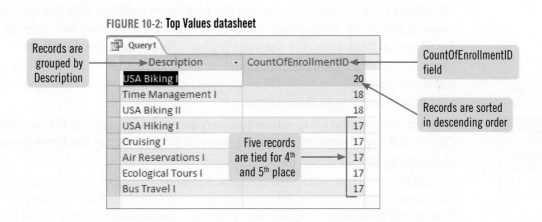

TABLE 10-1: Top Values options

action	displays
Click 5, 25, or 100 in the Top Values list	Top 5, 25, or 100 records
Enter a number, such as 10, in the Top Values box	Top 10, or whatever value is entered, records
Click 5% or 25% in the Top Values list	Top 5 percent or 25 percent of records
Enter a percentage, such as 10%, in the Top Values text box	Top 10 percent, or whatever percentage is entered, of records
Click All	All records

Create a Parameter Query

Learning Outcomes
• Enter parameter criteria
• Apply the Like operator

A **parameter query** displays a dialog box that prompts you for field criteria. Your entry in the dialog box determines which records appear on the final datasheet, just as if you had entered that criteria directly in the query design grid. You can also build a form or report based on a parameter query. When you open the form or report, the parameter dialog box opens. The entry in the dialog box determines which records the query selects in the recordset for the form or report. **CASE** ▶ *David Fox asks you to create a query to display the courses for an individual department that you specify each time you run the query. To do so, you copy the TopEnrollments query then modify it to remove the Top Values option and include parameter prompts.*

STEPS

1. **Right-click the TopEnrollments query in the Navigation Pane, click Copy, right-click a blank spot in the Navigation Pane, click Paste, type DeptParameter as the Query Name, then click OK**

   You modify the DeptParameter query to remove the top values and to include the parameter prompt.

   QUICK TIP
   You can also drag the Employees table from the Navigation Pane into Query Design View.

2. **Right-click DeptParameter, click Design View on the shortcut menu, click the Show Table button in the Query Setup group, double-click Employees, then click Close**

   The Employees table contains the EDepartment field needed for this query.

3. **Drag the title bar of the Courses field list to the left, then drag the title bar of the Enrollments field list to the right so that the relationship lines do not cross behind a field list**

   You are not required to rearrange the field lists of a query, but doing so can help clarify the relationships between them.

4. **Double-click the EDepartment field in the Employees field list, click the Top Values list arrow in the Query Setup group, click All, delete the Descending sort order in the EnrollmentID field, then click the View button ▦ to display the datasheet**

   The query now counts the EnrollmentID field for records grouped by course description as well as by employee department. Because you only want to query for one department at a time, however, you need to add parameter criteria to the Department field.

   QUICK TIP
   To enter a long criterion, right-click the Criteria cell, then click Zoom.

5. **Click the View button ▨ to return to Query Design View, click the EDepartment field Criteria cell, type [Enter department:], then click ▦ to display the Enter Parameter Value dialog box, as shown in FIGURE 10-3**

   In Query Design View, you enter parameter criteria within [square brackets], and it appears as a prompt in the Enter Parameter Value dialog box. The entry you make in the Enter Parameter Value dialog box is used as the final criterion for the field. You can combine logical operators such as greater than (>) or less than (<) as well as the keyword Like and wildcard characters such as an asterisk (*) with parameter criteria to create flexible search options. See **TABLE 10-2** for more examples of parameter criteria.

   QUICK TIP
   Query criteria are not case sensitive, so "marketing," "Marketing," and "MARKETING" all yield the same results.

6. **Type Marketing in the Enter department: text box, then click OK**

   Only those records with "Marketing" in the Department field are displayed, a portion of which are shown in **FIGURE 10-4**.

7. **Save and close the DeptParameter query**

FIGURE 10-3: Using parameter criteria for the EDepartment field

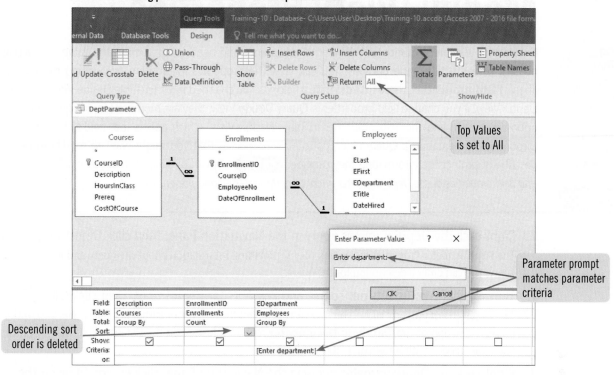

FIGURE 10-4: Datasheet for parameter query when EDepartment field equals Marketing

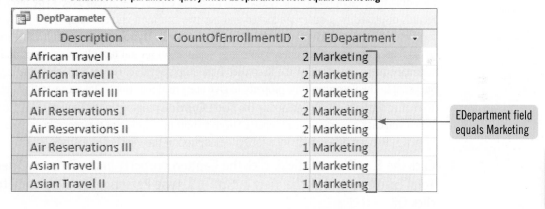

TABLE 10-2: Examples of parameter criteria

field data type	parameter criteria	description
Date/Time	>=[Enter start date:]	Searches for dates on or after the entered date
Date/Time	>=[Enter start date:] and <=[Enter end date:]	Prompts you for two date entries and searches for dates on or after the first date and on or before the second date
Short Text	Like [Enter the first character of the last name:] & "*"	Searches for any name that begins with the entered character
Short Text	Like "*" & [Enter any character(s) to search by:] & "*"	Searches for words that contain the entered characters anywhere in the field

Modify Query Properties

Learning Outcomes
- Modify the Description property
- Define the Recordset Type property
- Create a backup

Properties are characteristics that define the appearance and behavior of items in the database, such as objects, fields, sections, and controls. You can view the properties for an item by opening its Property Sheet. **Field properties**, those that describe a field, can be changed in either Table Design View or Query Design View. If you change field properties in Query Design View, they are modified for that query only (as opposed to changing the field properties in Table Design View, which affects that field's characteristics throughout the database). Query objects also have properties that you might want to modify to better describe or protect the information they provide. **CASE** *David Fox suggests that you modify the query and field properties of the DeptParameter query to better describe and present the data.*

STEPS

1. **Right-click the DeptParameter query in the Navigation Pane, then click Object Properties**

   The DeptParameter Properties dialog box opens, providing information about the query and a text box in which you can enter a description for the query.

2. **Type Counts enrollments per course and prompts for department, then click OK**

   The **Description** property allows you to better document the purpose or author of a query. The Description property also appears on **Database Documenter** reports, a feature on the Database Tools tab that helps you create reports with information about the database.

TROUBLE

The title bar of the Property Sheet always indicates which item's properties are shown. If it shows anything other than "Query Properties," click a blank spot beside the field lists to display query properties.

3. **Right-click the DeptParameter query in the Navigation Pane, click Design View on the shortcut menu, click the Property Sheet button in the Show/Hide group, then click a blank spot in the upper pane to show Query Properties in the Property Sheet**

   The Property Sheet for the query is shown in **FIGURE 10-5**. It includes a complete list of the query's properties, including the Description property that you modified earlier. The **Recordset Type** property determines if records displayed by a query are locked and has two common choices: Snapshot and Dynaset. **Snapshot** locks the recordset (which prevents it from being updated). **Dynaset** is the default value and allows updates to data. Because a summary query's datasheet summarizes several records, you cannot update the data in a summary query, regardless of the Recordset Type property value. For regular Select queries, you can specify Snapshot in the Recordset Type property to give users read (but not write) access to that datasheet.

   To change the field name, you modify the field's **Caption** property in the Property Sheet for field properties. When you click a property in a Property Sheet, a short description of the property appears in the status bar. Press [F1] to open Access Help for a longer description of the selected property.

4. **Click the EnrollmentID field, click the Caption property in the Property Sheet, type Total Enrollment, click the View button ▦, type Personnel as the parameter value, then click OK**

   The Total Enrollment Caption clarifies the second column of data, as shown in **FIGURE 10-6**, which displays a portion of the datasheet.

QUICK TIP

To add a description to a table, form, or other object, close it, right-click it in the Navigation Pane, then click View Properties on the shortcut menu.

5. **Save and close the DeptParameter query**

   The next few lessons work with action queries that modify data. In preparation for these lessons, you create a backup. A **backup** is a copy of the database that you could use if an error that cannot be fixed occurs in the current database. Businesses typically back up their database files each night.

6. **Click the File tab, click Save As, double-click Back Up Database, navigate to the location where you store your Data Files, then click Save**

   A copy of the database has been placed in the selected folder with the name Training-10_*current date*.accdb, and you are returned to the Training-10.accdb as shown in the title bar.

FIGURE 10-5: Query Property Sheet

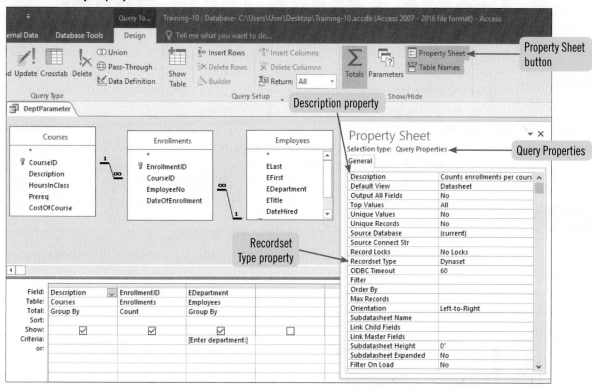

FIGURE 10-6: DeptParameter datasheet when EDepartment field equals Personnel

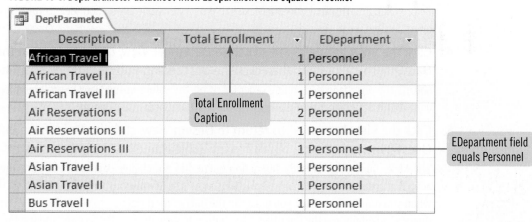

Creating an Alias

The **Alias** property renames a field list in Query Design View. An Alias doesn't change the actual name of the underlying object, but it can be helpful when you are working with a database that uses technical or outdated names for tables and queries. To create an alias, right-click the field list in Query Design View, click Properties on the shortcut menu, and then modify the Alias property.

Create a Make Table Query

Learning
Outcomes
• Define action
  queries
• Create a Make
  Table query

A **Select query** selects fields and records that match specific criteria and displays them in a datasheet. Select queries start with the SQL keyword **SELECT** and have many variations, such as summary, crosstab, top values, and parameter queries. Another very powerful type of query is the action query. Unlike Select queries that only select data, an **action query** changes all of the selected records when it is run. Access provides four types of action queries: Delete, Update, Append, and Make Table. See TABLE 10-3 for more information on action queries. A **Make Table query** is a type of action query that creates a new table of data for the selected datasheet. The location of the new table can be the current database or another Access database. Sometimes a Make Table query is used to back up data. **CASE** ▶ *David Fox asks you to use a Make Table query to archive the first quarter's records for the year 2017 that are currently stored in the Enrollments table.*

STEPS

1. **Click the Create tab, click the Query Design button, double-click Enrollments in the Show Table dialog box, click Close, then close the Property Sheet if it is open**
    Given that you cannot undo the changes made by an action query, it's a good idea to create a backup copy of the database before running an action query. You created a backup copy of the database in the last step of the previous lesson.

2. **Double-click the * (asterisk) at the top of the Enrollments field list**
    Adding the asterisk to the query design grid includes in the grid all of the fields in that table. Later, if you add new fields to the Enrollments table, they are also added to this query.

3. **Double-click the DateOfEnrollment field to add it to the second column of the query grid, click the DateOfEnrollment field Criteria cell, type >=1/1/17 and <=3/31/17, click the DateOfEnrollment field Show check box to uncheck it, then use the resize pointer ⟷ to widen the DateOfEnrollment column to view the entire Criteria entry, as shown in FIGURE 10-7**
    Before changing this query into a Make Table query, it is always a good idea to run the query as a Select query to view the selected data.

4. **Click the View button ▦ to switch to Datasheet View, click any entry in the DateOfEnrollment field, then click the Descending button in the Sort & Filter group**
    Sorting the records in descending order based on the values in the DateOfEnrollment field allows you to confirm that only records in the first quarter of 2017 appear in the datasheet.

5. **Click the View button ☑ to return to Design View, click the Make Table button in the Query Type group, type 1Q2017 in the Table Name text box, then click OK**
    The Make Table query is ready, but action queries do not change data until you click the Run button. All action query icons include an exclamation point in their buttons to remind you that they change data when you run them and that you must run the queries for the action to occur. To prevent running an action query accidentally, use the Datasheet View button to view the selected records, and use the Run button only when you are ready to run the action.

6. **Click the View button ▦ to double-check the records you have selected, click the View button ☑ to return to Query Design View, click the Run button to execute the make table action, click Yes when prompted that you are about to paste 143 rows, then save the query with the name Make1Q2017 and close it**
    When you run an action query, Access prompts you with an "Are you sure?" message before actually updating the data. The Undo button cannot undo changes made by action queries.

7. **Double-click the 1Q2017 table in the Navigation Pane to view the new table's datasheet as shown in FIGURE 10-8, then close the 1Q2017 table**

FIGURE 10-7: Creating a Make Table query

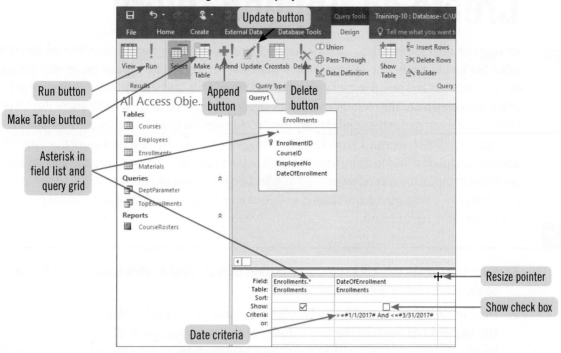

FIGURE 10-8: 1Q2017 table

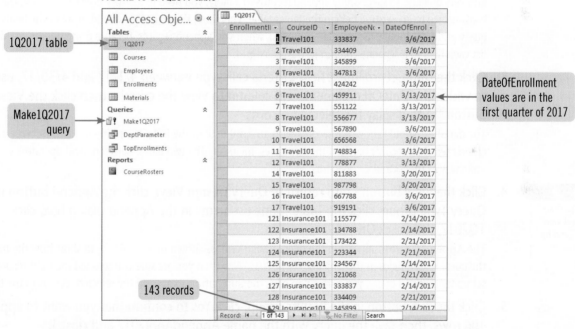

TABLE 10-3: Action queries

action query	query icon	description	example
Delete		Deletes a group of records from one or more tables	Remove products that are discontinued or for which there are no orders
Update		Makes global changes to a group of records in one or more tables	Raise prices by 10 percent for all products
Append		Adds a group of records from one or more tables to the end of another table	Append the employee address table from one division of the company to the address table from another division of the company
Make Table		Creates a new table from data in one or more tables	Export records to another Access database or make a backup copy of a table

Create an Append Query

Learning Outcomes
• Create an Append query

An **Append query** is an action query that adds selected records to an existing table. The existing table is called the **target table**. The Append query works like an export feature because the records are copied from one location and pasted in the target table. The target table can be in the current database or in any other Access database. The most difficult part of creating an Append query is making sure that all of the fields you have selected in the Append query match fields with the same data types in the target table. For example, you cannot append a Short Text field from one table to a Number field in another table. If you attempt to append a field to an incompatible field in the target table, an error message appears and you are forced to cancel the append process. **CASE** ▸ *David Fox wants you to use an Append query to append the records with a DateOfEnrollment value in April 2017 from the Enrollments table to the 1Q2017 table. Then you'll rename the 1Q2017 table.*

STEPS

1. **Click the Create tab, click the Query Design button, double-click Enrollments in the Show Table dialog box, then click Close**

2. **Double-click the title bar in the Enrollments table's field list to select all fields, then drag the highlighted fields to the first column of the query design grid**

   Double-clicking the title bar of the field list selects all of the fields, allowing you to add them to the query grid very quickly. To successfully append records to a table, you need to identify how each field in the query is connected to an existing field in the target table. Therefore, the technique of adding all of the fields to the query grid by using the asterisk does not work when you append records, because using the asterisk doesn't list each field in a separate column in the query grid.

3. **Click the DateOfEnrollment field Criteria cell, type Between 4/1/17 and 4/30/17, use ↔ to widen the DateOfEnrollment field column to view the criteria, then click the View button 📋 to display the selected records**

   The datasheet should show 106 records with an April date in the DateOfEnrollment field. **Between...and** criteria select all records between the two dates, including the two dates. Between...and operators work the same way as the >= and <= operators.

QUICK TIP
For Select queries, the Datasheet View button 📋 and the Run button do the same thing.

4. **Click the View button 📐 to return to Query Design View, click the Append button in the Query Type group, click the Table Name list arrow in the Append dialog box, click 1Q2017, then click OK**

   The **Append To row** appears in the query design grid, as shown in **FIGURE 10-9**, to show how the fields in the query match fields in the target table, 1Q2017. Now that you are sure you selected the right records and set up the Append query, you're ready to click the Run button to append the selected records to the table.

5. **Click the Run button in the Results group, click Yes to confirm that you want to append 106 rows, then save the query with the name AppendApril2017 and close it**

6. **Double-click the 1Q2017 table in the Navigation Pane, click any entry in the DateOfEnrollment field, then click the Descending button in the Sort & Filter group**

   The 106 April records are appended to the 1Q2017 table, which previously had 143 records for a new total of 249 records, as shown in **FIGURE 10-10**.

7. **Save and close the 1Q2017 table, right-click the 1Q2017 table, click Rename, type JanFebMarApr2017, then press [Enter]**

FIGURE 10-9: Creating an Append query

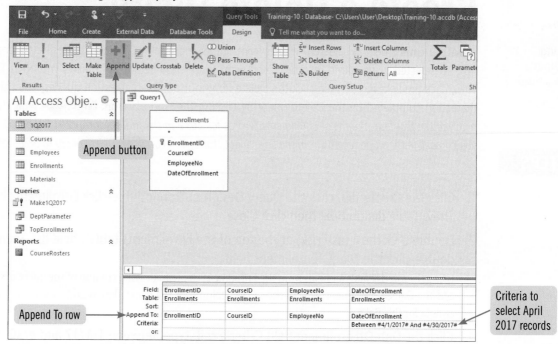

FIGURE 10-10: 1Q2017 table with appended records

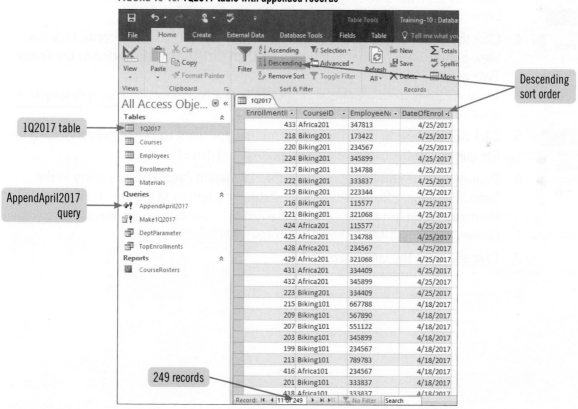

1900 versus 2000 dates

If you type only two digits of a date, Access assumes that the digits 00 through 29 are for the years 2000 through 2029. If you type 30 through 99, Access assumes the years refer to 1930 through 1999. If you want to specify years outside these ranges, you must type all four digits of the year.

Create a Delete Query

A **Delete query** deletes selected records from one or more tables. Delete queries delete entire records, not just selected fields within records. If you want to delete a field from a table, you open Table Design View, click the field name, then click the Delete Rows button. As in all action queries, you cannot reverse the action completed by the Delete query by clicking the Undo button. **CASE** *Now that you have archived the first four months of Enrollments records for 2017 in the JanFebMarApr2017 table, David Fox says you can delete the same records from the Enrollments table. You can use a Delete query to accomplish this task.*

STEPS

1. **Click the Create tab, click the Query Design button, double-click Enrollments in the Show Table dialog box, then click Close**

2. **Double-click the * (asterisk) at the top of the Enrollments table's field list, then double-click the DateOfEnrollment field**

   Using the asterisk adds all fields from the Enrollments table to the first column of the query design grid. You add the DateOfEnrollment field to the second column of the query design grid so you can enter limiting criteria for this field.

3. **Click the DateOfEnrollment field Criteria cell, type Between 1/1/17 and 4/30/17, then use ↔ to widen the DateOfEnrollment field column to view the criteria**

   Before you run a Delete query, be sure to check the selected records to make sure you selected the same 249 records that are in the JanFebMarApr2017 table.

QUICK TIP
The View button ▦ is always a safe way to view selected records for both Select and action queries.

4. **Click the View button ▦ to confirm that the datasheet has 249 records, click the View button ✎ to return to Design View, then click the Delete button in the Query Type group**

   Your screen should look like **FIGURE 10-11**. The **Delete row** now appears in the query design grid. You can delete the selected records by clicking the Run button.

QUICK TIP
Remember that the action taken by the Run button for an action query cannot be undone.

5. **Click the Run button, click Yes to confirm that you want to delete 249 rows, then save the query with the name DeleteJan-Apr2017 and close it**

6. **Double-click the Enrollments table in the Navigation Pane, click any entry in the DateOfEnrollment field, then click the Ascending button in the Sort & Filter group**

   The records should start in May, as shown in **FIGURE 10-12**. The Delete query deleted all records from the Enrollments table with dates between 1/1/2017 and 4/30/2017.

7. **Save and close the Enrollments table**

FIGURE 10-11: Creating a Delete query

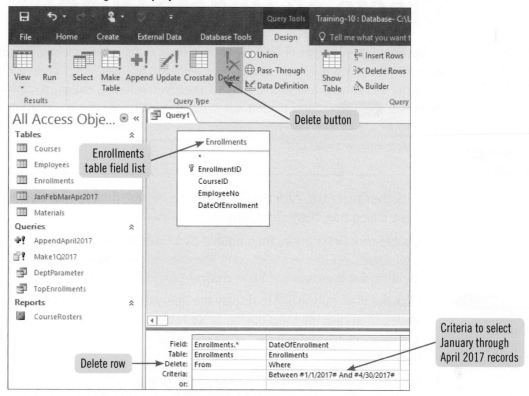

FIGURE 10-12: Final Enrollments table after deleting 249 records

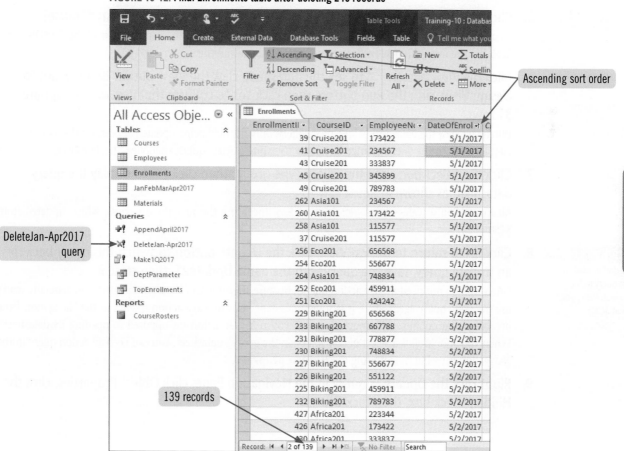

Create an Update Query

An **Update query** is a type of action query that updates the values in a field. For example, you might want to increase the price of a product in a particular category by 10 percent. Or you might want to update information such as the assigned sales representative, region, or territory for a subset of customers. **CASE** *David Fox has just informed you that the cost of continuing education is being increased by $25 for each class effective immediately. You can create an Update query to quickly calculate and update the new course costs.*

STEPS

1. **Click the Create tab, click the Query Design button, double-click Courses in the Show Table dialog box, then click Close**

2. **Double-click Description, then double-click CostOfCourse**

   Every action query starts as a Select query. Always review the datasheet of the Select query before initiating any action that changes data to double-check which records are affected.

3. **Click the View button [ ] to display the query datasheet and observe the CostOfCourse values, then click the View button [ ] to return to Design View**

   After reviewing the values in the CostOfCourse field, you're ready to change this Select query into an Update query.

4. **Click the Update button in the Query Type group**

   The **Update To row** appears in the query design grid. To add $25 to the values in the CostOfCourse field, you need to enter the appropriate expression in the Update To cell for the CostOfCourse field.

5. **Click the Update To cell for the CostOfCourse field, then type 25+[CostOfCourse]**

   Your screen should look like FIGURE 10-13. The expression adds 25 to the current value of the CostOfCourse field, but the CostOfCourse field is not updated until you run the query.

6. **Click the View button [ ] to see the datasheet, click the View button [ ] to return to Design View, click the Run button, then click Yes to confirm that you want to update 31 rows**

   When you view the datasheet of an Update query, only the field being updated appears on the datasheet. To view all fields in the query, change this query back into a Select query, then view the datasheet.

7. **Click the Select button in the Query Type group, then click [ ] to display the query datasheet, as shown in FIGURE 10-14**

   All CostOfCourse values have increased by $25, including the first three records, which updated from $450 to $475.

8. **Click [ ] to return to Design View, click the Update button to switch this query back to an Update query, save the query with the name Update25, then close it**

   Often, you do not need to save action queries because after the data has been updated, you generally won't use the same query again. Also, it is sometimes dangerous to leave action queries in the Navigation Pane because if you double-click an action query, you run that action (as opposed to opening its datasheet). When you double-click a Select query, you open the query's datasheet. You can keep an action query in the Navigation Pane but hide it using the **Hidden property**.

9. **Right-click the Update25 query in the Navigation Pane, click Object Properties, click the Hidden check box, then click OK**

Creating Advanced Queries

FIGURE 10-13: Setting up an Update query

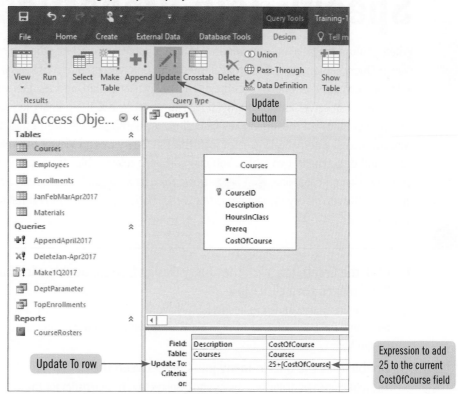

Update button

Update To row

Expression to add 25 to the current CostOfCourse field

FIGURE 10-14: Updated CostOfCourse values

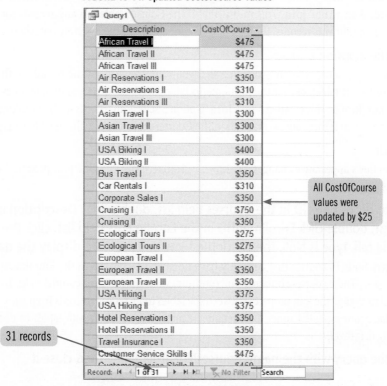

All CostOfCourse values were updated by $25

31 records

Restoring hidden objects

To view hidden objects, right-click a blank spot in the Navigation Pane, and then choose Navigation Options. In the Navigation Options dialog box, check the Show Hidden Objects check box, and then click OK.

Specify Join Properties

Learning Outcomes
• Create a left join
• Define left and right joins

When you use the Relationships window to define table relationships, the tables are joined in the same way in Query Design View. If referential integrity is enforced on a relationship, a "1" appears next to the field that serves as the "one" side of the one-to-many relationship, and an infinity symbol (∞) appears next to the field that serves as the "many" side. The "one" field is the primary key field for its table, and the "many" field is called the foreign key field. If no relationships have been established in the Relationships window, Access automatically creates **join lines** in Query Design View if the linking fields have the same name and data type in two tables. You can edit table relationships for a query in Query Design View by double-clicking the join line. **CASE** ▸ *David Fox asks what courses have been created but have never been attended. You can modify the join properties of the relationship between the Enrollments and Courses table to find the answer.*

STEPS

1. **Click the Create tab, click the Query Design button, double-click Courses, double-click Enrollments, then click Close**

   Because the Courses and Enrollments tables have already been related with a one-to-many relationship with referential integrity enforced in the Relationships window, the join line automatically appears in Query Design View.

2. **Double-click the one-to-many join line between the field lists**

   The Join Properties dialog box opens and displays the characteristics for the join, as shown in **FIGURE 10-15**. The dialog box shows that option 1 is selected, the default join type, which means that the query displays only records in which joined fields from both tables are equal. In **SQL (Structured Query Language)**, this is called an **inner join**. This means that if the Courses table has any records for which there are no matching Enrollments records, those courses do not appear in the resulting datasheet.

3. **Click the 2 option button**

   By choosing option 2, you are specifying that you want to see all of the records in the Courses table (the "one," or parent table), even if the Enrollments table (the "many," or child table) does not contain matching records. In SQL, this is called a **left join**. Option 3 selects all records in the Enrollments (the "many," or child table) even if there are no matches in the Courses table. In SQL, this is called a **right join**.

4. **Click OK**

   The join line's appearance changes, as shown in **FIGURE 10-16**. With the join property set, you add fields to the query grid.

5. **Double-click CourseID in the Courses field list, double-click Description in the Courses field list, double-click EnrollmentID in the Enrollments field list, click the EnrollmentID Criteria cell, type Is Null, then click the View button [▦] to display the datasheet**

   The query finds 16 courses that currently have no matching records in the Enrollments table, as shown in **FIGURE 10-17**. These courses contain a null (nothing) value in the EnrollmentID field. To select these records, you had to change the join property between the tables to include *all* records from the Courses table because the default join type, the inner join, requires a matching record in *both* tables to display a record in the resulting datasheet.

6. **Save the query with the name CoursesNoEnrollments, then close it**

FIGURE 10-15: Join Properties dialog box

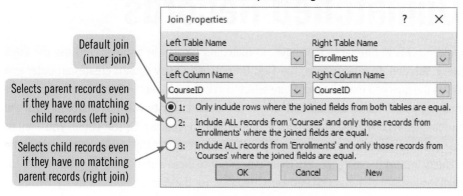

Default join (inner join)

Selects parent records even if they have no matching child records (left join)

Selects child records even if they have no matching parent records (right join)

FIGURE 10-16: Left join between tables

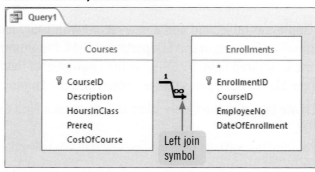

Left join symbol

FIGURE 10-17: Courses without matching enrollments

These courses have no matching records in the Enrollments table

EnrollmentID is null for each record

Null and zero-length string values

The term **null** describes a field value that does not exist because it has never been entered. In a datasheet, null values look the same as a zero-length string value but have a different purpose. A **zero-length string** value is a deliberate entry that contains no characters. You enter a zero-length string by typing two quotation marks ("") with no space between them. A null value, on the other hand, indicates unknown data. By using null and zero-length string values appropriately, you can later query for the records that match one or the other condition. To query for zero-length string values, enter two quotation marks ("") as the criterion. To query for null values, use **Is Null** as the criterion. To query for any value other than a null value, use **Is Not Null** as the criterion.

Find Unmatched Records

Another way to find records in one table that have no matching records in another is to use the **Find Unmatched Query Wizard**. In other words, the Find Unmatched Query Wizard creates an outer join between the tables in the query so that all records are selected in one table even if there is no match in the other table. Sometimes you inherit a database in which referential integrity was not imposed from the beginning, and unmatched records exist in the "many" table (orphan records). Or sometimes you want to find records in the "one" table that have no matching child records in the "many" table. You could use the Find Unmatched Query Wizard to create a query to answer either of these questions. **CASE** ▸ *David Fox wonders if any employees have never enrolled in a class. You can use the Find Unmatched Query Wizard to create a query to answer this question.*

STEPS

1. **Open the Employees table, and add a new record with *your name* in the ELast and EFirst fields, Information Systems in the EDepartment field, Programmer in the ETitle field, 1/1/17 in the DateHired field, 99-99-99 in the EmployeeNo field, and your school email address in the EEmail field, press [Enter], then close the Employees table**

2. **Click the Create tab, click the Query Wizard button, click Find Unmatched Query Wizard, then click OK**

   The Find Unmatched Query Wizard starts, prompting you to select the table or query that may contain no related records.

3. **Click Table: Employees, then click Next**

   You want to find which employees have no enrollments.

4. **Click Table: Enrollments, then click Next**

   The next question asks you to identify which field is common to both tables. Because the Employees table is already related to the Enrollments table in the Relationships window via the common EmployeeNo field, those fields are already selected as the matching fields, as shown in **FIGURE 10-18**.

5. **Click Next**

   You are prompted to select the fields from the Employees table that you want to display in the query datasheet.

6. **Click the Select All Fields button** `>>`

7. **Click Next, type EmployeesNoEnrollments, click Finish, then resize the columns of the datasheet to view all data**

   The final datasheet is shown in **FIGURE 10-19**. Three existing employees plus the record you entered in Step 1 have not yet enrolled in any class.

8. **Save and close the EmployeesNoEnrollments query, then close the Training-10.accdb database**

FIGURE 10-18: Using the Find Unmatched Query Wizard

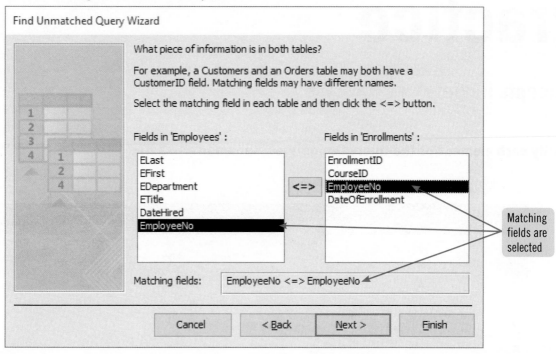

FIGURE 10-19: Employees without matching Enrollments records

ELast	EFirst	EDepartment	ETitle	DateHired	EmployeeN	EEmail
Fox	David	USA	Director	1/1/2011	11-22-44	dfox@r2g.com
Green	Kayla	USA	Director	1/1/2000	99-55-12	kgreen@r2g.com
Thomas	Jacob	Personnel	Staff Development Manage	1/2/2012	99-88-77	jthomas@r2g.com
Student Last	Student	Information System:	Programmer	1/1/2017	99-99-99	student@college.edu

Reviewing referential integrity

Recall that you can establish, or enforce, **referential integrity** between two tables when joining tables in the Relationships window. Referential integrity applies a set of rules to the relationship that ensures that no orphaned records currently exist, are added to, or are created in the database. A table has an **orphan record** when information in the foreign key field of the "many" table doesn't have a matching entry in the primary key field of the "one" table. The term "orphan" comes from the analogy that the "one" table contains **parent records**, and the "many" table contains **child records**. Referential integrity means that a Delete query would not be able to delete records in the "one" (parent) table that has related records in the "many" (child) table.

Find Duplicates Query Wizard

The Find Duplicates Query Wizard is another query wizard that is only available from the New Query dialog box. As you would suspect, the **Find Duplicates Query Wizard** helps you find duplicate values in a field, which can assist in finding and correcting potential data entry errors. For example, if you suspect that the same customer has been entered with two different names in your Customers table, you could use the Find Duplicates Query Wizard to find records with duplicate values in the Street or Phone field. After you isolated the records with the same values in a field, you could then edit incorrect data and delete redundant records.

Practice

Concepts Review

Identify each element of the Query Design View shown in FIGURE 10-20**.**

FIGURE 10-20

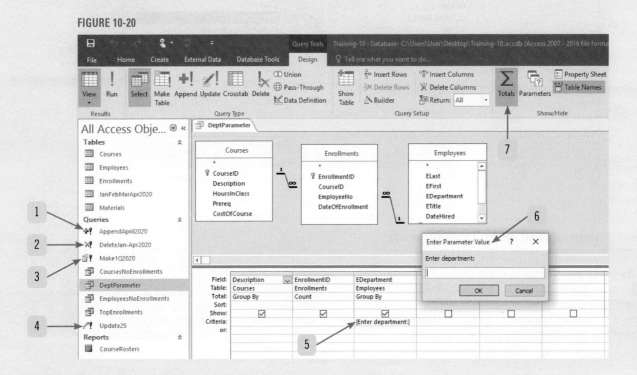

Match each term with the statement that best describes it.

8. **Parameter**
9. **Null**
10. **Inner join**
11. **Top Values query**
12. **Properties**
13. **Action query**

a. Characteristics that define the appearance and behavior of items within the database

b. Displays only a number or percentage of records from a sorted query

c. Displays a dialog box prompting you for criteria

d. Means that the query displays only records in which joined fields from both tables are equal

e. Makes changes to data

f. A field value that does not exist

Select the best answer from the list of choices.

14. Which join type selects all records from the "one" (parent) table?
- **a.** Inner
- **b.** Central
- **c.** Left
- **d.** Right

15. Which of the following is a valid parameter criterion entry in the query design grid?
- **a.** >={Type minimum value here: }
- **b.** >=[Type minimum value here:]
- **c.** >=(Type minimum value here:)
- **d.** >=Type minimum value here:

16. You cannot use the Top Values feature to:
- **a.** Update a field's value by 5 percent.
- **b.** Display a subset of records.
- **c.** Select the bottom 10 percent of records.
- **d.** Show the top 30 records.

17. Which of the following is not an action query?
- **a.** Make Table query
- **b.** Delete query
- **c.** Append query
- **d.** Union query

18. Which of the following precautions should you take before running a Delete query?
- **a.** Understand the relationships between the records you are about to delete in the database.
- **b.** Check the resulting datasheet to make sure the query selects the right records.
- **c.** Have a current backup of the database.
- **d.** All of the above

19. When querying tables in a one-to-many relationship with referential integrity enforced, which records appear (by default) on the resulting datasheet?
- **a.** All records from the "one" table and only those with matching values from the "many" side.
- **b.** Only those with matching values in both tables.
- **c.** All records from both tables will appear at all times.
- **d.** All records from the "many" table and only those with nonmatching values from the "one" side.

20. Which of the following is not a type of Select query?
- **a.** Crosstab
- **b.** Summary
- **c.** Update
- **d.** Parameter

Skills Review

1. Query for top values.
- **a.** Start Access, then open the Seminar-10.accdb database from the location where you store your Data Files. Enable content if prompted.
- **b.** Create a new query in Query Design View with the EventName field from the Events table and the RegistrationFee field from the Registration table.
- **c.** Add the RegistrationFee field a second time as the third field, then click the Totals button. In the Total row of the query grid, Group By the EventName field, Sum the first RegistrationFee field, then Count the second RegistrationFee field.
- **d.** Sort in descending order by the summed RegistrationFee field.
- **e.** Enter **3** in the Top Values list box to display the top three seminars in the datasheet, then view the datasheet.
- **f.** Save the query as **Top3Revenue**, then close the datasheet.

Skills Review (continued)

2. Create a parameter query.

  a. Create a new query in Query Design View with the AttendeeLastName field from the Attendees table, the RegistrationDate field from the Registration table, and the EventName field from the Events table.

  b. Add the parameter criteria **Between [Enter Start Date:] and [Enter End Date:]** in the Criteria cell for the RegistrationDate field.

  c. Specify an ascending sort order on the RegistrationDate field.

  d. Click the Datasheet View button, then enter **2/1/17** as the start date and **2/28/17** as the end date to find everyone who has attended a seminar in February 2017. You should view nine records.

  e. Save the query as **RegistrationDateParameter**, then close it.

3. Modify query properties.

  a. Right-click the RegistrationDateParameter query in the Navigation Pane, click Object Properties, then add the following description: **Prompts for a starting and ending registration date. Created by Your Name.**

  b. Close the RegistrationDateParameter Properties dialog box, then open the RegistrationDateParameter query in Query Design View.

  c. Right-click the RegistrationDate field in the query grid, then click Properties on the shortcut menu to open the Property Sheet for the Field Properties. Enter **Date of Registration** for the Caption property, change the Format property to Medium Date, then close the Property Sheet.

  d. View the datasheet for records between **1/1/17** and **1/31/17**, then widen the fields as needed to view the caption and the Medium Date format applied to the RegistrationDate field.

  e. Change Oxford to *your* last name, then print the RegistrationDateParameter datasheet if requested by your instructor.

  f. Save and close the RegistrationDateParameter query.

4. Create a Make Table query.

  a. Create a new query in Query Design View, add the Registration table, then select all the fields from the Registration table by double-clicking the Registration field list's title bar and dragging the selected fields to the query design grid.

  b. Enter **<=3/31/17** in the Criteria cell for the RegistrationDate field to find those records in which the RegistrationDate is on or before 3/31/2017.

  c. View the datasheet. It should display 23 records.

  d. In Query Design View, change the query into a Make Table query that creates a new table in the current database. Give the new table the name **BackupRegistration**.

  e. Run the query to paste 23 rows into the BackupRegistration table.

  f. Save the Make Table query with the name **MakeBackupRegistration**, then close it.

  g. Open the BackupRegistration table, view the 23 records to confirm that the Make Table query worked correctly, then close the table.

5. Create an Append query.

  a. Create a new query in Query Design View, add the Registration table, and select all the fields from the Registration table by double-clicking the Registration field list's title bar and dragging the selected fields to the query design grid.

  b. Enter **>=4/1/17 and <=4/30/17** in the Criteria cell for the RegistrationDate field to find those records in which the RegistrationDate is in April 2017.

  c. View the datasheet, which should display three records.

  d. In Query Design View, change the query into an Append query that appends records to the BackupRegistration table.

  e. Run the query to append the three records into the BackupRegistration table.

  f. Save the Append query with the name **AppendBackupRegistration**, then close it.

  g. Open the BackupRegistration table to confirm that it now contains the additional three April records for a total of 26 records, then close the BackupRegistration table.

Skills Review (continued)

6. Create a Delete query.

   a. Create a new query in Query Design View, add the Registration table, and select all the fields from the Registration table by double-clicking the Registration field list's title bar and dragging the selected fields to the query design grid.

   b. Enter **<5/1/17** in the Criteria cell for the RegistrationDate field to find those records in which the RegistrationDate is before May 1, 2017.

   c. View the datasheet, which should display 26 records—the same 26 records you added to the BackupRegistration table.

   d. In Query Design View, change the query into a Delete query.

   e. Run the query to delete 26 records from the Registration table.

   f. Save the query with the name **DeleteRegistration**, then close it.

   g. Open the Registration table in Datasheet View to confirm that it contains only three records, with a RegistrationDate value of 5/1/17 or later, then close the Registration table. (*Note*: Given that the Registration table now only contains three records, the Top3Revenue query, which is based on the Registration table, now only displays two records, summarized by the EventName field.)

7. Create an Update query.

   a. Create a query in Query Design View, add the Events table, then add the AvailableSpaces field in the query grid.

   b. View the datasheet, which should display seven records. Note the values in the AvailableSpaces field.

   c. In Query Design View, change the query to an Update query, then enter **100** in the AvailableSpaces field Update To cell to set the AvailableSpaces value to 100 for each record.

   d. Run the query to update the seven records.

   e. Save the query with the name **UpdateSpaces**, then close it.

   f. Open the Events table to confirm that the AvailableSpaces value for each of the seven records is 100, then close the Events table.

8. Specify join properties.

   a. Create a new query in Query Design View with the following fields: AttendeeFirstName and AttendeeLastName from the Attendees table, and EventID and RegistrationFee from the Registration table.

   b. Double-click the join line between the Attendees and Registration tables to open the Join Properties dialog box. Click the 2 option button to include all records from Attendees and only those records from Registration in which the joined fields are equal.

   c. View the datasheet, and change the record with Holly as the first name to *your* first name.

   d. In Query Design View, add **Is Null** criteria to the EventID field to select only those names of people who have never registered for an event.

   e. Save this query as **PeopleWithoutRegistrations**, then view and close the query.

9. Find unmatched queries.

   a. Start the Find Unmatched Query Wizard.

   b. Select the Events table, then the Registration table, to indicate that you want to view the Events records that have no related records in the Registration table.

   c. Specify that the two tables are related by the EventID field.

   d. Select all of the fields from the Events table in the query results.

   e. Name the query **EventsWithoutRegistrations**, then view the results. Change First National Bank of Fontanelle in the Location field to **Your Name College**, as shown in FIGURE 10-21.

   f. If requested by your instructor, print the EventsWithoutRegistrations query, then close the query, close the Seminar-10.accdb database, and exit Access.

FIGURE 10-21

Event I ·	Event Name	·	Location	·	Start Date ·	Available Sp ·
1	Estate Planning		Student Name College		4/29/2017	100
2	Planning a Will		Community Center of Greenfiel		4/30/2017	100
5	Wealth Management		Millen Civic Center		5/5/2017	100
6	Planning for College		Greenfield High School		5/6/2017	100
7	Live Debt Free		Wells Fargo Center		5/7/2017	100
* (New)						

Independent Challenge 1

As the manager of a college women's basketball team, you want to create several queries using the Basketball-10 database.

a. Start Access, then open the Basketball-10.accdb database from the location where you store your Data Files. Enable content if prompted.

b. Create a query in Query Design View with the FirstName and LastName fields from the Players table; the FG (field goal), 3P (three pointer), and FT (free throw) fields from the Stats table; and the Opponent and GameDate fields from the Games table.

c. Enter **Between [Enter start date:] and [Enter end date:]** in the Criteria cell for the GameDate field.

d. View the datasheet for all of the records between **12/1/17** and **12/31/17**. It should display 24 records.

e. Save the query with the name **StatsParameter**, change Lindsey Swift's name to *your name*, then print the datasheet if requested by your instructor.

f. In Query Design View of the StatsParameter query, insert a new calculated field named **TotalPoints** between the FT and Opponent fields with the expression **TotalPoints:[FG]*2+[3P]*3+[FT]**, then sort the records in descending order on the TotalPoints field.

g. Apply the 25% Top Values option, and view the datasheet for all of the records between **1/1/18** and **1/31/18**. It should display four records.

h. Use the Save Object As feature to save the revised query as **StatsParameterTopValues**. Print the datasheet if requested by your instructor, then close it.

i. Create a new query in Query Design View with the Opponent, Mascot, CycloneScore, and OpponentScore fields from the Games table, then add a new calculated field as the last field with the following field name and expression: **WinRatio:[CycloneScore]/[OpponentScore]**

j. View the datasheet to make sure that the WinRatio field calculates properly, and widen all columns as necessary to see all of the data. Because the CycloneScore is generally greater than the OpponentScore, most values are greater than 1.

k. In Query Design View, change the Format property of the WinRatio field to Percent and the Decimal Places property to **0**. View the datasheet, a portion of which is shown in FIGURE 10-22.

FIGURE 10-22

Opponent	Mascot	CycloneScore	OpponentScore	WinRatio
Northern Iowa	Panthers	81	65	125%
Creighton	Bluejays	106	60	177%
Northern Illinois	Huskies	65	60	108%
Louisiana Tech	Red Raiders	69	89	78%
Drake	Bulldogs	80	60	133%
Northern Iowa	Panthers	38	73	52%
Buffalo	Bulls	50	55	91%
Oklahoma	Sooners	53	60	88%
Texas	Longhorns	57	60	95%
Kansas	Jayhawks	74	58	128%

l. Save the query as **WinPercentage**, change the first opponent's name (Northern Iowa) and mascot to *your name* and a mascot of your choice, print the WinPercentage datasheet if requested by your instructor, then close the WinPercentage query.

m. Close the Basketball-10.accdb database, then exit Access.

Independent Challenge 2

As the manager of a college women's basketball team, you want to enhance the Basketball-10 database by creating several action queries.

a. Start Access, then open the Basketball-10.accdb database from the location where you store your Data Files. Enable content if prompted.

b. Create a new query in Query Design View, and select all the fields from the Stats table by double-clicking the field list's title bar and dragging the selected fields to the query design grid.

c. Add criteria to find all of the records with the GameNo field equal to **1**, **2**, or **3**, then view the datasheet. It should display 26 records.

d. In Query Design View, change the query to a Make Table query to paste the records into a table called **123Stats** in the current database.

e. Run the query to paste the 26 rows, save the query with the name **MakeStatsBackup**, then close it.

f. Open the datasheet for the 123Stats table to confirm that it contains 26 records, then close it.

g. In Query Design View, create another new query that includes all of the fields from the Stats table by double-clicking the field list's title bar and dragging the selected fields to the query design grid.

h. Add criteria to find all of the statistics for those records with the GameNo field equal to **4** or **5**, then view the datasheet. It should display 12 records.

i. In Query Design View, change the query to an Append query to append the records to the 123Stats table.

j. Run the query to append the 12 rows, save it with the name **AppendStatsBackup**, then close the query.

k. Open the 123Stats table to confirm that it now contains 38 records (26 original records plus 12 appended records), close it, and then rename it as **12345Stats**.

l. Close the Basketball-10.accdb database, then exit Access.

Independent Challenge 3

As the manager of a college women's basketball team, you want to query the Basketball-10 database to find specific information about each player.

a. Start Access, then open the Basketball-10.accdb database from the location where you store your Data Files. Enable content if prompted.

b. Create a query in Query Design View using the Players and Stats tables. Resize the field lists to view all of the fields in each table.

c. Double-click the join line to open the Join Properties dialog box, then change the join properties to option 2 to include all records from Players and only those from Stats where the joined fields are equal.

d. Add the FirstName and LastName fields from the Players table and the PlayerNo field from the Stats table.

e. Type **Is Null** in the Criteria cell for the PlayerNo field, as shown in FIGURE 10-23, then view the datasheet to find those players who do not have a related record in the Stats table. It should display one record.

FIGURE 10-23

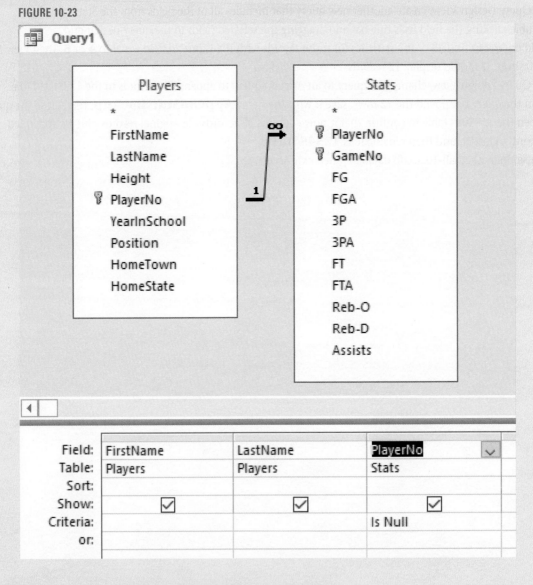

f. Save the query as **PlayersWithoutStats**, then close the query.

g. Close Basketball-10.accdb, then exit Access.

Independent Challenge 4: Explore

One way to use Access to support your personal interests is to track the activities of a club or hobby. For example, suppose you belong to a culinary club that specializes in cooking with chocolate. The club collects information on international chocolate factories and museums and asks you to help build a database to organize the information. (*Note*: To complete this Independent Challenge, make sure you are connected to the Internet.)

a. Start Access, then open the Candy-10.accdb database from the location where you store your Data Files. Enable content if prompted.

b. Open the Countries table, then add two more country records, allowing the CountryID field to automatically increment because it is an AutoNumber data type. Close the Countries table.

c. Create a query in Query Design View with the Country field from the Countries table and the PlaceName, City, and State fields from the Locations table.

d. Name the query **PlacesOfInterest**, double-click the join line between the Countries and Locations tables, then choose the 2 option that includes all records from the Countries table.

e. Save the PlacesOfInterest query and view the datasheet. Expand each column to show all of the data.

f. Print the PlacesOfInterest query if requested by your instructor, then close it.

g. Using the Internet, research a candy-related place of interest (a factory or museum/visitor center) for one of the countries you entered in Step b.

h. Open the Countries table, and use the subdatasheet for the country you selected to enter the data for the chocolate-related place of interest. Enter **F** for factory or **M** for museum in the FactoryorMuseum field.

i. Close the Countries table, and open the PlacesOfInterest query in Design View. Modify the link line to option 1 so that records that have a match in both tables are selected.

j. Save and open the PlacesOfInterest query in Datasheet View, as shown in FIGURE 10-24, and print the resulting datasheet if requested by your instructor. Note that the last record will show the unique data you entered.

k. Close Candy-10.accdb, then exit Access.

FIGURE 10-24

Country	PlaceName	City	State
Germany	Lindt factory	Aachen	
Germany	Imhoff Stollwerk Chocolate Museum	Cologne	
Switzerland	Lindt factory	Kilchberg	
Switzerland	Museum del Cioccolato Alprose	Caslano	Canton Ticino
Switzerland	Nestle	Broc	Canton Fribourg
France	Lindt Factory	Oloron	
France	Atelier Musee du Chocolat, Biarritz	Biarritz	
Italy	Lindt Factory	Induno	
Italy	Lindt Factory	Luserna	
Italy	Museo Storico della Perugina	Perugia	
Italy	Museo del Cioccolato Antia Norba	Norma	Latina Province
Austria	Lindt Factory	Gloggnitz	
USA	Lindt Factory	San Leandro	CA
USA	Lindt Factory	Stratham	NH
Belgium	Musee du Cacao et du Chocolat	Brussels	
Great Britian	Cadbury World	Bourneville	
Japan	Shiroi Koibito Park	Sapporo	

Visual Workshop

As the manager of a college women's basketball team, you want to create a query from the Basketball-10.accdb database with the fields from the Players, Stats, and Games tables as shown. The query is a parameter query that prompts the user for a start and end date using the GameDate field from the Games table. FIGURE 10-25 shows the datasheet in which the start date of **11/12/17** and end date of **11/15/17** are used. Also note that the records are sorted in ascending order first by GameDate, and then by LastName. Set these sort orders in Query Design View. The TotalRebounds field is calculated by adding the Reb-O (rebounds offense) and Reb-D (rebounds defense) values. Save and name the query **Rebounds**, change Lindsey Swift's name to *your name* if you have not already done so in a prior exercise, then print the datasheet if requested by your instructor.

FIGURE 10-25

GameDate	FirstName	LastName	Reb-O	Reb-D	TotalRebour
11/12/2017	Isten	Czyenski	2	2	4
11/12/2017	Denise	Franco	2	3	5
11/12/2017	Theresa	Grant	1	3	4
11/12/2017	Megan	Hile	1	2	3
11/12/2017	Amy	Hodel	5	3	8
11/12/2017	Ellyse	Howard	1	2	3
11/12/2017	Jamie	Johnson	0	1	1
11/12/2017	Student First	Student Last	1	2	3
11/12/2017	Morgan	Tyler	4	6	10
11/15/2017	Kristen	Czyenski	3	2	5
11/15/2017	Denise	Franco	5	3	8
11/15/2017	Sydney	Freesen	2	3	5
11/15/2017	Theresa	Grant	3	3	6
11/15/2017	Megan	Hile	1	5	6
11/15/2017	Amy	Hodel	1	4	5
11/15/2017	Ellyse	Howard	3	3	6
11/15/2017	Sandy	Robins	0	1	1
11/15/2017	Student First	Student Last	2	2	4
11/15/2017	Morgan	Tyler	3	6	9
11/15/2017	Abbey	Walker	2	4	6

Creating Advanced Reports

CASE David Fox, coordinator of training at Reason 2 Go, wants to enhance existing reports to more professionally and clearly present the information in the Training-11 database.

Module Objectives

After completing this module, you will be able to:

- Apply advanced formatting
- Control layout
- Set advanced print layout
- Create multicolumn reports
- Use domain functions
- Create charts
- Modify charts
- Apply chart types

Files You Will Need

Training-11.accdb   Basketball-11.accdb
LakeHomes-11.accdb

Apply Advanced Formatting

You use Print Preview to see how a report will fit on paper and to make overall layout modifications such as changes to margins and page orientation. You use Layout and Design Views to modify the layout and characteristics of individual controls on a report. For example, the **Format property** provides several ways to format dates and numbers. Dates may be formatted as **Medium Date** (19-Jun-17), **Short Date** (6/19/2017), or **Long Date** (Monday, June 19, 2017). Numbers may be formatted as **Currency** ($7), **Percent** (700%), or **Standard** (7). **CASE** ▶ *David Fox asks you to review the Departmental Summary Report to identify and correct formatting and page layout problems.*

STEPS

1. **Start Access, open the Training-11.accdb database from the location where you store your Data Files, enable content if prompted, then double-click DeptSummary in the Navigation Pane**

   Double-clicking a report in the Navigation Pane opens it in Report View, which doesn't show margins and page breaks. Switch to Print Preview to see how the report will look on paper.

2. **Right-click the Departmental Summary Report tab, then click Print Preview**

   Print Preview shows that data is cut off on the right side of the report. You fix this problem by modifying the margins and page orientation.

3. **Click the Margins button in the Page Size group, click the Narrow option, click the Page Setup button in the Page Layout group, select 0.25 in the Left margin box, then type 0.5, as shown in FIGURE 11-1**

   The Narrow margin option set all four margins to 0.25". To customize individual margin settings, you use the Page Setup dialog box.

4. **Click OK, then click the Landscape button in the Page Layout group**

   Now that the report fits nicely on the printed page, you want to make some modifications to the controls themselves. You want to widen the text box that contains the name expression and format the Cost fields to show a currency symbol.

5. **Right-click the Departmental Summary Report tab, click Design View, click the =[ELast]&", "&[EFirst] text box, then use ↔ to drag the right edge to the right to widen the text box**

   Many of the controls are grouped together in a report table layout, which means that resizing one control resizes the entire group. To modify an individual control in the group, you must first remove the layout.

6. **Click the Undo button ↩ on the Quick Access Toolbar, click the Arrange tab, click the Remove Layout button in the Table group, then use ↔ to drag the right edge of the name expression text box to the right to widen it to about the 4" mark**

   Your last improvement will be to modify the Format property of the four text boxes that display Cost information in the last column of the report to include a currency symbol, $.

7. **Click the CostOfCourse text box in the Detail section, press and hold [Shift], click the three =Sum([CostOfCourse]) text boxes in the footer sections, release [Shift], click the Design tab, click the Property Sheet button, click the Format property list arrow, click Currency, right-click the DeptSummary tab, click Print Preview, then move to the bottom of the last page of the report, as shown in FIGURE 11-2**

   The report is more professional and informative with the Cost values formatted as Currency.

8. **Save and close the report**

FIGURE 11-1: **Page Setup dialog box**

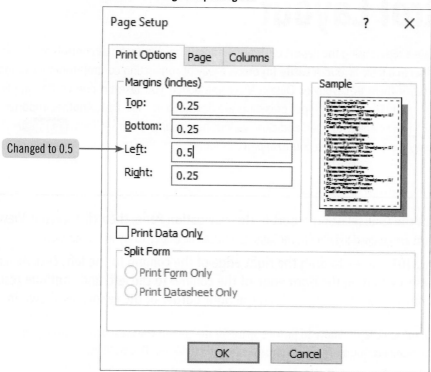

Changed to 0.5 →

FIGURE 11-2: **Applying the Currency format**

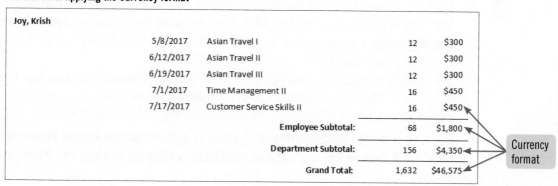

Access 2016

Control Layout

Learning Outcomes
- Change table layouts
- Open header and footer sections
- Insert page numbers

When you create a report using the Report button or Report Wizard, sometimes controls are automatically grouped together in a table layout. A **table layout** is a way of connecting controls together so that when you move or resize them in Layout or Design View, the action you take on one control applies to all controls in the layout. The different types of layouts are described in TABLE 11-1. Another important report modification skill is your ability to open and close various header and footer sections. **CASE** *David Fox asks you to modify the CourseListing report to improve its format.*

STEPS

TROUBLE
Close the Property Sheet if it opens.

1. **Right-click the CourseListing report in the Navigation Pane, then click Layout View**
   Controls that are grouped together in the same layout can be resized easily in Layout View.

2. **Click Africa101, use ↔ to drag the right edge of the column to the left, click African Travel I, use ↔ to drag the right edge of the column to the left, and continue resizing the columns so that they all fit within the right border of the report, as shown in FIGURE 11-3**
   Controls in the same layout move to provide space for the control you are moving. This report contains no title or page numbers. You add controls and open report sections in Design View.

3. **Right-click the CourseListing tab, then click Design View**
   You want to add a title to the Report Header section. Before you can add a label for the report title to the Report Header section, you must open it.

QUICK TIP
Recall that you open and close Group Header and Footer sections in the Group, Sort, and Total pane.

4. **Right-click the Detail section bar, click Report Header/Footer, click the Label button Aa on the Design tab, click at the 1" mark in the Report Header section, type Course Listing Report, press [Enter], click the Home tab, click the Font Color list arrow $\underline{A}$ in the Text Formatting group, then click Automatic (black) to make the title more visible**
   You also want to add page numbers to the Page Footer section. You can open the Page Footer section and insert the page number at the same time.

5. **Click the Design tab, click the Page Numbers button in the Header/Footer group, click the Page N of M option button, click the Bottom of Page [Footer] option button, click the Alignment list arrow, click Right in the Page Numbers dialog box as shown in FIGURE 11-4, then click OK**
   The Page N of M option creates the expression in the text box on the right side of the Page Footer, as shown in FIGURE 11-5. This expression displays the current page number and total pages in the Page Footer. Because neither the Page Header nor Report Footer sections have any controls, you close them.

6. **Use ↕ to drag the bottom edge of the report up to close the Report Footer section, then use ↕ to drag the top edge of the Detail section up to close the Page Header section**

QUICK TIP
You cannot see the Page Header or Page Footer sections in Report View. You must use Print Preview.

7. **Right-click the CourseListing report tab, click Print Preview, then zoom and navigate back and forth to observe the Report Header and the Page Footer**
   Always review your reports in Print Preview to see the contents of the Page Header and Page Footer sections, as well as to see how the report fits on a printed piece of paper.

8. **Save and close the CourseListing report**

FIGURE 11-3: Resizing columns in a layout

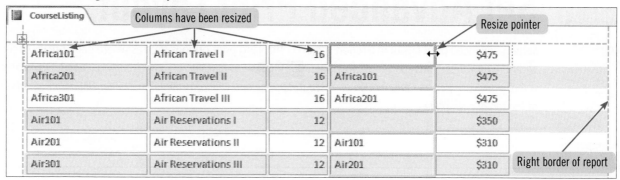

FIGURE 11-4: Page Numbers dialog box

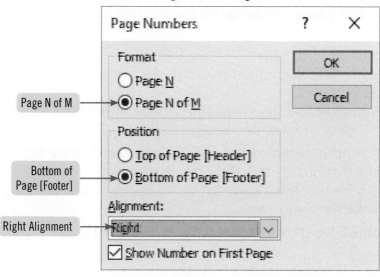

FIGURE 11-5: Opening sections in Design View

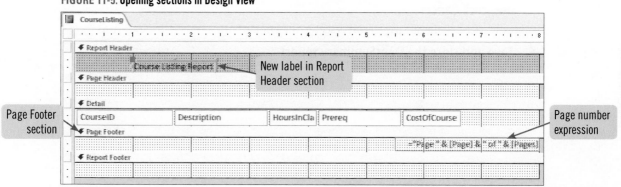

TABLE 11-1: Layouts

layout	description
Stacked	Labels are positioned to the left of the text box; most often used in forms
Tabular	Labels are positioned across the top in the Page Header section, forming columns of data with text boxes positioned in the Detail section; most often used in reports

Set Advanced Print Layout

Setting advanced print layout in a report means controlling print options such as where page breaks occur and how report sections span multiple pages. **CASE** ▶ *In the Departmental Summary Report, David asks you to print each person's information on a separate page and to repeat the EDepartment Header information at the top of each page.*

STEPS

1. **Right-click the DeptSummary report in the Navigation Pane, click Design View, double-click the EDepartment Header section bar to open its Property Sheet, double-click the Repeat Section property to change the property from No to Yes, then double-click the Force New Page property to change the property from None to Before Section, as shown in FIGURE 11-6**

   The control in the EDepartment Header section will now repeat at the top of every page.

2. **Click the EmployeeNo Footer section bar, click the Force New Page property list arrow, then click After Section**

   Access will format the report with a page break after each EmployeeNo Footer. This means that each employee's records will start printing at the top of a new page.

3. **Right-click the DeptSummary report tab, click Print Preview, then use the navigation buttons to move through the pages of the report**

   Previewing multiple pages helps you make sure that the department name repeats at the top of every page and that each employee starts on a new page.

4. **Navigate to page 2, then click the top of the page if you need to zoom in, as shown in FIGURE 11-7**

   To print only page 2 of the report, you use the Print dialog box.

5. **Click the Print button on the Print Preview tab, click the From box, enter 2, click the To box, enter 2, then if requested by your instructor to create a printout, click OK, but if not, click Cancel**

   Only page 2 of the 30+ page report is sent to the printer.

6. **Save and close the DeptSummary report**

FIGURE 11-6: Working with section properties in Report Design View

EDepartment Header section bar

EmployeeNo Footer section bar

Repeat Section set to Yes

Force New Page set to Before Section

FIGURE 11-7: Previewing the final Departmental Summary Report

Department	Name	Date	Description	Hours	Cost
Africa					
	Hosta, Boyd				
		5/2/2017	USA Biking II	12	$400
		5/29/2017	European Travel I	12	$350
		6/12/2017	Hotel Reservations I	12	$350
		7/10/2017	European Travel II	12	$350
		7/24/2017	European Travel III	12	$350
			Employee Subtotal:	60	$1,800

Department name repeats at the top of every page

Employee info starts at the top of every page

Create Multicolumn Reports

Learning Outcomes
• Modify a report for multiple columns
• Set column layout

A **multicolumn report** repeats information in more than one column on the page. To create multiple columns, you use options in the Page Setup dialog box. **CASE** ▶ *David asks you to create a report that shows employee names sorted in ascending order for each course. A report with only a few fields is a good candidate for a multicolumn report.*

STEPS

1. **Click the Create tab, click the Report Wizard button, click the Tables/Queries list arrow, click Table: Courses, double-click Description, click the Tables/Queries list arrow, click Table: Employees, double-click EFirst, double-click ELast, click Next, click Next to view the data by Courses, click Next to bypass adding any more grouping levels, click the first sort list arrow, click ELast, click Next, click the Stepped option button, click the Landscape option button, click Next, type Attendance List for the title, click Finish, then click the Last Page button ▶| on the navigation bar**

   The initial report is displayed in Print Preview. This report would work well as a multicolumn report because only three fields are involved. You also decide to combine the first and last names into a single expression.

2. **Right-click the report, click Design View, close the Property Sheet if it is open, click the ELast label, press [Delete], click the EFirst label, press [Delete], click the ELast text box, press [Delete], click the EFirst text box, press [Delete], click the Page expression text box in the Page Footer section, press [Delete], click the =Now() text box in the Page Footer section, press [Delete], then use ↔ to drag the right edge of the report as far to the left as possible**

   When designing a multicolumn report, Report Design View should display the width of only the first column. Your next task is to add a new text box to the Detail section with an expression that contains both the first and last names.

3. **Click the Text Box button |ab| in the Controls group, click at about the 0.5" mark of the Detail section to insert a new text box control, then delete the accompanying Text9 label**

   TROUBLE
   Do not forget to enter a space after the comma so the expression creates Dawson, Ron versus Dawson,Ron.

4. **Click the Unbound text box to select it, click Unbound, type =[ELast]&", "&[EFirst], press [Enter], use ↔ to widen the new control to about 2" wide, right-click the Attendance List report tab, then click Print Preview**

   With the information clearly presented in a single, narrow column, you're ready to specify that the report print multiple columns.

5. **Click the Page Setup button, click the Columns tab, double-click 1 in the Number of Columns box, type 3, then click the Down, then Across option button, as shown in FIGURE 11-8**

   The content of the report is now set to print in three newspaper-style columns. The Column Size Width value is based on 0.25" left and right margins, which leaves room for three 3" columns. The Height value is based on the Height property of the Detail section.

   QUICK TIP
   You must use Print Preview to view report columns. Report View doesn't display multiple columns.

6. **Click OK**

   The final Attendance List report is shown in FIGURE 11-9. By specifying that the report is three columns wide, the number of pages in the report is significantly reduced.

7. **Save and close the Attendance List report**

FIGURE 11-8: Page Setup dialog box

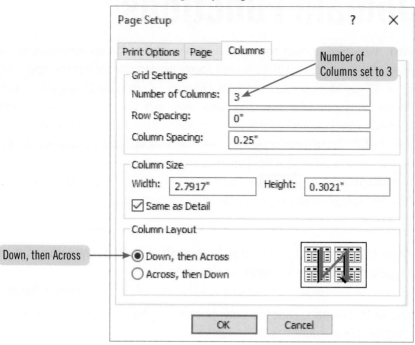

FIGURE 11-9: Attendance List report in three columns

Use Domain Functions

Domain functions, also called domain aggregate functions, are used in an expression to calculate a value based on a field that is not included in the Record Source property for the form or report. All Domain functions start with a "D" for "domain" such as DSum, DAvg, or DCount. The DSum, DAvg, and DCount functions perform the same calculations as their Sum, Avg, and Count function counterparts. The **DLookup** function returns or "looks up" a value from a specified domain. All domain functions have two required arguments: the field that is used for the calculation or "look up" and the domain. The **domain** is the table or query that contains the field. A third optional argument allows you to select records from the domain based on criteria you specify. **CASE** ▶ *David asks you to add a standard disclaimer to the bottom of every report. This is an excellent opportunity to use the DLookup function.*

STEPS

1. **Click the Create tab, click the Table Design button, then build a new table with the fields, data types, and primary key field, as shown in** FIGURE 11-10

    With the design of the Disclaimers table established, you add two records of standard text used at Reason 2 Go.

2. **Save the table as Disclaimers, click the View button** 🔳 **, then enter the two records and widen the StandardText column as shown in** FIGURE 11-11

    The first disclaimer is used with any report that contains employee information for Reason 2 Go, R2G. The second is added to all internal reports that do not contain employee information. With the data in place, you're ready to use the DLookup function on a report to insert standard text.

3. **Save and close the Disclaimers table, right-click the Attendance List report in the Navigation Pane, then click Design View**

    You can now add a text box using the DLookup function in an expression to return the correct disclaimer.

4. **Click the Text Box button** 📝**, click the Page Footer section, delete the Text11 label, click Unbound, type the expression =DLookup("[StandardText]","Disclaimers", "[ID]=1"), press [Enter], then widen the text box to about 3"**

    The expression is too wide to be completely displayed in Design View, but you must switch to Print Preview to see if it works anyway.

5. **Display the report in Print Preview and zoom and scroll to the Page Footer to view the result of the DLookup function, as shown in** FIGURE 11-12

    By entering standard company disclaimers in one table, the same disclaimer text can be consistently added to each report.

6. **Save and close the Attendance List report, double-click the Disclaimers table to open its datasheet, change R2G to Reason 2 Go in the first record for the ID of 1, close the Disclaimers table, right-click the Attendance List report, then click Print Preview**

    When the StandardText field is changed in the Disclaimers table, all reports that reference that value using the DLookup function in an expression are automatically updated as well.

7. **Close the Attendance List report**

Creating Advanced Reports

FIGURE 11-10: Disclaimers table

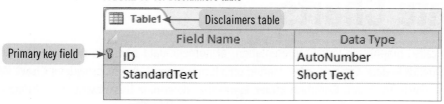

FIGURE 11-11: Records in the Disclaimers table

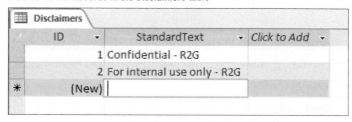

FIGURE 11-12: Standard disclaimer in Report Footer section created with DLookup expression

Adding page numbers or the date and time to a report

You can quickly add page numbers to a report by clicking the Page Numbers button on the Design tab of the ribbon. The Page Numbers dialog box prompts you for a page number format and whether you want to insert the information into the Page Header or Page Footer section. To quickly add the current date and time to the report, click the Date and Time button on the Design tab. Several date and time formats are available. Date and time information is always inserted on the right side of the Report Header section.

Creating Advanced Reports

Access 281

Access 2016

Create Charts

Learning Outcomes
- Define common chart types
- Add charts to a report

Charts, also called graphs, are visual representations of numeric data that help users see comparisons, patterns, and trends in data. Charts can be inserted on a form or report. Access provides a **Chart Wizard** that helps you create the chart. Common **chart types** that determine the presentation of data on the chart, such as column, pie, and line, are described in TABLE 11-2. **CASE** ▸ *David Fox wants you to create a chart of the total number of course enrollments by department.*

STEPS

1. **Click the Create tab, click the Query Design button, double-click Employees, double-click Enrollments, then click Close**

   The first step in creating a chart is to select the data that the chart will graph and collect those fields and records in one query object.

2. **Double-click EDepartment in the Employees field list, double-click EnrollmentID in the Enrollments field list, save the query with the name DeptEnrollments, then close it**

   Charts can be added to forms or reports.

   QUICK TIP
   You can also use the Chart Wizard to add a chart to a form in Form Design View.

3. **Click the Create tab, click the Report Design button, click the More button ⬇ in the Controls group on the Design tab, click the Chart button 📊, then click in the Detail section of the report**

   The Chart Wizard starts by asking which table or query holds the fields you want to add to the chart, then asks you to select a chart type.

4. **Click the Queries option button, click Next to choose the DeptEnrollments query, click the Select All Fields button ≫, click Next, click Next to accept Column Chart, then drag the EnrollmentID field from the Series area to the Data area, as shown in FIGURE 11-13**

   The **Data area** determines what data the chart graphs. If you drag a Number or Currency field to the Data area, the Chart Wizard automatically sums the values in the field. For Text or AutoNumber fields (such as EnrollmentID), the Chart Wizard automatically counts the values in that field.

   TROUBLE
   The chart in Design View is only a placeholder. You must switch to Print Preview to see the actual chart.

5. **Click Next, type Department Enrollment Totals as the chart title, click Finish, use ⬉ to drag the lower-right corner of the chart to fill the Detail section, right-click the Report1 tab, then click Print Preview**

   When charts are displayed in Design View or Layout View, they appear as a generic Microsoft chart placeholder. The chart in Print Preview should look similar to FIGURE 11-14. The chart is beginning to take shape, but some of the labels on the x-axis may not have room to display all of their text depending on the size of the chart. You enhance this chart in the next lesson.

Using the Blank Report button versus the Report Design button

Access provides several buttons on the Create tab to create a new report. The Blank Report button creates a new, blank report in Layout View. The Report Design button creates a new, blank report in Design View. The only difference between these two buttons is the initial view presented when you start building a new report. The same is true for the Blank Form button, which creates a new, blank form in Layout View, and the Form Design button, which creates a new, blank form in Design View.

FIGURE 11-13: Choosing the chart areas

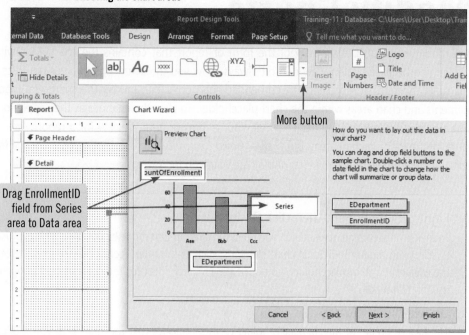

FIGURE 11-14: Initial Department Enrollment Totals column chart

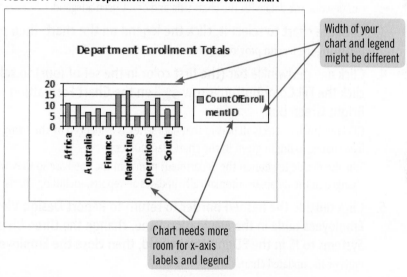

TABLE 11-2: Common chart types

chart type	chart icon	used to show most commonly	example
Column		Comparisons of values (vertical bars)	Each vertical bar represents the annual sales for a different product
Bar		Comparisons of values (horizontal bars)	Each horizontal bar represents the annual sales for a different product
Line		Trends over time	Each point on the line represents monthly sales for one product
Pie		Parts of a whole	Each slice represents total quarterly sales for a company
Area		Cumulative totals	Each section represents monthly sales by representative, stacked to show the cumulative total sales effort

Modify Charts

Learning Outcomes
- Define chart areas
- Modify a chart legend
- Modify chart bar colors

You modify charts in Design View of the form or report that contains the chart. Modifying a chart is challenging because Design View doesn't always show you the actual chart values but instead displays a chart placeholder that represents the embedded chart object. To modify the chart, you modify the chart elements and chart areas within the chart placeholder. To view the changes as they apply to the real data you are charting, return to either Form View for a form or Print Preview for a report. See TABLE 11-3 for more information on chart areas. **CASE** ▶ *David Fox wants you to resize the chart, change the color of the bars, and remove the legend to better display the values on the x-axis.*

STEPS

1. **Right-click the report, then click Design View**

   To make changes to chart elements, you open the chart in Edit mode by double-clicking it. Use **Edit mode** to select and modify individual chart elements, such as the title, legend, bars, or axes. If you double-click the edge of the chart placeholder, you open the Property Sheet for the chart instead of opening the chart itself in Edit mode.

2. **Double-click the chart**

   The hashed border of the chart placeholder control indicates that the chart is in Edit mode, as shown in **FIGURE 11-15**. The Chart Standard and Chart Formatting toolbars also appear when the chart is in Edit mode. They may appear on one row instead of stacked. Because only one series of bars counts the enrollments, you can describe the data with the chart title and don't need a legend.

   > **TROUBLE**
   > If you make a mistake, use the Undo button ↺ on the Chart Standard toolbar.

3. **Click the chart to select it, click the legend on the chart, then press [Delete] to remove it**

   Removing the legend provides more room for the x-axis labels.

   > **TROUBLE**
   > If you don't see the Fill Color button ⬜ ▾ on the Chart Formatting toolbar, drag the left edge of the toolbars to position them on two rows to show all buttons.

4. **Click any periwinkle bar (the first color in the set of four) to select all bars of that color, click the Fill Color button arrow ⬜ ▾ on the Chart Formatting toolbar, then click the Bright Green box**

   Clicking any bar selects all bars in that data series as evidenced by the sizing handle in each of the bars. The bars change to bright green in the chart placeholder.

   You also decide to shorten the department names in the database so they will better fit on the x-axis. Data changed in the database automatically updates all reports, including charts, that are based on that data.

5. **Click outside the hashed border to return to Report Design View, double-click the Employees table in the Navigation Pane, change the three instances of Information Systems to IS in the EDepartment field, then close the Employees table**

   Preview the updated chart.

   > **TROUBLE**
   > If your report doesn't look like **FIGURE 11-16**, return to Design View and resize it. Your report should also be only 1 page.

6. **Save the report as DeptChart, drag the sizing handles to expand the size of the chart to fill the width of the report as well as the blank space above the report, then display it in Print Preview**

   The final chart is shown in **FIGURE 11-16**.

FIGURE 11-15: Editing a chart placeholder

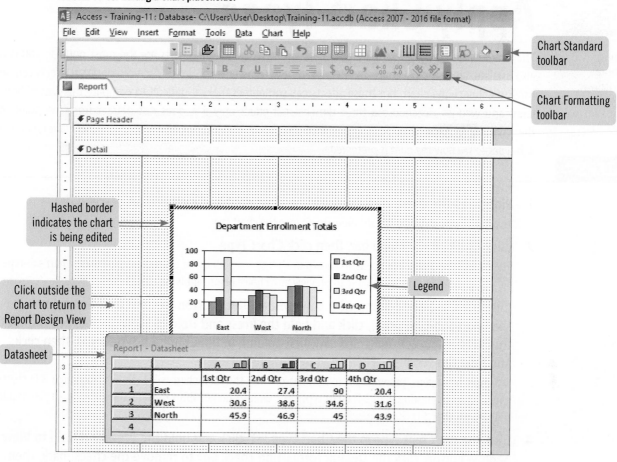

FIGURE 11-16: Final Department Enrollment Totals column chart

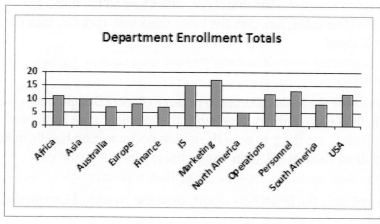

TABLE 11-3: Chart areas

chart area	description
Data	Determines what field the bars (lines, wedges, etc.) on the chart represent
Axis	The x-axis (horizontal axis) or y-axis (vertical axis) on the chart
Series	Displays the legend when multiple series of data are graphed

Apply Chart Types

Learning Outcomes
• Apply different chart types
• Describe 3-D chart types

The Chart Wizard provides 20 different chart types. While column charts are the most popular, you can also use line, area, and pie charts to effectively show some types of data. Three-dimensional effects can be used to enhance the chart, but those effects can sometimes make it difficult to compare the sizes of bars, lines, and wedges, so choose a three-dimensional effect only if it does not detract from the point of the chart. **CASE** *David Fox suggests that you change the existing column chart to other chart types and sub-types to see how the data is presented.*

STEPS

1. **Right-click the chart, click Design View, then double-click the chart placeholder**
   You must open the chart in Edit mode to change the chart type.

2. **Click Chart on the menu bar, then click Chart Type**
   The Chart Type dialog box opens, as shown in **FIGURE 11-17**. All major chart types plus many chart sub-types are displayed. A button is available to preview any choice before applying that chart sub-type.

3. **Click the Clustered column with a 3-D visual effect button (second row, first column in the Chart sub-type area), click and hold the Press and Hold to View Sample button, click the 3-D Column button (third row, first column in the Chart sub-type area), then click and hold the Press and Hold to View Sample button**
   A Sample box opens, presenting a rough idea of what the final chart will look like. Although 3-D charts appear more interesting than 2-D chart types, the samples do not show the data more clearly, so you decide to preview other 2-D chart types.

4. **Click the Bar Chart type in the Chart type list, click and hold the Press and Hold to View Sample button, click the Default formatting check box to remove the check mark, then click and hold the Press and Hold to View Sample button**
   Use the Default formatting option to quickly reapply default formats to the chart.

5. **Click OK to accept the bar chart type, click Chart on the menu bar, click Chart Options, click the Data Labels tab, click the Value check box, click OK, click the legend, then press [Delete]**
   With the modifications made to change the chart into a bar chart, you view it in Print Preview to see the final result.

6. **Click outside the hashed border to return to Report Design View, click the Label button Aa in the Controls group, click above the bar chart, type Enrollments by Department, press [Enter], use the ↕ to drag the middle bottom sizing handle down to make the chart about twice as tall, then display the report in Print Preview**
   The same departmental data, expressed as a bar chart, is shown in **FIGURE 11-18**.

7. **Save and close the DeptChart report, close the Training-11.accdb database, then exit Access**

Creating Advanced Reports

FIGURE 11-17: Chart Type dialog box

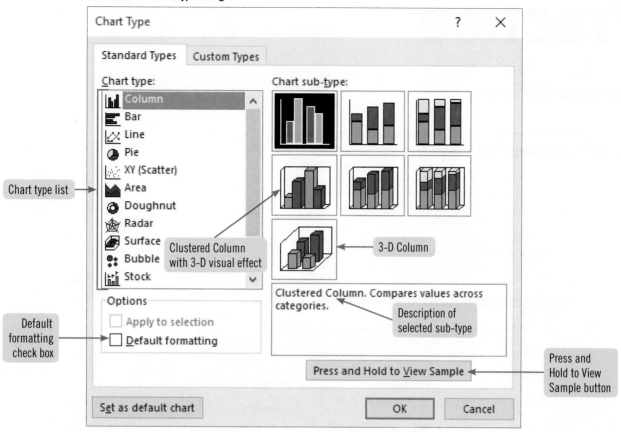

FIGURE 11-18: Department Enrollment Totals bar chart

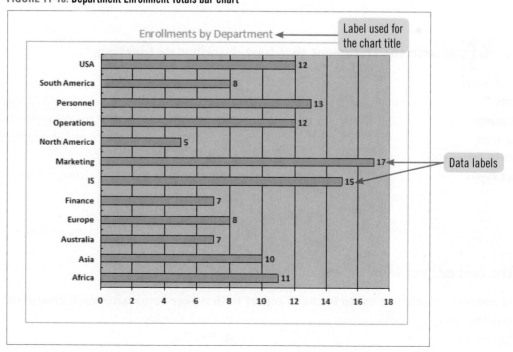

Practice

Concepts Review

Identify each element of Report Design View shown in FIGURE 11-19.

FIGURE 11-19

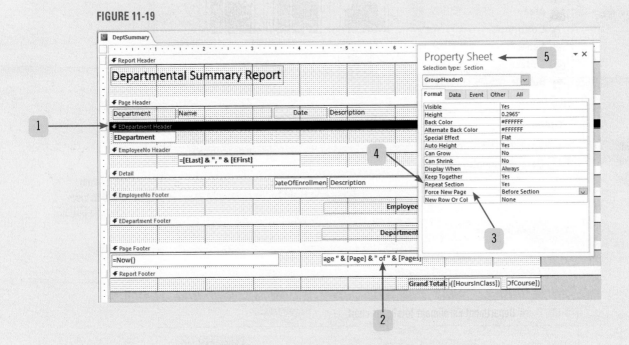

Match each term with the statement that best describes its function.

6. **Table layout**
7. **Charts**
8. **Edit mode**
9. **Data area**
10. **Domain functions**
11. **Chart types**

a. Visual representations of numeric data

b. A way of connecting controls so that when you move or resize them in Layout or Design View, the action you take on one control applies to all controls

c. Calculate a value based on a field that is not included in the Record Source property for the form or report

d. Used to select and modify individual chart elements, such as the title, legend, bars, or axes

e. Determines what data is graphed on the chart

f. Determine the presentation of data on the chart, such as column, pie, and line

Select the best answer from the list of choices.

12. **What property would you use to format a report with a page break after each group footer section?**
   a. Force Page Breaks
   b. Page Breaks
   c. Force New Page
   d. New Page

13. **To set a page break before a Group Header section on a report, you would modify the properties of the:**
   a. Report.
   b. Page Footer section.
   c. Group Header section.
   d. Detail section.

14. Which control layout is common for reports?

a. Datasheet

b. Stacked

c. Tabular

d. Gridlines

15. Which dialog box allows you to specify the number of columns you want to view in a report?

a. Columns

b. Print

c. Page Setup

d. Property Sheet

16. Which type of chart is best to show an upward sales trend over several months?

a. Scatter

b. Column

c. Pie

d. Line

Skills Review

1. Apply advanced formatting.

a. Start Access, then open the LakeHomes-11.accdb database from the location where you store your Data Files. Enable content if prompted. Change the name of Aaron Kelsey in the Realtors table to *your* name, then close the table.

b. Preview the AgencyListings report, noting the format for the SqFt and Asking fields.

c. In Report Design View, change the Format property for the SqFt text box in the Detail section to **Standard** and change the Decimal Places property to **0**.

d. In Report Design View, change the Format property for the Asking text box in the Detail section to **Currency** and change the Decimal Places property to **0**.

e. Preview the report to make sure your SqFt values appear with commas, the Asking values appear with dollar signs, and no decimal places are shown.

f. Change the top and bottom margins to **0.5"** and make sure the left and right margins are set to **0.25"**, then save the AgencyListings report.

2. Control layout.

a. Open the AgencyListings report in Design View.

b. Open the Group, Sort, and Total pane, then open the AgencyName Footer section.

c. Add a text box in the AgencyName Footer below the SqFt text box in the Detail section with the expression **=Sum([SqFt])**. Modify the new label to have the caption **Subtotals:**.

d. Add a text box in the AgencyName Footer below the Asking text box in the Detail section with the expression **=Sum([Asking])**. Delete the extra label in the AgencyName Footer section.

e. Format the =Sum([SqFt]) text box with **Standard** Format and **0** Decimals Places, format the =Sum([Asking]) text box with **Currency** Format and **0** Decimal Places, and then resize and align the text boxes under the fields they subtotal so that Print Preview looks similar to the last page of the report shown in FIGURE 11-20.

FIGURE 11-20

Skills Review (continued)

f. In Design View, insert the Page N of M page number format into the left side of the Page Footer.

g. Print preview several pages of the report, and work in Report Design View to remove extra space so that a blank page doesn't print between pages as needed. Save the AgencyListings report.

3. Set advanced print layout.

a. Open the AgencyListings report in Design View.

b. Modify the AgencyName Footer section to force a new page after that section prints.

c. Preview the report to make sure each agency prints on its own page.

d. Close and save the AgencyListings report.

4. Create multicolumn reports.

a. Use the Report Wizard to create a report with the AgencyName field from the Agencies table, the RFirst and RLast fields from the Realtors table, and the Type field from the Listings table. Be sure to select the fields from the table objects.

b. View the data by Listings, add AgencyName as the grouping level, sort the records in ascending order by RLast, use a Stepped layout and a Landscape orientation, and enter **Inventory** as the report title.

c. In Report Design View, delete the RLast and RFirst labels and text boxes.

d. Delete the page expression in the Page Footer section, delete the Type label in the Page Header section, and delete the AgencyName label in the Page Header section. Move the Type field in the Detail section to the left, just below the AgencyName text box.

e. Add a new text box to the right of the Type control in the Detail section with the following expression:
=[RLast]&", "&[RFirst]

f. Delete the label for the new text box, then widen the =[RLast]&", "&[RFirst] text box in the Detail section to be about 2" wide. Drag the right edge of the report as far as you can to the left so that the report is approximately 5" wide. Drag the top edge of the Page Footer section up to shorten the Detail section as much as possible.

g. Preview the report and use the Page Setup dialog box to change the Number of Columns setting to **2** and the column layout to Down, then Across. The report should look like **FIGURE 11-21**.

h. Save and close the Inventory report.

FIGURE 11-21

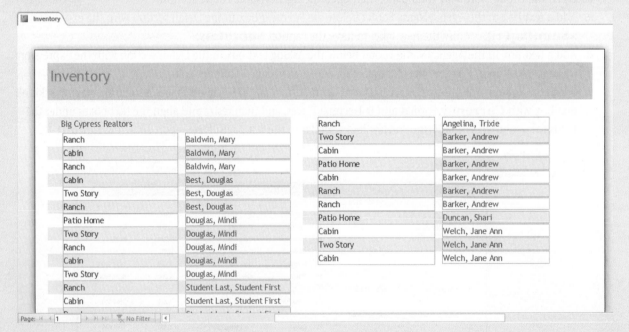

Skills Review (continued)

5. Use domain functions.

   a. Create a new table named **Legal** with two new fields: **LegalID** with an AutoNumber data type and **LegalText** with a Long Text data type. Make LegalID the primary key field.

   b. Add one record to the table with the following entry in the LegalText field: **The information in the listing is a preliminary estimate.** Widen the column of the LegalText field as needed. Note the value of the LegalID field for the first record (probably 1), then save and close the Legal table.

   c. Open the ListingReport in Design View, open the Report Footer section, then use a DLookup function in an expression in a text box in the Report Footer section to look up the LegalText field in the Legal table as follows: **=DLookup("[LegalText]","Legal","LegalID=1")**. Delete the accompanying label. (Note that the number in the expression must match the value of the LegalID field for the first record that you created in Step b.)

   d. Preview the report, then review the Report Footer. Switch back and forth between Report Design View and Print Preview to fix and widen the text box to be as wide as needed so that it clearly displays the entire expression, then save and close the ListingReport.

6. Create charts.

   a. Open the Inventory query in Query Design View, then add criteria to select only the **Ranch** (in the Type field) records.

   b. Save the query with a new name as **RanchHomes**, then close it.

   c. Start a new report in Report Design View.

   d. Insert a chart in the Detail section based on the RanchHomes query.

   e. Choose the RLast and Asking fields for the chart, choose a Column Chart, make sure the SumOfAsking field appears in the Data area, and move the RLast field from the Axis to the Series area.

   f. Title the chart **Ranch Listings**, do not display the legend, then preview the report to view the chart.

   g. Save the report with the name **RanchListings**.

7. Modify charts.

   a. Return to Report Design View for RanchListings report, and double-click the chart to open it in Edit mode.

   b. Double-click the y-axis values to open the Format Axis dialog box, click the Number tab, then choose the **Currency** format from the Category list, entering **0** for the Decimal Places.

FIGURE 11-22

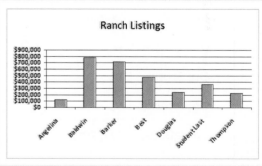

   c. Click the By Column button on the Chart Standard toolbar to switch the position of the fields in the x-axis and legend.

   d. Return to Report Design View, then switch to Print Preview. Resize the chart as necessary so it looks like FIGURE 11-22.

8. Apply chart types.

   a. Save and close RanchListings, then copy and paste it with the name **RanchListingsBar**.

   b. Open RanchListingsBar in Design View, open the chart in Edit mode, then change the chart type to a Clustered Bar.

   c. Switch between Report Design View and Print Preview, resizing the chart and changing the font sizes as needed so that all of the labels on each axis are displayed clearly. (*Hint*: To change the font sizes, double-click an axis label in Edit mode, then click the Font tab in the Format Axis dialog box.)

   d. Print RanchListingsBar if requested by your instructor, then save and close it.

   e. Close the LakeHomes-11.accdb database, and exit Access 2016.

Independent Challenge 1

As the manager of a college women's basketball team, you want to enhance a form within the Basketball-11.accdb database to chart the home versus visiting team scores. You will build on your report creation skills to do so.

a. Start Access, then open the database Basketball-11.accdb from the location where you store your Data Files. Enable content if prompted.

b. Open and then maximize the GameInfo form. Navigate through several records as you observe the Our Score and Opponent scores.

c. Open the form in Form Design View, then insert a chart on the right side of the form based on the Games table. Choose the CycloneScore and OpponentScore fields for the chart. Choose a Column Chart type.

d. Add the OpponentScore field to the Data area so that both SumOfCycloneScore and SumOfOpponentScore appear in the Data area, double-click the SumOfCycloneScore field, select None as the summarize option, double-click the SumOfOpponentScore field, then select None as the summarize option.

e. Click Next and choose GameNo as the Form Field and as the Chart Field so that the chart changes from record to record showing the CycloneScore versus the OpponentScore in the chart.

f. Title the chart **Scoring**, and do not display a legend.

g. Open the form in Form View, and view the record for GameNo 10, as shown in FIGURE 11-23. If requested by your instructor, print this record. To insert your name on the printout, add it as a label to the Form Header section.

h. Save the GameInfo form, close it, close the Basketball-11.accdb database, and exit Access 2016.

FIGURE 11-23

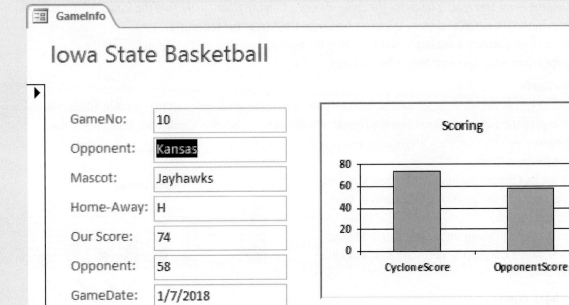

Independent Challenge 2

As the manager of a college women's basketball team, you want to build a report that shows a graph of total points per player per game.

a. Start Access, then open the database Basketball-11.accdb from the location where you store your Data Files. Enable content if prompted.

b. Open the Player Statistics report and study the structure. Notice that this report has the total points per player in the last column. You want to graph these values for the entire season. Open the Player Statistics report in Report Design View.

c. Double-click the edge of the far-right text box in the Detail section, and click the Data tab in the Property Sheet to study the Control Source property. The expression =[FT]+([FG]*2)+([3P]*3) adds one-point free throws [FT] to two-point field goals [FG] to three-point three-pointers [3P] to find the player's total contribution to the score. You will calculate the total point value in the underlying query instead of on the report to make it easier to graph.

d. Click the report selector button, then click the Build button for the Record Source property, which currently displays the PlayerStats query. In the first blank column, add a new field with the following expression: **TotalPts:[FT]+([FG]*2)+([3P]*3)**.

e. Save the query with the name **PlayerStats**, then close the query and return to Design View for the Player Statistics report. Open the Property Sheet for the GameNo Footer section. On the Format tab, change the Force New Page property to After Section.

f. Drag the bottom edge of the Report Footer section down so the height of the Report Footer section is about 3 inches, then insert a chart just below the existing controls in the Report Footer section.

g. In the Chart Wizard, choose the PlayerStats query to create the chart, choose the LastName and TotalPts fields for the chart, and choose the Column Chart type.

h. Use SumOfTotalPts in the Data area and the LastName field in the Axis area (which should be the defaults). Choose <No Field> for both the Report Fields and Chart Fields, and title the chart **Player Total Points**.

i. Widen the chart placeholder and report to be about 6" wide in Report Design View, delete the legend, then save and preview the report. The chart should look like FIGURE 11-24.

j. Save the Player Statistics report, add your name as a label to the Report Header section, print the first and last pages if requested by your instructor, then close the report.

k. Close the Basketball-11.accdb database, and exit Access 2016.

FIGURE 11-24

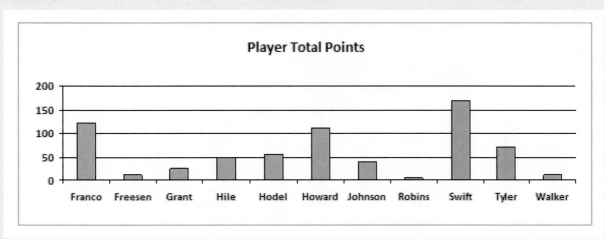

Independent Challenge 3

As the manager of a college women's basketball team, you want to create a multicolumn report from the Basketball-11.accdb database to summarize total points per game per player.

a. Start Access, then open the database Basketball-11.accdb from the location where you store your Data Files. Enable content if prompted.

b. Open the PlayerInfo query in Design View. In the first blank column, add a new field with the following expression: **TotalPts:[FT]+([FG]*2)+([3P]*3)**.

c. Save and close the PlayerInfo query.

d. Use the Report Wizard to create a new report from the PlayerInfo query with the fields **Opponent**, **GameDate**, **LastName**, and **TotalPts**. View the data by Games, do not add any more grouping levels, then sort the records in descending order by TotalPts.

e. Click the Summary Options button, then click the Sum check box for the TotalPts field.

f. Choose a Stepped layout and a Landscape orientation. Title the report **Point Production**, and preview it.

g. In Report Design View, delete the long text box with the Summary expression in the GameNo Footer section. Delete the LastName and TotalPts labels from the Page Header section.

h. Delete the page expression in the Page Footer section, then move the TotalPts and LastName text boxes in the Detail section to the left, just below the Opponent and GameDate text boxes in the GameNo Header section. Move any other text boxes to the left so that no control extends beyond the 4" mark on the horizontal ruler.

i. Drag the right edge of the report to the left so that it is no wider than 4", then right-align the values within the text boxes with the subtotal for total points in the GameNo Footer and the Report Footer sections and also right-align the right edges of these two text boxes.

j. Move and right-align the Sum and Grand Total labels closer to the text boxes they describe.

k. Preview the report, and in the Page Setup dialog box, set the report to **2** columns, then specify that the column layout go down, then across.

l. In Design View, add a horizontal line across the bottom of the GameNo Footer section to separate the records from game to game.

m. For the GameNo Footer section, change the New Row Or Col property to After Section.

n. Preview the Point Production report. It should structurally look like **FIGURE 11-25**. Print the first page of the report if requested by your instructor, adding your name as a label to the Report Header section if needed for the printout.

o. Close the Point Production report, close the Basketball-11.accdb database, then exit Access.

FIGURE 11-25

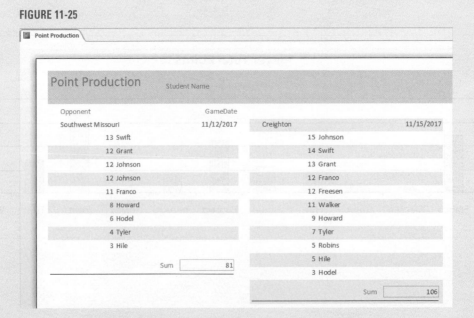

Independent Challenge 4: Explore

In your quest to become an Access database consultant, you want to know more about the built-in Microsoft Access templates and what you can learn about report design from these samples. In this exercise, you explore the reports of the Task management database. Note that templates are updated often, so you may need to alter these steps.

a. Start Access 2016, then select the Updated: Task management template. (*Hint*: Search for **task management** in the Search for online templates box.) Name the database **TaskMgmt**, save it in the location where you store your Data Files, then enable content if prompted.

b. If prompted with a Welcome or Getting Started window, read and close it, then expand the Navigation Pane if needed to review the objects in the database.

c. Open the Contacts table and add *your school name* in the Company field and *your name* in the Last Name and First Name fields. Fill in the rest of the record with fictitious but realistic data.

d. Add a second record in the Contacts table with your professor's information in the Last Name and First Name fields, using fictitious but realistic data in the rest of the record.

e. Expand the subdatasheet for your record and enter two task records with the titles **Web Site** and **SEO Project**. Do not change or enter data in any of the other fields, then close the Contacts table.

f. Preview each of the predeveloped reports going back and forth between Print Preview and Report Design View to study and learn about any new features or techniques these reports offer that you want to explore further.

g. Open the Contact Address Book in Print Preview and notice that the contacts are grouped by the first letter of their last name. To see how this was done, open the report in Design View and then open the Group, Sort, and Total Pane. Click the More button to reveal the characteristics of the Group on File As group. Click the list arrow for the "by first character" option to see more grouping options.

h. If requested by your instructor, print the Contact Address Book report, close the TaskMgmt.accdb database, and exit Access 2016.

Visual Workshop

As the manager of a college women's basketball team, you need to create a report from the Basketball-11.accdb database that lists information about each game played and that subtracts the OpponentScore from the CycloneScore field to calculate the number of points by which the game was won or lost in the Win/Loss column. Use the Report Wizard to start the report. Base it on all the fields in the Games table, and sort the records in ascending order on the GameDate field. Use a Tabular layout and a Landscape orientation, and name the report **Basketball Season**. Use Report Layout and Design View to move, resize, align, modify, and add controls as necessary to match FIGURE 11-26. (*Hint*: You must add a text box that calculates the Win/Loss value for each game.) If requested to print the report, add your name as a label to the Report Header section before printing.

FIGURE 11-26

GameDate	GameNo	Opponent	Mascot	Home-Away	Our Score	Opponent	Win/Loss
11/12/2017	1	Southwest Missouri	Patriots	A	81	65	16
11/15/2017	2	Creighton	Bluejays	H	106	60	46
11/22/2017	3	Northern Illinois	Huskies	H	65	60	5
11/29/2017	4	Louisiana Tech	Red Raiders	A	69	89	-20
12/10/2017	5	Drake	Bulldogs	H	80	60	20
12/18/2017	6	Northern Iowa	Panthers	A	38	73	-35
12/28/2017	7	Buffalo	Bulls	H	50	55	-5

Creating Macros

CASE ▶ Aaron Scout, the network administrator at Reason 2 Go, has identified several Access tasks that are repeated on a regular basis. He has asked you to help him automate these processes with macros.

Module Objectives

After completing this module, you will be able to:

- Understand macros
- Create a macro
- Modify actions and arguments
- Assign a macro to a command button

- Use If statements
- Work with events
- Create a data macro
- Troubleshoot macros

Files You Will Need

Equipment-12.accdb   Patients-12.accdb

Basketball-12.accdb   Candy-12.accdb

Understand Macros

Learning
Outcomes
• Describe the
benefits of macros
• Define macro
terminology
• Describe Macro
Design View
components

A **macro** is a database object that stores actions to complete Access tasks. Repetitive Access tasks such as printing several reports or opening and maximizing a form are good candidates for a macro. Automating routine tasks by using macros builds efficiency, accuracy, and flexibility into your database. **CASE** *Aaron Scout encourages you to study the major benefits of using macros, macro terminology, and the components of the Macro Design View before building your first macro.*

DETAILS

The major benefits of using macros include the following:

- Saving time by automating routine tasks
- Increasing accuracy by ensuring that tasks are executed consistently
- Improving the functionality and ease of use of forms by using macros connected to command buttons
- Ensuring data accuracy in forms by using macros to respond to data entry errors
- Automating data transfers such as collecting data from Excel
- Helping users by responding to their interactions within a form

Macro terminology:

- A **macro** is an Access object that stores a series of actions to perform one or more tasks.
- **Macro Design View** is the window in which you create a macro. **FIGURE 12-1** shows Macro Design View with an OpenForm action. See **TABLE 12-1** for a description of the Macro Design View components.
- Each task that you want the macro to perform is called an **action**. A macro may contain one or more actions.
- **Arguments** are properties of an action that provide additional information on how the action should execute.
- A **conditional expression** is an expression resulting in either a true or false answer that determines whether a macro action will execute. Conditional expressions are used in If statements.
- An **event** is something that happens to a form, window, toolbar, or control—such as the click of a command button or an entry in a field—that can be used to initiate the execution of a macro.
- A **submacro** is a collection of actions within a macro object that allows you to name and create multiple, separate macros within a single macro object.

Creating Macros

FIGURE 12-1: Macro Design View with OpenForm action

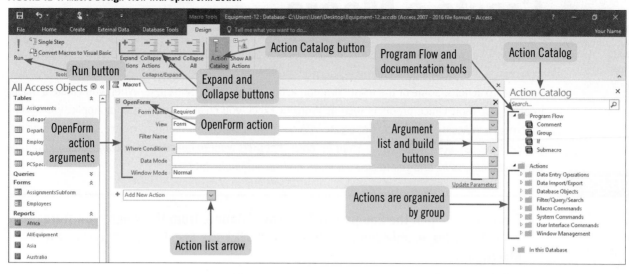

TABLE 12-1: Macro Design View components

component	description
Action Catalog	Lists all available macro actions organized by category. Use the Search box to narrow the number of macro actions to a particular subject.
If statement	Contains conditional expressions that are evaluated as either true or false. If true, the macro action is executed. If false, the macro action is skipped. If statements in Access 2016 may contain Else If and Else clauses.
Comment	Allows you to document the macro with explanatory text.
Arguments	Lists required and optional arguments for the selected action.
Run button	Runs the selected macro.
Expand and Collapse buttons	Allows you to expand or collapse the macro actions to show or hide their arguments.

Create a Macro

In Access, you create a macro by choosing a series of actions in Macro Design View that accomplishes the job you want to automate. Therefore, to become proficient with Access macros, you must be comfortable with macro actions. Some of the most common actions are listed in TABLE 12-2. When you create a macro in other Microsoft Office products such as Word or Excel, you create Visual Basic for Applications (VBA) statements. In Access, macros do not create VBA code, although after creating a macro, you can convert it to VBA if desired. **CASE** *Aaron Scout observes that users want to open the AllEquipment report from the Employees form, so he asks you to create a macro to help automate this task.*

STEPS

1. **Start Access, open the Equipment-12.accdb database from the where you store your Data Files, enable content if prompted, click the Create tab, then click the Macro button**

   Macro Design View opens, ready for you to choose your first action.

2. **Click the Action list arrow, type op to quickly scroll to the actions that start with the letters op, then scroll and click OpenReport**

   The OpenReport action is now the first action in the macro, and the arguments that further define the OpenReport action appear in the action block. The **action block** organizes all of the arguments for a current action and is visually highlighted with a rectangle and gray background. You can expand or collapse the action block to view or hide details by clicking the Collapse/Expand button to the left of the action name or the Expand and Collapse buttons on the Design tab in Macro Design View.

   The **OpenReport action** has three required arguments: Report Name, View, and Window Mode. View and Window Mode have default values, and if you start working with the OpenReport action's arguments but do not select a Report Name, the word "Required" is shown, indicating that you must select a choice. The Filter Name and Where Condition arguments are optional as indicated by their blank boxes.

3. **Click the Report Name argument list arrow, then click AllEquipment**

   All of the report objects in the Equipment-12.accdb database appear in the Report Name argument list, making it easy to choose the report you want.

4. **Click the View argument list arrow, then click Print Preview**

   Your screen should look like FIGURE 12-2. Macros can contain one or many actions. In this case, the macro has only one action.

5. **Click the Save button 🖫 on the Quick Access Toolbar, type PreviewAllReport in the Macro Name text box, click OK, right-click the PreviewAllReport macro tab, then click Close**

   The Navigation Pane lists the PreviewAllReport object in the Macros group.

6. **Double-click the PreviewAllReport macro in the Navigation Pane to run the macro**

   The AllEquipment report opens in Print Preview.

7. **Close the AllEquipment report**

FIGURE 12-2: Macro Design View with OpenReport action

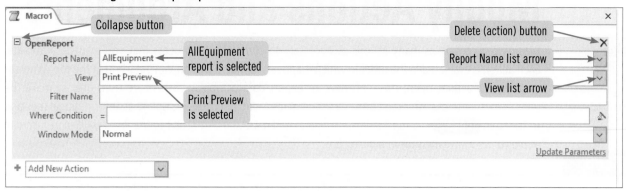

TABLE 12-2: Common macro actions

subject area	macro action	description
Data Entry Operations	DeleteRecord	Deletes the current record
	SaveRecord	Saves the current record
Data Import/Export	ImportExportSpreadsheet*	Imports or exports the spreadsheet you specify
	ImportExportText*	Imports or exports the text file you specify
	EMailDatabaseObject	Sends the specified database object through Outlook with specified email settings
Database Objects	GoToControl	Moves the focus (where you are currently typing or clicking) to a specific field or control
	GoToRecord	Makes a specified record the current record
	OpenForm	Opens a form in Form View, Design View, Print Preview, or Datasheet View
	OpenReport	Opens a report in Design View or Print Preview, or prints the report
	OpenTable	Opens a table in Datasheet View, Design View, or Print Preview
	SetValue*	Sets the value of a field, control, or property
Filter/Query/Search	ApplyFilter	Restricts the number of records that appear in the resulting form or report by applying limiting criteria
	FindRecord	Finds the first record that meets the criteria
	OpenQuery	Opens a select or crosstab query; runs an action query
Macro Commands	RunCode	Runs a Visual Basic function (a series of programming statements that does a calculation or comparison and returns a value)
	RunMacro	Runs a macro or attaches a macro to a custom menu command
	StopMacro	Stops the currently running macro
System Commands	Beep	Sounds a beep tone through the computer's speaker
	PrintOut*	Prints the active object, such as a datasheet, report, form, or module
	SendKeys*	Sends keystrokes directly to Microsoft Access or to an active Windows application
User Interface Commands	MessageBox	Displays a message box containing a warning or an informational message
	ShowToolbar*	Displays or hides a given toolbar
Window Management	CloseWindow	Closes a window
	MaximizeWindow	Enlarges the active window to fill the Access window

*Must click Show All Actions button on Ribbon for these actions to appear.

Modify Actions and Arguments

Learning
Outcomes
• Modify macro
 actions
• Modify macro
 arguments

Macros can contain as many actions as necessary to complete the process that you want to automate. Each action is evaluated in the order in which it appears in Macro Design View, starting at the top. Whereas some macro actions open, close, preview, or export data or objects, others are used only to make the database easier to use. **MessageBox** is a useful macro action because it displays an informational message to the user. **CASE** ▶ *Aaron Scout wants you to add a MessageBox action to the PreviewAllReport macro to display a descriptive message in a dialog box.*

STEPS

1. **Right-click the PreviewAllReport macro in the Navigation Pane, then click Design View on the shortcut menu**

   The PreviewAllReport macro opens in Macro Design View.

2. **Click the Add New Action list arrow, type me to quickly scroll to the actions that start with the letters me, then click MessageBox**

   Each action has its own arguments that further clarify what the action does.

3. **Click the Message argument text box in the action block, then type Click the Print button to print this report**

   The Message argument determines what text appears in the message box. By default, the Beep argument is set to "Yes" and the Type argument is set to "None."

4. **Click the Type argument list arrow in the action block, then click Information**

   The Type argument determines which icon appears in the dialog box that is created by the MessageBox action.

5. **Click the Title argument text box in the action block, then type To print this report...**

   Your screen should look like FIGURE 12-3. The Title argument specifies what text is displayed in the title bar of the resulting dialog box. If you leave the Title argument empty, the title bar of the resulting dialog box displays "Microsoft Access."

6. **Save the macro, then click the Run button in the Tools group**

   If your speakers are turned on, you should hear a beep, then the message box appears, as shown in FIGURE 12-4.

7. **Click OK in the dialog box, close the AllEquipment report, then save and close Macro Design View**

Creating Macros

FIGURE 12-3: Adding the MessageBox action

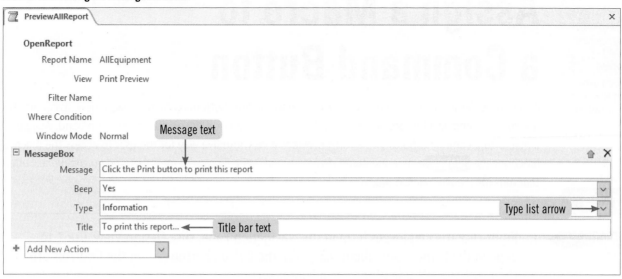

FIGURE 12-4: Dialog box created by MessageBox action

Assigning a macro to a key combination

You can assign a key combination such as [Shift][Ctrl][L] to a macro by creating a macro with the name **AutoKeys**. Enter the key combination as the submacro name. Use + for Shift, % for Alt, and ^ for Ctrl. Enclose special keys such as F3 in {curly braces}. For example, to assign a macro to [Shift][Ctrl][L], use +^L as the submacro name. To assign a macro to [Shift][F3], use +{F3} as the submacro name. Any key combination assignments you make in the AutoKeys macro override those that Access has already specified. Therefore, check the Keyboard Shortcuts information in the Microsoft Access Help system to make sure that the AutoKey assignment that you are creating doesn't override an existing Access quick keystroke that may be used for another purpose.

Assign a Macro to a Command Button

Learning Outcomes
• Tie a command button to a macro
• Describe trusted folders and files

Access provides many ways to run a macro: clicking the Run button in Macro Design View, assigning the macro to a command button, or assigning the macro to a Ribbon or shortcut menu command. Assigning a macro to a command button on a form provides a very intuitive way for the user to access the macro's functionality. **CASE** *You and Aaron decide to modify the Employees form to include a command button that runs the PreviewAllReport macro.*

STEPS

1. **Right-click the Employees form in the Navigation Pane, click Design View, use ↕ to expand the Form Footer about 0.5", click the Button button ▨ in the Controls group, then click the left side of the Form Footer section**

   The **Command Button Wizard** starts, presenting you with 28 actions on the right organized within 6 categories on the left. For example, if you want the command button to open a report, you choose the OpenReport action in the Report Operations category. In this case, you want to run the PreviewAllReport macro, which not only opens a report, but also presents a message. The Miscellaneous category contains an action that allows you to run an existing macro.

2. **Click Miscellaneous in the Categories list, click Run Macro in the Actions list as shown in FIGURE 12-5, click Next, click PreviewAllReport, click Next, click the Text option button, select Run Macro, type All Equipment Report, then click Next**

   The Command Button Wizard asks you to give the button a meaningful name. When assigning names, a common three-character prefix for command buttons is **cmd**.

3. **Type cmdAllEquipment, click Finish, then click the Property Sheet button in the Tools group to open the Property Sheet for the command button**

   The new command button that runs a macro has been added to the Employees form in Form Design View. You work with the Property Sheet to change the text color to differentiate it from the button color as well as to examine how the macro was attached to the command button.

4. **Click the Format tab in the Property Sheet, scroll down and click the Fore Color list arrow, click Text Dark, then click the Event tab in the Property Sheet, noting that the On Click property contains [Embedded Macro]**

   The PreviewAllReport macro was attached to the **On Click property** of this command button. In other words, the macro is run when the user clicks the command button. To make sure that the new command button works as intended, you view the form in Form View and test the command button.

5. **Close the Property Sheet, click the View button ▨ to switch to Form View, click the All Equipment Report command button in the Form Footer section, click OK in the message box, then close the AllEquipment report**

   The Employees form with the new command button should look like FIGURE 12-6. It's common to put command buttons in the Form Footer so that users have a consistent location to find them.

6. **Save and close the Employees form**

FIGURE 12-5: Adding a command button to run a macro

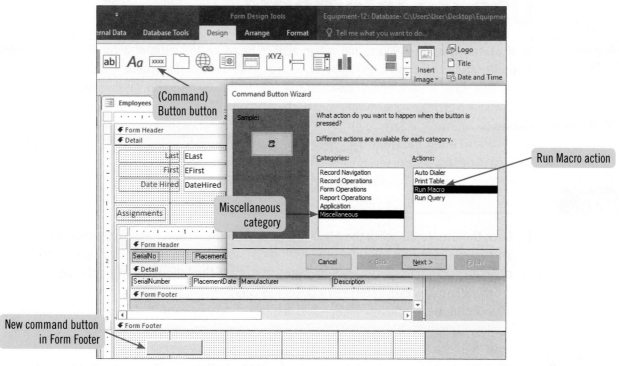

FIGURE 12-6: Employees form with new command button

Using a trusted database and setting up a trusted folder

A **trusted database** allows you to run macros and Visual Basic for Applications code (VBA). By default, a database is not trusted. To trust a database, click the Enable Content button on the Security Warning bar each time you open a database. To permanently trust a database, store the database in a **trusted folder**. To create a trusted folder, open the Options dialog box from the File tab, click the Trust Center, click the Trust Center Settings button, click the Trusted Locations option, click the Add new location button, then browse to and choose the folder you want to trust.

Use If Statements

Learning Outcomes
• Apply If statements to macros
• Enter conditional expressions

An **If statement** allows you to run macro actions based on the result of a conditional expression. A **conditional expression** is an expression such as [Price]>100 or [StateName]="MO" that results in a true or false value. If the condition evaluates true, the actions that follow the If statement are executed. If the condition evaluates false, the macro skips those actions. When building a conditional expression that refers to a value in a control on a form or report, use the following syntax: [Forms]![formname]![controlname], which is called **bang notation**. **CASE** ▶ At R2G, everyone who has been with the company longer than five years is eligible to take their old PC equipment home as soon as it has been replaced. Aaron asks you to use a conditional macro to help evaluate and present this information in a form.

STEPS

1. **Click the Create tab, click the Macro button, click the Action Catalog button in the Show/Hide group to toggle on the Action Catalog window if it is not already visible, double-click If in the Program Flow area, then type the following in the If box:**
   [Forms]![Employees]![DateHired]<Date()-(5*365)

   The conditional expression shown in FIGURE 12-7 says, "Check the value in the DateHired control on the Employees form and evaluate true if the value is earlier than 5 years from today. Evaluate false if the value is not earlier than 5 years ago."

2. **Click the Add New Action list arrow in the If block, then scroll and click SetProperty**

   The **SetProperty** action has three arguments—Control Name, Property, and Value.

3. **Click the Control Name argument text box in the Action Arguments pane, type LabelPCProgram, click the Property argument list arrow, click Visible, click the Value Property argument, then type True**

   Your screen should look like FIGURE 12-8. The **Control Name** argument must match the **Name property** in the Property Sheet of the label that will be modified. The **Property argument** determines what property is being modified. The **Value argument** determines the value of the **Visible property**. For properties such as the Visible property that have only two choices in the Property Sheet, Yes or No, you enter a value of False for No and True for Yes.

4. **Save the macro with the name 5Years, then close Macro Design View**

   Test the macro using the Employees form.

5. **Double-click the Employees form to open it, then navigate to the second record**

   The record for Ron Dawson, hired 2/15/2000, appears. Given that Ron has worked at R2G much longer than 5 years, you anticipate that the macro will display the label when it is run.

6. **Click the Database Tools tab, click the Run Macro button, verify that 5Years is in the Macro Name text box, then click OK**

   After evaluating the DateHired field of this record and determining that this employee has been working at R2G longer than five years, the LabelPCProgram label's Visible property was set to Yes, as shown in FIGURE 12-9. The LabelPCProgram label's **Caption property** is "Eligible for PC Program!"

7. **Navigate through several records and note that the label remains visible for each employee even though the hire date may not be longer than 5 years ago**

   Because the macro only ran once, the label's Visible property remains Yes regardless of the current data in the DateHired field. You need a way to rerun or trigger the macro to evaluate the data in the DateHired field for each employee.

8. **Close the Employees form**

FIGURE 12-7: Using an If statement to set a control's Visible property

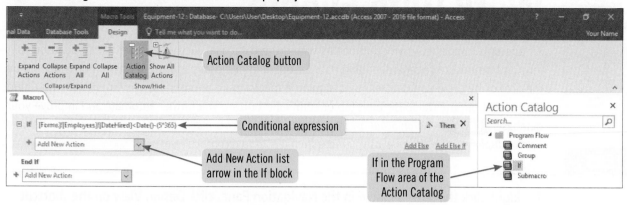

FIGURE 12-8: Entering arguments for the SetProperty action

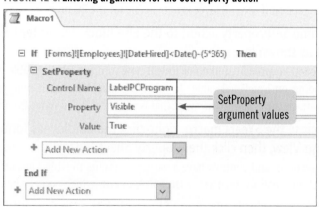

FIGURE 12-9: Running the 5Years macro

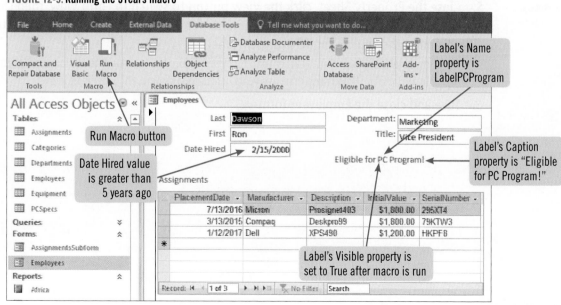

Work with Events

An **event** is a specific activity that occurs within the database, such as clicking a command button, moving from record to record, editing data, or opening or closing a form. Events can be triggered by the user or by the database itself. By assigning a macro to an appropriate event rather than running the macro from the Database Tools tab or command button, you further automate and improve your database. **CASE** ▶ *Aaron Scout asks you to modify the 5Years macro so that it evaluates the DateHired field to display or hide the label as you move from record to record.*

STEPS

1. **Right-click the 5Years macro in the Navigation Pane, click Design View on the shortcut menu, click anywhere in the If block to activate it, then click the Add Else link in the lower-right corner of the If block**

   The **Else** portion of an If statement allows you to run a different set of macro actions if the conditional expression evaluates False. In this case, you want to set the Value of the Visible property to False if the conditional expression evaluates False (if the DateHired is less than five years from today's date) so that the label does not appear if the employee is not eligible for the PC program.

   TROUBLE
   If your screen doesn't match **FIGURE 12-10**, use the Undo button ↺ to try again.

2. **Add the same SetProperty action to the Else block, but enter False for the Value argument as shown in FIGURE 12-10**

   With the second action edited, the macro will now turn the label's Visible property to True (Yes) or False (No), depending on DateHired value. To make the macro run each time you move to a new employee record, you attach the macro to the event that is triggered as you move from record to record.

3. **Save and close the 5Years macro, right-click the Employees form in the Navigation Pane, click Design View, then click the Property Sheet button**

   All objects, sections, and controls have a variety of events to which macros can be attached. Most event names are self-explanatory, such as the **On Click event** (which occurs when that item is clicked).

   TROUBLE
   Be sure you are viewing the Property Sheet for the form. If not, choose Form from the Selection Type list near the top of the Property Sheet.

4. **Click the Event tab in the Property Sheet, click the On Current list arrow, then click 5Years**

   Your Property Sheet should look like **FIGURE 12-11**. Because the **On Current event** occurs when focus moves from one record to another, the 5Years macro will automatically run each time you move from record to record in the form. Test your new macro by moving through several records in Form View.

5. **Close the Property Sheet, click the View button to switch to Form View, then click the Next record button ▶ in the navigation bar for the main form several times while observing the Eligible for PC Program! label**

   For every DateHired value that is earlier than five years before today's date, the Eligible for PC Program! label is visible. If the DateHired is less than five years before today's date, the label is hidden.

6. **Save and close the Employees form**

FIGURE 12-10: Adding an Else portion to an If block

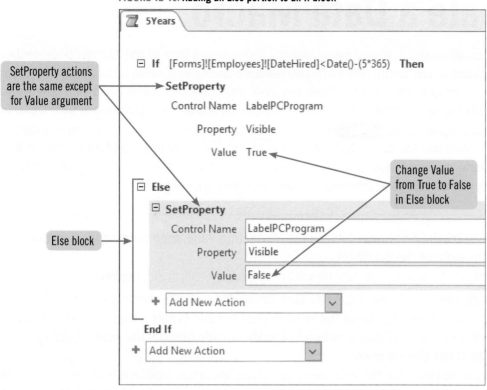

SetProperty actions are the same except for Value argument

Else block

Change Value from True to False in Else block

FIGURE 12-11: Attaching a macro to the On Current event of the form

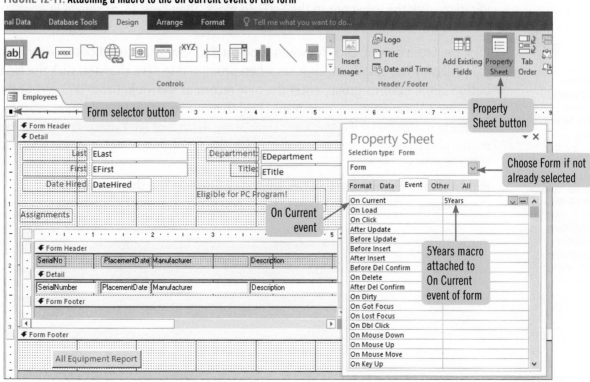

Form selector button

Property Sheet button

Choose Form if not already selected

On Current event

5Years macro attached to On Current event of form

Create a Data Macro

Learning Outcomes
- Describe the use of data macros
- Create a data macro

A data macro allows you to embed macro capabilities directly in a table to add, change, or delete data based on conditions you specify. Data macros are managed directly from within tables and do not appear in the Macros group in the Navigation Pane. You most often run a data macro based on a table event, such as modifying data or deleting a record, but you can run a data macro separately as well, similar to how you run a regular macro. **CASE** ▶ *R2G grants 10 days of regular vacation to all employees except for those in the Africa and Asia departments, who receive 15 days due to the extra travel requirements of their positions. Aaron asks you to figure out an automatic way to assign each employee the correct number of vacation days based on his or her department. A data macro will work well for this task.*

STEPS

1. **Double-click the Employees table in the Navigation Pane, then observe the Vacation field throughout the datasheet**

   Currently, the Vacation field contains the value of 10 for each record, or each employee.

2. **Right-click the Employees table tab, click Design View on the shortcut menu, click the Create Data Macros button in the Field, Record & Table Events group, click After Insert, then click the Action Catalog button in the Show/Hide group if the Action Catalog window is not already open**

   In this case, you chose the After Insert event, which is run after a new record is entered. See TABLE 12-3 for more information on table events. Creating a data macro is very similar to creating a regular macro. You add the logic and macro actions needed to complete the task at hand.

   QUICK TIP
   You can also drag a block or action from the Action Catalog to Macro Design View.

3. **Double-click the ForEachRecord data block in the Action Catalog to add a For Each Record In block, click the For Each Record In list arrow, click Employees in the list, click the Where Condition text box, type [EDepartment]="Africa" or [EDepartment]="Asia", double-click the EditRecord data block in the Action Catalog, double-click the SetField data action in the Action Catalog, click the Name box in the SetField block, type Vacation, click the Value box in the SetField block, then type 15, as shown in FIGURE 12-12**

   Test the new data macro by adding a new record.

   TROUBLE
   Be sure to tab to a completely new record to trigger the data macro attached to the After Insert event.

4. **Click the Close button, click Yes when prompted to save changes, click the View button to display the datasheet, click Yes when prompted to save changes, click the New button in the Records group, enter the new record as shown in FIGURE 12-13 except do not enter a Vacation value, then press [Tab] to move to a new record**

   The macro is triggered by the After Insert event of the record, and the Vacation field is automatically updated to 15 for the new record and all other records with Asia or Africa in the Department field, as shown in FIGURE 12-13.

   TROUBLE
   If your data macro doesn't work, click the Rename/Delete Macro button in Table Design View to delete it, and recreate the data macro.

5. **Right-click the Employees table tab, then click Close on the shortcut menu**

   Data is automatically saved when you move from record to record or close a database object.

Creating Macros

FIGURE 12-12: Creating a data macro

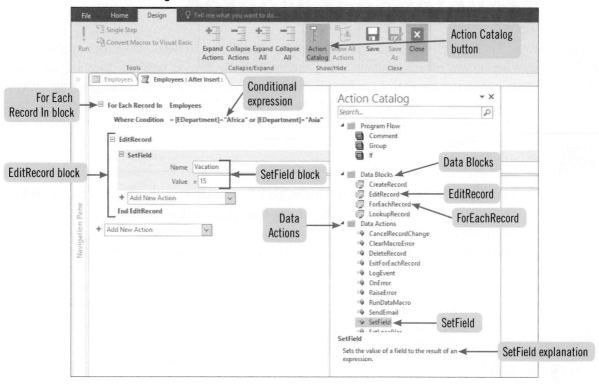

FIGURE 12-13: Running a data macro

TABLE 12-3: Table events

table event	runs...
After Insert	...after a new record has been inserted into the table
After Update	...after an existing record has been changed
After Delete	...after an existing record has been deleted
Before Delete	...before a record is deleted, to help the user validate or cancel the deletion
Before Change	...before a record is changed, to help the user validate or cancel the edits

Troubleshoot Macros

Learning
Outcomes
• Single step a
  macro
• Describe debug-
  ging techniques

When macros don't run properly, Access supplies several tools to debug them. **Debugging** means determining why the macro doesn't run correctly. It usually involves breaking down a dysfunctional macro into smaller pieces that can be individually tested. For example, you can **single step** a macro, which means to run it one action at a time to observe the effect of each specific action in the Macro Single Step dialog box. **CASE** *Aaron suggests that you use the PreviewAllReport macro to learn debugging techniques.*

STEPS

1. **Right-click the PreviewAllReport macro, click Design View on the shortcut menu, click the Single Step button in the Tools group, then click the Run button**

   The screen should look like FIGURE 12-14, with the Macro Single Step dialog box open. This dialog box displays information including the macro's name, the action's name, and the action's arguments. From the Macro Single Step dialog box, you can step into the next macro action, halt execution of the macro, or continue running the macro without single stepping.

2. **Click Step in the Macro Single Step dialog box**

   Stepping into the second action lets the first action run and pauses the macro at the second action. The Macro Single Step dialog box now displays information about the second action.

3. **Click Step**

   The second action, the MessageBox action, is executed, which displays the message box.

4. **Click OK, then close the AllEquipment report**

5. **Click the Design tab, then click the Single Step button to toggle it off**

   Another technique to help troubleshoot macros is to use the built-in prompts and Help system provided by Microsoft Access. For example, you may have questions about how to use the optional Filter Name argument for the OpenReport macro action.

6. **Click the OpenReport action block, then point to the Where Condition argument to view the ScreenTip that supplies information about that argument, as shown in FIGURE 12-15**

   The Access 2016 Macro Design View window has been improved with interactive prompts.

7. **Save and close the PreviewAllReport macro, close the Equipment-12.accdb database, then exit Access**

FIGURE 12-14: Single stepping through a macro

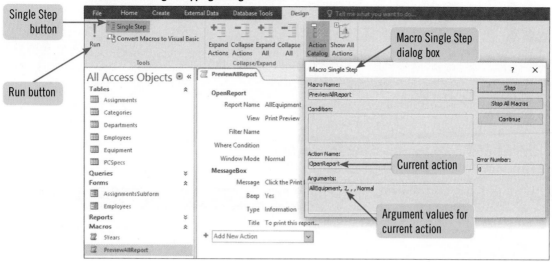

FIGURE 12-15: Viewing automatic prompts

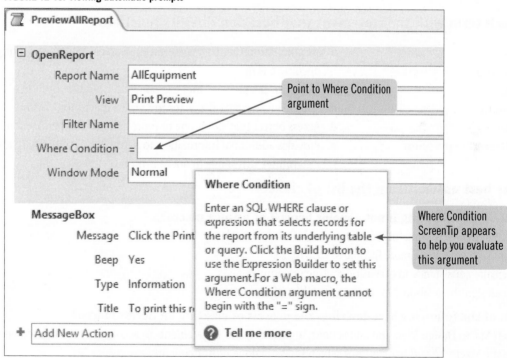

Access 2016

Practice

Concepts Review

Identify each element of Macro Design View shown in FIGURE 12-16.

FIGURE 12-16

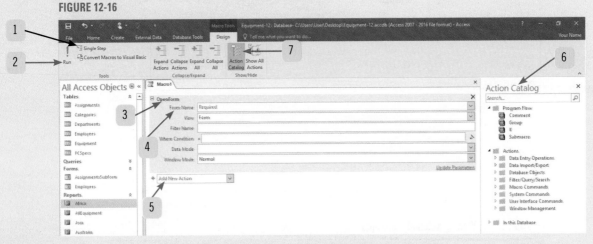

Match each term with the statement that best describes its function.

8. **Macro**
9. **Debugging**
10. **Action**
11. **Argument**
12. **Event**
13. **Conditional expression**

a. Specific action that occurs within the database, such as clicking a button or opening a form
b. Part of an If statement that evaluates as either true or false
c. Individual step that you want the Access macro to perform
d. Access object that stores one or more actions that perform one or more tasks
e. Provides additional information to define how an Access action will perform
f. Determines why a macro doesn't run properly

Select the best answer from the list of choices.

14. **Which of the following is not a major benefit of using a macro?**
    a. To save time by automating routine tasks
    b. To make the database more flexible or easy to use
    c. To ensure consistency in executing routine or complex tasks
    d. To redesign the relationships among the tables of the database

15. **Which of the following best describes the process of creating an Access macro?**
    a. Open Macro Design View and add actions, arguments, and If statements to accomplish the desired task.
    b. Use the Macro Wizard to determine which tasks are done most frequently.
    c. Use the single step recorder to record clicks and keystrokes as you complete a task.
    d. Use the macro recorder to record clicks and keystrokes as you complete a task.

16. **Which of the following would not be a way to run a macro?**
    a. Click the Run Macro button on the Database Tools tab.
    b. Double-click a macro action within the Macro Design View window.
    c. Assign the macro to a command button on a form.
    d. Assign the macro to an event of a control on a form.

17. **Which of the following is not a reason to run a macro in single step mode?**
    a. You want to observe the effect of each macro action individually.
    b. You want to run only a few of the actions of a macro.
    c. You want to change the arguments of a macro while it runs.
    d. You want to debug a macro that isn't working properly.

18. **Which of the following is not true of conditional expressions in If statements in macros?**
    a. Conditional expressions allow you to skip over actions when the expression evaluates as false.
    b. Macro If statements provide for Else and Else If clauses.
    c. More macro actions are available when you are also using conditional expressions.
    d. Conditional expressions give the macro more power and flexibility.

19. **Which example illustrates the proper syntax to refer to a specific control on a form?**
    a. [Forms] ! [formname] ! [controlname]   c. Forms ! formname. controlname
    b. {Forms} ! {formname} ! (controlname)   d. (Forms) ! (formname) ! (controlname)

20. **Which event is executed every time you move from record to record in a form?**
    a. On Move   c. New Record
    b. Next Record   d. On Current

Skills Review

1. **Understand macros.**
    a. Start Access, then open the Basketball-12.accdb database from the location where you store your Data Files. Enable content if prompted.
    b. Open the PrintMacroGroup macro in Macro Design View, then record your answers to the following questions on a sheet of paper:
       - What is the name of the first submacro?
       - How many macro actions are in the first submacro?
       - What arguments does the first action in the first submacro contain?
       - What values were chosen for these arguments?
       - Close Macro Design View for the PrintMacroGroup object.

2. **Create a macro.**
    a. Start a new macro in Macro Design View.
    b. Add the OpenQuery action.
    c. Select PlayerStats as the value for the Query Name argument.
    d. Select Datasheet for the View argument.
    e. Select Edit for the Data Mode argument.
    f. Save the macro with the name **ViewPlayerStats**.
    g. Run the macro to make sure it works, close the PlayerStats query, then close the ViewPlayerStats macro.

3. **Modify actions and arguments.**
    a. Open the ViewPlayerStats macro in Macro Design View.
    b. Add a MessageBox action as the second action of the query.
    c. Type **What a great season!** for the Message argument.
    d. Select Yes for the Beep argument.
    e. Select Warning! for the Type argument.
    f. Type **Iowa State Cyclones** for the Title argument.
    g. Save the macro, then run it to make sure the MessageBox action works as intended.
    h. Click OK in the dialog box created by the MessageBox action, close the PlayerStats query, then close the ViewPlayerStats macro.

Skills Review (continued)

   i. Open the PrintMacroGroup macro object in Design View.

   j. Modify the View argument for the OpenReport object of the PlayerStatistics submacro from Print to **Print Preview**.

   k. Modify the Message argument for the MessageBox object of the PlayerStatistics submacro to read **Click the Print button to send this report to the printer.**

   l. Save and close the PrintMacroGroup macro.

4. Assign a macro to a command button.

   a. In Design View of the Player Information Form, use the Command Button Wizard to the right of the FirstName text box. The new button should run the PlayerStatistics submacro in the PrintMacroGroup macro (PrintMacroGroup.PlayerStatistics).

   b. The text on the button should read **View Player Statistics**.

   c. The meaningful name for the button should be **cmdPlayerStatistics**.

   d. Test the command button in Form View, click OK in the message box, then close the PlayerStats report.

   e. Save and close the Player Information Form.

5. Use If statements.

   a. Start a new macro in Macro Design View, and open the Action Catalog window if it is not already open.

   b. Double-click If in the Action Catalog window to add an If block to the macro.

   c. Enter the following condition in the If box: **[Forms]![GameInfo]![CycloneScore]>[OpponentScore]**.

   d. Add the SetProperty action to the If block.

   e. Type **VictoryLabel** in the Control Name box for the SetProperty action.

   f. Select Visible for the Property argument for the SetProperty action.

   g. Enter **True** for the Value argument for the SetProperty action to indicate Yes.

   h. Click the Add Else link in the lower-right corner of the If block.

   i. Enter the same SetProperty action from the If statement under the Else clause.

   j. Use the same argument values for the second SetProperty action, but modify the Value property from True to **False** for the second SetProperty action.

   k. Save the macro with the name **VictoryCalculator**, compare it with **FIGURE 12-17**, make any necessary adjustments, then close Macro Design View.

FIGURE 12-17

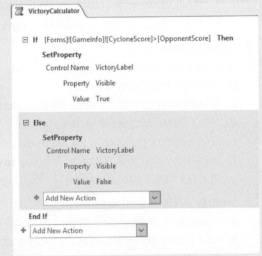

6. Work with events.

   a. Open the GameInfo form in Form Design View.

   b. Open the Property Sheet for the form.

   c. Assign the VictoryCalculator macro to the On Current event of the form.

   d. Close the Property Sheet, save the form, then open the GameInfo form in Form View.

   e. Navigate through the first four records. The Victory label should be visible for the first three records, but not the fourth.

   f. Add your name as a label in the Form Footer section to identify your printouts, print the third and fourth records if requested by your instructor, then save and close the GameInfo form.

7. Create a data macro.

   a. Open the Games table in Table Design View.

   b. Add a field named **RoadWin** with a Yes/No data type and the following Description: **Enter Yes if the Home-Away field is Away and the CycloneScore is greater than the OpponentScore**.

   c. Save the Games table and switch to Datasheet View to note that the RoadWin check box is empty (No) for every record.

   d. Switch back to Table Design View, then create a data macro based on the After Insert event.

Skills Review (continued)

e. Insert a ForEachRecord data block, and specify **Games** for the For Each Record In argument.

f. The Where Condition should be **[Home-Away]="A" and [CycloneScore]>[OpponentScore]**.

g. Add an EditRecord data block in the For Each Record In block, and a SetField data action. Be careful to add the EditRecord block within the For Each Record Block.

h. Enter **RoadWin** in the Name argument and **Yes** in the Value argument, as shown in FIGURE 12-18.

i. Save and close the data macro, save the Games table, switch to Datasheet View, then test the new data macro by entering a new record in the Games table as follows:

Opponent: **Johnson College**
Mascot: **Cavaliers**
Home-Away: **A**
CycloneScore: **100**
OpponentScore: **50**
GameDate: **3/2/2018**

FIGURE 12-18

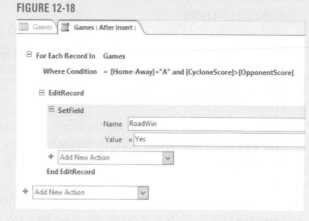

j. Tab to a new record. Six records where the Home-Away field is set to "A" and the CycloneScore is greater than the OpponentScore should be checked. Close the Games table.

8. Troubleshoot macros.

a. Open the PrintMacroGroup in Macro Design View.

b. Click the Single Step button, then click the Run button.

c. Click Step twice to step through the two actions of the submacro PlayerStatistics, then click OK in the resulting message box.

d. Close the PlayerStats report.

e. Return to Macro Design View of the PrintMacroGroup macro and click the Single Step button on the Design tab to toggle off this feature.

f. Save and close the PrintMacroGroup macro, close the Basketball-12.accdb database, then exit Access.

Independent Challenge 1

As the manager of a doctor's clinic, you have created an Access database called Patients-12.accdb to track insurance claim reimbursements. You use macros to help automate the database.

a. Start Access, then open the database Patients-12.accdb from the location where you store your Data Files. Enable content if prompted.

b. Open Macro Design View of the CPT Form Open macro. (CPT stands for Current Procedural Terminology, which is a code that describes a medical procedure.) If the Single Step button is toggled on, toggle it off.

c. On a separate sheet of paper, identify the macro actions, arguments for each action, and values for each argument.

d. In two or three sentences, explain in your own words what tasks this macro automates.

e. Close the CPT Form Open macro.

f. Open the Claim Entry Form in Form Design View.

g. The Form Footer of the Claim Entry Form contains several command buttons. Open the Property Sheet of the Add CPT Code button, then click the Event tab.

h. On your paper, write the event to which the CPT Form Open macro is assigned.

i. Open the Claim Entry Form in Form View, then click the Add CPT Code button in the Form Footer.

j. On your paper, write the current record number that is displayed for you.

k. Close the Patients-12.accdb database, then exit Access.

Independent Challenge 2

As the manager of a doctor's clinic, you have created an Access database called Patients-12.accdb to track insurance claim reimbursements. You use macros to help automate the database.

a. Start Access, then open the database Patients-12.accdb from the location where you store your Data Files. Enable content if prompted.

b. Start a new macro in Macro Design View, and open the Action Catalog window if it is not already open.

c. Double-click the Submacro entry in the Program Flow folder to add a submacro block.

d. Type **Preview Monthly Brown Report** as the first submacro name, then add the OpenReport macro action.

e. Select Monthly Brown for the Report Name argument, then select Print Preview for the View argument of the OpenReport action.

f. Double-click the Submacro entry in the Program Flow folder to add another submacro block.

g. Type **Preview Monthly Katera Report** as a new submacro name, then add the OpenReport macro action.

h. Select Monthly Katera for the ReportName argument, then select Print Preview for the View argument of the second OpenReport action.

i. Save the macro with the name **Preview Group**, then close Macro Design View.

j. Using the Run Macro button on the Database Tools tab, run the Preview Group.Preview Monthly Brown Report macro to test it, then close Print Preview.

k. Using the Run Macro button on the Database Tools tab, run the Preview Group.Preview Monthly Katera Report macro to test it, then close Print Preview.

l. Open the Preview Group macro in Macro Design View, then click the Collapse buttons to the left of the submacro statements to collapse the two submacro blocks.

m. Create one more submacro that previews the Monthly Winters report. Name the submacro **Preview Monthly Winters Report** as shown in FIGURE 12-19.

n. Save and close the Preview Group macro.

o. In Design View of the Claim Line Items Subform, add three separate command buttons to the Form Footer to run the three submacros in the Preview Group macro. Use the captions and meaningful names of **Brown** and **cmdBrown**, **Katera** and **cmdKatera**, **Winters** and **cmdWinters** to correspond with the three submacros in the Preview Group macro.

p. Change the font color on the new command buttons to black.

q. Select all three new command buttons and use the Size/Space and Align commands on the Arrange tab to precisely size, align, and space the buttons equally in the Form Footer section.

r. Save and close the Claim Line Items Subform, then open the Claim Entry Form in Form View, as shown in FIGURE 12-20. Test each of the new command buttons to make sure it opens the correct report.

s. Close the Claim Entry Form, close the Patients-12.accdb database, then exit Access

FIGURE 12-19

FIGURE 12-20

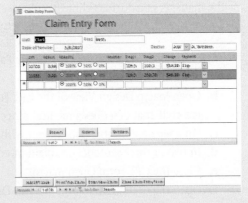

Independent Challenge 3

As the manager of a doctor's clinic, you have created an Access database called Patients-12.accdb to track insurance claim reimbursements. You use macros to help automate the database.

a. Start Access, then open the Patients-12.accdb database from the location where you store your Data Files. Enable content if prompted.

Independent Challenge 3 (continued)

b. Start a new macro in Macro Design View, then add an If statement.

c. Enter the following in the If box: **[Forms]![CPT Form]![RBRVS]=0**.

d. Select the SetProperty action for the first action in the If block.

e. Enter the following arguments for the SetProperty action: Control Name: **ResearchLabel**, Property: **Visible**, and Value: **True**.

f. Click the Add Else link, then select the SetProperty action for the first action of the Else clause.

g. Enter the following arguments for the SetProperty action: Control Name: **ResearchLabel**, Property: **Visible**, and Value: **False**.

h. Save the macro with the name **Research**, then close Macro Design View.

i. Open the CPT Form in Form Design View, then open the Property Sheet for the form.

j. Click the Research! label in the Detail section, and enter **ResearchLabel** as the Name property in the Property Sheet. (*Hint*: The Name property is on the Other tab in the Property Sheet.)

k. Assign the Research macro to the On Current event of the form.

l. Close the Property Sheet, save the form, then open the CPT Form in Form View.

m. Use the Next record button to move quickly through all 64 records in the form. Notice that the macro displays Research! only when the RBRVS value is equal to zero.

n. Save and close the CPT Form, then close the Patients-12.accdb database.

Independent Challenge 4: Explore

You are collecting information on international candy and chocolate factories, museums, and stores in an Access database. You tie the forms together with macros attached to command buttons.

a. Open the Candy-12.accdb database from the location where you store your Data Files, enable content if prompted, then open the Countries form in Form View. The database option to show overlapping windows versus tabbed documents has been set. Overlapping windows allows you to restore and size windows.

b. Click the New (blank) record button for the main form, then type **Poland** in the Country text box.

c. In the subform for the Poland record, enter **Cadbury-Wedel Polska** in the Name field, **F** in the Type field (F for factory), **Praga** in the City field, and **Lodz** in the StateProvince field. Close the Countries form. To maximize the windows of this database when they open, attach a macro to the On Load event of the form.

d. Open Macro Design View for a new macro, then add the MaximizeWindow action. Save the macro with the name **Maximize**, then close it. The Maximize macro helps you maximize windows if a database option is set to Overlapping Windows. To see this setting, click the File tab, click Options, click Current Database, and then view the Document Window Options section. When Tabbed Documents is selected, the windows are maximized and provide tabs for navigation. When Overlapping Windows is selected, windows can be any size.

e. Open the Countries form in Design View, add the Maximize macro to the On Load event of the Countries form, then open the Countries form in Form View to test it.

f. Save the Countries form and return to Design View.

g. In the Property Sheet for the form, click the On Load event, delete the Maximize macro entry, click the Build button, click Macro Builder, then click OK.

h. Add the MaximizeWindow action to the macro design window, then save and close it. Note that the Property Sheet now shows [Embedded Macro] for the On Load event vs. the Maximize macro.

i. Save the Countries form, open it in Form View, and resize it to something less than maximized. Close and reopen the form in Form View to test the embedded macro.

j. The Countries form should open maximized with either the embedded macro or the Maximize macro attached to the On Load event. Close the Candy-12.accdb database, then exit Access.

Visual Workshop

As the manager of a doctor's clinic, you have created an Access database called Patients-12.accdb to track insurance claim reimbursements. Develop a new macro called **Query Group** with the actions and argument values shown in FIGURE 12-21. Run both macros to test them by using the Run Macro button on the Database Tools tab, and debug the macros if necessary.

FIGURE 12-21

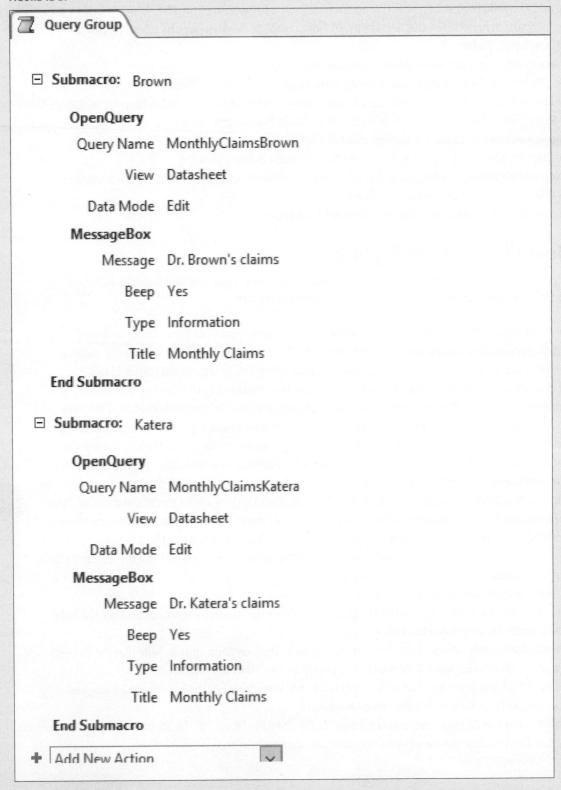

Creating Modules and VBA

CASE > You and Aaron Scout, the network administrator at Reason 2 Go, want to learn about VBA and create modules to enhance the capabilities of the Equipment-13 database for Reason 2 Go.

Module Objectives

After completing this module, you will be able to:

- Understand modules and VBA
- Compare macros and modules
- Create functions
- Use If statements

- Document procedures
- Build class modules
- Modify sub procedures
- Troubleshoot modules

Files You Will Need

Equipment-13.accdb   Insurance-13.accdb
Baseball-13.accdb   Basketball-13.accdb

Understand Modules and VBA

Learning Outcomes
• Define VBA terms
• Describe Visual Basic Editor components

Access is a robust and easy-to-use relational database program. Access provides user-friendly tools, such as wizards and Design Views, to help users quickly create reports and forms that previously took programmers hours to build. You may, however, want to automate a task or create a new function that goes beyond the capabilities of the built-in Access tools. Within each program of the Microsoft Office suite, a programming language called **Visual Basic for Applications (VBA)** is provided to help you extend the program's capabilities. In Access, VBA is stored within modules. A **module** is an Access object that stores Visual Basic for Applications (VBA) programming code. VBA is written in the **Visual Basic Editor (VBE)**, shown in FIGURE 13-1. The components and text colors of the VBE are described in TABLE 13-1. An Access database has two kinds of modules. **Standard modules** contain global code that can be executed from anywhere in the database. Standard modules are displayed as module objects in the Navigation Pane. **Class modules** are stored within the form or report object itself. Class modules contain VBA code used only within that particular form or report. **CASE** ▶ *Before working with modules, you ask some questions about VBA.*

DETAILS

The following questions and answers introduce the basics of Access modules:

• **What does a module contain?**

A module contains VBA programming code organized in procedures. A procedure contains several lines of code, each of which is called a **statement**. Modules can also contain **comments**, text that helps explain and document the code.

• **What is a procedure?**

A **procedure** is a series of VBA statements that performs an operation or calculates an answer. VBA has two types of procedures: functions and subs. **Declaration statements** precede procedure statements and help set rules for how the statements in the module are processed.

• **What is a function?**

A **function** is a procedure that returns a value. Access supplies many built-in functions, such as Sum, Count, Pmt, and Now, that can be used in an expression in a query, form, or report to calculate a value. You might want to create a new function, however, to help perform calculations unique to your database. For example, you might create a new function called Commission to calculate a sales commission using a formula unique to your business.

• **What is a sub?**

A **sub** (also called **sub procedure**) performs a series of VBA statements to manipulate controls and objects. Subs are generally executed when an event occurs, such as when a command button is clicked or a form is opened.

• **What are arguments?**

Arguments are constants, variables, or expressions passed to a procedure that the procedure needs in order to execute. For example, the full syntax for the Sum function is Sum(*expr*), where *expr* represents the argument for the Sum function, the field that is being summed. In VBA, arguments are declared in the first line of the procedure. They are specified immediately after a procedure's name and are enclosed in parentheses. Multiple arguments are separated by commas.

• **What is an object?**

In VBA, an **object** is any item that can be used or manipulated, including the traditional Access objects (table, query, form, report, macro, and module), as well as form controls and sections, existing procedures, and built-in VBA objects that provide functionality to your code.

• **What is a method?**

A **method** is an action that an object can perform. Procedures are often written to invoke methods in response to user actions. For example, you could invoke the GoToControl method to move the focus to a specific control on a form in response to the user clicking a command button.

FIGURE 13-1: Visual Basic Editor (VBE) window for a standard module

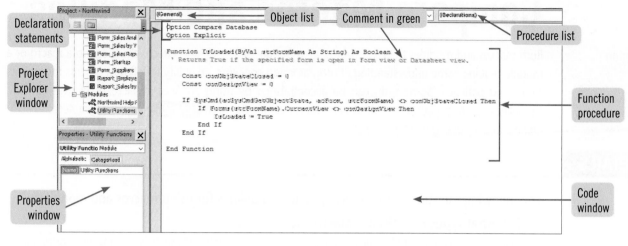

TABLE 13-1: Components and text colors for the Visual Basic Editor window

component or color	description
Visual Basic Editor, VBE	Comprises the entire Microsoft Visual Basic program window that contains smaller windows, including the Code window and Project Explorer window
Code window	Contains the VBA for the project selected in the Project Explorer window
Project Explorer window	Displays a hierarchical list of the projects in the database; a project can be a module object or a form or report object that contains a class module
Declaration statements	Includes statements that apply to every procedure in the module, such as declarations for variables, constants, user-defined data types, and external procedures in a dynamic-link library
Object list	In a class module, lists the objects associated with the current form or report
Procedure list	In a standard module, lists the procedures in the module; in a class module, lists events (such as Click or Dblclick)
Blue	Indicates a VBA keyword; blue words are reserved by VBA and are already assigned specific meanings
Black	Indicates normal text; black text is the unique VBA code created by the developer
Red	Indicates syntax error text; a red statement indicates that it will not execute correctly because of a syntax error (perhaps a missing parenthesis or a spelling error)
Green	Indicates comment text; any text after an apostrophe is considered documentation, or a comment, and is therefore ignored in the execution of the procedure

Compare Macros and Modules

**Learning
Outcomes**
• Contrast macros
and modules
• Define VBA
keywords

Both macros and modules help run your database more efficiently and effectively. Creating a macro or a module requires some understanding of programming concepts, an ability to follow a process through its steps, and patience. Some tasks can be accomplished by using an Access macro or by writing VBA. Guidelines can help you determine which tool is best for the task. **CASE** *You compare Access macros and modules by asking more questions.*

DETAILS

The following questions and answers provide guidelines for using macros and modules:

- **For what types of tasks are macros best suited?**

  Macros are an easy way to handle common, repetitive, and simple tasks such as opening and closing forms, positioning a form to enter a new record, and printing reports.

- **Which is easier to create, a macro or a module, and why?**

  Macros are generally easier to create because Macro Design View is more structured than the VBE. The hardest part of creating a macro is choosing the correct macro action. But once the action is selected, the arguments associated with that macro action are displayed, eliminating the need to learn any special programming syntax. To create a module, however, you must know a robust programming language, VBA, as well as the correct **syntax** (rules) for each VBA statement. In a nutshell, macros are simpler to create, but VBA is more powerful.

- **When must I use a macro?**

  You must use macros to make global, shortcut key assignments. **AutoExec** is a special macro name that automatically executes when the database first opens.

- **When must I use a module?**

  1. You must use modules to create unique functions. For instance, you might want to create a function called Commission that calculates the appropriate commission on a sale using your company's unique commission formula.

  2. Access error messages can be confusing to the user. However, by using VBA procedures, you can detect the error when it occurs and display your own message.

  3. Although Access macros have recently been enhanced to include more powerful If-Then logic, VBA is still more robust in the area of programming flow statements with tools such as nested If statements, Case statements, and multiple looping structures. Some of the most common VBA keywords, including If...Then, are shown in TABLE 13-2. VBA keywords appear blue in the VBE code window.

  4. VBA code may declare **variables**, which are used to store data that can be used, modified, or displayed during the execution of the procedure.

  5. VBA may be used in conjunction with SQL (Structured Query Language) to select, update, append, and delete data.

  Like macros, modules can be accessed through the Navigation Pane or embedded directly within a form or report. When embedded in a form or report object, the module is called a **class module**, like the one shown in FIGURE 13-2. If you develop forms and reports in one database and copy them to another, the class modules automatically travel with the object that stores it. Use class modules for code that is unique to that form or report. Use standard modules (also called **global modules**) to store code that will be reused in many places in the database application.

FIGURE 13-2: Visual Basic Editor window for a class module

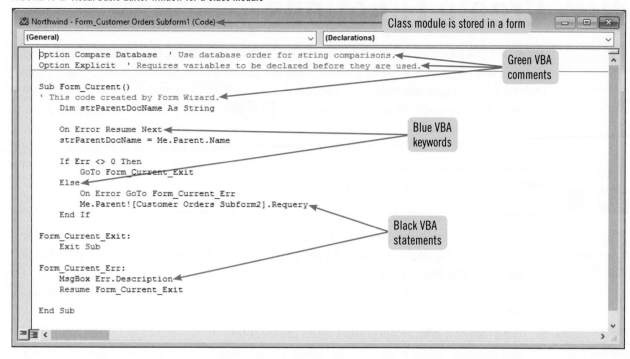

TABLE 13-2: Common VBA keywords

statement	explanation
Function	Declares the name and arguments that create a new function procedure
End Function	When defining a new function, the End Function statement is required as the last statement to mark the end of the VBA code that defines the function
Sub	Declares the name for a new Sub procedure; **Private Sub** indicates that the Sub is accessible only to other procedures in the module where it is declared
End Sub	When defining a new sub, the End Sub statement is required as the last statement to mark the end of the VBA code that defines the sub
If...Then	Executes code (the code follows the Then statement) when the value of an expression is true (the expression follows the If statement)
End If	When creating an If...Then...Else clause, the End If statement is required as the last statement
Const	Declares the name and value of a **constant**, an item that retains a constant value throughout the execution of the code
Option Compare Database	A declaration statement that determines the way string values (text) will be sorted
Option Explicit	A declaration statement that specifies that you must explicitly declare all variables used in all procedures; if you attempt to use an undeclared variable name, an error occurs at **compile time**, the period during which source code is translated to executable code
Dim	Declares a **variable**, a named storage location that contains data that can be modified during program execution
On Error GoTo	Upon an error in the execution of a procedure, specifies the location (the statement) where the procedure should continue
Select Case	Executes one of several groups of statements called a **Case** depending on the value of an expression; using the Select Case statement is an alternative to using **ElseIf** in **If...Then...Else** statements when comparing one expression with several different values
End Select	When defining a new Select Case group of statements, the End Select statement is required as the last statement to mark the end of the VBA code

Create Functions

Learning
Outcomes
• Create a custom
  function
• Use a custom
  function

Access and VBA supply hundreds of built-in functions such as Sum, Count, Ilf, First, Last, Date, and Hour. However, you might want to create a new function to calculate a value based on your company's unique business rules. You generally create new functions in a standard or global module so that it can be used in any query, form, or report throughout the database. **CASE** ▶ *Reason 2 Go allows employees to purchase computer equipment when it is replaced. Equipment that is less than a year old will be sold to employees at 75 percent of its initial value, and equipment that is more than a year old will be sold at 50 percent of its initial value. Aaron Scout, network administrator, asks you to create a new function called EPrice that determines the employee purchase price of replaced computer equipment.*

STEPS

1. **Start Access, open the Equipment-13.accdb database from the location where you store your Data Files, enable content if prompted, click the Create tab, then click the Module button in the Macros & Code group**

   Access automatically inserts the Option Compare Database declaration statement in the Code window. You will create the new EPrice function one step at a time.

2. **Type function EPrice(StartValue), then press [Enter]**

   This statement creates a new function named EPrice, which uses one argument, StartValue. The VBE automatically capitalized Function and added the **End Function** statement, a required statement to mark the end of the function. VBA keywords are blue.

3. **Press [Tab], type EPrice = StartValue * 0.5, then press [Enter]**

   Your screen should look like **FIGURE 13-3**. The EPrice= statement explains how the EPrice function will calculate. The function will return a value that is calculated by multiplying the StartValue by 0.5. It is not necessary to indent statements, but indenting code between matching Function/End Function, Sub/End Sub, or If/End If statements enhances the program's readability. When you press [Enter] at the end of a VBA statement, the VBE automatically adds spaces as appropriate to enhance the readability of the statement.

4. **Click the Save button 🖫 on the Standard toolbar, type basFunctions in the Save As dialog box, click OK, then click the upper Close button ⊠ in the upper-right corner of the VBE window to close the Visual Basic Editor**

   It is common for VBA programmers to use three-character prefixes to name objects and controls. This makes it easier to identify that object or control in expressions and modules. The prefix **bas** is short for Basic and applies to standard (global) modules. Naming conventions for other objects and controls are listed in **TABLE 13-3** and are used throughout the Equipment-13.accdb database. You can use the new function, EPrice, in a query, form, or report.

5. **Right-click the qryEmpPricing query in the Navigation Pane, then click Design View on the shortcut menu**

   You use the new EPrice function in the query to determine the employee purchase price of replaced computer equipment.

6. **Click the blank Field cell to the right of the InitialValue field, type Price:EPrice ([InitialValue]), then click the View button 🎟 to switch to Datasheet View**

   Your screen should look like **FIGURE 13-4**. In this query, you created a new field called Price that uses the EPrice function. The value in the InitialValue field is used for the StartValue argument of the new EPrice function. The InitialValue field is multiplied by 0.5 to create the new Price field.

7. **Save and then close the qryEmpPricing query**

Creating Modules and VBA

FIGURE 13-3: Creating the EPrice function

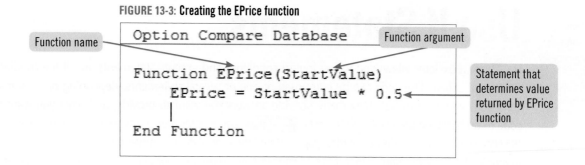

Function name → Option Compare Database ← Function argument

Function EPrice(StartValue)
    EPrice = StartValue * 0.5 ← Statement that determines value returned by EPrice function

End Function

FIGURE 13-4: Using the EPrice function in a query

ELast	Manufacture	Description	PlacementDat	InitialValue	Price
Dawson	Compaq	Deskpro99	3/13/2015	$1,800.00	900
Dawson	Micron	Prosignet403	7/13/2016	$1,800.00	900
Dawson	Dell	XPS490	1/12/2017	$1,200.00	600
Lane	Micron	Transtrek4000	8/29/2016	$1,900.00	950
Lane	HP	Deskjet 900XJ2	1/12/2017	$500.00	250
Wong	Compaq	Deskpro2099	5/7/2016	$1,700.00	850
Wong	Dell	Inspiron809	6/2/2017	$2,400.00	1200
Ramirez	Dell	XPS490	1/2/2012	$1,200.00	600
Latsky	Compaq	Deskpro99	4/12/2016	$2,000.00	1000
Latsky	Micron	Transtrek4000	8/29/2017	$1,800.00	900
Hoppengarth	Compaq	Deskpro99	4/12/2016	$1,800.00	900
Hoppengarth	Micron	Transtrek4000	8/29/2016	$1,800.00	900

qryEmpPricing

Calculated field, Price, uses EPrice custom function to multiply the InitialValue by 0.5

TABLE 13-3: Three-character prefix naming conventions

object or control type	prefix	example
Table	tbl	tblProducts
Query	qry	qrySalesByRegion
Form	frm	frmProducts
Report	rpt	rptSalesByCategory
Macro	mcr	mcrCloseInventory
Module	bas	basRetirement
Label	lbl	lblFullName
Text Box	txt	txtLastName
Combo box	cbo	cboStates
Command button	cmd	cmdPrint

Use If Statements

If...Then...Else logic allows you to test logical conditions and execute statements only if the conditions are true. If...Then...Else code can be composed of one or several statements, depending on how many conditions you want to test, how many possible answers you want to provide, and what you want the code to do based on the results of the tests. **CASE** *Aaron notes that you need to add an If statement to the EPrice function to test the age of the equipment and then calculate the answer based on that age. You want to modify the EPrice function so that if the equipment is less than one year old, the StartValue is multiplied by 75% (0.75) rather than by 50% (0.5).*

STEPS

1. **Scroll down the Navigation Pane, right-click the basFunctions module, then click Design View**

   To determine the age of the equipment, the EPrice function needs another argument: the purchase date of the equipment.

2. **Click just before the right parenthesis in the Function statement, type , (a comma), press [Spacebar], type DateValue, then press [↓]**

   Now that you established another argument, you can work with the argument in the definition of the function.

3. **Click to the right of the right parenthesis in the Function statement, press [Enter], press [Tab], then type If (Now() – DateValue) > 365 Then**

   The expression compares whether today's date, represented by the Access function **Now( )**, minus the DateValue argument value is greater than 365 days (1 year). If true, this indicates that the equipment is older than one year.

4. **Indent and type the rest of the statements exactly as shown in FIGURE 13-5**

   The **Else** statement is executed only if the expression is false (if the equipment is less than 365 days old). The **End If** statement is needed to mark the end of the If block of code.

5. **Click the Save button 🖫 on the Standard toolbar, close the Visual Basic window, right-click the qryEmpPricing query in the Navigation Pane, then click Design View on the shortcut menu**

   Now that you've modified the EPrice function to include two arguments, you need to modify the calculated Price field expression, too.

6. **Right-click the Price field in the query design grid, click Zoom on the shortcut menu, click between the right square bracket and right parenthesis, then type ,[PlacementDate]**

   Your Zoom dialog box should look like FIGURE 13-6. Both of the arguments used to define the EPrice function in the VBA code are replaced with actual field names that contain the data to be analyzed. Field names must be typed exactly as shown and surrounded by square brackets. Commas separate multiple arguments in the function.

7. **Click OK in the Zoom dialog box, then click the View button 🟦 to display the datasheet**

8. **Click any entry in the PlacementDate field, then click the Ascending button in the Sort & Filter group, as shown in FIGURE 13-7**

   The EPrice function now calculates one of two different results, depending on the age of the equipment determined by the date in the PlacementDate field.

9. **Save and then close the qryEmpPricing query**

FIGURE 13-5: Using an If...Then...Else structure

```
Function EPrice(StartValue, DateValue)     Second argument
   If (Now() - DateValue) > 365 Then       Then
        EPrice = StartValue * 0.5
   Else
        EPrice = StartValue * 0.75
   End If
End Function
```

If →
Else →
End If →

FIGURE 13-6: Using the Zoom dialog box for long expressions

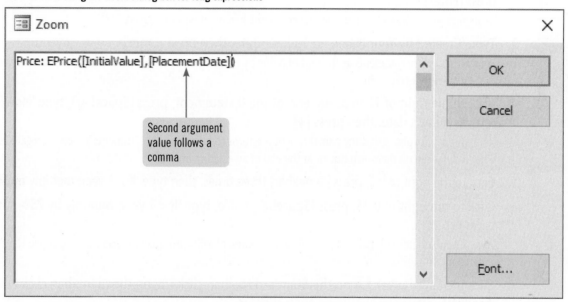

Zoom   ×

Price: EPrice([InitialValue],[PlacementDate])

                                                    OK

                                                    Cancel

    Second argument
    value follows a
    comma

                                                    Font...

FIGURE 13-7: Price field is calculated at 50% or 75% based on the age of equipment

qryEmpPricing

Sort in ascending order on PlacementDate

ELast	Manufacture	Description	PlacementDat	InitialValue	
Ramirez	Dell	XPS490	1/2/2012	$1,200.00	600
Dawson	Compaq	Deskpro99	3/13/2015	$1,800.00	1350
Greenfield	Compaq	Deskpro89	4/8/2015	$2,200.00	1650
Rock	Compaq	Deskpro2099	5/8/2015	$1,700.00	1275
Joy	Dell	Inspiron609	6/8/2015	$3,200.00	2400
Adair	Micron	Transtrek4000	12/30/2015	$1,900.00	1425
Rice	Micron	Prosignet403	1/8/2016	$1,700.00	1275
Arnold	Lexmark	Optra2000	1/13/2016	$2,000.00	1500
Orient	Lexmark	Optra2000	1/13/2016	$2,000.00	1500

InitialValue * 50%

InitialValue * 75%

Document Procedures

Learning Outcomes
- Add VBA comments
- Use the VBE toolbar

Comment lines are statements in the code that document the code; they do not affect how the code runs. At any time, if you want to read or modify existing code, you can write the modifications much more quickly if the code is properly documented. Comment lines start with an apostrophe and are green in the VBE. **CASE** *Aaron asks you to document the EPrice function in the basFunctions module with descriptive comments. This will make it easier for you and others to follow the purpose and logic of the function later.*

STEPS

QUICK TIP

You can also create comments by starting the statement with the rem statement (for remark).

1. **Right-click the** basFunctions module **in the Navigation Pane, then click** Design View

   The VBE window for the basFunctions module opens.

2. **Click the** blank line between the Option Compare Database and Function statements, **press [Enter], type 'This function is called EPrice and has two arguments, then press [Enter]**

   As soon as you move to another line, the comment statement becomes green.

TROUBLE

Be sure to use an ' (apostrophe) and not a " (quotation mark) to begin the comment line.

3. **Type 'Created by Your Name on Today's Date, then press [Enter]**

   You can also place comments at the end of a line by entering an apostrophe to mark that the next part of the statement is a comment.

4. **Click to the** right of Then at the end of the If statement, **press [Spacebar], type 'Now( ) returns today's date, then press [↓]**

   This comment explains that the Now() function returns today's date. All comments are green, regardless of whether they are on their own line or at the end of an existing line.

5. **Click to the** right of 0.5, **press [Spacebar] three times, then type 'If > 1 year, multiply by 50%**

6. **Click to the** right of 0.75, **press [Spacebar] twice, type 'If < 1 year, multiply by 75%, then press [↓]**

   Your screen should look like FIGURE 13-8. Each comment will turn green as soon as you move to a new statement.

7. **Click the** Save button 🖫 **on the Standard toolbar, click** File **on the menu bar, click** Print **if requested by your instructor, then click** OK

   TABLE 13-4 provides more information about the Standard toolbar buttons in the VBE window.

8. **Click** File **on the menu bar, then click** Close and Return to Microsoft Access

Creating Modules and VBA

FIGURE 13-8: Adding comments to a module

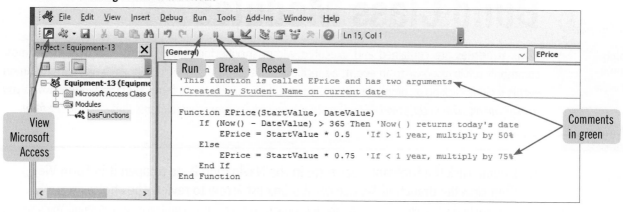

TABLE 13-4: Standard toolbar buttons in the Visual Basic window

button name	button	description
View Microsoft Access		Switches from the active Visual Basic window to the Access window
Insert Module		Opens a new module or class module Code window, or inserts a new procedure in the current Code window
Run Sub/UserForm		Runs the current procedure if the insertion point is in a procedure, or runs the UserForm if it is active
Break		Stops the execution of a program while it's running and switches to Break mode, which is the temporary suspension of program execution in which you can examine, debug, reset, step through, or continue program execution
Reset		Resets the procedure
Project Explorer		Displays the Project Explorer, which displays a hierarchical list of the currently open projects (set of modules) and their contents
Object Browser		Displays the Object Browser, which lists the defined modules and procedures as well as available methods, properties, events, constants, and other items that you can use in the code

Using comments for debugging

You can use comments to "comment out" or temporarily hide statements that you want to leave in your module but do not want to execute. "Commenting out" statements that do not work (versus editing the same broken statement(s) over and over) keeps a trail of every line of code that you have written.

This process makes development, debugging, and sharing your thought processes with other developers much more productive. When the code is working as intended, extra lines that have been "commented out" are no longer needed and can be deleted.

Build Class Modules

Learning
Outcome
• Build event
handlers

Class modules are contained and executed within specific forms and reports. Class modules most commonly run in response to an **event**, a specific action that occurs as the result of a user action. Common events include clicking a command button, editing data, and closing a form. **CASE** ► *Aaron wants you to examine an existing class module and create sub procedures connected to events that occur on the form.*

STEPS

1. **Double-click the frmEmployees form in the Navigation Pane to open it in Form View, then click the Branch of Service combo box list arrow to review the choices**

   A choice in the Branch of Service combo box only makes sense if an employee was a veteran. You'll set the Visible property for the Branch of Service combo box to True if the Veteran check box is checked and False if the Veteran check box is not checked.

TROUBLE
If the first line of your procedure is not Private Sub chkVeteran_ AfterUpdate( ), delete the stub, close the VBE, and repeat Step 2.

2. **Right-click the Employees form tab, click Design View on the shortcut menu, double-click the edge of the Veteran check box to open its Property Sheet, click the Event tab in the Property Sheet, click the After Update property, click the Build button [...], then click Code Builder and click OK if the Choose Builder dialog box opens**

   The class module for the frmEmployees form opens. Because you opened the VBE window from a specific event of a control on the form, the **stub**, the first and last lines of the sub procedure, were automatically created. The procedure's name in the first line, chkVeteran_AfterUpdate, contains the name of the control, chkVeteran, and the name of the event, AfterUpdate, that triggers this procedure. (The **Name property** of a control is on the Other tab in the control's property sheet. The **After Update property** is on the Event tab.) A sub procedure triggered by an event is often called an **event handler**.

QUICK TIP
Write your VBA code in lowercase. The VBE will automatically correct the case if your code is correct.

3. **Enter the statements shown in FIGURE 13-9**

   The name of the sub procedure shows that it runs on the AfterUpdate event of the chkVeteran control. (The sub runs when the Veteran check box is checked or unchecked.) The If structure contains VBA that makes the cboBranchOfService control visible or not visible based on the value of the chkVeteran control.

QUICK TIP
The **On Current** event of the form is triggered when you navigate through records.

4. **Save the changes and close the VBE window, click the View button [⊞], click the Veteran check box for the first record several times, then navigate through several records**

   Clicking the Veteran check box triggers the procedure that responds to the After Update event. However, you also want the procedure to run every time you move from record to record.

TROUBLE
If the Code window appears with a yellow line, it means the code cannot be run successfully. Click the Reset button [■] on the toolbar, then compare your VBA with FIGURE 13-10.

5. **Right-click the Employees form tab, click Design View on the shortcut menu, click the Form Selector button [▪], click the Event tab in the Property Sheet, click the On Current event property in the Property Sheet, click the Build button [...], click Code Builder and click OK if the Choose Builder dialog box opens, then copy or retype the If structure from the chkVeteran_AfterUpdate sub to the Form_Current sub, as shown in FIGURE 13-10**

   By copying the If structure to a second sub procedure, you create a second event handler. Now, the cboBranchOfService combo box will be visible or not based on updating the chkVeteran check box or moving from record to record. To test the new sub procedure, switch to Form View.

6. **Save the changes and close the VBE window, click [⊞] to switch to Form View, then navigate through several records to test the new procedures**

   Now, as you move from record to record, the Branch of Service combo box should be visible for those employees with the Veteran check box selected and not visible if the Veteran check box is not selected.

7. **Return to the first record for David Fox, click the Veteran check box (if it is not already selected), click the Branch of Service combo box list arrow, click Army as shown in FIGURE 13-11, then save and close the frmEmployees form**

Creating Modules and VBA

FIGURE 13-9: **Creating an event handler procedure**

Three-character prefixes in sub and control names enhance the meaning of the VBA

```
Private Sub chkVeteran_AfterUpdate()
    If chkVeteran.Value = True Then
        cboBranchOfService.Visible = True
    Else
        cboBranchOfService.Visible = False
    End If
End Sub
```

FIGURE 13-10: **Copying the If structure to a new event handler procedure**

Copy If structure from chkVeteran_AfterUpate sub to Form_Current sub

```
Private Sub chkVeteran_AfterUpdate()
    If chkVeteran.Value = True Then
        cboBranchOfService.Visible = True
    Else
        cboBranchOfService.Visible = False
    End If
End Sub

Private Sub Form_Current()
    If chkVeteran.Value = True Then
        cboBranchOfService.Visible = True
    Else
        cboBranchOfService.Visible = False
    End If
End Sub
```

FIGURE 13-11: **Branch of Service combo box is visible when Veteran box is checked**

David Fox record

Last: Fox
First: David
Date Hired: 1/1/2011
Assignments

Department: USA
Title: Director
Veteran: ☑ — Veteran check box is selected
Branch of Service: Army — Army is selected in Branch of Service combo box

Serial No	Placement Date	Manufacturer	Description	Initial Value
▶				

Modify Sub Procedures

Sub procedures can be triggered on any event in the Property Sheet such as **On Got Focus** (when the control gets the focus), **After Update** (after a field is updated), or **On Dbl Click** (when the control is double-clicked). Not all items have the same set of event properties. For example, a text box control has both a Before Update and After Update event property, but neither of these events exists for a label or command button because those controls are not used to update data. **CASE** ▶ *Aaron Scout asks if there is a way to require a choice in the Branch of Service combo box if the Veteran check box is checked. You use VBA sub procedures to handle this request.*

STEPS

QUICK TIP
If you select the Always use event procedures check box in the Object Designers section of the Access Options dialog box, you bypass the Choose Builder dialog box and go directly to the VBE.

1. **Right-click the frmEmployees form, click Design View on the shortcut menu, click the Before Update property in the Property Sheet, click the Build button** ▦ **, click Code Builder and click OK if the Choose Builder dialog box opens, then enter the code in FIGURE 13-12 into the Form_BeforeUpdate stub**

   Test the procedure.

2. **Close the VBE window, click the View button** ▦ **to switch to Form View, click the Last record button** ▶▌ **to navigate to the last record, click the Veteran check box to select it, then navigate to the previous record**

   Because the chkVeteran control is selected but the cboBranchOfService combo box is null, the MsgBox statement produces the message shown in FIGURE 13-13.

3. **Click OK, navigate back to the last record, then click the Veteran check box to uncheck it**

   The code produces the correct message, but you want the code to place the focus in the cboBranchOfService combo box to force the user to choose a branch of service when this condition occurs.

   DoCmd is a VBA object that supports many methods to run common Access commands, such as closing windows, opening forms, previewing reports, navigating records, setting focus, and setting the value of controls. As you write a VBA statement, visual aids that are part of **IntelliSense technology** help you complete it. For example, when you type the period (.) after the DoCmd object, a list of available methods appears. Watching the VBA window carefully and taking advantage of all IntelliSense clues as you complete a statement can greatly improve your accuracy and productivity in writing VBA.

TROUBLE
Be sure to type a period (.) after DoCmd.

4. **Right-click the Employees form tab, click Design View, click the View Code button in the Tools group, click after the MsgBox statement, press [Enter], then type docmd. (including the period)**

   Your sub procedure should look like FIGURE 13-14.

5. **Type gotocontrol, press [Spacebar] noting the additional IntelliSense prompt, type "cboBranchOfService", then press [↓] as shown in FIGURE 13-15**

   IntelliSense helps you fill out each statement, indicating the order of arguments needed for the method to execute. If IntelliSense displays more than one argument, the current argument is listed in bold. Optional arguments are listed in [square brackets]. The VBE also capitalizes the VBA it recognizes, such as DoCmd. GoToControl. Test the new procedure.

6. **Close the VBE window, click the View button** ▦ **to switch to Form View, navigate to the last record for Amanda Thomes, click the Veteran check box, then navigate to the previous record**

7. **Click OK to respond to the message box, choose Navy from the Branch of Service combo box, navigate to the previous record, then save and close the Employees form**

   VBA is a robust and powerful programming language. With only modest programming skills, however, you can create basic sub procedures that greatly help users work more efficiently and effectively in forms.

FIGURE 13-12: Form_BeforeUpdate sub

```
Private Sub Form_BeforeUpdate(Cancel As Integer)
    If chkVeteran = True Then
        If IsNull(cboBranchOfService.Value) Then
            MsgBox "Please select a branch of service"
        End If
    End If
End Sub
```

Form_BeforeUpdate sub

FIGURE 13-13: Message produced by MsgBox statement

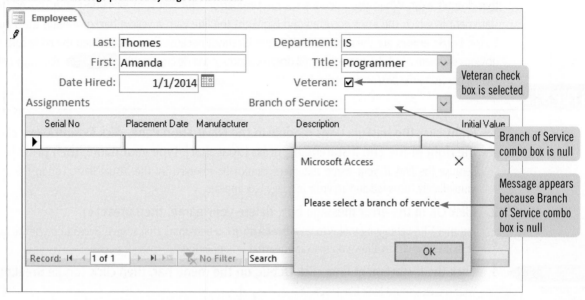

Veteran check box is selected

Branch of Service combo box is null

Message appears because Branch of Service combo box is null

FIGURE 13-14: IntelliSense technology prompts you as you write VBA statements

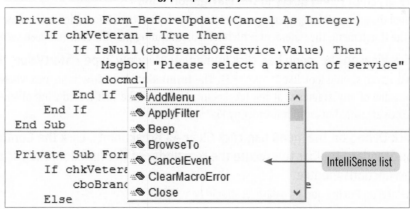

```
Private Sub Form_BeforeUpdate(Cancel As Integer)
    If chkVeteran = True Then
        If IsNull(cboBranchOfService.Value) Then
            MsgBox "Please select a branch of service"
            docmd.
        End If                AddMenu
    End If                    ApplyFilter
End Sub                       Beep
                             BrowseTo
Private Sub Forr             CancelEvent
    If chkVeter              ClearMacroError
        cboBranc             Close
    Else
```

IntelliSense list

FIGURE 13-15: New DoCmd statement

```
Private Sub Form_BeforeUpdate(Cancel As Integer)
    If chkVeteran = True Then
        If IsNull(cboBranchOfService.Value) Then
            MsgBox "Please select a branch of service"
            DoCmd.GoToControl "cboBranchOfService"
        End If
    End If
End Sub
```

New DoCmd statement

Access 2016

Creating Modules and VBA

Troubleshoot Modules

Learning Outcomes
• Set breakpoints
• Use the Immediate window

Access provides several techniques to help you **debug** (find and resolve) different types of VBA errors. A **syntax error** occurs immediately as you are writing a VBA statement that cannot be read by the Visual Basic Editor. This is the easiest type of error to identify because your code turns red when the syntax error occurs. **Compile-time errors** occur as a result of incorrectly constructed code and are detected as soon as you run your code or select the Compile option on the Debug menu. For example, you may have forgotten to insert an End If statement to finish an If structure. **Run-time errors** occur as incorrectly constructed code runs and include attempting an illegal operation such as dividing by zero or moving focus to a control that doesn't exist. When you encounter a run-time error, VBA will stop executing your procedure at the statement in which the error occurred and highlight the line with a yellow background in the Visual Basic Editor. **Logic errors** are the most difficult to troubleshoot because they occur when the code runs without obvious problems, but the procedure still doesn't produce the desired result. **CASE** *You study debugging techniques using the basFunctions module.*

STEPS

1. **Right-click the basFunctions module in the Navigation Pane, click Design View, click to the right of the End If statement, press [Spacebar], type your name, then press [↓]**

   Because the End If your name statement cannot be resolved by the Visual Basic Editor, the statement immediately turns red and an error message box appears.

2. **Click OK in the error message box, delete your name, then press [↓]**

   Another VBA debugging tool is to set a **breakpoint**, a bookmark that suspends execution of the procedure at that statement to allow you to examine what is happening.

   QUICK TIP
   Click the gray bar to the left of a statement to toggle a breakpoint on and off.

3. **Click the If statement line, click Debug on the menu bar, then click Toggle Breakpoint**

   Your screen should look like **FIGURE 13-16**.

4. **Click the View Microsoft Access button 🗝 on the Standard toolbar, then double-click the qryEmpPricing query in the Navigation Pane**

   When the qryEmpPricing query opens, it immediately runs the EPrice function. Because you set a breakpoint at the If statement, the statement is highlighted, indicating that the code has been suspended at that point.

   QUICK TIP
   Pointing to an argument in the Code window displays a ScreenTip with the argument's current value.

5. **Click View on the menu bar, click Immediate Window, type ? StartValue, then press [Enter]**

   Your screen should look like **FIGURE 13-17**. The **Immediate window** is an area where you can determine the value of any argument at the breakpoint. Note that the first record's InitialValue is 1200 when the records are sorted in ascending order by PlacementDate.

6. **Click Debug on the menu bar, click Clear All Breakpoints, click the Continue button ▶ on the Standard toolbar to execute the remainder of the function, then save and close the basFunctions module**

   The qryEmpPricing query's datasheet should be visible.

7. **Close the qryEmpPricing datasheet, close the Equipment-13.accdb database, then exit Access**

Creating Modules and VBA

FIGURE 13-16: Setting a breakpoint

```
Option Compare Database
'This function is called EPrice and has two arguments
'Created by Student Name on 2/1/2019

Function EPrice(StartValue, DateValue)
    If (Now() - DateValue) > 365 Then 'Now( ) returns today's date
        EPrice = StartValue * 0.5    'If > 1 year, multiply by 50%
    Else
        EPrice = StartValue * 0.75   'If < 1 year, multiply by 75%
    End If
End Function
```

Breakpoint

FIGURE 13-17: Stopping execution at a breakpoint

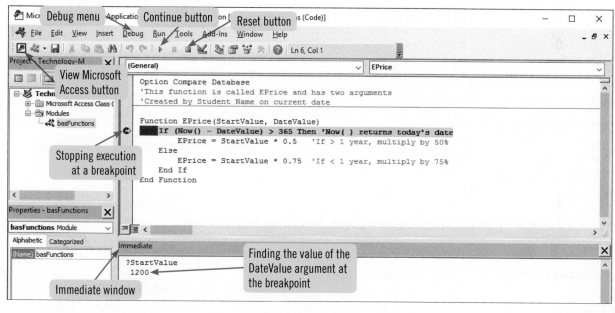

Debugging

Debugging is the process of finding and resolving bugs or problems in code. The term is generally attributed to Grace Hopper, a computer pioneer. Wikipedia (https://en.wikipedia.org/wiki/Debugging) states that while Grace was working at Harvard University in the 1940s, a moth was found in a relay component of the computer, which impeded operations. After the moth was removed, Grace remarked that they were "debugging" the system.

Practice

Concepts Review

Identify each element of the Visual Basic window shown in FIGURE 13-18.

FIGURE 13-18

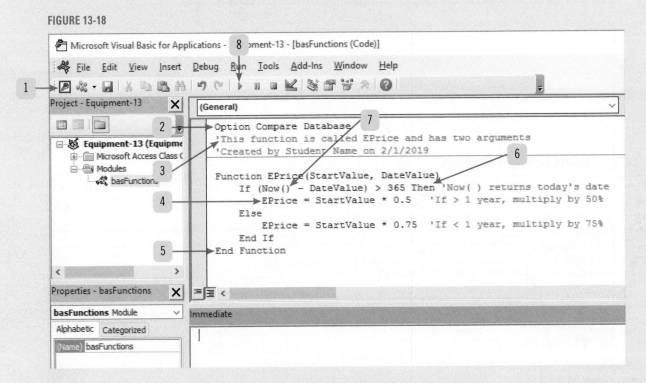

Match each term with the statement that best describes its function.

9. **Visual Basic for Applications (VBA)**
10. **Module**
11. **Debugging**
12. **If...Then...Else statement**
13. **Procedure**
14. **Class modules**
15. **Breakpoint**
16. **Arguments**
17. **Function**

a. Allows you to test a logical condition and execute commands only if the condition is true
b. The programming language used in Access modules
c. A line of code that automatically suspends execution of the procedure
d. A process to find and resolve programming errors
e. A procedure that returns a value
f. Constants, variables, or expressions passed to a procedure to further define how it should execute
g. Stored as part of the form or report object in which they are created
h. The Access object where VBA code is stored
i. A series of VBA statements that performs an operation or calculates a value

Skills Review

1. **Understand modules and VBA.**
   a. Start Access, then open the Baseball-13.accdb (not Basketball-13.accdb) database from the location where you store your Data Files. Enable content if prompted.
   b. Open the VBE window for the basFunctions module.

Skills Review (continued)

   c. Record your answers to the following questions about this module:

- What are the names of the functions?
- What are the names of the arguments for each function?
- What is the purpose of the End Function statements?
- Why are the End Function statements in blue?
- Why are some of the lines indented?

2. Compare macros and modules.

   a. If not already opened, open the VBE window for the basFunctions module.

   b. Record your answers to the following questions on a sheet of paper:

- Why was a module rather than a macro used to create these procedures?
- Why is VBA generally more difficult to create than a macro?
- Identify each of the VBA keywords or keyword phrases, and explain the purpose for each.

3. Create functions.

   a. If not already opened, open the VBE window for the basFunctions module.

   b. Create a function called **TotalBases** below the End Function statement of the Slugging function by typing the VBA statements shown in FIGURE 13-19. In baseball, total bases is a popular sta-

FIGURE 13-19

```
Function TotalBases(Base1, Base2, Base3, Base4)
    TotalBases = Base1 + (2 * Base2) + (3 * Base3) + (4 * Base4)
End Function
```

tistic because it accounts for the power of each hit. In the TotalBases function, each hit is multiplied by the number of bases earned (1 for single, 2 for double, 3 for triple, and 4 for home run).

   c. Save the basFunctions module, then close the VBE window.

   d. Use Query Design View to create a new query using the PlayerFName and PlayerLName fields from the tblPlayers table and the AtBats field from the tblPlayerStats table.

   e. Create a calculated field named **Batting** in the next available column by carefully typing the expression as follows: **Batting: BattingAverage([1Base],[2Base],[3Base],[4Base],[AtBats])**. (*Hint*: Use the Zoom dialog box to enter long expressions.)

   f. Create a second calculated field named **Slugger** in the next available column by carefully typing the expression as follows: **Slugger: Slugging([1Base],[2Base],[3Base],[4Base],[AtBats])**. (*Hint*: Use the Zoom dialog box to enter long expressions.)

   g. Create a third calculated field named **Bases** in the next available column by carefully typing the expression: **Bases: TotalBases([1Base],[2Base],[3Base],[4Base])**. (*Hint*: Use the Zoom dialog box.)

   h. View the datasheet, change Doug Schaller to *your* first and last name, save the query as **qryStats**, then close it.

4. Use If statements.

   a. Open the VBE window for the basFunctions module, then modify the BattingAverage and Slugging functions to add the If structure shown in FIGURE 13-20. The If structure

FIGURE 13-20

```
Function BattingAverage(SingleValue, DoubleValue, TripleValue, HRValue, AtBatsValue)
    If AtBatsValue = 0 Then
        BattingAverage = 0
    Else
        BattingAverage = (SingleValue + DoubleValue + TripleValue + HRValue) / AtBatsValue
    End If
End Function

Function Slugging(Base1, Base2, Base3, Base4, AtBats)
    If AtBats = 0 Then
        Slugging = 0
    Else
        Slugging = (Base1 + (2 * Base2) + (3 * Base3) + (4 * Base4)) / AtBats
    End If
End Function
```

prevents the error caused by attempting to divide by zero. The If structure checks to see if the AtBatsValue argument is equal to 0. If so, the BattingAverage function is set to 0. Otherwise, the BattingAverage function is calculated.

Skills Review (continued)

b. Save the basFunctions module, then close the VBE window.

c. Open the qryStats datasheet, then change the AtBats field value to **0** for the first record and press [Tab] to test the If statement. The Batting and Slugger calculated fields should equal 0.

d. Close the datasheet.

5. Document procedures.

a. Open the VBE window for the basFunctions module, and add the two statements above the End Function statement for the BattingAverage and Slugging functions, as shown in FIGURE 13-21. The statements use the Format function to format the calculation as a number with three digits to the right of the decimal point. The comments help clarify the statement.

b. Add a comment at the beginning of the VBA code that identifies *your name* and today's date, as shown in FIGURE 13-21.

FIGURE 13-21

```
Option Compare Database
'Created by Your Name on <insert today's date>
Function BattingAverage(SingleValue, DoubleValue, TripleValue, HRValue, AtBatsValue)
    If AtBatsValue = 0 Then
        BattingAverage = 0
    Else
        BattingAverage = (SingleValue + DoubleValue + TripleValue + HRValue) / AtBatsValue
    End If
    'Format as a number with three digits to the right of the decimal point
    BattingAverage = Format(BattingAverage, "0.000")
End Function

Function Slugging(Base1, Base2, Base3, Base4, AtBats)
    If AtBats = 0 Then
        Slugging = 0
    Else
        Slugging = (Base1 + (2 * Base2) + (3 * Base3) + (4 * Base4)) / AtBats
    End If
    'Format as a number with three digits to the right of the decimal point
    Slugging = Format(Slugging, "0.000")
End Function
```

c. Save the changes to the basFunctions module, print the module if requested by your instructor, then close the VBE window.

d. Open the qryStats query datasheet to observe how the values in the Batting and Slugger calculated fields are formatted with three digits to the right of the decimal point.

e. Print the qryStats datasheet if requested by your instructor, then close it.

6. Build class modules.

a. Open frmPlayerEntry in Form View, then move through several records to observe the data.

b. Switch to Design View, and on the right side of the form, select the Print Current Record button.

c. Open the Property Sheet for the button, click the Event tab, click the On Click property, then click the Build button to open the class module.

d. Add a statement using the MsgBox command after the DoCmd statement to send the following message to the user: "Printout sent to printer!"

e. Add a comment to the top of the module to show *your name* and the current date. Save the module, print it if requested by your instructor, then close the VBE window.

f. Test the code by switching to Form View and clicking the Print Current Record button on the form. (This action will send the current record in this form to the default printer.)

7. Modify sub procedures.

a. Open the frmPlayerEntry form in Form View, move through a couple of records to observe the txtSalary text box (currently blank), then switch to Design View.

b. The base starting salary in this league is $45,000. You will add a command button with VBA to help enter the correct salary for each player. Use the Button button to add a command button below the txtSalary text box, then cancel the Command Button Wizard if it starts.

Skills Review (continued)

c. Open the Property Sheet for the new command button, then change the Caption property on the Format tab to **Base Salary**. Change the Name property on the Other tab to **cmdBaseSalary**.

d. On the Event tab of the Property Sheet, click the On Click property, click the Build button, then click Code Builder if prompted. The stub for the new cmdBaseSalary_Click sub is automatically created for you.

e. Enter the following statement between the Sub and End Sub statements:

txtSalary.Value = 45000

f. Save the changes, then close the VBE window.

g. Close the Property Sheet, then save and open the frmPlayerEntry form in Form View.

h. Click the Base Salary command button for the first player, move to the second record, then click the Base Salary command button for the second player.

i. Save, then close the frmPlayerEntry form.

8. Troubleshoot modules.

a. Open the VBE window for the basFunctions module.

b. Click anywhere in the If AtBatsValue = 0 Then statement in the BattingAverage function.

c. Click Debug on the menu bar, then click Toggle Breakpoint to set a breakpoint at this statement.

d. Save the changes, then close the VBE window and return to Microsoft Access.

e. Open the qryStats query datasheet. This action attempts to use the BattingAverage function to calculate the value for the Batting field, which stops and highlights the statement in the VBE window where you set a breakpoint.

f. Click View on the menu bar, click Immediate Window (if not already visible), delete any previous entries in the Immediate window, type **?AtBatsValue**, then press [Enter]. At this point in the execution of the VBA, the AtBatsValue should be 0, the value you entered for the first record.

g. Type **?SingleValue**, then press [Enter]. At this point in the execution of the VBA code, the SingleValue should be 1, the value for the first record. (*Hint*: You can resize the Immediate window by dragging the top edge.)

h. Click Debug on the menu bar, click Clear All Breakpoints, then click the Continue button on the Standard toolbar. Close the VBE window.

i. Return to and close the qryStats query, close the Baseball-13.accdb database, then exit Access.

Independent Challenge 1

As the manager of a doctor's clinic, you have created an Access database called Insurance-13.accdb to track insurance claim reimbursements and general patient health. You want to modify an existing function within this database.

a. Start Access, then open the Insurance-13.accdb database from the location where you store your Data Files. Enable content if prompted.

b. Open the basBodyMassIndex module in Design View, and enter the **Option Explicit** declaration statement just below the existing Option Compare Database statement.

c. Record your answers to the following questions on a sheet of paper:

- What is the name of the function in the module?
- What are the function arguments?
- What is the purpose of the Option Explicit declaration statement?

d. Edit the BMI function by adding a comment as the first line of code with *your name* and today's date.

e. Edit the BMI function by adding a comment above the Function statement with the following information:
'A healthy BMI is in the range of 21-24.

Independent Challenge 1 (continued)

f. Edit the BMI function by adding an If clause that checks to make sure the height argument is not equal to 0. The final BMI function code should look like FIGURE 13-22.

g. Save the module, print it if requested by your instructor, then close the VBE window.

h. Create a new query that includes the following fields from the tblPatients table: **PtLastName**, **PtFirstName**, **PtHeight**, **PtWeight**.

FIGURE 13-22

```
'Student name and current date
Option Compare Database
Option Explicit

'A healthy BMI is in the range of 21-24.
Function BMI(weight, height)
    If height = 0 Then
        BMI = 0
    Else
        BMI = (weight * 0.4536) / (height * 0.0254) ^ 2
    End If
End Function
```

i. Create a calculated field with the following field name and expression: **BodyMassIndex: BMI([PtWeight], [PtHeight])**. (*Hint*: Use the Zoom dialog box for long expressions.)

j. Save the query as **qryPatientBMI**, view the qryPatientBMI query datasheet, then test the If statement by entering **0** in the PtHeight field for the first record. Press [Tab] to move to the BodyMassIndex field, which should recalculate to 0.

k. Edit the first record to contain *your* last and first names, print the datasheet if requested by your instructor, then close the qryPatientBMI query.

l. Close the Insurance-13.accdb database, then exit Access.

Independent Challenge 2

As the manager of a doctor's clinic, you have created an Access database called Insurance-13.accdb to track insurance claim reimbursements. You want to study the existing sub procedures stored as class modules in the Claim Entry Form.

a. Start Access, then open the Insurance-13.accdb database from the location where you store your Data Files. Enable content if prompted.

b. Open frmClaimEntryForm in Form View, then switch to Design View.

c. Open the VBE window to view this class module, then record your answers to the following questions on a sheet of paper:
  • What are the names of the sub procedures in this class module? (*Hint*: Be sure to scroll the window to see the complete contents.)
  • What Access functions are used in the PtFirstName_AfterUpdate sub?
  • How many arguments do the functions in the PtFirstName_AfterUpdate sub have?
  • What do the functions in the PtFirstName_AfterUpdate sub do? (*Hint*: You may have to use the Visual Basic Help system if you are not familiar with the functions.)
  • What is the purpose of the On Error command in the cmdEnterNewClaim_Click sub? (*Hint*: Use the Visual Basic Help system if you are not familiar with this command.)

d. Use the Property Sheet of the form to create an event-handler procedure based on the On Load property. Enter one statement using the Maximize method of the DoCmd object, which will maximize the form each time it is loaded.

e. Save the changes, close the VBE window and the Claim Entry Form, then open frmClaimEntryForm in Form View to test the new sub, which should automatically maximize the form in Form View.

f. Close frmClaimEntryForm, close the Insurance-13.accdb database, then exit Access.

Independent Challenge 3

As the manager of a doctor's clinic, you have created an Access database called Insurance-13.accdb to track insurance claim reimbursements that are fixed (paid at a predetermined fixed rate) or denied (not paid by the insurance company). You want to enhance the database with a class module.

a. Start Access, then open the Insurance-13.accdb database from the location where you store your Data Files. Enable content if prompted.

b. Open frmCPT in Form Design View.

c. Use the Command Button Wizard to add a command button in the Form Header section. Choose the Add New Record action from the Record Operations category.

d. Accept **Add Record** as the text on the button, then name the button **cmdAddRecord**.

e. Use the Command Button Wizard to add a command button in the Form Header section to the right of the existing Add Record button. (*Hint*: Move and resize controls as necessary to put two command buttons in the Form Header section.)

f. Choose the Delete Record action from the Record Operations category.

g. Accept **Delete Record** as the text on the button, and name the button **cmdDeleteRecord**.

h. Size the two buttons to be the same height and width, and align their top edges. Move them as needed so that they do not overlap.

i. Save and view frmCPT in Form View, then click the Add Record command button.

j. Add a new record (it will be record number 65) with a CPTCode value of **999** and an RBRVS value of **1.5**.

k. To make sure that the Delete Record button works, click the record selector for the new record you just entered, click the Delete Record command button, then click Yes to confirm the deletion. Close frmCPT.

l. In Design View of the frmCPT form, open the Property Sheet for the Delete Record command button, click the Event tab, then click the Build button beside [Embedded Macro]. The Command Button Wizard created the embedded macro that deletes the current record. You can convert macro objects to VBA code to learn more about VBA. To convert an embedded macro to VBA, you must first copy and paste the embedded macro actions to a new macro object. (*Hint*: You can widen the property sheet by dragging the left edge.)

m. Press [Ctrl][A] to select all macro actions, then press [Ctrl][C] to copy all macro actions to the Clipboard.

n. Close the macro window, then save and close frmCPT.

o. On the Create tab, open Macro Design View, then press [Ctrl][V] to paste the macro actions to the window.

p. Click the Convert Macros to Visual Basic button, click Yes when prompted to save the macro, click Convert, then click OK when a dialog box indicates that the conversion is finished.

q. Save and close all open windows with default names. Open the Converted Macro-Macro1 VBE window. Add a comment as the first line of code in the Code window with *your* name and the current date, save the module, print it if requested by your instructor, then close the VBE window.

r. Close the Insurance-13.accdb database, then exit Access.

Independent Challenge 4: Explore

(*Note*: To complete this Independent Challenge, make sure you are connected to the Internet.)

Learning a programming language is sometimes compared with learning a foreign language. Imagine how it would feel to learn a new programming language if English wasn't your primary language or if you had another type of accessibility challenge. Advances in technology are helping to break down many barriers to those with vision, hearing, mobility, cognitive, and language issues. In this challenge, you explore the Microsoft website for resources to address these issues.

a. Go to www.microsoft.com/enable, then print that page. Explore the website.

b. After exploring the website for products, demos, tutorials, guides, and articles, describe five types of accessibility solutions that might make a positive impact on someone. Identify both the problem and the solution.

c. Use bold headings for the five types of accessibility solutions to make those sections of your paper easy to find and read. Be sure to spell and grammar check your paper.

Visual Workshop

As the manager of a college basketball team, you are helping the coach build meaningful statistics to compare the relative value of the players in each game. The coach has stated that one offensive rebound is worth as much to the team as two defensive rebounds, and she would like you to use this rule to develop a "rebounding impact statistic" for each game. Open the Basketball-13.accdb (not Baseball-13.accdb) database, enable content if prompted, and use FIGURE 13-23 to develop a new function in a standard module. Name the new function **ReboundImpact** in a new module called **basFunctions** to calculate this statistic. Include *your* name and the current date as a comment in the first row of the function.

FIGURE 13-23

```
Function ReboundImpact(OffenseVal As Integer, DefenseVal As Integer) As Integer
    ReboundImpact = (OffenseVal * 2) + DefenseVal
End Function
```

Create a query called **qryRebounds** with the fields shown in FIGURE 13-24. Note that the records are sorted in ascending order on GameNo and LastName. The **ReboundPower** field is created using the following expression: **ReboundImpact([Reb-O],[Reb-D])**. Enter *your* first and last name instead of Kristen Czyenski, and print the datasheet if requested by your instructor.

FIGURE 13-24

GameN	FirstName	LastName	Reb-O	Reb-D	ReboundPower
1	Student First	Student Last	2	2	6
1	Denise	Franco	2	3	7
1	Theresa	Grant	1	3	5
1	Megan	Hile	1	2	4
1	Amy	Hodel	5	3	13
1	Ellyse	Howard	1	2	4
1	Jamie	Johnson	0	1	1
1	Lindsey	Swift	1	2	4
1	Morgan	Tyler	4	6	14
2	Student First	Student Last	3	2	8
2	Denise	Franco	5	3	13
2	Sydney	Freesen	2	3	7
2	Theresa	Grant	3	3	9
2	Megan	Hile	1	5	7
2	Amy	Hodel	1	4	6
2	Ellyse	Howard	3	3	9
2	Sandy	Robins	0	1	1
2	Lindsey	Swift	2	2	6
2	Morgan	Tyler	3	6	12
2	Abbey	Walker	2	4	8

Administering the Database

CASE Aaron Scout is the network administrator at Reason 2 Go corporate headquarters. You have helped Aaron develop a database to document R2G computer equipment. Now you can use Access to create a navigation form. You also examine several administrative issues, such as setting passwords, changing startup options, and analyzing database performance to protect, improve, and enhance the database.

Module Objectives

After completing this module, you will be able to:

- Create a navigation form
- Compact and repair a database
- Change startup options
- Analyze database performance

- Set a database password
- Back up a database
- Convert a database
- Split a database

Files You Will Need

Equipment-14.accdb   LakeHomes-14.accdb
Basketball-14.accdb   Music-14.accdb
Insurance-14.accdb

Create a Navigation Form

Learning
Outcomes
• Create a navigation
  form
• Add tabs to a
  navigation form

A **navigation form** is a special Access form that provides an easy-to-use database interface that is also web compatible. Being **web compatible** means that the form can be opened and used with a browser when the database is published to a SharePoint server. A **SharePoint server** is a special type of Microsoft web server that allows people to share and collaborate on information using only a browser such as Internet Explorer. Navigation forms can be used with any Access database, however, even if you don't publish it to a SharePoint server. **CASE** ▶ *Aaron Scout asks you to create a navigation form to easily access forms and reports in the Equipment-14 database.*

STEPS

1. **Start Access, open the Equipment-14.accdb database from the location where you store your Data Files, enable content if prompted, click the Create tab, click the Navigation button in the Forms group, click the Vertical Tabs, Left option, then close the Field List window if it opens**

   The new navigation form opens in Layout View. Vertical Tabs, Left is a **navigation system style** that determines how the navigation buttons are displayed on the form. Other navigation system styles include vertical tabs on the right, horizontal tabs at the top, or both horizontal and vertical tabs.

2. **Drag the frmEmployees form from the Navigation Pane to the first tab, which displays [Add New]**

   The frmEmployees form is added as the first tab, as shown in FIGURE 14-1, and a new tab with [Add New] is automatically created as well. The second and third tabs will display reports.

QUICK TIP
Click the object
expand ⌄
and collapse ⌄
buttons to display or
hide objects in the
Navigation Pane.

3. **Drag the rptAllEquipment report from the Navigation Pane to the second tab, which displays [Add New], then drag rptPCs to the third tab, which also displays [Add New]**

   With the objects in place, you rename the tabs to be less technical.

4. **Double-click the frmEmployees tab, edit it to read Employees, double-click the rptAllEquipment tab, edit it to read All Equipment, double-click the rptPCs tab, edit it to read PCs, right-click the Navigation Form tab, then click Form View on the shortcut menu to display the form in Form View, as shown in FIGURE 14-2**

   Test, save, and close the new navigation form.

5. **Click the All Equipment tab, click the PCs tab, click the Employees tab, click the Save button 🖫 on the Quick Access Toolbar, type frmNavigation, click OK, then close frmNavigation**

FIGURE 14-1: Creating a navigation form

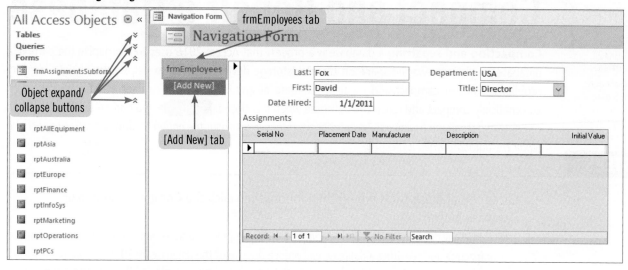

FIGURE 14-2: Final navigation form in Form View

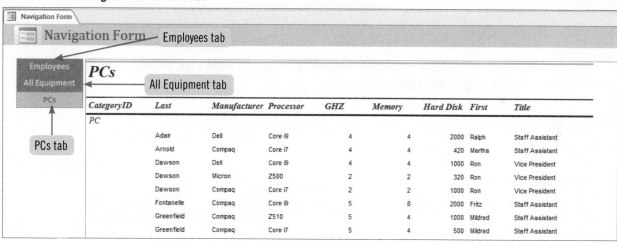

Setting navigation options

You can change the way the Navigation Pane appears by clicking the title bar of the Navigation Pane and choosing a different way to organize the objects (e.g., by Object Type, Created Date, or Custom Groups) in the upper portion of the menu. The lower portion of the menu lets you display only one object type (e.g., Tables, Queries, Forms, Reports, or All Access Objects). Right-click the Navigation Pane for more options on the shortcut menu, including Navigation Options, which allows you to create custom groups within the Navigation Pane.

Compact and Repair a Database

Compacting and repairing a database is a process that Access 2016 uses to reorganize the parts of a database to eliminate wasted space on the disk storage device, which also helps prevent data integrity problems. You can compact and repair a database at any time, or you can set a database option to automatically compact and repair the database when it is closed. **CASE** ➤ *You and Aaron Scout decide to compact and repair the Equipment-14 database and then learn about the option to automatically compact and repair the database when it is closed.*

STEPS

1. **Click the Database Tools tab on the Ribbon, then click the Compact and Repair Database button**

   Access closes the database, completes the compact and repair process, and reopens the database automatically.

   Compacting and repairing a database can reduce the size of the database by 10, 50, or even 75 percent because the space occupied by deleted objects and deleted data is not reused until the database is compacted. Therefore, it's a good idea to set up a regular schedule to compact and repair a database. You decide to change Access options to automatically compact the database when it is closed.

2. **Click the File tab on the Ribbon, then click Options**

   The Compact on Close feature is in the Current Database category of the Access Options dialog box.

3. **Click the Current Database category, then click the Compact on Close check box**

   Your screen should look like **FIGURE 14-3**. Now, every time the database is closed, Access will also compact and repair it. This helps you keep the database as small and efficient as possible and protects your database from potential corruption. The Access Options dialog box provides many important default options and techniques to customize Access, which are summarized in **TABLE 14-1**.

4. **Click OK to close the Access Options dialog box, then click OK when prompted to close and reopen the current database**

Trusting a database to automatically enable content

Trusting a database means to identify the database file as one that is safe to open. Trusted databases automatically enable all content, including all macros and VBA in modules, and, therefore, do not present the Enable Content message when they are opened. To trust a database, click the File tab, click Options, click Trust Center on the left, click the Trust Center Settings button, then use the Trusted Documents or Trusted Locations options to either trust an individual database file or an entire folder. To trust the folder, click Trusted Locations, click Add new location, click Browse to locate the folder to trust, select the desired folder, click the Subfolders of this location are also trusted check box to also trust subfolders, and then click OK to move through the dialog boxes and complete the process.

FIGURE 14-3: **Setting the Compact on Close option**

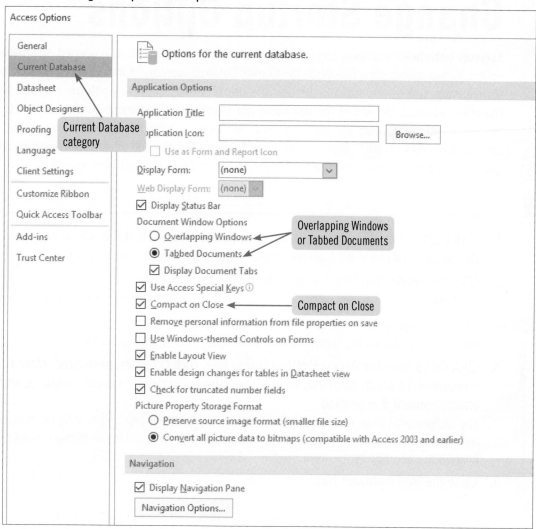

TABLE 14-1: **Access options**

category	description
General	Sets default interface, file format, default database folder, and username options
Current Database	Provides for application changes, such as whether the windows are overlapping or tabbed, the database compacts on close, and Layout View is enabled; also provides Navigation Pane, Ribbon, toolbar, and AutoCorrect options
Datasheet	Determines the default gridlines, cell effects, and fonts of datasheets
Object Designers	Determines default Design View settings for tables, queries, forms, and reports; also provides default error-checking options
Proofing	Sets AutoCorrect and Spelling options
Language	Sets Editing, Display, and Help languages
Client Settings	Sets defaults for cursor action when editing, display elements, printing margins, date formatting, and advanced record management options
Customize Ribbon	Provides an easy-to-use interface to modify the buttons and tabs on the Ribbon
Quick Access Toolbar	Provides an easy-to-use interface to modify the buttons on the Quick Access Toolbar
Add-ins	Provides a way to manage add-ins, software that works with Access to add or enhance functionality
Trust Center	Provides a way to manage trusted publishers, trusted locations, trusted documents, macro settings, and other privacy and security settings

Access 2016

Change Startup Options

Startup options are a series of commands that execute when the database is opened. You manage the default startup options using features in the Current Database category of the Access Options dialog box. More startup options are available through the use of **command-line options**, a special series of characters added to the end of the pathname (for example, C:\Documents\R2G.accdb /excl), which execute a command when the file is opened. See **TABLE 14-2** for information on common startup command-line options. **CASE** ▶ *You and Aaron Scout want to view and set database properties and then specify that the frmEmployees form opens when the Equipment-14.accdb database is opened.*

STEPS

1. **Click the File tab, click Options, then click Current Database if it is not already selected**
   The startup options are in the Application Options area of the Current Database category.

2. **Click the Application Title text box, then type Reason 2 Go**
   The Application Title database property value appears in the title bar instead of the database filename.

3. **Click the Display Form list arrow, then click frmEmployees**
   See **FIGURE 14-4**. You test the Application Title and Display Form database properties.

4. **Click OK to close the Access Options dialog box, click OK when prompted, close the Equipment-14.accdb database, then reopen the Equipment-14.accdb database and enable content if prompted**
   The Equipment-14.accdb database opens with the new application title, followed by the frmEmployees form, as shown in **FIGURE 14-5**. If you want to open an Access database and bypass startup options, press and hold [Shift] while the database opens.

5. **Close the frmEmployees form**

TABLE 14-2: Startup command-line options

option	effect
/excl	Opens the database for exclusive access
/ro	Opens the database for read-only access

FIGURE 14-4: Setting startup options

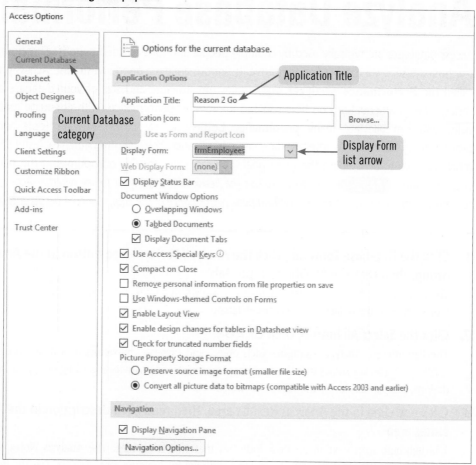

FIGURE 14-5: Display Form and Application Title startup options are in effect

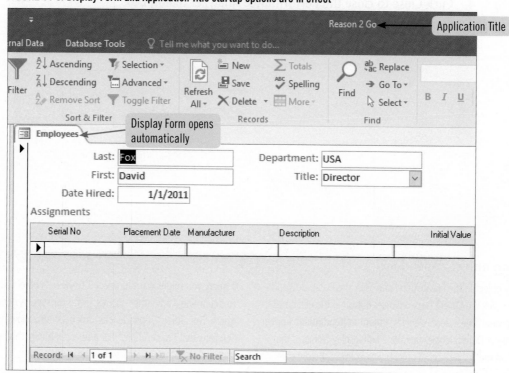

Analyze Database Performance

Access databases are typically used by multiple people and for extended periods. Therefore, spending a few hours to secure a database and improve its performance is a good investment. Access provides a tool called the **Performance Analyzer** that studies the structure and size of your database and makes a variety of recommendations on how you can improve its performance. With adequate time and Access skills, you can alleviate many performance bottlenecks by using software tools and additional programming techniques to improve database performance. You can often purchase faster processors and more memory to accomplish the same goal. See TABLE 14-3 for tips on optimizing the performance of your computer. **CASE** *You decide to use the Performance Analyzer to see whether Access provides any recommendations on how to easily maintain peak performance of the Equipment-14.accdb database.*

STEPS

1. **Click the Database Tools tab, click the Analyze Performance button in the Analyze group, then click the All Object Types tab**

   The Performance Analyzer dialog box opens, as shown in FIGURE 14-6. You can choose to analyze selected tables, forms, other objects, or the entire database.

2. **Click the Select All button, then click OK**

   The Performance Analyzer examines each object and presents the results in a dialog box, as shown in FIGURE 14-7. The key shows that the analyzer gives four levels of advice regarding performance: recommendations, suggestions, ideas, and items that were fixed.

3. **Click each line in the Analysis Results area, then read each description in the Analysis Notes area**

   The lightbulb icon next to an item indicates that this is an idea. The Analysis Notes section of the Performance Analyzer dialog box gives you additional information regarding the specific item. All of the Performance Analyzer's ideas should be considered, but they are not as important as recommendations and suggestions.

4. **Click Close to close the Performance Analyzer dialog box**

Viewing object dependencies

Click any object in the Navigation Pane, click the Database Tools tab, then click the Object Dependencies button in the Relationships group to view object dependencies. **Object dependencies** appear in the Object Dependencies task pane and display "Objects that depend on me" (the selected object). For example, before deleting a query you might want to select it to view its object dependencies to determine if any other queries, forms, or reports depend on that query. The Object Dependencies task pane also allows you to view "Objects that I depend on." For a selected query, this option would show you what tables are used in the query.

FIGURE 14-6: Performance Analyzer dialog box

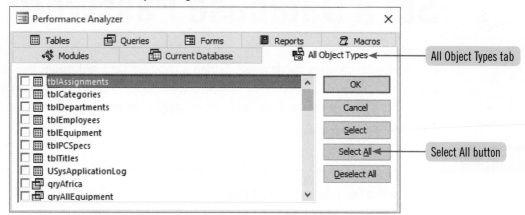

All Object Types tab

Select All button

FIGURE 14-7: Performance Analyzer results

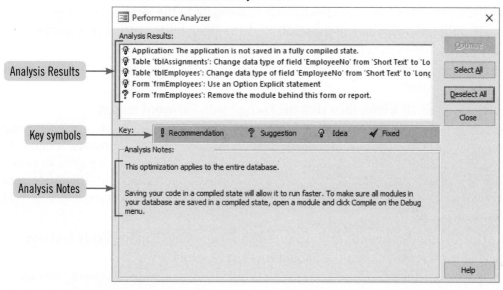

Analysis Results

Key symbols

Analysis Notes

TABLE 14-3: Tips for optimizing performance

degree of difficulty	tip
Easy	Close all applications that you don't currently need
Easy	Eliminate unneeded memory-resident programs, such as complex screen savers, email alert programs, and virus checkers
Easy	If you are the only person using a database, open it in Exclusive mode
Easy	Use the Compact on Close feature
Moderate	Add more memory to your computer
Moderate	If others don't need to share the database, load it on your local hard drive instead of the network's file server (but be sure to back up local drives regularly, too)
Moderate	Split the database so that the data is stored on the file server but other database objects are stored on your local (faster) hard drive
Moderate to difficult	Move the database to an uncompressed drive
Moderate to difficult	Run Performance Analyzer on a regular basis, examining and appropriately acting on each recommendation, suggestion, and idea
Moderate to difficult	Make sure that all PCs are running the latest versions of Windows and Access
Essential	Make sure your database is normalized correctly and that appropriate one-to-many relationships are established in the Relationships window.

Set a Database Password

Learning Outcomes
- Open the database in Exclusive mode
- Set a password and encryption

A **password** is a combination of uppercase and lowercase letters, numbers, and symbols that the user must enter to open the database. Setting a database password means that anyone who doesn't know the password cannot open the database. Other ways to secure an Access database are listed in **TABLE 14-4.** **CASE** ▶ *Aaron Scout asks you to apply a database password to the Equipment-14.accdb database to secure its data.*

STEPS

1. **Click the File tab, then click Close**

   The Equipment-14.accdb database closes, but the Access application window remains open. To set a database password, you must open the database in Exclusive mode using the Open dialog box.

   TROUBLE
   You cannot use the Recent list to open a database in Exclusive mode.

2. **Click the Open Other Files link, click Browse to navigate to the location where you store your Data Files, click Equipment-14.accdb, click the Open button arrow, as shown in FIGURE 14-8, click Open Exclusive, then enable content if prompted**

   Exclusive mode means that you are the only person who has the database open, and others cannot open the file during this time.

   QUICK TIP
   It's always a good idea to back up a database before creating a database password.

3. **Click the File tab, click Info, then click the Encrypt with Password button**

   Encryption means to make the data in the database unreadable by other software. The Set Database Password dialog box opens, as shown in **FIGURE 14-9.** If you lose or forget your password, it cannot be recovered. For security reasons, your password does not appear as you type; for each keystroke, an asterisk appears instead. Therefore, you must enter the same password in both the Password and Verify text boxes to make sure you haven't made a typing error. Passwords are case sensitive, so, for example, Cyclones and cyclones are different.

   QUICK TIP
   Check to make sure the Caps Lock key is not selected before entering a password.

4. **Type GoISU! in the Password text box, press [Tab], type GoISU! in the Verify text box, click OK, then click OK if prompted about row-level security**

   Passwords should be easy to remember but not as obvious as your name, the word "password," the name of the database, or the name of your company. **Strong passwords** are longer than eight characters and use the entire keyboard, including uppercase and lowercase letters, numbers, and symbols. Microsoft provides an online tool to check the strength of your password. Go to www.microsoft.com and search for password checker.

5. **Close, then reopen Equipment-14.accdb**

   The Password Required dialog box opens.

6. **Type GoISU!, then click OK**

   The Equipment-14.accdb database opens, giving you full access to all of the objects. To remove a password, you must exclusively open a database, just as you did when you set the database password.

   TROUBLE
   You must browse for the file to open it exclusively.

7. **Click the File tab, click Close, click the Open Other Files link, click Browse to navigate to the location where you store your Data Files, single-click Equipment-14.accdb, click the Open button arrow, click Open Exclusive, type GoISU! in the Password Required dialog box, then click OK**

8. **Click the File tab, click Info, click the Decrypt Database button, type GoISU!, then click OK**

FIGURE 14-8: Opening a database in Exclusive mode

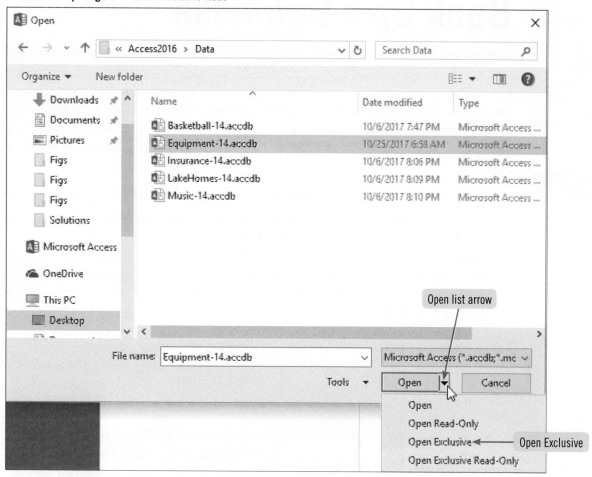

FIGURE 14-9: Set Database Password dialog box

TABLE 14-4: Methods to secure an Access database

method	description
Password	Restricts access to the database and can be set at the database, workgroup, or VBA level
Encryption	Makes the data indecipherable to other programs
Startup options	Hides or disables certain functions when the database is opened
Show/hide objects	Shows or hides objects in the Navigation Pane; a simple way to prevent users from unintentionally deleting objects is to hide them in the Navigation Pane by checking the Hidden property in the object's Property Sheet
Split a database	Separates the back-end data and the front-end objects (such as forms and reports) into two databases that work together; splitting a database allows you to give each user access to only those front-end objects they need as well as add security measures to the back-end database that contains the data

Back Up a Database

Backing up a database refers to making a copy of it in a secure location. Backups are important to protect those who rely on a database from the problems created when the database is corrupted, stolen, or otherwise compromised. Database threats and solutions are summarized in TABLE 14-5. Backups can be saved on an external hard drive, the hard drive of a second computer, or a web server such as OneDrive. Because most users are familiar with saving and copying files to hard drives, the new technology streamlines the effort of backing up a database. **CASE** ▶ *Aaron Scout asks you to review the methods of backing up the database.*

STEPS

1. **Click the File tab, click Save As, click the Save Database As option if it is not selected, click Back Up Database, then click the Save As button, as shown in** FIGURE 14-10

   The Save As dialog box is shown in FIGURE 14-11. When using the Back Up Database option, the current date is automatically added to the database filename. However, any copy of the entire database with any filename also serves as a valid backup of the database. The **Save Database As** option saves the entire database, including all of its objects, to a completely new database file. The **Save Object As** option saves only the current object (table, query, form, report, macro, or module).

   The Save As window shown in FIGURE 14-10 allows you to save the database in an older 2000 database format (.mdb file extension), a database template file (.accdt file extension), or an executable database (.accde file extension).

   The Save As dialog box shown in FIGURE 14-11 allows you to save the database to external locations such as an FTP (File Transfer Protocol) server, Dropbox folder, OneDrive folder, or SharePoint site. Your locations will vary based on the resources available to you on the computer you are using.

2. **Navigate to the location where you store your Data Files, then click Save**

   A copy of the Equipment-14.accdb database is saved in the location you selected with the name Equipment-14-*currentdate*.accdb, and the original Equipment-14.accdb database is open.

   Yet another way to make a backup copy of an Access database is to use your Windows skills to copy and paste the database file in a File Explorer or Windows Explorer window. If you choose this backup method, however, make sure the database and Access are closed before copying the database file.

   If you want to copy only certain objects from a backup database to a production database, use the Access button in the Import & Link group of the External Data tab to select and import specific objects from the backup database.

Using portable storage media

Technological advancements continue to make it easier and less expensive to store large files on portable storage devices. **Secure digital (SD)** and **micro SD cards** slip directly into a computer and typically store around 32 to 64 **GB** (**gigabyte**, a million bytes or a thousand megabytes). **CompactFlash (CF) cards** are slightly larger and also store around 16 GB to 64 GB. **USB (Universal Serial Bus) drives** (which plug into a computer's USB port) are also popular. USB drives are also called thumb drives, flash drives, and travel drives. USB devices typically store anywhere from 4 GB to 128 GB of information. Larger still are **external hard drives**, sometimes as small as the size of a cell phone, that store anywhere from 20 GB to about 4 **TB** (**terabyte**, a trillion bytes or a thousand gigabytes) of information and connect to a computer using either a USB or FireWire port.

FIGURE 14-10: Save As options

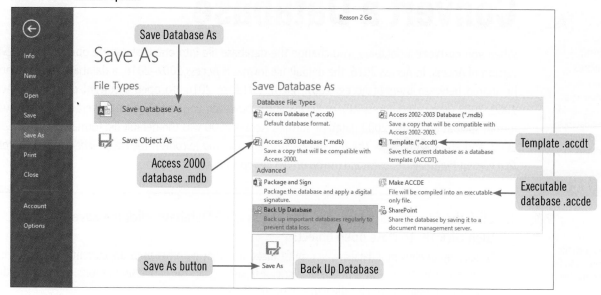

Save Database As

Save As

File Types

Save Database As

Save Object As

Save Database As

Database File Types

Access Database (*.accdb)
Default database format.

Access 2002-2003 Database (*.mdb)
Save a copy that will be compatible with Access 2002-2003.

Access 2000 Database (*.mdb)
Save a copy that will be compatible with Access 2000.

Template (*.accdt)
Save the current database as a database template (ACCDT).

Template .accdt

Access 2000 database .mdb

Advanced

Package and Sign
Package the database and apply a digital signature.

Make ACCDE
File will be compiled into an executable-only file.

Executable database .accde

Back Up Database
Back up important databases regularly to prevent data loss.

SharePoint
Share the database by saving it to a document management server.

Save As button

Save As

Back Up Database

FIGURE 14-11: Save As dialog box to back up a database

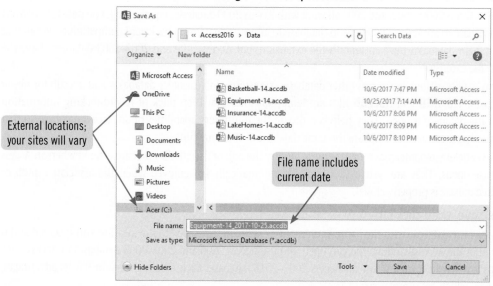

External locations; your sites will vary

File name includes current date

TABLE 14-5: Database threats and solutions

incident	what can happen	appropriate actions
Virus	Viruses can cause a wide range of harm, from profane messages to corrupted files	Purchase the leading virus-checking software for each machine, and keep it updated
Power outage	Power problems such as construction accidents, **brownouts** (dips in power often causing lights to dim), and **spikes** (surges in power) can damage the hardware, which may render the computer useless	Purchase a **UPS (uninterruptible power supply)** to maintain constant power to the file server. Purchase a **surge protector** (power strip with surge protection) for each user
Theft or intentional damage	Computer thieves or other scoundrels steal or vandalize computer equipment	Place the file server in a room that can be locked after-hours. Use network drives for user data files, and back them up on a daily basis. Use off-site storage for backups. Set database passwords and encrypt the database so that stolen files cannot be used; use computer locks for equipment that is at risk, especially laptops

Convert a Database

When you **convert** a database, you change the database file into one that can be opened in a previous version of Access. In Access 2016, the default file format is Access 2007–2016, a database format that can be shared between users of Access 2007, 2010, 2013, or 2016. To open a current database in Access 2000, 2002 (also called Access XP), or Access 2003, however, you first need to convert it to a previous file format such as an Access 2000 database format. Access 2000 was the default file format for Access 2000, 2002, and 2003. **CASE** *The Training Department asks you to convert the Equipment-14.accdb database to a version that they can open and use on an old laptop with Access 2003.*

STEPS

1. **Click the File tab, click Save As, click Access 2000 Database, click the Save As button, then click Yes to close open objects**

   To back up or convert a database, you must make sure that no other users are currently working with it. Because you are the sole user of this database, it is safe to start the conversion process. The Save As dialog box opens, prompting you for the name of the database.

2. **Navigate to the location where you store your Data Files, then type Equipment-14-2000.mdb in the File name text box, as shown in FIGURE 14-12**

   Because Access 2000, 2002, and 2003 all work with Access 2000 databases equally well, you decide to convert this database to an Access 2000 version database to allow for maximum backward compatibility. Recall that Access 2016 databases have an **.accdb** file extension, but Access 2000 and 2002–2003 databases have the **.mdb** file extension.

   You may occasionally see two other database extensions, .ldb for older databases and .laccdb for newer databases. The **.ldb** and **.laccdb** files are temporary files that keep track of record-locking information when the database is open. They help coordinate the multiuser capabilities of an Access database so that several people can read and update the same database at the same time.

   Never delete, rename, move, or otherwise modify the .ldb or .laccdb files that are created when an Access database opens. They are system files and will automatically be removed when the associated .mdb or .accdb database is properly closed.

3. **Click Save, then click OK**

   A copy of the database with the name Equipment-14-2000.mdb is saved to the location you specified and is opened in the Access window. You can open and use Access 2000 and 2002–2003 databases in Access 2016 just as you would open and use an Access 2007–2016 database. Each database version has its advantages, however, which are summarized in TABLE 14-6.

4. **Close the database**

FIGURE 14-12: Save As dialog box for Access 2000 file format

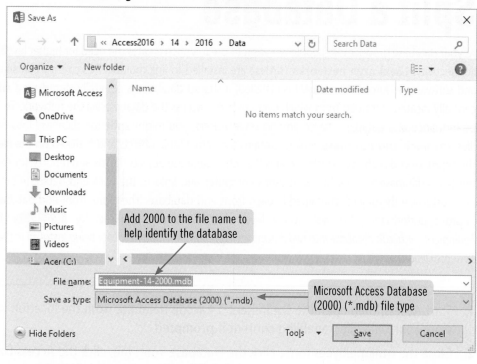

Add 2000 to the file name to help identify the database

File name: Equipment-14-2000.mdb

Save as type: Microsoft Access Database (2000) (*.mdb)

Microsoft Access Database (2000) (*.mdb) file type

TABLE 14-6: Differences between database file formats

database file format	file extension	Access version(s) that can read this file	benefits
2000	.mdb	2000, 2002, 2003, 2007, 2010, 2013, and 2016	Most versatile if working in an environment where multiple versions of Access are still in use; however, some .mdb files cannot be opened in Access 2013 and 2016
2002–2003	.mdb	2002, 2003, 2007, 2010, 2013, and 2016	Most reliable version if multiple versions of Access are still in use
2007	.accdb	2007, 2010, 2013, and 2016	Supports multivalued fields Provides excellent integration with SharePoint and Outlook Provides more robust encryption

Split a Database

As your database grows, more people will want to use it, which creates the need for higher levels of database connectivity. **Local area networks (LANs)** are installed to link multiple PCs so they can share hardware and software resources. After a LAN is installed, a shared database is generally stored on a **file server**, a centrally located computer from which every user can access the database via the network. To improve the performance of a database shared among several users, you might **split** the database into two database files: the **back-end database**, which contains the actual table objects and is stored on the file server, and the **front-end database**, which contains the other database objects (forms and reports, for example). The front-end database is stored on each user's computer and links to the back-end database tables. You can also customize the objects contained in each front-end database. Therefore, front-end databases not only improve performance, but also add a level of customization and security. **CASE** *You split the Equipment-14.accdb database into two databases in preparation for a new LAN being installed in the Information Systems Department.*

STEPS

1. **Start Access, then open the Equipment-14.accdb database from the location where you store your Data Files, enabling content if prompted**

2. **Close the frmEmployees form, click the Database Tools tab, click the Access Database button in the Move Data group, read the dialog box, then click Split Database**

   Access suggests the name of Equipment-14_be.accdb for the back-end database in the Create Back-end Database dialog box.

3. **Navigate to the location where you store your Data Files, click Split, then click OK**

   Equipment-14.accdb has now become the front-end database, which contains all of the Access objects except for the tables, as shown in FIGURE 14-13. The tables have been replaced with links to the physical tables in the back-end database.

TROUBLE
The path to your
back-end database
is different from
FIGURE 14-14.

4. **Click the Tables expand button ⊻ to open the table section in the Navigation Pane, point to several linked table icons to read the path to the back-end database, right-click any of the linked table icons, then click Linked Table Manager**

   The Linked Table Manager dialog box opens, as shown in FIGURE 14-14. This allows you to select and manually update tables. This is useful if the path to the back-end database changes and you need to reconnect the front-end and back-end database.

5. **Click Cancel**

   Linked tables work just like regular physical tables, even though the data is physically stored in another database.

6. **Close the Equipment-14.accdb database and exit Access**

FIGURE 14-13: Front-end database with linked tables

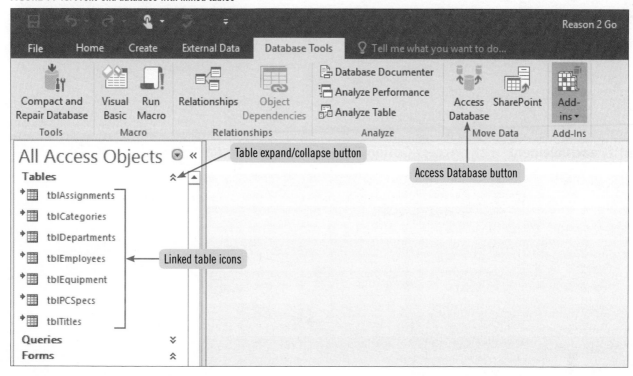

FIGURE 14-14: Linked Table Manager dialog box

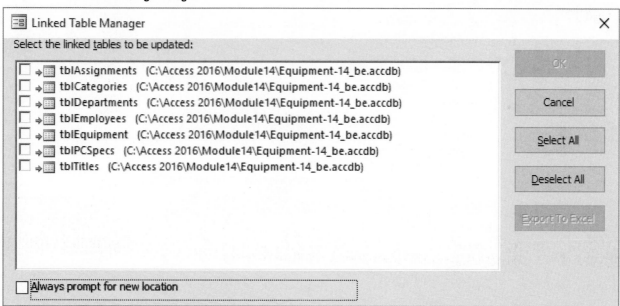

Databases and client/server computing

Splitting a database into a front-end and a back-end database that work together is an excellent example of client/server computing. **Client/server computing** can be defined as two or more information systems cooperatively processing to solve a problem. In most implementations, the **client** is defined as the user's PC and the **server** is defined as the shared file server, minicomputer, or mainframe computer. The server usually handles corporate-wide computing activities, such as data storage and management, security, and connectivity to other networks. Within Access, client computers generally handle those tasks specific to each user, such as storing all of the queries, forms, and reports used by a particular user. Effectively managing a client/server network in which many front-end databases link to a single back-end database is a tremendous task, but the performance and security benefits are worth the effort.

Practice

Concepts Review

Identify each element of the Access Options dialog box in FIGURE 14-15.

FIGURE 14-15

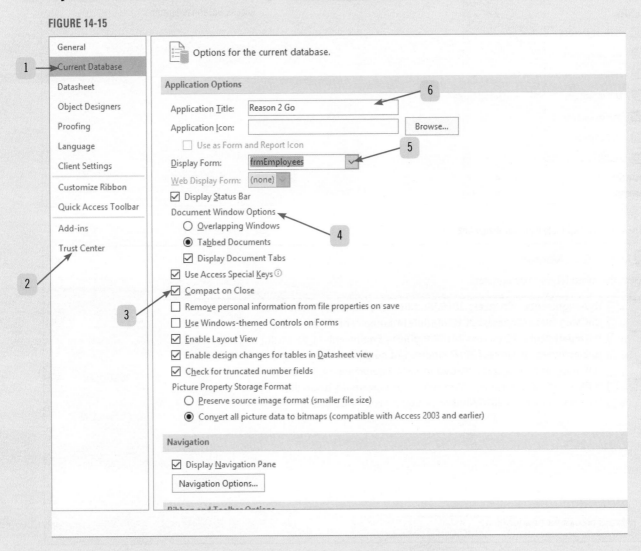

Match each term with the statement that best describes its function.

7. **Exclusive mode**
8. **Performance Analyzer**
9. **Navigation form**
10. **Back-end database**
11. **Encrypting**

a. Scrambles data so that it is indecipherable when opened by another program
b. Studies the structure and size of your database and makes a variety of recommendations on how you can improve its speed
c. Contains database tables
d. Provides an easy-to-use database interface
e. Means that no other users can have access to the database file while it's open

Select the best answer from the list of choices.

12. Changing a database file so that a previous version of Access can open it is called:

   a. Splitting.

   b. Encrypting.

   c. Analyzing.

   d. Converting.

13. Which is not a strong password?

   a. 1234$College=6789

   b. 5Matthew14?

   c. password

   d. Lip44Balm*!

14. Which character precedes a command-line option?

   a. !

   b. ^

   c. /

   d. @

15. Client/server computing is defined as:

   a. Making sure that the database is encrypted and secure.

   b. Creating an easy-to-use interface for a database application.

   c. Analyzing the performance of the database.

   d. Two or more information systems cooperatively processing to solve a problem.

16. Compacting and repairing a database does not help with which issue?

   a. Identifying unused database objects

   b. Preventing data integrity problems

   c. Eliminating wasted space

   d. Making the database as small as possible

17. Which of the following is not an item that you can "trust"?

   a. Database table

   b. Folder that stores the database

   c. Database file

   d. You can trust all of the above.

18. Which of the following is not a reason to create a backup?

   a. Protect against theft

   b. Minimize damage caused by an incident that corrupts data

   c. Improve performance of the database

   d. Safeguard information should a natural disaster destroy the database

19. Why might you split a database?

   a. To make access to the database more secure

   b. To improve performance

   c. To customize the front-end databases

   d. All of the above

20. Which phrase best defines a SharePoint server?

    a. A UNIX-based web server

    b. A special type of Microsoft web server

    c. An online learning management system

    d. An academic wiki website

Skills Review

1. Create a navigation form.

    a. Start Access, open the Basketball-14.accdb database from the location where you store your Data Files, and enable content if prompted.

    b. Create a navigation form using the Horizontal Tabs style.

    c. Close the Field List.

    d. Add the frmGameInfo form, the frmGameSummaryForm, and the frmPlayerInformationForm to the tabs.

    e. Rename the tabs to **Games**, **Summary**, and **Players**.

    f. Display the form in Form View, then test each tab.

    g. Save the form with the name **frmNavigation**, then close it.

2. Compact and repair a database.

    a. Compact and repair the database using an option on the Database Tools tab.

    b. Open the Access Options dialog box, and check the Compact on Close option in the Current Database category.

3. Change startup options.

    a. Open the Access Options dialog box.

    b. Type **Iowa State Cyclones** in the Application Title text box, click the Display Form list arrow, click the frmNavigation form, then apply the changes.

    c. Close the Basketball-14.accdb database, then reopen it to check the startup options. Notice the change in the Access title bar.

    d. Close the frmNavigation form that automatically opened when the database was opened.

4. Analyze database performance.

    a. On the Database Tools tab, click the Analyze Performance button.

    b. On the All Object Types tab, select all objects, then click OK.

    c. Read each of the ideas and descriptions, then close the Performance Analyzer and the database.

5. Set a database password.

    a. Start Access and open the Basketball-14.accdb database in Exclusive mode. (*Hint*: Remember you must browse for a database from within Access to open it in Exclusive mode.)

    b. Encrypt the database and set the password to **Ames!Iowa**. (*Hint*: Check to make sure the Caps Lock key is not selected because passwords are case sensitive.) Click OK if prompted about row level locking.

    c. Close the Basketball-14.accdb database, but leave Access open.

    d. Reopen the Basketball-14.accdb database to test the password. Close the Basketball-14.accdb database.

    e. Reopen the Basketball-14.accdb database in Exclusive mode. Type **Ames!Iowa** as the password.

    f. Unset the password and decrypt the database.

    g. Close the frmNavigation form.

6. Back up a database.

    a. Click the File tab, click Save As, then use the Back Up Database option to save a database backup with the name **Basketball-14-currentdate.accdb** in the location where you store your Data Files.

Skills Review (continued)

7. **Convert a database.**

   a. Click the File tab, click Save As, and save the database backup as an Access 2000 database with the name **Basketball-14-2000.mdb** in the location where you store your Data Files.

   b. Notice that the frmNavigation no longer works correctly because the navigation form is a feature that is only compatible with Access 2007 database file formats. Close frmNavigation.

   c. Open the Access Options dialog box.

   d. Click the Display Form list arrow, select (none), then apply the changes.

   e. If the Navigation Pane displays only tables, click the arrow to the right of Tables in the Navigation Pane title bar, and then click All Access Objects.

   f. Close the Basketball-14-2000.mdb database and click OK if prompted about a collating sequence.

8. **Split a database.**

   a. Start Access, open the Basketball-14.accdb database from the location where you store your Data Files, and enable content if prompted.

   b. Close frmNavigation.

   c. On the Database Tools tab, click the Access Database button and split the database.

   d. Name the back-end database with the default name **Basketball-14_be.accdb** and save it in the location where you store your Data Files.

   e. Point to the linked table icons to observe the path to the back-end database.

   f. Close the Basketball-14.accdb database and exit Access.

Independent Challenge 1

As the manager of a doctor's clinic, you have created an Access database called Insurance-14.accdb to track insurance claims. You want to set a database password and encrypt the database, as well as set options to automatically compact the database when it is closed.

   a. Start Access. Open Insurance-14.accdb in Exclusive mode from the location where you store your Data Files. Enable content if prompted.

   b. Encrypt the database with a password.

   c. Enter **2-your-health** in the Password text box and the Verify text box, then click OK. Click OK if prompted about row level locking.

   d. Close the Insurance-14.accdb database, but leave Access running.

   e. Reopen the Insurance-14.accdb database, enter **2-your-health** as the password, then click OK.

   f. In the Access Options dialog box, check the Compact on Close option.

   g. Close the Insurance-14.accdb database and Access.

Independent Challenge 2

As the manager of a doctor's clinic, you have created an Access database called Insurance-14.accdb to track insurance claims. You want to analyze database performance.

   a. Open the Insurance-14.accdb database from the location where you store your Data Files, and enable content if prompted.

   b. Enter **2-your-health** as the password if prompted.

Independent Challenge 2 (continued)

c. Use the Analyze Performance tool on the Database Tools tab to analyze all objects.

d. Click each item in the Performance Analyzer results window, and read the Analysis Notes in the Performance Analyzer dialog box.

e. Click Close in the Performance Analyzer dialog box and apply the first suggestion by double-clicking the basBodyMassIndex module. Choose Debug on the menu bar, then Compile. Save and close the VBE and run the Performance Analyzer again.

f. Click each item in the Performance Analyzer results window, and read the Analysis Notes in the Performance Analyzer dialog box.

g. Click Close in the Performance Analyzer dialog box and apply the suggestion about Option Explicit by double-clicking the basBodyMassIndex module. Enter **Option Explicit** as the second declaration statement, just below the Option Compare Database statement. Save and close the VBE and run the Performance Analyzer again.

h. Click each item in the Performance Analyzer results window, and read the Analysis Notes in the Performance Analyzer dialog box.

i. Click Close in the Performance Analyzer dialog box and consider the suggestion about tblClaimLineItems by opening the tblClaimLineItems table in Datasheet View. The suggestion was to change the Data Type of the Diag1 field from Short Text to Number with a Field Size property value of Double. Given that those values represent codes and not quantities, Short Text is a better description of the data and you will not implement this suggestion. Close the tblClaimLineItems table.

j. Run the Performance Analyzer for all objects again. To implement the MDE suggestion, close the Performance Analyzer dialog box, click the File tab, click Save As, click Make ACCDE, then click the Save As button. Save the Insurance-14.accde file to the location where you save your Data Files. An accde file is a database file that can be used just like an accdb file, but many of the objects cannot be modified in Design View.

k. Close the Insurance-14.accde database, then close Access.

Independent Challenge 3

As the manager of a residential real estate listing service, you have created an Access database called LakeHomes-14.accdb to track properties that are for sale. You want to analyze how the compact and repair feature affects a database.

a. Open File or Windows Explorer depending on your version of Windows, then open the folder that contains your Data Files.

b. Change the view to Details to view the Name, Date modified, Type, and Size of the file. Record the Size value for the LakeHomes-14.accdb database.

c. Double-click LakeHomes-14.accdb to open it, right-click the frmListingsEntryForm, and then click Delete.

d. Close the LakeHomes-14.accdb database and return to File Explorer or Windows Explorer. Record the Size value for the LakeHomes-14.accdb database.

e. Double-click LakeHomes-14.accdb to open it, click the Database Tools tab, then click the Compact and Repair Database button.

f. Close the LakeHomes-14.accdb database and return to File Explorer or Windows Explorer. Record the Size value for the LakeHomes-14.accdb database.

Independent Challenge 4: Explore

Trusting a database means to identify the database file as one that is safe to open. Trusted databases automatically enable all content, including all macros and VBA in modules, and, therefore, do not present the Enable Content message when they are opened. In this exercise you will learn how to trust a folder and all subfolders and files within it.

a. Open LakeHomes-14.accdb or any other database file in your Module 14 Data Files folder.

b. Click the File tab, click Options, click Trust Center on the left, then click the Trust Center Settings button.

c. Click the Trusted Locations option, click Add new location, click Browse, locate the Access2016 folder or whatever folder contains all of the subfolders for each module in this book, then click OK in the Browse dialog box.

d. Click the Subfolders of this location are also trusted check box to also trust subfolders, and then click OK in the Microsoft Office Trusted Location dialog box.

e. Click OK in the Trust Center dialog box.

f. Click OK in the Access Options dialog box.

g. Close the database, then reopen it. You should no longer be prompted to Enable Content for this database or any others in your data files folder.

h. Close the LakeHomes-14.accdb database and close Access.

Visual Workshop

As the manager of a music store, you have created an Access database called Music-14.accdb that tracks musical instrument rentals to schoolchildren. Use the Performance Analyzer to generate the results shown in FIGURE 14-16 by analyzing all object types. Save the database as an ACCDE file, but do not implement the other ideas. In a Word document, explain why implementing the last three ideas might not be appropriate.

FIGURE 14-16

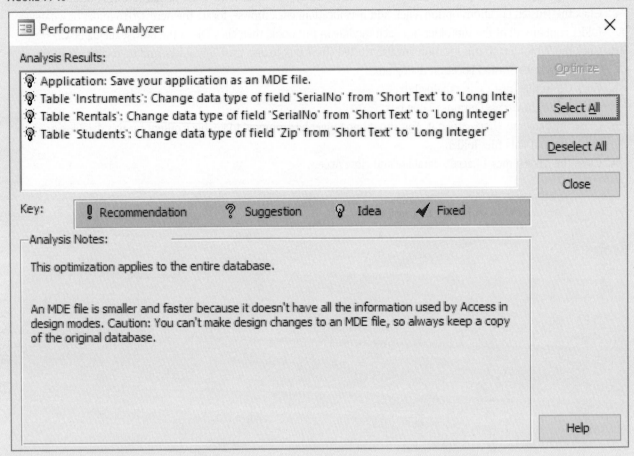

Administering the Database

Using Access and the Web

CASE ▶ Aaron Scout is the network administrator at R2G corporate headquarters. Aaron asks about ways that Access can participate with web technologies. You work with Aaron to explore and use the web technologies that complement an Access database.

Module Objectives

After completing this module, you will be able to:

- Create a hyperlink field
- Create a hyperlink control
- Use HTML tags to format text
- Export to HTML and XML
- Import from HTML and XML
- Save and share a database with OneDrive
- Understand Access web apps
- Create an Access web app

Files You Will Need

R2G-15.accdb

Scouts.docx

Newsletter.docx

NewCustomers.html

NewTrips.xml

NewTrips.xsd

Basketball-15.accdb

Cardinals.png

NextSeason.html

NewPlayers.xml

NewPlayers.xsd

Module15Skills Review.docx

Insurance-15.accdb

Music-15.accdb

Create a Hyperlink Field

Learning Outcomes
• Create a hyperlink field
• Enter hyperlink data for a webpage or file

A **hyperlink field** is a field with the **Hyperlink** data type. Use the Hyperlink data type when you want to store a link to a webpage or file. The file can be located on the Internet, on your company's local area network, or on your own computer. **CASE** ▸ *You create two hyperlink fields to store linked information about each Trip record in the Trips table. The first hyperlink field will link to a webpage that provides information about the Trip location. The second hyperlink field will link to a Word document that contains a Trip flyer.*

STEPS

1. **Start Access, open the R2G-15.accdb database from where you store your Data Files, enable content if prompted, then double-click the Trips table to open it in Datasheet View**

   You can add new fields in either Datasheet View or Design View.

2. **Click the *Click to Add* placeholder to the right of the Price field, click Hyperlink in the drop-down list, type WebPage as the new field name, then press [Enter]**

   The new WebPage field will store a hyperlink to the webpage address for that Trip. Before you enter those values, you will create another hyperlink field to link to a local Word document that contains a flyer for the Trip.

3. **Click the *Click to Add* placeholder to the right of the WebPage field if the placeholder is not selected, click Hyperlink, type Flyer, press [Enter], then click the WebPage field for the first record**

   The Trips datasheet should look like FIGURE 15-1. With the new hyperlink fields in place, you'll use them to further describe the Vail Biking Trip record. Hyperlink values such as webpage addresses may be typed directly in the field.

4. **Click the WebPage field for the Boy Scout Project record (TripNo 4), type www.vail.com, then press [Enter]**

   To store the link to a local Word document, you browse for the file.

5. **Right-click the Flyer field for the Boy Scout Project record (TripNo 4), click Hyperlink, click Edit Hyperlink, scroll down and click Scouts.docx, then click OK in the Insert Hyperlink dialog box as shown in FIGURE 15-2**

   The Insert Hyperlink dialog box lets you link to an existing file, webpage, or email address. Test your hyperlinks.

6. **Click the www.vail.com hyperlink, close the browser to return to Access, click the Scouts.docx hyperlink, click Yes if prompted about a security concern, then close Word to return to Access**

   Note that your mouse pointer becomes a **hyperlink pointer** 🖑 and displays the path to the resource when you hover over a hyperlink. Also note that the hyperlink changes colors, from blue to purple, once the hyperlink has been visited, as shown in FIGURE 15-3.

7. **Right-click the Trips table tab, then click Close**

   Hyperlink fields store paths to files and webpages, not the files or webpages themselves. If the location of the hyperlink file or database changes, the Hyperlink value must be changed in the Edit Hyperlink dialog box to reflect the new path as well.

FIGURE 15-1: Creating hyperlink fields

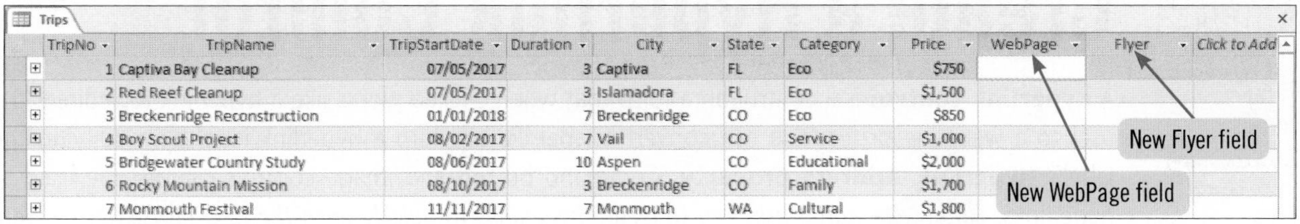

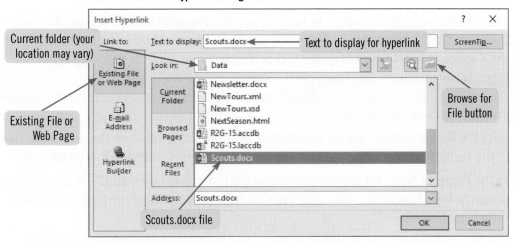

FIGURE 15-2: Insert Hyperlink dialog box

FIGURE 15-3: Trips datasheet with visited hyperlinks

Access 2016

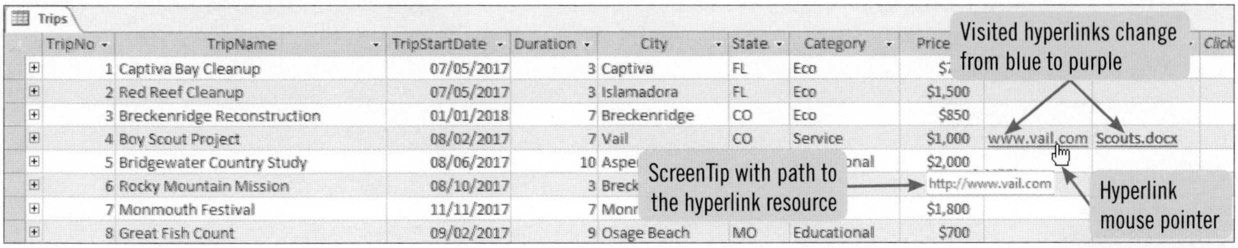

Create a Hyperlink Control

Learning Outcomes
- Modify a command button to be a hyperlink
- Modify a label to be a hyperlink

A **hyperlink control** is a control on a form that when clicked works like a hyperlink to redirect the user to a webpage or file. You can convert a label control into a hyperlink label by modifying the label's **Hyperlink Address property**. Command button and image controls can also be used as hyperlinks. **CASE** ▸ *Aaron asks you to create hyperlinks to quickly open the R2G newsletter (a Word document) as well as the www.mapquest.com website from the Trip Entry form. You will create a hyperlink command button for each link.*

STEPS

1. **Right-click the TripEntry form in the Navigation Pane, then click Design View**
   You will add two new hyperlink controls in the Form Header, just to the left of the existing command buttons.

2. **Click the Button in the Controls group, click at about the 4.5" mark on the horizontal ruler in the Form Header section, then click Cancel to close the Command Button Wizard**
   You work with the command button's Property Sheet to modify it into a hyperlink control.

3. **Click the Property Sheet button to toggle open the Property Sheet if it is closed, click the Format tab in the Property Sheet if it is not already selected, select Command19 in the Caption property, type Mapquest, click the Hyperlink Address property, type http://www.mapquest.com, then press [Enter]**
   The command button's Property Sheet should look like FIGURE 15-4. Now you will add another command button hyperlink for the newsletter.

4. **Click the Button in the Controls group, click at about the 3" mark on the horizontal ruler in the Form Header section, then click Cancel to close the Command Button Wizard**

5. **In the Property Sheet for the new command button, select Command20 in the Caption property, type Newsletter, click the Hyperlink Address property, type Newsletter.docx, then press [Enter]**
   With the new hyperlink command buttons in place, you will align them for a more professional look.

6. **Click the Property Sheet button to close the Property Sheet, drag a selection box through all four command buttons in the Form Header section, click the Arrange tab on the Ribbon, click the Align button, then click Top to align the top edges of the four buttons, as shown in FIGURE 15-5**
   Test the hyperlinks in Form View.

7. **Right-click the TripEntry form tab, click Form View, click the Newsletter link, click Yes if prompted about unsafe content, close Word to return to Access, click the Mapquest link, close your browser to return to Access as shown in FIGURE 15-6, close the TripEntry form, then click Yes when prompted to save it**

FIGURE 15-4: Property Sheet for hyperlink command button

Property Sheet for Command Button control

Format tab

Caption property

Hyperlink Address property

Property Sheet
Selection type: Command Button

Command19

Format | Data | Event | Other | All

Caption	Mapquest
Picture Caption Arrangement	No Picture Caption
Visible	Yes
Picture Type	Embedded
Picture	(none)
Width	1"
Height	0.25"
Top	0.125"
Left	4.4583"
Back Style	Normal
Transparent	No
Use Theme	No
Back Color	Accent 1, Lighter 40%
Border Style	Solid
Border Width	Hairline
Border Color	Accent 1, Lighter 40%
Hover Color	#FFFFFF
Pressed Color	#FFFFFF
Hover Fore Color	#FFFFFF
Pressed Fore Color	#FFFFFF
Font Name	Calibri (Detail)
Font Size	11
Alignment	Center
Font Weight	Normal
Font Underline	Yes
Font Italic	No
Fore Color	Hyperlink Color
Hyperlink Address	http://www.mapquest.com
Hyperlink SubAddress	
Hyperlink Target	
Gridline Style Top	Transparent

FIGURE 15-5: Aligning new command buttons

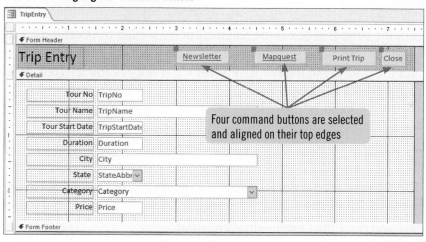

Four command buttons are selected and aligned on their top edges

FIGURE 15-6: TripEntry form with hyperlink command buttons

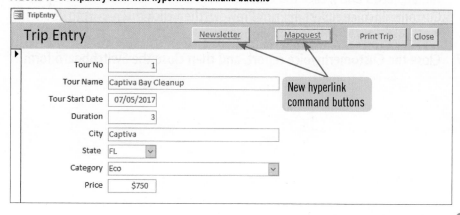

New hyperlink command buttons

Use HTML Tags to Format Text

HTML is the language used to describe content in a traditional webpage. HTML stands for **Hypertext Markup Language**. HTML **tags** are the codes used to identify or "mark up" the content in the page. Tags are entered into an HTML file in <angle brackets>, and many HTML tags are used in pairs to mark the beginning and end of the content they identify. For example, you would use the <b> tag to mark where bold starts. The same tag with a slash, </b>, marks where bold ends. See TABLE 15-1 for more examples of common HTML tags you can use with the Rich Text format. **Rich Text** is a Text Format property that allows you to mix formatting of text displayed by a text box on a form or a report. With a little bit of HTML knowledge, you can transform a large block of text on a report into a paragraph with multiple formatting embellishments. **CASE** ▶ *Aaron asks you to review the CustomerInvoice report. He wants you to format the payment disclaimer paragraph so it is more readable. You will use HTML tags to format the text.*

STEPS

1. **Double-click the Switchboard form to open it in Form View, click the FIND Customer Invoice combo box arrow, click the Alman, Jacob entry, click the Preview Invoice command button to open the Customer Invoice report in Print Preview, then click the report to zoom in on it**

   You want to better format the sentences in the large text box that starts with "Thank you for your order."

2. **Right-click the CustomerInvoice tab, then click Design View to open the report in Design View**

   The first step in formatting text in a text box is to change the Text Format property to Rich Text.

3. **Click the large text box in the SalesNo Footer section to select it, click the Property Sheet button to open the Property Sheet for the text box if it is not already visible, click the Data tab in the Property Sheet if it is not already selected, click the Text Format property, click the Text Format list arrow, then click Rich Text**

   With the Text Format property set to Rich Text, you can mark up the text with HTML tags.

4. **Edit the text box entry, as shown in FIGURE 15-7**

   Note that all HTML tags are surrounded by <angle brackets>. The beginning of the text to format is marked with an **opening tag** such as <b> for start bold. The end of the text to format is marked with a **closing tag**, which is identified with a forward slash such as </b> for end bold. **Empty tags** such as <br> are those that are a single tag, not paired.

5. **Save and close the CustomerInvoice report**

   Test the new Rich Text box with HTML formatting tags.

6. **On the Switchboard form, click the FIND Customer Invoice combo box arrow, click the Alman, Jacob entry, click the Preview Invoice command button to open the CustomerInvoice report in Print Preview, then click the report to zoom in**

   The final report should look like FIGURE 15-8.

7. **Close the CustomerInvoice report, and then close the Switchboard form**

FIGURE 15-7: Using HTML tags to format Rich Text

="<font size=6><b>Thank you for your order.</font></b>

 Payment Notes: 10% deposit is due at time of booking.

<i> 50%, nonrefundable deposit is due two weeks prior to departure date.</i>

 <font color=red> The full balance is due 2 days prior to departure date.</font>"

HTML tags must be entered precisely as shown

FIGURE 15-8: Formatted CustomerInvoice report

Customer Invoice

There is a ....

reason to go!

Invoice No: 34

Invoice Date: 6/30/2017

Jacob Alman   (555) 111-6931
2505 McGee St
Des Moines, IA 50288

Trip Number	Trip Name	Trip Start Date	Duration	Destination City	State	Price
2	Red Reef Cleanup	07/05/2017	3	Islamadora	FL	$1,500

Thank you for your order.

Payment Notes: 10% deposit is due at time of booking.

50%, nonrefundable deposit is due two weeks prior to departure date.

The full balance is due 2 days prior to departure date.

Rich Text formatted with HTML tags

TABLE 15-1: Common HTML tags

HTML tag	description	example
p	paragraph	<p>The p tag marks the beginning and ending of a paragraph of text. </p>
br	Marks a line break	 or (*Note:* The br tag is not a paired tag. One single tag creates the line break. Unpaired tags are also called empty tags.)
b	Marks the beginning and end of bold text	We <b>**appreciate**</b> your business.
i	Marks the beginning and end of italic text	Product may be returned for a full refund <i>*within 30 days.*</i>
code	Marks the beginning and end of monospaced text	<code>`Terms and Conditions`</code>
font	Identifies the color, font face, and size of the marked content	<font color=red>Merry Christmas!</font> <font font_family=Arial>Purchase Order</font> <font size=16>Inventory Report</font>

HTML5

HTML5 is the latest version of HTML as defined by the leading international standards committee on fundamental web technologies, the **W3C**, or **World Wide Web Consortium**, at www.w3c.org. HTML5 has **deprecated** (retired due to new, better technologies) the HTML <font> tag in favor of a much more powerful, flexible, and productive way to define webpage formatting and presentation called **CSS, Cascading Style Sheets**. Therefore, it would not be appropriate or professional to use the HTML font tag in traditional webpage development. Given that there is no current way to apply CSS technology to a Rich Text control in an Access form or report, however, the HTML formatting tags such as <font> still have a meaningful role for this situation.

Export to HTML and XML

Learning Outcomes
- Export data to HTML
- Export data to XML
- Compare HTML and XML files

Given the widespread use of the web to share information, you may want to export Access data to a format that works well with existing web technologies. For example, you might want to view data stored in an Access database using a common browser such as Firefox, Chrome, or Edge. Access allows you to export data to two common web-related formats: HTML and XML. Recall that HTML files are webpages that use HTML tags to mark up content stored in the file. **XML**, short for **Extensible Markup Language**, is a language used to mark up structured data so that the data can be more easily shared between different computer programs. The process of exporting a report to an HTML or XML file is very similar. **CASE** > *You use Access to export data to both an HTML file as well as an XML file to compare them.*

STEPS

TROUBLE
Click the More button in the Export group and not in the Import & Link group.

1. **Click the Customers table in the Navigation Pane, click the External Data tab, click the More button in the Export group, then click HTML Document**

   The Export - HTML Document dialog box opens, prompting you for a name and location of the HTML file it is about to create, as shown in FIGURE 15-9.

TROUBLE
If prompted with more than one option to open the HTML file, choose any current browser. You may also have to switch to the browser window to see the Customers .html file.

2. **Click the Export data with formatting and layout check box, click the Open the destination file after the export option is complete check box, click Browse, navigate to where you store your Data Files, click Save in the File Save dialog box, click OK in the Export - HTML Document dialog box, then click OK in the HTML Output Options dialog box**

   The webpage created by the export process automatically opens in the program that is associated with the HTML file extension, which is probably your default browser, such as Edge, Chrome, or Firefox. An HTML file format works well when you want to present the information as a webpage for a human to read. If you want to pass the data to another program, however, the XML file format does a better job of describing the individual fields of data for a program to read.

TROUBLE
Be sure to click the XML File button in the Export group and not in the Import & Link group.

3. **Close the window with the Customers.html file to return to Access, click Close in the Export - HTML Document dialog box if it is not already closed, click the Trips table in the Navigation Pane, click the XML File button in the Export group, click Browse, navigate to where you store your Data Files, click Save in the File Save dialog box, click OK, click OK in the Export XML dialog box, then click Close in the Export - XML File dialog box**

   The Export - XML File dialog box doesn't have an option to automatically open the exported XML file, but you can find and double-click the Trips.xml file to review its contents.

TROUBLE
If you are prompted to select a program, choose Notepad.

4. **Start File Explorer or Windows Explorer, navigate to where you store your Data Files, then double-click the Trips.xml file to open it**

   Trips.xml opens in the program associated with the .xml file extension as shown in FIGURE 15-10. This is a good choice when your goal is to share data between programs because XML files separate and describe the raw data in one file (**XML**), place a description of the data's characteristics into another file (**XSD**), and place an optional description of how the data should be formatted into a third file (**XSL**).

5. **Close the Trips.xml file and return to Access**

   The decision on which file format to choose when exporting Access data is dictated by the needs of the person or program that is receiving the file. You can export Access data just as easily to an HTML or XML file format as you previously experienced with other common file formats, such as Excel and PDF in Module 9.

FIGURE 15-9: Export - HTML Document dialog box

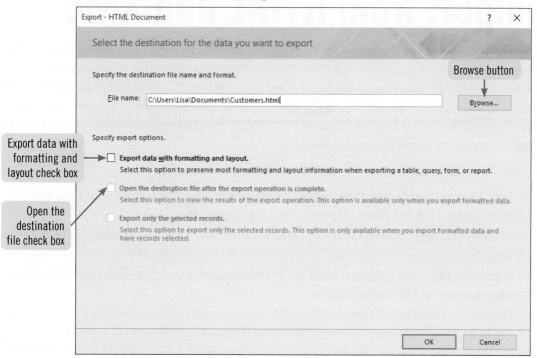

Browse button

Export data with formatting and layout check box

Open the destination file check box

FIGURE 15-10: Trips.xml file

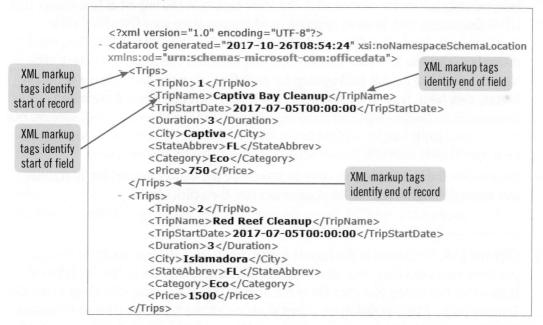

XML markup tags identify start of record

XML markup tags identify start of field

XML markup tags identify end of field

XML markup tags identify end of record

XML, XSD, and XSL files

When you export data as an XML file, you are prompted to export two helper files, XSD and XSL. The **XSD** file stores the schema of data stored in the XML file. The **schema** of the data is a description of the fields and their properties. The **XSL** file describes how to display an XML file. Therefore, if you're using the XML file to pass data from one computer application to another, the XSD file provides information about the data types and properties that can be used to describe and ensure the integrity of the data. The XSL file isn't used to pass data from one computer to another, but if you want to retain any styles or formatting information, include an XSL file in the export.

Import from HTML and XML

Learning Outcomes
• Import data from HTML
• Import data from XML

Importing brings data into the database from an external file. You can import data directly from an HTML file provided the data is structured in the HTML file with HTML table tags so that Access knows where each field and record starts and stops. If the data is stored in an XML file, it is by definition already structured into fields and records with XML tags. **CASE** *You use Access import features to import new customer data from an HTML file that the Marketing Department created. You also import new Trip data from an XML file that the Information Systems Department created.*

STEPS

1. **Start File Explorer or Windows Explorer, navigate to where you store your Data Files, then double-click the NewCustomers.html file to open it**

   The NewCustomers.html file opens in the program associated with viewing HTML files, which is probably a browser as shown in **FIGURE 15-11**. View the HTML stored in the page to see how the data is structured.

   > **TROUBLE**
   > The Developer Tools window is also commonly docked on the bottom of the screen.

2. **Right-click the NewCustomers.html file in the browser, then click View source (or View page source) on the shortcut menu**

   The NewCustomers.html file opens in the program associated with creating and editing HTML files, which may be a text editor program such as Notepad or the Developer Tools window, as shown in **FIGURE 15-12**. HTML table tags separate the data using HTML **tr** tags to separate the records and **td** tags to separate each field. HTML table tags are further described in **TABLE 15-2**.

   > **TROUBLE**
   > Be sure to click the More button in the Import & Link group and not in the Export group.

3. **Close all windows that display the NewCustomers.html file to return to Access, click the External Data tab on the Ribbon, click the More button in the Import & Link group, click HTML Document, click Browse, navigate to where you store your Data Files, click NewCustomers.html, click Open, click OK in the Get External Data - HTML Document dialog box, click the First Row Contains Column Headings check box, click Next, click Next to accept the default field options for each field, click the No primary key option button, click Next, type NewCustomers, click Finish, then click Close if prompted**

   The records in the NewCustomers.html file are imported to a new Access table named NewCustomers. That gives you the ability to view the imported data in Access to make sure the import was successful and then use an Append query to combine the records from the imported table to an existing table.

4. **Double-click the NewCustomers table to make sure the import process for 10 records was successful, right-click the NewCustomers tab, then click Close**

   Confident that the data in the HTML file was successfully imported into the Access database as a new table, you import the XML file.

   > **TROUBLE**
   > Be sure to click the XML File button in the Import & Link group and not in the Export group.

5. **Click the XML File button in the Import & Link group, click Browse, navigate to where you store your Data Files, click NewTrips.xml, click Open, click OK in the Get External Data – XML File dialog box, click OK in the Import XML dialog box, click Close in the Get External Data - XML File dialog box, then double-click the NewTrips table to make sure that the seven new trip records were imported successfully**

   The NewTrips.xml data imported successfully. Switch to Design View to see more information about each field.

6. **Right-click the NewTrips tab, then click Design View**

   The TripNo and Duration fields were created as Number fields, the NewTripStartDate field was created with a Date/Time data type, and the Price field has a Currency data type. The import process made these intelligent choices because of the information about the fields stored in the schema file, the XSD file.

7. **Right-click the NewTrips tab, then click Close**

FIGURE 15-11: NewCustomers.html file opened in a browser

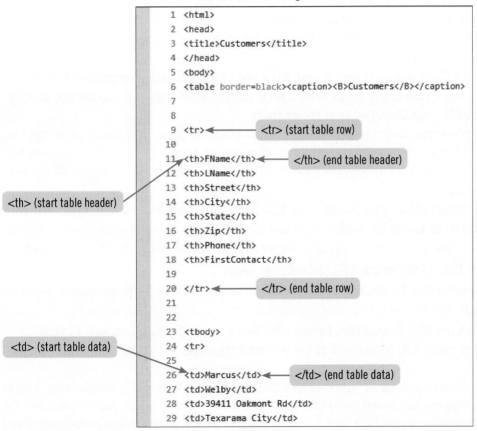

FIGURE 15-12: NewCustomers.html tags

```
 1  <html>
 2  <head>
 3  <title>Customers</title>
 4  </head>
 5  <body>
 6  <table border=black><caption><B>Customers</B></caption>
 7
 8
 9  <tr>
10
11  <th>FName</th>
12  <th>LName</th>
13  <th>Street</th>
14  <th>City</th>
15  <th>State</th>
16  <th>Zip</th>
17  <th>Phone</th>
18  <th>FirstContact</th>
19
20  </tr>
21
22
23  <tbody>
24  <tr>
25
26  <td>Marcus</td>
27  <td>Welby</td>
28  <td>39411 Oakmont Rd</td>
29  <td>Texarama City</td>
```

- <tr> (start table row) → line 9
- </th> (end table header) → line 11
- <th> (start table header) → line 11
- </tr> (end table row) → line 20
- <td> (start table data) → line 26
- </td> (end table data) → line 26

TABLE 15-2: HTML table tags

tag	description
<table> </table>	Marks the beginning and end of the entire table
<tr> </tr>	Marks the beginning and end of a table row (a table row in HTML becomes a table record in Access)
<th> </th>	Marks the beginning and end of a table header entry (a table header entry in HTML becomes a field name in Access)
<td> </td>	Marks the beginning and end of a table data entry (a table data entry in HTML becomes a field value in Access)

Save and Share a Database with OneDrive

Learning Outcomes
• Create a OneDrive folder
• Save a database to OneDrive
• Share a database from OneDrive

OneDrive is a cloud-based storage and file-sharing service provided by Microsoft. Saving files to OneDrive means that you can access those files from any computer connected to the Internet. You can also share the files with other people or create **shared folders** in your OneDrive to organize shared files. OneDrive is particularly helpful to students who work on many different computers. The shared file and folder feature is very useful to anyone who works on group projects in which the same file or files need to be constantly accessible to several team members. **CASE** ▶ *Aaron Scout asks you to create a folder on your OneDrive to save and share the R2G-15 database.*

STEPS

TROUBLE
You must be signed in to your Microsoft account to access your OneDrive. See the "Getting Started with Microsoft Office 2016" module. If you do not see OneDrive in Step 1, continue to Step 2 to access it directly and sign in.

1. **Click the File tab on the Ribbon, click Save As, click the Save As button, click OneDrive in the left pane or navigate to your OneDrive, then click Save**

   A copy of the R2G-15.accdb database can be saved to your personal OneDrive if it is available in the Save As dialog box. OneDrive works just like your hard drive but is available to you on any computer connected to the Internet.

2. **Close the R2G-15 database and Access 2016, start Microsoft Edge or another browser, type OneDrive.com in the Address box, press [Enter], then sign in if you are not already connected to your OneDrive.com server space**

   The contents of your OneDrive appear. From here, you can upload, delete, move, download, or copy files, similarly to how you work with files on your local computer. You want to share the R2G-15 database with your instructor. You decide to first create a folder for the database. That way, your OneDrive will stay more organized.

QUICK TIP
You can use OneDrive to create Word, Excel, PowerPoint, and OneNote files. See the "Getting Started with Microsoft Office 2016" module.

3. **Click the New button, click Folder, type R2G Shared Files as the new folder name, then press [Enter] to create the folder, as shown in FIGURE 15-13**

   Now you're ready to open the R2G Shared Files folder and then upload the R2G-15 database file into it.

4. **Drag the R2G-15 file to the R2G Shared Files folder**

   With the R2G-15 database stored in an appropriate folder on the OneDrive, you're now ready to invite your instructor to share it.

5. **Right-click the R2G Shared Files folder, click Share, enter the email address of your instructor, enter R2G Module 15 as the personal message, then click Share as shown in FIGURE 15-14**

   To review the share permissions, right-click the R2G-15 file and click Share on the shortcut menu. A list of the individuals who have permission to view and or edit the file is listed on the left, and you can modify the permissions or delete people from the list. You can also share the entire folder, which automatically shares all files stored in that folder.

6. **Click Close, then close the OneDrive.com browser window**

FIGURE 15-13: Creating an R2G Shared Files folder

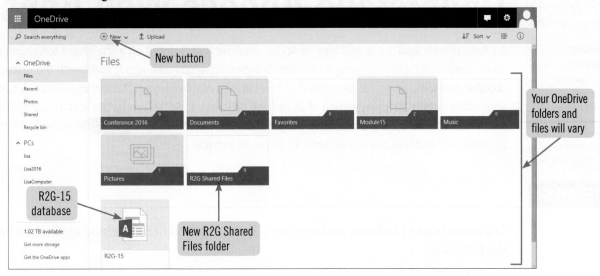

FIGURE 15-14: Sharing a OneDrive folder

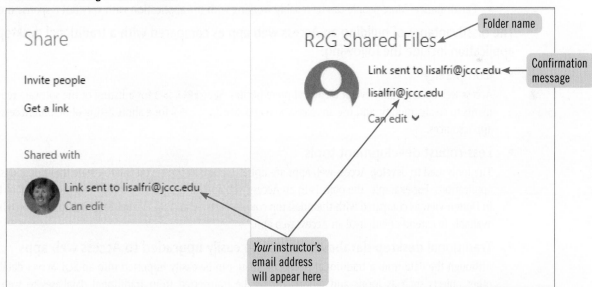

Understand Access Web Apps

Learning
Outcomes
• Describe the
advantages and
disadvantages of
an Access web app
• Define the software
requirements for
an Access web app

An **Access web app** is a special type of Access database that is stored on a SharePoint server and allows users to enter and edit data using a common browser. An Access web app is saved with the extension of **.accdw**. See TABLE 15-3 for a description of the software requirements to create and use an Access web app, which include a current version of SharePoint, SQL Server, Access, and a browser. FIGURE 15-15 shows how those software tools are used to develop and use an Access web app. **CASE** ▶ *Aaron Scout asks you to review the benefits of and requirements for an Access web app.*

DETAILS

The advantages of building an Access web app over a traditional desktop application include the following:

- **Access is not required for the user**

  A copy of Microsoft Access on each client computer is not required for each user. An Access web app is available to any user with a current browser.

- **A local connection to the database is not required for each user**

  An Access web app is available to any user with an Internet connection.

- **Access web app data is stored in a back-end SQL Server database**

  Storing data in SQL Server tables versus embedded Access tables provides these benefits:
  - **User-level security:** The data is more secure because it can be password protected at a user level.
  - **Scalability:** Much larger amounts of data can be stored and managed.
  - **Performance:** More people can be reliably working with the application with very fast response times.

The disadvantages of building an Access web app as compared with a traditional desktop application include the following:

- **Complexity**

  Access web apps require several technical prerequisites. See TABLE 15-3 for a listing of the software requirements to create, modify, and use an Access web app. See TABLE 15-4 for a short listing of helpful Access web app resources.

- **Less-robust development tools**

  The tools used to develop Access web apps are not as mature as those you use to create traditional desktop applications. For example, the objects in an Access web app do not provide a full set of development tools in Design View as compared with their desktop counterparts. Also, VBA (Visual Basic for Applications) is not available to extend or enhance an Access web app.

- **Traditional desktop databases cannot be easily upgraded to Access web apps**

  Although the data from a traditional Access database can be easily imported into an SQL Server database, other objects such as forms and reports cannot be transferred from traditional databases to web app applications.

  In conclusion, Access web apps are a powerful new tool to deploy Access database applications across the Internet. By marrying the fast, easy application developments of Microsoft Access with the power, speed, and ubiquity of SQL Server and the Internet, Access web apps provide a fast way to deploy secure relational database applications across the Internet.

FIGURE 15-15: Software required to develop and use an Access web app

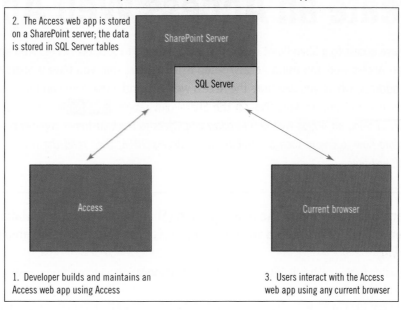

2. The Access web app is stored on a SharePoint server; the data is stored in SQL Server tables

SharePoint Server

SQL Server

Access

Current browser

1. Developer builds and maintains an Access web app using Access

3. Users interact with the Access web app using any current browser

TABLE 15-3: Software required to create, modify, and use an Access web app

software	description
SharePoint	An Access web app is deployed to a file server loaded with SharePoint. **SharePoint** is a Microsoft software product that is loaded on a file server to help a company organize and share files and data across its business. SharePoint can be purchased separately and is also included in the Microsoft Office 365 Small Business Premium and Office 365 Enterprise plans.
SQL Server	**SQL Server** is a Microsoft software product used to store and manage a relational database. All Access web apps use SQL Server to manage the data. No tables are created or managed by Access.
Access	Access is required to make modifications to Access web apps.
Web browser	A browser is required for users to view and enter data into an Access web app.

TABLE 15-4: Reference material for Access web apps

type of resource	title	author	location
Article	Create an Access App	Microsoft	https://support.office.com/en-gb/Article/ Create-an-Access-app-25f3ab3e-510d-44b0-accf-b976c0813e71 (or search for this article by title on support.office.com)
Article	New in Access for Developers	Microsoft	http://msdn.microsoft.com/en-us/library/office/jj250134.aspx (or search for this article by title on microsoft.com)

Create an Access Web App

Learning Outcome
• Create an Access web app

If you have access to a SharePoint server that is configured to support Access web apps, you can quickly create an Access web app using Access. Setup issues require that you have a SharePoint server location (a web address) where you will store the Access web app and a username and password that has already been given permission to save files on the SharePoint server. **CASE** *Aaron asks you to explore the possibility of using an Access web app to allow employees to track customer comments, concerns, and issues. You explore how to create such a database using Access 2016, then read the rest of the process from the Microsoft website.*

STEPS

QUICK TIP
The template icons with a globe in the background are web app templates.

1. **Start Access 2016, click the Issue tracking (SharePoint web app) database template, then click OK if prompted with an error message about not being able to connect to a server**

   The Issue tracking (SharePoint web app) template information window opens, as shown in FIGURE 15-16, to provide a quick preview of what types of tables the template will create (Issues, Customers, and Employees) and what the List View for the Issues table will look like. Note that SharePoint is required and that you can customize the web app after it is created. You are also prompted for an App Name and web location.

TROUBLE
If you do not have access to a SharePoint server, close the Issue tracking window and continue to Step 5.

2. **Type Customer Feedback as the App Name, enter the web location of your SharePoint server in the SharePoint or Office 365 site URL box, click Create, then enter your username and password when prompted**

   Access and SharePoint work together to create the web app. Three tables—Issues, Customers, and Employees—are created automatically. Two **views** (called forms in a traditional desktop database) of each table, named **List** and **Datasheet**, are also automatically created to give you a fast way to quickly enter and edit data.

3. **Close Access 2016, open Edge or another browser, enter the web location for your new Access web app, then enter your username and password when prompted**

TROUBLE
Access templates including web apps often change. You may have to navigate through the app to find the Customers table.

4. **Click the Customers table in the Navigation Pane, enter your name and fictitious but realistic data for the rest of the record, click the Save button, then click the Datasheet button to observe your new record in that view**

   At this point, you could continue to enter data into one of the three tables using either the List or Datasheet views created by the Issue tracking web app template. To modify the interface (the views), however, you have to download the web app and open it in Access.

5. **Go to http://msdn.microsoft.com/en-us/library/office/jj249372.aspx or go to www.microsoft.com and search for how to create a web app in Access**

TROUBLE
Although the article is for Access 2013, the information is still helpful for Access 2016.

6. **Read the Microsoft article about how to create and customize an Access web app, as shown in FIGURE 15-17**

7. **Close your browser and Access 2016 if it is still open.**

FIGURE 15-16: Issue tracking web app template information window

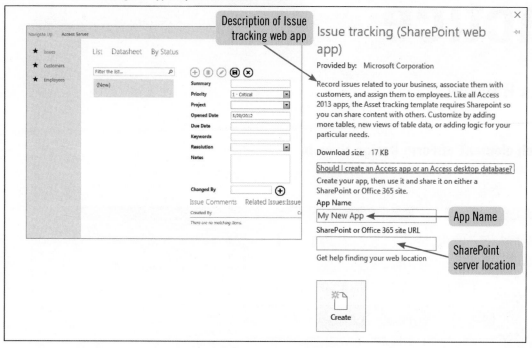

FIGURE 15-17: How to: Create and customize a web app in Access article

Practice

Concepts Review

Identify each element of Form Design View in FIGURE 15-18.

FIGURE 15-18

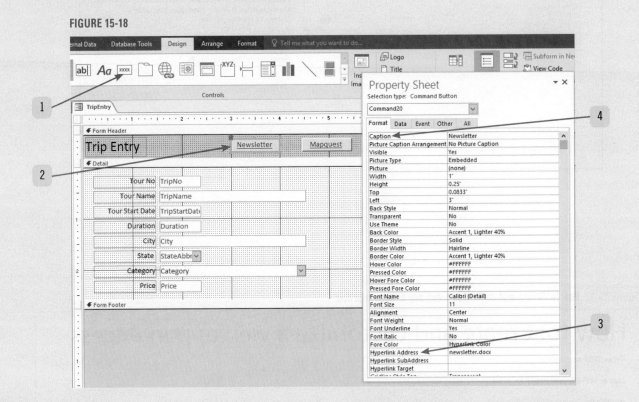

Match each term with the statement that best describes its function.

5. OneDrive
6. SQL Server
7. Access web app
8. Hyperlink data type
9. XML
10. HTML

a. The language used to describe content in a traditional webpage
b. A cloud-based storage and file-sharing service
c. Used to store a link to a webpage or file
d. A language used to mark up structured data
e. A Microsoft relational database management program
f. A special type of Access database that is stored on a SharePoint server

Select the best answer from the list of choices.

11. **If you wanted to create a field that stored email addresses, which data type would work best?**
    a. Hyperlink
    b. Short Text
    c. Long Text
    d. Memo

12. **Which of the following is not used to work with Access web apps?**
    a. SharePoint Server
    b. Access
    c. SQL Server
    d. All are used.

Using Access and the Web

13. **Where is an Access web app stored?**
   a. On a SharePoint server
   b. In the Downloads folder on your local hard drive
   c. In the Data Files folder on your local hard drive
   d. In a OneDrive folder

14. **What is the HTML tag to create a line break?**
   a. <cf>
   b. <break>
   c. <lf>
   d.

15. **Which HTML tags would you use to identify the start and end of a paragraph?**
   a. <p> </p>
   b.
   c.
   d. <start text> </end text>

16. **Which of the following form controls is not a common candidate for a hyperlink?**
   a. Image
   b. Combo box
   c. Command button
   d. Label

17. **What are forms called in an Access web app?**
   a. Layouts
   b. Views
   c. Tables
   d. Reports

18. **Where is data stored in an Access web app?**
   a. Access tables
   b. OneDrive folders
   c. SQL Server tables
   d. XML files

19. **Which of the following is not a reason to use OneDrive?**
   a. To access your files from any computer connected to the Internet
   b. To deploy an Access web app
   c. To share files with others
   d. To eliminate the problems associated with losing a flash drive

20. **HTML tags are also called:**
   a. Selectors
   b. Properties
   c. Attributes
   d. Elements

Skills Review

1. **Create a hyperlink field.**
   a. Start Access, open the Basketball-15.accdb database from where you store your Data Files, and enable content if prompted.
   b. Open the tblGames table and add two fields, each with a Hyperlink data type: **SchoolWebSite** and **Logo**.
   c. Save the tblGames table and switch to Datasheet View. Enter a new record with *your* school name in the Opponent field, **Cardinals** in the Mascot field, **H** in the Home-Away field, no scores, and today's date in the GameDate field. Enter the webpage address for *your* school's home page in the SchoolWebSite field. Browse for the file named **Cardinals.png** where you store your Data Files, then insert it in the Logo field.
   d. Click both hyperlinks to test that they locate and display the desired resource. The SchoolWebSite hyperlink should open a browser that takes you to the home page for your school. The Cardinals.png hyperlink should display the Cardinals.png image.
   e. Close the tblGames table.

2. **Create a hyperlink control.**
   a. Open the frmPlayerInformation form in Form Design View, then open the Form Header section by dragging the top edge of the Detail section down about 0.5".
   b. Add a command button to the left side of the Form Header section, then cancel the Command Button Wizard.

Skills Review (continued)

c. Open the Property Sheet for the new command button and make these property modifications:

Caption: **ESPN**

Hyperlink Address: **http://www.espn.com**

d. Add a second command button on the right side of the Form Header section, then cancel the Command Button Wizard.

e. In the Property Sheet for the new command button, make these property modifications:

Caption: **Point Production**

Hyperlink Address: Click the Build button, click Object in This Database on the left, expand the Reports section on the right, click rptPointProduction, then click OK. (*Note:* You can also directly type **Report rptPointProduction** in the Hyperlink SubAddress property.)

f. Save the frmPlayerInformation form, test both of the new command buttons in Form View, close the ESPN webpage, close the rptPointProduction report, then close the frmPlayerInformation form.

3. Use HTML tags to format text.

a. Right-click the rptCodeOfConduct report, then click Print Preview to review the Player Code of Conduct. Although this is an unbound report (it does not display data from the database and the Record Source property is blank), you want to keep the information in the Basketball-15 database.

b. Switch to Report Design View, select the text box that contains the code of conduct text, then change the Text Format property to **Rich Text**.

c. Use HTML tags to format the report as follows:

- Increase the size of the Player Code of Conduct title with the font tag: **<font size=8>**Player Code of Conduct**</font>**

- Increase the size of four introductory phrases with the font tags:
  - **<font size=6>** As a college player, I recognize that: **</font>**
  - **<font size=6>** I therefore pledge that: **</font>**
  - **<font size=6>** I understand that: **</font>**
  - **<font size=6>** The consequences for any such behavior could be: **</font>**

- Add two line breaks to create spaces between the lines with two line break tags at the end of every line or sentence: **

**

- Format Player Name in red, bold text with the font tags: **<font color=red><b>**Player Name**</b></font>**

d. Save and preview the rptCodeOfConduct report, as shown in **FIGURE 15-19**.

e. Close the rptCodeOfConduct report.

4. Export to HTML and XML.

a. Select the tblPlayers table in the Navigation Pane, then export it to an HTML document named **Players.html** in the location where you store your Data Files.

b. Select the qryFieldGoalStats query, then export it to an XML document named **FieldGoals.xml** in the location where you store your Data Files. Export both the XML and XSD files.

FIGURE 15-19

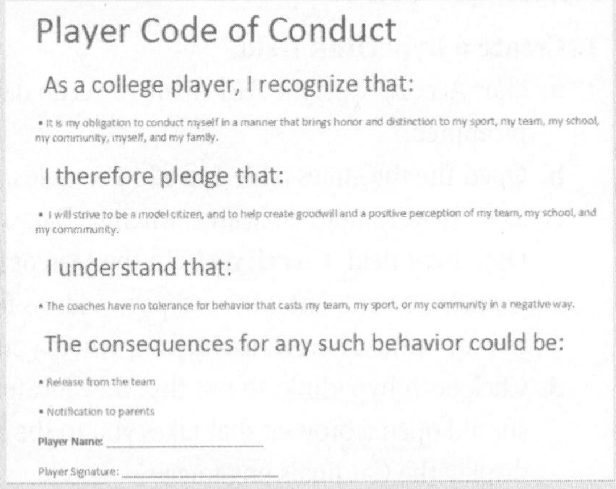

Player Code of Conduct

As a college player, I recognize that:

- It is my obligation to conduct myself in a manner that brings honor and distinction to my sport, my team, my school, my community, myself, and my family.

I therefore pledge that:

- I will strive to be a model citizen, and to help create goodwill and a positive perception of my team, my school, and my community.

I understand that:

- The coaches have no tolerance for behavior that casts my team, my sport, or my community in a negative way.

The consequences for any such behavior could be:

- Release from the team
- Notification to parents

Player Name: _____

Player Signature: _____

5. Import from HTML and XML.

a. Import the NextSeason.html file into the database. The first row does *not* contain column headings.

b. In the Import HTML Wizard, use the Field Name box in the Field Options area to rename Field1 through Field4: **Opponent**, **Mascot**, **HomeOrAway**, and **GameDate**. Let Access add the primary key, then import the data to a new table named **tblNextSeason**.

c. Import the NewPlayers.xml file into the database.

d. After Access imports the data into a table named tblPlayers1, rename the tblPlayers1 table to **tblNewPlayers**.

Skills Review (continued)

6. **Save and share a database with OneDrive.**

   a. Save the Basketball-15.accdb database to your OneDrive using the Save As option on the File tab or by going directly to the OneDrive through a browser (see Step b).

   b. Close Access, open Edge or another browser, then go to **www.onedrive.com** and sign in as needed.

   c. Create a new folder named **Module15** in OneDrive, then move the Basketball-15.accdb database to the Module15 folder. (*Hint*: Be sure Access is closed. Closing Access guarantees that the local Basketball-15.accdb database is closed on your machine, which impacts how it is handled by OneDrive.)

   d. Share the Module15 folder with your instructor, using your instructor's email address. Type **Module 15 Basketball** for the message.

   e. Close the browser, close the Basketball-15.accdb database, then exit Access 2016 if it is still open.

7. **Understand Access web apps.**

   a. Start Word and open the Module15SkillsReview.docx document from the location where you store your Data Files.

   b. Complete the header information to identify your name, the current date, the class, and the instructor's name.

   c. Respond to the following three instructions in the document using complete sentences, proper grammar, and spelling.

      1. Briefly describe the difference between the purpose for an Access web app and an Access traditional desktop database.

      2. Briefly describe the different software requirements for an Access web app and an Access traditional desktop database.

      3. Why do you think Microsoft uses the word desktop to describe traditional Access databases?

   d. Save the document, close it, then close Word 2016.

8. **Create an Access web app.**

   a. Start Access 2016 and click the Contacts (SharePoint web app) template. (*Note*: If you do not have access to a SharePoint server, watch a video that demonstrates Step 8 by going to www.youtube.com or www.microsoft.com and searching for a video that shows how to create an Access web app. The resources you find may reference Access 2013 instead of Access 2016, but web apps work essentially the same in those two versions of Access.)

   b. Enter **Alumni Contacts** as the App Name, enter your SharePoint server web location, then click Create.

   c. Enter *your* username and password as prompted.

   d. Click the Contacts table icon on the left, click the Navigation Pane button, then double-click the Contacts table.

   e. Add a field named **Pledge** with a Currency data type to the end of the field list, then save and close the table.

   f. Click the Launch App button to view the Access web app in your browser and sign in if prompted. Enter *your* information in the First Name, Last Name, and Email fields. Enter realistic but fictitious information in the other fields. Enter **5000** in the Pledge field, then click the Save button.

   g. Close the browser, then close Access 2016.

Independent Challenge 1

As the manager of a doctor's clinic, you have created an Access database called Insurance-15.accdb to track insurance information. You need to create two hyperlink fields to reference the patient's employer and insurance company. You also want to add some hyperlink command buttons to a form to link the form to medical reference guides on the web.

   a. Start Access 2016, then open the Insurance-15.accdb database from where you store your Data Files. Enable content if prompted.

   b. Open the tblPatients table in Design View. Add the following two new fields at the bottom of the list, each with the Hyperlink data type: **Employer**, **Insurance**.

   c. Save the tblPatients table, then switch to Datasheet View. Enter **http://www.iastate.edu** for the Employer field in the first record for PatientSequence 20. Enter **http://www.bcbs.com** for the Insurance field for PatientSequence 20.

Independent Challenge 1 (continued)

d. Enter *your* school's website address in the Employer field for the second record for PatientSequence 21. Research and enter the website address for a common health insurance company in your state in the Insurance field. (*Note*: Copying website addresses from documents and pasting them into the datasheet can lead to inconsistent address results. Be sure to enter the complete website address into the field from the keyboard starting with http:// to ensure consistent results.)

e. Test all four hyperlinks to make sure they work correctly, close all browser windows to return to Access, then save and close the tblPatients table.

f. Open frmClaimEntryForm in Design View, then add a command button to the upper-right corner of the Form Header. (See **FIGURE 15-20** for the button placement.) The Hyperlink Address property for the button should be **http://www.bcbs.com**. The Caption property should be **Blue Cross**.

g. Add a second command button to the upper-right corner of the Form Header section. The Hyperlink Address property for the button should be **https://www.humana.com**. The Caption property should be **Humana**.

h. Save frmClaimEntryForm, then test both of your new hyperlink command buttons as shown in **FIGURE 15-20**.

i. Close all browser windows and return to Access, close the Insurance-15 database, then close Access 2016.

FIGURE 15-20

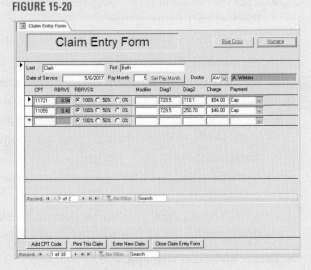

Independent Challenge 2

As the manager of a doctor's clinic, you have created an Access database called Insurance-15.accdb. You are in the process of expanding the database to include information about employees. One of the first documents a new employee must read and sign is the Employee Pledge, which you have partially completed and stored as an Access report. Your employer wants you to format certain words with red and bold text. You use a Rich Text format and HTML tags to format the pledge.

a. Open the Insurance-15.accdb database from the location where you store your Data Files, then enable content if prompted.

b. In the Navigation Pane, double-click the rptPledge report to open it in Report View. Open the rptPledge report in Report Design View, select the large text box in the Detail section, open the Property Sheet, then change the Text Format property on the Data tab to **Rich Text**.

c. Use HTML tags as follows to format and space the following phrases with red, bold text and line breaks:

To the best of my ability, I pledge to:**

**

arrive and begin work **<font color=red>**on time**</font>

**

focus on my work and the **<font color=red>**patients while on the job**</font>

**

maintain a **<font color=red>**positive attitude**</font>

**

continue to **<font color=red>**learn and improve**</font>

**

be **<font color=red>**honest and trustworthy **</font>

**

treat everyone with **<font color=red>**respect**</font>

**

limit all personal communication to a minimum while on the job**

**

follow the law and regulations**

**

<b> not complain about the job I agreed to take**</b>

**

Signature: _____ **

**

Independent Challenge 2 (continued)

d. Save and preview the rptPledge report, as shown in FIGURE 15-21. Switch between Report Design View and Print Preview as needed to perfect the report.

e. Close the rptPledge report, close the Insurance-15 database, then close Access 2016.

FIGURE 15-21

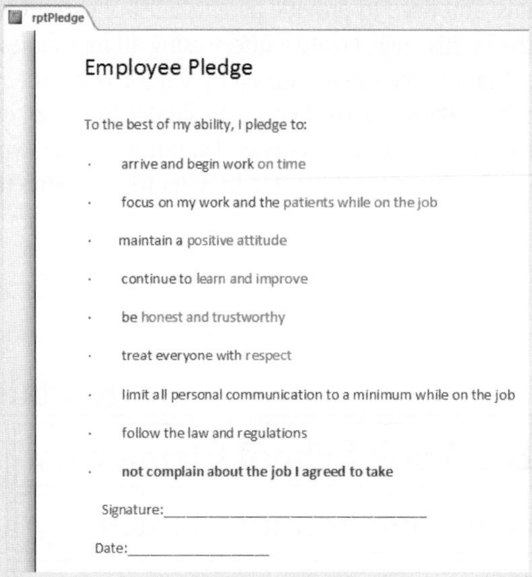

Employee Pledge

To the best of my ability, I pledge to:

· arrive and begin work on time

· focus on my work and the patients while on the job

· maintain a positive attitude

· continue to learn and improve

· be honest and trustworthy

· treat everyone with respect

· limit all personal communication to a minimum while on the job

· follow the law and regulations

· **not complain about the job I agreed to take**

Signature:_____

Date:_____

Independent Challenge 3

In this exercise, you will create a OneDrive folder and share all of the databases you used to complete the end-of-module exercises for Module 15 with your instructor.

a. Open a browser window, then open your OneDrive folder by going to **www.onedrive.com**.

b. If you completed all steps of the Skills Review, you have already created a OneDrive folder named Module15 and shared it with your instructor. If that is the case, add the Insurance-15.accdb database to the shared Module15 folder using the OneDrive Upload button.

c. If you have not completed all of the steps of the Skills Review, complete Skills Review Step 6 to create the shared OneDrive Module15 folder with the Basketball-15.accdb database. After you have completed Independent Challenges 1 and 2, add the Insurance-15.accdb database to the shared Module15 folder.

d. After you have completed Independent Challenge 4, add the WebBasedBenefits document to the shared Module15 folder.

e. After you have completed the Visual Workshop, add the Music-15.accdb file to the shared Module15 folder.

f. Close the browser window that displays your OneDrive.

Independent Challenge 4: Explore

Developing software solutions in a proprietary technology such as Microsoft Access is a simpler, faster solution for the developer because he or she only has to work with one software product for both the developer and user. As soon as an application is deployed to the Internet, the work becomes more difficult because multiple software products are typically involved. To create and deploy an Access web app, for example, the developer needs Access, SharePoint, SQL Server, and a web browser. However, there are also many benefits to making your application web accessible. In this exercise, you'll research the web to document five benefits of web-based applications.

a. Using a browser and your favorite search engine, search for **benefits of web-based applications**.

b. In a Word document, enter your name and the current date on the first line. Below your name, create a table with three columns and six rows. Enter these column headings in the first row: **Benefit**, **Description**, **Source**.

c. Complete the table with five more rows that identify and describe five benefits of a web-based application over a traditional desktop Access database application. In the first column, identify the benefit. In the second column, briefly describe the benefit using one to two sentences. In the third column, copy and paste the web address of the source you are citing for that benefit. The five benefits should reference at least three different sources.

d. Save your document with the name **WebBasedBenefits** to the location where you save your Data Files, and then close Word.

Visual Workshop

As the manager of a music store, you have created an Access database called Music-15.accdb that tracks musical instrument rentals. You need to provide parents a list of current rentals posted as a webpage, a portion of which is shown in FIGURE 15-22. To create this page, create a query using all four tables in the database to select the fields in the order shown in the webpage. Note that the records are sorted by SchoolName, then by LastName, then by SerialNo. Save the query with the name **RentalsBySchool**. Export the RentalsBySchool query with the name **RentalsBySchool.html** to the location where you store your Data Files. Do not select the Export data with formatting and layout check box. Open the RentalsBySchool.html file in a browser to make sure that the export was successful.

FIGURE 15-22

RentalsBySchool

Blackbob School Elementary	Eagan	55442	Viola
Blackbob School Elementary	Eagan	7714	Clarinet
Blackbob School Elementary	Eagan	7715	Clarinet
Blackbob School Elementary	Eagan	90	Bass
Blackbob School Elementary	Jupiter	12999	Trumpet
Blackbob School Elementary	Jupiter	89	Bass
Blackbob School Elementary	Shering	1234570	Cello
Blackbob School Elementary	Shering	12997	Trumpet
Blue Eye Elementary	Andrews	9988776	Violin
Blue Eye Elementary	Scott	12998	Trumpet
Blue Eye Elementary	Scott	55443	Viola
Blue Eye Elementary	Thompson	1234567	Cello
Blue Eye Elementary	Thompson	1234569	Cello
Blue Eye Elementary	Thompson	888335	Saxophone
Naish Middle School	Douglas	888334	Saxophone
Naish Middle School	Douglas	9988775	Violin
Naish Middle School	Friend	7713	Clarinet

Completing a Database Application

CASE You work with Aaron Scout, network administrator, and David Fox, director of staff development, at Reason 2 Go to improve and complete the Training database application.

Module Objectives

After completing this module, you will be able to:

- Normalize data
- Analyze relationships
- Evaluate tables
- Improve fields

- Use subqueries
- Modify joins
- Create a switchboard form
- Pass criteria to a report from a form

Files You Will Need

Training-16.accdb   LakeHomes-16.accdb

R2G-16.accdb   Jobs-16.accdb

Basketball-16.accdb   Scuba-16.accdb

Personnel-16.accdb

Normalize Data

Learning Outcomes
• Describe normalization
• Create Lookup fields

Normalizing data means to structure and link the tables in a well-designed relational database. A normalized database reduces inaccurate and redundant data, decreases storage requirements, improves database speed and performance, and simplifies overall database maintenance. **CASE** ▶ *Aaron and David ask you to study and improve the Training-16 database.*

STEPS

1. **Open the Training-16.accdb database from the location where you store your Data Files, then enable content if prompted**

2. **Double-click the Employees table in the Navigation Pane**

   The EDepartment and ETitle fields both contain repeating data. You decide to further normalize the database by creating lookup tables for these fields. A **lookup table** is a small table that stores values used in a field of another table.

3. **Close the Employees datasheet, click the Create tab, click the Table Design button in the Tables group, type Department as the field name, press [Tab], click the Primary Key button in the Tools group, save the table with the name Departments, then open it in Datasheet View and enter the values shown in FIGURE 16-1**

QUICK TIP
Use the ↔ pointer to resize columns.

4. **Close the Departments datasheet, click the Create tab, click the Table Design button in the Tables group, type Title as the field name, press [Tab], click the Primary Key button in the Tools group, save the table with the name Titles, then open it in Datasheet View and enter the values shown in FIGURE 16-2**

5. **Save and close the Titles datasheet, right-click the Employees table in the Navigation Pane, then click Design View**

   Next, you use the Lookup Wizard to establish a one-to-many relationship between the Department field in the Departments table and the EDepartment field in the Employees table. The Lookup Wizard also creates a drop-down list of values for the Lookup field.

TROUBLE
If you receive an error message, compare the values in your Departments table to **FIGURE 16-1**, then redo Step 6.

6. **Click the EDepartment field Short Text list arrow, click Lookup Wizard, click Next to look up values in a table, click Table: Departments, click Next, double-click Department as the selected field, click Next, click the first sort arrow, click Department, click Next, click Next, click the Enable Data Integrity check box, click Finish, then click Yes**

   The Departments and Employees tables are now linked in a one-to-many relationship with referential integrity enforced.

TROUBLE
If you receive an error message, compare the values in your Titles table to **FIGURE 16-2**, then redo Step 7.

7. **Click the ETitle field Short Text list arrow, click Lookup Wizard, click Next to look up values in a table, click Table: Titles, click Next, double-click Title as the selected field, click Next, click the first sort arrow, click Title, click Next, click Next, click the Enable Data Integrity check box, click Finish, click Yes, then click Yes again**

   The Titles and Employees tables are now linked in a one-to-many relationship with referential integrity enforced.

8. **Click the View button ▦ to switch to Datasheet View, click any value in the EDepartment field, click the list arrow as shown in FIGURE 16-3, click any value in the ETitle field, then click its list arrow to test its Lookup properties as well**

   Lookup properties mean that data entry will be faster, more consistent, and more accurate.

FIGURE 16-1: Departments datasheet

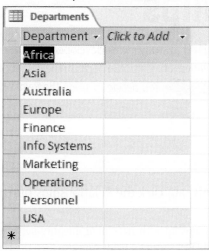

FIGURE 16-2: Titles datasheet

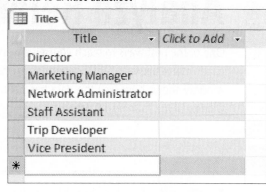

FIGURE 16-3: EDepartment field of the Employees table has Lookup properties

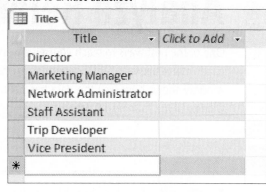

Understanding third normal form

The process of normalization can be broken down into degrees, which include **first normal form (1NF)**, a single two-dimensional table with rows and columns; **second normal form (2NF)**, where redundant data in the original table is extracted, placed in a new table, and related to the original table; and **third normal form (3NF)**, where calculated fields (also called derived fields) such as totals or calculated taxes are removed. In an Access database, calculated fields can be created "on the fly" using a query, which means that the information in the calculation is automatically produced and is always accurate based on the latest updates to the database. Strive to create databases that adhere to the rules of third normal form.

Analyze Relationships

Learning Outcomes
- Analyze table relationships
- Analyze junction tables

One of the best ways to teach yourself advanced database skills is to study a well-developed database. The relationships between tables determine the health and effectiveness of a database because the Relationships window shows how well the data has been normalized. **CASE** *You decide to study the Relationships window of the Training-16 database.*

STEPS

1. **Close the Employees table, click the Database Tools tab, click the Relationships button, then click the All Relationships button**

   You used the Lookup Wizard to create a one-to-many relationship with referential integrity between the Departments and Employees tables using the Department and EDepartment fields. You also used the Lookup Wizard to create a one-to-many relationship with referential integrity between the Titles and Employees tables using the Title and ETitle fields. Move the field lists to better view the relationships.

2. **Drag and resize the field lists in the Relationships window so they look like** FIGURE 16-4

   When the relationship lines are clear, the database design is easier to read. Putting the "one" table of a one-to-many relationship on the left side also makes the relationships slightly easier to read.

   A **many-to-many relationship** exists when two tables are related to the same intermediate table, called the **junction table**, with one-to-many relationships. The Employees and Courses tables have a many-to-many relationship (one employee can take many courses, and one course can be taken by many employees). This relationship is resolved with the junction table, Enrollments.

3. **Click the Relationship Report button, click the Landscape button in the Page Layout group as shown in** FIGURE 16-5**, right-click the Relationships for Training-16 report tab, click Close, click Yes, then click OK to save the report with the default name**

   The report is a valuable tool when you are creating other objects or expressions given that it provides all of the table and field names and the relationships between the tables.

4. **Right-click the Relationships tab, click Save, right-click the Relationships tab again, then click Close**

Multivalued fields

Access allows you to store multiple values in one field by setting the **Allow Multiple Values property** to Yes. This property is found on the Lookup tab in Table Design View. For example, you might be tempted to create an Ingredients field in a Products table to list all of the major ingredients for each product. A better way to handle this, however, is to create an Ingredients table and relate it to the Products table using a one-to-many relationship. The latter approach may take a little more time up front, but it respects fundamental database design rules and gives you the most flexibility in the long run.

FIGURE 16-4: Training-16.accdb relationships

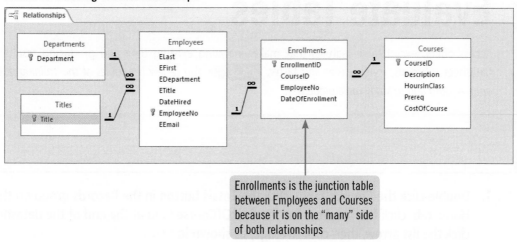

Enrollments is the junction table between Employees and Courses because it is on the "many" side of both relationships

FIGURE 16-5: Relationships for Training-16.accdb report

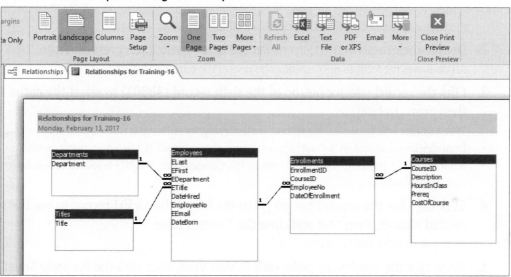

More about Cascade options

When referential integrity is enforced on a relationship, two options become available in the Edit Relationships dialog box, as shown in **FIGURE 16-6**: Cascade Update Related Fields and Cascade Delete Related Records.

Checking the **Cascade Update Related Fields** check box means that if you change the primary key field value in the table on the "one" side of a one-to-many relationship, all foreign key field values in the "many" table automatically update as well. Checking the **Cascade Delete Related Records** check box means that if you delete a record in the table on the "one" side of a relationship, all related records in the "many" table are automatically deleted as well. Therefore, the cascade options both automatically change data in the "many" table based on changes in the "one" table.

FIGURE 16-6: Edit Relationships dialog box

Edit Relationships | ? | X

Table/Query: Related Table/Query:

Departments   Employees

Department	EDepartment

☑ Enforce Referential Integrity

☑ Cascade Update Related Fields

☐ Cascade Delete Related Records

Relationship Type: One-To-Many

OK

Cancel

Join Type..

Create New..

Evaluate Tables

Learning Outcomes
- Apply the Total row in a datasheet
- Modify table properties

Access offers several table features that make analyzing existing data and producing results, such as datasheet subtotals, much easier and faster. **CASE** ▸ *You review the tables of the Training database to analyze data and to study table properties.*

STEPS

1. **Double-click the Courses table, click the Totals button in the Records group on the Home tab, click the Total cell for the CostOfCourse field at the end of the datasheet, click the list arrow, then click Average, as shown in FIGURE 16-7**

   The average cost of an R2G course, $358, appears in the Total cell for the CostOfCourse field. You can calculate the Average, Sum, Count, Maximum, Minimum, Standard Deviation, or Variance statistic for a numeric field. If you were working with a Text field, you could Count the field values. Notice that the Current Record box displays the word "Totals" to indicate that you are working in the Total row. You can use the Current Record box to quickly move to a record.

2. **Double-click Totals in the Current Record box, type 6, then press [Enter]**

   Access moves the focus to the CostOfCourse field of the sixth record (Air301).

3. **Click the record selector button of the sixth record (Air301) to select the entire record, then press [Delete]**

   When using a relational database with referential integrity enforced on all relationships, you are prevented from deleting a record in a "one" (parent) table if the record is related to many records in a "many" (child) table. In this case, the sixth record in the Courses table (Air301) is related to seven records in the Enrollments table.

4. **Click OK, click the expand button ⊞ to the left of the Air301 record to see the seven related records, then save and close the Courses table**

   Next, you examine table properties.

5. **Right-click the Employees table, click Design View, then click the Property Sheet button in the Show/Hide group**

   For the Employees table, you can prevent data entry errors by specifying that the DateHired field value is always greater than the DateBorn field value.

6. **Click the Validation Rule box, type [DateHired]>[DateBorn], click the Validation Text box, type Hire date must be greater than birth date as shown in FIGURE 16-8, click the Save button 🖫 on the Quick Access Toolbar, click Yes, then click the View button ▦ to switch to Datasheet View**

   Test the new table validation rule.

7. **Tab to the DateHired field, type 1/5/61, then press [↓]**

   A dialog box opens, displaying the text entered in the Validation Text property.

8. **Click OK, then press [Esc] to remove the incorrect hire date entry for the first record**

FIGURE 16-7: Courses datasheet with Total row

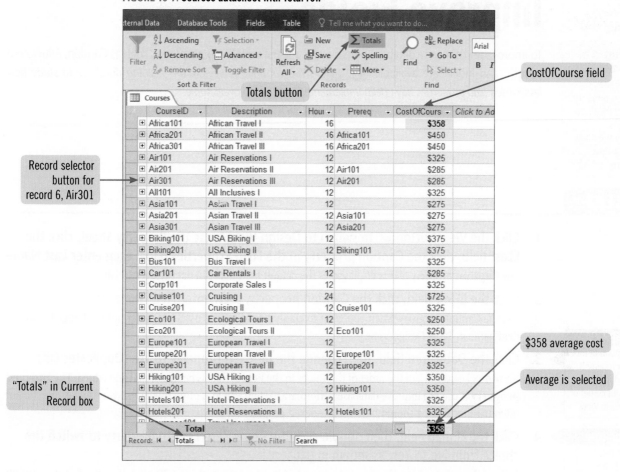

FIGURE 16-8: Property Sheet for the Employees table

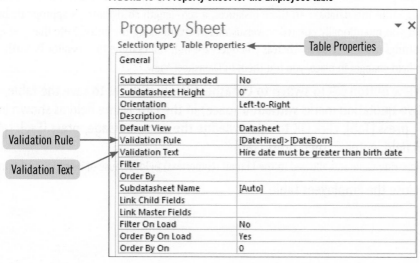

Modifying fields in Datasheet View

When working in Table Datasheet View, the Fields tab on the Ribbon contains buttons that allow you to add or delete a field or change the name or data type of an existing field. You can also modify certain field properties such as Caption, Field Size, Format, Required, Validation Rule, and Validation Text. For full access to all of the properties for a field, however, work in Table Design View.

Access 2016

Improve Fields

Learning Outcomes
- Modify the Caption property
- Modify the Index property
- Modify the Allow Zero Length property

To improve and enhance database functionality, several useful field properties, such as Caption, Allow Zero Length, and Index, are available. **CASE** *You continue to review the Training database to study how lesser-used field properties have been implemented in the Employees table.*

STEPS

1. **Click the View button [] to switch to Design View, close the Property Sheet, click the ELast field, click the Caption property in the Field Properties pane, then enter Last Name**

   The **Caption** property text is displayed as the default field name in datasheets and labels.

2. **Click the EFirst field, click the Caption property, then enter First Name**

   Use the Caption property when you want to clarify a field for the users but prefer not to change the actual field name in Table Design View.

3. **Click the DateHired field, then change the Indexed property to Yes (Duplicates OK)**

   An **index** keeps track of the order of the values in the field as data is being entered and edited. The **Indexed property** is used to improve database performance when a field is often used for sorting. Fields that are not often used for sorting should have their Indexed property set to No.

4. **Click the EEmail field, then double-click the Allow Zero Length property to switch the choice from No to Yes, as shown in FIGURE 16-9**

   If the **Allow Zero Length property** is set to No, zero-length strings ("") are not allowed. A zero-length string is an intentional "nothing" entry (as opposed to a **null** entry, which also means that the field contains nothing but doesn't indicate intent). For example, some employees might not want their email address entered into this database. In those instances, a zero-length string entry is appropriate because it indicates that you intentionally entered "" versus merely overlooking the entry. Note that you query for zero-length strings using "" criteria, whereas you query for null values using the operator **Is Null**.

   With the field changes in place, you test them in Datasheet View.

5. **Click the View button [] to switch to Datasheet View, click Yes to save the table, enter "" (two quotation marks without a space) in the Last Name field as shown in FIGURE 16-10, press [Tab], click OK to acknowledge the error message, press [Esc], tab to the EEmail field, enter "", then press [Tab]**

   A zero-length string value was allowed in the EEmail (Hypertext) field because of its property settings.

6. **Save and close the Employees table**

FIGURE 16-9: Changing field properties in the Employees table

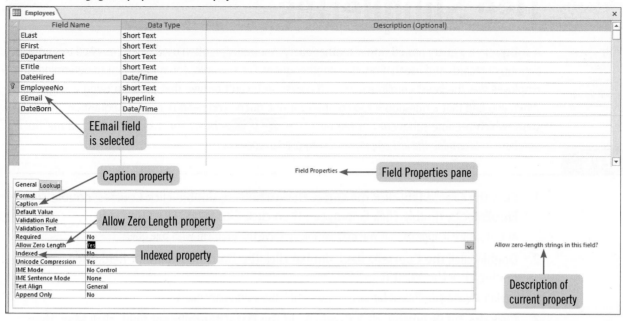

FIGURE 16-10: Testing field properties in the Employees table

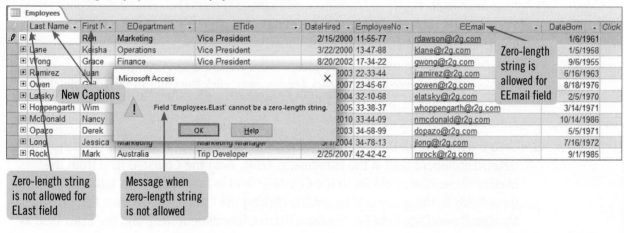

Using Long Text fields

Use Long Text fields when you need to store more than 256 characters in a field, which is the maximum Field Size value for a Short Text field. Fields that store comments, reviews, notes, or other ongoing conversational information are good candidates for the Long Text data type. Set the **Append Only** property to Yes to allow users to add data to a Memo field but not to change or remove existing data. The Append Only property is available for Long Text fields in Access 2007-2016 databases.

Use Subqueries

A **subquery** is a query nested within another query. A subquery is often used when you need to summarize a group of records and use that result in another query. For example, you might want to determine which employee was the latest enrollment in each course. You can't resolve that problem using a single query. When you find that a question is too complex for one query, you need to break the question into smaller steps, which become subqueries to the next step. **CASE** ▶ *David Fox asks you to work in the Training database to determine the last employee who enrolled in each course.*

STEPS

1. **Click the Create tab, click the Query Design button, double-click Courses, double-click Enrollments, double-click Employees, then click Close**

   At first glance it appears that you may be able to solve the problem with one query.

2. **Double-click the CourseID field, double-click the DateOfEnrollment field, then double-click the ELast field**

   To find the last enrollment for each course, you'll use a summary query.

3. **Click the Totals button, click Group By in the DateOfEnrollment field, click Max, then click the View button** 🔲

   This query shows several records for each course description because the records are also grouped by the ELast field. There's no way to tell the query to select *only* the ELast field for the record with the maximum DateOfEnrollment value. This can be resolved by breaking the problem into two steps.

4. **Click** 🔲**, click the Employees field list title bar, press [Delete], then click** 🔲 **to review the datasheet**

   The query now displays 32 records as shown in FIGURE 16-11 for the last enrollment date for each course offered. This query will serve as the subquery to the next step.

5. **Right-click the Query1 tab, click Save, type MaxEnrollmentDate as the query name, click OK, close the query, click the Create tab, click the Query Design button, double-click Employees, double-click Enrollments, click the Queries tab, double-click MaxEnrollmentDate, then click Close**

   You use the MaxEnrollmentDate subquery to constrain this query to only those records.

6. **Drag the MaxOfDateOfEnrollment field from the MaxEnrollmentDate field list to the DateOfEnrollment field in the Enrollments table, drag the CourseID field from the MaxEnrollmentDate field list to the CourseID field in the Enrollments table, then add three fields to the query grid by double-clicking the CourseID field from the MaxEnrollmentDate field list, the MaxOfDateOfEnrollment field, and the ELast field as shown in FIGURE 16-12**

   The relationships between the MaxEnrollmentDate subquery and the Enrollments table select only the records that are in both tables.

7. **Click Ascending as the sort order for the CourseID field, then click** 🔲 **to view the resulting datasheet as shown in FIGURE 16-13**

   The datasheet now displays the same 32 records that were in the MaxEnrollmentDate query plus the ELast field from the Employees table.

8. **Save and close the query as MaxEnrollmentDate2**

FIGURE 16-11: Building a subquery

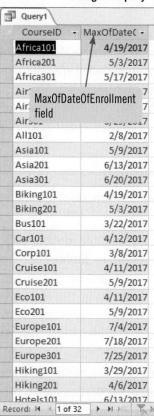

MaxOfDateOfEnrollment field

FIGURE 16-12: Using a subquery

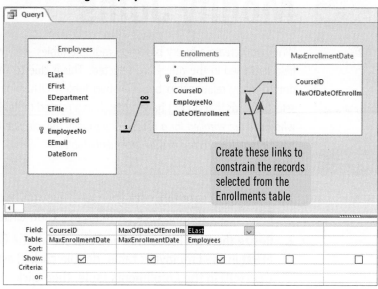

Create these links to constrain the records selected from the Enrollments table

FIGURE 16-13: Final datasheet

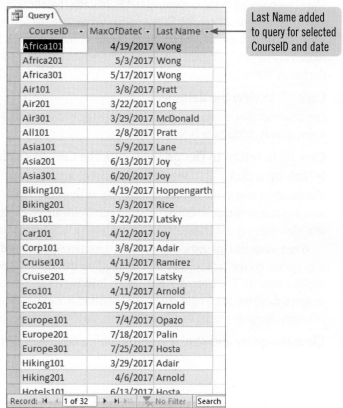

Last Name added to query for selected CourseID and date

Modify Joins

When you create a query based on multiple tables, only records that have matching data in each of the field lists used in the query are selected. This is due to the default **inner join** operation applied to the one-to-many relationship between two tables. Other join types are described in TABLE 16-1. They help select records that do not have a match in a related table. **CASE** *David Fox wants to identify employees who have not enrolled for a course. You modify the join line to find records in the Employees table that do not have a matching record in the Enrollments table.*

STEPS

1. **Click the Create tab, click the Query Design button in the Queries group, double-click Employees, double-click Enrollments, then click Close**

2. **Resize the field list so that you can see all the fields in the Employees table, double-click EFirst in the Employees table, double-click ELast in the Employees table, double-click CourseID in the Enrollments table, then click the View button 🔲 to view the datasheet**

   This query selects 403 records using the default inner join between the tables. An inner join means that records are selected only if a matching value is present in both tables. Therefore, any records in the Employees table that did not have a related record in the Enrollments table would not be selected. You modify the join operation to find those employees.

3. **Click the View button 🔲 to switch to Design View, then double-click the middle of the one-to-many relationship line between the tables to open the Join Properties dialog box shown in FIGURE 16-14**

   The Join Properties dialog box provides information regarding how the two tables are joined and allows you to change from the default inner join (option 1) to a left outer join (2) or right outer join (3).

4. **Click the 2 option button, then click OK as shown in FIGURE 16-15**

   The arrow pointing to the Enrollments table indicates that the join line has been modified to be a left outer join. With join operations, "left" always refers to the "one" table of a one-to-many relationship regardless of where the table is physically positioned in Query Design View. A **left outer join** means that all of the records in the "one" table will be selected for the query regardless of whether they have matching records in the "many" table.

5. **Click 🔲 to view the datasheet**

   The datasheet now shows 407 records, 4 more than when an inner join operation was used. To find the 4 new records quickly, use Is Null criteria.

6. **Click 🔲 to return to Design View, click the Criteria cell for the CourseID field, type Is Null, then click 🔲 to view the datasheet again**

   The datasheet now contains only four records, as shown in FIGURE 16-16, the four employees who do not have any matching enrollment records. Left outer joins are very useful for finding records on the "one" side of a relationship (parent records) that do not have matching records on the "many" side (child records).

   When referential integrity is enforced on a relationship before data is entered, it is impossible to create new records on the "many" side of a relationship that do not have matching records on the "one" side (orphan records). Therefore, a **right outer join** is very useful to help find orphan records in a poorly designed database, but a right outer join operation would not be useful in the Training database because referential integrity was applied on all relationships before any records were entered.

7. **Close the query and save it with the name EmployeesWithoutEnrollments**

FIGURE 16-14: **Join Properties dialog box**

Left table, "one" table → Employees

Right table, "many" table → Enrollments

Primary key field → EmployeeNo

Foreign key field → EmployeeNo

Inner join → ○ 1: Only include rows where the joined fields from both tables are equal.

Left outer join → ○ 2: Include ALL records from 'Employees' and only those records from 'Enrollments' where the joined fields are equal.

Right outer join → ○ 3: Include ALL records from 'Enrollments' and only those records from 'Employees' where the joined fields are equal.

FIGURE 16-15: **Left outer join line**

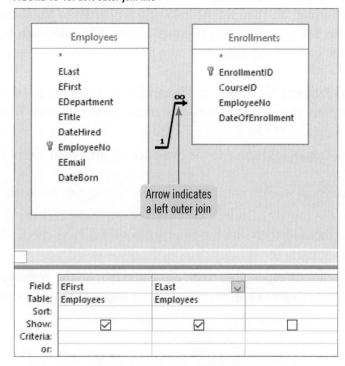

Arrow indicates a left outer join

FIGURE 16-16: **Employees without enrollments**

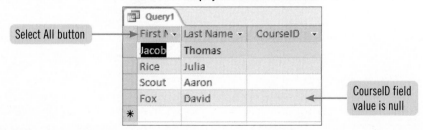

Select All button

CourseID field value is null

TABLE 16-1: **Join operations**

join operation	description
inner	Default join; selects records from two related tables in a query that have matching values in a field common to both tables
left outer	Selects all the records from the left table (the "one" table in a one-to-many relationship) even if the "one" table doesn't have matching records in the related "many" table
right outer	Selects all the records from the right table (the "many" table in a one-to-many relationship) even if the "many" table doesn't have matching records in the related "one" table

Create a Switchboard Form

Learning
Outcomes
•Work with form
  properties
•Create a
  switchboard form
•Hide the
  Navigation Pane

In a fully developed database, users generally do not work with individual objects or the Navigation Pane. Rather, they use a startup form sometimes called a **switchboard form** with command buttons to guide all of their activities. Well-designed forms make it easy to navigate and work with the data in the underlying database. **CASE** *Aaron Scout asks you to create a switchboard form to automatically open and to hide the complexity of the Training database application. Given that this form will not be used for data entry, you'll first modify some of the form's properties to change its appearance from that of a data entry form to a switchboard form.*

STEPS

QUICK TIP
Any form can act
as a startup
switchboard form,
not just one named
Switchboard.

1. **Right-click the** Switchboard form, **click** Design View, **click the** Property Sheet button, **click the** Format tab, **then set the following properties to No:** Record Selectors, Navigation Buttons, Scroll Bars (Neither), Control Box, **and** Min Max Buttons (None)

   The elements on a form that allow you to move between records or resize the window are not helpful on a switchboard form.

2. **Close the Property Sheet, save the form, click** 🗔 **to switch to Form View to observe the form property changes, then click each of the three** command buttons **to test them**

   A switchboard form can have as many command buttons, labels, or other controls as needed.

3. **Close the Employees form and the two open reports, then return to the Switchboard form**

   Use Access options to set the Switchboard form as the opening form and to hide the Navigation Pane.

4. **Click the** File tab, **click** Options, **click** Current Database, **click the** Display Form list arrow, **click** Switchboard, **then click the** Display Navigation Pane check box **to uncheck it as shown in** FIGURE 16-17

QUICK TIP
Press and hold the
[Shift] key while
opening a database
to bypass the startup
options.

5. **Click** OK, **click** OK **again, then save, close, and reopen the Training-16 database**

   The Training-16 database opens to the Switchboard form with the Navigation Pane closed as shown in FIGURE 16-18.

FIGURE 16-17: Access startup options

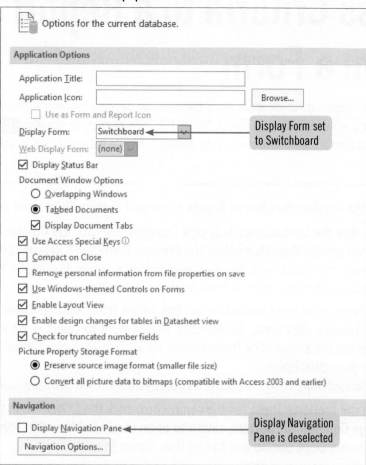

FIGURE 16-18: Switchboard opens automatically and Navigation Pane is hidden

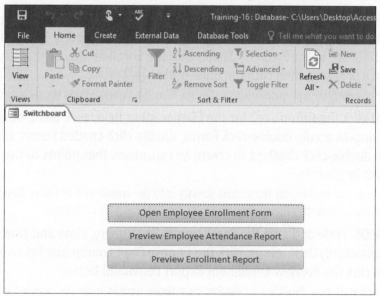

Reviewing Microsoft databases

Microsoft provides several fully developed, well-designed database examples as templates. Click the File tab, click New, then search for desktop templates. The Northwind database template is very popular and tracks worldwide orders for a specialty food wholesale business.

Pass Criteria to a Report from a Form

In a fully developed database application, the database designer provides the user flexible and easy ways to find data without having to create his or her own queries or reports. **CASE** > *You modify the Switchboard form to create flexible reports by passing criteria to the report from a combo box.*

STEPS

1. **Click the Preview Enrollment Report command button, then scroll through the report**

2. **Right-click the Switchboard tab, click Design View, click the Combo Box control in the Controls group, then click below the Preview Enrollment Report command button**

   The Combo Box Wizard opens. You want the combo box to list the departments. You also want the selected department to determine the records displayed on the Enrollment report.

3. **Click Next to let the combo box get the values from another table, click Table: Departments, click Next, double-click Department to select it, click Next, click the first sort order list arrow, click Department, click Next, click Next, type Choose Dept: as the label, then click Finish**

   With the combo box in place, you'll give it a more meaningful name to make it easier to identify in the query.

4. **Open the Property Sheet for the combo box, click the Other tab in the Property Sheet, change Combo5 to cboDept, save and open the Switchboard in Form View, then click the Choose Dept combo box to test it as shown in** FIGURE 16-19

   The interface is almost complete, but you still need to tie the choice in the combo box to the query that supports the report. The Record Source property of a report identifies the recordset (table or query) on which the report is based.

5. **Click the Preview Enrollment Report command button to open the report, right-click the EnrollmentByDept tab, click Design View, open the Property Sheet for the report, click the Data tab of the Property Sheet, click the EnrollmentByDept query in the Record Source property, then click the Build button** [...]

   The EnrollmentByDept query opens in Design View. This query selects the records for the report.

6. **Right-click the Criteria cell for the EDepartment field, click Build, double-click Training-16.accdb, double-click Forms, double-click Loaded Forms, click Switchboard, then double-click cboDept to create an expression that points to the combo box as shown in** FIGURE 16-20

   Although you could enter the criteria directly into the criteria cell of Query Design View, the Expression Builder helps you with the **syntax**, the rules, to enter complex criterion.

7. **Click OK, close and save the EnrollmentByDept query, close and save the EnrollmentsByDept report, click the Choose Dept combo box list arrow, click USA, then click the Preview Enrollment Report command button**

   The report is now modified to display only those records from the selected department as shown in FIGURE 16-21.

8. **Save and close all objects, close the Training-16 database, then close Access**

FIGURE 16-19: Adding a Choose Dept: combo box

FIGURE 16-20: Expression Builder dialog box

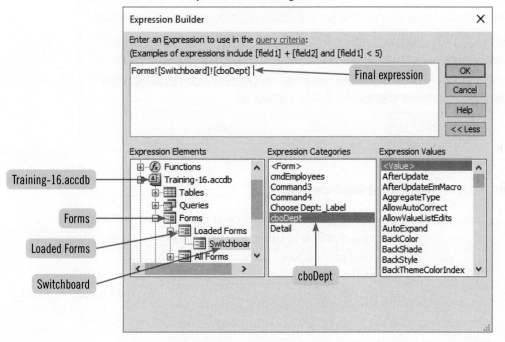

FIGURE 16-21: Report displays USA department records

Practice

Concepts Review

Identify each element of the Join Properties dialog box in FIGURE 16-22.

FIGURE 16-22

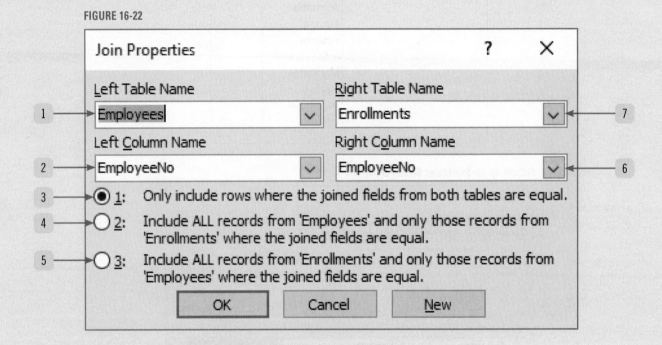

Match each term with the statement that best describes it.

8. **Zero-length string**
9. **Index**
10. **Caption**
11. **Normalization**

a. Displayed as the default field name at the top of the field column in datasheets as well as in labels that describe fields on forms and reports

b. An intentional "nothing" entry

c. The process of structuring data into a well-formed relational database

d. Keeps track of the order of the values in the indexed field as data is entered and edited

Select the best answer from the list of choices.

12. **Which of the following is not a benefit of a well-designed relational database?**
    a. Is easier to create than a single-table database
    b. Reduces redundant data
    c. Has lower overall storage requirements
    d. Improves reporting flexibility

13. **First normal form can be described as:**
    a. A well-functioning, fully developed relational database
    b. A series of queries and subqueries
    c. Any collection of data in any form
    d. A single two-dimensional table with rows and columns

14. Which of the following activities occurs during the creation of second normal form?

  a. Redundant data is removed from one table, and relationships are created.

  b. Calculated fields are removed from tables.

  c. All data is organized in one master table.

  d. Additional calculated fields are added to tables.

15. Which of the following activities occurs during the creation of third normal form?

  a. Calculated fields are removed from tables.

  b. Additional calculated fields are added to tables.

  c. Redundant data is removed from one table, and relationships are created.

  d. All data is organized in one master table.

16. What is a common name for the first form that opens when the database opens?

  a. Start   **c.** Switchboard

  b. Open   **d.** Pane

17. Which of the following is a good candidate for lookup properties?

  a. A foreign key field   **c.** A primary key field

  b. An AutoNumber field   **d.** A Date/Time field

18. Which of the following is not true for the Caption property?

  a. The value of the Caption property is the default label that describes a field on a report.

  b. It is the default field name at the top of the field column in datasheets.

  c. The value of the Caption property is the default label that describes a field on a form.

  d. It is used instead of the field name when you build expressions.

19. Which of the following fields would most likely be used for an index?

  a. ApartmentNumber   **c.** FirstName

  b. MiddleName   **d.** LastName

20. Which of the following phrases best describes the need for both null values and zero-length strings?

  a. They look different on a query datasheet.

  b. Having two different choices for "nothing" clarifies data entry.

  c. They represent two different conditions.

  d. Null values speed up calculations.

Skills Review

1. Normalize data.

  a. Start Access, open the R2G-16.accdb database from the location where you store your Data Files, then enable content if prompted.

  b. Open the Relationships window, show all relationships, then move and resize the tables as shown in FIGURE 16-23.

FIGURE 16-23

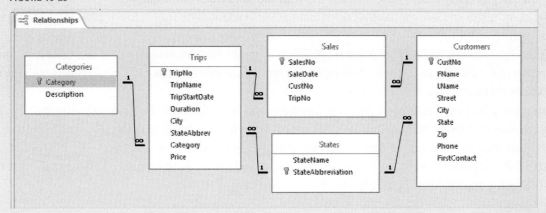

Skills Review (continued)

c. Open the Customers table to view its datasheet, and then click the State field. Notice that the State field in the Customers table does not have lookup properties. Close the Customers table and open the Trips table in Datasheet View. Click the State field and again notice that it does not have Lookup properties. Close the Trips table.

d. In the Relationships window, delete the one-to-many relationship between the States and Customers and the States and Trips tables, then save and close the Relationships table.

e. Open the Customers table in Design View. Start the Lookup Wizard for the State field to look up values from the States table. Choose both the StateName and StateAbbreviation fields and sort in ascending order on the StateName field. Do not hide the primary key field, select StateAbbreviation when asked which field contains unique data, accept the State label, enable data integrity, and respond to the prompts to save the table. Display the Customers table in Datasheet View and test the State field's lookup properties.

f. Save and close the Customers table, and then repeat Step e for the State field in the Trips table, again using State as the label. Test the Lookup properties of the State field in the Trips datasheet, then save and close the Trips table.

2. Analyze relationships.

a. Open the Relationships window, then create a Relationship report. Use landscape orientation so that the report is only one page long, and insert your name as a label in the Report Header using black text and a 12-point font size. Save and close the report using the default name, **Relationships for R2G-16**.

b. Use the table to the right to identify the tables joined in a many-to-many relationship. Two relationships are many-to-many relationships in this database.

c. Save and close the Relationships window.

Table 1	Junction Table	Table 2
Employees	Orders	Customers

3. Evaluate tables.

a. Open the datasheet for the Trips table, then click the Totals button to open the Total row at the end of the datasheet.

b. Use the Total row to find the average value of the Price field, then save and close the Trips table.

4. Improve fields.

a. Open the Trips table in Design View, then change the Caption property for the TripName field to **Name**.

b. Change the Caption property for the TripStartDate field to **Start Date**.

c. Change the Indexed property for the TripName field to **Yes (No Duplicates)**.

d. Change the Allow Zero Length property to **No** for the TripName, City, State, and Category fields.

e. Save and close the Trips table.

5. Use subqueries.

a. Create a query in Query Design View, then add the Trips and Sales tables to the query.

b. In the query design grid, add the SaleDate field from the Sales table and the TripNo and TripName fields from the Trips table.

c. Click the Totals button, and select Max instead of Group By for the SaleDate field. View the datasheet to see the 17 records that are displayed. This datasheet represents the last sale date for each trip. Save the query with the name **MaxSaleDate** and close it.

d. Create a query in Query Design View. Show the Customers and Sales tables and the MaxSaleDate query.

e. Drag the MaxOfSaleDate field from the MaxSaleDate field list to the SaleDate field in the Sales table. Drag the TripNo field from the MaxSaleDate field list to the TripNo field in the Sales table.

f. Add the following fields to the query design grid: the FName and LName fields from the Customers table and the MaxOfSaleDate and TripName fields from the MaxSaleDate query.

g. Save the query as **MaxSaleDate2** and display the datasheet. The datasheet has 35 records versus 17 because the maximum sale date is connected with several customers for several trips. For example, 4 different customers are related to the same max sale date value of 5/4/2017 for the Golden Hands Venture trip.

h. Save and close the MaxSaleDate2 query.

6. Modify joins.

a. Open the Customers table in Datasheet View, and enter a record using your own name. Enter realistic but fictitious data for the rest of the record, then close the Customers table.

b. Create a query in Query Design View, and add FName and LName from the Customers table and SaleDate from the Sales table. Add an ascending sort on the LName field, then view the datasheet. The datasheet has 105 records and your name is not included.

c. Return to Query Design View, then change the join properties to option 2, which will select all Customers records even if they don't have matching data in the Sales table.

d. View the datasheet, and note that it now contains 109 records.

e. Return to Query Design View, and add **Is Null** criteria to the SaleDate field.

f. View the datasheet, noting that four records in the Customers table do not have a related record in the Sales table, including the record with your name.

g. Save the query with the name **CustomersWithoutSales**, then close it.

7. Create a switchboard form.

a. Open the Switchboard form in Form View. It contains five command buttons and two combo boxes. Modify its properties to make it appear more like a navigation form and less like a data entry form by making these form property changes in Form Design View: Record Selectors: **No**, Navigation Buttons: **No**, Scroll Bars: **Neither**, Control Box: **No**, Close Button: **No**, Min Max Buttons: **None**.

b. Save and close the Switchboard form.

c. Set the Switchboard form to open and do not display the Navigation Pane when the database opens.

d. Save all objects, close the database, and reopen it to test your new startup options.

8. Pass criteria to a report from a form.

a. Click the Trip Listing command button. Enter **CA** when prompted. You want to replace that parameter prompt with a choice from the "FIND Trips for this State" combo box.

b. Open the TripListing report in Design View. Open the Property Sheet for the report, click the Data tab, click the Record Source property, then click the Build button.

FIGURE 16-24

c. Delete the parameter prompt [Enter desired state], right-click the State criteria cell, then click Build.

d. In the Expression Builder, choose the cboFindState control on the Switchboard form as shown in **FIGURE 16-24**.

e. Save and close the TripListing query and TripListing report. Use the FIND Trips for this State combo box on the Switchboard form to select MO Missouri, then click the Trip Listing command button. The six trips in the state of Missouri should appear.

f. Save and close all open objects, close the R2G-16 database, and exit Access.

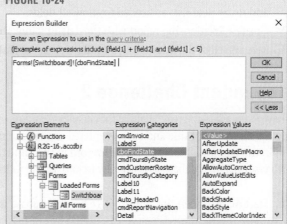

Independent Challenge 1

As the manager of a basketball team, you have created an Access database called Basketball-16.accdb to track players, games, and statistics. You have recently learned how to create lookup tables to better control the values of a field that contains repeated data and to apply your new skills to your database.

a. Start Access, open the Basketball-16.accdb database from the location where you store your Data Files, and enable content if prompted.

b. Double-click the Players table to view its datasheet. Notice the repeated data in the YearInSchool and Position fields. You will build lookup tables to better describe and manage the values in those fields. Close the Players datasheet.

c. In Table Design View, create a two-field table with the field names **PositionID** and **PositionDescription**. Both fields should have a Short Text data type. Set PositionID as the primary key field. Save the table with the name **Positions**, and enter the data in the datasheet shown in FIGURE 16-25. Save and close the Positions table.

FIGURE 16-25

PositionID	PositionDescription
C	Center
F	Forward
G	Guard
*	

d. Open the Players table in Design View, click the Position field, then choose Lookup Wizard using the Data Type list arrow.

e. Choose the "I want the lookup field to get the values..." option, choose Table: Positions, choose both fields, choose PositionDescription for an ascending sort order, hide the key column, accept the Position label, click the Enable Data Integrity check box, finish the Lookup Wizard, then click Yes to save the table. Close the Players table.

FIGURE 16-26

ClassRankID	RankDescription	SortOrder
Fr	Freshman	1
So	Sophomore	2
Jr	Junior	3
Sr	Senior	4
*		0

f. Repeat Step c, creating a **ClassRanks** table instead of a Positions table using the field names and data shown in FIGURE 16-26. The RankDescription and ClassRankID fields are both Short Text fields. The SortOrder field is a Number field. Make the ClassRankID field the primary key field, then close the ClassRanks table.

g. Repeat Step d by using the Lookup Wizard with the YearInSchool field in the Players table to look up data in the ClassRanks table. Choose all three fields, choose the SortOrder field for an ascending sort order, hide the key column, accept the YearInSchool label, click the Enable Data Integrity check box, finish the Lookup Wizard, then click Yes to save the table.

h. Click the Lookup tab and change the Column Widths property to 0;1;0 to hide the SortOrder field, then save the Players table.

i. Open the Players table datasheet to test the drop-down lists for the YearInSchool and Position fields.

j. Open the Relationships window, click the All Relationships button to make sure you're viewing all relationships, and resize field lists as needed to show all fields.

k. Create a Relationship report with the default name **Relationships for Basketball-16**.

l. Save and close the Relationships window, close the Basketball-16.accdb database, then exit Access.

Independent Challenge 2

You have been asked to create a query that displays employees as well as their manager in the same datasheet. Because each employee, regardless of title and rank, is entered as a record in the Employees table, you know that you will need to relate each record in the Employees table to another record in the same table to show the employee–manager relationship. You will work in the Personnel-16 database to learn how to join a table to itself in order to answer this challenge.

a. Start Access, open the Personnel-16.accdb database from the location where you store your Data Files, then enable content if prompted. This database contains only one table at this point, the Employees table.

b. Create a query in Query Design View. Add the Employees table, and then add the Employees table a second time. Right-click the Employees_1 field list, click Properties to open the Property Sheet for the Employee_1 field list, select Employees_1 in the Alias text box, type **Managers**, press [Enter], then close the Property Sheet.

Independent Challenge 2 (continued)

c. Resize both field lists to see all fields, then drag the EmployeeID field from the Managers field list to the ReportsTo field in the Employees table because each employee reports to another employee whose EmployeeID value has been entered in the ReportsTo field. By creating this relationship using the primary key field of the Managers table, one record in the Managers table can be related to many records in the Employees table.

d. In the Managers field list, double-click the LastName field, then double-click the FirstName field.

e. In the Employees field list, double-click the LastName field, then double-click the FirstName field.

f. Add an ascending sort order on both LastName fields, and identify the manager names using ManLast: and ManFirst: fieldnames as shown in FIGURE 16-27.

g. Display the query datasheet, then widen each column to display all data. The datasheet should show that one person reports to Portillo, four employees report to Tesdahl, and three report to Vera.

FIGURE 16-27

Field:	ManLast: LastName	ManFirst: FirstName	LastName	FirstName
Table:	Managers	Managers	Employees	Employees
Sort:	Ascending		Ascending	
Show:	☑	☑	☑	☑
Criteria:				
or:				

h. Save the query as **ManagerList**, close the query, then close the Personnel-16 database and exit Access.

Independent Challenge 3

As the manager of a regional real estate information system, you track offers for each real estate listing in a database. Create a table to track the offers and relate it to the rest of the database in a one-to-many relationship.

a. Start Access, open the LakeHomes-16.accdb database from the location where you store your Data Files, and enable content if prompted.

b. Create a table named **Offers** with the fields, data types, descriptions, and primary key shown in FIGURE 16-28.

FIGURE 16-28

	Field Name	Data Type	Description
🔑	OfferID	AutoNumber	primary key field
	ListingNo	Number	foreign key field to Listings table
	OfferDate	Date/Time	date of offer
	OfferAmount	Currency	dollar value of the offer
	Buyer	Short Text	last name or company name of entity making the offer
	AcceptanceDate	Date/Time	date that the offer was accepted

c. Use the Lookup Wizard on the ListingNo field in the Offers table to connect the Offers table to the Listings table. Select all the fields from the Listings table; sort in ascending order on the Type, Area, and SqFt fields; do not hide the key column; store the ListingNo value in the field; accept the ListingNo label for the lookup field; enable data integrity; and finish the wizard. Save the table when prompted.

d. In Table Design View, on the Lookup tab (Field Properties) for the ListingNo field, change the value for the Column Heads property from No to Yes.

e. In Table Design View, on the Lookup tab (Field Properties) for the ListingNo field, change the value for the List Rows property from 16 to **100**.

f. Save the table, click Yes when asked to check the data, then display it in Datasheet View.

g. Enter the record shown in the first row of FIGURE 16-29 using the new combo box for the ListingNo field as shown.

FIGURE 16-29

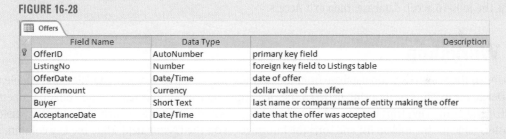

OfferID	ListingNo	OfferDate	OfferAmour	Buyer	AcceptanceDate	Click to Add
1	12	5/1/2017	$375,000.00	Student Last Name	5/20/2017	

ListingNo	Type	Area	SqFt	LakeFt	BR	Bath	Garage	Pool	Asking	RealtorNo	ListingDate
4	Cabin	Horseshoe Ber	1200	102	4	3	2	No	$150,000.00	2	2/28/2017
22	Cabin	Kimberling City	1350	50	2	2	2	No	$127,900.00	5	1/3/2017

h. Close the Offers table, close the LakeHomes-16.accdb database, then exit Access.

Independent Challenge 4: Explore

An Access database can help record and track your job search efforts. In this exercise, you work with a database that tracks employers and job positions to better normalize and present the data.

    a. Start Access, open the Jobs-16.accdb database from the location where you store your Data Files, and enable content if prompted.

    b. Open both the Employers and Positions tables in Datasheet View to review the data. One employer may offer many positions, so the tables are related by the common EmployerID field. You decide to add Lookup properties to the EmployerID field in the Positions table to better identify each employer in this view.

    c. Close both table datasheets, open the Relationships window, right-click the join line between the Employers and Positions tables, then click Delete. Click Yes to delete the relationship. Before you can start the Lookup Wizard on the EmployerID field in the Positions table, all existing relationships to that field must be deleted.

    d. Save and close the Relationships window, then open the Positions table in Design View.

    e. Start the Lookup Wizard for the EmployerID field to look up values in the Employers table. Select all fields, sort in ascending order on the CompanyName field, hide the key column, select EmployerID if asked to select the field containing the value you want to store, use the EmployerID label, enable data integrity, finish the wizard, then save the table.

    f. Display the Positions table in Datasheet View, then test the new Lookup properties on the EmployerID field by changing the EmployerID for the "Technician" position to **JCCC**.

    g. Close the Positions table, then start a new query in Query Design View. Add both the Employers and Positions tables.

    h. Add the CompanyName field from the Employers table and the Title and CareerArea fields from the Positions table.

    i. Modify the join line to include all records from Employers, then view the datasheet.

    j. Save the query with the name **AllEmployers**, then close it.

    k. Close the Jobs-16.accdb database, then exit Access.

Visual Workshop

Start Access, open the Scuba-16.accdb database from the location where you store your Data Files, and enable content if prompted. Delete the existing relationship between the DiveTrips and DiveMasters tables. Add Lookup properties to the DiveMasterID field of the DiveTrips table to achieve the result shown in FIGURE 16-30, which looks up every field from the DiveMasters table for the lookup list and sorts the information on the LName field. Hide the key column, accept the DiveMasterID label, and enforce data integrity. You'll also want to modify the Lookup properties of the DiveMasterID field so that Column Heads is set to **Yes** and List Rows is set to **100**. The final DiveTrips datasheet with Lookup properties applied to the DiveMasterID field will look like FIGURE 16-30.

FIGURE 16-30

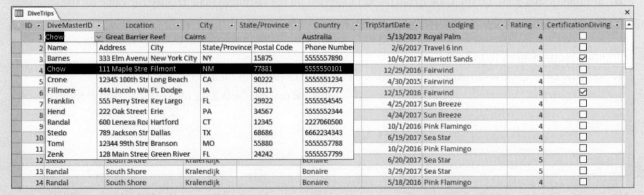

Glossary

.accdb The file extension that means the database is an Access database, created with Access 2007, 2010, 2013, or 2016.

.accdw The file extension for an Access web app file.

.jpg The filename extension for JPEG files.

.laccdb The file extension for a temporary file that keeps track of record-locking information when a .accdb database is open. It helps coordinate the multiuser capabilities of an Access database so that several people can read and update the same database at the same time.

.ldb The file extension for a temporary file that keeps track of record-locking information when a .mdb database is open. It helps coordinate the multiuser capabilities of an Access database so that several people can read and update the same database at the same time.

.mdb The file extension for Access 2000 and 2002–2003 databases.

Access web app A special type of Access database that is stored on a SharePoint server and allows users to enter and edit data using a common browser.

Action Each task that you want a macro to perform.

Action block In Macro Design View, the area of the window that organizes all of the arguments for a current action.

Action query A query that changes the selected records when it is run. Access provides four types of action queries: Delete, Update, Append, and Make Table.

Active The currently available document, program, or object; on the taskbar, when more than one program is open, the button for the active program appears slightly lighter.

Add-in Software that works with an installed app to extend its features.

Adobe Reader software A software program provided free of charge by Adobe Systems for reading PDF (portable document format) files.

After Update A property that specifies an action to perform after an object or control is updated.

Aggregate function A function such as Sum, Avg, and Count used in a summary query to calculate information about a group of records.

Alias A property that renames a field list in Query Design View.

Alignment command A command used in Layout or Design View for a form or report to left-, center-, or right-align a value within its control using the Align Left, Center, or Align Right buttons on the Home tab. In Design View, you can also align the top, bottom, right, or left edge of selected controls using the Align button.

Allow Multiple Values A Lookup field property that lets you create a multivalued field.

Allow Value List Edits A Lookup field property that determines whether users can add to or edit the list of items in a lookup field.

Allow Zero Length A field property that determines whether to allow zero-length strings (""). Zero-length strings are intentional "nothing" entries, such as a intentionally entering "" into a Phone Number field.

Alternate Back Color property A property that determines the alternating background color of the selected section in a form or report.

Anchoring A layout positioning option that allows you to tie controls together so you can work with them as a group.

AND criteria Criteria placed in the same row of the query design grid. All criteria on the same row must be true for a record to appear on the resulting datasheet.

Animation emphasis effect In Sway, a special effect you can apply to an object to animate it.

Append To add records to an existing table.

Append Only A field property available for Long Text fields. When enabled, the property allows users to add data to a Long Text field, but not change or remove existing data.

Append query An action query that adds selected records to an existing table called the target table.

Append To row When creating an Append query, a row that appears in the query design grid to show how the fields in the query match fields in the target table.

Application developer The person responsible for building and maintaining tables, queries, forms, and reports for all of the database users.

Application Part An object template that creates objects such as tables and forms.

Argument Information that a function uses to create the final answer. Multiple arguments are separated by commas. All of the arguments for a function are surrounded by a single set of parentheses.

Asterisk (*) A wildcard character used to search for any number of characters in query criteria.

Attachment A field data type for adding one or more files, such as images, to database records.

Attachment field A field that allows you to attach an external file such as a Word document, PowerPoint presentation, Excel workbook, or image file to a record.

AutoExec A special macro name that automatically executes when a database opens.

Autofilter A feature that lets users quickly sort or filter a datasheet by a particular field.

AutoKeys A macro designed to be assigned a key combination (such as [Shift][Ctrl][L]).

AutoNumber A field data type in which Access enters a sequential integer for each record added into the datasheet. Numbers cannot be reused even if the record is deleted.

Avg function A built-in Access function used to calculate the average of the values in a given field.

Backup A copy of the database.

Back up (*v*) To create a duplicate copy of a database that is stored in a secure location.

Back-end database Part of a split database that contains the table objects and is stored on a file server that all users can access.

Background image An image that fills an entire form or report, appearing "behind" the other controls; also sometimes called a watermark.

Backstage view Appears when the File tab is clicked. The navigation bar on the left side contains commands to perform actions common to most Office programs, such as opening a file, saving a file, and closing the file.

Backward-compatible Software feature that enables documents saved in an older version of a program to be opened in a newer version of the program.

Bang notation A format that separates the object type from an object name and from a control name by using [square brackets] and exclamation points (!).

bas An abbreviation for Basic that is sometimes used to prefix the names of standard (global) modules.

Between...and Criteria that selects all records between the two dates, including the two dates. Between...and criteria work the same way as the >= and <= operators.

Bound control A control used in either a form or report to display data from the underlying field; used to edit and enter new data in a form.

Breakpoint A VBA debugging tool that works like a bookmark to suspend execution of the procedure at that statement so you can examine what is happening.

Brown-out A power problem caused by a dip in power, often making the lights dim.

Byte A field size for Number fields that allows entries only from 0 to 255.

Calculated field A field created in Query Design View that results from an expression of existing fields, Access functions, and arithmetic operators. For example, the entry Profit:[RetailPrice]-[WholesalePrice] in the field cell of the query design grid creates a calculated field called Profit that is the difference between the values in the RetailPrice and WholesalePrice fields.

Calculation A new value that is created by an expression in a text box on a form or report.

Calendar Picker A pop-up calendar from which you can choose dates for a date field.

Caption A field property that specifies the text to display in place of the value of the Name property for an object, control, or field.

Card A section for a particular type of content in a Sway presentation.

Cascade Delete Related Records A relationship option that means that if a record in the "one" side of a one-to-many relationship is deleted, all related records in the "many" table are also deleted.

Cascade Update Related Fields A relationship option that means that if a value in the primary key field (the field on the "one" side of a one-to-many relationship) is modified, all values in the foreign key field (the field on the "many" side of a one-to-many relationship) are automatically updated as well.

Cascading Style Sheets (CSS) A powerful, flexible, and productive way to define webpage formatting and layout.

Case In VBA, a programming structure that executes one of several groups of statements depending on the value of an expression.

Chart A visual representation of numeric data that helps users see comparisons, patterns, and trends in data. Also called a graph.

Chart type A category of chart layouts that determines the presentation of data on the chart such as column, pie, or line.

Chart Wizard A wizard that guides you through the steps of creating a chart in Access.

Child record A record contained in the "many" table in a one-to-many relationship.

Child table The "many" table in a one-to-many relationship.

Class module An Access module that is contained and executed within specific forms and reports.

Client In client/server computing, the user's PC.

Client/server computing Two or more information systems cooperatively processing to solve a problem.

Clip A short segment of audio, such as music, or video.

Clipboard A temporary Windows storage area that holds the selections you copy or cut.

Closing tag In HTML, the tag used to mark the end of text to be identified or formatted, such as </b> for end bold.

Cloud computing Using an Internet resource to complete your work such as saving a database to Microsoft OneDrive or maintaining Microsoft Office 365.

cmd A common three-character prefix for command buttons.

Code window Contains the VBA for the selected form, report, or module.

Column separator The thin line that separates field names to the left or right in a datasheet or the query design grid.

Combo box A bound control used to display a drop-down list of possible entries for a field in which you can also type an entry from the keyboard. It is a "combination" of the list box and text box controls.

Combo Box Wizard A wizard that helps you create a combo box control on a form.

Comma-separated values (CSV) A text file where fields are delimited, or separated, by commas.

Command button An unbound control commonly called a button, used to provide an easy way to initiate an action on a form.

Command Button Wizard A wizard that organizes the most common command button actions within several categories.

Command-line option A special series of characters added to the end of the path to the file (for example, C:\R2G.accdb /excl), and execute a special command when the file is opened.

Comment Text in a module that helps explain and document the code. Comments in VBA start with an apostrophe (') or the keyword rem (short for remark).

Comment line In VBA, a statement in the code that documents the code; it does not affect how the code runs. Comments in VBA start with an apostrophe (') or the keyword rem (short for remark).

Compact and repair To reorganize the parts of the database to eliminate wasted space on the disk storage device, which also helps prevent data integrity problems.

Compact Flash (CF) card A card about the size of a matchbook that you can plug into your computer to store data. Current compact flash cards store anywhere from 128MB to about 4GB of data.

Compatibility The ability of different programs to work together and exchange data.

Compile time The period during which source code is translated to executable code.

Compile-time error In VBA, an error that occurs as a result of incorrectly constructed code and is detected as soon as you run your code or select the Compile option on the Debug menu.

Conditional expression An expression resulting in either a true or false answer that determines whether a macro action will execute. Conditional expressions are used in VBA If statements.

Conditional formatting Formatting that is based on specified criteria. For example, a text box may be conditionally formatted do display its value in red if the value is a negative number.

Constant In VBA, an value that doesn't change throughout the execution of the code.

Contextual tab A tab that appears only when a specific task can be performed; contextual tabs appear in an accent color and close when no longer needed.

Control Any element on a form or report such as a label, text box, line, or combo box. Controls can be bound, unbound, or calculated.

Control Name A property that specifies the name of a control on a form or report.

Control Source property A property of a bound control in a form or report that determines the field to which the control is connected.

Convert To change the database file into one that can be opened in another version of Access such as an Access .mdb file for Access 2003.

Cortana The Microsoft Windows virtual assistant that integrates with Microsoft Edge to find and provide information.

Creative Commons license A public copyright license that allows the free distribution of an otherwise copyrighted work.

Criteria Entries (rules and limiting conditions) that determine which records are displayed when finding or filtering records in a datasheet or form, or when building a query.

Criteria syntax Rules by which criteria need to be entered. For example, text criteria syntax requires that the criteria are surrounded by quotation marks (" "). Date criteria are surrounded by pound signs (#).

Crosstab query A query that represents data in a cross-tabular layout (fields are used for both column and row headings), similar to PivotTables in other database and spreadsheet products.

Crosstab Query Wizard A wizard used to create crosstab queries and which helps identify fields that will be used for row and column headings, and fields that will be summarized within the datasheet.

Crosstab row A row in the query design grid used to specify the column and row headings and values for the crosstab query.

CSV *See* comma-separated values.

Currency A numeric format within the Format property that displays numbers with a currency symbol.

Current record The record that has the focus or is being edited.

Data area When creating a chart, the area in the Chart Wizard that determines what data the chart graphs.

Data cleansing The process of removing and fixing orphan records in a database.

Data macro A type of macro that allows you to embed macro capabilities directly in a table to add, change, or delete data based on conditions you specify.

Data type A required property for each field that defines the type of data that can be entered in each field. Valid data types include AutoNumber, Short Text, Long Text, Number, Currency, Yes/No, Date/Time, and Hyperlink.

Database administration The task of making a database faster, easier, more secure, and more reliable.

Database designer The person responsible for building and maintaining tables, queries, forms, and reports.

Database Documenter A feature on the Database Tools tab that helps you create reports containing information about the database.

Database template A tool that can be used to quickly create a new database based on a particular subject such as assets, contacts, events, or projects.

Database user The person primarily interested in entering, editing, and analyzing the data in the database.

Datasheet A spreadsheet-like grid that displays fields as columns and records as rows.

Datasheet View A view that lists the records of an object in a datasheet. Tables, queries, and most form objects have a Datasheet View.

Date function A built-in Access function used to display the current date on a form or report; enter the Date function as Date().

Debug To determine why a macro or program doesn't run correctly.

Declaration statement A type of VBA statement that precedes procedure statements and helps set rules for how the statements in the module are processed.

Default View property A form property that determines whether a subform automatically opens in Datasheet or Continuous Forms view.

Delete query An action query that deletes selected records from one or more tables.

Delete row When creating a Delete query, a row that appears in the query design grid to specify criteria for selecting which records to delete.

Delimited text file A text file that typically stores one record on each line, with the field values separated by a common character such as a comma, tab, or dash.

Delimiter A common character, such as a comma, tab, or dash.

Deprecate To retire the usage of some type of technology in the current standard. For example the <font> tag has been deprecated in the latest HTML standards.

Description A query property that allows you to better document the purpose or author of a query.

Design View A view in which the structure of an object can be manipulated. Every Access object (table, query, form, report, macro, and module) has a Design View.

Desktop database A traditional Access database available to users who work with Access on their computers over a local area network.

Dialog box launcher An icon you can click to open a dialog box or task pane from which to choose related commands.

Dim A VBA keyword that declares a variable.

DLookup A domain function that returns, or "looks up," a value from a specified table or query.

DoCmd A VBA object that contains many methods to run common Access commands such as closing windows, opening forms, previewing reports, navigating records, and setting the value of controls.

Docs.com A Microsoft website designed for sharing Sway sites.

Document window Most of the screen in Word, PowerPoint, and Excel, where you create a document, slide, or worksheet.

Domain The recordset (table or query) that contains the field used in a domain function calculation.

Domain function A function used in an expression to calculate a value based on a field that is not included in the Record Source property for a form or report. Also called domain aggregate function.

Drawing canvas In OneNote, a container for shapes and lines.

Dynaset A property value for the Recordset Type query property that allows updates to data in a recordset.

Edit List Items button A button you click to add items to a combo box list in Form View.

Edit mode When working with Access records, the mode in which Access assumes you are trying to edit a particular field, so keystrokes such as [Ctrl][End], [Ctrl][Home], [←], and [→] move the insertion point within the field. When working with charts, a mode that lets you select and modify individual chart elements such as the title, legend, bars, or axes.

Edit record symbol A pencil-like symbol that appears in the record selector box to the left of the record that is currently being edited in either a datasheet or a form.

Element A pair of HTML tags and its contents, such as <p>paragraph text</p>.

Else The part of an If statement that allows you to run a different set of actions if the conditional expression evaluates False.

ElseIf In VBA, a keyword that executes a statement depending on the value of an expression.

Empty tag In HTML, a single, unpaired tag that ends with a forward slash, such as <br /> for line break or <hr /> for a horizontal rule (line).

Enabled property A control property that determines whether the control can have the focus in Form View.

Encryption To make the data in the database unreadable by tools other than opening the Access database itself, which is protected by a password.

End Function In VBA, a required statement to mark the end of the code that defines the new function.

End If In VBA, a statement needed to mark the end of the If block of code.

End Select When defining a new Select Case group of VBA statements, the End Select statement is required as the last statement to mark the end of the VBA code.

End Sub When defining a new sub in VBA, the End Sub statement is required as the last statement to mark the end of the VBA code that defines the sub.

Error indicator An icon that automatically appears in Design View to indicate some type of error. For example, a green error indicator appears in the upper-left corner of a text box in Form Design View if the text box Control Source property is set to a field name that doesn't exist.

Event A specific activity that happens, such as the click of a command button or an entry in a field, that can be used to initiate the execution of a macro or VBA procedure.

Event handler A procedure that is triggered by an event. Also called an event procedure.

Exclusive mode A mode indicating that you are the only person who has the database open, and others cannot open the file during this time.

Export To copy Access records to another database, spreadsheet, or file format.

Expression A combination of values, functions, and operators that calculates to a single value. Access expressions start with an equal sign and are placed in a text box in either Form Design View or Report Design View.

Extensible Markup Language (XML) A open source markup language mainly used to identify and share data across a wide range of applications.

External hard drive A portable storage device that typically plugs into a computer using either a USB or FireWire port.

Field In a table, a field corresponds to a column of data, a specific piece or category of data such as a first name, last name, city, state, or phone number.

Field list A small window that lists the fields in a table for a query or the fields in the record source for a form or report.

Field name The name given to each field in a table.

Field properties Characteristics that further define the field. Field properties are displayed in Table Design view.

Field Properties pane The lower half of Table Design View, which displays field properties.

Field selector The button to the left of a field in Table Design View that indicates the currently selected field. Also the thin gray bar above each field in the query grid.

Field Size property A field property that determines the number of characters that can be entered in a field.

File A stored collection of data; in Access, the entire database and all of its objects are in one file.

File server A centrally located computer from which every user can access the same information via the network.

Filter A way to temporarily display only those records that match given criteria.

Filter By Form A way to filter data that allows two or more criteria to be specified at the same time.

Filter By Selection A way to filter records for an exact match.

Find Duplicates Query Wizard A wizard used to create a query that determines whether a table contains duplicate values in one or more fields.

Find Unmatched Query Wizard A wizard that guides you through the steps of creating a query that finds records in one table that do not have matching records in a related table.

First normal form (1NF) The first degree of normalization, in which a table has rows and columns with no repeating groups.

Focus The property that indicates which field would be edited if you were to start typing.

Force New Page A property that forces a report section to start printing at the top of a new page.

Foreign key field In a one-to-many relationship between two tables, the foreign key field is the field in the "many" table that links the table to the primary key field in the "one" table.

Form An Access object that provides an easy-to-use data entry screen that generally shows only one record at a time.

Form Header The section of a form that appears at the beginning of a form and typically displays the form title.

Form section A location in a form that contains controls. The section in which a control is placed determines where and how often the control prints.

Form View View of a form object that displays data from the underlying recordset and allows you to enter and update data.

Form Wizard An Access wizard that helps you create a form.

Format Painter A tool you can use when designing and laying out forms and reports to copy formatting characteristics from one control to another.

Format property A field property that controls how information is displayed and printed.

Formatting Enhancing the appearance of information through font, size, and color changes.

Free response quiz A type of Office Mix quiz containing questions that require short answers.

FROM A SQL keyword that determines how tables are joined.

Front-end database Part of a split database application that contains the database objects other than tables (it contains the queries, forms, reports, macros, and modules), and which links to the back-end database tables.

Function A special, predefined formula that provides a shortcut way to make a calculation. SUM, COUNT, and IIF are examples of built-in Access functions. You can create custom functions using VBA.

Gallery A visual collection of choices you can browse through to make a selection. Often available with Live Preview.

Get External Data – Excel Spreadsheet A dialog box used to import data from an external file into an Access database.

Gigabyte (GB or G) One billion bytes (or one thousand megabytes).

Global module Modules that store code that may be reused many places in the database application.

Graphic image *See* Image.

Grouping A way to sort records in a particular order, as well as provide a section before and after each group of records.

Groups Each tab on the Ribbon is arranged into groups to make features easy to find.

Hidden property A property you can apply to an object to hide the object in the Navigation Pane.

HTML5 The latest version of HTML as defined by the leading international standards committee on fundamental web technologies, the W3C, www.w3c.org.

Hub A pane in Microsoft Edge that provides access to favorite websites, a reading list, browsing history, and downloaded files.

Hyperlink Address property A control property that allows the control to behave like a hyperlink.

Hyperlink control A control on a form that when clicked, works like a hyperlink to redirect the user to a webpage or file.

Hyperlink data type A data type for fields that store a link to a webpage, file, or email address.

Hyperlink field A field with the Hyperlink data type.

Hyperlink pointer A mouse pointer that looks like a pointing hand when it is positioned over a hyperlink.

Hypertext Markup Language (HTML) The language used to describe content in a traditional webpage.

If statement A statement in a macro that allows you to run macro actions based on the result of a conditional expression.

If...Then In VBA, a logical structure that executes code (the code that follows the Then statement) when the value of an expression is true (the expression follows the If statement).

If...Then...Else In VBA, a logical structure that allows you to test logical conditions and execute statements only if the conditions are true. If...Then...Else code can be composed of one or several statements, depending on how many conditions you want to test, how many possible answers you want to provide, and what you want the code to do based on the results of the tests.

Image A nontextual piece of information such as a picture, piece of clip art, drawn object, or graph. Because images are graphical (and not numbers or letters), they are sometimes referred to as graphical images.

Immediate window In the Visual Basic Editor, a pane where you can determine the value of any argument at the breakpoint.

Import To quickly convert data from an external file into an Access database. You can import data from one Access database to another—or from many other data sources such as files created by Excel, SharePoint, Outlook, or text files in an HTML, XML, or delimited text file format such as CSV (comma separated values).

Import Spreadsheet Wizard A wizard that guides you through the steps of importing data from Excel into an Access database.

Index A field property that keeps track of the order of the values in the field. If you often sort on a field, the Index property should be set to Yes to improve performance (because the order of the records has already been created by the index).

Indexed property A field property that can be changed to determine whether a field is indexed.

Infinity symbol The symbol that indicates the "many" side of a one-to-many relationship.

Ink to Math tool The OneNote tool that converts handwritten mathematical formulas to formatted equations or expressions.

Ink to Text tool The OneNote tool that converts inked handwriting to typed text.

Inked handwriting In OneNote, writing produced when using a pen tool to enter text.

Inking toolbar In Microsoft Edge, a collection of tools for annotating a webpage.

Inner join A type of relationship in which a query displays only records where joined fields from *both* tables are equal. This means that if a parent table has any records for which there are no matching records in the child table, those parent records do not appear in the resulting datasheet.

Input Mask A field property that provides a visual guide for users as they enter data.

Insertion point A blinking vertical line that appears when you click in a text box; indicates where new text will be inserted.

Integrate To incorporate a document and parts of a document created in one program into another program; for example, to incorporate an Excel chart into a PowerPoint slide, or an Access report into a Word document.

IntelliSense technology In VBA, visual aids that appear as you write a VBA statement to help you complete it.

Interface The look and feel of a program; for example, the appearance of commands and the way they are organized in the program window.

Is Not Null An operator you use to query for any value other than a null value.

Is Null An operator you use to query for null values.

Join line The line identifying which fields establish the relationship between two related tables. Also called a link line.

JPEG (Joint Photographic Experts Group) Acronym for Joint Photographic Experts Group, which defines the standards for the compression algorithms that allow image files to be stored in an efficient compressed format. JPEG files use the .jpg filename extension.

Junction table A table created to establish separate one-to-many relationships to two tables that have a many-to-many relationship.

Key symbol The symbol that identifies the primary key field in each table.

Label control An unbound control that displays text to describe and clarify other information on a form or report.

Label Wizard A report wizard that precisely positions and sizes information to print on a vast number of standard business label specifications.

Landscape orientation A printout that is 11 inches wide by 8.5 inches tall.

Launch To open or start a program on your computer.

Layout A way to group several controls together on a form or report to more quickly add, delete, rearrange, resize, or align controls.

Layout View An Access view that lets you make some design changes to a form or report while you are browsing the data.

Left function An Access function that returns a specified number of characters, starting with the left side of a value in a Text field.

Left join A type of relationship in which a query displays all of the records in the "one" (parent) table, regardless of whether they have matching records in the "many" (child) table. Also called a left outer join.

Len function Built-in Access function used to return the number of characters in a field.

Like operator An operator used in a query to find values in a field that match the pattern you specify.

Limit to List A combo box control property that allows you to limit the entries made by that control to those provided by the combo box drop-down list.

Line A graphical element that can be added to a report to highlight information or enhance its clarity.

Link To connect an Access database to data in an external file such as another Access database table; an Excel or other type of spreadsheet; a text file; an HTML file; or an XML file.

Link Child Fields A subform property that determines which field serves as the "many" link between the subform and main form.

Link line The line identifying which fields establish the relationship between two related tables.

Link Master Fields A subform property that determines which field serves as the "one" link between the main form and the subform.

Link Spreadsheet Wizard A wizard that guides you through the steps of linking to a spreadsheet.

List box A bound control that displays a list of possible choices for the user. Used mainly on forms.

List Rows A control property that determines how many items can be displayed in a list, such as in a combo box.

Live Preview A feature that lets you point to a choice in a gallery or palette and see the results in the document or object without actually clicking the choice.

Local area network (LAN) A type of network installed to link multiple PCs together so they can share hardware and software resources.

Locked property A control property specifies whether you can edit data in a control on Form View.

Logic error In VBA, an error that occurs when the code runs without obvious problems, but still doesn't produce the desired result.

Logical view The view of a query that shows the selected fields and records as a datasheet.

Long Date A date format provided by the Format property that displays dates in the following format: Friday, June 19, 2017.

Long Integer The default field size for a Number field.

Lookup field A field that has lookup properties. Lookup properties are used to create a drop-down list of values to populate the field.

Lookup properties Field properties that allow you to supply a drop-down list of values for a field.

Lookup table A small table that stores values used in a field of another table.

Lookup Wizard A wizard used in Table Design View that allows one field to "look up" values from another table or entered list. For example, you might use the Lookup Wizard to specify that the Customer Number field in the Sales table display the Customer Name field values from the Customers table.

M

Macro A database object that stores actions to complete Access tasks.

Macro Design View An Access window in which you create and modify macros.

Mail merge A way to export Access data by merging it to a Word document. Data from an Access table or query is combined into a Word form letter, label, or envelope to create mass mailing documents.

Mail merge task pane A pane that appears in the Word window to step you through the mail-merge process.

Main document In a mail merge, the document used to determine how the document and Access data are combined. This is the standard text that will be consistent for each document created in the mail merge process.

Main form A form that contains a subform control.

Main report A report that contains a subreport control.

Make Table query An action query that creates a new table of data for a selected datasheet. The location of the new table can be the current database or another Access database.

Many-to-many relationship The relationship between two tables in an Access database in which one record of one table relates to many records in the other table and vice versa. You cannot directly create a many-to-many relationship between two tables in Access. To relate two tables with such a relationship, you must establish a third table called junction table that creates separate one-to-many relationships with the two original tables.

Margin The space between the outer edge of the control and the data displayed inside the control.

Medium Date A date format provided by the Format property that displays dates in the dd-Mmm-yy format, such as 19-Jun-17.

Megabyte (MB or M) One million bytes (or one thousand kilobytes).

Merge field A code in the main document of a mail merge that is replaced with the values in the field that the code represents when the mail merge is processed.

MessageBox A macro action that displays an informational message to the user.

Method An action that an object can perform. Procedures are often written to invoke methods in response to user actions.

Microsoft Excel The spreadsheet program in the Microsoft Office suite.

Microsoft OneNote Mobile app The lightweight version of Microsoft OneNote designed for phones, tablets, and other mobile devices.

Microsoft Word Mail Merge Wizard A wizard that guides you through the steps of preparing to merge Access data with a Word document.

Module An Access object that stores Visual Basic for Applications (VBA) programming code.

Multicolumn report A report that repeats the same information in more than one column on the page.

Multiuser A characteristic that means more than one person can enter and edit data in the same Access database at the same time.

Multivalued field A field that allows you to make more than one choice from a drop-down list.

Name property The property that determines the name of a control or object. The Name property value is used in VBA to reference and work with the control.

Navigation buttons Buttons in the lower-left corner of a datasheet or form that allow you to quickly navigate between the records in the underlying object as well as add a new record.

Navigation form A special Access form that provides an easy-to-use database interface to navigate between the objects of the database.

Navigation mode A mode in which Access assumes that you are trying to move between the fields and records of the datasheet (rather than edit a specific field's contents), so keystrokes such as [Ctrl][Home] and [Ctrl][End] move you to the first and last field of the datasheet.

Navigation Pane A pane in the Access program window that provides a way to move between objects (tables, queries, forms, reports, macros, and modules) in the database.

Navigation system style In a navigation form, a style that determines how the navigation buttons will be displayed on the form.

Normalize To structure data for a relational database using appropriate one-to-many relationships between related tables.

Note In OneNote, a small window that contains text or other types of information.

Notebook In OneNote, the container for notes, drawings, and other content.

Now() An Access function that displays today's date.

Null Means that a value has not been entered for the field.

Null entry The state of "nothingness" in a field. Any entry such as 0 in a numeric field or a space in a text field is not null. It is common to search for empty fields by using the Null criterion in a filter or query. The Is Not Null criterion finds all records where there is an entry of any kind.

Object A table, query, form, report, macro, or module in a database. In VBA, any item that can be identified or manipulated is an object, including the traditional Access objects (table, query, form, report, macro, module) as well as other items that have properties such as controls, sections, and existing procedures.

Object list In a VBA class module, lists the objects associated with the current form or report.

ODBC *See* open database connectivity.

OLE A field data type that stores pointers that tie files, such as pictures, sound clips, or spreadsheets, created in other programs to a record.

On Click A property of a control such as a command button that triggers an event when the control is clicked.

On Current An event that occurs when focus moves from one record to another in a form.

On Dbl Click An Access event that is triggered by a double-click.

On Error GoTo Upon an error in the execution of a procedure, the On Error GoTo statement specifies the location (the statement) where the procedure should continue.

On Got Focus An Access event that is triggered when a specified control gets the focus.

OneDrive A Microsoft storage system that lets you easily save, share, and access your files from any device with Internet access.

One-to-many line The line that appears in the Relationships or query design window and shows which field is used between two tables to serve as the linking field. The one-to-many line displays a "1" next to the field that serves as the "one" side of the relationship and displays an infinity symbol next to the field that serves as the "many" side of the relationship when referential integrity is specified for the relationship. Also called the one-to-many join line.

One-to-many relationship The relationship between two tables in an Access database in which a common field links the tables together. The linking field is called the primary key field in the "one" table of the relationship and the foreign key field in the "many" table of the relationship.

Online collaboration The ability to incorporate feedback or share information across the Internet or a company network or intranet.

Open database connectivity (ODBC) A collection of standards that govern how Access connects to other sources of data.

Opening tag In HTML, the tag used to mark the beginning of text to be identified or formatted, such as <p> to start a paragraph.

OpenReport action A macro action that opens a specified report.

Option button A bound control used to display a limited list of mutually exclusive choices for a field, such as "female" or "male" for a gender field in form or report.

Option Compare Database A VBA declaration statement that determines the way string values (text) will be sorted.

Option Explicit A VBA declaration statement that specifies that you must explicitly declare all variables used in all procedures; if you attempt to use an undeclared variable name, an error occurs at compile time.

Option group A bound control placed on a form that is used to group together several option buttons that provide a limited number of values for a field.

Option Value An option button property that determines the values entered into a field when the option button is selected.

OR criteria Criteria placed on different rows of the query design grid. A record will appear in the resulting datasheet if it is true for any single row.

ORDER BY A SQL keyword that determines how records in the query result are sorted.

Orphan record A record in the "many" table of a one-to-many relationship that doesn't have a matching entry in the linking field of the "one" table. Orphan records cannot be created if referential integrity is enforced on a relationship.

Padding The space between the outside borders of adjacent controls.

Page In OneNote, a workspace for inserting notes and other content, similar to a page in a physical notebook.

Parameter criteria Text entered in [square brackets] that prompts the user for an entry each time the query is run.

Parameter query A query that displays a dialog box to prompt users for field criteria. The entry in the dialog box determines which records appear on the final datasheet, similar to criteria entered directly in the query design grid.

Parameter report A report that prompts you for criteria to determine the records to use for the report.

Parent record A record contained in the "one" table in a one-to-many relationship.

Parent table The "one" table in a one-to-many relationship.

Password A combination of uppercase and lowercase letters, numbers, and symbols that when entered correctly, allow you to open a password-protected database.

Percent A number format provided by the Format property that displays numbers with a percent symbol.

Performance Analyzer An Access tool that studies the structure and size of your database and makes a variety of recommendations on how you can improve its performance.

Pixel (picture element) One pixel is the measurement of one picture element on the screen.

Pmt function Built-in Access function used to calculate the monthly payment on a loan; enter the Pmt function as Pmt([Rate],[Term],[Loan]).

Portable Document Format (PDF) A file format developed by Adobe Systems that has become the standard format for exchanging documents.

Portrait orientation A printout that is 8.5 inches wide by 11 inches tall.

Previewing Prior to printing, seeing onscreen exactly how the printout will look.

Primary key field A field that contains unique information for each record. A primary key field cannot contain a null entry.

Print Preview An Access view that shows you how a report or other object will print on a sheet of paper.

Private Sub A statement that indicates that a sub procedure is accessible only to other procedures in the module where it is declared.

Procedure A series of VBA statements that performs an operation or calculates an answer. VBA has two types of procedures: functions and subs.

Procedure list In a VBA standard module, lists the procedures in the module; in a class module, lists events (such as Click or Dblclick).

Project In VBA, a module object or a form or report object that contains a class module.

Project Explorer window In the Visual Basic Editor, a window you use to switch between objects that can contain VBA code.

Property A characteristic that defines the appearance and behavior of items in the database such as objects, fields, sections, and controls. You can view the properties for an item by opening its Property Sheet.

Property Sheet A window that displays an exhaustive list of properties for the chosen control, section, or object on a form or report.

Property Update Options A Smart Tag that applies property changes in one field to other objects of the database that use the field.

Query An Access object that provides a spreadsheet-like view of the data, similar to that in tables. It may provide the user with a subset of fields and/or records from one or more tables. Queries are created when the user has a "question" about the data in the database.

Query Datasheet View The view of a query that shows the selected fields and records as a datasheet. Query Datasheet View is displayed when you run a query.

Query design grid The bottom pane of the Query Design View window in which you specify the fields, sort order, and limiting criteria for the query.

Query Design View The window in which you develop queries by specifying the fields, sort order, and limiting criteria that determine which fields and records are displayed in the resulting datasheet.

Question mark (?) A wildcard character used to search for any single character in query criteria.

Quick Access Toolbar A small toolbar on the left side of a Microsoft application window's title bar, containing icons that you click to quickly perform common actions, such as saving a file.

Read-only An object property that indicates whether the object can read and display data, but cannot be used to change (write to) data.

Reading view In Microsoft Edge, the display of a webpage that removes ads and most graphics and uses a simple format for the text.

Record A row of data in a table.

Record Source A property of a form or report that identifies the table or query containing the data to display.

Recordset Type A property that determines if and how records displayed by a query are locked. The Recordset Type settings are Snapshot and Dynaset.

Referential integrity A set of Access rules that govern data entry and help ensure data accuracy. Setting referential integrity on a relationship prevents the creation of orphan records.

Relational database software Software such as Access that is used to manage data organized in a relational database.

Relationship report A printout of the Relationships window that shows how a relational database is designed and includes table names, field names, primary key fields, and one-to-many relationship lines.

Report An Access object that creates a professional printout of data that may contain such enhancements as headers, footers, and calculations on groups of records.

Report Design View An Access view that allows you to work with a complete range of report, section, and control properties.

Report Wizard An Access wizard that helps you create a report.

Resize bar A thin gray bar that separates the field lists in the query design grid.

Responsive design A way to provide content so that it adapts appropriately to the size of the display on any device.

Ribbon Appears below the title bar in every Office program window, and displays commands you're likely to need for the current task.

Rich Text A Text Format property that allows you to mix formatting of text displayed by a text box on a form or a report.

Rich Text Format (RTF) A file format for exporting data to a text file that can be opened and edited in Word.

Right function Built-in Access function used to return the specified number of characters from the end of a field value.

Right join A type of relationship in which a query selects all records in the "many" (child) table even if there are no matches in the "one" (parent) table. Also called a right outer join.

Row Source A property that defines the values to display in a list, such as in a Lookup field or combo box.

RTF *See* Rich Text Format.

Ruler A vertical or horizontal guide that appears in Form and Report Design View to help you position controls.

Run a query To open a query and view the fields and records that you have selected for the query presented as a datasheet.

Run-time error In VBA, an error that occurs as incorrectly constructed code runs and includes attempting an illegal operation such as dividing by zero or moving focus to a control that doesn't exist. When you encounter a run-time error, VBA will stop executing your procedure at the statement in which the error occurred and highlight the line with a yellow background in the Visual Basic Editor.

Sandbox A computer security mechanism that helps to prevent attackers from gaining control of a computer.

Save As command A command on the File tab that saves the entire database (and all objects it contains) or only the current object with a new name.

Save Database As An Access command that saves an entire database including all of its objects to a completely new database file.

Save Object As An Access command that allows you to save the current object, such as a table, query, form, report, macro, or module with a new name.

Saved Exports An option provided in Access that lets you quickly repeat the export process by saving the export steps.

Saved Imports An option provided in Access that lets you quickly repeat the import process by saving the import steps.

Schema A description of the fields and their properties stored in XML data.

Screen capture An electronic snapshot of your screen, as if you took a picture of it with a camera, which you can paste into a document.

Screen clipping In OneNote, an image copied from any part of a computer screen.

Screen recording In Office Mix, a video you create by capturing your desktop and any actions performed on it.

Scrub the database To remove and fix orphan records and otherwise improve the quality and consistency of data in the database.

Second normal form (2NF) The second degree of normalization, in which redundant data from an original table is extracted, placed in a new table, and related to the original table.

Section A location in a form or report that contains controls. The section in which a control is placed determines where and how often the control prints.

Section properties Characteristics that define each section in a report.

Section tab In OneNote, a divider for organizing a notebook.

Secure digital (SD) card A type of small external storage device that slips directly into a computer with an SD card reader slot.

SELECT A SQL keyword used to create select queries.

Select Case In VBA, executes one of several groups of Case statements depending on the value of an expression.

Select query A query that selects fields and records matching specific criteria and displays them in a datasheet.

Server In client/server computing, the shared file server, mini, or mainframe computer. The server usually handles corporate-wide computing activities such as data storage and management, security, and connectivity to other networks.

SetProperty A macro action that allows you to manipulate the property value of any control on a form.

Shape effect A special visual impact (such as shadow, glow, soft edges, and bevel) applied to command buttons.

Shared folder A folder created online, such as on OneDrive, which you allow others to open and access.

SharePoint server A server computer that runs Microsoft SharePoint, software that allows an organization to host Web pages on an intranet.

Short Date A date format provided by the Format property that displays dates in the mm/dd/yyyy format, such as 6/19/2017.

Simple Query Wizard An Access wizard that prompts you for information it needs to create a new query.

Single step To run a macro one line (one action) at a time to observe the effect of each specific action in the Macro Single Step dialog box.

Sizing handles Small squares at each corner of a selected control in Access. Dragging a handle resizes the control. Also known as handles.

Slide Notes In Office Mix, the written and displayed version of notes typically used to recite narration while creating a slide recording.

Slide recording In Office Mix, a video you create by recording action with a webcam, a camera attached or built into a computer.

Smart Tag A button that provides a small menu of options and automatically appears under certain conditions to help you work with a task, such as correcting errors. For example, the AutoCorrect Options button, which helps you correct typos and update properties, and the Error Indicator button, which helps identify potential design errors in Form and Report Design View, are smart tags.

Snapshot A property value for the Recordset Type query property that locks the recordset (which prevents it from being updated).

Sort To reorder records in either ascending or descending order based on the values of a particular field.

Spike A surge in power, which can cause damage to the hardware.

Split To separate the tables into one database and the other database objects into another.

Split form A form split into two panes; the upper pane allows you to display the fields of one record in any arrangement, and the lower pane maintains a datasheet view of the first few records.

SQL (Structured Query Language) A language that provides a standardized way to request information from a relational database system.

SQL View A query view that displays the SQL code for the query.

Standard A number format provided by the Format property that displays numbers with no symbols or decimal places.

Standard module A type of Access module that contains global code that can be executed from anywhere in the database. Standard modules are displayed as module objects in the Navigation Pane.

Startup option One of a series of commands that execute when the database is opened.

Statement A single line of code within a VBA procedure.

Storyline In Sway, the workspace for assembling a presentation.

Strong password A password longer than eight characters that uses a combination of uppercase and lowercase letters, numbers, and symbols.

Stub In the Visual Basic window, the first and last lines of a procedure.

Sub (sub procedure) A procedure that performs a series of VBA statements, but it does not return a value and cannot be used in an expression like a function procedure. You use subs to manipulate controls and objects. They are generally executed when an event occurs, such as when a command button is clicked or a form is opened.

Subdatasheet A datasheet that is nested within another datasheet to show related records. The subdatasheet shows the records on the "many" side of a one-to-many relationship.

Subform A form placed within a form that shows related records from another table or query. A subform generally displays many records at a time in a datasheet arrangement.

Submacro A collection of actions within a macro object that allows you to name and create multiple, separate macros within a single macro object.

Subreport A control that displays a report within another report.

Suite A group of programs that are bundled together and share a similar interface, making it easy to transfer skills and program content among them.

Sum function A mathematical function that totals values in a field.

Summary query A query used to calculate and display information about records grouped together.

Summary report A report that calculates and displays information about records grouped together.

Surge protector A power strip with surge protection.

Sway site A website Sway creates to share and display a Sway presentation.

Switchboard form A special Access form that provides command buttons to help users navigate throughout a database.

Sync In OneNote, to save a new or updated notebook so that all versions of the notebook, such as a notebook on OneDrive and a copy on a hard drive, have the same contents.

Syntax Rules for entering information such as query criteria, property values, and programming statements.

Syntax error In VBA, an error that occurs immediately as you are writing a VBA statement that cannot be read by the Visual Basic Editor. Syntax errors are displayed in red text.

Tab control An unbound control used to create a three-dimensional aspect to a form so that other controls can be organized and shown in Form View by clicking the "tabs."

Tab Index property A form property that indicates the numeric tab order for all controls on the form that have the Tab Stop property set to Yes.

Tab order property A form property that determines the sequence in which the controls on the form receive the focus when the user presses [Tab] or [Enter] in Form view.

Tab Stop property A form property that determines whether a field accepts focus.

Table A collection of records for a single subject, such as all of the customer records; the fundamental building block of a relational database because it stores all of the data.

Table Design View The view in which you can add, delete, or modify fields and their associated properties.

Table layout A way of connecting controls together so that when you move or resize them in Layout or Design View, the action you take on one control applies to all the controls in the layout.

Tabs Organizational unit used for commands on the Ribbon. The tab names appear at the top of the Ribbon and the active tab appears in front.

Tag In HTML, the codes used to identify or "mark up" the content in a webpage such as <p>....</p> tags to markup a paragraph.

Target table The table to which an Append query adds records.

td An HTML table data tag <td>...</td> that separates each field of data in a table.

Template A sample file, such as a database provided within the Microsoft Access program. In OneNote, a page design you can apply to new pages to provide an appealing background, a consistent layout, or elements suitable for certain types of notes, such as meeting notes or to-do lists.

Terabyte (TB) One triillion bytes (or one thousand gigabytes).

Text Align property A control property that determines the alignment of text within the control.

Text box The most common type of control used to display field values.

Theme A predefined set of colors, fonts, line and fill effects, and other formats that can be applied to an Access database and give it a consistent, professional look.

Third normal form (3NF) The third degree of normalization, in which calculated fields (also called derived fields) such as totals or taxes are removed. Strive to create databases that adhere to the rules of third normal form.

Title bar Appears at the top of every Office program window; it displays the document or database name and program name.

To Do tag In OneNote, an icon that helps you keep track of your assignments and other tasks.

Top Values A feature in Query Design View that lets you specify a number or percentage of sorted records that you want to display in the query's datasheet.

Total row Row in the query design grid used to specify how records should be grouped and summarized with aggregate functions. Total row also refers to the last row of a datasheet where the values in a field may be summarized in a number of ways such as summed or counted.

tr An HTML table row tag <tr>...</tr> that separates each record in a table.

Trusted database When opened, a trusted database that allows you to run its macros and VBA without prompts.

Trusted folder A folder specified as a trusted folder is used for storing databases with macros and VBA. When opened, databases in a trusted folder allow you to run their macros and VBA without prompts.

Unbound control A control that does not change from record to record and exists only to clarify or enhance the appearance of the form, using elements such as labels, lines, and clip art.

Update query An action query that updates the values in a field.

Update To row When creating an Update query, a row that appears in the query design grid to specify criteria or an expression for updating records.

UPS (Uninterruptible Power Supply) A device that provides constant power to other devices, including computers.

USB (Universal Serial Bus) drive A device that plugs into a computer's USB port to store data. USB drives are also called thumb drives, flash drives, and travel drives.

User interface A collective term for all the ways you interact with a software program.

Validation Rule A field property that helps eliminate unreasonable entries by establishing criteria for an entry before it is accepted into the database.

Validation Text A field property that determines what message appears if a user attempts to make a field entry that does not pass the validation rule for that field.

Value argument In a macro, the argument that determines the value of a property or field.

Variable In VBA, a named location that stores data that can be used, modified, or displayed during the execution of the procedure.

VBA *See* Visual Basic for Applications.

VBE *See* Visual Basic Editor.

View Each Access object has different views for different purposes. For example, you work with data in Datasheet View. You modify the design of the object in Layout and Design Views. You preview a printout in Print Preview. Common views include Datasheet View for a table or query, or Design View for any Access object.

Visible property A property that determines whether a control such as a label is visible in a form or report.

Visual Basic Editor (VBE) Comprises the entire Microsoft Visual Basic program window that contains smaller windows, including the Code window and Project Explorer window.

Visual Basic for Applications (VBA) A programming language provided within each program of the Microsoft Office suite to help you extend the program's capabilities. In Access, VBA code is stored within modules.

Web compatible An Access object that can be opened and used in a browser.

Web Note In Microsoft Edge, an annotation on a webpage.

Wildcard A special character used in criteria to find, filter, and query data. The asterisk (*) stands for any group of characters. For example, the criteria M* in a State field criterion cell would find all records where the state entry was Massachusetts, Missouri, Montana, MA, MO, MT, and any other entry that starts with M. The question mark (?) wildcard stands for only one character. In this example, M? would only find MA, MO, or MT.

Word wrap A feature in word processing programs that determines when a line of text extends into the right margin of the page and automatically forces the text to the next line without you needing to press Enter.

World Wide Web Consortium (W3C) The leading international standards committee on fundamental web technologies.

XML Short for Extensible Markup Language, a language used to mark up structured data so that the data can be more easily shared between different computer programs.

XML file A text file containing XML tags that identify field names and data. *See also* Extensible Markup Language (XML).

XSD A file that stores the schema of data stored in an XML file.

XSL A file that describes how to display the data in an XML file.

Zero-length string A deliberate entry that contains no characters. You enter a zero-length string by typing two quotation marks ("") with no space between them.

Zooming in A feature that makes a printout appear larger but shows less of it on screen at once; does not affect the actual size of the printout.

Zooming out A feature that shows more of a printout on screen at once but at a reduced size; does not affect the actual size of the printout.

Index

frm prefix, AC 327
FROM keyword, AC 140
front-end databases, AC 360
function(s), AC 88, AC 146, AC 147, AC 322
  aggregate, AC 148, AC 149
  creating, AC 326–327
  domain, AC 280–281
Function statement, AC 325

G

galleries, OFF 6
GBs (gigabytes), AC 356
General option, Access Options dialog box, AC 349
Get External Data - Excel Spreadsheet dialog box, AC 218, AC 220, AC 221
gigabytes (GBs), AC 356
global modules, AC 324
Go To button, AC 35
GoToControl macro, AC 301
GoToRecord macro, AC 301
graph(s). *See* chart(s)
graphic images, inserting in forms, AC 68–69
greater than operator (>), AC 36, AC 143
greater than or equal to operator (>=), AC 36, AC 143
Group Footer section, AC 84
  reports, AC 191
Group Header section, AC 84
  reports, AC 191
grouping records in reports, AC 86–87

H

handwriting, converting to text, PA 3–4
hard drives, external, AC 356
Help system, OFF 14, OFF 15
hidden objects, restoring, AC 257
Hidden property, AC 256
hiding fields in datasheets, AC 30
  objects in Navigation Pane, AC 346
HTML. *See* Hypertext Markup Language (HTML)
HTML Document dialog box, AC 376, AC 377

HTML elements. *See* HTML tags
HTML tags
  common, AC 375
  empty, AC 374
  formatting text, AC 374–375
  opening and closing, AC 374
  table, AC 378, AC 379
HTML5, AC 375
Hub, Edge, PA 14
Hyperlink Address property, AC 372
hyperlink controls, AC 372–373
Hyperlink data type, AC 7, AC 370
Hyperlink dialog box, AC 370, AC 371
hyperlink fields, AC 370–371
hyperlink pointer, AC 370
Hypertext Markup Language (HTML)
  exporting to, AC 376–377
  formatting text with HTML tags, AC 374–375
  HTML5, AC 375
  importing from, AC 378–379

I

<i> tag, AC 375
If statements, macros, AC 306–307
If...Then statement, AC 325
If...Then...Else statement, AC 325, AC 328–329
Immediate window, AC 336
Import Spreadsheet Wizard, AC 218, AC 219
ImportExportSpreadsheet macro, AC 301
ImportExportText macro, AC 301
importing
  from another database, AC 233
  data from Excel, AC 218–219
  file formats Access can link to, import, and export, AC 223
  from HTML and XML, AC 378–379
In operator, AC 143
indentation, readability of code, AC 328
index(es), AC 400
Indexed property, AC 400
infinity symbol, AC 12
Ink to Text button, PA 3
inked handwriting, PA 3
Inking toolbar, PA 15
inner joins, AC 258, AC 404, AC 405

Input Mask property, AC 114, AC 115
Insert Module button, AC 331
insertion point, OFF 8
integrating, OFF 2
IntelliSense technology, AC 334, AC 335
intentional damage, AC 357
interfaces, OFF 2
Is Not Null criterion, AC 36, AC 258
Is Not Null operator, AC 143
Is Null criterion, AC 36, AC 258

J

join(s), modifying, AC 404–405
join lines, AC 32, AC 258
Join Properties dialog box, AC 258, AC 259, AC 404, AC 405
JPEG (Joint Photographic Experts Group), AC 122
.jpg file extension, AC 122
junction table, AC 106, AC 396

K

key combinations, assigning macros, AC 303
key fields, AC 9
key symbols, AC 12, AC 108
keyboard shortcuts
  Edit mode, AC 17
  Navigation mode, AC 15
keywords, VBA, AC 325

L

label(s)
  forms, AC 63
  prefix for naming, AC 327
label controls, AC 54
Label Wizard, AC 94, AC 95
.laccdb file extension, AC 358
landscape orientation, AC 80, AC 81
Language option, Access Options dialog box, AC 349
Last function, AC 149
launchers, OFF 6

U

unbound controls, AC 61
Undo button, AC 168, AC 284
unfreezing fields in datasheets, AC 30
unhiding fields in datasheets, AC 30
Universal Serial Bus (USB) drives, AC 356
Update queries, AC 251, AC 256–257
Update To row, AC 256
USB (Universal Serial Bus) drives, AC 356
Use Control Wizards button, AC 304
user(s), databases, AC 54
user interfaces, OFF 6

V

Validation Rule property, AC 120–121
Validation Text property, AC 120–121
Value argument, AC 306
Value field, AC 150
Var function, AC 149
variables, AC 324, AC 325
VBA. *See* Visual Basic for Applications (VBA)
VBE. *See* Visual Basic Editor (VBE)
video clips, capturing, PA 11
view(s), AC 384, OFF 12, OFF 13
    logical, AC 138
    objects, AC 10
    reports, AC 83
    switching between, AC 66

View button, AC 254
View Microsoft Access button, AC 331
viewing
    Page Footer section, AC 274
    Page Header section, AC 274
    selected records for queries, AC 254
virtual assistant, Edge, PA 14–15
viruses, AC 357
Visible property, AC 306
Visual Basic Editor (VBE), AC 322, AC 323
    standard toolbar buttons, AC 331
Visual Basic for Applications (VBA), AC 322, AC 323
    keywords, AC 325
    syntax, AC 324

W

W3C (World Wide Web Consortium), AC 375
web app(s). *See* Access web apps
web app templates, AC 384
web browsers, AC 383. *See also* Microsoft Edge
web compatibility, forms, AC 346
Web Note tools, PA 15
webpages
    annotating, PA 15
    live, inserting in slides, PA 12
wildcard characters, AC 36, AC 145

Word. *See* Microsoft Word 2016
word wrap, AC 224
World Wide Web Consortium (W3C), AC 375

X

XMD files, AC 376, AC 377
XML (Extensible Markup Language), AC 228, AC 376
    exporting to, AC 376–377
    importing from, AC 378–379
    tags, AC 218
XML files, AC 218
XSD files, AC 376, AC 377

Y

yellow line, Code window, AC 332
Yes/No data type, AC 7

Z

zero-length string values, AC 258
Zoom In button, Microsoft Office 2016, OFF 6, OFF 7
Zoom Out button, Microsoft Office 2016, OFF 6, OFF 7